REVISE
HISTORY

1750–1992
British Political and Social

A COMPLETE REVISION COURSE FOR

GCSE

Peter Lane
Formerly Head of History, Coloma College of Education

BPP Letts Educational Ltd

First published 1982

Revised 1986, 1987, 1989, 1992
Reprinted 1988

Prints
Hulton Picture Library: pp 105.
Mansell Collection: pp 24, 70 79, 91, 122.
Mary Evans Picture Library: pp 42, 68, 120.

British Library Cataloguing in Publication Data

Lane, Peter, 1925—
    Revise History (1750–1992: a complete revision
    course for GCSE.—4th ed.—(Letts study aids)
    1. Great Britain — History —18th century —
    Examinations, questions, etc. 2. Great
    Britain —History — 19th Century —
    Examinations, questions, etc. 3. Great
    Britain —History — 20th Century —
    Examinations, questions, etc.
    I. Title
    909.07´076   DA470

    ISBN 1 85758 009 5

Acknowledgements

Thanks go to the following Examination Groups for their
permission to use GCSE examination material:

    London East Anglian Group
    Midland Examining Group
    Northern Examining Association
    Northern Ireland Schools Examinations and Assessment Council
    Welsh Joint Education Committee

The author would also like to thank his colleagues Richard Maples (teaching
for the Midland and London-based Groups), Joan Kennedy (teaching for the
Southern Group and, previously, an assistant examiner for the London
Association) and Richie Greig (an assistant examiner for the Scottish
Examination, for which he also prepares pupils).

Printed and bound in Great Britain by
Staples Printers St Albans Limited

CONTENTS

INTRODUCTION

A Guide to Using this Book

This book has been written to help candidates for GCSE and similar examinations to gain the knowledge and to develop the skills which will enable them to give their best performance in the History examination. It has been written with the help of several examiner-teachers and under the guidance of experienced teachers. The author and the team of examiners and teachers have taken into account the material published by the various Examining Boards. On p.v you will find an outline of the Aims which these Boards have set for our subject. More importantly you will also find the Assessment Objectives (1-4) which candidates have to bear in mind when studying and when answering examination papers: you will see that various papers in your examination have been designed to test one or more of these Objectives: it is obviously important that you should understand what these are and how you may achieve them.

In unit 58 of this book you will find a selection of the types of questions set by the various Examining Boards. You should use these are part of your revision. The long experience of examiners has shown that many candidates become nervous and lack confidence in the examination room because of inexperience and poor preparation for the examination. As a result they do less well than they, and their schools, expect. This book aims to provide the preparation which will allow candidates to approach the examination with more understanding and greater confidence.

The Examination Syllabuses

It is important that you study the table on pp. xiv-xvii. Find the columns which refer to the examination for which you are preparing. If you are in any doubt, check with your teacher or, if you are a private student, write to the Board for a copy of the syllabus. You will find the addresses of the Boards on p.xiii.

In the relevant column in the table of analysis you will find:
▶ the number of examination papers to be taken;
▶ the topics which make up the syllabus for your particular examination and, for many Boards, the papers in which these will be examined. Not all Boards require knowledge of all the 57 topics covered in the core section. Various symbols in the column indicate whether a topic is included in your syllabus. Please read the *Notes on the Table of Analysis of Examination Syllabuses* (pp. viii–xii), which contain additional and relevant information on the syllabuses and examinations of the various Boards.

Studying material in the core units

Work you way through as many of the necessary units as possible. Your teacher will advise you on which units have been chosen for study by your school.

Preparing for the Examination

Study the examination hints provided by experienced examiner-teachers (p. vii) and, in particular, note the advice about last-minute preparation.

Understanding the questions

In unit 58 you will find examples of the kinds of questions set by your Board. Broadly these are divided into:
▶ structured questions based on one or more pieces of evidence. Some of the questions may be answered in one word (e.g. 58.1, question 9); others may be answered in a sentence (e.g. 58.1, question 1); others, the majority, by a paragraph or two. Candidates for the London East Anglian Group have also to answer an unstructured essay question (e.g. 58.1, question 1(b));
▶ structured questions (or above) which also call for some source evaluation;
▶ questions based on a number of sources requiring evaluation and interpretation.

Even if your Board does not use all the kinds of questions to be found on these various pages, you will still benefit from a study of these pages as part of the revision of your subject.

Coursework

See pp. vi-vii.

GCSE

THE AIMS OF THE EXAMINATION

Each History course has to aim to achieve:
▶ the stimulation of interest in and enthusiasm for the study of the past;
▶ the development of a feeling for the past;
▶ the acquisition of knowledge and understanding of human activity in the past, linking it, as appropriate, with the present;
▶ an understanding of the nature and use of historical evidence;
▶ an understanding of the development over time of social and cultural values, particularly in those courses or parts of courses on British History;
▶ an understanding of the nature of cause and consequence, continuity and change, similarity and difference;
▶ the development of essential study skills such as the ability to locate and extract information from primary and secondary sources; to detect bias; to analyse this information and to construct a logical argument;
▶ the furthering of methods for the discovery, interpretation and communication of knowledge about the past;
▶ the provision of a sound basis for further study and the pursuit of personal interests.

Assessment objectives

It is essential that you study these Objectives. You will see from the table of analysis of syllabuses that different papers are set to test a candidate's level of achievement of these Objectives.
The examination will assess a candidate's ability to:
1 recall, evaluate and select knowledge relevant to the context, to analyse and synthesize such knowledge, and to deploy it in a clear and coherent form;
2 make use of and understand the concepts of cause and consequence, continuity and change, similarity and difference;
3 show an ability to look at events and issues from the perspectives of people in the past;

4 show the skills necessary to study a wide variety of historical evidence such as primary and secondary written sources, statistical and visual material, artefacts, textbooks and orally transmitted information;

▶ by comprehending and extracting information from it;

▶ by interpreting and evaluating it – distinguishing between fact, opinion and judgment; pointing to deficiencies in the material as evidence, such as gaps and inconsistencies; detecting bias.

▶ by comparing various types of historical evidence and reaching conclusions based on this comparison.

What Grade will I get?

The grade awarded to each candidate will depend upon the extent to which the candidate has met the Assessment Objectives. It might conceal weakness in one aspect of the examination which is balanced by above average performance in some other. If you study carefully the material below, you will see that to obtain a high grade (Grade C) you will have to have done very different quality work compared to the work required for the award of a low grade (Grade F). You will see this almost immediately if you compare the requirements for each Grade under the requirement numbered '7' in each case.

Grade descriptions

Grade descriptions are provided to give a general indication of the standards of achievement likely to have been shown by candidates awarded particular grades. The grade awarded will depend upon the extent to which the candidate has met the Assessment Objectives overall and it might conceal weakness in one aspect of the examination which is balanced by above average performance in some other.

Grade C

Candidates will be expected:

1 to recall and use historical knowledge, accurately and relevantly, in support of a logical and evaluative argument; to distinguish between cause and occasion of an event; to show some capacity both to analyse and to synthesise historical problems; to show that change in history is not necessarily linear or 'progressive'; to compare and contrast people, events, issues and institutions;

2 to be able to look at events and issues from the perspective of other people in the past; to understand the importance of looking for motives; to display sufficient imagination in seeing the past through the eyes of those living at the time;

3 to demonstrate comprehension of a range of evidence either by translating from one form to another (e.g. explaining accurately the information contained in a bar graph) or by summarizing information given in a document; to answer accurately questions demanding specific information to be extracted from the evidence;

4 to demonstrate adequately the limitations of a particular piece of evidence, e.g., point to the use of emotive language and to generalizations based on little or no evidence; to identify deficiencies in sources and to indicate other types of evidence that the historian would need to consult in relation to the topic and period in question;

5 to compare and contrast two or more different types of evidence, showing where they contradict or support each other, and write a coherent conclusion based on them, even though all aspects may not be taken into account;

6 to communicate clearly and coherently in a substantially accurate manner.

Grade F

Candidates will be expected:

1 to recall and display a limited amount of accurate and relevant historical knowledge; to show a basic understanding of the historical concepts of cause and consequence, continuity and change, sufficiently supported by obvious examples; to identify difference and similarity;

2 to show occasional insights into why and how people acted as they did in the past;

3 to show ability to comprehend straightforward evidence; to extract partial and/or generalized information;

4 to demonstrate obvious limitations of a particular piece of evidence; to list some of the evidence needed to reconstruct a given historical event;

5 to make simple comparisons between pieces of evidence; to list the major features of two or more pieces of evidence, without drawing conclusions from them;

6 to communicate in an understandable form.

■ Coursework ■

Each of the Examining Groups requires candidates for GCSE to submit coursework. In the table of analysis on pp. xii-xiv you will see the marks assigned to this work by your Board, as well as the Assessment Objectives which this work is meant to examine. Each Board has its own requirements concerning this work and it is important that you understand what your particular Board demands. However, there is some practical advice which will help you, no matter which examination you are taking. I am grateful to examiner-teachers for these important suggestions.

ORGANIZATION OF COURSEWORK

▶ Jotter—if using a jotter, use a separate one for each unit of work.

▶ 'Science-type' note books will prove useful as permanent holders of all notes and pupil tasks. However, you may find that it is difficult, if not impossible, to insert new material into such a book.

▶ Loose-leaf A4 ring-binders have the benefit that you will be able to add new material to previous work, which may also be improved on or discarded at a later date. This updating or improving on your work during the year may well be an important feature of your coursework. Diagrams and/ or slides can be inserted into the ring-binder in see-through folders. However, note that you are NOT allowed to submit your final work in a ring-binder.

THE LAYOUT OF THE WORK

▶ Headings should be used to differentiate aspects of each topic: you might illustrate these or pick them out in red capital letters.

▶ Use paragraphs (each separated by a space) for each item of information, detailed at some length.

▶ Sentences and not a series of notes must be used. Make sure that each sentence is complete and full and that it is factually accurate.

▶ Highlighting of important points by underlining of certain words or phrases will improve the appearance of your work.

▶ Summarize your conclusions with a single page at the end of your work.

▶ Contents: use a series of headings at the start of your work to show the examiner the logical way in which you have laid out the work which follows.

▶ Illustrations should be used to enhance your written work. If you are drawing a diagram, make sure you use a ruler when drawing straight lines. If you are using coloured pens or shading, make sure that this work is done neatly. Do not forget to add explanatory notes to photographs or slides and other illustrative material.

SKILLS TO BE DEVELOPED

▶ You have to develop your ability to write a sustained answer. Examples of such writing should be a part of your coursework.

▶ As well as such written work, examples of slides, videos and computer programmes may be attempted. You may submit tapes of oral reports or photographs of artefacts, with accompanying descriptions and commentary.

▶ Interviewing skills can be shown by, for example, a taped interview of a person being asked pre-arranged questions intended to provide you with specific information.

▶ Historical diaries and records of visits should be encouraged. Each item used in such work should be detailed and follow a logical sequence: for example, an account of a visit to a museum should show:
● what you hoped to gain from the visit;
● what you saw;
● how far the experience of the visit was relevant to the topic being pursued.
▶ Handling of sources: your coursework should show your ability to interpret various types of source material, and to use these as bases for arguments you wish to make. In developing your argument, you will be expected to show an ability to arrange work logically, to explain it fully and to arrive at correct conclusions.

CONSULT YOUR TEACHER

Before you decide what work you wish to do, consult your teacher and be guided by his or her advice. Teachers will know whether the examiners will accept some work or not (e.g. they will not necessarily accept the 'story' of your local football team, although you may find it interesting). Teachers will know what sources are easily available that will be useful for you.

Your teacher will help you to improve your work during the years. Make sure that you follow any suggestions which may be made.

DOING THE WORK – ON TIME

Make sure that you keep up to date with your coursework, by doing the work regularly. Try not to get behind with it. You cannot do good work if you leave most of it until the last few months or weeks. Start it at the beginning of the (one or) two-year period of study for the examination, and make sure that you have each piece completed in good time to be accepted by your teacher. There is a deadline – a date by which the whole of the completed coursework has to be submitted to your examiners. Find out from your teacher what that date is, and aim to have your coursework ready well before that date.

MAKE YOUR WORK AS GOOD AS POSSIBLE

Do take a great deal of care with your coursework and make it as good as you can. Unlike the examination – where you have a limited time in which to show the examiners what you understand and can do – you can normally take as much time as you like with your coursework. Because the mark for this work is added to the marks you gain in the written examination your final grade can often be better than it would otherwise have been if you obtain a high mark for your coursework.

EXAMINING GROUPS DIFFER

Make sure that you understand what your Group demands – as to length and number of assignments, the Assessment Objectives being examined in each piece and the total value of coursework. Your teacher will provide this information; if you are a private candidate you can get the information from the syllabus, which is available from the address shown on p. xiii.

A Revision Programme

Why Revise?

You may know people who do not seem to do much preparation before examinations, yet who still obtain high marks. You may also know people who spend a great deal of time at revision, some even studying up to the day of the examination.

It is impossible to define 'the best method' for all candidates, because people are different and what suits one may not do for another. But long experience has shown teachers and examiners that most people learn more, gain in confidence and perform better in examinations after they have made suitable preparations by a sensible programme of revision.

Planning Your Revision

Some people prefer to read a unit several times before testing themselves to see whether they can remember the work they have studied. Others prefer to make notes as they read and to use these notes for revision purposes. Almost everyone learns best by tackling small portions of work. Study one unit, test yourself on it and then decide whether you have understood the unit. By the time you have gone through all the necessary units you should have a list of topics which need further revision to help you overcome your weaknesses.

A Revision Timetable

A complete revision requires a good deal of time and needs sensible planning. The following timetable is based on the assumptions that the examination will take place in mid-June. If your examination takes place in May, November or January, obviously you will need to change the suggested dates.

▶ **End of March**
● Check how well you did in the mock examination so that you can see which topics you need to study carefully.
● Make up a timetable using the units in this book and any other topics which you need to study.
● The timetable should cover April and May and you should plan to do extra work during the Easter holidays.
● The timetable should be drawn up to allow you to finish your revision by the end of May. This will give you two weeks for further revision of your weaker points and a final revision of the main points in the days before the examination.

▶ **April and May**
● Allow yourself about one hour every day for history revision.

▶ **June**
● Revise the main points, using the examination questions in Unit 58. Make a list of the main points needed to answer any of the questions in that section.

▶ **Examination day**
● Make sure that you arrive at the examination in time and that you have with you all the things you think you might need – pens, pencils, ruler, crayons and eraser.

Taking the Examination

▶ **Read the paper carefully**
Almost every Report made by examiners complains that candidates did not understand the questions asked or failed to use the information supplied in the examination paper. If the examiners ask you to 'Give an account of Gladstone's domestic policies', they expect less analysis than they expect from answers to 'Account for Gladstone's defeat in the Election of 1874'. If you are asked to 'Give an account of Disraeli's domestic policy in his ministry of 1874-80', do not waste time by offering accounts of his foreign and imperial policies.

▶ **Tick off the questions you intend to do**
As you read through the paper tick off the questions which you think you could answer. Then check the instructions at the head of your examination paper to see how many questions you have to do, and from which sections, if the paper is sub-divided into sections.

Having ticked off a number of questions, go back through the paper and choose those which you intend to do. As you do this, number the questions – 1, 2 and so on – to remind yourself which question you intend to tackle first, which next and so on to the end. Always do first the question which you think you can answer best; this will give you confidence to go on with the rest of the paper.

▶ **Plan each answer before you start**

This refers to those questions which require you to write either an essay or a brief note on some item. It does not refer to the fixed-response questions.

▶ **Time yourself**

If you only answer half the questions asked for, you cannot expect to get more than 50 per cent even if you get full marks for each answer. It is important to attempt to answer the required number of questions. To help you do this you should:

● **Before the examination**, practise doing questions in the time allocated. This is important because you have to find out how much you can write in the 25 or 30 minutes which you can spend on a question in the examination.

● **In the examination room**, make a note of the time which you will allow for each question. If, for example, you have to do four questions in two hours you will have 100 minutes in which to write your answers (if you have spent 20 minutes on planning). This means that each answer should take 25 minutes. So if you start writing at 2.00 pm you should finish your answer to your first question at 2.25 pm, your second answer should be finished at 2.50 pm and so on.

● **When answering the paper**, keep an eye on your proposed timing and on the clock. When you get to the end of the time allocated to an answer, stop writing, even if you have not completed the answer. Leave a space and, if you have time, complete the answer later. It is better to have answered all five questions (if that is the number required), even if the answers are incomplete, than to answer only three – which you might do if you take five minutes more for this answer and a further five minutes for another.

▶ **Answering the questions**

You should remember that examiners have to mark a large number of papers. They will appreciate it if your work is neat, although they will not object if you have crossed out such things as plans for answers. They will object to a sort of shorthand which some candidates use, such as 'Pam' for Palmerston or 'Dizzie' for Disraeli. They will not give you any credit for the use of 'etc.' since they will think that this means you do not know any more. If you really do know more, then you should write it down so that the examiners can award the marks you deserve.

 ## Notes on the Table of Analysis

It is important that you read the section which follows which refers to the Board whose examination you intend to take These notes will help you to understand the table of analysis on pp. xiv-xvii.

LONDON EAST ANGLIAN GROUP

Assessment

The scheme of assessment is common to the two syllabuses outlined.

Paper 1 (40 per cent of the total mark) comprises questions based on a piece of source material. Each question will be divided into two parts. The first part comprises FIVE write-a-sentence/paragraph questions intended to test Objective 1. The second part comprises short essay questions intended to test Objective 4.

Paper 2 (30 per cent of total mark) comprises questions that require the analysis of pieces of evidence, and is intended to test Objective 3. A variety of forms of evidence will be used. Usually, each question will comprise a series of sub-questions based on one or more pieces of evidence.

Coursework (30 per cent of the total mark). Candidates will be required to submit THREE assignments aimed at testing Objectives 2, 3 and 4. These assignments may be related to any of the topics on the syllabus. No assignment should be longer than 1500 words and the total for the three assignments should be about 4000 words.

Syllabus B: British and European History from the mid-18th century

In spite of the title of this syllabus, candidates do not have to study both British and European History. They have to answer questions on TWO sections of the TEN listed in the syllabus. This book contains material on FIVE sections. You should note that, if you concentrate on British History, you have to choose chronologically adjacent topics, i.e. you have to take Topic B if you choose to study Topic A but, if you choose to study Topic B, you may choose EITHER Topic A or Topic C. Notice that in Paper 2, the Nominated Topics are relevant to the Topics chosen in Paper 1.

If you choose to study both British *and* European History, you should notice that you have to take TWO sections (one from British and one from European History) which cover, roughly, the same period of time, e.g. if you take Topic C from this book, you would also have to study Europe, 1870-1918 from the European section. Material for THREE of the European Topics may be found in the companion book, *Revise GCSE World History 1870-1992*.

Paper 1 consists of TEN sections, each with THREE questions. Candidates have to answer THREE questions taken from TWO sections.

Paper 2 consists of TEN sections, each of ONE question, on nominated topics. Candidates have to answer TWO questions. Note that the nominated topics will be changed every two years.

Coursework may be related to any of the topics on the syllabus.

Syllabus C: British Economic and Social History from the mid-18th century

There are four different syllabus schemes, all of them examined in the same examination. These are called Scheme A, Scheme B, Scheme C and Scheme D. In the table of analysis on p. xiv the schemes are shown as C(A), C(B), C(C) and C(D). Note that the study of Industry is central to all four schemes.

Scheme A. Candidates have to study Topic A1 (The Industrial Revolution, c. 1760-1870) and SEVEN other pre-1870 topics chosen from NINE options EIGHT of which are listed in the table on p. xiv.

Scheme B. Candidates have to study Topic B1 (Industrial Development since c. 1870) and SEVEN others listed in the analysis table.

Scheme C. Candidates have to study Topic C1 (The Industrial Revolution, c. 1760–1870 and Industrial Development since c. 1870) and THREE of the other EIGHT listed in the table of analysis.

Scheme D. Permits

either (i) the study of ONE topic for both pre-1870 (Scheme A) and post-1870 (Scheme B) periods and SIX other topics all chosen from *either* the pre-1870 period or the post-1870 period.

or (ii) the study of TWO topics for both the pre-and post-1870 periods and FOUR other topics all chosen from *either* the pre-1870 period *or* the post-1870 period. Candidates are required to study Topic A1 and/or Topic B1.

The topic coverage across Papers 1 and 2 for 1993 will be:

	Paper 1 Topics	*Paper 2 Topics*
Summer 1993	A1, B2, A3, A4, B5, B6, A7, B8, B9, A10	B1, A2, B3, B4, A5, A6, B7, A8, A9, B10

Paper 1 Ten questions of which candidates answer any THREE.

Paper 2 Ten questions of which candidates answer any TWO.

Coursework assignments may be related to any of the topics on the syllabus.

MIDLAND EXAMINING GROUP

Assessment

The scheme of assessment is common to all the syllabuses offered by the Group.

Paper 1 (40 per cent of the total mark) will test the Core Content (listed as C1–C3 in the table of analysis). It will consist of SIX structured questions, of which candidates must answer ANY THREE. Questions may make use of source material, but no evaluation of sources will be required. TWO questions will be set on EACH of the THREE Core Units, but candidates may choose to answer questions on only TWO Core Units if they wish.

Paper 2 (30 per cent of the total mark) will consist of ONE question set on each of the Optional Topics (listed in the table of analysis), and candidates must answer TWO questions. All questions will make use of source material. All questions will be structured and will include sub-questions requiring the evaluation and analysis of the source material provided.

Coursework (30 per cent of the total mark). Candidates will be required to submit either ONE piece of work or TWO shorter pieces of work on a subject related to the syllabus they are following. Each piece may consist of several shorter pieces of work related to a common theme, provided that the finished assignment has between 2000 and 4500 words.

Syllabus 1606: British Social and Economic History

Paper 1 will examine the Core Content 'Developments from 1750 to 1850' in:

1 Agriculture (C1 in the table of analysis)
2 Industry (C2)
3 Transport (C3)

Paper 2 will examine the NINE Optional Topics listed as TA–TJ in the table. Candidates have to answer questions on TWO of these Topics.

Coursework See above on assessment.

Syllabus 1611 (D): British and European History, 1685–1815

Despite the title of this Syllabus, candidates do not have to study European History: there is enough choice in the examination to allow them to concentrate on British History if they wish to do so. Candidates should also notice that they do not have to answer questions on each of the Core Content Units. There are TWO questions set on EACH of the THREE Core Content Units and candidates have to answer ANY THREE questions, although they may, if they wish, choose to study only TWO of the Core Content Units.

Paper 1 will examine the Core Content (British History):
1 The Glorious Revolution, 1685-1701. This topic is NOT covered in this book
2 Agricultural and Industrial Change, c. 1700-1815 (C2 in the table of analysis)
3 Britain and the French Revolution (C3).

Paper 2 will examine Optional Topics. Candidates have to answer questions on TWO of FIVE Topics listed in the Syllabus. In this book there is material on THREE Topics (listed TA – TC in the table of analysis).

Coursework. See above on assessment.

Syllabus 1612 (E): British and European History, 1789– 1914

In spite of the title of this Syllabus, candidates do not have to study European History: there is enough choice in the examination to allow them to concentrate on British History – if they wish.

Paper 1 will examine the Core Content (British History):
1 Britain and the French Revolution (C1 in the table of analysis)
2 The Demand for Political Reform (C2)
3 The Improvement of Social Conditions (C3)
Paper 2 will examine Optional Topics. Candidates have to answer questions on TWO of the SEVEN Topics listed in the syllabus. In this book there is material on FOUR Topics (listed TA–TD in the table). Additional material on Topic TD (The Origins of the First World War) may be found in the companion book, *Revise GCSE World History 1870 – 1992*.

Coursework. See p. ix on assessment.

Syllabus 1613 (F): British and European History, 1867 to the Present Day

In splite of the titles of this Sullabus, candidates do not have to sutdy European History: there is enough choice in the examination to allow them to concentrate on British History – if they wish.

Paper 1 will examine the Core Content (British History):

1 Political Change, 1867–1931 (C1 in the table of analysis)
2 Employment and unemployment in the Inter-War Period (C2)
3 Social change (C3)

Paper 2 will examine Optional Topics. Candidates have to answer questions on TWO of the SIX Topics listed in the Syllabus. In this book there is material on THREE Topics (listed TA–TC in the table). There is material on the other (following) Topics in the companion book, *Revise GCSE World History 1870–1992*:

1 Russia, 1917 – 41
2 Germany, 1919 – 45
3 The Origins of the First World War
4 Cooperation in Western Europe from 1945

Coursework. See above on assessment.

NORTHERN EXAMINING ASSOCIATION

Assessment

The scheme of assessment will consist of three components.

Paper 1 (30 per cent of the total mark). This will be based on the subject content for Themes 2 and 3. Four questions will be set, one on each of the two main parts of each theme. Candidates will have to answer two questions; one on *either* Trade Unions (T2A) *or* Political Representation (T2B), the other on *either* Social Welfare (T3A) *or* Education (T3B).

Paper 2 (40 per cent of the total mark). Candidates have to answer FOUR questions of which THREE will be compulsory. The fourth question must be taken from a choice of three.

Coursework (30 per cent of the total mark). Candidates will be expected to submit a minimum of THREE and a maximum of SIX assignments based on the themes outlined in the syllabus. At least ONE assignment must be based on EACH of the three themes. At least ONE assignment must be based on a local aspect or aspects of ONE of these three themes. In total, the assignments should consist of at least 3000 written words but should not contain more than 6000 words.

Syllabus

Theme 1: Industrialization and Urbanization

(a) Agriculture (T1A)
(b) Industry (T1B)
(c) Transport (T1C)
(d) Trade (T1D)
(e) Population (T1E)
(f) Urbanization (T1F)
Theme 2: Responses to Industrialization. Candidates will be required to answer a question on either section (a) or section (b):

either
(a) Trade Unions (T2B(i))
or (b) Political Representation (T2B(ii))
Theme 3: Social Improvements. Candidates will be required to answer a question on either section (a) or section (b)
either
(a) Social Welfare (T3A)
or (b) Education (T3B).

NORTHERN IRELAND SCHOOLS EXAMINATIONS AND ASSESSMENT COUNCIL

Assessment

This Board's examination syllabus contains some material on World History. For an assessment scheme relevant to sections which deal with World History, see the companion volume *Revise GCSE World History 1870-1992.*

Paper 1 (consists of TWO sections, A and B, each carrying 25% of the total marks)
Section A A Modern World Study. You have to answer questions on ONE of the following:
1 Israel and the Arab World
2 The USA in the Modern World
3 Great Britain and Northern Ireland in the Modern World
4 Modern Ireland
   Material relevant to 1 and 2 will be found in the companion volume *Revise GCSE World History 1870-1992.*
   In the examination there will be one compulsory source-based question. A number of questions will be set relating to a selection of source materials.
One essay (choice of three).
Section B A study in depth of ONE of:
1 Germany, 1919–39
2 Russia, 1905–29
3 China, 1934–53
   All these topics are dealt with in the companion volume *Revise GCSE World History 1870-1992.*

Paper 2 A study in development of *either* Medicine through time *or* Energy through time – which are not dealt with in either of the two *Revise* volumes. (This paper carries 20% of the total mark.)
Coursework (which carries 30% of the total mark) given for work associated with a local study.
Candidates may submit *either* four assignments, each linked with specific assessment objectives *or* a single piece of work which meets those objectives.

SOUTHERN EXAMINING GROUP

Syllabus 1 (1167): Aspects of British Social and Economic History since 1750.

Paper 1 has questions on EIGHT themes (marked 1 – 8 under Paper 1 in the Analysis on page xvi). Candidates must study AT LEAST TWO themes, but are advised to study FOUR.
The eight themes are:
1 Industry, 1750–1875
2 Industry since 1875
3 Agriculture, 1750–1875
4 Agriculture since 1875
5 Transport, 1750–1875
6 Transport since 1875
7 Social changes, 1750–1875
8 Social changes since 1875.
Section A *(15% of the total mark)* has one compulsory question on theme 1, based on an array of sources and consisting of a number of sub-questions requiring brief responses. This question is concerned with Assessment Objective 4.
Section B *(25% of the total mark)* has eight questions, one on each of the eight themes. Two questions have to be answered. Candidates may answer only one of the two questions set on Industry, (themes 1 – 2): they may decide to answer neither of these two questions. All questions are

structured, based on stimulus material and primarily concerned with Assessment Objective 2, but they also involve Assessment Objectives 1 and 4.
Paper 2 has questions on EIGHT topics (marked 1 – 8 under Paper 2 in the Analysis on page xvi). Candidates must study TWO topics but may study more if they wish. The eight topics are:
1 Religion and Society, 1750–1820
2 Slavery and its abolition, 1760–1840
3 The Poor Law, 1790–1850
4 Chartism, 1832–60, and its results
5 Medicine, 1840–1900
6 Trade Unions, 1880–1930
7 The role and status of women, 1880–1930
8 Population trends and the multi-cultural society in Britain since 1900.

Section A *(15% of the total mark)* has EIGHT questions, one on each topic. The questions are structured and based on stimulus material and are primarily concerned with Assessment Objective 2 but also involve Assessment Objective 1.

Section B *(15% of the total mark)* has EIGHT questions, one on each topic. These questions are structured, based on one or more brief sources and concerned with Assessment Objectives 2, 3 and 4.
Advice Candidates are advised to study *linked* themes and topics. The following are examples of such links, but other linked combinations are equally valid.

Paper 1	Paper 2
(a) Themes 1,3,5,7	Topics 3 and 4
(b) Themes 1,2,6,8	Topics 1 and 8
(c) Themes 1,2,7,8	Topics 6 and 7

Coursework (30% of the total mark). Candidates have to submit TWO assignments, one concerned with Assessment Objective 3 and one with Assessment Objective 4.

Syllabus 4 (1172) Aspects of British History, 1850–1979

Paper 1 is based on FOUR themes (marked 1–4 under Paper 1 in the Analysis on page xvi).
Paper 2 is based on SIX topics (marked 1–6 under Paper 2 in the Analysis on page xvi). These themes and topics are:

Paper 1: Themes	**Paper 2: Topics**
1 The working classes, 1815–80	1 The Eastern Question, 1821–56
2 The working classes, 1880–1951	2 Education, 1833–1944
3 Political change and society, 1815–1900	3 Ireland, 1868–1922
4 Political change and society, 1900–79	4 Britain's involvement in India, 1848–1947
	5 Britain's involvement in the First World War 1914–18
	6 Britain's involvement in the Second World War, 1939–45

For Paper 1 candidates must study TWO themes, choosing either themes 1 and 3 or themes 2 and 4. For Paper 2 candidates must study TWO topics.
   It is anticipated that candidates will not extend their studies beyond TWO themes and TWO topics, though they are free to do so if they wish.
   Candidates are strongly recommended to study linked themes and topics. The links will usually be chronological but might also relate to issues. For example, a study of topics 5 and 6 might help candidates when they are studying the consequences of the two World Wars in themes 2 and 4. Similarly, it might be interesting for candidates to study political change in different countries combining theme 3 or 4 with topic 3 or 4. Other linked permutations are equally valid.

Paper 1 This paper contains THREE sections.

Section A *(15% of the total mark)* This section contains TWO questions, one being set on each of themes 1 and 2. ONE question is to be answered. Each question is based on an array of sources and consists of a number of sub-questions requiring brief responses. The questions are concerned with Assessment Objective 4. Both questions carry equal marks.

Sections B and C *(25% of the total mark)* Each section contains FOUR questions. In Section B TWO questions are set on each of themes 1 and 2. In Section C TWO questions are set on each of themes 3 and 4. Candidates are to answer ONE question from Section B and ONE question from Section C. All questions are structured and are based upon stimulus material. They are primarily concerned with Assessment Objective 2 but also involve Assessment Objective 1. All eight questions carry equal marks.

Paper 2 This paper contains 12 questions, two being set on each of topics 1 – 6. TWO questions are to be answered, but from different topics. All questions are structured and are based upon stimulus material. They are concerned with Assessment Objectives 1,2 and 4. All 12 questions carry equal marks.

Coursework (30% of the total mark) Candidates are required to submit TWO written assignments produced during the course. ONE assignment must be concerned with Assessment Objective 3. The other assignment must be concerned with Assessment Objective 4, with particular emphasis on a variety of types of historical sources. Each assignment must relate to a theme or topic in the syllabus.

Syllabus 5 (1173) Aspects of British, European and World History, 1862–1974

The examination papers are based on 14 topics, listed below. Some of the topics are covered in this book (namely topics 3, 4, 7, 9, and (in part) 11–14). Most of the topics, including topics 11–14, are covered in *GCSE Revise World History, 1870–1992*.

Paper 1: Topics	Paper 2: Topics
1 Russia, 1894–1924 2 Germany, 1862–90 3 Britain, 1867–94 4 Britain 1895–1918 5 Russia, 1924–53 6 Germany 1918–45 7 Britain, 1919–45 8 The USA 1919–45 9 Britain 1945–74 10 The USA, 1945–74	*Section A* 11 The relationships between the European Powers, 1871–1914 12 The relationships between the European Powers, 1919–39 *Section B* 13 The First World War, 1914–18 14 The Second World War, 1939–45

For *Paper 1* candidates must study at least two topics and are advised to study four. In Section A, candidates must answer on either topic 1 or topic 7.

For *Paper 2* candidates must study one topic from Section A and one topic from Section B. Candidates are strongly recommended to combine topics 11 and 13 or, alternatively, topics 12 and 14.

It is anticipated that candidates will not extend their studies beyond six topics overall (four for Paper 1 and two for paper 2), though they are free to do so if they wish.

Candidates are strongly recommended to study six linked topics. Some topics are linked by chronology, others by country. The following are examples of combinations of linked topics, and other linked combinations are equally valid.

Paper 1	*Paper 2*
(a) Topics 1 – 4	Topics 11 and 13
(b) Topics 5 – 8	Topics 12 and 14
(c) Topics 1, 4, 5, 7	Either pair
(d) Topics 2, 6, 7, 9	Either pair
(e) Topics 7 – 10	Topics 12 and 14
(f) Topics 1, 5, 8, 10	Topics 12 and 14

Paper 1 contains TWO sections.

Section A *(15% of the total mark)* This section contains TWO questions, ONE being set on topics 1 and 7. ONE question is to be answered. Each question is based on an array of sources an consists of a number of sub-questions requiring brief responses. The questions are concerned with Assessment Objective 4. Both questions carry equal marks.

Section B *(25% of the total mark)* This sections contains TEN questions, ONE being set on each of topics 1–10. Any TWO questions are to be answered. All questions are structured and are based upon stimulus material. They are primarily concerned with Assessment Objective 2 but also involve Assessment Objectives 1 and 4. All ten questions carry equal marks.

Paper 2 contains TWO sections.

Section A *(15% of the total mark)* This section contains FOUR questions, TWO being set on each of topics 11–12. ONE question is to be answered. All questions are structured and may be based upon stimulus material. They are primarily concerned with Assessment Objective 2 but also involve Assessment Objective 1. All four questions carry equal marks.

Section B *(15% of the total mark)* This section contains FOUR questions, TWO being set on each of topics 13–14. ONE question is to be answered. All questions are structured and may be based upon stimulus material. They are primarily concerned with Assessment Objective 2 but also involve Assessment Objective 1. All four questions carry equal marks.

Coursework (30% of the total mark) Candidates are required to submit TWO written assignments produced during the course. ONE assignment must be concerned with Assessment Objective 3. The other assignment must be concerned with Assessment Objective 4, with particular emphasis on a variety of types of historical sources.

SCOTTISH EXAMINATION BOARD

Standard Grade

Assessment

Note that this is liable to amendment. You should consult your teacher as to the current scheme. At the time of writing the scheme consists of THREE papers designated as Foundation, General and Credit which will be offered as follows:

Paper	Grades assessed	Prescribed Units assessed
Foundation	6 and 5	1 *or* 2 *or* 3
General	4 and 3	1, 2 and 3
Credit	2 and 1	1, 2 and 3

You will have to ask your teacher which Level or Levels, you are to be entered for, and which Units you will be examined on. Candidates have to know the level for which they have been entered: Foundation (F), General (G), or Credit (C). The level for which you have been entered determines the number and nature of the papers which you have to take in the examination. School assess-ments will be used as a guide for deciding which level and how many papers you may take in the examination.

Syllabus

The course is based on FOUR units of study.

Unit 1 Changing Life in Scotland and Britain.
Candidates have to study ONE of the periods:

A 1750s–1850s (A in the table of analysis)
B 1830s–1930s (B)
C 1880s–to the present day (C)

Unit 2 International Cooperation and Conflict.
Candidates have to study ONE of the periods:

A 1790s–1820s (A in the table of analysis)
B 1890s–1920s (B)
C 1930s–60s (C)

Additional material on this Unit will be found in the companion volume, *Revise GCSE World History 1870– 1992.*

Unit 3 People and Power.
Candidates have to study ONE of the following:

A USA 1850–80
B India 1917–47
C Russia 1914–41
D Germany 1918–39

Material for this Unit will be found in the companion volume *Revise GCSE World History 1870–1992.*

Unit 4 Historical Investigation.
This is to be undertaken on the advice of your teacher.

WELSH JOINT EDUCATION COMMITTEE

Assessment

Candidates have to answer one written paper (55 per cent of the total mark), and submit coursework (45 per cent of the total mark).

Written Paper (55 per cent of the total mark) consists of three sections (A, B and C).

Section A *(15 per cent)*. Candidates have to write a paragraph (100 words or so) on FIVE of EIGHT items. This section is designed to test syllabus coverage.

Section B *(25 per cent)*. Candidates have to answer ONE of TWO evidence-based questions which are designed to test Assessment Objectives 1, 2 and 3 (see p. v).

Section C *(15 per cent)*. Candidates have to choose ONE of TWO questions requiring an imaginative and understanding written response. This is designed to test, in particular, Assessment Objective 3.

Coursework (45 per cent of the total mark). This will consist of THREE written assignments, each of 1500 words maximum, and each to be marked out of 15 per cent of the total mark.

ONE assignment must be based on EACH of the THREE thematic sections. At the time of writing the nominated areas on which these assignments are to be based are:

A Coal mining developments (in relation to one specified area of Wales or England)
B Social conditions in the new industrial towns, with specific reference to one named Welsh town or one named English town
C Chartism in England and Wales

Candidates should ensure that they know which areas have been nominated by the examiners for the year in which they are taking the examination.

Syllabus C: A Social and Industrial History of England and Wales, 1760–1875

The syllabus is presented in THREE thematic sections, each sub-divided into a number of defined areas:

A Aspects of Industrial Change, 1760–1875 (A in the table of analysis)
B The Social Implications of Industrialization (B)
C Popular Protest and Reaction to Change (C)

Note. Candidates will be expected to be able to relate the material contained in the relevant sections of this book to the Welsh situation. However, there is sufficient material in the Units indicated in the table of analysis, and in the examination questions, to ensure that candidates who have understood that material will do well in the examination paper.

Examination Boards: Addresses

To obtain syllabuses, past examination papers and further details, write to your Examining Group.

Northern Examination Association (NEA)

JMB Joint Matriculation Board
Devas Street, Manchester M15 6EU

ALSEB Associated Lancashire Schools Examining Board
12 Harter Street, Manchester M1 6HL

NREB Northern Regional Examinations Board
Wheatfield Road, Westerhope, Newcastle upon Tyne NE5 5JZ

NWREB North-West Regional Examinations Board
Orbit House, Albert Street, Eccles, Manchester M20 0WL

YHREB Yorkshire and Humberside Regional Examinations Board
Harrogate Office – 31-33 Springfield Avenue, Harrogate HG1 2HW
Sheffield Office – Scarsdale House, 136 Derbyshire Lane, Sheffield S8 8SE

Midland Examining Group (MEG)

Cambridge University of Cambridge Local Examinations Syndicate
Syndicate Buildings, 1 Hills Road, Cambridge CB1 2EU

O & C Oxford and Cambridge Schools Examination Board
Purbeck House, Purbeck Road, Cambridge CB2 1PU and Elsfield Way, Oxford OX2 7BZ

WMEB West Midlands Examinations Board
Mill Wharf, Mill Street, Birmingham B6 4BU

EMREB East Midland Regional Examinations Board
Robins Wood House, Robins Wood Road, Aspley, Nottingham NG8 3NR

London East Anglian Group (LEAG)
(now known as University of London Examinations and Assessment Council)

London office Stewart House, 32 Russell Square, London WC1B 5DN

Colchester office The Lindens, Lexden Road, Colchester CO3 3RL

Southern Examining Group (SEG)

AEB The Associated Examining Board
Stag Hill House, Guildford GU2 5XJ

OSEB Oxford School Examinations Board
Ewert House, Ewert Place, Summertown, Oxford OX2 7BZ

SEG Southern Regional Examinations Board
Unit 23, Monksbrook Industrial Park, Chandlers Ford, Eastleigh SO5 3RA

South-East Regional Examinations Board
Beloe House, 2-10 Mount Ephraim Road, Tunbridge Wells TN1 1EU

South-Western Examinations Board
23-29 Marsh Street, Bristol BS1 4BP

Wales

WJEC Welsh Joint Education Committee
245 Western Avenue, Cardiff CF5 2YZ

Northern Ireland

NISEAC Northern Ireland Schools Examinations and Assessment Council
Beechill House, 42 Beechill Road, Belfast BT8 4RS

Scotland

SEB Scottish Examination Board
Ironmills Road, Dalkeith, Midlothian EH22 1BR

Table of Analysis of Examination Syllabuses

		LEAG														
	Syllabus	B			C(A) See cycle on page ix			C(B) See cycle on page ix			C(C) See cycle on page ix			C(D) See cycle on page ix		
	Paper	1	2	C/W	1	2	C/W	1	2	C/W	1	2	C/W	1	2	C/W
	Fixed-response	•			•			•			•			•		
	Structured essays	•			•			•			•			•		
	Evidence-based	•	•		•	•		•	•		•	•		•	•	
	Source evaluation															
	Assessment objectives (see pp v–vi)	1+4	3	2–4	1+4	3	2–4	1+4	3	2–4	1+4	3	2–4	1+4	3	2–4
	European component	Opt	Opt	Opt												
1	George III 1760–1782	A		•												
2	Population changes 1760–1986	A		•	A3	A2	•	B3	B3	•	C3	C3	•			
3	The Agricultural Revolution 1760–1820	A	A	•	A2	A2	•									
4	The Transport Revolution 1760–1820	A		•	A4	A4	•				C4	C4	•			
5	The Industrial Revolution 1760–1850	A		•	A1	A1	•				C1	C1	•	•		
6	The American War of Independence	A		•												
7	William Pitt the Younger 1783–1793	A		•												
8	William Pitt the Younger 1793–1806	A		•												
9	The defeat of Napoleon 1806–1815	A		•												
10	Religion and the Humanitarians	A		•												
11	Domestic policy 1815–1822	B		•												
12	Domestic policy 1822–1830	B		•	A6	A6	•									
13	Foreign affairs 1815–1827	B		•												
14	Parliamentary reform 1830–1832	B		•												
15	Whig governments 1833–1841	B	B	•	A6	A6	•									
16	Chartism 1837–1850	B		•	A5	A5	•				C5	C5	•			
17	Factory reform 1833–1878	B		•	A6	A6	•									
18	Public health and medical science	B		•	A3/7	A3/7	•	B3	B3	•	C3	C3	•			
19	Sir Robert Peel	B		•												
20	Free trade and the Anti-Corn Law League	B		•	A2	A2	•									
21	Palmerston 1830–1865	B		•												
22	The Eastern Question 1820–1856	B		•												
23	Ireland 1760–1850	B		•												
24	The British Empire 1760–1860	A/B		•												
25	Trade Unions 1760–1867	B		•	A5	A5	•	B5	B5	•	C5	C5	•			
26	Railways and steam shipping 1820–1914	B	A	•	A4	A4	•	B4	B4	•	C4	C4	•			
27	Agriculture 1846–1914	B		•	A2	A2	•	B2	B2	•	C2	C2	•			
28	Industrial progress and Tariff Reform	B		•	A1	A1	•	B1	B1	•	C1	C1	•	•		
29	Gladstone: Part 1, to 1874	C		•												
30	Disraeli	C		•												
31	Gladstone: Part 2, 1880–1894	C		•												
32	The Eastern Question 1870–1914	C		•												
33	Ireland 1860–1966	C/D		•												
34	Joseph Chamberlain	C		•				B6	B6	•						
35	Conservative governments 1886–1905	C		•												
36	Foreign affairs 1890–1914	C		•												
37	The Liberals 1906–1914	C	C	•				B6	B6	•						
38	Parliamentary reform 1860–1928	B/C		•												
39	Trade Unions 1867–1980	C		•				B5	B5	•	C5	C5	•			
40	The rise of the Labour Party 1893–1924	C		•				B5	B5	•	C5	C5	•			
41	The changing role of women	C		•	A9	A9	•	B9	B9	•	C9	C9	•			
42	State education 1760–1986	C		•	A8	A8	•	B8	B8	•	C8	C8	•			
43	The First World War 1914–1918	C		•												
44	Peacemaking: the effects of the war on Britain	C		•												
45	Domestic affairs 1918–1924	D		•				B6	B6	•						
46	Industry and trade 1919–1939	D	D	•				B1	B1	•	C1	C1	•	•		
47	Baldwin and the General Strike	D		•				B5/6	B5/6	•	C5	C5	•			
48	The second Labour government 1929–1931	D		•				B6	B6	•						
49	Domestic affairs 1931–1939	D		•							C1	C1	•			
50	Foreign affairs 1919–1939	D		•												
51	The Second World War 1939–1945	D		•				B6	B6	•						
52	Labour governments 1945–1951	E		•				B1,5,6	B1,5,6	•	C5	C5	•	•		
53	Conservative governments 1951–1964	E		•				B5,6	B5,6	•	C5	C5	•			
54	Foreign and imperial affairs 1945–1988	E	E	•				B2	B2	•	C2	C2	•			
55	Domestic affairs 1964–1979	E		•				B1,5,6	B1,5,6	•	C5	C5	•	•		
56	The Thatcher decade	E		•				B1,5,6	B1,5,6	•	C5	C5	•	•		
57	Modern communications 1900–1988	E		•				B4	B4	•	C1,4	C1,4	•			

Consult the Syllabus on page ix and choose options from C(A) or C(B)

MEG												NEA			NISEAC				
1606			1611(D)			1612(E)			1613(F)			C							
1	2	C/W	1	2	C/W	1	2	C/W	1	2	C/W	1	2	C/W	1A	1B	2	C/W	
•	•		•	•		•	•		x	•		•	•		•	•			
•	•		•	•		•	•		•	•		•			•	•			
				•			•								•	•			
1+2	1,2+4	1–4	1+2	1,2+4 Opt	1–4	1+2	1,2+4 Opt	1–4 Opt	1+2	1,2+4 Opt	1–4 Opt	1,2+4	1–4	C/W	1–4	1–4	1–4	1–4	
																			1
							TB	•					T1E						2
C1		•	C2		•								T1A						3
C3		•	C2		•								T1C						4
C2		•	C2		•								T1B						5
				TB	•														6
			C3		•	C1		•					T1D						7
			C3		•	C1		•											8
			C3		•	C1		•											9
	TA	•	C3	TC	•	C1		•				T3A							10
C1		•	C3		•	C1/2		•											11
						C2		•											12
																			13
						C2		•											14
	TC	•				C3		•				T3A							15
	TD	•				C2		•				T2B							16
C2		•				C3		•											17
C2	TB	•	C2		•	C3		•					T1F						18
																			19
C1		•											T1D						20
																			21
																			22
							TA	•											23
				TA	•														24
	TD	•										T2A							25
C3	TH	•					TB	•					T1C						26
C1	TG	•					TB	•					T1A						27
							TB	•					T1D						28
																			29
							TC	•		TA	•		T1F						30
							TC	•		TA	•								31
							TD	•		TB	•								32
							TA	•							A4				33
							TC	•		TA	•		T1F						34
							TC	•		TA	•								35
							TD	•		TB	•								36
	TC	•				C3		•	C3		•	T3A							37
						C2		•	C1		•	T2B							38
	TD	•										T2A							39
	TD	•							C1		•	T2B							40
	TE	•				C2		•	C1/3		•								41
	TA	•				C3		•				T3B							42
																			43
	TD	•							C1/2		•	T2B			A3				44
									C1		•	T2B							45
	TD/H	•							C2		•		T1B		A3				46
	TD	•							C1/2		•	T2A							47
									C1		•				A3				48
									C2		•		T1		A3				49
																			50
	TC	•							C3	TC	•	T3A			A3				51
	TC/D	•							C3		•	T3A	T1B		A3				52
	TD	•													A3				53
	TD/G/H	•											T1D						54
	TD/G	•							C3		•	T2A			A3				55
	TD/G	•							C3		•	T2A	T1		A3				56
	TI/J	•							C3		•		T1C		A3				57

Material for this section is NOT covered by the Revise GCSE History books

Material for this section will be found in the companion book Revise GCSE World History 1870–1992

Table of Analysis of Examination Syllabuses

	SEG														
	1 (1167)					**4(1172)**					**5 (1173)**				
Paper	1A	1B	2A	2B	C/W	1A	1B	1C	2	C/W	1A	1B	2A	2B	C/W
Fixed-response	•					•					•				
Structured essays		•	•				•	•	•			•	•	•	
Evidence-based	•	•	•	•	•	•	•	•	•	•	•	•	•	•	•
Source evaluation	•	•		•	•	•			•	•	•	•			•
Assessment objectives (see pp v–vi)	4	1,2+4	1–2	1,2+4	3–4	4	1–2	1–2	1,2+4	3–4	4	1,3+4	1–2	1–2	3–4
European component											•	•	•	•	•
1 George III 1760–1782															
2 Population changes 1760–1986			7+8	7+8								9			
3 The Agricultural Revolution 1760–1820		3													
4 The Transport Revolution 1760–1820		5													
5 The Industrial Revolution 1760–1850	1														
6 The American War of Independence															
7 William Pitt the Younger 1783–1793															
8 William Pitt the Younger 1793–1806		3	3	3											
9 The defeat of Napoleon 1806–1815															
10 Religion and the Humanitarians			1	1											
11 Domestic policy 1815–1822		3				1–3	1–3	1–3							
12 Domestic policy 1822–1830															
13 Foreign affairs 1815–1827									1						
14 Parliamentary reform 1830–1832			4	4		3	3	3							
15 Whig governments 1833–1841			2–3	2–3		1	1	1							
16 Chartism 1837–1850			4	4		1	1	1							
17 Factory reform 1833–1878		6				1	1	1				3			
18 Public health and medical science	1	6	5	5		1	1	1							
19 Sir Robert Peel															
20 Free trade and the Anti-Corn Law League		3				1	1	1							
21 Palmerston 1830–1865									1						
22 The Eastern Question 1820–1856									1						
23 Ireland 1760–1850															
24 The British Empire 1760–1860									4						
25 Trade Unions 1760–1867						1	1	1							
26 Railways and steam shipping 1820–1914	1	5													
27 Agriculture 1846–1914		3–4										3			
28 Industrial progress and Tariff Reform		2										3			
29 Gladstone: Part 1, to 1874												3			
30 Disraeli												3			
31 Gladstone: Part 2, 1880–1894											7	3–4			
32 The Eastern Question 1870–1914															
33 Ireland 1860–1966										3		3			
34 Joseph Chamberlain												3			
35 Conservative governments 1886–1905												3			
36 Foreign affairs 1890–1914															
37 The Liberals 1906–1914		8				2	2	2				4			
38 Parliamentary reform 1860–1928			7	7		3–4	3–4	3–4				3			
39 Trade Unions 1867–1980		8	6	6		2	2	2				3			
40 The rise of the Labour Party 1893–1924						2–3	2–3	2–3				4			
41 The changing role of women			7	7		3–4	3–4	3–4				4–9			
42 State education 1760–1986		6+8							2						
43 The First World War 1914–1918									5						
44 Peacemaking: the effects of the war on Britain		2+6	6	6		2	2	2	5			4		13	
45 Domestic affairs 1918–1924						4	4	4			7			13	
46 Industry and trade 1919–1939		2				2	2	2			7				
47 Baldwin and the General Strike			6	6		2	2	2			7				
48 The second Labour government 1929–1931						4	4	4			7				
49 Domestic affairs 1931–1939		2									7				
50 Foreign affairs 1919–1939									4						
51 The Second World War 1939–1945		8				2	2	2	2–6		7			14	
52 Labour governments 1945–1951						2	2	2				9			
53 Conservative governments 1951–1964												9			
54 Foreign and imperial affairs 1945–1988		4				4	4	4	4						
55 Domestic affairs 1964–1979												9			
56 The Thatcher decade															
57 Modern communications 1900–1988		6													

Material for this section (SEG 5 (1173), paper 2A) will be found in the companion book Revise GCSE World History 1870–1992.

SEB							WJEC		
Standard							C		
1			2			3	1	C/W	
							•		
•	•	•	•	•	•		•		
•	•	•	•	•	•		•		
1–4	1–4	1–4	1–4	1–4	1–4	1–4	1–4	1–4	
									1
A	B	C					B		2
A									3
A									4
A	B						A	•	5
									6
									7
			A						8
A			A						9
									10
			A				C		11
			A						12
			A						13
A									14
							B		15
	B						C	•	16
A	B						B		17
A	B						B	•	18
									19
A	B								20
									21
									22
									23
									24
							B		25
	B	C							26
	B								27
	B						A		28
									29
									30
									31
									32
									33
									34
									35
			B						36
									37
	B								38
		C					B		39
		C							40
	B	C							41
									42
			B						43
			B	C					44
		C							45
		C							46
									47
									48
		C							49
					C				50
					C				51
					C				52
									53
					C				54
									55
									56
		C							57

Material for this section will be found in the companion book *Revise GCSE World History 1870–1992*

1 GEORGE III, 1760–82

1.1 The First 'English' Hanoverian

The first two Hanoverian Kings–George I (1714–27) and George II (1727–60)–had been born in the German state of Hanover. They knew little English, preferred Hanover to England and enjoyed being Kings of England mainly for the money which this gave them. George III's father, Frederick, Prince of Wales, had died in 1751 hated by and hating his own father, George II. The young George had been brought up by his mother, Augusta, the Princess of Wales, who had appointed the Scottish Marquess of Bute to be his tutor. (In ballads and pamphlets, Bute was portrayed as Augusta's lover). Both tutor and mother taught the Prince that the first Hanoverians had allowed the Whig politicians too much power. They urged him to 'be a king'. He was proud of the fact that, unlike the first two Georges, he was truly an Englishman.

THE GOVERNMENT OF BRITAIN, 1760

You will not understand the importance of George III's career unless you understand the way in which the country was governed.

The King had the right to:
▶ appoint and to dismiss Ministers, although he had to make sure that those he appointed had the support of the House of Commons (see below);
▶ lay down government policy, but he had to get Parliament to agree with his policies. Because George III believed that the first two Georges had handed too much over to the Whig politicians, one of his aims was to break the power of the Whigs; another was to get back for the Crown those powers which he thought it had lost between 1714 and 1760. It is important to note that no one argued against this, until his policies regarding America had so obviously failed and until he himself became mentally unstable.

The King's Ministers

Ministers were appointed from the Houses of Lords and Commons. Few Members of Parliament (MPs) were anxious to become Ministers or to hold office. Most, however, had a great interest in government policies, supporting those which they thought would benefit the country and the people who elected them to the Commons. The small number who were anxious to hold office tended to follow one of the important political figures–Walpole, Townshend, Pelham and Pitt–each of whom had his own small group of supporters. To form a successful government, such politicians had to win the support of other important men (and their followers) and then follow policies which would win the support of the majority of the disinterested MPs.

The House of Commons

This consisted of 558 MPs. About 100 were sons or relations of members of the House of Lords and would vote as their lordly relatives told them to. About 60 were in the Army or Navy, using their vote in the Commons to persuade a Minister to give them a promotion. Others sold their votes to Ministers in return for some reward–a title or honour, a job for a relative, a contract for their firm or a relative's firm, or sometimes for a simple money bribe. Walpole had said, 'Every man has his price' and the King's Ministers were usually able to pay that price.

MPs had been elected in the unreformed system (which was to be changed in 1832) (see unit 14). The electoral system was a corrupt one with many MPs being returned only by the owner of a borough. Others were returned by maybe two or three voters, and most were returned by voters who had been bribed or forced to vote as the neighbouring landowner or government agent told them to vote.

Political Parties did not exist as we understand them today when every Member of Parliament belongs to a party. There were small groups which believed that the King ought to have more power than he was allowed by the constitution; their opponents called them **Tories**–the slang term for Irish bandits. There was another and larger group which believed that Parliament ought to be at least as important as the King. The Tories called these **Whigs**–a slang term for Scottish bandits. But, as we have seen, most MPs were more interested in their career–their future as members of the Lords, or their job–than they were in politics. These so-called **Independent**, or **Country MPs** would usually vote for whichever Minister happened to be in power–provided they liked his policies.

GEORGE III's FIRST GOVERNMENT, 1760–62

When George III came to the throne, Britain was fighting a war against France–in Europe, in Canada, in India and in the West Indies. The government was led by William Pitt, who looked after the war, and by the Duke of Newcastle (Thomas Pelham), whose task was to get MPs to support government policy.

George III's former tutor, Bute, persuaded him that Newcastle and Pitt were the sort of Whig politicians who had taken power away from the first two Georges. He got himself appointed a Minister–equal in power to Pitt–and he had the support of most of the 45 Scottish MPs in the Commons and 16 Scottish Lords.

THE FALL OF NEWCASTLE AND PITT, 1762

By 1761 the war against France was going well for Britain–Wolfe had taken Quebec, Clive had defeated the French in India, Rodney and other Admirals had defeated the French in the West Indies and had captured several islands. But Pitt knew that Spain would not stand aside and watch this onward march of British power. He knew that she would join France to help her defeat Britain. He therefore proposed to attack Spain before she was ready to go to war.

Bute was against this. He and the King wanted to make peace as soon as they could, so that they could get on with the task of winning back those lost powers. Pitt argued against making peace until France was heavily defeated and until Britain's European ally, Frederick of Prussia, had agreed on a peace treaty. When the King insisted on an end to the war Pitt resigned and Bute took command. He stopped the supply of money going to Frederick–and Newcastle resigned in protest. Bute was now completely in charge.

1.2 John Wilkes and Bute

BUTE'S GOVERNMENT, 1762–63

Bute arranged a truce with France and in a magazine called *The Briton* he published the terms of the peace which he hoped to arrange with France. Many people agreed with him; traders wanted a chance to get on with trade without danger of attack by French ships, taxpayers were worried abut the cost of the war.

John Wilkes, MP for Aylesbury since 1757 and once a close friend of Bute, disagreed. In June 1762, in his magazine, *The North Briton* (a sly reference to the Scottish

Bute) Wilkes attacked the peace proposals. But the King and Bute, with the help of Henry Fox, got Parliament to agree to the Peace of Paris.

In December 1762 the Commons voted 319 to 65 in support of the King and the Peace.

Number 45 of *The North Briton*

When opening a new session of Parliament in April 1763, the King claimed that Frederick of Prussia was delighted with the Peace of Paris. Wilkes claimed that this was untrue and, in Number 45 of *The North Briton,* called the King and Bute (who must have written the King's speech) liars. We will see the importance of this in a moment, but here we have to notice that during April 1763 Bute was forced to resign—in spite of the fact that the King wanted him to be Chief Minister.

Because of the cost of the Seven Years War, the King had been forced to put up the taxes on land and on such things as cider. The higher land tax made him unpopular with the landowners and with many MPs: the increased taxes on goods made him unpopular with the mob, which did not have the vote but which could frighten those who did and could frighten MPs. Bute had a nervous breakdown in the face of the opposition inside and outside Parliament and was forced to resign.

GRENVILLE'S GOVERNMENT, 1763–65

George III asked Pitt to come back as Chief Minister, but he refused. Newcastle agreed to take office only if he had the right to appoint Whigs as his fellow-Ministers, but the King refused to agree to this. This forced the King to turn to another Whig, Grenville, and it was he who had to try to deal with the problem of the American colonies (unit 6) and with the problems caused by John Wilkes.

WILKES UNDER ATTACK

Wilkes and Bute had been friends and members of the Hell Fire Club, where they and other members gambled heavily, drank a great deal, swopped pornographic pictures and writings and thoroughly earned the name of hellrakers. When Bute became Chief Minister he put one member of the Club, the Earl of Sandwich, in charge of the Navy, but did not give Wilkes a place in the government. This was one reason for the appearance of *The North Briton.* When Number 45 appeared with its attack on the King and the Peace of Paris, Grenville was in power.

It was Grenville's government which issued a general warrant for the arrest of everyone connected with the magazine—printers, writers and publishers. Such warrants were legal under an Act of 1695 but few had been issued because it was agreed that they gave the authorities too much power. Almost anyone who criticised the government might be imprisoned under such a warrant.

WILKES AND LIBERTY

Wilkes was arrested and put into the Tower of London. In May 1763 the Lord Chief Justice, Pratt, discharged him, arguing that as an MP he ought to be free to criticise the government. On his release he demanded the return of papers which had been taken when his home was searched. When the government refused to hand them back, Wilkes took the Ministers to Court (December 1763) and the Lord Chief Justice awarded him the case, imposed damages on the government of £1000 and decided that general warrants were illegal. This was a major step in the battle for the liberty of the people and in 1766 Parliament passed an Act which repealed the Act of 1695.

GEORGE III AND WILKES

In November 1763 the King and Grenville persuaded MPs to vote that Number 45 of *The North Briton* was a piece of 'seditious libel' and that Wilkes could not claim parliamentary privilege for writing such an article. Wilkes realised that he would be arrested again, so he fled to Paris.

In January 1764, in his absence, Parliament voted to expel him from membership of the Commons.

In November 1764 his former friend, Sandwich, produced *An Essay on Woman,* which Wilkes had written for the enjoyment of his Hell Fire Club friends. The Courts declared that this was an obscene piece of pornography, and ordered the arrest of its author, Wilkes.

WILKES AND THE COMMONS

Wilkes stayed in Paris until February 1768, when all the fuss had died down. He came back for the Election in which he won the Middlesex seat. But he still feared that he might be arrested if he went back to the Commons. So he gave himself up in April 1768, refused to accept the bail offered and was, again, put into prison.

The London mob, which had enjoyed Wilkes's attacks on the King and Bute and had sniggered over the pornographic essay, rioted when it heard of his arrest. The government had no police force with which to control the crowd of about 20 000 which gathered outside the prison. The army had to be brought in and on 10th May five people were shot by Scottish soldiers trying to restore order. This 'St George's Field Massacre' only made the crowd even more angry.

In June, Wilkes was brought to Court where he was found guilty of issuing a seditious libel (Number 45 of *The North Briton*) and of writing and publishing an obscene piece (*An Essay on Woman*). He was fined £1000 and sentenced to 22 months in prison.

By this time Wilkes had been elected MP for Middlesex. The King persuaded the Commons (February 1769) to expel Wilkes from its membership. However, even while in prison, he was re-elected at the three elections held to find a new member. The King and Commons decided, after the fourth election, that Wilkes's defeated opponent, Luttrell, should be allowed to take his seat instead.

In April 1770 Wilkes was released from prison. While in prison he had been chosen by the London councillors to be an Alderman of the City. In this post he became involved in a new struggle with the King.

WILKES AND THE FREEDOM OF THE PRESS

For a long time it had been forbidden to publish reports of Parliamentary debates in newspapers. Some people ignored this ban and in 1771 the Commons sent messengers to the City of London to arrest two printers and publishers, Wheble and Thompson. These two men were brought before the City Aldermen-magistrates, one of whom was Wilkes. He and his fellow magistrates released the men, arguing that their arrest was a breach of the privileges of the City of London. The Lord Mayor also imprisoned the Commons' messenger for having issued a warrant for arrest without the permission of the City's magistrates.

The Commons then imprisoned the Lord Mayor and another Alderman. This led to rioting all over London and the mob cried again in favour of 'Wilkes and Liberty'. The final result of this squabble was that although it was still forbidden to report Parliamentary debates, no attempt was made ever again to interfere with the freedom of the Press.

In 1774 Wilkes was elected Lord Mayor of London and in the General Election of that year was again elected MP for Middlesex. He was allowed to take his seat, and although he supported the American colonists in their fight against the British government (unit 6) and helped the campaign for Parliamentary Reform (unit 14), he became an accepted member of the Commons. He rode out as an Alderman on belhalf of the government to put down the Gordon Riots (pp. 3, 27) and became an ardent supporter of the younger William Pitt (unit 7).

By then Wilkes he had won a place in history as the champion of liberty. His struggles put an end to general warrants, maintained the freedom of the Press and defended the rights of electors to have the man of their choice as their Member of Parliament.

1.3 Governments 1765–83

THE ROCKINGHAM GOVERNMENT, 1765–66

In following the career of Wilkes we have moved ahead of our study of George III's governments. By 1765 Grenville had roused opposition in the Commons because of his American policy (p. 16) and his inability to bring down taxes. He had also quarrelled with the King over the exclusion of the Dowager Princess of Wales from the list of a Regency Council which would be set up if the King's nervous breakdown made it impossible for him to play his part in the government. Grenville was forced to resign.

Lord Rockingham, another Whig Lord, had the support of the followers of the Duke of Newcastle and had his own supporters elected for estates which he owned in Yorkshire. He tried to win popularity by abolishing the hated cider tax and the unpopular general warrants. But like all George III's governments, this one fell because of the failure of its American policy (p. 16).

CHATHAM'S GOVERNMENT, 1766–68

William Pitt had refused to serve in the governments of Grenville and Rockingham. However, in August 1766 he accepted the King's invitation to lead the government. He made a mistake when he accepted the title of the Earl of Chatham, since this took him from the Commons, whose support was essential. He was also unlucky in that before the end of 1766 he was a very sick man, so that he did not really lead the government. But, again, it was because of his American policy (p. 16) that the government fell.

THE GRAFTON GOVERNMENT, 1768–70

Grafton, a former supporter of Chatham, became Chief Minister in 1768. He had to deal with the problem of Wilkes and of the American colonies. In neither case was the government successful and its fall in 1770 was no surprise.

LORD NORTH'S GOVERNMENT, 1770–82

Lord North had been a junior Minister in previous governments. He was 37 years old when he accepted the King's invitation to be Chief Minister. He had no large body of supporters, as had Chatham and Rockingham.

He had, however, the support of the many MPs who wanted to see the country with a settled government in which the King's policies might be put into practice. There were also a group of MPs who would support any government in return for a bribe of some sort—a job, a title, a contract or money. These two groups of MPs became known as **The King's Friends**, and it was on their support that North relied.

At first, North was a successful Minister. He quietly settled the long-running Wilkes affair. He lowered taxes, which made his government popular with the taxpayers. However, it also meant that there was less money for government spending on such items as the army and navy. The decline of the Navy was to have an important bearing on the outcome of the American War (p. 18).

North also seemed to have sorted out the problem of the government of India, by his Regulating Act of 1773 (p. 57).

But the government was less successful in three important matters:

▶ It failed to answer the demands made by MPs and others for a reform of the corrupt Parliamentary system.

▶ It failed to deal energetically with the **Gordon Riots** of June 1780. These riots had their origin in the **Catholic Relief Bill** which North pushed through Parliament in 1778 to make life a little easier for Catholics. Opposition to the proposals first appeared in Scotland and there was anti-government and anti-Catholic rioting in Edinburgh and Glasgow. In London, a **Protestant Association** was formed with the half-mad MP, Lord George Gordon, as its president. Gordon whipped up support among the London rabble against the new new law:

● because he hated North, whom he saw as a 'failed Prime Minister' after the disasters in America; and

● he was violently anti-Catholic.

The London mob followed Gordon not so much because it was opposed to relaxing laws against Catholics, but because of its anger at the economic and political effects of the American War. There was large-scale **unemployment** owing to the fall in trade with the warring colonies and there were countrywide demands for **parliamentary reform**, by people who hoped that a reformed Parliament would somehow make life better.

On 2nd June, Gordon led the mob to the Commons, bringing with them a petition for the repeal of the Relief Bill. Thousands of common people besieged Parliament, attacked members, pillaged Catholic chapels, burned private homes, demolished Newgate prison freeing prisoners, and tried to storm the Bank of England. The London magistrates were afraid to take action, fearing that there might be a repetition of the 'St George's Field Massacre' (p. 2). For a week the mob roamed freely throughout the City of London. In the end it was the King who ordered troops into the City on 9th June. Cavalry charged, while the infantry put the mob to flight, leaving London looking 'like a city put to fire and sword'.

▶ The government failed to cope with the American problem (p. 16). The failure to win the War led to increased criticism from the Opposition, while North's wish to make peace with the American rebels led the King to demand his resignation.

AFTER NORTH

In December 1783 William Pitt the Younger, son of Chatham, formed a government. But in the 22 months between the fall of North and the coming to power of Pitt there had been three short-lived governments. We will examine their records on pp. 18–19.

Unit 1 Summary

▶ How was Britain governed in the eighteenth century?
▶ What was 'rotten' about the Parliamentary system? (unit 14 also).
▶ How far, if at all, did George III try to 'turn back the clock'?
▶ The importance of the career of John Wilkes.
▶ Why did Lord North's government (1770–1782) (i) last so long; (ii) fall from power?

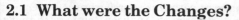
2.1 What were the Changes?

In 1700 there were about 5½ million people living in England and Wales; by 1911 there were about 36 million; today there are about 56 million.

In 1700 most of the people worked in farming and lived in small villages. Today most people live in large towns. There has been a change in the distribution of the population.

WHAT ARE THE QUESTIONS TO BE STUDIED?

▶ When did the population start to grow rapidly?

▶ Why did this great change take place?

▶ Why did the population of some areas grow more rapidly than did the population of other areas?

▶ What were the main results of the changes in:

● the growth population;

● the change in distribution?

2.2 Population Figures, 1700

▶ **Size**: there were about 5½ million people in England and Wales.

▶ **Change in size**: this depends on the rate of natural increase, that is, the difference between birth rates and death rates:

● **Birth rates**: as in most agricultural countries, the annual birth rate in England and Wales before the Industrial Revolution was somewhere between 30 and 40 births for every 1000 of the population.

▶ **Death rates**: these tended to be slightly lower that birth rates – generally being between 25 and 35 per 1000.

● So, in the predominantly agricultural country, the population tended to grow at an **annual rate** of between one half and 1 per cent a year.

▶ **Interference with growth**: pre-industrial societies often suffered sudden and very high death rates. These might have been cause by:

● an epidemic, such as the Black Death of the fourteenth century or the Great Plague of the 1660s;

● wars, such as the Civil Wars of the twelfth century when King Stephen fought Queen Matilda, and the Wars of the Roses of the fifteenth century when the Yorkists fought the Lancastrians;

● a succession of harvest failures, which could double or treble the normal death rate. Harvest failure often led to the onset and spread of diseases as people moved in search of food.

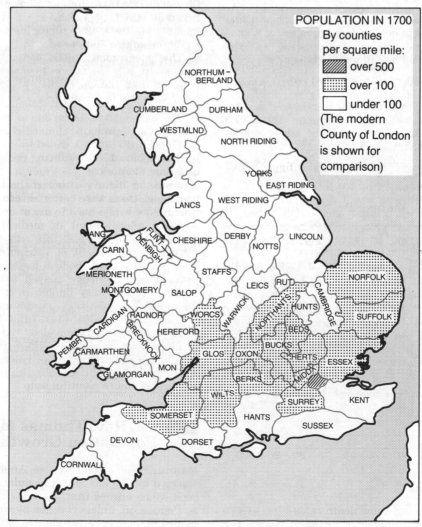

Fig. 2.2 Population distribution in England and Wales in 1700

THE DISTRIBUTION OF THE POPULATION, 1700

Where did the people live?

Look at fig 2.2. This shows that the most heavily populated regions were in the South, the South-West and the East Anglian region.

But you should take care; Middlesex (in 1700) had the sort of population distribution that you would find in modern Devon; most of the people lived in small villages.

What caused this population distribution?

▶ **Agriculture**: England and Wales were underdeveloped and agricultural countries. About 90 per cent of the people had their living in farming and tended to live in the most fertile areas, near rivers (such as the Severn) and near markets (such as London, Norwich and Bristol) where they could sell their produce.

▶ **The woollen industry** was Britain's main industry. People bred large flocks of sheep in the Cotswolds region, in East Anglia and in the West Riding of Yorkshire. Here, too, there developed the centres for the marketing of wool and cloth.

▶ Ports developed in the South and in East Anglia to cater for trade with, particularly, Europe, although London, Bristol and Liverpool grew to cater for trade with North America and the West Indies. But take care; in 1700, the population of London was only about 500,000, that of Bristol about 30,000 and that of Liverpool about 20,000.

■ 2.3 The Increase in Population, 1700–1801

John Rickman (1771–1840) was a government official appointed to prepare the first official census (1801). As preparation for that census, he produced estimates of changes in population since 1700 (see table 2.3).

Table 2.3 Population of England and Wales

1700	5,475,000	1730	5,796,000	1770	7,428,000
1710	5,240,000	1740	6,064,000	1780	7,953,000
1720	5,565,000	1759	6,467,000	1790	8,675,000

1801 Census Figures: 8,893,000

Gregory King (1648–1712) was a statistician and government official who, in 1695, drew up an estimate of the size of the population of England and Wales. His figures, and Rickman's estimates for the eighteenth century, were based on:

▶ **Hearth-tax returns**: the problem with these is that

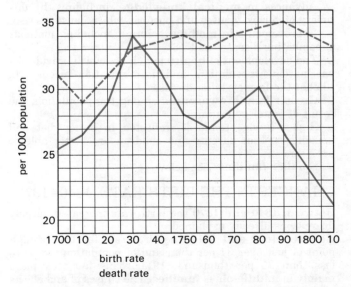

birth rate
death rate

Fig. 2.3 Changes in the birth and death rates 1700–1800. The figures relate to the number of births or deaths per 100 of the population. Examiners expect an understanding of the reasons for the changes illustrated by the graph.

they are unreliable:
● some people avoided the tax by telling lies about the size of their homes and families;
● local officers often cheated to please relations and friends.

▶ **Parish registers** of baptisms, burials and marriages. The weaknesses with this source were:
● they only referred to Anglican services, so that they do not include the births, marriages and deaths of Non-conformists.
● many Anglican records were incomplete; some had been destroyed (fires, floods, carelessness), others were illegible.

Modern historians have tried to add to our knowledge by studies of particular districts and by comparing these with the figures produced by Rickman for these districts. They then amend Rickman's overall figures in the light of their own detailed study. The weakness of this is that we have no guarantee that a change in one district was matched by changes elsewhere.

Conclusions that we can make, in the light of present knowledge, are that:
▶ the population did increase;
▶ we do not know, definitely, by how much.

BIRTH RATE AND DEATH RATES,

Look at fig. 2.3. Remember that these are only estimates, based on the work of Rickman and modern historians. The figures show that, while there were small changes in the birth rate, there was a more important change in the death rate.

Birth rate changes

▶ **Good harvests** (1730–60). This led to increased demand for workers and to higher wages, which encouraged people to marry.
▶ **Earlier marriages.** More women married while they were of child-bearing age.

Death rate changes

▶ The unexplained disappearance of the plague-carrying black rat which had carried the germ of the Great Plague, bubonic plague and other virulent epidemics.
▶ The decline of malaria, due to domestic hygiene, swamp drainage and, perhaps, climatic changes.
▶ **Good harvests** which led to:
● higher incomes for working people;
● falling food prices;
● a rise in dietary standards, which meant that child-bearing mothers were better able to bring up their children, over half of whom used to die at or soon after childbirth.
▶ Some improvement in medical knowledge, the most important of which was the work of Edward Jenner who discovered the benefit of vaccination as a guard against smallpox. However, medical historians argue that changes in medical knowledge played little part in population changes; it was very limited in its scope and even more limited in its application to ordinary people.

The changes in agriculture (unit 3) and transport (unit 4) and industry (unit 5) provided:
▶ more work for skilled workers and farm workers;
▶ a better distribution of food along the canals;
▶ cheaper, washable clothing, as cotton replaced linen;
▶ cheaper, more plentiful soap.

■ 2.4 Rev. Thomas Malthus and Population Growth

Malthus (1766–1834) was an Anglican vicar who became alarmed by the increase in population. In 1798 he wrote a book which argued that:
▶ Population, unless checked by wars, famines or plagues, tended to increase at geometric rates (1-2-4-8 or 1-3-9-27).
▶ Food output, even in favourable circumstances, increased only in arithmetic proportions (1-2-3-4 and so on).

▶ Life would always be a desperate struggle for survival. His work was welcomed by:

▶ Employers, who used it to justify the long hours and harsh conditions in which their employees worked (unit 17)

▶ Taxpayers opposed to the Speenhamland system (unit 15), who argued that a generous poor law system helped keep the poor alive (so that they could have children). They wanted a harsher system – and presumably, the deaths of potential parents.

Malthus was proved wrong, at least in the short run. British farmers responded to the growth in population by making better use of their land (units 3 and 27), and the increased population provided the workforce for British factories which produced a greater quantity of goods of ever-increasing quality at falling prices. These factory-produced goods led to:

▶ increased incomes for the increasing population;

▶ increased exports to pay for imported food – which was even cheaper than British-produced food (unit 27).

2.5 Population Changes, 1800–1986

THE CONTINUED GROWTH OF POPULATION, 1800–1911

Censuses were taken every ten years starting in 1801.

Table 2.5 The changes in the population of Great Britain

1801	11.9 million	1841	20.2 million	1881	31.0 million
1811	13.4 million	1851	22.3 million	1891	34.3 million
1821	15.5 million	1861	24.5 million	1901	38.2 million
1831	17.8 million	1871	27.4 million	1911	42.1 million

You should notice that the increase between 1811 and 1821 (2.1 million) was, proportionately, a greater increase than that which took place between 1891 and 1901 (3.9 million). **The rate of increase had slowed down** – we will see why later on.

Changes in the death rate (fig. 2.5A) were the result of:

▶ **Public water supplies** replacing insanitary well-water in towns (unit 18).

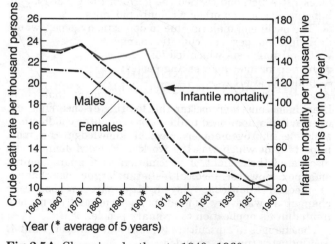

Fig 2.5A Changing death rate 1840–1960

▶ Improvements in **midwifery** which halved infant death rate by 1830.

▶ **Public health services** taken over by town councils after the Municipal Reform Act, 1835 (unit 15) and the first Public Health Act of 1848 (unit 18). Drainage, paving, refuse collection and slum clearance became widespread.

▶ **Better diet,** in quantity, quality and variety, with the import of foreign food (unit 27).

▶ **Cheap and washable clothing.**

▶ **Medical improvements** (unit 18).

INFANT MORTALITY

In 1730, over half the children died before reaching the age of two years.

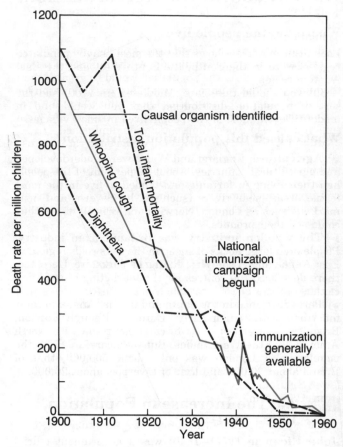

Fig. 2.5B Infant mortality 1900–60

In 1842, a Report by Edwin Chadwick showed that infant mortality was still very high (unit 18).

In 1901, about 20 per cent of children died before they were five years of age. This was a great improvement on the figures for 1730 and 1842. But, in 1901, thousands of children died every year from 'killer diseases' such as enteric fever, measles, scarlet fever, whooping cough and diphtheria. The graph (fig. 2.5B) shows the sharp decline in infant deaths from two diseases. Similar graphs could be drawn to show falls in deaths from scarlet fever, measles and other diseases.

The causes of these sharp falls

▶ Advances in **medical knowledge,** including the discovery of germs, viruses and bacteria which cause disease.

▶ Improvements in **medical science**, including methods of combating disease (unit 18).

▶ The development of **health services**, which provide the vaccination, inoculation and immunization needed to combat the former 'killer diseases'.

▶ Greater **health awareness** among the population, the result of better education.

● Higher living standards, reflected in better diet and housing, so that parents and children are better able to fight illness.

▶ **Smaller families** – see below.

CHANGES IN THE BIRTH RATE, 1840–1970

Between 1840 and 1870 the birth rate increased, largely for reasons already explained.

Between 1870 and 1914, the birth rate fell from a high point of just over 34 per thousand of population (1871) to less than 25 per thousand (1911). This fall took place mainly in **middle-class families.** The causes of and effects of this fall are explained in unit 41.

Between 1920 and 1939 there was a further fall in the birth rate, from about 26 per thousand (1920) to about 15

per thousand (1930). The causes and effects of this fall are studied in unit 41. The fall in the birth rate between 1920 and 1939 was so great that there were fears that the population of Great Britain would:

▶ decline, since deaths would exceed births;
▶ becoming an ageing population, as the number of people in the older section of the population would be greater than the number in the younger section. This was one reason for the introduction of Family Allowances (unit 51).

Between 1945 and 1965, there was a rise in the birth rate and fears of a declining population diminished.

Since 1970, there has been a fall in the birth rate because of:

▶ greater knowledge of, and availability of, contraception;
▶ easier access to legal abortion,
▶ the continued ambition of more women to have a career;
▶ economic recession, which makes it more difficult for families to bring up children.

■ 2.6 Changing Family Size ■

The fall in the birth rate which began in the 1870s and which spread to the working classes in the 1920s, is reflected in the changing size of families. Figure 2.6 shows that:

▶ in 1870–9, some 611 families per thousand had five or more children;
▶ in 1900–9, some 725 families per thousand had four or fewer children;
▶ in 1925, some 667 families per thousand had two or fewer children.

The effects of this fall in family size are studied in unit 41.

■ 2.7 The Changing Distribution of the Increased Population

Look again at fig. 2.2 and remind yourself of where the majority of people lived before the Industrial Revolution. Now look at fig. 2.7A, which shows the distribution of the population in 1911. You will see that, leaving London aside, the heavily populated areas lie to the north of a line from Bristol to the Wash.

You will know, if you have done geography, or if you have studied unit 5 and unit 18, that these heavily populated regions lie on the coalfields, the centres of industrial development in the nineteenth century.

This growth is reflected in fig. 2.7B where you will see how some old towns (e.g. Bath) hardly grew at all, how some

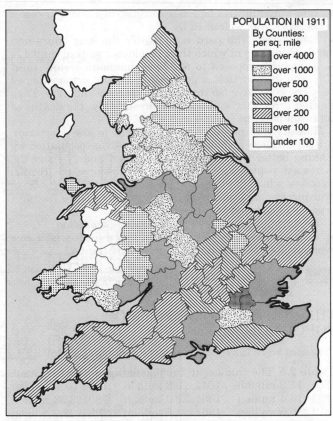

Fig. 2.7A Population distribution in England and Wales in 1911

(e.g. Nottingham) grew only lately and how some (e.g. Liverpool, Birmingham and Manchester) grew very rapidly.

The problems connected with this rapid urban development are examined in:

▶ units 14 and 38, where we study political effects;
▶ units 15, 16 and 17, where we study some social effects;
▶ units 15 and 18, where we study the growth of local government;
▶ unit 20, where we study the effect of the growth of an important industrial middle class.

SOME RECENT CHANGES IN THE DISTRIBUTION OF POPULATION, 1920–86

There has been a drift back to the South and South-East, for reasons explained in unit 46.

In the 1930s the government became alarmed at the

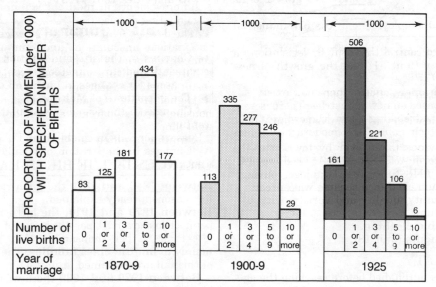

Fig. 2.6 Changes in family size 1870–1925

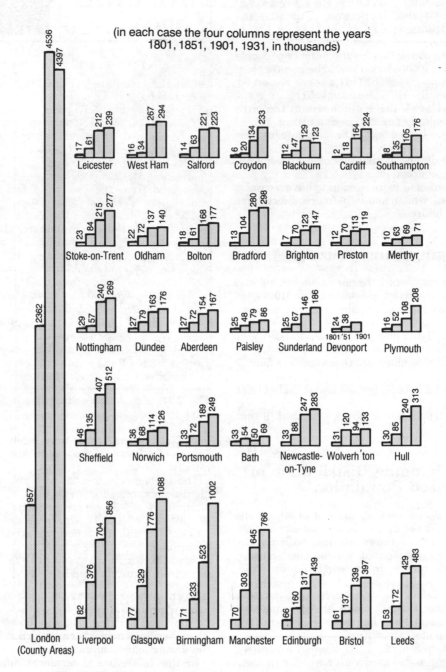

(in each case the four columns represent the years
1801, 1851, 1901, 1931, in thousands)

Fig. 2.7B The growth of major towns and cities 1801–1931

effect of this drift on unemployment in the old, industrial areas.

Efforts were made to control this drift by legislation on the location of industry (unit 51) and the growth of new towns (unit 52).

But, in spite of government efforts, there now exist:

▶ Prosperous areas, based on new industries. There is a so-called 'silicon valley', stretching from somewhere near London, to Bristol, which houses the modern electronics industries.

▶ Depressed areas, based on the declining industries such as shipbuilding, steel, textiles and coal.

Unit 2 Summary

▶ Changes in the size and location of population in the eighteenth and early nineteenth centuries (see 2.2 also).
▶ Reasons for changes in birth and death rates.
▶ The importance of Malthus.
▶ Changes in the size of the population in the nineteenth century.
  Reasons for falls in the birth and death rates since 1870.
▶ Changes in the location of population in the twentieth century.

3 THE AGRICULTURAL REVOLUTION, 1760–1820

3.1 Its Causes

There was an increased demand for food and from the growing population. Even before this, falling prices – which were the result of very good harvests – had forced some farmers to look for ways of improving their methods, so as to cut their costs and increase the productivity of their land.

After 1760, when the rise in population began to have an effect on the demand for food, there was a steady rise in food prices. This made the farmers anxious to produce as much as they could to get the benefits from higher prices.

Many of the older landowners sold off all or parts of their large estates to merchants and other successful businessmen who wanted country estates as a sign that they were now as important as the landowners. These new owners had made their money in commerce; they brought the habit of money-making to the countryside and looked for new and profit-making methods.

There was the emergence of new ideas about farming. Some of these, such as the use of root crops, came from Holland. Others, such as new ideas on stockbreeding, were the result of a growth in scientific knowledge.

THE OPEN FIELDS AND LARGE COMMONS

In 1700, throughout the Midlands and eastern England, each village or estate had three main fields. Each farmer and tenant farmer had a strip or a number of strips in each of these fields. In this way, everyone shared in the good land and the poor, in the land which was well watered and that which was, for example, stony. But the system was very wasteful:

▶ Room had to be left between each strip so that ploughing teams could turn. This meant that a great deal of land was unused.

▶ There were no hedges around the fields, so that animals could wander freely, eating crops and otherwise doing damage.

▶ Every farmer was expected to follow tradition in what he grew in his different strips. No one was encouraged or, in some places, even allowed, to experiment with a new crop which might have improved the quality of his land.

▶ Because of the lack of knowledge about fertilizers, one of the three great fields had to be allowed to lie unused (or fallow) every year. This meant that one-third of the land was unproductive. Perhaps the most serious defect in the old system of farming was the existence of the common lands. Each village had its common, which was often as much as 4000 acres in size, or about the size of 40 average farms today. Here were the woods and forests, the grazing land for animals, the fruit bushes and rabbits – a source of food for village people. But, for the business-minded owners, here were huge areas of land which could be ploughed up and made to produce food – and profit.

3.2 Enclosures

From about 1760 onwards, a movement grew up which supported the idea of turning the separate strips into compact holdings, each enclosed behind its own hedge. Those who led the movement believed that it would save time and land. They also wanted to divide up the commons so that these too might become part of compact and enclosed farms. Sometimes such enclosures were carried out by agreement between the various people concerned. However, if the more forward-looking landowners could not persuade the less well-off to agree to a change, then they had to go to Parliament and get an Enclosure Act. This cost about £6000. But before the Act could be passed, certain steps had to be taken:

▶ Three-quarters of the owners of the land involved had to agree to the enclosure. If only two or three people owned the land concerned, then such agreement might not be too difficult to achieve.

▶ For three Sundays a notice had to be put on the Church door telling the other farmers – mostly tenants who rented their land from the owners – about the proposals. Sometimes there were riots and notices were pulled down by angry people who feared the change.

▶ Then the proposals, in the form of a Parliamentary Bill, were presented to a Committee of the House of Commons which heard evidence for and against them. The poor could not afford to go to London to give evidence, so generally the Committee only heard from the rich owners.

▶ When the Committee was satisfied, the Bill went to the Houses of Parliament and, in time, became an Act.

▶ Parliament then appointed a number (between three and seven) of Commissioners to go to the village, map out the land, check each person's claims to a part of it, divide it up and settle all the arguments about fencing, pasture and ownership of the woods. Between 1760 and 1793, 1355 Enclosure Acts were passed and another 1934 were passed between 1793 and 1815. The demand for Private Acts became so great that Parliament passed a General Enclosure Act in 1801 and thousands of enclosures took place under its terms.

LOSERS AND GAINERS

Many tenant farmers lost as a result of the enclosures because:

▶ Some could not prove to the Commissioners that they had any legal claim to their strips. These customary tenants had merely inherited their family's traditional right to farm certain strips. Having no legal documents to prove their rights (such as those held by freeholders and copy leaseholders) they lost everything.

▶ Some, who got a compact holding, found that they could not afford their share of the costs of the Act and the cost of fencing and hedging. These often sold their small farm (if they were freeholders) or handed it back to the owner (if they were leaseholders).

▶ Some less efficient farmers found, in time, that they could not produce food at the prices charged by the more efficient and larger farmers. They, too, were driven out of business.

But the main losers were the many who had depended on the commons – for firewood, fruits and nuts, food for pigs and other animals and, in the case of the cottars (who lived in squalid huts on the edges of commons) the right to grow crops on a small patch of land. The loss of the commons affected almost everyone except the more prosperous farmers.

So while the British people gained from a larger food supply of a more varied sort, many villagers suffered. Some remained behind to become labourers – breaking up the newly-enclosed commons, building fences or putting in the hedges. Others left the countryside and went to find work in the growing industrial towns.

3.3 The New Farming

Most enclosures took place in eastern England and it was here that the new system of farming was seen at its best. For this reason it often became known as the Norfolk System, while one of its best examples was found on the estates of Lord 'Turnip' Townshend, brother-in-law of Prime Minister Walpole and himself a prominent politician. The Norfolk System consisted of:

▶ Granting tenants a long lease of, say, 21 years, so that they might be encouraged to do the draining, hedging and other work, knowing that they would share in the prosperity of their enclosed farms.

▶ Changing to a four-field system instead of the old three-field. Each year a different crop was grown in each field. On newly-ploughed common, turnips or some other root crop would be sown. These root crops helped to break up the land and were left in the ground where, during the winter, they were eaten by sheep or cattle, whose manure helped to make the ground more fertile. Then in Year 2 a barley crop would be sown, followed in Year 3 by a clover or grass crop which restored the soil and also provided winter food for animals. In Year 4 wheat was grown to provide the farmer with a second cash crop (after barley).

▶ Building the new roads which would be needed to carry the larger crops to market more efficiently than had been done before.

You can imagine that the Norfolk System cost a great deal of money and needed people with a progressive view. Not everyone was prepared to be so adventurous.

NEW MACHINERY

Several new machines were produced in the eighteenth century, including the new ploughs such as the Rotherham plough, reapers and threshing machines. Two important machines were invented by Jethro Tull, a Berkshire farmer, best remembered for his seed drill invented in 1701 and his horse-drawn hoe, which he described in a book published in 1731. But, as with the Norfolk System, only the richer and more venturesome farmers used these machines.

STOCK BREEDING

The new root crops (turnips, swedes and mangels), as well as the new grass crops (clover and rye), provided a great supply of winter food for animals. This meant that fewer animals had to be killed off in the autumn than had previously been the case. There was, therefore, a greater supply of fresh meat available throughout the year, and people's health benefited from this.

With the improved animal-food supply, some people began to experiment with scientific stockbreeding. Farmers mated healthy male animals with healthy female ones to improve the quality of their stock—and so the supply of meat. Robert Bakewell had great success with his New Leicester sheep and his Dishley long-horn cattle. The Earl of Leicester, better known as Thomas Coke of Holkham Hall, bred strong strains of Southdown sheep. The Colling brothers were other notable stockbreeders at the time. Such men rented out their bigger animals and so helped improve the strains of other farmers' stock.

SPREADING THE NEWS

There were three main ways in which news of the new techniques reached farmers in other parts of the country:

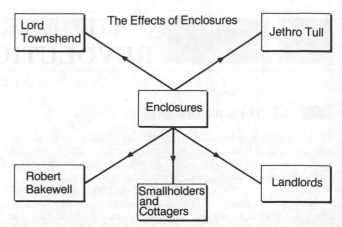

Fig. 3.3 The effect of enclosures. Examiners expect an understanding of the relationship, and an ability to explain the causes and effects of enclosure.

▶ Some large landowners held demonstrations on their estates. The Bedfords at Woburn held an annual sheep-shearing event which attracted thousands of visitors who were able to see the evidence of the new breeding system and also hear speakers explaining the new farming.

▶ In many areas, local agricultural societies were formed, which produced pamphlets outlining the new methods. Larger societies organized shows such as the Bath and West (1777) where the visiting farmer could hear about the new methods and see evidence of their success.

▶ There was royal encouragement for such new farming, with George III boasting of his title of 'Farmer George' in his model farm at Windsor. But above all, perhaps, it was the writings of Arthur Young which did most to spread the good news. Young had failed as a farmer, but could see the benefits of the new system. He travelled thousands of miles visiting successful farmers; he wrote at great length about what he saw and so helped to spread the knowledge which otherwise might have remained localized in Norfolk. It was fitting that he became the first Secretary of the Board of Agriculture, when it was set up in 1793.

▨ 3.4 Later Developments ▨

▶ **1793–1815**: see unit 9.2 and fig. 9.2;
▶ **1815–30**: see unit 11.1;
▶ **the Corn Laws**: see unit 11.3;
▶ **Huskisson and the Corn Laws**: see unit 12.2;
▶ **the Anti-Corn Law League**: see unit 20;
▶ **1846–1914**: see unit 27.

▨ Unit 3 Summary ▨

▶ The causes of the eighteenth-century agricultural revolution.

▶ The good and bad effects of enclosures.

▶ The work of the agricultural pioneers, e.g. Tull, Townshend, Bakewell, Coke and Young.

4 THE TRANSPORT REVOLUTION, 1760–1820

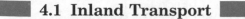

4.1 Inland Transport

Most goods were carred either on horse-back or in horse-drawn waggons. Packhorses were used to carry coal, wool, clay and other products along rough roads where waggons could not go. Waggons pulled by two, four or more horses carried china, cloth, iron and other goods along what roads there were. The slow and difficult movement of goods was hardly suitable even for a pre-industrial country. Carts and waggons often overturned, destroying fragile articles and damaging others. It is not surprising that many people used the sea, rivers and man-made canals instead of the roads (see below).

4.2 The Roads

By 1700 little had been added to the road system left by the Romans. In theory, every parish was supposed to maintain its roads. In practice, the parish authorities were unwilling to force people to work on the roads which, in any case, were mostly used by strangers and not by parishioners.

TURNPIKE TRUSTS

In the late seventeenth and eighteenth centuries the government handed the task of road maintenance and building to private companies known as turnpike trusts (in the USA people still refer to main roads as turnpikes).

Such trusts employed men to build and maintain roads, put toll-gates at various stages along the road and charged road users as they went through. The trusts only built roads along which many people, waggons or animals were likely to pass. They built a series of main roads which helped Britain's industrial development in a small way.

THE BUILDERS

The turnpike trusts employed road engineers to plan and supervise the building of their roads. The most important of these were:
▶ **John Metcalf** (1717–1810), also known as Blind Jack of Knaresborough. He was engineer for the Harrogate-Boroughbridge Trust in 1763. Over the next 30 years he built roads in Yorkshire, Lancashire, Cheshire and Derbyshire. He made his men dig deep ditches on either side of the proposed roadway, putting the earth on to the roadway where it was beaten down and covered with stones. He piled earth and stones higher at the centre of the road so that the rainwater could drain away into the ditches.
▶ **Thomas Telford** (1757–1834) was a stone mason who became the first great civil engineer, building roads, canals and bridges such as the Menai Bridge which carries the road from the mainland to Anglesey. He also built viaducts to carry roads and aqueducts to carry his canals across valleys.

Telford was a better engineer than Metcalf. He planned his roads so that there was never a steep climb; he laid drains under the foundations to carry off the rainwater. He built a raised, curved foundation on which he put carefully cut stones, narrower at the top that the bottom. The spaces between these stones were packed with smaller stones. Over this base he laid small broken stones to a depth of six inches. Then he laid a final layer of gravel about one inch thick. Telford's roads became noted for their firm, dry surfaces, which rarely needed repairing.
▶ **John Rennie** (1761–1821) was another road engineer, now best remembered for his bridges across the Thames; Waterloo (demolished in 1937), London (demolished in the 1970s) and Southwark, which is still in use.

▶ **John Macadam** (1756–1836) used some of Metcalf's ideas (making a curved surface) and some of Telford's (foundations of stone). But he also had his own idea for a surface of very small stones which became bound together by the mixture of rain and dust and the pressure from traffic. Today we commemorate his name in 'tarmac' or 'macadamized' roads.

STAGE COACHES

The improvement in the main roads led to the development of new coaches in which the Royal Mail and rich passengers travelled between main towns. Such journeys were broken into stages, marked by coaching inns where passengers ate and stayed overnight, hence the name 'stage coach'.

4.3 Water Transport

Even the best road system could not have carried the traffic created by industrialization and the growth of towns. In the past, people had used the navigable rivers and the sea as a way of carrying goods. Wedgwood's china clay came from Cornwall in coastal vessels as far as Liverpool and then by pack horses from there. Some people had made rivers more navigable by building 'by-passes' (or canals) around such obstacles as waterfalls.

THE BRIDGEWATER CANAL

The first important canal was built for the Duke of Bridgewater, who owned coal mines at Worsley about ten miles from Manchester. He wanted a cheap, quick way of getting the coal into the growing town. He employed a millwright, James Brindley, to build this canal.

Brindley had to design a series of tunnels to carry the canal through hills, a massive aqueduct to take it across the River Irwell, lock gates to carry it up and down slopes and a system of 'puddling' the bottom with heavy clay to stop the water draining away.

The canal was a great success. The price of coal in Manchester fell from 60p a ton to 30p, so industrialists and other coal-consumers gained. The Duke, who sold his coal and carried other people's goods on his canal, became even richer and other industrialists were encouraged to build canals.

Josiah Wedgwood financed the building of a canal from Liverpool to the Potteries. Before long this was linked with Bridgewater's canal. With about 20 others being built every year from 1780 to 1810, the industrial Midlands, Lancashire and Yorkshire were soon covered with a network of canals.

Most of these canals were built by joint stock companies in which people joined together to provide the money needed for the building of the canal. The stockholders, or shareholders, shared the profits although many companies in the south made little profit.

THE BENEFITS OF THE CANAL SYSTEM

It provided a cheap method of carrying:
▶ coal from mines to ports and towns;
▶ raw materials to industrial towns;
▶ finished articles to markets and ports;
▶ food and other consumer goods to growing towns;
▶ fertilizers and machinery to farming districts;
▶ building materials needed for the expansion of towns.

DEFECTS OF THE SYSTEM

The canal system was a major factor in the early industrial expansion which took place between 1760 and 1830. But

when men had learned how to build and use railways (unit 26), the canals became much less used. The main defects from which the canal system suffered were:
▶ Each company had its own ideas about width and depth. This made it difficult to organize through-traffic, which was what railways quickly achieved with their common gauge.
▶ Factory owners and industrialists built along the canal banks, which made it difficult and expensive to consider widening them, when this proved essential if they were to compete with railways.
▶ Railway companies often bought up a link in the canal chain in an area, and then let that link fall into disrepair, or imposed such high charges that people refused to use it. In this way the whole chain of canals became less profitable and less used.

It is significant that historians choose to use the date 1830 as one which marks a major stage in industrial development. This was the year in which the Liverpool-Manchester railway was opened, the first major railway in the world. Britain had entered into a new world, one dominated by the railway.

4.4 Later Developments

▶ **Eighteenth-century railways**: see unit 26.1
▶ **Railway development, 1800–70**: see unit 26.1–4.
▶ **Railway mania in the 1840s**: see unit 26.2.
▶ **Nineteenth-century steamshipping**: see unit 26.5.

Unit 4 Summary

▶ The reasons for and effects of the building of better roads and canals.
▶ The work of the builders and navigators.

---

5 THE INDUSTRIAL REVOLUTION, 1760–1860

5.1 Why did it take place in Great Britain?

WAR

In 1760 Great Britain was fighting a war against France; her ally was Prussia, which was fighting against France's ally, Austria. Great Britain was not, at that time, the strongest or richest country in Europe. But by 1830 she was both the richest and the strongest because only she had gone through the first stages of the Industrial Revolution.

Why did it take place in Great Britain?

By winning India, Canada and more islands in the West Indies in the war, which ended in 1763, Great Britain increased the markets for British goods. At the same time there was an increased demand for goods from the growing population at home. The old system of production could not meet that demand and had to change.

SOCIAL CONDITIONS

In Great Britain (but not, for example, in France or Italy) **people were free to experiment** without being afraid of being arrested for breaking some law or other. This gave scientists a chance to get on with their work and the early inventors a chance to produce their new machines.

There were many **rich people** in Britain who had become used to investing their money – in their own land (unit 3), in government stocks and in overseas trading companies. When industrialists wanted money to build a new factory or new machinery, there were plenty of people in Britain who understood the benefits of such investment and who were prepared to lend the money. These included:
▶ **The landowning aristocracy** with high incomes from their estates. The Earls of Durham, the Marquesses of Londonderry and of Bute were among those who provided industrial capital for development in the North-East and in South Wales.
▶ **Rich farmers** with increasing incomes from their improved farms (unit 3). Having seen the benefit of investing capital in their own land, they were prepared to become lenders to industrialists.

▶ **Trading merchants** who made profits from overseas trade. In particular there were those who were involved in trade with the East Indies, the West Indies and, above all, the very profitable slave trade (unit 10).

The influence of Puritanism and Calvinism

Religious belief was an important factor in the acquisition of capital and in industrial development. Indulgence in worldly pleasures was condemned and Puritans, Calvinists, Quakers, Methodists and other Noncomformists did not spend their money on grand houses, splendid clothes or luxurious living. This self-denial helped them save money, which was then available for industrial investment. At the same time their religious beliefs taught them that God would approve of success in business, so that they were almost forced to try to succeed.

British banks

Towards the end of the seventeenth century banks had developed to handle the financial business of the land-owning aristocracy, rich farmers and merchants. They were important channels along which capital could flow from those who were ready to invest it (for example in agricultural East Anglia) to those who wanted to borrow the money (in the industrial North-West, for example).

In France, the majority of people 'belonged' to estate owners and were not free to leave to find work elsewhere. In Germany there were over 300 separate small states, each with its own government, trade laws and import duties. This made internal trade a very difficult and expensive affair. In Great Britain people and goods could move freely all over the country.

Great Britain was fortunate in that she had many of the raw materials needed for the Industrial Revolution – coal and iron for example – or could get them from her colonies. Other countries did not have these benefits (fig. 5.2).

5.2 Traditional Industries

THE PRE-INDUSTRIAL IRON INDUSTRY

There had been an iron industry in Britain for many centuries. The ore was smelted in furnaces heated by charcoal got from burning the trees of the forests which once covered the country. This explains why the industry was located in the Weald of Kent and the Forest of Dean.

The Darby family

The iron industry faced a number of problems:
► Charcoal was becoming scarcer and more expensive, which meant it was cheaper to import iron from Sweden than to make it here.
► The furnaces were very small so that they could be pulled down and rebuilt when people moved to a new source of charcoal. It was the Darby family of Coalbrookdale who changed the nature of the iron industry by:
● the discovery in 1709 that while coal could not be used as a furnace fuel, coke could. This meant that the industry could now be located on the coal fields where, fortunately, there was also a supply of iron-ore;
● the building of the first iron bridge at Coalbrookdale (1777) which showed that there were more uses for the product than man had thought of before.

Henry Cort and wrought iron

The Darby family and other ironmasters produced pig iron (so called because the molten metal ran into moulds called pigs) or cast iron which, though strong, was brittle and easily broken. The more refined and purer wrought iron could not be made with coke furnaces until Henry Cort developed his puddling process. In a coke-fired reverberatory furnace he extracted the carbon from the pig iron and produced a purer iron.

Other people invented new methods of rolling the hot iron into bars and saved time and fuel by using big mechanical hammers.

Blast furnaces

In the older iron foundries, and in those where Darby and Cort made their discoveries, water-wheels were used to drive the bellows which helped create the great heat needed in the blast furnaces. The invention of the rotary steam-engine in 1783 provided a new way of driving the bellows. It also meant that iron-masters could now build their plants away from the riversides. This helped complete the shift of the industry from its old centres to the coalfields of Scotland, Yorkshire and South Wales.

COAL

The coal industry was another old industry. But the demand for coal in the new iron industry, as well as in the textile industry after the invention of the steam-driven machinery, led to many changes in this expanding industry.

Men had to go deeper down to get coal. This exposed them to danger from flooding and created the need for more efficient steam pumps to get the water out.

In the deeper mines there was also increasing danger from the explosive gas 'fire-damp'. This exploded when it came into contact with the candles stuck into miners' hats. The invention of Sir Humphrey Davy's safety lamp meant that men could work without danger in the deeper mines.

New and stronger wire ropes were produced to get the coal up from the deeper mines.

THE PRE-INDUSTRIAL TEXTILE INDUSTRY

It may seem strange to start the study of the Industrial Revolution with iron and coal rather than with textiles, for this was Britain's most important industry after agriculture. British woollen cloth was known throughout the world, while in the eighteenth century there was also the start of a new textile industry – cotton.

The older woollen industry was run on the domestic system. In this a merchant or clothier bought the raw material (wool) from individual farmers or at a wool market and took it around the small cottages of the country workers, who worked on the raw wool by:
► sorting the long strands from the short;
► washing it in a stream to get the dirt out;
► carding or combing it so that all the fibres lay the same way;
► spinning it on a distaff or a spindle or simple wheel.

This work could be done in the workers' cottages because no machinery was involved except the simple spinning-wheel and it was said 'every cottage had its wheel'. The merchant would then collect the spun yarn when he delivered the next lot of raw wool. He would pay the people for the work they had done and then take the yarn to the local weavers who, maybe in their cottages or maybe in a special workshop, would weave the cloth. The woven cloth then went to the fuller who, using a mixture of fuller's earth and water, soaked the cloth to thicken it, after which it was stretched on frames called tenters until it was dry. The dried and thickened cloth was then brushed with the prickly teasels to bring up any loose ends before it was given to the cropper who used a long pair of shears to cut these ends and give the cloth a smooth finish.

Not all these jobs could be done in cottages. There were workshops and mills under the control of merchants who also employed dyers who used plants, either grown in Britain or imported, to make the dyes which gave each cloth its special colour.

Advantages and disadvantages of the domestic system

For the workers the system had several advantages:
► They could work on the wool when there was no work to be done on the land, so adding to their incomes.
► Child workers worked under the direction of their parents so that it was likely that they were treated kindly.
► They could work at their own pace and stop when they wanted to.

But there were many disadvantages to the system:
► Workers were often cheated by merchants who argued that they had handed over such-and-such a weight of wool, and only paid what they thought was a right amount. If the workers became troublesome the merchant could simply stop supplying them with wool – there were plenty of cottages willing to do this work.

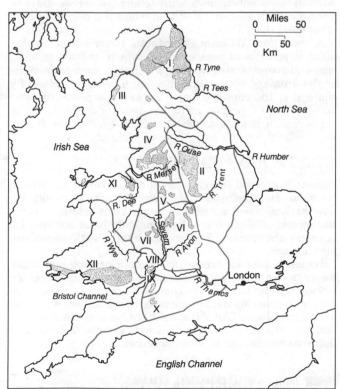

Fig. 5.2 The main coalfields of England and Wales. Examiners expect an ability to name the industries which grew up on the various coalfields.

▶ There was no individual wage paid in this system; the parents got the money from the merchant. This made it difficult for young people to save money to get married. In towns this was not so, which helps to explain the earlier marriages there (p. 5).

▶ People had to work and live in the same room, and this was often unhealthy.

5.3 Developments and Inventions

THE GROWTH OF THE COTTON TRADE

The woollen industry was Britain's traditional industry. One might have expected it to be the leader in industrialization. This was not so, however, because:

▶ There was a plentiful supply of workpeople in the cottages, so that machinery was less needed here than in cotton where there was no traditional labour force. If that industry were to expand it had to be mechanized.

▶ It was easy to increase the supply of cotton. This was achieved by sowing more in the fields of the USA or India. This was especially so after the American, Eli Whitney, developed the **cotton gin** to help the producers of raw cotton. But it was very difficult to increase the supply of wool; lambs take time to mature. It was not until the development of Australian sheep farming in the nineteenth century that the supply of wool was greatly increased.

▶ There were a number of groups in the traditional woollen industry opposed to change; the merchant guilds as well as the workers in the journeymen guilds blocked attempts to bring machinery into the industry. The cotton industry had no such traditional obstacles to overcome.

So the textile revolution took place in the cotton industry which grew up near the port of Liverpool, through which the supply of raw cotton was imported, and near the rivers flowing down the Pennines which provided the power to drive the first machines. When steam-driven machinery was introduced the industry did not have to move, because there was a supply of coal available from the Lancashire coalfields.

The spinning sector

One weaver could deal with the yarn provided by ten spinners. This explains why most of the early inventions were in the spinning side of the industry. There were:

▶ James Hargreaves's **spinning jenny** (1764) which could work a number of spindles at once. This was, at first, a simple, wooden machine which could be used in workers' cottages. By 1775 larger jennies worked as many as 120 spindles.

▶ Richard Arkwright's **water-frame** (1769), a spinning machine driven by water-power. This could not be housed in workers' homes, so factories had to be built. The first, at Cromford, was built in 1771 driven by water from the Derwent. Arkwright won the title of 'father of the factory system'.

▶ Richard Arkwright's **carding-engine** (1775) to comb out the fibres.

▶ Samuel Crompton's **mule** (1779), so called because it was a cross between the jenny and the frame. This made thread as fine as that produced on the jenny and as strong as that produced on the frame. At first it was a hand-driven machine, but by 1790 it was being driven by steam-engine and housed in factories.

The weaving sector

In 1733 John Kay invented a **fly shuttle** which had a system of springs and strings to enable the weaver to work more quickly. But this machine was little used at first, because the weavers could handle all the yarn then being produced by the spinners.

The increased supply of spun yarn (from the new machinery) meant that in the 1770s handloom weavers were very busy, earned high wages and lived well.

In 1785 Edward Cartwright invented the **power-loom**, a steam-driven machine which had to be housed in a factory. At first merchants were slow to adopt this machine and hand-loom weavers continued to prosper. But gradually the machine was adopted. This led to a fall in the price of cloth, a sharp fall in the wages of hand-loom weavers and a good deal of hardship for them and their families. Even as late as 1850, however, some of them were still trying to make a living at their old craft.

Other sectors of the industry

Other sectors became increasingly mechanized as the supply of material increased. Dyeing, once a domestic chore, now became factory-based. Croppers were replaced by shearing machines in the 1880s and gave rise to the Yorkshire Luddite movement.

THE STEAM-ENGINE

Here we have a good example of the steady improvement in things because of the new demands in other parts of industry.

▶ In 1698 **Thomas Savery** invented a steam pump to pump water out of Cornish tin and copper mines.

▶ In 1711 **Thomas Newcomen**, a Cornish blacksmith, improved on Savery's work and produced a more efficient engine. It was this engine which was used by the Darby family. By 1770 over 170 of them were in use in various industries.

▶ **James Watt's** first experiments with the steam-engine involved an attempt to repair a Newcomen engine. By 1775 he had invented a more efficient model, using less fuel and producing more power.

WATT AND BOULTON

Watt entered into a partnership with Matthew Boulton, whose factory produced mechanical toys and other objects. Helped by Boulton's money and marketing experience, Watt designed new engines, using the cylinders made by another famous ironmaster, **John Wilkinson**.

Between 1775 and 1800 they built over 500 new engines – a reminder of the spread of industrialization. But all these engines were only pumps with to-and-fro action. Only in 1783 did Watt discover a way of using the engine to turn other machinery.

A colleague, **William Murdock**, showed him how to build in a series of cogs and wheels, which Watt called a 'sun and planet' system that would change the motion of the engine from merely to-and-fro action into rotary action. By the end of the century Watt's **rotary steam-engine** was being used in textile factories, ironworks, coal mines, breweries, flour mills, potteries and other industries. It may be seen as the real start of industrialization.

WEDGWOOD AND POTTERY

Josiah Wedgwood founded his pottery firm at Etruria in Burslem. He employed high quality artists to design his famous Wedgwood ware. He also sent out salesmen to all the capitals of Europe to sell his goods to royal families. He opened a showroom in London to attract attention from rich people there.

He used china clay from Devon and Cornwall and flints, for grinding, from the Thames Valley. Transporting the heavy clay and the delicate china Wedgwood played a large part in the development of the canal system. Wedgwood was a rich man, and like Arkwright, he was made a knight ('Sir') – a sign that in Great Britain, success in trade and industry was no bar to social progress.

5.4 The Effects of the Industrial Revolution

▶ There was a great increase in the output of goods.

▶ This helped many people to become very rich. Some of their money they spent on more industrial development, some of it they spent on their own homes and families.

▶ Towns grew up around the mines, factories and ports and by 1851 there were more people living in large towns (over 50 000 population) than in the traditional villages. These new towns created their own problems – of housing, public health and factory conditions. Laws on these matters led to the development of strong local government and, later, to the development of the welfare state, which was paid for out of the increased wealth of industrial Britain.

▶ The coming together of many workpeople in the new towns led to the growth of the trade union movement and, later, to the demand for a reform of the Parliamentary system.

▶ As Britain became the richest country in the world, its politicians were able to play a larger part in world affairs. Palmerston, for example, could dominate world affairs because of the industrial and military power of the country. In politics as in welfare, in standards of living as in national prosperity, industrial development was the key which enabled Britain to lead the world in the nineteenth century.

5.5 Later Developments

▶ **The effects of railways**: see unit 26.3.
▶ **The growth of shipbuilding**: see unit 26.5.
▶ **The workshop of the world**: see unit 28.1–2.
▶ **Britain invests overseas**: see unit 28.2.
▶ **Nineteenth-century industrial progress**: see unit 28.2.
▶ **The growth of foreign competition**: see unit 28.3.
▶ **Evidence of Britain's decline**: see unit 28.3.
▶ **The demand for Tariff Reform, 1900–06**: see unit 28.4.

Unit 5 Summary

▶ The merits and defects of the domestic system.
▶ Reasons for the industrial revolution in textiles, iron and coal.
▶ The development of the steam engine.
▶ The work of inventors and improvers, e.g. the Darby family, Cort, Davy, Newcomen, Watt, Murdock, Hargreaves, Arkwright, Crompton, Kay and Cartwright.
▶ The career of Josiah Wedgwood.

6 THE AMERICAN WAR OF INDEPENDENCE

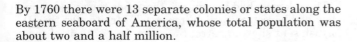

6.1 The 13 Colonies

By 1760 there were 13 separate colonies or states along the eastern seaboard of America, whose total population was about two and a half million.

LIFE STYLES

In the southern states, where tobacco and cotton could be grown, there were many large estates on which the owners (including Washington) had slaves to work in the fields.

In the northern states the land was divided into smaller farms and, as in Britain, people tended to live in small villages.

In the larger towns the colonists had set up their universities and colleges. They had established industry and they enjoyed the sort of life enjoyed by people in towns such as Bristol and Exeter.

THEIR GOVERNMENT

Each colony had its own government in the form of a State Assembly (or Parliament). In most states the Assembly was elected by a wide manhood suffrage. In some there was a property qualification which prevented poorer white men getting on to the electoral roll, although in others women were allowed to vote (which made these colonies more democratic that Britain). However, not even in these 'democratic' states were black people allowed to vote, nor did the colonists' claim for 'rights' for 'every man' extend to black Americans.

The State Assemblies had many powers, so that the colonists saw them as true Parliaments. They could impose taxes and bring in proposals for changes in the law. In each state there was a British-appointed governor, who had the power to set aside any decisions made by the Assembly. This was a major source of conflict between the colonists and the British government.

THE IMPORTANCE OF THE COLONIES TO BRITAIN

In 1772 the 13 colonies took about one-quarter of all Britain's exports – as much as was being taken by the West Indies and India combined. Tools, weapons, nails, steel, clothes, dishes and furniture were exported.

6.2 American Discontent

REMOTE CAUSES OF AMERICAN DISCONTENT

Mercantilism

By 1760 the first of the colonies was over 100 years old and the descendants of the early settlers resented the old Colonial System whereby the colonies were supposed to exist for the benefit of the Mother Country. This was part of the theory known as mercantilism. Mercantilism influenced British governments, which insisted that the colonists should not develop any industry that might lead to competition with a British industry. This meant they were not allowed to develop an iron or cloth-making industry which might have led to a fall in imports from Britain. Britain argued that this system also benefited the Americans because it offered them secure markets for their goods (rice, tobacco, timber and furs) and helped the development of ship-building in the colonies which were allowed to share in carrying the trade of the Empire.

Navigation Acts 1650, 1651 and 1660

Trade to and from the colonies had to be carried in British ships or ships belonging to the colonists. This was an attempt to break the power of the Dutch, who had a large merchant fleet and, at the same time, to expand the British merchant fleet which would provide the sailors needed for the Royal Navy in the event of a war.

Changed circumstances

Earlier colonists had accepted such regulations of their trade and industry because they depended on the British government to defend them against possible attacks from the French (in Canada), the Spanish (in Louisiana and Florida) and the Indians of the interior. But by 1765 these old arguments had lost their strength because:

► Many of the descendants of the earlier settlers felt they were American rather than British. Others, who did not share this nationalist feeling, saw themselves as 'Englishmen abroad', and were conscious of their political rights, including 'no taxation without representation'.

► The more venturesome wanted a chance to develop their own industries and the freedom to trade with whoever they wished.

► The more educated resented the control exercised by the British-appointed governors over the Assemblies.

► Most importantly, the French had been defeated by the British and, by the Peace of Paris (1763), Canada became British. There was now little danger of attack from France, and so less need for dependence on the British government.

THE GROWTH OF DISCONTENT, 1765–70

The British had spent a good deal of money in their wars against France. By 1763 the government had a national debt of £138 million on which it had to pay interest each year. Part of that money had been spent defending the colonists against the French. Some British politicians felt it right that the colonists should be asked to pay towards their own defence in the future, even if they were not asked to pay for the wars.

A British Army was still in the colonies to defend them against the possibility of attacks from the Indians. In 1763 an Indian chief, Pontiac, had united a number of tribes who were opposed to the way in which the colonists were expanding into their lands. The British Army had put down the Pontiac rising, but at a cost of £350,000. It was felt that the colonists should meet the cost of the resident army.

Successive governments tried to find a way of raising that money from the colonists. As we have seen in unit 1, the American problem dominated the rise – and the fall – of each of George III's governments between 1765 and 1782.

► **1764** Grenville imposed a **Sugar Act**, which increased the tax on all sugar imported into the colonies from the West Indies. This provided about £45 000 a year. Although the colonists were angry at it, they did not rebel because it was seen as part of that long-established system by which Britain controlled external trade with the colonies.

► **1765** Grenville imposed a **Mutiny Act**, which forced the colonists to pay for the everyday needs of the British Army stationed in the colonies as a defence against possible Indian attack. This was resented by the colonists, but at least the tax collected would be spent in the colonies. So, reluctantly, it was paid.

► **1765** Grenville then asked Parliament to pass the **Stamp Act**, which required that a government stamp be fixed on newspapers, packs of playing cards, legal documents, and newsapaper advertisements. The government hoped to raise £100 000 a year from this Act.

► **1765–66** There was widespread opposition to the Stamp Act, which was an attempt by the government to impose an internal tax on colonists who had only reluctantly accepted regulation of their external trade. Although there were 13 separate states, none of whom had, in the past, united to fight against Indian attacks, the Stamp Act managed to bring them together.

► **1765** Delegates from various states met in New York to debate the Stamp Act, and it was here that they coined the slogan 'No taxation without representation', arguing that it was against the principles of Magna Carta for them to be taxed by a Parliament in which they were not represented. Protest meetings followed. Stamp collectors were attacked, their offices raided and burnt; merchants boycotted British goods, which led to unemployment in Britain.

► **1766** Grenville was sacked and replaced by Rockingham who tried to please the colonists by repealing the Stamp Act. He then went on to push through the **Declaratory Act** which claimed that the British had the right to impose internal taxes if they wanted to.

► **1767** Rockingham's government fell, to be replaced by Chatham's in which Townshend was Chancellor of the Exchequer. Townshend tried to raise £40 000 a year by putting import taxes on various goods exported from Britain to the colonies – glass, paper, lead, paint and tea. This was an attempt to get the money by expanding the principle contained in the Sugar Act – namely that such taxes dealt with external trade and were not, like the Stamp Act, an attempt to impose internal taxes.

The colonists did not see it like that. Again they raised the cry of 'no taxation without representation'. But there was a major change in the protest. The State Parliament (or Assembly) of the colony of Massachusetts sent a letter to all the other Assemblies, asking them to unite in a boycott of British goods. American unity was being forged in the fire of opposition. The British government responded to this by announcing that the Massachusetts Assembly was dismissed. This angered the other states because it was an interference with internal government. There was widespread rioting against British property, especially in Boston, the capital of Massachusetts. Juries were unwilling to punish rioters and law and order seemed to have broken down.

6.3 Lord North's Attempts to Deal with the Problem

North became Chief Minister in 1770. He repealed all the Townshend duties, except the one on tea, to show that Britain had the right to impose taxes if she wished.

This was followed by rioting in Boston, where British soldiers had been sent to guard the Customs Commissioners. In March 1770 a soldier on sentry duty was attacked. Shots were fired and four Bostonians were killed in what became known as the **Boston Massacre**. This raised the tension between the colonists and the British.

The colonists had to smuggle the goods they needed once they had boycotted British imports. To try to stop this, the British sent ships to patrol the coast. In 1772 one of these, the *Gaspée*, ran aground off Providence, Rhode Island and the colonists burnt the ship.

In 1773, North introduced a **Tea Act** under which the colonists could import their tea directly from India, instead of via Britain. This brought down the price of tea, but North insisted that the hated Tea Tax should remain. The colonists remained opposed to this tax and, in December 1773, 150 men disguised as American Indians boarded three tea ships in Boston harbour and threw overboard tea worth £18 000, in what became known as the **Boston Tea Party**.

In 1774, after the defeat of the French in Canada, the government had to face the problem of the French settlers in that colony. The government pushed through the Quebec Act, under which the French people living in Canada were allowed to keep their Catholic religion, their language and their existing system of government. This angered the colonists in the American states, who saw it as an attempt to stop them expanding to the north, while the New England Puritans saw it as a threat to their religious liberties.

LORD NORTH AND THE INTOLERABLE ACTS, 1774

While dealing with the French Canadians, North also had to deal with the Bostonians who had held their Tea Party. He got Parliament to pass a series of Acts which:

► closed the port of Boston;
► removed the Customs House to Salem;
► insisted that the people of Boston had to provide barracks for the British troops sent to deal with the troubles;

▶ banned public meetings;
▶ increased the powers of the British governor, who could now send Bostonian prisoners to Britain for trial;
▶ annulled (or abolished) the Charter of Massachusetts so that, instead of being a self-governing colony, Massachusetts became a Crown Colony. This was seen by the colonists in other states as a drastic interference with the political and legal freedom of the people of Massachusetts, who had already lost their Assembly.

6.4 The Outbreak of War

FLASHPOINTS, 1774–75

The Philadelphia Congress

In 1774, delegates from all colonies except Georgia met in Philadelphia to discuss their policies towards Britain. This first Colonial Congress:
▶ re-affirmed the loyalty of the colonists to the Crown;
▶ drew up a Declaration of Rights, demanding the repeal of all Acts passed since 1763;
▶ decided to form local association committees in the various colonies to collect military supplies, raise local armies and lead resistance to the 'Intolerable Acts'.

Not all the colonists agreed with these steps, which would have meant the end of the old Colonial System and of Britain's control over her colonies. But most people supported these moves towards a demand for greater freedom.

Lexington

General Gage of Britain had been sent to take charge of the government of Massachusetts and to close the port of Boston. In April 1775 he sent troops to destroy a store of ammunition at Concord. On the way they met colonial resistance, and 244 soldiers were killed at the Battle of Lexington.

The Second Colonial Congress

Congress assembled in Philadelphia in May 1775, appointed Washington as commander of the colonial army and adopted the name of 'The United Colonies'.

Bunker Hill, June 1775

The colonists tried to get control of Boston and in so doing clashed with British troops at Bunker Hill. The British won the battle but suffered such heavy losses that the Americans were encouraged to continue the struggle. At the same time there was a reluctance to go the whole way and separate themselves from the Mother Country. Congress sent an **Olive Branch Petition** to George III, asking him to agree to settle the colonists' grievances peacefully. But the King refused.

THE WAR ON THE AMERICAN MAINLAND

Stage One, 1775–76

After the Battle of Bunker Hill, the colonists attacked Montreal and Quebec but were defeated by **General Burgoyne** who had arrived from Britain.

Washington's troops drove the British from Boston; **General Howe** withdrew his troops to Halifax. This encouraged the colonists to issue their **Declaration of Independence** (4th July 1776), drawn up by Thomas Jefferson, which said that the colonies were free and independent states and attacked George for his offences against them. It said that all men were created equal and outlined the aims of the new government which would guarantee equality and liberty for all men.

In the autumn of 1776 Howe's troops drove a colonial army from New York and reoccupied the port. Howe then wasted the opportunity to chase after Washington: by remaining in New York he allowed Washington to escape.

Stage Two, 1776–78

The British were in a strong position. From New York, Howe controlled the sea approaches to the colonies;

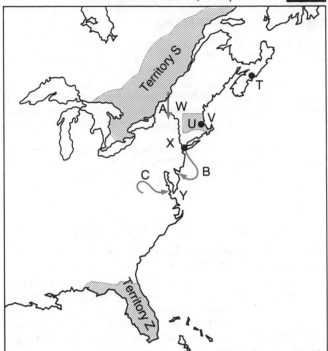

Fig. 6.4 A sketch map showing some of the important places in the American colonies. Examiners expect candidates to be able to name the men who followed routes A, B and C, the towns marked V and X, the battles marked W and Y and the territories marked S, U and Z.

Burgoyne was preparing to march south from Canada along the Hudson and Champlain river valleys. Howe was to march north from New York, link up with Burgoyne and isolate the northern (New England) colonies. The defeat of these colonies could have led to a quick end to the war.

Messages did not always get through from Britain, however. Nor were the commanders always as competent as they might have been. Howe did not wait for Burgoyne to march. Instead, in September 1777 he defeated Washington at **Brandywine**–although again allowing Washington to escape to Valley Forge. He then marched on to capture Philadelphia. Meanwhile, Burgoyne, having reached **Saratoga** found himself outnumbered by the rebel army. He surrendered, which was a moral booster for the colonists, particularly after the defeat at Brandywine.

Stage Three, 1778–83

The defeat at Saratoga was welcome news in Europe. In 1778 France declared war on Britain, hoping to get revenge for earlier defeats. In 1779 Spain joined France, while in 1780 Britain declared war on Holland for supplying the colonists with arms. In addition, the League of Armed Neutrality (Prussia, Russia, Denmark and Sweden) was formed to resist British claims to search neutral ships going to and from America.

Having failed to win the battle in the north, the British switched their attention to the south. General Cornwallis defeated small rebel armies in Georgia and then marched into Virginia. Here the rebels were much stronger and Cornwallis marched to **Yorktown** to await reinforcement from Britain.

But now the British paid the price for tax-cutting at home. The British Navy was not as strong as it might have been, while the combined navies of France, Spain and the League of Armed Neutrality meant that Britain no longer controlled the seas. The French defeated the British at **Chesapeake Bay**, ensuring their control of the coast. The British reinforcements did not arrive at Yorktown, where in October 1781 Cornwallis surrendered. This was the end of the fighting in America. When the news of the defeat reached Britain, North resigned and his Whig successors agreed first to a truce and then to the Treaty of Versailles (see below).

THE WAR ELSEWHERE

▶ In Europe the French captured Minorca (1782) and attacked Gibraltar (1779–82) but the defence under the command of General Elliott held out.

▶ In the West Indies the French fleet under De Grasse captured some British-held islands, but in 1782 Admiral Rodney defeated De Grasse at the **Battle of the Saints**, which saved Jamaica and restored British sea power in the area.

▶ In India the French encouraged Hyder Ali, the King of Mysore, to rise against the British in the Carnatic. Warren Hastings and Admiral Hughes kept the French at bay and put down the rising (see unit 24).

6.5 American Victory

WHY DID THE AMERICANS WIN?

Inefficient leadership

Lord Sandwich, in charge of the Navy, and Lord George Germaine, the War Minister, were inefficient. They did not appreciate the nature of the colonial war, so that too few troops were sent at the outset. The early successes encouraged the colonists, who might have been defeated by a massive effort at the start.

The navy

The Navy had suffered from the economies of North and previous governments. It was unable to meet all the demands made on it – in India, Europe, the West Indies and America. One result was that the French were able to ensure the surrender of Cornwallis at Yorktown.

The generals

The British generals were not accustomed to the sort of war in which they were engaged. They were not ready for the guerrilla warfare waged by the colonists, who used small groups of untrained men to ambush British columns. They lacked that intimate knowledge of the countryside which the colonists had. They insisted that their men wore red uniforms, powdered their hair and generally behaved as if they were on parade, making their men easier targets for the sharpshooting Americans.

The mercenaries

The British generals also suffered because they led a force consisting in the main of German (Hessian) mercenaries who had little enthusiasm for the fight and were more interested in looting. This turned even the moderate colonists against them. The Americans, on the other hand, enjoyed the leadership of Washington whose force of character kept his armies together even in the most difficult period.

Distance

The British were hampered by the long sea journey which had to be made if reinforcements and orders were to get through. The Americans, on the other hand, had short internal lines of communication.

THE TREATY OF VERSAILLES, 1783

▶ This recognized the independence of the states. Their territory was defined as that which lay between the Mississippi and the Great Lakes.

▶ The French regained the island of St Lucia and Tobago in the West Indies. Britain regained most of the other West Indian islands.

▶ France gained Senegal in West Africa.

▶ Spain retained Minorca and Florida but gave Louisiana to France.

THE LONG TERM EFFECTS OF THE WAR

▶ Those colonists who had opposed the war (nicknamed 'Tories' by rebels but 'Loyalists' by the British) left the colonies to live in Canada. This created fresh problems in that colony (unit 24).

▶ British trade with independent America quickly recovered so that by 1797 America was taking one-third of Britain's total exports.

▶ George III was never again as confident or ambitious as he had been before the War.

▶ Ordinary people in Britain became interested in the idea of 'no taxation without representation' and began to demand a reform of the British political system (unit 14).

▶ Britain had to find a new overseas penal settlement to which prisoners could be sent. This led to the development of Australia (unit 24).

▶ French soldiers took back ideas of equality and liberty and added to the problems of the ancien régime. The French Revolution (unit 8) was, in one sense, a natural consequence of French participation in the American War.

Unit 6 Summary

▶ The eighteenth-century colonial system, mercantilism and Navigation Acts.

▶ The growth of colonial discontent.

▶ Reasons for and effects of the colonists' victory.

7 WILLIAM PITT THE YOUNGER, 1783–93

7.1 Political Confusion after North's Resignation, 1782

North's government faced much opposition in the Commons, from one group led by **Charles James Fox** and another made up of former supporters of **Chatham**, both of which wanted a peace with the warring colonists. But, on the other hand, there was another group which wanted the government to fight the war more vigorously. The defeat at Yorktown led to North's resignation in the face of this opposition.

The only person who could command a majority in the Commons was the Whig, Rockingham. The King asked him to form a government, although he knew that this government would propose a peace treaty with the colonists and would also try to change the Parliamentary system to lessen the King's influence.

Fox became Foreign Secretary in the Rockingham government and he recalled Rodney after the victory in the Battle of the Saints. This prevented the capture of several French islands and led some people to suspect Fox of not being a patriot.

Rockingham died before a truce had been arranged with the colonists. The King then appointed Shelburne as his Chief Minister. He sacked Fox but appointed the young William Pitt to the post of Chancellor of the Exchequer. In January 1783 this government signed a truce with the colonists, which meant that the fighting stopped while a peace treaty was arranged.

In February 1783 Shelburne's government was defeated in the Commons because a majority of MPs thought that the terms of the truce were too lenient to the colonists and because many Whigs were opposed to Shelburne's close friendship with the King. Other Whigs, led by Fox, wanted the Commons, and not the King, to have the right to decide who should be the Chief Minister.

THE FOX–NORTH COALITION, 1783

Fox (the Whig) and North (George III's favourite Minister) had been bitter enemies, quarrelling over such issues as the power of the King and the claims of the colonists. Consequently it was a great surprise when they agreed to join a new government under the Duke of Portland – one which George III had to appoint, since no other Minister could command a majority in the Commons.

The fall of the Fox–North coalition, December 1783

The **Portland government**, better known as the Fox–North Coalition, signed the Treaty of Versailles (p. 18). Many people were surprised at this because North had opposed Shelburne when he had signed the truce in January 1783. Now North was willing to sign a peace treaty with the colonists.

People were angered when the government brought in the **India Bill** in December 1783 (p. 58). The Bill aimed at dealing with the problems of governing large parts of India. It proposed that the political work of the East India Company should be controlled by seven commissioners appointed by the government. This would have given Fox and North more political influence; which MPs would sell their votes in return for being one of the commissioners?

The Commons passed the Bill but the King used his influence to get it rejected in the Lords. The government resigned, and a week before Christmas 1783 the King appointed William Pitt, then only 24, to be his Chief Minister.

THE MINCE PIE ADMINISTRATION, 1783

Fox boasted that the government would be dismissed once the mince pies of 1783 had been eaten. Many people agreed with him because Pitt was so young and had no large following in the Commons, as did Fox, Shelburne and Portland.

But Pitt had a number of advantages over his great rivals:
▶ He was obviously more honest than Fox, who had united with his great rival, North, simply to get into power.
▶ He had the support of the King, who had a great deal of influence over many MPs and over the Lords.
▶ Many independent MPs were bribed, by Robinson, the former Treasury Secretary, to side with Pitt. Fox called these 'Robinson's Rats' who left his sinking ship to side with Pitt.
▶ Many MPs and many voters remembered the great days when Pitt's father led the country to greatness against France. They hoped that the son might be 'a chip off the old block' and bring the country back to greatness after the humiliation of the defeat in America.

THE ELECTION, MARCH 1784

▶ Pitt held on to his office in spite of much opposition. When he thought that public opinion was favourable to himself, he asked the King to dismiss Parliament and to call a general election.

▶ Fox argued that the King had no right to do this, claiming that the Parliament elected in 1780 ought to sit for its full seven years. At the same time, he argued that the King ought to allow Parliament to choose the man it wanted to be the Chief Minister, hoping that it would choose him.
▶ But the election was held. To Fox's surprise there was a good deal of support for Pitt and a good deal of opposition to himself and his supporters. This was because of the India Bill, Fox's change of attitude towards North, and his too obvious ambition. About 80 of Fox's supporters lost their seats, and became known as 'Fox's Martyrs'. Pitt's supporters won enough seats to give him a majority in the Commons.

7.2 Pitt's Domestic Policy

PITT AND TRADE, 1784–93

One immediate result of the American War was a drop in trade with the former colonies, which led to a recession and unemployment. It was Pitt's first task to try to restore the prosperity of the country.

Pitt was influenced by the ideas of **Adam Smith**, who was the Scottish writer of *The Wealth of Nations*, the first economics text book. Smith argued that if every country did away with import and export duties, there would be a rise in the volume of trade since more people would be able to afford the cheaper goods. This would lead to the creation of more employment and to general prosperity. Pitt followed Smith's proposals by:
▶ **Cutting import duties**. The duty on sugar was cut from 119 per cent to 20 per cent, that on tea from 100 per cent to 12½ per cent. One result of this was that smuggling became less profitable, another was a fall in the cost of living in Britain.
▶ The **Eden treaty** with France (1786). Manufactured goods from both countries would be allowed in on easier terms than before and duties on other goods (e.g wine and silk) would be lowered. This brought down prices in Britain and opened the French market to more British goods.
▶ Setting up more **bonded warehouses** in which could be stored those colonial goods (tobacco, spices and furs) meant for re-export to Europe. Before Pitt's time, import taxes had to be paid on such goods when they entered British ports. In the bonded warehouses the goods were kept under government guard until they were re-exported without having paid the import duty. This kept their prices down and so more were sold, which increased the profits of British merchants.
▶ Pitt knew that **smuggling** had been common before 1784. He hoped to make it less profitable by his cuts in import duties. He also passed the **Hovering Act** (1787) which said that foreign ships had to anchor at least 12 miles out at sea unless they intended entering a British port. This would make the job of the smuggler more difficult.

PITT AND FINANCE, 1784–93

The reduction in import duties meant that the government had a lower income. To make up for this Pitt:
▶ Introduced new taxes on luxuries such as racehorses, carriages, hair powder and wigs, servants and windows – people with more than three windows in their homes had to pay a tax on the other windows.
▶ Reorganized the customs and excise system so that, in place of the different rates of taxes on each item imported, a single tax was applied to all imports. This gave rise to a new book of rates being used by the customs authorities. This made the system simple and therefore easier for merchants to understand.
▶ Reorganized the internal tax system. Until 1786 each separate tax, for example, on cider or sugar, was put into a separate account. Each time the government spent money – on ships, soldiers' pay or a new office – each piece of spending was put against a particular tax. This was very complicated and was one reason why some officials were

able to steal a good deal of money and not get caught. In 1786 Pitt set up the **Consolidated Fund**. All taxes were paid into a single account and all spending taken out of that account. This cut down on the work of the Treasury and made it difficult for dishonest clerks and officials to cheat.

▶ Cut down on the number of government posts in which people were paid without being expected to do any work. Edmund Burke had brought in the **Economical Reform Act** (1782) which had abolished dozens of such sinecures. Pitt carried on this process and so cut down the amount of government spending.

▶ Pushed through an Act which created the **Sinking Fund** (1786), by which each year £1 million was handed to a Board of Commissioners set up to buy back government stock owned by people who had loaned money to the government. These loans made up the national debt which had grown as a result of the wars of the eighteenth century. The government had to pay interest on this stock each year. Pitt hoped that by buying back the stock he would be able to abolish the national debt and would not have to collect the taxes needed to pay that interest. This policy succeeded during the years of peace, when improving trade brought increased revenue to the government; the Fund's Commissioners bought back much stock. But once war started in 1793 (p. 21) the government had to borrow even more money to help fight the war, which further increased the size of the national debt.

PITT THE REFORMER, 1784–93

In 1782 before becoming Prime Minister, Pitt had introduced a **Parliamentary Reform Bill**, but this had been defeated. In 1785 he brought in another such Bill, which would have abolished 36 'rotten boroughs' and would have given these seats to some of the growing industrial towns. But the Commons rejected this Bill. Once the French Revolution had broken out, Pitt gave up ideas on such reform. Indeed, as we shall see (p. 23) he brought in many Acts against reform and reformers.

Through his friend, **William Wilberforce** (p. 28), Pitt became aware of the evils of the slave trade and of slavery. In 1791 Pitt set up a Parliamentary Committee to examine the slave trade. As a result, one Act was passed to improve conditions on slave-carrying ships. But two others, which would have abolished the trade, were defeated in the Commons. Pitt might have continued with his campaign against the slave trade but, once again, the French Revolution may be seen as the reason for his refusing to do so.

THE REGENCY BILL, 1788

In 1788 George III seemed to be on the point of death, and had already been declared insane. His son (later the Prince Regent and then George IV) hoped that he would be asked to take his fathers' place. So did Fox, who was the Prince's friend. Pitt was determined not to let Fox get back into power. There was a good deal of political haggling, with Pitt agreeing to bring in a Bill which would allow the Prince to sign Bills and otherwise take the place of the King, but which would not allow him to appoint Ministers. In fact the King recovered and the Bill was dropped. But the rivalry between Fox and Pitt was further increased by the arguments over the Regency question.

IRELAND, 1798–1801

We shall study this question on p. 56.

7.3 Pitt's Foreign Policy, 1784–93

When Pitt came to power, Britain had no friends in Europe and had just lost the War of American Independence. Pitt wanted to restore Britain to a place of power in Europe while, at the same time, ensuring a period of peace during which trade could improve. He achieved these objects by:

▶ **The Triple Alliance**, 1788. The Emperor Joseph II of Austria ruled over the Austrian Netherlands (now called Belgium). He wanted to make it into a trading centre. To do this he had to try to force the Dutch to allow him to use the River Scheldt, which would enable him to build up the port of Antwerp. The British did not want to see another rival to London; the Dutch did not want a threat to their port, Rotterdam. When Austrian forces attacked Holland, France announced that she would side with Holland. To try to limit French influence over Holland, Pitt signed a treaty with Frederick of Prussia (an enemy of Austria) in which Britain and Prussia agreed that they would help Holland. The government of Holland preferred to rely on Britain and Prussia rather than on France, and signed the Triple Alliance in 1788.

▶ **Opposing Russia**, 1790. Russia was anxious to extend her territory both north and south. In 1790 she tried to conquer Sweden and was helped by Denmark, Sweden's traditional enemy. The Triple Alliance powers forced Denmark to withdraw from the attack on Sweden. In 1790 Russia signed a peace treaty which left Sweden free and meant that Pitt had succeeded in stopping Russia making the Baltic Sea into a Russian lake.

▶ **Opposing Spain**, 1790. English fishermen had created a harbour at **Nootka Sound** on the shores of Vancouver Island. The Spaniards claimed all the territory on the west coast of America. In 1789 a Spanish force was sent to capture Nootka Sound, seizing British ships and ejecting British settlers. Britain protested, received promises of help from her partners in the Triple Alliance but did not have to go to war since Spain withdrew from the Sound.

In later units we will see how Pitt dealt with the problems of the growing Empire – in Canada, India and Australia. But you should know enough to realize that he was a very successful Minister during these ten years. However, he failed to check Russian advance into:

▶ **The Black Sea Coastal Region**. In 1791 Russia seized Ochakov; Pitt protested, but Russia ignored him and held on to her conquest.

▶ **Poland**, which was partitioned by Austria, Prussia and Russia in 1793 and again in 1795. Pitt was powerless to prevent this Russian expansion into Europe.

7.4 Pitt and the Empire

▶ **India**: see unit 24.2.
▶ **Canada**: see unit 24.7.
▶ **Australia**: see unit 24.8.

Unit 7 Summary

▶ The importance of political events, 1782–84 on the careers of Pitt and Fox and on constitutional development.
▶ The work of Pitt the reformer.
▶ The importance of the Regency Crisis, 1788.

8 WILLIAM PITT THE YOUNGER, 1793–1806

8.1 The French Revolution

SOME CAUSES OF THE FRENCH REVOLUTION

The French had spent a great deal of money fighting wars – mainly against Britain. Unlike the British, they had nothing to show for it, whereas Britain had gained an Empire.

By 1787 the French government was bankrupt and did not know how to get the money needed to run the country. King Louis XVI asked the nobility to help him reform the system of government and taxation. They refused, in 'the revolt of the nobility', 1787–89.

This forced the King to call a meeting of the **States-General**, which had not been called together for 175 years. This body was divided into three separate parts, or estates; the first formed by representatives of the nobility, a second representing the clergy, while the third was elected by the common people. The States-General met in May 1789 after two years of bad harvests which had created discontent in the country.

Many delegates in the third estate had read the writings of philosophers such as Rousseau and Voltaire, and wanted France to have a more democratic form of government. In addition, many Frenchmen had fought for the American colonists against Britain. Back in France they, too, began to demand reforms. If it was right to fight for the colonist with their slogan 'no taxation without representation', then maybe it was right to demand that in France, too, that slogan should be put into practice.

SOME STAGES IN THE REVOLUTION

The States-General assembled at the Royal Palace in Versailles in **May 1789**. It spent the first two months arguing with the King, who wanted it to meet as three separate Houses. He expected that the nobility and the clergy would tend to vote against the common people's House, so giving him a majority of 2–1 in any vote. The delegates in the third estate wanted a single Assembly, in which they would have the majority and so be able to force change on an unwilling King.

The Paris mob, hungry because of the poor harvests, and impatient with the States-General, finally rioted on the **14th July** and attacked **the Bastille**, a state prison which was a symbol of the King's power. The seven prisoners were freed and the Parisian mob stole the guns and ammunition from the prison armoury.

The King gave in to the third estate and ordered that the three estates should meet as one Assembly, which in August 1789 abolished all the nobles' feudal privileges and unequal taxation and issued the **Declaration of the Rights of Man** which said that all men were equal.

This did not satisfy the Parisians. In **October** they marched to Versailles and brought the King and Queen back to Paris. The royal couple were virtually prisoners of the mob until **June 1791** when they tried to flee from France to join their relations and friends in Austria. They were caught at Varennes and dragged back to Paris again.

In **September 1791** fresh elections gave extremists control of the Assembly. This new Assembly announced, in **October 1791**, that French nobles who had fled from France would be sentenced to death if they did not return immediately.

When the nobles did not return, the French felt a sense of grievance against Emperor Leopold of Austria and Frederick William of Prussia who were sheltering the nobles. These monarchs had issued their **Declaration of Pillnitz** (August 1791) claiming that the changes taking place in France were a matter of concern to all the rulers of Europe. The French thought that these monarchs were preparing to attack France and to undo all that had happened since 1789.

On 20th April 1792 the French declared war on Austria, and Prussia announced that she would join with Austria. The French invaded the Austrian Netherlands in the first campaign of the Revolutionary War.

BRITAIN AND THE REVOLUTION

Pitt welcomed the news that France had been thrown into confusion in 1789 because this meant that France would not be a threat to European peace. Even as late as 1792 Pitt claimed that Europe could look forward to 15 years of peace, during which British trade and industry would have a chance to prosper.

Fox and many Whigs thought that the attack on the King's power in 1789 was a French imitation of the Glorious Revolution of 1688–89, in which the British asserted the power of the people as represented in Parliament.

Dissenters such as the Nonconformists, Quakers and other religious groups welcomed the French Revolution. They were suffering from religious persecution in Britain and they hoped that in the face of the great upheaval in France, Britain might be forced to change its laws and allow greater freedom to Dissenters.

It was a Dissenter, **Dr Price**, who preached a famous sermon on 'The love of our country' which started off the long debate on the merits and demerits of the French Revolution.

Edmund Burke, one of the Rockingham Whigs, had supported the American colonists in their revolt. But in answer to Dr Price he wrote *Reflections on the Revolution in France* (1790) in which he prophesied that the Revolution would lead to bloodshed, war and the rising of a military dictator. Many people in the upper class – both Tory and Whig – agreed with this. They feared that the British people might rise as the French had done, and demand major changes in the way in which Parliament was elected.

Tom Paine, a radical, wrote *The Rights of Man* (1791) supporting the Revolution and demanding radical change in Britain.

Corresponding Societies were formed by various groups which supported the Revolution. In 1791 some nobles formed the **Society of the Friends of the People** and produced pamphlets calling for reform – of Parliament for example. In 1792 the **London Corresponding Society** was formed by lower-class people led by Thomas Hardy, a shoemaker. Its demands were more far-reaching, and frightened the ruling class.

8.2 Britain at War with France, February 1793

Within a year of making his 'fifteen years of peace' speech, Pitt found himself at war with France because of:

▶ **The Edict of Fraternity**, November 1792. The French government, at war with Austria and Prussia, called on all lower-class people in Europe to rise against their rulers and to side with France. Pitt's government was afraid that the British lower classes might take notice of such a demand and act upon it.

▶ **The Opening of the Scheldt**, November 1792. The Austrians and Prussians had been driven from France, whose armies had then invaded the Austrian Netherlands.

The French threatened to open up the Scheldt to world trade and to build up the port of Antwerp. The British had already shown that they were not prepared to allow this challenge to London's power (p. 20).

▶ **The Terror**, September – October 1792. There was general disgust in Britain at the news of the butchery of thousands of people after mock trials. This horror reached a peak in January 1793 when the King was executed.

A SURVEY OF PITT'S WARTIME POLICIES

Pitt hoped that the war which started in 1793 would be a short one. This explains why he continued the Sinking Fund, even though he was being forced to borrow vast sums of money and so increase the national debt.

Subsidies were provided for foreign allies who used the money to buy the arms and hire mercenaries to fight the war. Pitt hoped to avoid having to maintain a large British army in Europe.

The colonies in India and the West Indies were valuable markets. Pitt concentrated the main British effort on maintaining and, if possible, expanding these colonies.

The Navy was the major force which Britain used against France, before and after Pitt's death in 1806. It fulfilled a number of roles in that it:

▶ **blockaded France** to make it more difficult for the French to import the goods they needed;

▶ **maintained British trade** and so ensured that Britain had the materials and money with which to fight France;

▶ **attacked the French coast** at places such as Toulon;

▶ prevented a French **invasion** of Britain which seemed likely once Napoleon had become master of Europe;

▶ ensured that British troops on the Continent were properly supplied. This was vital during the Peninsular War (unit 9).

THE FIRST COALITION, 1793 – 97

The members of this Coalition were Sardinia, Holland, Austria, Prussia, England and Spain (SHAPES from their initials) and Russia. Although this appeared to be a strong alliance, it failed to defeat the French, largely because:

▶ Russia, Prussia and Austria were more interested in the division of **Poland** than in fighting France.

▶ Prussia and Austria were traditional enemies and did not provide the united leadership which a coalition needed.

On the other hand the French were fortunate in that:

▶ They found great leaders. **Danton** was a successful political leader (1793 – 94) who kept French enthusiasm going. **Carnot** was a great military organiser who managed to get almost everyone in France involved in fighting against the hated foreigners.

▶ There was a high degree of enthusiasm for the ideas of the Revolution – liberty, equality and fraternity – which were being attacked by the European monarchs and their armies. This gave the French a sense of mission and determination in fighting.

▶ Surprisingly, after the flight of most officers, Carnot found a number of able leaders from among the ordinary people.

Britain and the first coalition

▶ **1793**: A combined military and naval force attacked the French port of **Toulon**, hoping to come to the aid of a small group of anti-revolutionaries in the south of France. The attack was badly planned, poorly led and failed completely.

▶ **September 1793**: The Duke of York (made famous in the nursery rhyme) led the British in an attack on Dunkirk. The French victory in the Battle of Honschoote led to British withdrawal, and Dunkirk was recaptured.

▶ **1793**: Naval clashes took place between English and French in the West Indies.

▶ **1794**: An expedition was sent to attack the French sugar islands in the **West Indies**. By 1798 over 100 000 men had died, mostly from yellow fever. Some islands were captured in 1795, but were lost again later on.

▶ **1795**: Britain captured the Cape of Good Hope, which had been part of the Dutch Empire. This was a valuable port of call for British ships trading with India.

▶ The Navy blockaded the French coast and had some success. On 'the Glorious First of June' 1794, Howe's fleet defeated a French fleet, but failed to prevent corn ships from getting into Brest. This was, therefore, a mixed success.

The end of the coalition

▶ In **1795** Prussia, anxious about her interests in Poland and Spain, made peace with France.

▶ In **1797** Austria, after suffering a defeat at **Rivoli**, concluded a peace treaty at **Campo Formio**.

▶ In **1796** Spain and Holland declared war on Britain, hoping to gain something for themselves out of the general warfare into which France had plunged Europe.

Fortunately the **Navy** once again saved Britain by victories at:

▶ **Cape St Vincent** (1797) where Nelson was second-in-command to Jervis, whose fleet defeated the Spanish;

▶ **Camperdown** (1797) where Duncan's fleet defeated the Dutch.

1797 – A YEAR OF CRISIS

▶ The Coalition finally broke up.

▶ In **Ireland** there was the threat of an uprising, which actually did not take place until 1798 (p. 56).

▶ The **Navy** was weakened by the mutinies which broke out at the Nore and Spithead. Sailors were angered at the way in which they had been **press-ganged** (i.e. kidnapped) into serving and by the **cruelty** of many of their **incompetent officers**, who also stole much of the money which ought to have been spent on **food**.

The mutinies did not last very long; the leaders were arrested and some were executed. Officers were then warned to take account of the men's complaints and conditions slowly improved as some leaders began to treat their men as well as did Nelson and other more popular commanders.

THE SECOND COALITION, 1799 – 1801

In 1799 Britain, Russia, Austria and Turkey (BRAT) formed a Second Coalition. It had a short life during which:

▶ A combined Austrian and Russian army drove the French from Italy.

▶ A Russian and British expedition to the Netherlands failed.

Russia withdrew from the Coalition (1799) to help form the **Armed Neutrality** (1800) along with Denmark and Sweden. This was aimed at Britain's imports of timber, hemp and tar from the Baltic – essential to her Navy. **Austria** was left to fight the land battles against France and after a series of defeats she signed the Treaty of **Luneville** (1801) and withdrew from the struggle. Once again, Britain was on her own.

THE PEACE OF AMIENS, 1802

Pitt had resigned in 1801 over the question of Catholic Emancipation (p. 56). His successor, Addington, was anxious to make peace. The Peace of Amiens was signed in March 1802. In it:

▶ Britain returned all the colonial conquests she had gained from France, Spain and Holland, except Trinidad (from Spain) and Ceylon (from Holland).

▶ The French withdrew from Rome, Naples and Egypt.

▶ Britain promised to hand back Malta to its previous rulers, the Knights of St John.

THE THIRD COALITION, 1804 – 05

The Peace of Amiens was only a breathing space. Napoleon was now the ruler of France, determined to defeat Britain which, in turn, was unwilling to stand by and watch him gain too much power. When his armies conquered northern Italy and invaded Switzerland, Britain decided to declare war (May 1803). Pitt was brought back into office (April 1804) and he organized yet another coalition with Russia and Austria, but:

▶ The **Austrians** suffered a number of crushing defeats, ending with the defeat at Ulm and Napoleon's triumphal entry into Vienna (1805).

▶ The combined armies of Russia and Austria were defeated at **Austerlitz** (1805). Napoleon redrew the map of Europe, creating a modern Holy Roman Empire and new kingdoms for various of his relations.

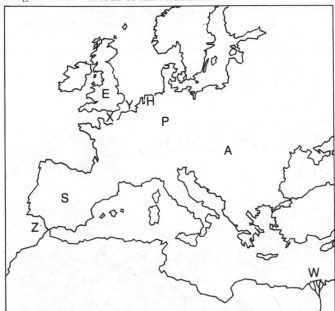

Fig. 8.2 A sketch map of Europe during the wars against Revolutionary France. Examiners expect candidates to name the countries marked A, E, H, P and S, and to be able to explain the importance of the events which took place at W, X, Y and Z.

▨ 8.3 Naval Success, 1798–1806 ▨

While the French armies were succeeding, so too was the British Navy. In particular there were the victories at:

▶ **Aboukir Bay**, or the **Battle of the Nile**, 1798. Napoleon, not yet the dictator of France, had sent an army to conquer Egypt – the gateway to India. On the way he had captured the island of **Malta**. Nelson, commanding the fleet in the Mediterranean, chased after the French and defeated their fleet at Aboukir Bay. The French army, then isolated, was defeated at the **Battle of Acre** by troops supported by a fleet commanded by Sir Sydney Smith.

▶ **Malta**, which was captured in 1800.

▶ **Copenhagen**, 1801 where the British fleet was commanded by Hyde Parker. It was here that Nelson defied his commander's orders and sailed into the harbour to sink the Danish fleet, so putting an end to the threat of the Armed Neutrality.

TRAFALGAR, 1805

Napoleon now began to plan the invasion of Britain. Armies were prepared and fleets of invasion barges assembled in northern ports waiting for the arrival of the French fleet from the Mediterranean ports. **Villeneuve**, commander of the French fleet, escaped from the British blockade and sailed to the West Indies to link up with another French and Spanish fleet. Nelson failed to catch him on his way to and from the West Indies, but blockaded the fleet in **Cadiz** where it had put in for a refit. When Villeneuve's fleet came out, Nelson won the victory at **Trafalgar** which ensured that the invasion would not take place and that, while Napoleon was the master on land, Britain remained mistress of the seas.

Nelson died during this battle and shortly after it ended (January 1806) Pitt also died, worn out by his exertions.

THE IMPORTANCE OF NELSON'S CAREER

This is a favourite topic with examiners. You should note:

▶ Born in Norfolk in 1758, he went to sea as a midshipman in 1771. He served in the East and West Indies and the Arctic.

▶ Ill health forced him to give up active service and he was at home, on half-pay, when the Revolutionary War began in January 1793.

▶ **January 1793** He was given command of the **Agamemnon** in Hood's Mediterranean fleet which:

● protected British trading routes and vessels;

● attacked and captured French shipping;

● attacked French garrisons. In July 1794, in the attack on Calvi, Nelson lost the sight of his right eye;

● in a battle off Genoa (March 1795) he first showed the ability and decisiveness in action which led to great fame.

▶ **June 1796** In command of the *Captain* in Jervis's fleet, he took part in the **Battle of Cape St Vincent** (February 1797). Nelson made a major contribution to this victory over the Spanish fleet and was promoted to Rear Admiral.

▶ **1797** In an attack on a Spanish treasure ship near Teneriffe he lost his right arm.

▶ **Naval Mutinies** (p. 22) Nelson was not involved in the mutinies at the Nore and Spithead because he was at sea at the time. But you ought to notice that he (and many other officers, such as Collingwood) had always treated their men fairly so that they won the loyalty of their crews. Nelson was one who attacked the bad habits of some of his fellow officers which were part of the cause of the mutinies.

▶ **1798** His success at **Aboukir Bay** prevented Napoleon from going ahead with his attack on British India, and gained Nelson the title of Baron (or Lord).

▶ **1801** After a further period of ill-health, he was promoted to the rank of Vice-Admiral and sent to the Baltic as second-in-command to Hyde Parker. His success at the **First Battle of Copenhagen** in April 1801 ended the threat of **the Armed Neutrality**. He was made a Viscount and, on Parker's recall, was promoted to Commander-in-Chief of the Baltic Fleet.

▶ **1802** He was recalled to take command of the anti-invasion fleets assembled because of Napoleon's preparations to invade England.

▶ **May 1803** Appointed Commander-in-Chief of the Mediterranean Fleet, his flagship being the *Victory*. He blockaded Villeneuve's fleet in Toulon (1803–04) and, after Villeneuve's escape led his fleet of 27 ships to victory over 33 French ships at **Trafalgar** ensuring British naval supremacy.

▨ 8.4 Pitt's Domestic Policies, 1793–1805

Pitt had been a reforming minister between 1783 and 1793. But once Britain became involved in the wars against France he was convinced that ideas of reform were dangerous, and he pushed through a number of repressive Acts:

▶ **1793: The Aliens Act** to stop foreigners entering England.

▶ **1794: Habeas Corpus** was suspended so that anyone suspected of any crime could be arrested and imprisoned without trial. The leaders of the **Corresponding Societies** were arrested in 1794. Tom Paine, author of *The Rights of Man*, fled to France. Some of the leaders of the Societies were brought to trial and acquitted; others were found guilty and the Scottish leaders, Muir and Palmer, were deported to Botany Bay in Australia. Such attacks on freedom of speech and on those demanding reform led to a decline in the reform movement.

▶ **1795: The Seditious (or Treasonable) Practices Act** was passed after an attack on the King's coach as he was on his way to open Parliament. This led to the government to pass an Act which:

● forbade any criticism in print or speech of the King or his government, and

● forbade meetings of more than 50 people.

▶ **1799 and 1800**: The government feared that the working class might prove to be revolutionary-minded. So it passed the **Combination Acts** which forbade the formation of trade unions.

INCOME TAX, 1798

Pitt had to borrow large sums of money to pay for British armaments and to provide subsidies to the Coalition Allies. He tried to find some of the money he needed by introducing a 'temporary tax' on incomes. The tax had to be paid by anyone earning more than £60 a year and it was graduated on incomes between £60 and £200 a year. People earning more than £200 a year had to pay a tax of 10 per cent of their incomes. This **direct tax** was very unpopular with the rich who had to pay it and they were determined that as soon as the war ended, so too would income tax (p. 30).

Unit 8 Summary

▶ Varying British views on the French Revolution, 1789–91.
▶ Why Britain went to war against France, 1793.
▶ Pitt as a war minister; the end of his reforming period.
▶ The failure of successive coalitions against France.
▶ The important role of the navy; the career of Nelson.

9 THE DEFEAT OF NAPOLEON, 1806–15

9.1 Politics after Pitt's death

▶ Grenville became Prime Minister of the 'Ministry of all the talents'. He appointed Fox as Foreign Secretary, who tried to make peace with France but failed.

▶ Fox died in September 1806 but his supporters managed to put through an Act abolishing the slave trade (March 1807).

▶ Grenville resigned when the King again (1807) refused to agree to Catholic Emancipation (p. 56).

▶ Then there were governments led by Portland (1807–09) and by Perceval (1809–12) who was murdered by a madman in the lobby of the House of Commons.

▶ Jenkinson, later Lord Liverpool, became Prime Minister in 1812 and stayed in power until his death in 1827.

THE WAR AFTER PITT'S DEATH, 1806–07

Britain, Russia and Prussia were allies in the Third Coalition. Prussia withdrew, however, after the defeat at Jena (1806), and Alexander I, the Tsar of Russia, met Napoleon on a raft in the River Nemen and agreed to the Treaty of Tilsit (1807), by which Russia agreed to join an alliance against Britain.

Napoleon hoped to force Sweden and Denmark to join the new Allies in an embargo on trade with Britain; he also hoped to be able to use the Danish fleet in his war against Britain.

Canning, Foreign Secretary under Portland, learned about this, and ordered the fleet into **Copenhagen** to capture the Danish fleet in the Second Battle of Copenhagen, 1807.

9.2 The Continental System

Napoleon realized that he could not defeat Britain at sea, and he decided to try to defeat 'the nation of shopkeepers' by attacking British trade. He did this by:

▶ **The Berlin Decree** (1806) which said that no British goods would be allowed into any country in Europe;

▶ **The Milan Decree** (1807) which said that neutral ships which entered British ports would be seized by the French when they came out to sea again.

To try to make this System work, Napoleon got the support of Alexander I at Tilsit and could therefore impose his decision on Prussia, Austria and most other European countries.

Fig. 9.2 A cartoon, drawn in 1795, showing Pitt as the butcher and the poorer classes as John Bull, the customer, obviously suffering from the high price of food. You will find the word *journeyman* explained on p. 61, and you should know that in the year in which the cartoon was drawn (1795) the Speenhamland System was started (p. 39).

CONDITIONS IN BRITAIN

The Industrial Revolution went on at an increasing rate. The huge demand for **munitions** led to increased demand for **iron** and **coal**. By 1800 over 16 million tons of coal were being dug out each year – the first product to measure its output in millions of tons.

Watt's **steam-engine** was used in more factories, iron-works, breweries, potteries and coal mines.

Textiles were in great demand, for uniforms and for exports to the Empire. But the more productive machinery meant that there was unemployment among hand-workers. This was especially true of the hand-loom weavers, who suffered after the introduction of the power-loom (p. 14).

In **Yorkshire** the croppers (p. 13) attacked the factories in which owners used the new **shearing machines** (p. 14). In the **Nottingham and Derby** region, workmen attacked the factories using the new **stocking-knitting** machinery. In both cases the attackers claimed that they were led by a character called Ned Ludd, after whom they were nicknamed **Luddites**.

The Continental System interfered with trade and led to some unemployment. But merchants looked for new markets in South America, which was to prove important in the 1820s.

Farmers benefited from the drop in the volume of food imported into Britain when Europe became involved in the War after 1793. This drop led to **increased prices** for bread and other food. For the workers this was disastrous, particularly in years when unemployment was high and wages low. It is not surprising that there were years during which there were food riots (1810), machine wrecking (1812) and even the murder of the Prime Minister (1812).

BRITAIN'S ANSWER TO THE CONTINENTAL SYSTEM

The government realized that if the System succeeded, Britain would have to make peace on Napoleon's terms. So the **Orders in Council** (1807) were issued, which said that Britain would seize any ship trying to enter or leave French ports.

The **Navy** now came into its own. The European coast was blockaded so that goods in Europe became scarce, manufacturers were unable to export their products and unemployment spread across France. So difficult did life become in Europe that Napoleon was forced to allow some British goods to be brought in.

NAPOLEON AND THE IMPOSITION OF THE SYSTEM

In spite of the difficulties that he faced, Napoleon tried to ensure that the system worked. The country which caused him the most trouble was **Portugal**, a long-time friend to Britain and one with a long coastline.

■ 9.3 The Peninsular War ■

THE ORIGINS OF THE PENINSULAR WAR

Portugal refused to obey the Continental System. This forced Napoleon to invade **Spain** to give his armies access to Portugal. This, in turn, angered the Spaniards who were further enraged when Napoleon made his brother, Joseph, the King of Spain.

THE GUERRILLA WAR IN SPAIN

There were very **few good roads** in Spain, a mountainous country. This made it difficult for the French armies to maintain contact with France.

Spain was also a poor country. French armies had been used to getting the **supplies** they needed from the countries through which they moved. This was not possible in Spain.

Although the Spanish army was no match for the French, the people were able to organize themselves into small groups (called **guerrillas**) to attack the French struggling across the mountains. Napoleon summed up the situation when he said that Spain was a country in which large armies would starve while small armies would be beaten.

BRITAIN ENTERS THE PENINSULAR WAR, 1808

In June 1808 a small army under Sir Arthur Wellesley (later Lord Wellington) was sent to help the Portuguese against the French.

In August 1808 he defeated the French at **Rolica** and **Vimiero**. The French then signed the Convention (or agreement) of **Cintra** agreeing to leave Portugal, while the British agreed to let them take away their arms and equipment. This lenient treatment angered some people in Britain and Wellesley was recalled.

Sir John Moore was sent to replace him, while Napoleon himself took charge of the French forces in Spain, where the Spaniards had driven Joseph from Madrid. In August 1808 Napoleon captured Madrid and put Joseph back on the throne.

Moore decided to lead his army to help the Spaniards but when he heard about the capture of Madrid he turned north hoping to cut off Napoleon's army as it retreated to France. This failed and Moore took his army to **Corunna** where he was attacked by the French. He died after managing to get most of his army on to British ships and to safety. The Navy had once again saved the day.

WELLINGTON AND THE PENINSULAR WAR, 1809–13

After Moore's death Napoleon left Spain and appointed Marshal Soult as Commander of the French in Spain. In April 1809 Wellesley was sent as British Commander. His campaigns in the Peninsula fall into three stages:

▶ **1809**, the year of his appointment. In April he defeated Soult at **Oporto** in Portugal and at **Talavera** in Spain – after which victory he was made Viscount Wellington of Talavera. Soult was replaced by Marshal Massena who brought fresh armies from France. This forced Wellington to retreat to **Torres Vedras** near Lisbon, where there were three strong lines of defence to protect him from French attack.

▶ **1809–10** During the winter of 1809–10 Massena laid seige to Torres Vedras, but had to call off the siege when his supplies ran out. Wellington's men were better supplied because the **Navy** brought in supplies.

▶ **1810–13** During these years, Wellington drove Massena from Portugal, from Spain and over the Pyrenees into France. His success was marked by a number of famous victories: **Fuentes d'Onoro** (1811), **Almeida** (1811) and **Albeura** (1811). These victories enabled him to go on to take his main objectives, **Badajoz** (1812) and **Ciudad Rodrigo** (1812), which commanded the two routes from Lisbon to Madrid.

In 1812 Wellington captured **Madrid**, and in June 1813 he had another string of victories, at **Burgos, Vittoria, San Sebastian** and **Pamplona**, and drove the French out of Spain.

WHY DID WELLINGTON DEFEAT THE FRENCH?

▶ His armies were better supplied because of the **Navy**.
▶ The strong lines of defence at **Torres Vedras** prevented a French victory in 1809.
▶ The Spanish and Portuguese **guerrillas** hampered the French effort, attacked their supplies and forced commanders to use men who might otherwise have been fighting the British.

■ 9.4 Napoleon's Downfall ■

THE WAR WITH THE USA, 1812–14

As part of its campaign against the Continental System, the British insisted on their right to search merchant ships of any country. This was meant to prevent goods going to or from France.

The Americans claimed the right to trade as they wanted, and declared war on Britain, hoping to conquer Canada. An American army invaded Canada, burnt down part of York (now Toronto) but then retreated.

A British army led by General Ross invaded the USA, attacked Washington and set fire to some important buildings, including the home of the US President. Later the house was whitewashed to hide the marks of the fire, and so became known as the White House.

There were several naval encounters – in Chesapeake Bay as well as in the English Channel – in which the Americans proved that they were as good as the British. But they did not have the power to defeat Britain, while Britain wanted to get on with the more serious business of defeating Napoleon.

Both sides agreed to end the fighting in the **Treaty of Ghent** (1814). which ignored the question of the right to search but which did lead to the appointment of four Commissioners to examine the problems of the boundary between Canada and the USA.

NAPOLEON AND RUSSIA, 1812–15

Napoleon described the Peninsular War as 'the Spanish ulcer' which drained away men and material. Even more disastrous for him was the Russian campaign, which was forced on him by Alexander I's decision to break the Treaty of Tilsit (p. 24), and abandon the Continental System (December 1810) – a sign of Russia's need for British goods.

In June 1812 Napoleon led 600 000 French troops, supported by Austrians and Prussians into Russia. In September he defeated the Russians at **Borodino**, but lost 100 000 men in so doing.

A week later he entered **Moscow**, a deserted and burning city as part of the Russian policy of 'scorched earth'. In October Napoleon left Moscow. Heavy losses were incurred by the retreating army by:
▶ **the attacks of the Russian cavalry;**
▶ **the severe weather;**
▶ **the lack of food and supplies.**

When he finally left Russia, Napoleon had lost over 500,000 men. This failure led to a general uprising against him throughout Europe in 1813.

THE FOURTH COALITION, 1813–15

In 1813 the British Foreign Secretary, Lord Castlereagh,

arranged a Coalition between Britain, Russia, Austria and Prussia. Britain, again, gave the Allies the money they needed, a proof of Britain's wealth derived from her industrial power. The Allies enjoyed continual success:
▶ Britain's Allies defeated the French at the Battle of the Nations at Leipzig (1813);
▶ Wellington won a battle at **Toulouse**, 1814.
▶ Both armies then marched on **Paris**, which fell in March 1814.

THE HUNDRED DAYS, MARCH – JUNE 1815

Napoleon gave up the French throne in April 1814 and went to live in exile on the island of Elba.

The Allied Powers then arranged a Conference in Paris to hammer out a peace treaty in which they meant to reward themselves, punish the French, restore the French monarchy and redraw the map of Europe. In January 1815 the peacemakers left Paris for Vienna. The Treaty which ended the War is usually described as having been made by the **Congress of Vienna**.

After ten months in exile, Napoleon left Elba, returned to France, raised new armies and entered Paris in triumph in March 1815. This forced the Allies to get down again to the work of defeating Napoleon.

In June 1815 Napoleon left Paris to campaign in the Netherlands where he was outnumbered by the Allied Troops led by **Blucher** and **Wellington**. On June 18th the armies met at **Waterloo**, and after a hard day's fighting Napoleon's army was put to flight.

Napoleon returned to Paris, gave up the throne again then travelled to the coast where he surrendered to the captain of a British ship, the **Bellerophon**. When this ship reached Plymouth Napoleon was told that the Allies had decided to exile him to the lonely island of St Helena. He died there in May 1821.

Unit 9 Summary

▶ The course of the war against Napoleon.
▶ The Continental System and its effects on British life.
▶ The importance of the Peninsular War.
▶ The career of the Duke of Wellington.
▶ Reasons for the defeat of Napoleon.

---

10 RELIGION AND THE HUMANITARIANS

10.1 The Church of England and the Crown

DISSENTERS

The Church of England – the Anglican Church – had been founded during the Tudor Reformation and the break with Rome. The Monarch was, and is, the Head of that Church.

From the beginning there were some people who thought the Anglican Church was still too much like the Roman Catholic Church. They wanted even more extreme changes. Because they dissented from (or disagreed with) the Anglicans they were called **Dissenters**.

In the sixteenth and seventeenth centuries the Kings and government thought that those who dissented in religion

were disloyal to the Throne. So Dissenters and Catholics were punished and made to suffer for their religion.

Penal Laws against the Catholics

Even in the middle of the eighteenth century, by law:
▶ Priests could be fined £200 and tried for high treason for saying the Mass.
▶ Catholics who refused to attend the local Anglican Church were fined £20 a month.
▶ No Catholic was allowed to hold any civil, naval or military post, sit in Parliament or on a local council, become a doctor or a lawyer or travel more than five miles from home without a licence.

During the second half of the century these laws were

relaxed. In 1778 and 1779 Catholic Relief Acts abolished some of the Penal Laws, but when the government tried to introduce these laws into Scotland there was a riot in Edinburgh, while a half-mad Scottish nobleman, Lord George Gordon, led the London mob into a week of rioting (pp. 2, 3).

In 1791 the laws were further relaxed, and Catholics who were prepared to take an oath of loyalty to the King were allowed to become lawyers, attend Mass and enter religious orders.

Penal Laws against the Non-Catholic Dissenters

The Dissenters had been persecuted under the Stuarts. Some of them had escaped on the **Mayflower** and founded a colony in New England in America.

Under Charles II the **Clarendon Code** was brought into operation to stop Dissenting clergymen from preaching, teaching or holding meetings in established towns. In addition, **the Test Acts** were passed, allowing only communicating Anglicans to hold official posts or attend the only universities in England, Oxford and Cambridge.

THE GROWTH OF TOLERATION

William III and Queen Mary were put on the throne when Parliament led a rebellion against the Catholic James II in 1688. William was a **Calvinist** and the overthrow of James II has been supported by English Dissenters.

As a reward for this support, Parliament passed the **Toleration Act** (1689) allowing Dissenters to hold religious services. In 1718 and 1719 Parliament, although dominated entirely by Anglicans, passed Acts to allow Dissenters to stand for election to town councils and to send their children to Dissenting schools. Finally, in 1728 Walpole persuaded Parliament to pass the first **Annual Indemnity Act** which cancelled the political restrictions on Dissenters; they could now sit in Parliament.

Other restrictions remained, however, until the repeal of the Test Acts in 1827–28.

A BROADMINDED CHURCH OF ENGLAND

The **Jacobite** risings (1715 and 1745) which were in favour of the Stuarts, frightened the English government. They realized that the people were not entirely united in support of the Hanoverian Kings.

If the government had appointed Bishops with strict religious views, there might have been a renewal of the religious quarrels which had divided the country in the seventeenth century. This might have given the Jacobites another chance to rise.

Consequently the government appointed Bishops who were more politicians than dedicated clergymen. They spent most of their time in London and did not interfere with the local clergy, who were then free to practise whatever services they wanted. Some followed an almost Catholic form of service, while others were more like Dissenters with their concentration on the sermon.

Many parish clergy, freed from a bishop's supervision, became careless about their work. Some did not hold regular services, others were more interested in hunting and fishing than about religion. Many of the better-off clergy got themselves appointed to a number (or a **plurality**) of parishes. They could not serve all their parishes and they appointed poorly paid, often poorly educated curates to do their work.

The result of this was that the Church of England lost much of its influence over the people in the villages and older towns. It also had little influence in the growing industrial towns, where there were no churches at first.

The decline of religion led to a decline in morals and standards of behaviour. Drunkenness, gambling, robbery and violence became more common – and the absence of organized police forces made life easy for the wrongdoers.

▮ 10.2 John Wesley, 1703–91 ▮

John Wesley was the son of an Anglican clergyman. In 1720 he went to Oxford University and later was ordained a clergyman. He acted as his father's curate for two years before going back to Oxford, where his younger brother, **Charles** had started a religious society.

John Wesley joined this group and, as the only ordained clergyman, he soon became its leader. The group held regular meetings, spent many hours each day in prayer, religious study and good works, such as visiting the poor and prisoners. Some people mocked them for the regular pattern of life and nicknamed them the **Methodists**.

Charles Wesley (1707–88) helped his brother, particularly by writing over 6000 hymns which became popular with Methodists and many of which have been accepted and used by other Christian denominations.

WESLEY AND THE SPREAD OF METHODISM

In 1736 Wesley accepted an invitation to serve in the new colony of **Georgia**. But he did not get on with the Indians or the colonists, and was forced to leave.

While travelling back from America he met a group of **Moravians** (German Protestants) who invited him to attend their church in London. At one of these services, in 1738, Wesley had a great religious experience which changed his way of life.

He decided that he had to spend his life bringing back the people to God. He went on a series of **journeys** throughout the Kingdom. By the end of his life he had travelled 250 000 miles. He preached over 40 000 **sermons**, averaging 15 a week.

At first he preached in the local **Anglican Church**. But soon the majority of clergy turned against him, maybe because they realized that they, too, ought to be doing what Wesley was doing. They refused to let him use their Churches so that he had to preach out of doors, in village squares, at pit heads and at factory gates. Some clergymen and Anglican gentlemen led mobs against him; he was often attacked and several times nearly killed.

Wesley helped his followers to form a **society** in every town, so that they would continue to meet when he left. The members of the society continued to meet in prayer under the leadership of a **layman**.

The Bishops refused to help him in his work. In **1784** he wanted three ministers to be ordained to serve in America. No Bishop would perform an ordination, so Wesley 'ordained' his own clergymen, so separating himself from the Anglican Church. Until then he had been careful to organize the meetings of his societies so that they did not clash with the times of Anglican services. But in **1786** a Conference of Methodists decided to hold services at the same time as the Parish Church.

THE IMPORTANCE OF WESLEY'S WORK

Many Anglican clergy adopted some of Wesley's methods (see below.) His insistence that, while people were unequal in terms of wealth and worldly goods, they were equal before God, led many of his supporters to become 'other wordly', i.e. they took little part in the demand for social and political reform. Many historians claim that it was the spread of Methodism that saved Britain from following the French example in 1789 when France embarked on its Revolution (unit 8).

Later, in the nineteenth century, many Methodists argued that, if men were equal before God, then that equality should be a feature of their life in this world. They became the leaders of the demand for social and economic reform. In particular, Methodists made a major contribution to the development of trade unionism (unit 25).

Although some Methodists were industrialists and wealthy men, the majority were working people. In Methodist chapels in the industrial areas many of them learned to organize themselves in order to raise money for the chapel, to run Sunday schools and to supervise the work of their local chapel. Others became preachers. One result of these activities was to help some working men to develop so that they were able to organize non-Church societies such as the local Cooperative (unit 17) and the local Labour Party (unit 40).

10.3 Anglican Evangelicals

Wesley's success in the new industrial towns, and in the industrial areas of Cornwall and Wales, stirred the consciences of some Anglican clergymen who decided that Wesley was right and that the slack behaviour of the Bishops, clergy and laypeople in the Anglican Church was wrong.

In the north, the Midlands and the west, clergymen began to imitate Wesley, preaching lively sermons, asking people to give their lives to God and showing how this might be done by the way in which they lived. Because they lived according to the Gospels written by the four Evangelists, and because they wanted to spread these Gospels, they became known as Evangelicals.

Amongst the more important Evangelicals were Wilberforce, Hannah More, Robert Raikes and John Howard. They and other Evangelicals led the movement to improve not only the morals of the people, but the conditions of life of the less fortunate.

WILLIAM WILBERFORCE, 1759–1833

Wilberforce was a friend of the Younger Pitt (p. 18) and MP for Hull. He became an Evangelical after a journey to Milan in the company of **Isaac Milner** (1784), a Cambridge clergyman who influenced many students.

He had influential friends in the Clapham parish, where the Evangelical clergyman was **John Venn**. These men formed what became known as the **Clapham Sect**, which campaigned to get better-off people to take a close interest in politics, the lives of the less well-off and in reforms that were needed. In particular they helped form the anti-slavery movement. But this did not make them Radicals. Wilberforce was the first MP who put forward the motion that trade unions should be banned – a motion which led his friend, Prime Minister Pitt, to bring in the Combination Acts (p. 61). Wilberforce was also opposed to Factory Reform (unit 17). This led one reformer, Oastler, to attack him as a hypocrite who opposed slavery in the colonies but who did nothing about the slavery in his constituency (Hull in Yorkshire) where children worked in conditions which Oastler described as 'Yorkshire Slavery'.

The slave trade

Since Elizabethan times, English merchants had played a part in the slave trade. This was given recognition in the **Treaty of Utrecht** (1713), which said that British merchants had the right to sell African slaves in the Spanish colonies of Central and South America.

The growth of the southern colonies in **British America** led to an expansion of that trade, since slave labour was needed to work the tobacco plantations and the cotton fields. The development of the sugar industry in the **West Indies** led to a further increased demand for African slaves.

British merchants bought their slaves in the slave markets of the **West African** coast where Europeans, Africans and Arabs brought men, women and children captured in the interior.

The slaves were taken on board the 'slavers' (slave-carrying ships) where they were crowded together, often handcuffed and chained to stop them attacking the crews. They were punished by whippings if they proved difficult, and were badly fed by captains anxious to make a profit on the long journey to the Americas.

Bristol and **Liverpool** grew rich on the proceeds of the

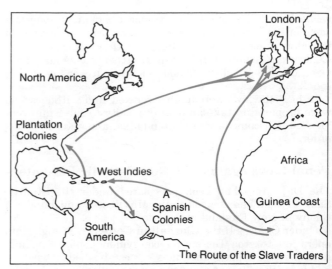

Fig. 10.3 A sketch map to illustrate the routes taken by slave traders, who left London, Liverpool or Bristol to pick up slaves on the west coast of Africa and to sail on the 'Middle Passage' (marked 'A') to work in plantations in America, the West Indies and Spanish America.

slave trade, while the profits made by merchants in this trade provided some of the finance needed for the early industrial revolution.

The Campaign against the Slave Trade

The evils of the slave trade became well known because of the work of various groups of reformers. There were **Quakers** such as Thomas Clarkson who got their information from sailors and slaver-captains.

But these people had no voice in Parliament. In **1787** Wilberforce and the rest of the Clapham Sect set up a Society for the Abolition of the Slave Trade. In **1788** Pitt, as Prime Minister, set up a Commons' Committee to examine the slave trade. In **1789** Wilberforce brought in his first motion for the abolition of the trade, but failed to get the support of the Commons.

The campaign continued, and in **1807** succeeded in getting Parliament to abolish the slave trade. This still left unsolved the problem of slavery in the Empire. Wilberforce continued his campaign but had to wait until 1833 – when he was dying – before that campaign succeeded (p. 38).

HANNAH MORE (1745–1833) AND EDUCATING THE POOR

Hannah More was a well-known playwright and a member of high society until she decided that God wanted more from her. She spent the rest of her life trying to help the poor to lead better lives. She opened her first school in 1789 in Cheddar where she provided classes for the women as well as the children. Many people attacked her for this, claiming that she was giving the poor ideas above their station, such that they might become willing to support a revolution in Britain. She argued that she only taught the catechism, used the Bible, the Prayer Book and religious tracts for reading lessons and taught the people their duties – obedience to masters and being content with their station in life.

ROBERT RAIKES, 1755–1811

Raikes was a Gloucester journalist who spent his time and money founding Sunday schools for the education of working children. He knew about these kinds of school because Wesley and other Dissenters had been running them for a long time.

JOHN HOWARD, 1726–90

Howard became High Sheriff for Bedfordshire in 1773 and became aware of the horrible conditions in prisons. In 1777

he published an account of his survey of prisons in England and Wales. This showed that:
▶ Men, women and children often shared cells, with hardened criminals being put in the same cells as young children.
▶ Most prisons were overcrowded and dirty.
▶ There was often a poor water supply and lack of sanitation.
▶ Because the authorities did not want to spend much money on prisoners, the food was deficient in quantity and quality, and clothing and bedding was rarely changed or washed.
▶ Disease was common and many prisoners died from one or other of the epidemics which flourished in these conditions. Howard went on to campaign for prison reform but had little success, although an Act passed in 1784 dealt with some of the worst evils. However, his work went on after his death, and even today his name is commemorated in the Howard League for Penal Reform, which continues to campaign for improved treatment of prisoners.

ELIZABETH FRY, 1780–1845

Elizabeth Fry was the wife of a banker-relative of the Frys, the Bristol chocolate manufacturers. She took a particular interest in the condition of women prisoners. In 1813 she began to visit the women in **Newgate** prison, teaching them to read and write and providing work for them and their children to do. She hoped that this might help them while in prison and make it easier for them to find work when they were released. In 1817 she got other people to join her in this work. She formed an Association and extended her work to other prisons. Her demands for reform were ignored until long after her death.

Unit 10 Summary

▶ The legal position of Catholics and Nonconformists in the eighteenth and early nineteenth centuries.
▶ The decline in the influence of the Anglican Church, and the growth of Methodism.
▶ The career of Wesley.
▶ The growth of, and importance of the Evangelical Movement.
▶ The work of important figures such as Hannah More, Elizabeth Fry, Robert Raikes and John Howard.
▶ The campaign against the slave trade and slavery.

---

11 DOMESTIC POLICY, 1815–22

11.1 Understanding the Problem

The period 1815–22 is sometimes described as 'the years of distress', and you should (i) understand the reasons for that distress, (ii) see how the people of the country behaved in these hard times and (iii) examine the ways in which the government dealt with the problems facing the country.

You will not understand the causes of the distress unless you remember that British history did not start in 1815 – although, for some students, their study does begin at that date. The government under Lord Liverpool had led the country in the final days of the struggle against Napoleon (unit 9). This struggle had its beginnings in the wars against the French Revolutionary government (unit 8) which started in 1793. These long wars had their effects on life in Britain after 1815.

During the period 1793–1815 the country had also been going through the later stages of the revolutions in industry (unit 5) and agriculture (unit 4). As we shall see, these revolutions also had their effects on life in Britain after 1815.

So there were many causes of that distress from which the people and the country suffered after 1815. It is important that you should study these under three headings: (i) the effects of the industrial and agricultural revolutions; (ii) the effects of the war and the end of the war; (iii) the effects of government policies before and after 1815.

11.2 The Industrial Revolution

On p. 14 we considered the changes in industry which had taken place after 1760. You read about the power-driven machinery which could be worked by women and children and which produced much more than had the old-fashioned hand-worker in the domestic system. This revolution had gone on during the wars against France. In particular there had been the introduction of the steam-driven power loom on which women and children wove that cloth for which Britain was famous. The success of this machine meant that:
▶ Handloom weavers – once the best paid of all workers – had to accept lower prices for the work they did, if they got any work at all.
▶ Unemployment spread from the spinning to the weaving towns of Lancashire and Yorkshire.
▶ The factory system – in spinning and weaving – forced men, women and children to work long hours for low wages in dirty and dangerous conditions.
▶ Because of their low pay, millions of people had to live in overcrowded housing conditions where they had a poor diet, which led to a high death rate.

WORKING-CLASS REACTION TO THESE CONDITIONS

Some working people, led by such men as Francis Place, tried to get the government to allow them to form trade unions so that they might be better able to get higher wages and better working conditions from their employers. The government passed the Combination Acts to make trade unions illegal. Some middle-class Radicals, such as Cobbett, Hunt and Robert Owen, tried to lead the people in protest against the effects of the industrial revolution. We shall see how the government dealt with these men and the protests they organized.

Some working men took the law into their own hands. Under the pretended leadership of 'Ned Ludd' they attacked factory owners, smashed machines and tried to prevent the introduction of the machines which created unemployment.

The government sent the army to deal with such gangs and encouraged magistrates and judges to pass harsh sentences against any Luddites who were captured.

11.3 The Agricultural Revolution

In the countryside the agricultural revolution had also gone on during the long wars.
► The General Enclosure Act of 1801 (p. 9) allowed the completion of the enclosure movement.
► On their bigger farms the new owners brought in new machinery, which meant less work for farmworkers. The end of the domestic system in the textile trades meant that these workers also lost their second source of income.
► Those who lost their jobs drifted to the industrial towns in the search for work.
► Those working had to take wage cuts or face dismissal.
► Some of them tried to take the law into their own hands, although the agricultural riots did not become too serious until 1830, which is outside the dates for this unit.

It is clear that there would have been a good deal of distress and hardship in 1815, even if the country had not been involved in the long wars between 1793 and 1815. But these wars made things much worse.

THE GOVERNMENT AND CORN

During the war it had not been possible to import foreign corn. This had led to an expansion of British wheat farming and to high prices for wheat and other grain (unit 3). These high prices had led to high incomes for farmers and to high rents for landowners who let their land to tenant farmers.

Once the war was over these people were frightened that the import of foreign corn would lead to lower prices, falling incomes and lower rents. The landowners controlled the corrupt and unreformed Parliamentary system and pushed through the Corn Laws, which said that no corn could be imported until the prices of home-grown corn had reached the wartime price of £4 a quarter. This kept the price of bread high and meant an even harder life for the low-paid who had to pay those higher prices.

11.4 The Cost of the Wars

The governments under Pitt and Liverpool had paid huge sums of money to Britain's allies to help them in the fight against France. Huge sums had also been spent on Britain's own war effort – paying for munitions, ships, uniforms, soldiers' pay, waggons, horses and food.

This spending at home and abroad meant that the government had to put up taxes. It brought in a new form of tax called income tax (p. 24).

Taxation did not bring in all the money needed, so the government had to borrow about £700 million from rich people in this country, and had to pay them interest each year on the money borrowed. This interest had to come from taxation so that, again, taxes had to be increased.

THE WAR AND PRICES

During the war most people had a job, since the employers were able to sell their goods to the government. This meant that **prices rose**, since there was too much money (from wages and profits) chasing too few goods in the shops. This was especially hard on those who had no job or who had low wages.

But **once the war had ended** the government cut its orders to the munitions and other industries. Employers now found that they had too many goods on their hands, so they dismissed their workpeople – which added to the problem of unemployment. **Prices of goods now fell** sharply, which frightened those businessmen who might have been thinking of building a factory. This meant that there was less employment than there might have been.

THE END OF THE WAR

The end of the war had several effects on life in Britain:
► The government immediately **demobilized** over 300 000 soldiers and sailors. These had no jobs to go to and joined the ranks of the unemployed.
► The government **cut its orders to industry**, which led to a cut in industry's demand for coal, iron, machinery and raw material. Many people lost their jobs in this way.
► Those who had work were forced to accept **lower wages**, or face dismissal.
► Because people had less to spend there was a **fall in the demand** for clothing, furniture, pots and pans and other things they might have bought. This led to **unemployment** in the industries which might have made these goods. So, for all those reasons there was a high level of unemployment and for those in work, low wages. Nor was this the end.

THE GOVERNMENT AND TAXES

The selfishness of the landowners in Parliament was also responsible for the abolition of Pitt's income tax (unit 8). They argued that it had been a wartime and a temporary tax. Once the war was over, they said, the tax ought to be abolished – and that was done in 1816.

The government had to get money from somewhere. This meant that other taxes had to be put up – on candles, beer, sugar, salt, clothing and other goods bought by ordinary people as well as by the rich. This meant that the less well-off had to pay higher prices for these goods so that they had less money to spend on other things.

11.5 Popular Discontent

POLITICAL AND LEGAL REPRESSION

Some people wanted to change the Parliamentary system so that ordinary people would have a hand in the electing of MPs. They hoped that this would force Parliament to think about the problems of ordinary people and, perhaps, pass laws to help them. William Cobbett argued for Parliamentary reform in his *Weekly Register*. To try to end the influence of such papers the government brought in a paper duty which pushed the price up to 1 shilling (5p). This meant that fewer such papers were bought.

What were ordinary people to do when faced with such harsh conditions, when they had no chance to get Parliament to listen to their complaints? It is not surprising that many of them turned to violence in their search for a solution to their problems.

DEMONSTRATIONS

Figure 11.5 shows the places where the violence was most serious. In particular there were:
► The activities of the **Luddites**.
► In years of bad harvests there were **'bread riots'**.
► **1816** A riot followed a meeting at **Spa Fields** where Henry Hunt had got the crowd to support a resolution in favour of Parliamentary Reform. After the meeting some of the men broke into a gunsmith's shop and marched on the Royal Exchange where they confronted the Lord Mayor with their demands. They were dispersed by armed soldiers.
► **1817** The London mob stoned the Prince Regent's carriage when he went to open Parliament.
► **1817** Unemployed cotton workers from Manchester set out to march to London where they hoped to persuade the Prince Regent (p. 20) to get Parliament to change the laws on wages and working conditions. Because they carried blankets for use at night they were nicknamed **'the Blanketeers'**.
► **1817** The **Derby Insurrection** which followed the collapse of the Blanketeers' march near Derby.
► **1819 The Peterloo Massacre.** Henry Hunt arranged to address Lancashire workers assembled at St Peter's Fields in Salford. The Manchester magistrates were frightened by the size of the crowd and feared that there

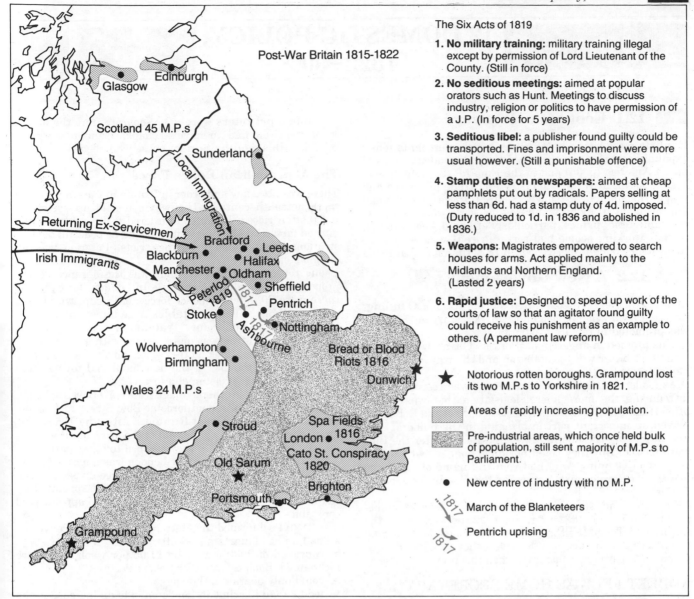

The Six Acts of 1819

1. **No military training:** military training illegal except by permission of Lord Lieutenant of the County. (Still in force)

2. **No seditious meetings:** aimed at popular orators such as Hunt. Meetings to discuss industry, religion or politics to have permission of a J.P. (In force for 5 years)

3. **Seditious libel:** a publisher found guilty could be transported. Fines and imprisonment were more usual however. (Still a punishable offence)

4. **Stamp duties on newspapers:** aimed at cheap pamphlets put out by radicals. Papers selling at less than 6d. had a stamp duty of 4d. imposed. (Duty reduced to 1d. in 1836 and abolished in 1836.)

5. **Weapons:** Magistrates empowered to search houses for arms. Act applied mainly to the Midlands and Northern England. (Lasted 2 years)

6. **Rapid justice:** Designed to speed up work of the courts of law so that an agitator found guilty could receive his punishment as an example to others. (A permanent law reform)

★ Notorious rotten boroughs. Grampound lost its two M.P.s to Yorkshire in 1821.

▨ Areas of rapidly increasing population.

▦ Pre-industrial areas, which once held bulk of population, still sent majority of M.P.s to Parliament.

● New centre of industry with no M.P.

March of the Blanketeers

Pentrich uprising

Fig. 11.5 Notice the centres of unrest, some of the causes of that unrest and, on the right-hand side, the Six Acts.

might be a riot such as happened at Spa Fields. They did not have a police force to keep order or to help break up the crowd. They did have the local yeomanry and some soldiers under their control once they had read the Riot Act and told the crowd to disperse. When the crowd stayed to listen to Hunt, the military were ordered to charge. About a dozen people were killed and 500 seriously wounded. The action was nicknamed 'Peterloo' in mockery of the army's last success at Waterloo. The magistrates were congratulated by the government and by the Prince Regent.

▶ **1820** At **Cato Street** in London a half-mad nobleman, Lord Thistlewood, plotted to kill the members of the Cabinet. His plot was discovered and he and his gang were arrested. But it is a sign of the times that such a plot was even considered.

THE IMPORTANT MEMBERS OF THE GOVERNMENT

▶ **Lord Liverpool,** who continued as Prime Minister until 1827.

▶ **Castlereagh,** as Foreign Secretary, was also leader of the House of Commons and was blamed for much of the repressive legislation that was introduced.

▶ **Eldon,** the Lord Chancellor, was the leader of the 'Ultras'–those Tories who were opposed to any reform.

▶ **Sidmouth,** the Home Secretary, was responsible for putting most of the repressive laws into operation.

THE GOVERNMENT'S ANSWER TO THE DISCONTENT

You have to remember that the government had led the country during the long Wars. It is not surprising that some of the Ministers feared that the British working men might start a French-style revolution of their own. This helps to explain the hard line that the government took during this period.

▶ **1817** Following an attack on the Prince Regent's coach, the government abolished the **Habeas Corpus Act**, so that people could be arrested and imprisoned without being brought to trial.

▶ **1819** The government persuaded Parliament to pass the **Six Acts**. After this, there was a drop in the level of unrest. There was also a slow improvement in trade at home and abroad which led to more work and some improvement in the conditions in which some of the people lived. But, until 1822, there was no change in government policy towards Parliamentary Reform, trade unionism and the demand for social reform.

Unit 11 Summary

▶ The reasons for discontent, 1815–22.
▶ The government's response to that discontent.
▶ The reasons for, and effects of, the Corn Laws.

12 DOMESTIC POLICY, 1822-30

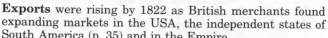

12.1 Economic Recovery

Exports were rising by 1822 as British merchants found expanding markets in the USA, the independent states of South America (p. 35) and in the Empire.

Employment rose as industry and trade prospered and **wages** began to rise slowly, so that there was a small improvement in living standards for some workpeople. At the same time, **prices**, particularly of bread, began to fall, so that working people had a rise in **real wages**, that is, their money bought more goods in 1822 than it had in 1816.

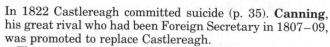

12.2 A New Government

In 1822 Castlereagh committed suicide (p. 35). **Canning**, his great rival who had been Foreign Secretary in 1807-09, was promoted to replace Castlereagh.

This promotion angered most of the 'Ultras' who disliked Canning's bitter wit, his ambition and the way in which he had opposed Castlereagh.

As leader of the Commons, Canning was responsible for introducing the more liberal legislation that was passed after 1822. Other ministers (Huskisson, Peel and Robinson) played an important part in bringing in these liberal Bills and in putting the liberal laws into practice after the Bills were passed. But they could not have done so without the support of Canning, who had won the name of being the leader of the reforming Tories, or the Young (or Liberal) Tories.

Canning had supported the repressive legislation between 1815 and 1822. But in 1822 he convinced the majority of Tory MPs that they could not go on governing the country with such a repressive policy. They had to be prepared to pass reforming laws when this proved necessary.

ROBERT PEEL AS HOME SECRETARY

The death penalty

In 1822 people could be hanged for over 100 crimes, including stealing articles worth 5 shillings (25p) or for scribbling on Westminster Bridge.

Other people had tried to reform this severe system. In **1808 Samuel Romilly** had brought a Bill to Parliament which would have abolished the law requiring pickpockets to be hanged. But Parliament threw out that Bill.

In 1818 **James Mackintosh** brought in another reforming Bill. He showed that juries were unwilling to convict people brought to Court on minor offences carrying the death penalty. This made a nonsense of the law. He also showed that a man committing only a minor offence might commit murder if he though he was going to be in danger of being caught. 'As well to be hanged for a sheep as a lamb' was the proverb that illustrated this behaviour.

In **1823 Peel** had the active support of Canning and the support of the majority of MPs when he proposed the abolition of the death penalty for most crimes. Later on there were further reforms so that by 1838 people could only be hanged for murder or for treason.

Prison reform

Peel accepted the evidence which had been produced by Howard and Elizabeth Fry (p. 29) about prison conditions. He began a reform of the prison system by ordering that:
▶ **gaolers were to be paid** by the government instead of relying on getting money from the prisoners themselves;
▶ **magistrates were to inspect** prisons to see that conditions were sanitary and humane;

▶ **women prisoners** were to be separate from the m
▶ each prison had to have a chaplain and teacher provide a **basic education** for those who needed it.

The Metropolitan Police Force

There was little law and order in Britain in the early pa the nineteenth century. Highwaymen held up travel mobs often rioted, Luddites murdered factory owners burned factories. Meetings which began as peaceful der strations often ended in savage riots. Peterloo wa example of this.

One reason for this behaviour was the absence of proper police force in the country. In London, for exar there were 70 different police forces, each supervised parish authority. The **constables** were unpaid and se for one year as a public duty. **Watchmen** were appointed to patrol the dark streets at night, armed with a rattle and a staff. Only old men took on this work and they were unable to deal with criminals. In the new industrial towns there was not even this skeleton of a force.

The **Fielding** brothers, magistrates at Bow Street in London, had set up a paid force at Bow Street in London, known as the **Bow Street Runners**. After the 1750s, this group frightened many gangs out of the area, but it was not allowed to pursue them if they escaped to other parts.

In **1792** the police system for London was improved by an Act which divided London into seven police divisions, each under the control of three paid magistrates appointed by the Home Secretary. These had the power to appoint paid constables.

In 1829 Peel formed the Metropolitan Police force which:
▶ had its headquarters at Scotland Yard;
▶ consisted of 3000 men, paid £1.05 per week, who were nicknamed 'Bobbies' after Sir Robert Peel;
▶ could only operate in London;
▶ led to a fall in crime in London and to an increase in the number of those caught committing crimes;
▶ caused other towns to follow London's example by setting up their own forces.

The 'spy' system

This had been used by the government between 1815 and 1822 in its campaigns against those responsible for popular demonstrations. Men paid by the government would behave as if they were supporters of reform, trade unionism or some other radical proposal. They provoked people to support such proposals, hence their French name of *agents provocateurs*. When the people had chosen their leaders or planned a demonstration, the 'spies' would inform the magistrates who could then more easily arrest the leaders. Peel ended this system of paid 'spies'.

WILLIAM HUSKISSON AT THE BOARD OF TRADE

Huskisson, one of Canning's supporters and, like him, an MP for Liverpool, was responsible for the more important reforms made by this government. He, Canning and Peel (the son of a cotton manufacturer) realized the importance of trade to Britain's prosperity. Britain was now the world's leading industrial power and needed to find larger markets for her products.

Huskisson persuaded **Robinson, the Chancellor of the Exchequer**, to bring in a budget (1824) which lowered import duties on raw wools and raw silks. In later budgets he lowered the duties on cotton, woollen goods, coffee, cocoa, lead and iron. All this led to a fall in prices, which made it easier to sell British goods abroad. It also led to increased employment in Britain and to a rise in living standards. It is not surprising that the Chancellor became known as 'Prosperity' Robinson.

Huskisson brought in a series of Acts by which:

▶ **duties on raw materials** were cut; the duty on cotton was cut from about 50 per cent to 10 per cent. This helped reduce the price of cotton manufactured goods, led to increased sales at home and abroad, encouraged an expansion of the textile industry and helped create more employment;

▶ **duties on imported manufactured goods** were cut, with the government hoping to bring them down, on average to 20 per cent. The duty on woollen goods fell from about 60 per cent to only 18 per cent; the duty on linen goods fell from over 100 per cent to 25 per cent while the duty on silk imports was fixed at 30 per cent.

Huskisson was following the policies started by Pitt as regards import duties (p. 19). He also followed the example of Pitt's trade treaty with France (p. 19) by getting Parliament to pass the **Reciprocity Act** (1825) which gave him power to lower the duties on goods coming from countries which lowered their import duties on British goods.

He negotiated changes in the **Navigation Acts** (p. 15) so that goods could be brought from foreign countries in foreign ships. This led to a further increase in trade with foreign countries. However, he insisted that trade between countries in the Empire had to be carried on British ships only. The Navigation Acts were not totally repealed until 1849.

Huskisson and trade unions, 1824–25

Until 1824 British workmen were forbidden to emigrate. Governments feared that they might take abroad the secrets of the steam-engine and other machinery. By 1824 Huskisson thought that Britain did not need to fear foreign competition and that it did not need such a law, so he set up a Committee of the Commons to examine this law. **Joseph Hume**, a Radical MP, and **Francis Place** (p. 61) persuaded him to allow the Committee to examine the question of the Combination Acts which forbade the formation of trade unions.

The Committee decided that men should be free to form unions and in 1824 Huskisson got Parliament to pass an Act **repealing the Combination Acts**. However, this led to the formation of many unions and the calling of many strikes. In 1825 Huskisson had an Act passed which forbade strikes, although trade unions were still legal.

Huskisson and corn

Since 1816 there had been a campaign against the Corn Laws by:

▶ **employers** who argued that they kept the price of bread too high and so forced them to pay too-high wages;

▶ **manufacturers** who argued that if it was right to lower the duties on manufactured goods and raw materials, it must also be right at least to lower the duty on imported corn;

▶ **working-class leaders** such as Place who argued that the high price of bread left the people with less money to spend on other things. This reduced the demand for goods which they might have bought if bread were cheaper.

Huskisson knew all this but he was a member of a government and a Parliament controlled by landowners. So he could not support the abolition of the Corn Laws. He did, however, propose a **sliding scale** so that when the price of British corn rose (because of a poor harvest) the tax on imported corn should be cut. If the price of British corn fell (because of a good harvest) then the tax would rise. This would have given the British farmer a good market and a sure income, but it would also have led to a fall in bread prices, at least in years of bad harvests. The landowners would not agree until 1828, by which time Huskisson had resigned.

12.3 Catholic Emancipation and Canning

Canning called himself 'a Pittite' because he agreed with the policies of the Younger Pitt, who had tried to bring in Catholic Emancipation in 1801 and had resigned when the King refused to agree.

Canning supported Emancipation but could not get his Cabinet colleagues to agree when he was only leader of the House.

In February 1827, however, Liverpool had a stroke and resigned, and Canning became Prime Minister. Wellington, Peel and Eldon resigned because they feared that he would try to bring in an Emancipation Bill.

Unfortunately he died in August 1827 before he could do so.

A DIVIDED TORY PARTY, 1827–30

The resignation of Wellington and Peel in January 1827 had split the Tory party and angered the Canningites. After Canning's death, Lord **Goderich**, previously Robinson, became Prime Minister but was unable to hold the Cabinet together and resigned in January 1828.

Wellington then became Prime Minister, determined not to bring in an Emancipation Bill. Peel was appointed Home Secretary again, with his record of having once been an anti-Catholic Chief Secretary for Ireland.

Some Canningites, including **Huskisson**, tried to get the Cabinet to agree to Emancipation. When they failed, they resigned. The Tory party was now split again. many of the Canningites drifted to the Whig party where Palmerston and Melbourne, for example, became outstanding leaders.

THE FALL OF WELLINGTON

In unit 23 we shall see that the election of O'Connell for County Clare forced the Wellington government to bring in an Emancipation Bill in 1829, or risk civil war in Ireland.

While this did not win back the support of the Canningites, it led to a further division in the Tory party. The 'Ultras' regarded Wellington and Peel as traitors for having given in over the Catholic question.

In November 1830 the government's many Tory opponents – Canningites and 'Ultras' – combined with the Whigs to defeat the government on its tax proposals.

The King, William IV, was forced to ask the Whig leader, Grey, to form a government and it was that government which reformed Parliament (unit 14).

12.4 The Economy and Politics

In 1830 the Liverpool–Manchester railway was opened. This was the longest railway line ever planned at that time. It linked two of the important industrial centres.

Its opening marked a new stage in the Industrial Revolution. It was, in a sense, fitting that a new, reforming government should come to office in that year. Politics and economic development marched hand in hand.

At its opening, Huskisson was knocked down by the engine as he was crossing the line to go to speak to Wellington. Some people think that he was about to try to reach an agreement with the Prime Minister so that the Canningites would come back into the government. His death as a result of this accident meant that no such agreement was reached and the Canningites moved into the Whig Party.

Unit 12 Summary

▶ The work of the 'liberal' Tories – Peel, Huskisson, Robinson – for legal and prison reform, freer trade and trade unionism.
▶ Attempts to reform the Corn Laws.
▶ The problem of Catholic Emancipation; the break up of the Tory Party after Canning's death.

13 FOREIGN AFFAIRS, 1815–27

13.1 Castlereagh and Canning

During this period the two Foreign Ministers were Castlereagh (until 1822) and Canning, who died in August 1827. It used to be thought that there were great differences between their policies but modern research has shown that this was not so. While historians still show some differences between their policies, they also see that the two men had much in common.

CASTLEREAGH, A GOOD 'EUROPEAN'

Castlereagh was Foreign Minister from 1812 until his death in 1822. During this period he had helped form the final Coalition against Napoleon and had come to know the leaders of the European Powers with whom he worked. He realized that Britain had a major part to play in Europe's affairs. He also succeeded in re-establishing friendly relations with the USA after the war of 1812–14.

13.2 The Congress of Vienna, 1815

The leaders of the Allied Powers who met–first at Paris then in Vienna–to draw up the Treaty to bring the French Wars to their final end, had two main aims:
► to make sure that France did not present a threat to European peace in the future as she had done since 1792;
► to punish France and those States which had sided with her and to reward the Allies–Russia, Austria and Prussia–with territorial gains. Castlereagh claimed that Britain did not want any such rewards–overlooking the gains Britain had made during the war itself.

If you are studying European History you have to know that the Allies were guilty of ignoring:
► the **national** feelings of European people whose territories were divided up to satisfy the ambitions of the Allied rulers;
► the growth of **liberal** feeling since 1789, although it has to be said that liberalism was still much less important in 1815 than it was to become by 1830.

THE CONGRESS SYSTEM AND THE QUADRUPLE ALLIANCE

The Allied Powers agreed that they would hold meetings from time to time and would also come together whenever it seemed that there was a threat to European peace. They signed the **Quadruple Alliance** (November 1815), Article VI of which contained the agreement on future meetings.

THE HOLY ALLIANCE

It is important to note the difference between the **Quadruple Alliance** and the **Holy Alliance**. The first was drawn up by the Allied Powers and owed a good deal to the work of Castlereagh and of Metternich, the Chancellor of Austria. The Holy Alliance was produced by Alexander I of Russia, but unlike the Quadruple Alliance, with its practical ideas on future meetings, it:
► made those who signed it promise that they would agree to live together in the spirit of Christian brotherhood– whatever that might mean in practice (Castlereagh called the document 'a piece of sublime mysticism and nonsense', while Metternich thought it ought never have been produced, calling it a 'loud-sounding nothing');

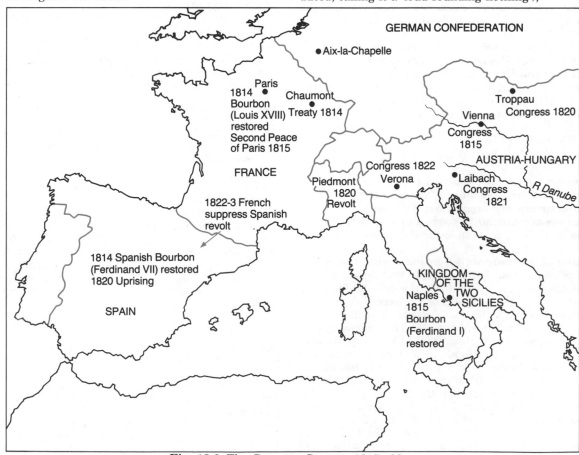

Fig. 13.2 The Congress System, 1815–22.

► was supposed to be signed by every ruler in Europe. **The Pope**, then political ruler of much of Central Italy, refused to do so; the **Sultan of Turkey**, a Muslim, would have nothing to do with 'the spirit of Christian brotherhood'; Castlreagh argued that **the King** could not sign it since he was already insane, while the **Prince Regent** could not sign it since he was not yet the ruler of the country.

At first few people saw this Alliance as a threat. It was not until Metternich used its ideas (after 1820) that it was criticized.

13.3 The Congress of Aix-La-Chapelle, 1818

In 1818 the four Allied Powers held their first peace-time Congress. They agreed to take their armies of occupation out of France, which seemed to be firmly under the rule of the restored Bourbon King. France was admitted to the Alliance, which then became the Quintuple Alliance.

13.4 European Revolutions 1818–22

Many Europeans did not like the ways in which the Allied Powers had put back pre-Revolutionary rulers on their thrones without finding out whether their peoples wanted them back, and there were Liberal risings in Spain, Portugal, Piedmont and Naples.

Alexander wanted to send Russian troops to put these risings down. Metternich opposed this, fearing that Alexander might be tempted to try to acquire European territory for himself.

INTERVENTION IN NAPLES

Metternich had a special interest in the rising in Naples, because Lombardy and Venetia were part of the Austrian Empire and the rulers of other small Italian states were related to the Austrian Emperor.

Castlreagh agreed that Naples might be considered a 'domestic' affair of Austria, and he did not oppose Metternich's plan to send troops to put down the rising there (1820).

13.5 The State Paper, 1820

Castlereagh wrote an important Paper in which he stated:
► If European peace was ever threatened, then Britain would play her part in keeping the peace, as she had done in the past.
► Some uprisings might, at some time, appear to be likely to lead to a wider rising and, maybe, to general war. In such a case, there might be a case for intervention.
► There could not be any case for agreeing to all interventions against liberal risings. Britain, for example, had had its civil wars in the seventeenth century when it had executed one King and removed another from the throne. It would be wrong for Britain to forbid other people the same freedom.

THE CONGRESS OF TROPPAU, 1820

Few people knew about this Paper, and even fewer understood its arguments, including Metternich, who thought that Castlereagh, having agreed to the intervention in Naples, would support him in his wish to intervene elsewhere. In 1820 the Powers held their second Congress, to which Castlereagh sent a delegate. At Troppau, Metternich persuaded the rulers of Russia and Prussia to sign the **Troppau Protocol** in which they agreed to intervene whenever and wherever a rising took place against a 'legitimate' ruler.

Castlereagh withdrew the British delegate and sent a letter to all British Ambassadors explaining his State Paper and asking them to likewise explain it to foreign governments.

THE CONGRESS OF LAIBACH, 1821

Metternich ignored Castlereagh's warning. He called a third Congress at which the three countries (Russia, Austria and Prussia) agreed to send troops to put down the liberal rising in Piedmont. Castlereagh protested. The unit of Europe which he had done much to create was now broken – although you should notice that he only protested at the intervention and did not take any military action against his former Allies.

THE DEATH OF CASTLEREAGH, 1822

Many Radicals blamed Castlereagh for the government's repressive policy. Some people, such as the popular poet, Byron, accused him of being under Metternich's thumb. We have seen that there was no truth in this.

While suffering from such attacks Castlereagh was also being blackmailed on a personal matter, and the pressure finally drove him to suicide.

13.6 George Canning

Canning had been Foreign Secretary (1807–9) and was the obvious choice when Castlereagh died. Unlike Castlereagh, Canning had never worked with the European Ministers and Kings. He was much less of a 'European' than was Castlereagh. He was also more fortunate.

We have seen that by 1822 the economy had begun to recover (p. 32) and that this allowed the government to adopt new policies at home. The growth in Britain's industrial power allowed Canning to pursue a more forceful policy than Castlereagh.

VERBAL OPPOSITION, 1822

At their fourth Congress, held in **Verona** in 1822, the three Allied Powers agreed to use French troops to put down the liberal rising in Spain. Canning wrote to Wellington, the British delegate, telling him to oppose such an intervention. But the intervention went ahead and Canning only protested – as Castlereagh had done in 1821. He did not send an army or navy to defend the Spanish liberals.

13.7 The Spanish-American Colonies

These colonies had been in revolt since 1809, and independent governments had been set up in Bolivia, Brazil and other former colonies. Metternich proposed that, having put down the liberal rising in Spain, the Allied Powers should win back the colonies for Spain.

Canning threatened to use the British navy to stop any such attempt, since many British merchants had a prosperous trade with the former colonies.

President Monroe of the USA issued a warning that any attempt to send European armies to anywhere in the Americas would be resisted by the USA. This **Monroe Doctrine** (1823) was aimed as much at Britain as at the European Powers.

The intervention did not take place and the former colonies achieved their independence.

13.8 Portugal, 1826

In 1820 King John VI of Portugal was living in Brazil, a Portuguese colony. A liberal rising in Portugal caused him to agree to give Portugal a more democratic form of government ('the constitution of 1822'). When John died in 1826, his daughter, the seven-year-old Maria, became ruler of Portugal together with her uncle, Miguel, as Regent.

Miguel asked the King of Spain to send in an army to support his claim to the throne and to abolish the democratic constitution. Canning sent a fleet and 4500 troops to Lisbon to help the young Monarch and the Spanish withdrew, leaving Maria as Queen.

13.9 The Greek Revolt, 1821–25

Greece was part of the Turkish Empire. By 1820 the rulers of Turkey had become corrupt and were unable to control their European and African Empire.

When the Greek people rose in revolt in 1821, the European Powers faced a major problem; were they to help their fellow-Christians in their rebellion or were they to treat this rising as they had treated those in Naples, Piedmont and Spain?

Metternich wanted to put down the rebellion. Otherwise, he argued, the idea of liberal revolutions would spread to other parts of Europe.

Alexander I wanted to help the Greeks (and so perhaps win influence in the Balkan area for Russia). But he was persuaded by Metternich not to do so and Russia remained neutral.

Alexander died in 1825. His successor, Nicholas I, decided to help the Greeks.

CANNING AND THE GREEK QUESTION

At first **Canning** had played no part in this question although many people, such as the poet Byron, thought that England and other Europeans, heirs to Greek civilization, ought to help the Greeks.

Nicholas I's decision forced Canning to act. He persuaded the Tsar to sign a Protocol under which:
▶ the Greeks would gain their independence as a state inside the Turkish Empire;
▶ Russia and Britain promised not to try to gain any

territory for themselves in the Balkan area.

The Sultan of Turkey refused to agree to these proposals. He had the help of one of his subjects. Mehemet Ali, the Viceroy of Egypt, who sent an army and navy to help him put down the rebellion.

Britain, Russia and France signed the **Treaty of London** (1827) which contained the ideas expressed in the earlier Protocol. To try to persuade the Sultan to accept its terms. Canning sent a fleet under the command of Admiral Codrington to the eastern Mediterranean.

In October 1827 Codrington found the Turkish and Egyptian fleets at **Navarino**, where there took place an 'accidental' battle in which these fleets suffered heavy losses.

THE GREEK QUESTION
AFTER CANNING'S DEATH

Canning was dead before the Battle of Navarino took place. **Wellington** apologized to the Turks for what he called 'an untoward event' and recalled the British fleet.

Russia invaded Moldavia and Wallachia in the northern part of the Turkish Empire and in 1829 the Turks were forced to agree to the **Treaty of Adrianople**, which gave the Greeks partial independence.

Wellington feared that Greece would become a pawn in Russia's hands. Britain and France demanded the complete independence of Greece, which was agreed in 1832.

Unit 13 Summary

▶ Castlereagh, the Congress System (1815–22) and the Holy Alliance.
▶ Canning continues and develops Castlereagh's policies, 1815–27.
▶ The first stages of the Eastern Question.

---

14 PARLIAMENTARY REFORM, 1830–32

14.1 Understanding the Words We Use

▶ A **constituency** is part of the country (or the people living in that part of the country) represented by a Member of Parliament (MP).
▶ The **franchise** is the right to vote. Each of us lives in a constituency and almost everyone over the age of 18 has the right to vote.

14.2 The Situation Before 1832

Constituencies

The majority of MPs were elected for constituencies in the southern part of England. One-quarter of them represented constituencies in the four south-western counties. This was because, when the constituencies were named in Charles II's reign, England was mainly an agricultural country.

The franchise
In 1830 there was a complex and bewildering system:
▶ **County MPs** Each county was represented by two MPs,

elected by the male freehold owners of land which, for rating purposes, was valued at 40 shillings (£2) a year.
▶ **Borough (or town) franchises** Here there was no simple franchise. In different boroughs the franchise was given to:
● all the **free men** of the town – a very small number;
● the members of the **town council** (or **corporation**);
● men who paid the local **scot and lot** rates;
● **potwallopers**, the nickname given to those who occupied certain houses which had a large fireplace;
● **every male householder.**

There was a great deal of corruption which allowed rich men and the government to control some of these boroughs. In particular there were:
▶ **rotten boroughs** such as Old Sarum and Dunwich, where no one lived, but which had two MPs chosen by the local landowners;
▶ **pocket boroughs** in which the voting was completely controlled by a rich patron, e.g. the government, West Indian trading merchants or East India traders. These 'borough mongers' bribed the small number of voters to ensure the return of their candidates.
▶ **open-air stands (or hustings)** to which voters had to

go and vote publicly – which made it easier for agents to check that they had done as they were told.

WHAT WAS WRONG WITH THE SYSTEM IN 1830?

The constituencies

Large industrial towns (Manchester, Birmingham, Leeds and Sheffield for example) were not represented in Parliament, while East Looe had two MPs and West Looe had another two. A heavily populated county (Yorkshire) and a small county (Rutland, with only 600 voters) each had two MPs.

The franchise

In most **counties** the elections were controlled by the large landowners, who bought up all the freehold land and leased it to their tenants. Many rich farmers were excluded from the franchise because they were only leaseholders.

In the **boroughs** the confused franchises excluded many people from voting, and a man who had the right to vote in one borough lost it if he moved to another with a different franchise.

Rotten and pocket boroughs gave too much political power to a small number of men, some of whom already had seats in the House of Lords.

WHO DEMANDED CHANGE?

▶ As early as 1780 there was a demand by some MPs that King George III should not be able to control Parliament as he did. **John Dunning** proposed in Parliament that 'the influence of the Crown has increased, is increasing and ought to be diminished' (1780). **Edmund Burke** (1782) and the **Younger Pitt** (1785) tried to get Reform Bills through, but failed.

▶ At that time there was also a demand outside Parliament for reform. **Wilkes, Major Cartwright** and others wrote pamphlets proposing reform. In 1780 the **Yorkshire Association** was formed by Christopher **Wyvill** whose proposals for reform won the support of many industrialists.

▶ During and after the French Revolution the idea of reform was supported by **Radicals** such as Hunt.

▶ By 1830 the **new middle class** of industrialists, financiers, canal-owners, merchants and engineers had grown sufficiently large and confident to challenge the political power of the landowners. Some of them formed **Political Unions**, such as the Birmingham Political Union led by Thomas Attwood.

▶ The **Whigs** were not in favour of democracy, but they realized that after the Industrial Revolution it was wrong to exclude great cities and industrialists. Some feared that, if there was no reform, these middle-class men might lead a revolution to overthrow the unreformed Parliament.

▶ The **working class** hoped that a reform would force Parliament to consider working-class complaints.

WHO WAS OPPOSED TO REFORM?

▶ The **Tories**, including the liberal Canningites (p. 33), thought that the existing system was the best possible one.

▶ The **landowners** feared that reform would end their power which had allowed them to pass the Corn Laws. 'He who controls the system gets the laws he wants.'

▶ **Traditionalists** argued that the old system had worked. The Younger Pitt had got into Parliament via a pocket borough. Was there any guarantee that he would have been elected by a more democratic franchise?

▶ The **King**, William IV, having seen the revolution in France (July 1830) feared that reform might turn into revolution and lead to the overthrow of the Monarchy.

14.3 Earl Grey's Government, 1830

After Wellington's defeat in November 1830, Earl Grey, the Whig leader, was asked to form a government.

Eleven of his 13 ministers were aristocrats; he hoped to prove that the rich could govern well. He asked Lord John Russell to draw up a Reform Bill.

THE FIRST BILL, MARCH 1831

Russell presented his Bill to the Commons on **1st March 1831** and the Commons approved it by one vote (302–301) on the **31st March**.

▶ The Bill went into Committee and was defeated in **April**.

▶ Grey then asked the King to hold a General Election.

14.4 The Election, 1831

Grey was supported by the Radicals, the middle class and the working class. Attwood and other leaders of Political Unions led demonstrations for 'the Bill, the whole Bill and nothing but the Bill'.

Bribery was commonplace and fear of the mobs forced many voters to support Whig candidates. The result was a majority of over 100 for the government.

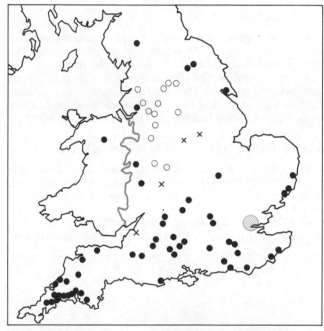

Fig. 14.4 A sketch map of England and Wales in 1831. showing (i) rotten boroughs marked as black dots, (ii) large towns, not represented in Parliament in 1831, marked as circles, and (iii) towns where riots took place in 1831, marked by crosses.

THE SECOND BILL, JUNE 1831

Russell's new Bill was slightly different from the first; it was passed by the Commons in **September**, but the Lords rejected it in **October** by a majority of 41. Twenty-one Bishops voted against the Bill.

This led to widespread unrest throughout the country. In Derby, Nottingham and Bristol gaols were broken open and fires were started in violent anti-Tory demonstrations.

THE THIRD BILL, DECEMBER 1831

Russell brought in a slightly amended Bill in **December 1831** and this went to the Lords on the **26th March 1832**.

The Lords threatened to reject this Bill, and Grey resigned. For a week Wellington tried to form a government to bring in a Reform Bill. He found that:

▶ Peel and other Tories refused to serve;

▶ public opinion was against the Tories and Wellington feared that if he persisted there might be a civil war.

The King had to ask Grey to take office again and had to promise that, if necessary, he would create new peers to ensure the Bill's passage through the Lords.

Wellington then persuaded the Tories in the Lords to abstain and allow the Bill through. The Bill passed its final reading in the Lords in June 1832.

14.5 The Terms of the Reform Act

The constituencies

▶ 56 boroughs with less than 2000 inhabitants lost both their MPs;
▶ 31 boroughs with populations less than 4000 lost one of their MPs;
▶ 143 seats were distributed by giving:
● 65 to the more populous counties in England and Wales;
● 8 extra seats to Scotland;
● 5 extra seats to Ireland;
● 21 to smaller towns which gained representation for the first time;
● 44 to 22 larger towns which were to be represented by two MPs.

The franchise

In the **boroughs** there was a simple qualification. Any male occupier (owner or tenant) of a house valued (for rating purposes) at £10 a year received the franchise.

In the **counties** the franchise was extended to (a) **copyholders** (i.e. tenants of farms which were traditionally handed from father to son) of property valued at £10 a year and to (b) **leaseholders** of land worth £50 a year.

WHAT DID THESE CHANGES MEAN?

▶ The number of voters went up from about 440 000 to about 657 000. The £10 qualification for the borough vote meant that only the richer industrialists and merchants got the vote.
▶ The Commons continued to be dominated by MPs from the south; only a small number of seats were redistributed.

▶ Bribery and intimidation continued during elections, until the Ballot Act, 1872 and the Corrupt Practices Act, 1883 (unit 38).

WHO GAINED FROM THE CHANGES

▶ Some of the **middle class**. They learned 'to call the tune' and the Repeal of the Corn Laws in 1846 was the economic outcome of the Reform Act.
▶ **The Whigs** gained the reputation of being 'reformers', while the Tories suffered as 'anti-reformers'.

WHO WERE DISAPPOINTED WITH THE REFORM?

▶ **The Radicals** had expected much wider changes.
▶ **The working class** got nothing from the Bill for which they had campaigned.

WHAT WAS THE IMPORTANCE OF THE ACT?

When the Act was finally passed, the anti-reformers realized that it was not as bad as they feared, while many of the supporters of reform found that the changes it made were not very great. But the Act was important because it made the first break in the unreformed system and paved the way for further changes in 1867 and 1884–85.

By increasing the power of the middle class and of the Commons, the Act created the probability of a clash between the Commons and the Lords. We will see that such clashes occurred in 1860, 1893 and 1909 and that the final outcome was a victory for the Commons by the Parliament Act of 1911 (unit 38).

14.6 Summary

▶ The demand for reform of the Parliamentary system.
▶ The course of the Reform Bill through Parliament.
▶ The nature of the changes made by the 1832 Reform Act.

15 WHIG GOVERNMENTS, 1833–41

 ## 15.1 The Great Reformers

There were two important groups in Parliament:
▶ The **Evangelical Humanitarians**, the successors of people such as Howard and Fry (p. 29) who campaigned for the abolition of slavery and for factory reform.
▶ The **'Economists'**, who supported Adam Smith's ideas. These were summed up in the term **'laissez-faire'**, meaning 'leave alone'. They thought the government should not be involved in the social or economic life of the country and that everything should be left to **natural laws of economics**. Leading economists were:
● **David Ricardo** (1772–1823) who thought wage increases caused falls in profits and less investment and progress.
● **Thomas Malthus** (1766–1834) who, in his *Essay on Population,* argued that populations grew more rapidly than good production. This meant that famines and hardship were inevitable unless people married at a later age and had smaller families.
● **Jeremy Bentham** (1748–1832) who thought that every

institution (such as Parliament or the Church) and every law ought to be examined to see if it produced 'the greatest happiness for the greatest possible number of people'. He thought that this greatest happiness would come if everyone were left as free as possible to do whatever they wanted. He and his supporters became known as Utilitarians, because of every law and institution they asked the question 'What use is it?'

 ## 15.2 The Work of the Whig Governments

THE ABOLITION OF SLAVERY, 1833

The slave trade had been abolished in 1807, but the campaign against slavery continued. In 1833 Parliament passed the Abolition Act which said that:
▶ slaves under the age of six were freed immediately;
▶ other slaves remained part-slaves and part-free for four years. During that time they had to be paid a wage for the work they did in the quarter of the week when they were 'free';

slave owners were compensated for the loss of their 'property', the former slaves. The government paid £20 million – about £37.50 for each slave.

Opposition to Abolition was led by MPs representing Bristol and Liverpool, and by Gladstone, son of a Liverpool ship owner. They claimed it would ruin the sugar industry in the West Indies.

In the **West Indies** the freed slaves were unwilling to work for the low wages offered by their former owners, whose plantations were no longer as profitable as they had been. The West Indies faded in importance as a market for British exports.

In the **Cape of Good Hope** the Dutch settlers were already angry with British leniency towards black Africans. After Abolition they went on the Great Trek from the Cape, across the Vaal River. They set up two new states – the Transvaal and the Orange Free State – where they could continue to own slaves.

FACTORY REFORM, 1833

Children had worked in the domestic system, and continued to be employed in the industrial factories. Some were orphans sent by Poor Law authorities. Factory owners had to house such pauper children. Others were sent to work by their parents who wanted the small income (30 pence or so) which the children could earn.

In **1802** Robert Owen, a factory owner, persuaded Parliament to pass an Act limiting the working day of **pauper children** to 12 hours. In **1819** Sir Robert Peel, father of the future Prime Minister, persuaded Parliament to extend that Act to all children. After the 1819 Act:
▶ no child under the age of nine could be employed in cotton mills;
▶ children between 9 and 12 were only to work 12 hours a day.

These Acts, which only applied to cotton mills, were ineffective because the government left it to local magistrates to see that the Act was obeyed. Many of these magistrates were also factory owners. Others were related to, or friendly with, factory owners.

Michael Sadler, MP and Humanitarian, persuaded Parliament to set up a Commission to investigate working conditions. From its Report in 1831–32 we know about the conditions in which children worked. Anthony Ashley Cooper (later Lord Shaftesbury) took up the cause of child workers when Sadler lost his seat in 1832.

Opposition to reform was led by the 'Economists', who wanted the government to let factory owners get on with their own business.

The 1833 Act, introduced by Lord Althorp, said that, in textile mills:
▶ no child under the age of nine was to be employed;
▶ children aged between 9 and 13 were not to work for more than 9 hours a day and more than 48 hours a week;
▶ children between the aged of 13 and 18 were not to work more than 12 hours a day and 69 hours a week;
▶ no nightwork was to be done by anyone under 18;
▶ the government would appoint four inspectors so see that the terms of the Act were obeyed.

The Act only applied to children in textile mills, except silk and lace-making mills. It did not apply to mines, brickyards and other places.

You should note that the Whig government, which was responsible for this Factory Act and which appeared to be concerned about the working conditions of townspeople, showed no concern for the conditions of work and life of the people in the countryside, where the Whig landowners had their estates. Indeed, they tried to suppress movements which aimed at improving the harsh conditions in which the rural poor worked and lived. As examples of the repression you should note:
▶ the putting down of the labourers' revolt in 1830, when the army was used against agricultural workers who were demonstrating against unemployment and low wages;
▶ the case of the Tolpuddle Martyrs, 1834 (unit 25).

THE EDUCATION GRANT, 1833

A clause in the Factory Act said that children working in mills had to have two hours a day in school. This made the government take some interest in children's schooling. We will study this in unit 42. Here we ought to note that:
▶ in **1833** the government provided £20 000 to help the voluntary societies to provide schools;
▶ in **1839** it increased the grant to £30 000 and it also set up a Cabinet Committee to supervise the spending of this money.

THE POOR LAW AMENDMENT ACT, 1834
The old Poor Law

Since Tudor times, parish authorities had had to look after the poor of the parish – the old, the handicapped, the sick, widows, orphans or children of widows. Such help led to:
▶ the collection of a Poor Rate in each parish;
▶ the building of workhouses where the poor might be housed and where work might be provided for them.

The Speenhamland system

By 1795 the price of food had risen (p. 24), yet many workers received low wages. The magistrates at the parish of Speenhamland in Berkshire decided that they would give money to poorly-paid workers.

The amount of help would vary with the price of bread and married men would get an allowance for their wives and each of their children.

Critics argued that:
▶ it increased the poor rates;
▶ it encouraged larger families, and so increased the probability of food shortage;
▶ it encouraged employers to offer lower wages than they might otherwise have done.

This system was widely adopted in the agricultural districts of southern England.

A **Poor Law Commission** was set up in 1833 to examine the working of the Poor Law system throughout the country. In its Report (1834) it made several recommendations to Parliament, which went on to pass the **Poor Law Amendment Act** which said:
▶ no fit (or 'able-bodied') person was to receive money or other help from the Poor Law authorities except in a workhouse;
▶ conditions in workhouses were to be made very harsh ('less desirable'), to discourage people;
▶ workhouses were to be built in each parish or, if parishes were too small, in unions of parishes;
▶ ratepayers in each parish or union had to elect a Board of Guardians to supervise the workhouse, to collect the Poor Rate and to send reports to the Central Poor Law Commission;
▶ this Commission, of three men appointed by the government, had an office in Whitehall and had to supervise the working of the Amendment Act throughout the country. Edwin Chadwick was its Secretary.

The Poor Law Amendment Act in operation after 1834

▶ The **Andover Scandal**, 1845–46, was caused by an outcry when it was learned that the poor in the Andover Workhouse had been driven by hunger to eat rotting bone marrow. Many Boards of Guardians spent too little on the inmates of workhouses.
▶ **Bastilles** (p. 21) was the nickname given to the workhouses by the opponents of the reformed system. It was shown that families were split up when they entered the workhouse.
▶ **Richard Oastler,** a land agent, led the workers in Yorkshire in attacks on workhouses.

Changes in the system

Trade depressions caused large-scale unemployment. The Guardians could not take all the people into their workhouses. The Commissioners were forced to allow them to give help to people who continued to live outside the workhouses.

The Poor Law Board was set up in 1847 to replace the Commissioners and in 1871 this was united with the Public Health Board (p. 45) to become the **Local Government Board**, which advised Guardians to treat people more kindly.

The Reform Acts of 1867 and 1884 gave some working-class men the franchise and they demanded an improvement in the system. After 1867 **working-class men and some women** could become Guardians. They had a more sympathetic attitude.

Regulations were changed to allow visiting, an allowance of tobacco for men and of snuff for women. But it was not until the twentieth century that politicians started to look for humane ways of dealing with poverty.

MUNICIPAL CORPORATIONS ACT, 1835

There were 178 chartered boroughs in England and Wales, old boroughs which had received a Charter to allow the townspeople to have their own council (or Corporation). There were no such councils in the new and growing industrial towns.

The 178 councils were undemocratic. In Bath, for example, 110 of the 38 000 inhabitants elected a council of 30. **Dissenters** were often excluded from voting and from being candidates for election.

The **1835 Act** changed the system. It said that:
▶ **all ratepayers** should have a vote in council elections;
▶ each town was to be divided into **wards**, with councillors being elected for each ward;
▶ the elected **councillors** were to choose **aldermen**, who would form one-quarter of the council;
▶ the council was to elect a **mayor**;
▶ the council might, if it wished, take over the powers now being exercised by **Improvement Commissioners** and other bodies which looked after such matters as the water supply;
▶ the council had to form a **Watch Committee** and to organize a police force;
▶ inhabitants of **towns without councils** could ask Parliament to allow them the right to have a council. Manchester did this in 1839;
▶ councils were allowed to borrow money from the public, but the borrowing (by loans) and the ways in which the money was spent had to be audited (or examined) by a government-appointed official.

REGISTRATION OF BIRTHS AND DEATHS, 1836

This Act compelled people to register every birth and death with an officer appointed by the Registrar General. Only after this could people be certain of a child's age, and so ensure that the Factory Act was being obeyed.

THE PENNY POST, 1840

Rowland Hill had proposed a system of pre-paid postage in 1837. In 1839 he was employed by the government to advise them on how to make it work, and the modern postal system was started in 1840.

IRELAND AND CANADA

The Whig government was supported by O'Connell and other Irish MPs, who hoped that the 'great Reformers' would either give Ireland its own Parliament and independent government or, at least, try to improve conditions in Ireland. (There is more about this part of Whig policy on p. 56). The government was also responsible for sending out Lord Durham to examine conditions in the Canadian colonies (and there is more about this on p. 59).

15.3 What did the Whigs fail to do?

Free Trade had been one of the policies of the Liberal Tories (p. 33). The Whigs had the support of the industrialists and merchants. It is surprising that they did nothing about Free Trade.

Trade depressions occurred in 1837 and 1839–40, when foreign buyers were unable to buy all the goods produced by British factories. Unemployment rose, profits fell and government revenue – from indirect taxes and import and export duties – also fell. One result of this was a **budget deficit**, since the government was spending more than it was collecting by taxation. It was left to Peel to restore the country's finances.

15.4 Why were the Whigs unpopular in 1840?

▶ The **middle class** was angered by the Whigs' failure to deal with the trade problem.
▶ The **Radicals** were angered by the Poor Law Amendment Act, which also annoyed the **working class**.
▶ The **government**, which had started off with a rush of laws after 1832, seemed to have run out of steam after 1835 and had little to offer the country.

Unit 15 Summary

▶ The demand for widespread economic and social reform.
▶ What the Whigs did for factory reform, education, local government and the abolition of slavery.
▶ The Poor Law Amendment Act, 1834 and the end of the Speenhamland System of poor relief.
▶ The failure of the Whigs to deal with trade recessions.

16.1 Working-Class Discontent, 1830–50

▶ **Living conditions:**
● housing conditions;
● diet;
● the environment – streets, refuse and water supply.
▶ **Working conditions:**
● hours and conditions of work;
● wage rates;
● child labour.
▶ **The 1832 Act:** the working class had hoped that Reform would give it a share in the electoral system. Its anger after 1832 was a major cause of the Chartist movement.
▶ **The Poor Law Amendment Act, 1834:** this seemed to blame the poor for their poverty and led to support for Chartism.
▶ **Trade Unions** (p. 61): some men had hoped to gain better conditions by **industrial action**. The collapse of trade unions, as shown by the case of the **Tolpuddle Martyrs** (p. 62), convinced many workers that improvements could best be gained by **political action** – hence their support for Chartism.

TRADE DEPRESSIONS AND CHARTISM

Trade depressions occurred when there was over-production of goods, when foreign demand fell, and because of poor harvests, people had a lower income and so bought fewer goods.

When manufacturers could not sell their goods they closed down their factories or kept the workers on part-time. This led to a fall in family income, and to a drop in workers' living conditions (see above).

Such depressions occurred in 1837, 1839 and 1843 and support for Chartism grew in those years.

THE CHARTER
The six points

1 A vote for every man over 21 years of age.
2 A secret ballot.
3 No property qualifications for MPs, so that working men might stand as candidates.
4 Payment of MPs.
5 Equal constituencies, so that each MP would represent roughly the same number of constituencies.
6 Annual Parliaments so that MPs would have to take more account of their constituents' wishes.

POLITICAL CHANGE AND WORKERS' DISCONTENT

The working class had a number of grievances, most of which could only be satisfied by new laws – on housing and factory conditions.

Such laws would have to be passed by Parliament, and Chartists believed that if the workers had control of the Parliamentary system these laws would be passed.

A DIVIDED WORKING CLASS
Trade Unionism

In spite of the failure of the GNCTU (p. 61), many working-class leaders thought that the development of a strong trade union movement would be the best way to gain improvements. They argued that industrial action could achieve better wages, which would enable working people to afford better housing, food, clothing and schooling for their children. This was in line with the widespread belief in **self-help** (p. 70).

The Six Points OF THE PEOPLE'S CHARTER.

1. A VOTE for every man twenty-one years of age, of sound mind, and not undergoing punishment for crime.
2. THE BALLOT.—To protect the elector in the exercise of his vote.
3. No PROPERTY QUALIFICATION for Members of Parliament —thus enabling the constituencies to return the man of their choice, be he rich or poor.
4. PAYMENT OF MEMBERS, thus enabling an honest tradesman, working man, or other person, to serve a constituency, when taken from his business to attend to the interests of the country.
5. EQUAL CONSTITUENCIES, securing the same amount of representation for the same number of electors, instead of allowing small constituencies to swamp the votes of large ones.
6. ANNUAL PARLIAMENTS, thus presenting the most effectual check to bribery and intimidation, since though a constituency might be bought once in seven years (even with the ballot), no purse could buy a constituency (under a system of universal suffrage) in each ensuing twelvemonth; and since members, when elected for a year only, would not be able to defy and betray their constituents as now.

Fig. 16.1 A Chartist handbill. Examiners expect an explanation of the words used and accounts of when and how five of those points were achieved.

Moral force

William Lovett, a leading figure in the movement, believed that the Chartists could gain their victory by peaceful means. Pamphlets and peaceful demonstrations would, he thought, convince MPs. This ignored the fact that:
▶ most MPs were quite satisfied with the electoral system after 1832; they did not want a more democratic system;
▶ social improvements would cost a great deal of government money – and better-off MPs were opposed to increases in taxation;
▶ if there were more laws – on housing and factories – there would have to be an increase in government activity. This was contrary to the widespread belief in **laisser-faire** (p. 38). You should remember in this connection:
● the opposition to the Public Health Act of 1848 (p. 45);
● even Radicals such as John Bright were totally opposed to such reforms as the Ten-Hour Day (p. 43).

There was little support among politicians in the 1830s and 1840s for the sort of legislation that the Chartists had in mind.

Physical force

Feargus O'Connor and other leaders of the movement realised that 'moral force' would not succeed. They called for violent action – or 'physical force'. Weapons were collected, men were armed, small groups drilled in preparation for an uprising. But such 'physical force' could never have succeeded, because the majority of workers would not support it. The 'rising' would only have been a small-scale affair, and the army was well able to deal with such outbreaks.

Reports of arming and drilling frightened the middle class, whose support was needed if Parliament was to pass the political reforms demanded by the Charter.

Apathy

The majority of workers took no interest in the activities of the Chartists because:
► their religious beliefs taught them to accept their conditions. Religion was a much stronger influence in the nineteenth century than it is today;
► they had neither the time nor the energy to give to Chartism because of their deprived conditions;
► they did not see the link between political reforms and their conditions. They saw much more easily the importance of the Anti-Corn Law movement (unit 20).

16.2 The Course of Chartism, 1837–50

► **William Lovett,** a skilled cabinet-maker, led a group of politically minded working men in the formation of the London Working Men's Association in **1836**.
► **1837** Feargus O'Connor founded *The Northern Star* as the Chartists' newspaper. Five hundred delegates from Chartist groups throughout the country met in Birmingham to draw up the **National Petition** in which they complained about the 1832 Reform Act and demanded further political reforms.
► **1838** In Birmingham there were riots led by Chartists. London police went to deal with the trouble.
► **1839** This was an important year for the movement because:
● **Thomas Attwood,** the founder of the Birmingham Political Union (p. 37) presented the National Petition to Parliament, pointing to the 1 280 000 signatures supporting it;
● led by John Frost, miners and ironworkers in the valleys of East Wales marched to try to free their Chartist leader, Henry Vincent, who was imprisoned in Monmouth. They clashed with the army in **Newport** and confirmed middle-class fears about the movement.
► **1842** After the unrest of 1839 the movement declined in the face of a revival in trade. But another depression saw:
● so-called **Plug Riots** in Preston, where men tried to prevent steam-engines working by pulling out the plugs which kept the steam under pressure;
● the **Rebecca Riots** in Wales, which were also aimed against toll-gates, Corn Laws and English rule;
● the presentation of a **second Charter** to Parliament.
► **1843–47** While there were many local meetings, the movement declined because of:
● improved trade – a result of Peel's free trade policies (p. 48);
● the railway boom (p. 65) which provided much employment;
● falls in living costs because of Peel's policies which, together with the increased employment, led to a rise in living standards.

It was this slight improvement in conditions which led to an increase in self-help activities, such as the founding of the first cooperative society (p. 44) at Rochdale. O'Connor founded a cooperative community at New Harmony, but this failed.

1848 AND THE COLLAPSE OF THE MOVEMENT

In 1848 there were revolutions throughout Europe; many kings lost their thrones and democratically elected governments came to power. One reason for this widespread unrest was that Europe suffered from a food shortage because of poor harvests. Another reason was widespread unemployment created during the beginnings of the industrial revolution. It was also the year in which the Chartist movement made its major demonstration, one which proved to be its last.
► A new Petition was prepared.
► A mass rally was held on Kennington Common to support the presentation of the Petition. The leaders planned a march from the Common across the Bridge into London.
► The government feared that this might lead to riots, so the army was brought in to guard London; a special constabulary was recruited to help safeguard property.
► On the day of the rally it rained and this affected the numbers of those who turned out, and their enthusiasm. The police allowed only the leaders to cross the Bridge. The mass of the demonstrators were unable to join forces with Chartists north of the river.
► The massive Petition, containing two million signatures, was presented peacefully, but many of the signatures proved to be forgeries ('Queen Victoria') or laughably stupid ('Pug Nose').
► Parliament rejected the demands contained in the Petition which was mocked in the newspapers.

THE END

A trade revival began in 1849 and continued throughout most of the 1850s, with Britain gaining the title of 'workshop of the world'. This provided more employment and higher wages.

Working people once again turned from **political action** and Chartism to **industrial action**, and formed new, stronger and successful trade unions (unit 25).

Lovett abandoned the movement and became a teacher. O'Connor and a handful of Radicals tried to persuade Londoners to rise in revolt in 1848–49 but received no support. O'Connor became insane, was arrested in 1852 and sent to Chiswick asylum.

THE ACHIEVING OF FIVE OF THE SIX POINTS

By 1850 the movement was dead with none of its aims achieved. Over the next 60 years, however, some of the Six Points were granted by Parliament. The political reforms will be studied later but here you ought to note:
► **The Reform Acts** of 1867, 1884 and 1918 which enlarged the electorate. After 1918 every adult male had a vote.
► 1872 saw the passing of the **Ballot Act**.
► 1911 saw the first **payment to MPs.**
► The re-distribution of seats in 1867 and 1884–85 led to the creation of **more equal constituencies**.
► The **property qualification** was abolished and working men were elected to Parliament in 1874.
► In 1911 the Parliament Act **shortened the life of future Parliaments**. Elections had to be held at least every five years.

16.3 Summary

► The economic and social causes of Chartism.
► The Six Points of the Charter.
► The weaknesses of the Chartist Movement; a comparison with the Anti-Corn Law League.
► The collapse of the Movement after 1848 but the fulfilment of its aims in later years.
► The work of individuals, notably Lovett and O'Connor.

17 FACTORY REFORM, 1833-78

17.1 The Arguments in Favour of Reform

▶ **Oastler,** a land agent, argued that child workers were worse treated than West Indian slaves. If it was right to campaign against slavery, then it was right to work for factory reform.

▶ **Shaftesbury** and other Evangelicals thought it wrong that people should be forced to work for such long hours. They campaigned for the **Ten-Hour Day.** They also thought that children needed special protection and factory laws.

▶ **Workers** wanted a shorter working day so that they might enjoy some sort of social life.

▶ Some **factory owners** were among the reformers because:

● it was only a minority of owners who forced their workers to work overlong hours, so gaining an advantage;

● the success of the 1833 Act (p. 39) had shown that workers produced as much in the shorter day as in the longer one.

THE ARGUMENTS AGAINST REFORM

▶ **Laissez-faire** had its supporters, who said that the government had no right to interfere.

▶ **Self-help** was almost a by-product of **laissez-faire.** Its supporters claimed that Britain had become great because inventors and merchants had been free to do as they liked. They believed that workers should help themselves and that factory owners should be given complete freedom.

▶ John Bright was a Radical MP who campaigned against the Corn Laws (unit 20) and for Parliamentary Reform (unit 38). But he was a powerful opponent of factory reform. He and others feared that British owners would lose out in competition with foreigners, who had no such laws to hinder them.

THE CAMPAIGN FOR REFORM, 1833-50

The **1833 Act** had several favourable effects. **Inspectors** presented their Reports to Parliament and helped in the campaign for more reform (on such things as the fencing of dangerous machinery). These Reports also showed that owners were not ruined when they obeyed the Act.

Many workers were distracted from this campaign, however, by Chartism, the Anti-Corn Law League and the development of cooperatives (see below).

Shaftesbury continued to press for further reforms, and a **Royal Commission** on conditions in the mines was set up. In its report (1842) it showed that in British mines:

▶ **children** as young as four years old worked underground;

▶ **boys**, known as trappers, worked in the dark for 12 hours a day opening and closing the ventilation doors;

▶ **boys and girls** aged about 12 years dragged heavy loads to the mine-shaft so that they could be taken to the surface (fig. 17.1);

▶ **children** were left in charge of the engines which winched miners to the surface. There were many accidents because of the children's inability or carelessness;

▶ **Scottish miners** were forced to sign documents which bound them to the owners of a particular mine, so that they were virtually slaves with no rights or privileges.

The **Mines Act 1842** said that:

▶ boys under 10, women and girls were not to work underground;

▶ boys under 15 were not to be left in charge of engines;

LETTING CHILDREN DOWN A COAL MINE
From a Plate in the *Westminster Review*

Fig. 17.1 An illustration from the Report of the Commission on conditions in British mines (1840) showing children being lowered down a mine shaft. Accidents were frequent and you should be able to say why.

▶ government inspectors were to be appointed.

This Act said nothing about the length of the working day.

The ten hour day

Shaftesbury and working-class leaders knew that the government would not grant such a short day to men. They also knew that textile factories depended on the work of women and children and they concentrated on getting a shorter day for these.

The **1844 Act** said that in textile factories:

▶ **children** under 13 were not to work more than six and a half hours a day;

▶ **women and young people** under 18 were not to work more than 12 hours a day;

▶ **dangerous machinery** had to be fenced in.

This Act disappointed the campaigners for the Ten Hour Day.

The **1847 Act** said that children between 13 and 18 and women were not to work more than ten hours a day and 58 hours a week. This should have meant that factories could not operate for more than ten hours a day. But many owners side-stepped the Act by employing women and children on shift systems.

Inspectors prosecuted many owners who got around the Act. **Judges** agreed with the Inspectors and punished such owners.

The **1850 Act** said that:

▶ women and young people (13 to 18) were to work 60 hours a week – and not 58 as laid down in the 1847 Act;

▶ hours of opening were to be limited to 12 for Mondays to

Friday, with one and a half hours off for meals, and Saturday closing time at 2 pm.

▶ This gave women and young people a working day of ten and a half hours on weekdays and seven and a half hours on Saturday.

Some workers were angry at this slight lengthening of the day for women and young people. Shaftesbury argued that the Act meant a ten and a half hour working day for all workers.

17.2 Later Reforms, 1867–1914

The **1867 Factories and Workshops Act** extended the working of existing Acts to all places of manufacturing employing more than five people, but excluded agriculture and domestic service.

The **1878 Consolidating Act** passed during Disraeli's Ministry (p. 73) brought into one Act and code all the regulations affecting factories and workshops.

'Sweatshops', particularly those employing the tailors and seamstresses in London's clothing trade, were outside the terms of these Acts because there were fewer than five workers or because, in theory, the people who worked there were self-employed workers. These had to wait for the setting up of **Trade Boards** by the Liberal government of 1906–14 (p. 91).

SHAFTESBURY AND WORKING CHILDREN

Until 1851, Shaftesbury (as Lord Ashley) had led the campaign for factory reform as a member of the House of Commons. He became a member of the House of Lords when he inherited the earldom in 1851 and became Lord Shaftesbury.

Shaftesbury was also a supporter of the **'Ragged Schools'** which supplied free education and sometimes food and clothing for poor children. The first such school had been started in 1820 by John Porter, a Portsmouth shoe-maker. In Scotland Dr Guthrie developed such schools around 1850. Shaftesbury became chairman of the Ragged Schools Union, set up to find the money needed to run these schools.

Climbing boys were employed by chimney sweeps to climb up inside the huge chimneys of the large Victorian houses. Charles Kingsley wrote about these children in *The Water Babies*. Various Acts were passed to try to control the employment of such children, and Shaftesbury led the campaign.

▶ **Acts** passed in 1834 and 1840 had little effect, because of the difficulty in inspecting the children at work.

▶ *The Water Babies* was published in 1863 and led to an outcry.

▶ Shaftesbury promoted the **1864 Act** which said that:

● Sweeps were forbidden to employ children under ten;

● No child under 16 was to be sent up inside the chimney.

▶ Many sweeps evaded this Act – and were employed (along with their illegal 'water babies') by respectable Victorians.

▶ The **1875 Act** said that:

● Sweeps had to apply for an annual licence. This gave local magistrates some control over the trade.

● The police were to be responsible for enforcing the regulations on ages and hours affecting sweeps.

THE CAMPAIGN AGAINST 'TRUCK'

Many employers paid their workmen **in kind rather than cash**. Some handed over articles made in their factories; others gave out coupons to be exchanged for goods in shops owned by the employer (called **tommy shops** by the workers); some made their own token coinage to be used only in the tommy shops.

▶ **Employers** argued that this allowed them to use their money to expand their businesses and create employment.

▶ **Workers** argued that this system meant that they either got inferior goods or had to pay higher prices at tommy shops.

Acts against this system had been passed in the 1820s, but were ignored by employers and not enforced by magistrates. More detailed, more effective and better enforced Acts were passed in 1854 and 1871. The fact that an Act had to be passed in 1871 shows how ineffective earlier Acts had been.

After 1871 it became illegal to pay wages other than in cash. Some employers then insisted on paying wages only in public houses which they owned – and so ensured that much of the cash 'flowed' back to them.

THE COOPERATIVE MOVEMENT

Some workers tried to overcome the truck system by forming cooperative stores, as did the **Rochdale Pioneers**.

In 1844, 28 weavers in Rochdale each put £1 into a fund, hired the ground floor of a warehouse in Toad Lane, and opened a retail shop. They bought food and other goods from manufacturers and warehouses. They sold the goods at the normal retail prices and so made the same profits as other shopkeepers. The Rochdale Pioneers handed back a share of the profits to the shoppers in proportion to the amount they had spent during the year. Most customers left their share (or dividend) in the business as a form of saving. This enabled the business to expand and to become even more profitable. The example of the Pioneers was followed by working people in many other towns.

You should notice that this was in keeping with ideas of **self-help** which also led workmen to help themselves by forming trade unions (unit 25), friendly societies, building societies, mechanics' institutes and clubs and the like. It was not only the middle class that believed in self-help.

Unit 17 Summary

▶ The arguments for and against reform.
▶ The importance of the work of Shaftesbury.
▶ The achievement of the ten-hour day.
▶ Who gained what from various Factory Acts and Mines Acts.

18.1 Industrial Towns

As a result of the industrial revolution, new industrial towns grew very rapidly. The population of Manchester doubled from 50 000 (1788) to 100 000 (1802) and more than tripled to 350 000 by 1844 (fig. 2.7b).

None of these new towns had town councils nor, as a result, did they have adequate supervision of the ways in which houses were built or services (water, refuse collection and street cleaning) were provided.

Even if there had been active councils, there would have been little they could have done about town development because there was no legislation about such things as housing and water supply.

The government, under the influence of the doctrine of **laissez-faire** thought that town development, like industrial development should be left to private enterprise. This, after all, did supply the factories, ports, railways and mines; and so it could supply the houses, and provide other essential services.

PRIVATE ENTERPRISE AND HOUSING

House builders did provide adequate housing for the better-off factory owners and merchants. However, they did not provide adequate housing for the workers. In their defence it ought to be noted that:
► they built in order to make a profit;
► workers earned less than £1 a week in 1830;
► rent was only one of the weekly expenses facing working people;
► the average rent which workers could afford was four shillings (20p), or about one-quarter of their weekly wage;
► the house builder then had to provide the accommodation for which he could charge that sort of rent and still make a profit.

It is not surprising tht the result was narrow streets, overcrowded housing, lack of essential services – and dirt.

18.2 Disease and Death

A result of this lack of adequate housing and services was a high death rate. This is illustrated by the figures on p. 188 where you can see that: country people (living in Rutland) had a longer expectation of life than people in industrial towns. Better-off people in towns had a longer life expectancy than did the less well-off, with the poor having the lowest life expectancy.

One reason for the low average life expectancy was the **very high death rate**. You should notice that about one-third of all children died before reaching the age of one year, while about one-half of working-class children died before they were one year old. This high rate of **infant mortality** was the result of the mother's ill-health (so she could not feed her baby properly) and of the dirt in which people lived. Babies became victims of many diseases which flourished in these insanitary conditions.

Many people, of all ages, died from one or other of the many diseases which flourished in the dirty conditions. There were common epidemics of typhoid and cholera in the first half of the nineteenth century.

HEALTH REFORMERS

Improvement Commissioners were elected in those industrial towns whose inhabitants had obtained a Private Act of Parliament to allow the setting up of a body to insist on improvements in housing and services.

Liverpool paid for a Private Act which allowed it to appoint a council to provide drainage, paving, sewerage and street cleansing, while also allowing it to appoint the first-ever Medical Officer of Health (William Duncan). **London** appointed Dr John Simon as its Medical Officer of Health in 1848 and slowly other towns followed this example.

Manchester had a number of Private Acts allowing it to build a council-owned water supply and in 1847 **Liverpool** began to build its own water supply.

Chadwick and the Poor Law Commissioners (p. 39) became concerned at the cost to the poor of the rate of disease and death which left many widows and orphans to be looked after and which left many families to be looked after when the wage earner became too ill to work.

The Commissioners were responsible for the publication in 1842 of a **Report on Sanitary Conditions**, which showed the effects and costs of disease.

Parliament refused to take any notice of the Report.

CHOLERA AND THE 1848 PUBLIC HEALTH ACT

In 1848 there was a fresh outbreak of cholera. Thousands of people died, thousands more were made too ill to work and the cost to the poor was very great.

Most of the victims lived in the slum areas of the industrial towns, showing the link between disease and dirt, but many people from these areas came into contact with the better-off – as servants, delivery men and workers. This took disease into the better-off areas.

There was a widespread campaign for government action, which led to the 1848 Public Health Act. This said that:
► A Board of Health was to be set up in London. Its three original members were Lord Morpeth, Lord Shaftesbury and Edwin Chadwick.
► Local Boards of Health were to be set up in towns where the death rate in any one year was more than 2.3 per cent of the population.
► A local Board might be set up when the ratepayers voted in favour of a petition for such a Board.
► Local Boards had powers to set up systems of street cleansing and refuse collection, and could force house-builders to put in water supplies and sewerage systems.
► The local Boards could collect a Health Rate.

OPPOSITION TO THE HEALTH ACT

► The outbreak of cholera ended late in 1848.
► Many people then opposed the Boards of Health.
► Many resented the rates imposed by local Boards.
► Chadwick annoyed many people by his stubborn determination to get reforms through.
► **Laissez-faire** influenced both people and Parliament.

In 1854 Parliament dismissed Chadwick and the Central Board became weaker. In 1858 the Board was abolished, although its work was handed over to the Privy Council which appointed Dr John Simon as its first Officer of Health.

CONTINUING REFORM

In spite of the strong opposition, the work of reform went ahead – because of a handful of reformers and because all the evidence showed the value of health reform.

Parliament passed many Acts which allowed, but did not force, local councils to make by-laws about housing, refuse collection, water supplies and street cleansing.

By 1879 only 69 towns owned their water supplies. At the end of the nineteenth century only 5000 of Bristol's 30 000 houses were linked to a water supply, while only in 1898 did Manchester insist on flush toilets in private homes.

18.3 More Effective Councils, 1868–75

▶ **The Torrens Act** (1868) allowed councils to pay for the pulling down of houses condemned as unfit by a Medical Officer of Health. Few councils took this step.

▶ **The Local Government Board** (1871) took over the duties once performed by the Board of Health and by the Poor Law Commission. There was now a government board to supervise the workings of local councils.

▶ **The Cross Act** (1875), also known as the **Artisans Dwellings Act**, allowed councils to condemn whole areas as unfit for human habitation. Councils could then buy up a district, pull down the slum housing and put up decent housing.

▶ **The Public Health Act** (1875) compelled councils to appoint a Medical Officer of Health and an Inspector of Nuisances. It also allowed councils to build sewers, street drainage, new reservoirs, public parks, libraries, swimming baths and public lavatories.

COUNCILS AND HEALTH

Most councils refused to use the powers, not wishing to increase local rates.

Joseph Chamberlain (p. 83) as leader of the Birmingham Council used all the powers of all the Acts so that between 1873 and 1876 he boasted that he had 'parked, paved, gas-and-watered and improved' the city. But by 1884 even the active Chamberlain had come to see that there was a limit to the increases in rates which could be imposed.

Even in Birmingham only 40 acres of slums had been cleared in 1884, for the building of Corporation Street Shopping Centre. The working people forced to leave the condemned housing merely crowded together in other districts.

PRIVATE HELP FOR HOUSING THE POOR

▶ **George Peabody** was a rich American who came to live in England in 1837. In 1869 he set up the Peabody Trust to which he gave £500 000. The Trust built blocks of Peabody Buildings, the first of which opened in Spitalfields in 1864. Flats were rented out to working-class people.

▶ **Octavia Hill** was the granddaughter of Dr Southwood Smith, a notable reformer in the 1830s and 1840s. In 1864 she bought three cottages in Marylebone and spent money improving them. She rented out the improved cottages at a rent which covered her costs. She encouraged friends to follow her example.

▶ **Sir Titus Salt** was a Yorkshire textile manufacturer who built a new town, Saltaire, for his employees. The town contained decent housing, parks, libraries and a social club – but no public house. **W. H. Lever**, the soap manufacturer, imitated Salt and built Leverhulme, while **George Cadbury**, the chocolate manufacturer, built Bournville (1879).

▶ In 1898 Ebenezer Howard wrote a book in which he called on the government to imitate their example by building Model Towns. In 1902 he wrote *Garden Cities of Tomorrow,* in which he showed that it was possible to build small towns which could combine the advantages of living in both town and country. **Letchworth** (1903) was the first such garden city, followed by **Hampstead Garden Suburb**.

The **Town Planning Act** (1909) was the result of Howard's influence on politicians. It gave councils the right to insist that new housing estates had to be properly laid out.

18.4 Medical Science

Operations and anaesthetics

Until the 1840s hospitals were dirty and dangerous places, and patients often died from wound infections or shock after operations. Changes were made because of the work of:

▶ **Sir Humphrey Davy,** who discovered that nitrous oxide ('laughing gas') removed pain. He suggested it be used during operations.

▶ **Michael Faraday,** Davy's assistant, who discovered (1838) that ether had the same effects as nitrous oxide. But doctors paid no attention to the work of these two eminent scientists.

▶ **Sir James Simpson,** professor of midwifery at Edinburgh University, who used chloroform as a painkiller during childbirth. His new anaesthetic became popular once it became known that Queen Victoria used it for the birth of her seventh child, Prince Leopold.

Pasteur and germs

Louis Pasteur discovered that disease was caused by germs. This led him to experiment until he produced a cholera vaccine (1879) in which he imitated the early work of the Englishman, Edward Jenner, who had discovered an antidote to smallpox in 1798. Pasteur went on to produce vaccines against typhoid, plague, yellow fever and typhus. The modern practice of **vaccination** had begun.

Joseph Lister and antiseptics

Lister was professor of surgery at Glasgow University. He studied Pasteur's work and realized that it was germs which infected the open wounds of patients in hospitals. In **1864** he used carbolic acid as an antiseptic, wiping everything that came into contact with the patient. The result was a drop in the numbers of those who died from infections of wounds.

▶ **Florence Nightingale** had gone to nurse in the Crimea (p. 54). She was responsible for:
● the reforms in the Army Medical Services (p. 55);
● the setting up of the first training schools for nurses at St Thomas's Hospital, London.

▶ **Sir Ronald Ross** entered the Indian Medical Service in 1881. By 1898 he had discovered that malaria was transmitted by mosquitoes. The destruction of the breeding-grounds of mosquitoes (by draining swampy places or by covering pools of standing water with a thin film of oil) led to the eradication of this disease.

▶ The **Curies**, Marie and Pierre, discovered the element **radium**, which provided doctors with another weapon in their fight against disease.

▶ **Röntgen** discovered X-rays (1895), which allow doctors to 'see' a patient's internal organs and structure and which enable doctors to make better diagnoses and to prescribe more suitable remedies.

18.5 A Decline in the Death Rate

The **discovery** of the causes of diseases led to the development of vaccines against many of them. This has continued in the twentieth century, and diphtheria and other killer-diseases have almost been eradicated (figs. 2.5A and 2.5B, p. 6).

▶ New **medicines and drugs** helped fight sickness and disease. Fleming's discovery of penicillin was a major step in this field.

▶ **Better living conditions** – housing, water supplies, street cleansing and the like – considerably reduced the incidence of disease.

▶ Better **wages** provided people with a chance to buy more and varied food, clothing, warmth and housing so that they were better able to fight disease.

► **Education** in schools, newspapers, radio and TV programmes has helped make people more health-conscious, so that diseases are less easily transmitted, and the consequences for one's health of smoking and over-drinking have been made clear.

► Improved **medical training** ensures that doctors are better able to understand their work, while **technology** provides them with the **drugs, instruments** and **machines** they need to do it.

► The development of the National Health Service ensured that people get the treatment they need.

It is worth noting that none of this would have been possible without an industrial revolution—the key to progress.

Unit 18 Summary

► The growth of insanitary towns and the spread of disease.
► Early attempts at sanitary reform; the importance of the work of Chadwick and of the 1842 Report.
► The 1848 Public Health Act and later reforms.
► Housing legislation 1867–75; the work of Joseph Chamberlain.
► The work of philanthropists – Peabody, Hill, Salt and Cadbury.
► Howard and the growth of the Model Towns movement.
► Development in medical science and the importance of the work of pioneers such as Simpson, Pasteur, Lister, Ross, the Curies and Röntgen.
► The decline in the death rate in the late nineteenth century.

19 SIR ROBERT PEEL

19.1 Peel's Family

Peel's grandfather had helped found a large textile firm. His father, the first Sir Robert, had enlarged the business and had given his son the sort of education that previously only the sons of landed gentlemen had enjoyed.

The first Sir Robert had promoted the Factory Act, 1819.

19.2 Peel's Early Career

After his education at Harrow and Oxford, Peel became an MP.

► **1812–28** Lord Liverpool (p. 32) appointed him Secretary of State for Ireland, where he opposed the Catholic demands for freedom.

► **1822–27** He was a reforming Home Secretary (p. 32).
Canning became Prime Minister early in 1827 and Peel refused to serve under him (p. 33).

► **1827–28 Wellington** became Prime Minister and Peel served in his Ministry – with its opposition to Emancipation.

► **1828–29** The election of O'Connell in County Clare forced Wellington and Peel to bring in an Emancipation Bill, which helped to divide further the Tory Party (p. 33).

19.3 Peel as Party Leader 1834–41

In **November 1834** Earl Grey resigned and William IV asked Peel to form a government. He called an election.

The Tamworth Manifesto is the name given to the letter which Peel wrote to his constituents. In it he explained his policy on:

► the **1832 Reform Act**, which he had opposed but which he now agreed to accept as a final settlement;

► the **spirit of reform**. He agreed that it would be necessary to examine institutions (the Church, local government and Parliament) and to reform where abuses could be proved to exist.

This was an important document, because it showed that the Tory Party was now willing to give a lead in reforms in some directions. This is why Peel is sometimes considered to be the founder of a new Party, one which he said would 'conserve the interest of the country' and which became known as **Conservative** rather than Tory Party.

Peel lost the election held in April 1835, so that his first Ministry was a short one.

The economic scene, 1837–41

The Whig government under Melbourne had been unable to cope with the growing problems presented by trade depressions and budget deficits (p. 41). When Melbourne resigned in 1841 Peel became Prime Minister for the second time.

19.4 Peel's Domestic Policy

PEEL AND SOCIAL REFORM

Between 1841 and 1846 the government was responsible for:

► **The Mines Act, 1842** (p. 43);
► **The Factory Act, 1844** (p. 43);
► Royal Commissions, to examine the **Health of Towns**, whose Reports led to the passing of the **Public Health Act 1848** (p. 45).

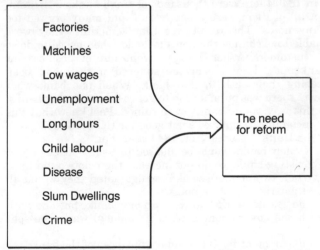

Factories
Machines
Low wages
Unemployment
Long hours
Child labour
Disease
Slum Dwellings
Crime

→ The need for reform

Fig. 19.4 A diagram showing some of the social problems found in Britain in the middle of the nineteenth century. Peel's government played a part in the campaign to find answers to these problems.

PEEL AND THE RAILWAYS

Unit 26 examines the development of the railway system and the many contributions which that system made to British life.

Peel, unlike the Whigs, realized the importance of the railway system. Gladstone, his minister at the Board of Trade, was responsible for the **Railway Act 1844**, which said that every railway company had to send at least one train every day to carry third-class passengers. It also said that the fare should not be more than 'one penny for each mile travelled'. This is sometimes known as the **Parliamentary mile**. This Act was important because it showed that the government was ready to intervene in the economic life of the country–against **laissez-faire** and it provided cheap travel for ordinary people.

PEEL AND TRADE, 1842–45

The trade depressions of 1837 and 1839–40 had been among the causes of the rise of Chartism (p. 41). Peel, son of a manufacturer, wanted to improve the economy, providing more employment for workpeople and more profits for industrialists. At the Board of Trade he was responsible for **The Budget, 1842** in which import duties were reduced to:
► a maximum of 5 per cent on raw materials;
► 12 per cent on semi-manufactured goods;
► 20 per cent on manufactured goods.

This was in keeping with the Free Trade policies followed by Pitt (p. 19) and Huskisson (p. 32), but ignored by the Whigs after 1832. The results of these changes in duty were:
► lower prices for finished goods;
► increased demand for those cheaper goods;
► more employment, because more people were needed to make the goods.

The success of the free-trade policy was so obvious that between 1843 and 1845 Peel reduced tariffs again so that after the 1845 budget there was only a 10 per cent duty on manufactured goods. Raw materials and semi-manufactured goods came in duty-free.

PEEL AND INCOME TAX

The reduction in tariffs led to a fall in government revenue. To make up for this Peel imposed a 'temporary' tax on incomes. People earning more than £150 a year had to pay 7d (3p) on each pound.

THE BANK CHARTER ACT, 1844

Anyone could open a Bank. They could ask people to lend them gold, which was described as 'cash'. They could print their own banknotes to lend to other customers to buy raw materials, build a factory or develop a firm.

In 1840 there were thousands of small banks in Britain. Not all of them were properly run and many printed too many notes. The result was that sometimes they were unable to exchange the notes for gold when asked to do so by customers. When a bank went out of business (or 'bankrupt'), local businesses suffered if they had been keeping their cash in that bank. When one bank went down, there was often a rush to get cash out of other banks. In this way, many banks were ruined. Peel knew that this financial uncertainty was not good for the economy.

The **Bank Charter Act, 1844** said that:
► No new banks would be allowed to issue notes.
► Existing banks could not increase their note issue.
► When two or more banks amalgamated they would all lose their right to issue notes.
► The **Bank of England** (a private bank, but one with which the government banked its money) was to be split into:
● a department for the ordinary business of the bank;
● an **Issue Department** to deal with the printing and issuing of bank notes. All these notes had to be covered by gold in the bank's vaults, except for £14 million, known as the fiduciary (or 'on trust') issue.

The effects of the Bank Charter Act

There was a fall in the number of note-issuing banks. As industry grew and firms became larger, there was a demand for larger sums of money and larger loans. Small banks could not provide enough. Many amalgamated–and lost their right to issue notes. The last note-issuing bank amalgamated with Lloyds in 1921.

Before 1844 the Bank of England had been only one out of many banks. This Act gave it a special position. Its notes became the normal currency of the country. There were fewer bank failures after 1844 which gave a boost to business confidence, savings and investments.

The limiting of the note-issue would have led to a slowing-down in the rate of business growth, but bankers developed the **cheque system** which enables business to be carried on without 'cash' (gold) or notes changing hands.

19.5 Foreign Policy, 1841–46

Peel's Foreign Minister was Lord Aberdeen. He was much less forceful than his predecessor, the Whig Minister, Lord Palmerston (unit 21). Aberdeen believed in negotation and was responsible for:
► **The Treaty of Nanking**, 1842, which brought the Opium War to an end (p. 51). It also brought Hong Kong into the British Empire and forced China to open five other 'treaty' ports to foreign trade.
► **The Ashburton Treaty**, 1841, which settled the frontier between Canada and the USA on the eastern seaboard.
► **The Oregon Treaty**, 1846, which settled the rest of the frontier between Canada and the USA. It named the 49th parallel as the frontier.
► Settling the dispute with the French concerning Tahiti, which some English missionaries wanted the government to annex, but which was annexed by France (1846).

PEEL AND IRELAND

This subject forms part of unit 23, but here you ought to note:
► Peel's links with Ireland in 1812–18 and 1827–29;
► The Maynooth grant;
► O'Connell's arrest (p. 56);
► **The Famine**, which was a cause of Peel's decision to repeal the Corn Laws in 1846 (p. 57).

19.6 A Summary of Peel's Ministry

The **working classes** benefited from:
► the Mines and Factory Acts;
► the fall in prices because of cuts in tariffs–their living standards rose;
► the increase in employment after tariff cuts;
► the growth in confidence, which helped employment.

They were also going to gain, later on, from Peel's interest in the conditions of the industrial towns.

The **industrialists** benefited from:
► the cuts in tariffs, since their business expanded;
► the development of railways (unit 26);
► the growth in business confidence.

It was during this Ministry that Britain gained the title of 'Workshop of the World'.

Farmers and **landowners** benefited from the rising incomes of the increasing populations of industrial towns. Greater quantities of more varied food were bought, having been carried to the towns on the railway system. But there was the **Anti-Corn Law League** which asked why it was right (and beneficial) to cut tariffs on raw materials and yet not right (according to the government) to abolish the Corn Laws. That question will be examined in the next unit.

Unit 19 Summary

► The role of Peel as Party leader, social and financial reformer.
► The achievement of Free Trade.
► Who gained and who lost because of Peel's work?

20 FREE TRADE AND THE ANTI-CORN LAW LEAGUE

20.1 The Free Trade 'Stream'

We have already seen the emergence of the Free Trade movement and its development because of:
► **Adam Smith,** who explained the benefits of Free Trade in *The Wealth of Nations* (p. 19).
► **William Pitt,** who had followed Smith's policies (p. 19).
► **William Huskisson** (p. 32).
► **Peel's** budgetary policy.

20.2 Industrialists and the Corn Laws

The Corn Laws had been imposed in 1815 to protect British farmers and landowners (p. 30). Huskisson had wanted to amend the laws by a sliding scale, but had failed to gain support for this until 1828 (p. 33).

The **1832 Reform Act** had given industrialists a share in the political system. **Trade depressions** in 1837 and 1839–41 led to the closure of many firms, short-time working for many more – and a decline in profits. Industrialists argued that:
► The Corn Laws resulted in high prices for food so that they had to pay higher wages than would be required if there were no such protection.
► If corn were allowed in, foreigners would have money to buy British goods – and so help overcome the depressions.

Peel's cuts in tariffs led many industrialists to ask why only corn (and farmers) should be protected.

20.3 The Anti-Corn Law League

By 1838 there were a number of local Anti-Corn Law Societies. **The League** was formed as a result of a meeting of delegates from such Societies. The meeting took place at the York Hotel, Manchester on the 10th January 1839. Its aim was simple – the abolition of the Corn Laws.

ADVANTAGES OF THE LEAGUE OVER THE CHARTIST MOVEMENT

Money

The League's supporters provided the money needed to pay for:
► **lecturers** who had to travel, for whom halls had to be hired and whose appearances had to be advertised;
► **pamphlets** which had to be printed and distributed;
► **postage** required for distributing propaganda. Notice the importance of the Penny Post (p. 40) and of the development of the railway network, which allowed speakers to travel and post to be delivered quickly.

Votes

After 1832 many of those who came to support the League had a vote. The leaders of the League worked to:
► make sure that such voters were **registered** on electoral lists so that they could vote at elections;
► **canvass at elections** to gain votes for Anti-Corn Law candidates in order to give the League more voices in the Commons.

Crowd appeal

The League appealed to the working class who hoped that cheap food would lead to a rise in living standards.

Parliamentary attention

The Commons could either ignore Chartist petitions or simply vote against them by large majorities. There were few MPs prepared to speak in support of that Movement. In the case of the League there were:
► **Richard Cobden,** the leading spirit in the formation of the League. A cotton manufacturer, Cobden supported Peel's Free Trade policy – and then continued to ask for a similar freedom for the trade in corn. Peel acknowledged that his conversion to Repeal and the abolition of the Corn Laws was due very largely to Cobden's persuasive arguments.
► **John Bright,** another of the founders of the League and an outstanding orator. Bright won the support of the crowds outside Parliament and of the MPs who had been elected by Anti-Corn Law voters.
► **Peel,** who was always open to conversion. He had changed his mind in 1829 over Emancipation (p. 33); the evidence of Royal Commissions made him a Factory Reformer (p. 47). His willingness to change his mind was a help to the Repealers.
► **Russell and the Whigs,** who, having done nothing about the Corn Laws when in office (1833–41), were won over by Cobden and Bright to support Repeal.

20.4 The Irish Famine, 1845–49

The potato was the main diet of the Irish peasant farmers. A blight of the crop in 1845 spread through the country so that millions of families faced terrible hardship.

Peel allowed into Ireland an importation of maize from Turkey – duty-free. He hoped that this might provide the food needed by the starving poor. The Turkish maize made a breach in the barrier against the importing of cheap food.

At the same time thousands of tons of corn and hundreds of cattle and sheep were being exported from Ireland.

When the Irish continued to suffer in the winter of 1845 Russell and the Whigs, Cobden and the MPs elected by the supporters of the League, as well as Peel, came to see that further breaches would be needed if the Irish were not to suffer even more. As the Duke of Wellington said, 'It was the rotten potatoes that did it'.

20.5 The Repeal of the Corn Laws

► **22nd November 1845** Russell wrote an open letter from **Edinburgh** to his constituents in the City of London announcing his conversion to Repeal.
► **2nd December 1845** Peel announced his decision to bring in a Repeal Bill. Many of the Cabinet refused to support him. He resigned so that Russell might be invited to form a Repealing government. Russell refused because many of his colleagues refused to help form a government.
► **20th December 1845** Peel was back in office. The great landowners, who controlled many seats, opposed him and ordered the resignation from the government of MPs from their 'pocket boroughs'.
► **January 1846** In the Commons the attack on Peel was led by Bentinck and Disraeli, who claimed that Peel was sacrificing the interests of the farmers to those of industry.
► **25th June 1846** The third reading of Peel's Bill to reduce the duty on imported corn to a nominal shilling. It was passed.

That same night the government was defeated over a proposal to bring in a Coercion Bill for Ireland. The Whigs, the Radicals, the followers of Bentinck and Disraeli combined in 'a blackguard combination'. But the Corn Laws had been repealed.

AGRICULTURE IN A FREE TRADE COUNTRY

From **1846** to **1873** British farming enjoyed a 'Golden Age' (unit 27). In **1873**, however, the importation of cheap American corn during a period of poor harvests in Britain led to the decline in the wheat farming sector of British agriculture (p. 66).

So in the short run the fears of the Tories were not realized. This helps to explain why in the 1850s Disraeli said that the Corn Laws were 'dead and damned' and, when in office, he made no attempt to bring them back.

 ### 20.6 Further Developments of Free Trade

Gladstone had worked with Peel on the development of Free Trade between 1841 and 1845. **After 1846** Gladstone and other 'Peelites' (supporters of Peel) tended to vote with the Whigs. Gladstone served as Chancellor of the Exchequer in Whig-Peelite governments.

Gladstone wanted to complete Peel's work, so:
▶ **1853** In his first Budget, Gladstone abolished 140 duties, lowered another 150, put income tax to 7d (just over 2½p) in the pound and planned for the abolition of income tax within seven years. However, on the outbreak of the Crimean War this tax was immediately doubled. Among the duties abolished were those on soap (which led to lower

prices and to the greater cleanliness of the people) and on paper (which led to lower prices for newspapers and books, and to an extension of readership among the masses).
▶ **1860** He supported Cobden's successful attempts to negotiate a trade treaty with France. The **Cobden Treaty** (1860) abolished many French duties on British goods and lowered others in return for the British abolition of many duties on French goods.
▶ **The Budget, 1860,** was designed to incorporate the terms of the Cobden Treaty. It also removed the duties on 371 articles, including paper. Only 48 articles were now subject to import duties and in each case the duty was not aimed at protection but was used to bring in government revenue.

THE SUCCESS OF FREE TRADE

From 1846 Britain enjoyed continuing prosperity. Gladstone argued that this prosperity was due to Free Trade. This helps to explain why many came to see Free Trade as 'natural' while for others it came to be treated as a 'gospel', as if it were a religious truth. When Free Trade proved less successful after 1879 (p. 68) it was impossible to get wide enough support for its abolition and for the imposition of a system of tariffs (unit 28).

Unit 20 Summary

▶ The Anti-Corn Law League – its supporters and their arguments.
▶ Comparisons between the League and Chartism.
▶ The repeal of the Corn Laws, 1846.
▶ The completion of Free Trade under Gladstone.

21 PALMERSTON, 1830–65

 ### 21.1 A Canningite

▶ **1807** Palmerston entered Parliament as a Tory MP.
▶ **1809–28** He was Secretary of State for War.
▶ **1828** He resigned with Huskisson from Wellington's government.
▶ **1829** With Melbourne and other Canningites he joined the Whigs.
▶ **1830** He was appointed Foreign Secretary. Like Canning, he thought 'the interests of England ought to be the aims of his policy'.

21.2 Palmerston's Foreign Policy

PALMERSTON THE NATIONALIST – BELGIUM

Belgium was linked with Holland, at the Congress of Vienna, to create a strong country on France's border. It was an unhappy union, however, because:
▶ there were differences in religion – the Belgians being Catholic;
▶ there were differences in occupation – Belgium being industrialized;
▶ most government posts went to the Protestant Dutch;
▶ most taxes were organized to help Dutch agriculture.

In July 1830 the French revolted and put Louis Philippe on the throne. This breaking of the terms of the Congress of Vienna encouraged the Belgians to rise to try to get their independence.

Metternich saw this as a reason for intervention under the terms of the Troppau Protocol (p. 35). The Belgians asked for French help.

Palmerston, newly appointed to office, decided:
▶ to oppose the Holy Alliance – as Canning might have done;
▶ to stop France from gaining influence in Belgium because of the possible security threat to Britain.

He used British naval power to force the Dutch to hand Antwerp to the Belgians, while he offered to cooperate with France against the Holy Alliance if its forces should invade.

He then persuaded the Belgians to give their Crown to Leopold of Saxe-Coburg, a relation of the British Royal Family, instead of giving it to the son of Louise Philippe, King of France.

In the Treaty of London, 1839, Palmerston persuaded the major powers to agree that Belgium would be permanently a neutral country. This Treaty was partly responsible for drawing Britain into war in 1914 (p. 89).

PALMERSTON THE LIBERAL – SPAIN AND PORTUGAL, 1834

▶ **1828** Dom Miguel illegally seized the throne of Portugal during the infancy of the rightful Queen, Donna Maria.

▶ **1834** Don Carlos challenged the claims of Queen Isabella to the throne of Spain.

▶ **1834** Palmerston sent troops to help expel the Miguelists from Portugal and the Carlists from Spain.

He persuaded France, Spain and Portugal to sign a **Quadrilateral Alliance** with Britain, as 'a powerful counterpoise to the Holy Alliance of the east', as Palmerston wrote when describing it as 'A capital hit and all my own doing'.

PALMERSTON THE BULLYING MERCHANT – THE OPIUM WAR, 1839–42

In the 1830s the British banned the sale of opium in India, so the Indian opium growers then exported the drug to China.

The Chinese government was opposed to this because:
▶ the drug was harmful;
▶ it was expensive, and cost China a good deal of gold;
▶ the British merchants often insulted the Chinese customs officials who thought the British 'barbarians'.

There were many clashes between Chinese and British. In **1839** Chinese officials destroyed British ships and a brief war followed.

Under the terms of **the Treaty of Nanking**, 1842, China had to cede Hong Kong to Britain and five ports – Canton, Amoy, Foochow, Nangpo and Shanghai – had to be open to foreign shipping.

PALMERSTON THE ANTI-RUSSIAN – MEHEMET ALI, 1830–41

We will study this subject in unit 22.

PALMERSTON THE CAUTIOUS LIBERAL – THE 1848 REVOLUTIONS

Palmerston became Foreign Secretary in the Russell government formed after Peel's resignation (p. 49). Palmerston warned the European rulers that if they did not give some concessions to their peoples, then they would have to face the threats of revolutions.

In 1848 a series of revolutions broke out in Europe. Many people hoped that Palmerston would help the rebels, but he refused to do so. He was anxious for peace, fearing that Russia might take advantage of the unrest to extend her power.

He was anxious that Austria should remain a strong power and therefore an obstacle to Russian advance, and he was glad when, in 1849 and 1850, the old rulers, with the aid of their armies, got back to their thrones.

He welcomed the exiled liberals from France, Austria, Prussia and Hungary, and approved of the rough treatment given to General Haynau who was attacked by London brewery workers during a visit to Britain.

PALMERSTON THE PATRIOTIC BULLY AND DON PACIFICO

Don Pacifico was a Gibraltarian-born Jew with stores and other property in Athens in Greece. During anti-government riots in Athens in 1847 his property was destroyed. He asked the Greek government for compensation.

The government ignored his exaggerated claims and he appealed to the British government.

In December 1849 Palmerston ordered a fleet to Athens, threatening to bombard the city if the Greeks did not give Don Pacifico the compensation demanded.

The Greeks gave way to this show of force (1850), although in the Commons the action was challenged by the Radicals led by Cobden, Bright and Gladstone.

Palmerston defended himself. He claimed that the Romans had defended anyone who could claim **Civis Romanus Sum** ('I am a Roman citizen') so Britain ought to look after anyone who could claim **Civis Britannicus Sum**.

Most people in the country welcomed this strong action.

PALMERSTON THE REVENGE-TAKER OVER FRANCE, 1846

Louis Philippe and Palmerston had cooperated over the Belgian Question and over Spain and Portugal, but in 1839–41 they quarrelled over Mehemet Ali (p. 53).

In 1843 they agreed about the marriage plans for the young Queen Isabella of Spain and her younger sister, Louisa. The French King's son was to marry Louisa, after the Queen married and had an heir. Palmerston feared a French-born heir to the Spanish throne.

In 1846 Louis Philippe broke that agreement; he arranged a marriage for the Spanish Queen – to an old man who would not be able to produce an heir. This meant that his son's children would take the Spanish throne.

Palmerston did not forgive this breach of an agreement.

PALMERSTON THE CONSERVATIVE AND LOUIS NAPOLEON

The French Revolution of 1848 led to a Republic, in which socialists and conservatives shared power and Louis Napoleon became President for four years. In 1851 Louis Napoleon used his powers to get the people to elect him President for 10 years.

Palmerston had feared that socialism and radicalism might take over in France – and provided the example for extremists in other countries.

He thought Louis Napoleon could provide strong government to hold socialism and radicalism in check. He told the French Ambassador in London that he approved of the way in which Louis Napoleon had seized power.

This brought to a head the conflict between Queen Victoria and Palmerston. The Queen argued that the Foreign Minister was wrong in discussing this affair without first getting her approval. She forced his resignation from Russell's government in 1851.

21.3 In and Out of Office, 1852–55

Within two months of his dismissal, Palmerston had organized a majority in the Commons against Russell's proposals for the formation of a local militia. Russell resigned and Palmerston told his wife, 'I have had my tit-for-tat'.

NOW FOR IT !

A Set-to between "Pam, the Downing Street Pet," and "The Russian Spider."

Fig. 21.3 A cartoonist's view of the accession of Palmerston to the office of Prime Minister during the Crimean War.

Derby and Disraeli failed to form a government, and the Peelite, Aberdeen, became Prime Minister and appointed Palmerston Home Secretary.

Aberdeen's government was soon involved in the dispute which led to the Crimean War (unit 22).

During the negotiations preceding the outbreak of the war, Palmerston resigned. The government failed to pursue the war vigorously. It became unpopular and in 1855 Aberdeen was forced to resign (p. 54).

Queen Victoria had to make Palmerston Prime Minister.

The conclusion of the Crimean War
See unit 22.

21.4 China Again, 1856–60

The Treaty of Nanking satisfied neither the Chinese nor the British. Clashes were frequent.

In 1851, during a peasant uprising against the Chinese government, some Europeans were murdered. In 1856, while the uprising continued, customs officials seized the Hong Kong ship the **Arrow**, and accused the captain of piracy.

Palmerston ordered the Royal Navy to bombard Canton, and a joint French and British army invaded China in 1857. This defeated the Chinese army, already weakened by the peasant uprising.

In June 1858 the Treaty of Tientsin was signed which forced the Chinese to open more ports to foreign trade, but the peasants refused to allow the use of the new ports.

The French and British continued their war in China. In 1860 their armies entered the Chinese capital Peking. The government was then forced to sign the Treaty of Peking which confirmed the Treaty of Tientsin. Eleven new ports were open to trade.

21.5 Italy

ORSINI

In 1855 there was no 'Italy' but several separate states. Some were under Austrian rule, or the rule of Austrian-dominated rulers. The Papal States cut right across Central Italy. The Kingdom of Piedmont sent help to the Allies in the Crimean War.

▶ Napleon III (as Louis Napoleon had become in 1852) wanted a united Italy, but he feared that the loss of the Papal States might lose him the support of French Catholics.

▶ Palmerston favoured Italian unification, provided it could be achieved without a major European war.

▶ In 1858 an Italian refugee called **Orsini** threw a bomb in Paris at Napoleon III because he had not yet helped the Italians.

▶ Napoleon was unhurt but Orsini fled to England where the bomb had been made and where other conspirators lived.

▶ French newspapers attacked Britain and Palmerston brought in the **Conspiracy to Murder Bill** to allow the government to order the arrest of Orsini.

▶ The Bill was attacked by Palmerston's opponents. It was defeated and Palmerston resigned.

▶ The Tories formed a government but in the 1859 Election failed to gain a majority. Palmerston became Prime Minister.

ITALIAN UNIFICATION, 1859–61

▶ **May 1859** Napoleon declared war on Austria in Italy.

▶ Britain opposed this, fearing a general war.

▶ French troops defeated the Austrians.

▶ The Treaty of Villafranca ended the war. The Italians made little progress towards unification and Palmerston and his Foreign Minister, Russell, encouraged the Italians to continue their war against Austria.

▶ Napoleon then persuaded the Austrians to change the terms of the Treaty of Villafranca. Piedmont was enlarged.

▶ Garibaldi led his red-shirted troops from Genoa to Sicily and defeated the Austrian-dominated ruler of Naples and Sicily. His success depended on British naval support.

▶ Garibaldi handed Naples and Sicily to the King of Piedmont in January 1861.

21.6 The American Civil War

▶ In 1861 the slave-owning states of the USA tried to break away to form their own Federation.

▶ President Lincoln declared war on these rebel states, and Gladstone and many liberal-minded MPs supported Lincoln. So too did the working class of Lancashire, although they suffered from the fall in imports of raw cotton.

▶ Palmerston sympathized with the southerners, however.

▶ Lincoln's government claimed the right to search ships trading with the southerners. One of their ships stopped a British vessel, the *Trent*, which was carrying two delegates from the south to Britain.

▶ Palmerston wrote a bitter note to Lincoln. This might well have forced Lincoln to declare war on Britain. But Prince Albert, the Prince Consort, altered its wording so that it was less insulting.

▶ The British government allowed the southern states to pay a Birkenhead shipyard to build the *Alabama*. It was used to destroy northern shipping. The Lincoln government claimed compensation.

▶ Palmerston refused this. The ill-feeling between the two countries was ended only when Gladstone settled this matter (unit 29).

21.7 Palmerston and Bismarck

Bismarck was the Chancellor of Prussia, a powerful and industrialized state, which he wanted to become the centre of a unified Germany. In 1864 Bismarck planned a war against Denmark so that he could seize the Duchies of Schleswig and Holstein.

Palmerston promised the Duchies that if they went to war, they would have the help of Britain. War was declared; Britain did not help the Duchies, which were seized by Austria and Prussia.

This showed that Britain could not run world affairs as she had done in, for example, the Middle East or China.

Palmerston's death in 1865 marked the end of an era.

Unit 21 Summary

▶ Palmerston's policies, 1830–41 – Belgium, Spain and Portugal, China (the Opium War).
▶ Britain and the 1848 Revolutions in Europe.
▶ The Don Pacifico affair ('Civis Britannicus Sum').
▶ Palmerston and France – Louis Philippe and Louis Napoleon.
▶ The Second Chinese War.
▶ Palmerston's relations with Italy, the USA and Bismarck.

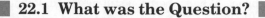
22.1 What was the Question?

There were three questions:
▶ **Turkey**, by 1800, seemed unable to control her large Empire. A Viceroy ruled in Egypt; elsewhere there were Christians rebelling against their Muslim rulers. One question was **'Can Turkey survive?'**
▶ A second question was, **'What will happen to its Empire?'** Would the various peoples form independent states? Or would some other Power step in to replace Turkey?
▶ The third question was **'What would the Powers do if Turkey crumbled?'** Would they help the rebels get their independence? Would they use them as satellites? Would they seize power?

22.2 Turkish Problems

THE GREEK REBELLION, 1812−30

Led by the **Hypsilanti family**, the Greeks were in rebellion. In the early 1820s they were winning, and the Turks asked their vassal, Mehemet Ali of Egypt, to send an army and navy to help put down the Greeks. He was promised Syria as a reward. **Nicholas I** decided to help the Greeks; Canning feared this. The **Battle of Navarino** ensured Greek independence.

UNKIAR SKELESSI, 1833

The Turks refused to hand over Syria. Mehemet Ali sent an army from Egypt to invade Syria and talked of founding an independent kingdom. The British Ambassador at Constantinople was Stratford Canning, a nephew of the great Canning. He feared that Russia would take advantage of Ali's invasion to win power for herself.

Because of the unrest over the Reform Bill, Britain was unable to take any action in 1831−32. This forced Turkey to ask for Russian help.

The price was the Treaty of Unkiar Skelessi. This said:
▶ Russian warships could sail from Russian ports on the Black Sea through the Dardanelles into the Mediterranean. This Treaty gave Russia a virtual protectorate over the area.
▶ No other foreign warships would be allowed through the Dardanelles into the Black Sea.

MEHEMET ALI, 1839−41

In **1839** the Sultan of Turkey decided to attack Ali. Ali's army defeated the Turks and invaded Syria. **Louis Philippe** promised to support Ali, to gain French influence in North Africa and Syria.

Palmerston wanted to keep Turkey as a bulwark against Russian expansion and to keep France out of the area.

Fig. 22.2 A sketch map illustrating Russian foreign policy in the 19th century. Notice the threats to British interests in the Mediterranean (marked 4 and 5), in India (marked 6 and 7) and, later in the century, in the Far East (marked 8).

The **London Conference, 1840**, was organized by Palmerston. Austria, Russia, Prussia and Britain agreed that Ali would have to give up the territory he had taken from Turkey. Ali, with the support of France, refused.

The British navy bombarded Beirut in North Syria and the army defeated the Egyptians at the Battle of Acre (November 1840).

The **Straits Convention, 1841** was then signed by Britain, Austria, Russia, Turkey, Prussia and France (now back in line). It said that the Dardanelles would be closed to all foreign warships so long as Turkey was at peace. Unkiar Skelessi was undone.

AN UNEASY PEACE, 1841–52

Stratford Canning had feared Russian policy in 1833. **Nicholas I** suggested to Canning, and later to the government in London, that Britain and Russia ought to agree over Turkey: the 'sick man' talks.

'**The sick man**' was Nicholas's description of Turkey. He suggested that the property of that 'sick man' ought to be divided peacefully between the Powers, rather than allowed to be the cause of war between them.

Canning, Palmerston and the British in general were even more suspicious of Russia after these talks (fig. 22.2).

■ 22.3 The Holy Places ■

The Turkish Empire contained many places of religious significance to Christians, who were allowed to build churches, hostels and hospitals in Jerusalem and other centres.

France, once the leading Catholic country, had earlier acted as Guardian to the pilgrims visiting the Holy Places. She had let that right lapse, however, and in 1774 Turkey had signed a Treaty (Kutchuk Kainardji) which recognized Russia as the Guardian of the Holy Places.

NAPOLEON III AND THE HOLY PLACES

Napoleon III was anxious to keep the support of French Catholics. In 1853 he reminded the Turks of French claims to be the Guardians of the Holy Places. This claim was supported by the British who hoped to weaken Russian influence in the area.

In **February 1853** the Russians asked the Turks to agree that the Treaty of 1774 still operated, and that Russia was the Guardian of the Holy Places.

■ 22.4 The Drift to War, 1853 ■

Canning (who had become Lord Stratford de Redcliffe in 1852) represented the British government at talks in February 1853, held to resolve the subject of the Guardianship.

Turkey accepted Russia's claim to the Guardianship of the Holy Places, but rejected her wider claims to be the Guardian of Christians throughout the Empire.

In **June**, to give support to the Turkish refusal to accept Russia's wider claims, a British and French fleet was sent to the Dardanelles. Meanwhile, to try to force Turkey to grant her claims, Russia invaded the Danubian Provinces of Moldavia and Wallachia.

Palmerston, who was Home Secretary in Aberdeen's government, wanted the fleets to go into the Black Sea to threaten the Russian ports. Other ministers refused.

In **September** British, French, Austrian and Prussian delegates met at Vienna to discuss the Turkish problem. They issued the **Vienna Note** which asked:
▶ Russia to withdraw her army from the Provinces;
▶ Turkey to agree to discuss Russia's claim.

Canning persuaded Turkey to reject this Note and promised British help in a war with Russia.

TO FIGHT OR NOT?

Turkey declared war on Russia on 4th October 1853. **Aberdeen's** government was divided. Aberdeen hoped that the matter could be settled by negotiations. **Palmerston** thought that it could only be settled by war.

In **November 1853** a Russian fleet destroyed a Turkish fleet at Sinope. When Aberdeen still hesitated, Palmerston resigned (p. 52).

In **January 1854 Aberdeen** ordered the fleet into the Black Sea, and in **March 1854** Britain finally declared war.

THE CRIMEAN WAR

A fleet attacked Russia's northern ports. Troops were landed in Finland to invade northern Russia, but there seemed little chance of success in these frozen wastes.

In **September 1854** troops were landed at Calamity Bay to help in the capture of Sebastopol. They won the **Battle of Alma** and surrounded Sebastopol.

Allied fleets attacked Sebastopol from the sea, but **General Menshikoff** repulsed this attack.

In **October** Menshikoff's army met the Allied armies at **Balaclava**, where there took place the futile **Charge of the Light Brigade**.

In **November** the armies met again at the **Battle of Inkerman**, after which the Russians retreated back into Sebastopol.

GENERAL WINTER AND THE ALLIES

The allies failed to defeat Russia because they were led by incompetent generals who quarrelled, and they were badly armed and clothed because of the incompetence of the supply department of the War Office. During the winter of 1854–55 many men died because of lack of food, medicine, clothing and adequate shelter.

W. H. Russell was *The Times'* reporter in the Crimea. His reports – of the stupidity of the generals, conditions of hospitals, incompetence of supply departments and needless sufferings and deaths these caused – led to demands for a public enquiry into the conduct of the war.

Florence Nightingale was appalled at the reports of conditions in Crimean hospitals. She gathered a group of nursing nuns and other women with nursing experience and went to **Scutari** where she challenged the army's attitude towards the sick and wounded. Her hospital at Scutari was the first efficient military hospital in which men did not die of infected wounds or of the many fevers which had swept through the insanitary and unorganized hospitals of the past.

■ 22.5 A Change of Government ■

In **January 1855** Aberdeen's conduct of the war was condemned by Parliament. He was forced to resign. The Queen asked Palmerston to form a government. People hoped for a great and speedy victory.

Britain and France then sent delegates to a Conference at Vienna where, under Austria's leadership, an agreement was worked out by which the Allies and Austria hoped to limit Russian power in the Crimea and the Danube Basin. Russia rejected the proposals, so the war continued.

Cavour (Prime Minister of Piedmont) sent a contingent of soldiers to fight alongside the Allies, hoping that this would give him a seat (and influence over Napoleon III) at the peacemaking Conference which would follow the end of the war. Sweden entered into an anti-Russian alliance with Britain and France.

A three-month attack on Sebastopol, from June to August, ended with the Russians abandoning the fortress, which actually fell on 8th September 1855.

THE END OF THE WAR

Nicholas I died in 1855. Alexander II, the new Tsar, wanted peace so that he could bring some reforms to Russia.

Palmerston realized that it was going to be impossible to win any quick or great victory.

THE PEACE OF PARIS, 1856

Britain, France and Russia negotiated this Treaty at a Conference in Paris at which Cavour, the Prime Minister of Piedmont, was also a participant. The Treaty said that:

▶ Russia would not re-build Sebastopol as a fortress;
▶ Russia would not build a new fleet in the Black Sea;
▶ the two provinces, Moldavia and Wallachia, were to be independent but had to acknowledge Turkish sovereignty;
▶ the Danube was to be brought under international control, while Russia had to surrender Bessarabia at the mouth of the Danube;

The Sultan agreed to treat his Christian subjects more kindly than in the past, while Russia had to abandon her claim to protect Christians inside the Turkish Empire.

22.6 The Effects of the War on Britain

▶ **Palmerston** was confirmed as the country's hero.

▶ **Army reform** (unit 29).
▶ **The Army hospital service was reorganized.**
▶ **Florence Nightingale** carried the development of a good nursing service into civilian life.
▶ Many British regiments went from India to the Crimea. This was a cause of the **Indian Mutiny** (p. 58).
▶ **New words** entered the language. Lord **Cardigan** gave his name to a new woollen jacket; **Balaclava** gave its name to a woollen helmet.
▶ **The Victoria Cross** was instituted as a reward for bravery. The first crosses were made from the metal of guns captured at Sebastopol.

Unit 22 Summary

▶ Meaning of the 'Question' and its development.
▶ Canning and the Greek question, 1827.
▶ The importance of (i) the Treaty of Unkiar Skelessi and (ii) Mehemet Ali.
▶ Britain's hostility to Russia.
▶ Steps leading to the Crimean War; the role of Palmerston.
▶ The effects of the Crimean War.

23 IRELAND, 1760–1850

23.1 Ireland's Four Grievances, 1760

Political

▶ **The Irish Parliament** met in Dublin, but had little power because of **Poynings' Law** (1494–5) which said:
● no decision by the Irish Parliament could become law until approved by the Westminster Parliament;
● every Act passed by Westminster applied to Ireland. Ireland was subject to the Navigation Acts (p. 15).
▶ **Catholics** could not vote nor stand as candidates.
▶ **The Chief Secretary** for Ireland was always a British politician, such as Castlereagh (p. 34) or Peel (p. 47). He and the Viceroy of Ireland paid little attention to the Irish Parliament.

Economic

Irish Protestants hated the English control of their politics. Even more, they disliked the way in which their economy was treated.
▶ **No industry** was allowed if this would compete with an English industry. This meant that flax could be woven, but no wool.
▶ **Trade** was subject to the Navigation Acts.
▶ **Pitt** had made a trade treaty with France in 1786 (p. 19) but Parliament would not allow one for Ireland.

Religious

The majority of the Irish were Catholics. They were angered at the attacks on their religion. They were further angered because the Anglican Church was the Established Church, to which they had to pay tithes.

The Penal Laws drawn up in the seventeenth century meant that no Catholic could legally practise his religion, send his children to school, vote or own land, become an

officer in the services, a lawyer, a town councillor or an MP. Priests found guilty of saying Mass could be fined and imprisoned.

Land

Various laws made it almost impossible for Catholics to own land. Three-quarters of Irish land was owned by absentee British landlords, whose estates were run by bailiffs or agents. The estates were split into small plots and rented out to Catholic peasants. If tenants failed to pay rent, they were evicted.

23.2 Ireland and the American War of Independence

▶ **No taxation without representation:** the Irish were controlled by a Parliament over which they had no control.
▶ **The French menace** after 1778 (p. 18) led to the formation of the Protestant Irish Volunteers organized to defend Ireland.

The continued success of the Americans encouraged the Irish to ask for the relaxation of laws which they disliked. Fear of an Irish uprising while the American War was going on persuaded the British to relax or repeal some of those laws. By 1777 Britain had removed the worst of the Penal Laws, although Catholics were still not allowed to vote.

▶ **Henry Grattan**, an MP in the Irish Parliament, demanded complete freedom for Ireland. Britain feared a Protestant rebellion.
▶ In **1780** the worst features of the Navigation Acts were repealed. Some Irish industry could now be developed.
▶ In **1782** the Irish Parliament became independent and the Acts of 1494 and 1714 were repealed. However, through the corrupt electoral system, the British controlled many seats while through the system of patronage, the Crown could 'buy' the votes of many Irish MPs.

▓ 23.3 Irish Government, 1782–92

The Irish Parliament could legislate freely, but the Chief Secretary and the Viceroy controlled many boroughs and bribed many other MPs, so Britain still controlled Parliament.

Pitt failed to get a trade treaty for Ireland in 1786 and the religious and land problems remained almost untouched.

▓ 23.4 Ireland and the French Revolution

▶ **1791** Wolfe Tone, a Belfast Protestant lawyer, founded a society called the **United Irishmen**. Catholics and Protestants joined; they hoped to force Pitt to give more freedom to Ireland.
▶ **1792** More Penal Laws were repealed.
▶ **1793** Catholics allowed to vote – but not to be candidates.
▶ **1795** Tone went to Paris to ask for help from the French.
▶ **1796** Hoche brought a French fleet to Bantry Bay but was driven away by a storm before a landing could be made.

In **1798** an Irish Rising took place, mainly in Ulster and Wexford. It failed in Ulster, where the Protestants formed the Orange Society and turned on the Catholics. Many atrocities occurred. It also failed in Wexford, where the peasants were badly armed, poorly led and easily beaten by the English forces. The rising was helped by a French invasion. An army led by Humbert landed at Killala (1798) and defeated a Protestant militia at Castlebar, but surrendered at Ballinasloe.

▓ 23.5 Pitt and Ireland, 1798–1800

Pitt feared another (and successful) rising. He wanted to pacify the Catholics by giving them Emancipation, which would allow Catholics to stand in elections, but he knew that the Protestants were frightened of the idea of a Catholic Parliament in Dublin. Pitt's solution was to propose the Union.

THE UNION, 1800–01

▶ Irish Protestants (a minority in their own country) would be part of a majority in a United Kingdom.
▶ Irish Catholics (a majority in Ireland) would be a minority in a United Kingdom. If they were allowed to become MPs, Catholic MPs would have little influence over the British Parliament.

THE ACT OF UNION, 1800–01

▶ The Irish Parliament was abolished and Ireland was split into 100 constituencies.
▶ Four Protestant Irish bishops and 28 Irish noblemen had seats in the Lords.
▶ Trade would be completely free and Ireland would be treated in the same way as Wales or Scotland.

THE UNION AND THE CATHOLICS

Pitt hoped to please the Catholics by getting Parliament to pass an Emancipation Act for Catholics. George III refused to allow this. Pitt resigned in 1801 (p. 22).

▓ 23.6 Daniel O'Connell, 1812–28

O'Connell was a Catholic lawyer. In **1823** he formed the Catholic Association. Its members paid 1d per month to his agents, who used churches as collecting centres for the **Catholic Rent**, as he called it. In **1825** The Association was made illegal. He reformed it, however, and toured the country to rouse and unite the people against the Union.

O'CONNELL AND THE CLARE ELECTION, 1828

▶ Wellington had rejected Catholic Emancipation (p. 33).
▶ O'Connell stood at a by-election in County Clare; since most of the voters were Catholics, he won.

Wellington and Peel now had a choice:
▶ they could declare the election illegal and order a fresh one. Wellington feared a Catholic rising in which the Whigs and Canningites might side with the Catholics;
▶ they could allow him into Parliament. This meant going back on the promises made when they replaced Canning.

O'CONNELL THE LIBERATOR

In **1829**, the Roman Catholic Emancipation Act gave Catholics complete civil, political, legal and economic freedoms – except that, because of older laws, no Catholic could become Regent, Viceroy of Ireland or India, or Lord Chancellor, nor could a member of the royal family marry a Catholic without giving up any claim to the throne.

O'Connell took his seat in the Commons.

O'CONNELL AND THE WHIGS, 1830–41

O'Connell wanted a repeal of the Union. He hoped the Whigs might give Ireland this self-rule and supported them, playing a part in bringing down the Tories in 1835 and 1839 (p. 47). The agreement between O'Connell and the Whigs is called the **Lichfield House Compact**.

In **1838** the government abolished the system by which Catholics had been forced to pay tithes to Protestant clergymen; but the Whigs failed to do any more.

O'CONNELL AND PEEL, 1841–43

Peel thought Ireland's main problem was religious; the increase in the Maynooth Grant from £9000 to £26 000 was one way by which he hoped to ease that problem (p. 48).

The main problems, however, were land and politics (home rule). O'Connell toured Ireland to get support for home rule. Prayers were said for him in every church; vast crowds turned out to hear him speak.

Peel feared that O'Connell, like Tone, might lead a rising, and in **1843** Peel banned a national demonstration which O'Connell planned to hold at Clontarf.

O'Connell agreed not to march, but Peel arrested him. His release was ordered by the House of Lords, but O'Connell was a broken man. He retired and later died in May 1847.

▓ 23.7 The Famine ▓

In **1841** the Census showed that there were about nine million people in Ireland, half of whom lived in 'windowless mud cabins of a single room'. The **potato** was their main crop: they sold part of it to get the money for rent and lived off the rest.

In **1845** a fungus attacked the Irish potato crop. Within six months most people were penniless and starving.
▶ **Evictions** took place when rents were not paid.
▶ **Diseases**, such as cholera and typhus, followed the famine.
▶ **Death** accounted for the loss of about one million people.
▶ **Emigration** accounted for the loss of about two million who left Ireland to live in Britain, Australia, New Zealand, Canada and, above all, the USA.

PEEL AND THE FAMINE

There was no attempt to interfere with 'natural' laws. Poor Law Guardians were allowed to give help to the poor and starving – if they collected the money. Landlords were encouraged to provide work for the starving. Walls were built around estates by men working for 1d (less than ½p) a day.
▶ **Food** was exported to England from the prosperous

estates of the 'gentry'. The penniless people could not have bought it even if the government had forbade its export.

▶ **Charity** was provided by Quakers at soup kitchens.

▶ **Maize** was allowed in from Turkey.(p. 49).

▶ The **Corn Laws** were repealed by an opportunist Parliament. Russell and the Whigs allied with the Peelites to get repeal through Parliament. But this did not help the Irish who continued to starve, die or emigrate through four more years of famine.

23.8 Young Ireland, 1848

Many people said that O'Connell had failed when he allowed himself to be arrested in 1843. There were many others, however, who realized that the English had failed to help Ireland during the Famine Years of 1845–8.

In **1848** Europe was torn by revolution (p. 51), while England went throught the Chartist crisis. Radical Irishmen, many of them journalists and poets, wanted Ireland to rebel.

The young radicals, known as **Young Ireland**, called on the people to rise. The 1848 rising was a badly organized and poorly led affair. It was easily suppressed and its leaders were shot or exiled. Some, in exile in the USA, helped promote an even more violent, richer, more popular movement called the **Fenians**, a society named in memory of the ancient **fianna** or **feinne**, a legendary band of warriors in the heroic age of Irish history. It was the Fenians who were to provide the crisis with which Gladstone had to deal when he came to power in 1868 (units 29 and 33).

Unit 23 Summary

▶ Ireland's various grievances, 1760.

▶ Ireland's parliamentary independence, 1782.

▶ The influence of the French Revolution on Irish affairs.

▶ The work of Wolfe Tone; Pitt and the Act of Union, 1801.

▶ The career of O'Connell and the campaign for Catholic Emancipation.

▶ The Irish Famine and the growth of the Young Ireland movement.

24 THE BRITISH EMPIRE, 1760–1860

24.1 The East India Company

From 1600 onwards British merchants sent out ships to trade with the islands of the East Indies. These merchants formed the East India Company, which built warehouses, offices and housing for clerks and officials on various islands and formed a private army to defend its property.

In the 1660s the Company was driven from the East Indies by the Dutch. The British then went to India. Here they found that **the Emperor of India** (or Mogul) once a powerful ruler, by 1700 was unable to control his people. The last able Mogul, Aurungzeb, died in 1707 and his death led to the break-up of the Mogul Empire. In his place, **local Princes** tried to set themselves up as independent rulers.

The Company took advantage of this situation by helping Princes to win local power in return for a monopoly of trade. Clive's victory over Surrajahdowlah at Plassey (1757) was not only a revenge for the Black Hole of Calcutta, but was the means of ensuring British control of Bengal.

Similar efforts by a French Company in the Carnatic (the region around Madras) and Bengal were thwarted by the Company.

THE PEACE OF PARIS, 1763

This ended the Seven Years War (p. 1). In India it left the Company in control of the **Carnatic**, most of **Bengal** and the island of **Bombay**.

THE REGULATING ACT, 1773

The government decided that it was wrong for a trading company to have political control of such large areas. In 1773 North's government passed the Regulating Act, by which:

▶ **the Company** had to appoint an official as Governor-General of Bengal, who ruled over all the districts controlled by the Company;

▶ **the British government** appointed a **Council of Four** to advise the Governor-General;

▶ **British judges** would administer justice in Company districts.

24.2 Warren Hastings, 1772–85

Hastings had been Governor of Bengal since 1772. He became Governor-General in 1774. His difficulties included: **the Council**, which came out to India in 1774. They thought that Hastings, like other Company officials was dishonest, and the Council criticized everything Hastings did.

In spite of this Hastings was successful in:

▶ setting up a **Civil Service** to replace Company officials;

▶ appointing British tax collectors to replace the more dishonest local people;

▶ defending British interests during the American War of Independence. This involved him with:

● **the Mahrattas**, a warlike tribe in Central India. In 1778 the French persuaded them to rise against the British. Hastings sent an army across India, defeated the Mahrattas and saved Bombay. He took Mahratta land for Britain.

● **Hyder Ali**, the King of Mysore. In 1780 he attacked the Carnatic. Hastings sent Sir Eyre Coote with an army from Bengal. Coote defeated Ali at Porto Novo and saved the Carnatic.

HASTINGS AND THE EXPANSION OF BRITISH INDIA

▶ Hastings extended British influence over Mahratta land.

▶ The ruler of Oudh had a treaty with the Company, which had a monopoly of trade in Oudh and maintained law and order there. He asked for help when his female relatives (the **Begums**) seized his jewels and treasures. Hastings sent an army to punish the Begums and regain the treasure. **The Council** was to accuse him of taking a bribe over this.

PITT'S INDIA ACT, 1784

Philip Francis, one of the Council of Four, was the leader of a campaign against Hastings.

▶ **In 1780** he returned to England and persuaded politicians that Hastings and other officials were dishonest.

▶ **In 1783** North and Fox brought in an India Bill, one of the causes of their fall from power (p. 19).

▶ **In 1784** Pitt's India Act was passed. This said:

● The work of trading had to be separated from the work of governing British India.

● The company could keep control of trade.

● The British government should appoint a London-based Board of Control to appoint a Governor-General and other officials. An **Amending Act** passed in 1786 increased the power of the Governor-General by giving him power to overrule his council. This Act lapsed when the East India Company was abolished in 1858.

HASTING'S TRIAL

Because of Francis's influence Hastings was recalled, accused of accepting bribes and of cruelty to the Begums, and put on trial. His trial lasted from 1788 to 1795, when he was found innocent.

■ 24.3 Other Governors-General ■

WELLESLEY, 1798–1805

The Marquess of Wellesley was Governor-General while Britain was at war with France in Europe. The government sent out an army to defend British interests in India. Among the officers sent out was Arthur Wellesley, brother to the Governor-General and the future Duke of Wellington. During this period the British:

▶ made alliances with the weaker rulers, promising to defend them in return for the right to trade;

▶ attacked and defeated **Tippoo of Mysore** and appointed a 'puppet' to rule Mysore;

▶ forced the Nizam (or ruler) of **Hyderabad** to dismiss his army and submit to a treaty with Britain;

▶ made war on the **Mahrattas**, who tried to drive the British from the west coast;

▶ conquered the whole of the **Carnatic** on the east coast and large areas around Bombay in the west.

THE MARQUESS OF HASTINGS, 1813–28

The Marquess of Hastings extended the work of Wellesley by finally destroying the power of **the Mahrattas** and annexing **Poona**, forcing the Hindu chiefs to admit defeat.

He defeated **the Gurkhas of Nepal** and destroyed the **Pindaris**, the robber bands which threatened the peace of Central India.

He extended British power during **the First Burmese War** (1823), the first step in the acquisition of that country. Between **1823 and 1857** Britain annexed the coast and southern part of Burma and completed its annexation in **1886** when King Thibaw was found to have been intriguing with the French.

BENTINCK, 1828–35

With British power established throughout India, the new Governor-General tried to make it a peaceful country. Bentinck attacked **the thugees**, who, in the name of religion, murdered and robbed travellers along the long Indian roads. He also attacked the practice of **suttee**, by which the widow of a deceased Hindu burned herself to death on the fires cremating the husband's body. He was also responsible for setting up **English language schools** for Indian children, so that they might get jobs with the government and the company, and he admitted Indians to the lower ranks of the **Civil Service**.

LORD AUCKLAND, 1836–41

The British conquest of India and the further extension of its power into Burma alarmed the people of Afghanistan and the Sikh rulers of the Punjab. **Afghanistan** was a buffer state between Russia and British India where the Persians (influenced by the Russians) interfered to try to create an anti-British feeling.

The First Afghan War (1839–41) was the result of a British invasion, aimed at protecting British interests. After initial success, the British were driven from Afghanistan, only one man surviving from the force of 4000 which has been stationed at **Kabul** in Afghanistan.

Afghanistan was to be a problem for Disraeli and Gladstone later in the century.

The Sind and the Punjab

In **1843** the British annexed the Sind in order to control the route through the Bolan Pass into India. The Sikhs ruled **the Punjab**, which included **the Khyber Pass**, the other route into India. They feared that the British might try to annex their country. Having seen the British failure in Afghanistan (1841) they invaded India (1845), which led to the **First Sikh War** and, some years later to **the Second Sikh War** (1848–49), after which the victorious British annexed the Punjab.

LORD DALHOUSIE, 1848–56

Dalhousie was Governor-General when the Punjab was annexed (1849) and when Lower Burma was conquered (1852). Dalhousie annoyed the people of India by:

▶ **seizing the territories of rulers** whom he declared to be inefficient, such as the rulers of Oudh;

▶ inventing **the doctrine of lapse**, to allow the seizure of states whose rulers died without heirs;

▶ **introducing railways and the telegraph**, which brought economic benefits to British traders, but which Indians saw as attempts to Westernize their country. The railways in particular were seen as an attempt to destroy the caste system by obliging people of all castes to travel together.

■ 24.4 The Indian Mutiny, 1857 ■

Dalhousie welcomed his successor, Canning, with the promise that India was 'in a state of perfect tranquility'. Within a year India was rocked by a Mutiny owing to:

▶ **The Centenary of Plassey**, Clive's great victory in 1757 in revenge for the Black Hole of Calcutta. In 1856 and 1857 agitators claimed that a great ruler would lead them against the British who had deposed many rulers, attacked their religious beliefs and taken great wealth from India.

▶ **The Indian Army**, which consisted of a few British and many Indian troops (sepoys). Some of the sepoys resented the changes, such as the attack on suttee, the Westernization of education and the seizing of territory. But they particularly resented being sent across the sea to fight in Burma. This offended the Hindu caste system, as did railway travel in which there was no room for the many demarcations of the complicated caste system.

▶ **The Crimean War**, which led to the withdrawal of many British troops for service in the Crimea. This increased the proportion of sepoys in the Indian Army. British failure during that War reminded the Indians of the failure to conquer Afghanistan; the British were not invincible.

▶ **Religious agitators**, who argued that the British had overthrown Indian rulers, stamped out traditional practices and brought in the telegraph, railway and Western education. What was to stop them forcing the Indians to convert to Christianity?

▶ **The cartridges:** the new Enfield rifle required soldiers to bite the end off the cartridge. The cartridges were covered in grease. Some said it was cow fat (which offended Hindus); some said it was pig fat (which offended Muslims).

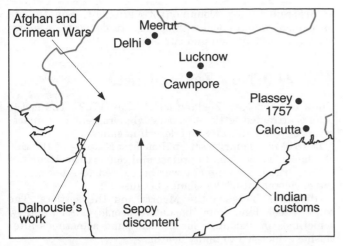

Fig. 24.4 A diagram showing some of the causes and main centres of the Indian Mutiny.

THE AREA AND COURSE OF THE MUTINY

It is incorrect to talk of an Indian Mutiny, since it was a rising only of some troops and people in only three regions.
▶ In **May, 1857**, in **Meerut** the sepoys massacred the British and marched to Delhi to proclaim the re-establishment of the Indian Empire.
▶ At **Cawnpore** a Mahratta chief led another massacre.
▶ Sir John Lawrence had kept the Sikhs of the Punjab loyal. He led an army to recapture **Delhi** in September, 1857. This marked the beginning of the end of the Mutiny.
▶ **Lucknow** endured a long seige until it was relieved by Sir Colin Campbell in November, 1857.
▶ The end of the Crimean War allowed the return of British troops to suppress the rebellion.
By June 1858 the rebellion was over.

'CLEMENCY' CANNING

While the mutiny still raged, Canning sent orders that no one was to take revenge on any Indians. In addition the government decided that **reforms** would be introduced more slowly and that **more troops** would be sent to serve in India. The British, who had once mixed freely with the Indians, now cut themselves off.

24.5 The Government of India Act, 1858

This abolished the East India Company and put India firmly under British government control. It said that the East India Company was abolished, its territories going to the Crown, and that a Secretary of State for India was to control Indian affairs.

A Council of 15 members was appointed to help the Secretary of State and the Governor-General, to be renamed the Viceroy, would represent the Queen.

24.6 South Africa

After taking the Cape of Good Hope from the Dutch, the government encouraged settlers to migrate to the Cape and allowed missionaries to go to work among the black population.

The Dutch settlers, or **Boers**, hated the British because:
▶ they had taken control of 'their' land. The British also made English the official language and introduced British taxation (both in 1821);
▶ British missionaries treated the blacks kindly;
▶ British judges gave blacks and whites equal treatment in court, mainly because of the influence of British missionaries both in Africa and, through their missionary societies, in Britain itself.
The Abolition of Slavery, 1833 (p. 38), was the final

straw. The Boers could not now have slaves to run their farms. In **1836** about 5000 Boers set out on the **Great Trek** to the north.

They founded two new states – the Orange Free State and the Transvaal. Britain recognized these as independent states by agreements with the Transvaal people (1852) and with those of the OFS (1854). But there would be trouble between British and Boers later in the century (unit 35).

24.7 Canada

CANADA, 1791–1848

Britain gained French Canada in 1763 as a result of the Seven Years' War.

During and after the American War from **1777–83** (p. 18) many colonists (**Loyalists**) migrated to Canada.

In **1791** Parliament passed the Canada Act which divided Canada into Lower Canada (based on Quebec) and Upper Canada (based on Ontario).
▶ **Lower Canada** was dominated by the original French settlers, who were allowed to practise their own religion and to use their own language. They disliked the British-appointed Governor-General and his power to overrule decisions of the democratically elected Assembly.
▶ **Upper Canada** was English-speaking and Protestant. Here too, the settlers resented a British Governor-General.

1837–39

In 1837 there were rebellions in both Provinces. The Whig government sent out Lord Durham to settle matters. He produced the **Durham Report 1839** which said that:
▶ the two Canadas should be united;
▶ the united Canada should be given self-government with Ministers being responsible to a Canadian Parliament.

1840–48

The recommendations of the Report were put into operation:
▶ in **1840** the British passed **the Reunion Act** which united the two Provinces;
▶ in **1848** the Governor of Canada (**Lord Elgin**, Durham's son-in-law) allowed the Canadian Parliament to choose its own ministers and, after they took office, he did not overrule any of their decisions. Canada had achieved responsible government.

CANADA, 1848–67

Emigrants came from Scotland and other parts of Britain, and **new Provinces** were founded in Nova Scotia (1848), New Brunswick (1848), Prince Edward Island (1851) and British Columbia (1858).

Railways pushed into the interior, opening up the prairies, allowing the formation of new settlements which, later, became Provinces. The simultaneous expansion of the USA and its economic growth led to a movement for the union of Canada (old and new Provinces) with its powerful neighbour.

To forestall such a development, **Sir John Macdonald** proposed the union of the Provinces of British North America. This led to the passing of the **British North America Act, 1867**, in which:
▶ four Provinces (Ontario, Quebec, Nova Scotia and New Brunswick) formed a federal union named the **Dominion of Canada**;
▶ each Province had its **local Parliament** to deal with local affairs;
▶ the **Union Parliament** (for the whole Dominion) had more power than the local Parliaments;
▶ provision was made for **the expansion of the Union**. The Hudson Bay territory joined in 1869, Manitoba in 1870, British Columbia in 1871 (on condition that the Canadian Pacific Railway was built – it was completed in 1885). Prince Edward Island joined in 1871 and new Provinces formed after the completion of the railway joined later.

The boundaries between the USA and the expanding Canada were settled by the **Ashburton** and **Oregon Treaties** (p. 48).

24.8 Australia

Captain Cook explored the coast of Australia in three voyages (1768–79) and took possession of New South Wales in the name of Britain.

Botany Bay was used as a dumping ground for convicts, the first of whom arrived in 1786, guarded by troops led by **Captain Phillip**. Other convict settlements were established at Hobart (1803) and Brisbane (1824).

Gibbon Wakefield encouraged the setting up of free settlements and suggested that emigrants should be helped to buy land for farming. By 1839 there were more free settlers than convicts.

Various **difficulties** affected the development of Australia:
▶ the laziness and insubordination of convicts;
▶ the Eastern Highlands proved difficult to cross, so that settlement was, at first, limited to the coastal regions;
▶ the climate of much of the interior was unfavourable, much of it being too dry for agriculture;
▶ difficulties of communication between the various settlements made a unified administration impossible;
▶ many of the early free settlers (attracted by grants of free land) failed to make a success of farming until sheep were introduced.

The development of sheep farming followed from the introduction of Spanish merino sheep to the coastlands (1803) and the exploration of the grazing lands of the Murray-Darling Basin after the discovery of a pass through the mountains in 1813. The growth of the Yorkshire woollen industry depended almost entirely on the vast quantities of wool exported from Australia.

Free settlements were established in:
▶ Western Australia, along the Swan River (1829). This colony only prospered when convict labour was sent to help landowners (1849);
▶ South Australia (1836), which was colonized on lines suggested by Wakefield, who advocated the sale of land to those who could afford to buy. The price fixed was too high and few emigrants arrived.

THE GOVERNMENT OF AUSTRALIA

With the growth of the number of free settlers, the convict system came to an end and, following the principles of the Durham Report, Britain gave the peoples of the individual states their own representative governments (between 1842 and 1850) and, later, responsible government (1855).

The discovery of gold in New South Wales and Victoria and the development of agriculture, especially of sheep farming, led to an increase in immigration and a growth in the population. New states were formed with their own responsible government – Queensland (1859) and Western Australia (1890).

The growth of the number of individual states, each jealous of its independence from the others, led to various difficulties: different states had varying gauges for their **railways**, each state had **tariff barriers** against imports from the others, and no single state could raise the money needed for **the development of the whole country** – but common policy was ruled out by states' jealousies.

Fear of foreigners forced the states to consider the need for unity. **Germany's acquisition** of part of New Guinea and of the Pacific Islands as well as the rise of Japan showed the need for a common defence policy. The possibility that people from India, China and Japan might settle in the hot and harsh Far North, provided the spur needed for the creation of **a common policy on coloured immigration**. **The Commonwealth of Australia Act, 1900** established the federal Dominion of Australia in which:
▶ each state had its own Parliament and government to deal with local affairs and such matters as were not dealt with by the Dominion Parliament and government;

▶ the central (or Dominion) government, Senate and Parliament were to deal with defence, trade, postal systems, railways, immigration and currency.

24.9 New Zealand

Cook claimed New Zealand for Britain (1769). The fertile islands attracted settlers, traders, whalers, sealers, convicts escaped from Australia and deserting sailors.

In **1814** missionaries set up their first station – at the Bay of Islands. They came to protect and convert the Maoris.

The British government was persuaded to intervene in the development of the islands because of:
▶ **disputes** between the Maoris and the settlers. The settlers took land from the native people, often unfairly, sometimes in exchange for firearms and sometimes after clashes which led to many deaths;
▶ the danger that a newly established **French Company** might try to annex the South Island;
▶ the arguments of **Gibbon Wakefield**. He formed the New Zealand Company to buy land on which to settle emigrants in what he called 'the fittest country in the world for colonization'.

In 1840 the Governor of New South Wales was told to take over the colony of New Zealand.

Captain Hobson arranged the **Treaty of Waitangi** with the Maoris. This said that:
▶ the Maoris accepted British rule;
▶ Britain guaranteed them their lands and estates;
▶ only the government was allowed to buy land from the Maoris.

The First Maori War, 1843, was caused by the Maori chiefs' anger at their people's loss of land which the increasing number of settlers forced the Maoris to sell. The war was ended when Governor-General Sir George Grey (1848–53) bought the land in the South Island (which was then settled by Anglican and Scottish Presbyterian emigrants).

Grey advised that the colony should be given the right to elect its own Parliament. In **1852** it was given representative government which in **1856** became responsible government.

The continuing increase in the number of settlers put pressure on Maori holdings, particularly in the North Island. The New Zealand Parliament confiscated Maori land and, in retaliation, the Maoris united under an elected king. Clashes between Maoris and white settlers led to the Second Maori War, which began in 1860 and lasted until 1871. Grey was brought back as Governor-General to settle the problem. The Maoris were allowed half the land in North Island, the rest being assigned for British settlement.

THE DOMINION OF NEW ZEALAND

In 1901 New Zealand refused to join the newly formed Commonwealth of Australia. In 1907 New Zealand was given the status of a Dominion. By that time the British had acquired large areas of Africa which presented them with fresh problems (unit 35).

Unit 24 Summary

India

▶ The development of British control of India.
▶ The Regulating Act (1782) and the India Act (1784).
▶ The work of Warren Hastings; Wellesley; the Marquess of Hastings; Bentinck; Auckland; Dalhousie.
▶ The causes and effects of the Indian Mutiny.

Other colonies

▶ The development of colonies in South Africa, Canada, New Zealand and Australia.

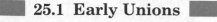 25.1 Early Unions

JOURNEYMEN GUILDS

In medieval times craftsmen formed guilds. The guilds controlled the training of apprentices by master craftsmen.

After completing his apprenticeship a man worked as a daily-paid worker (**journeyman** – from the French **le jour**, meaning 'day'). A journeyman became a master craftsman upon presentation of his masterpiece to the guild's officials.

From the seventeenth century onwards, however, it became increasingly difficult for ordinary workers to become masters. The existing masters put up the fees, insisted on the buying of expensive clothing (or **livery**) and so made it hard for men to get on. This gave rise to **journeymen guilds** for the workers.

FRIENDLY SOCIETIES

These guilds were, in many ways, what were called friendly societies in the nineteenth century. In return for a weekly subscription a man would get payment when ill, a retirement pension, help for a widow and children and expenses when he travelled to find work in a strange town. Friendly societies were a form of social security for members.

WAGE FIXING BEFORE 1760

Since Tudor times, wages and prices were fixed by government or by the local magistrates. From about 1700, journeymen guilds tried to get employers to negotiate on wages and conditions. This was condemned by governments and made illegal.

INDUSTRIALIZATION AND WORKING PEOPLE

Towns grew at a rapid rate (p. 15) and workers were employed in vast numbers, which meant that the old wage-fixing system could not work properly.

Workers were grouped in thousands and met large numbers of their fellows, which they had not done in villages and small towns. They found common grievances in social and working conditions.

EARLY UNIONS, 1760–1800

Older guilds or societies expanded – as did the woolcombers and the brushmakers, both of them national organizations. New ones sprung up, sharing common features:
▶ they were **local** societies. Because of the lack of good communications only local people could combine easily;
▶ they were for men of one **craft** only – spinners, weavers, carpenters;
▶ they had **friendly society** arrangements.

Unlike the older guilds and societies these new unions demanded the right to negotiate with employers on wages.

25.2 Government, Owners and Unions

▶ **Owners** regarded their men as just another part of the manufacturing process. They could do as they wished with machinery and they expected the same rights over their employees.
▶ **Government** wanted no change in the old methods of wage fixing.
▶ **The French Revolution** led to the fear that British working men might overturn society.

THE COMBINATION ACTS, 1799–1800

▶ **1797** The Navy mutinies (p. 22).
▶ **1798** The Irish risings (p. 56).
▶ In **1799** Wilberforce, the abolitionist, demanded laws to prevent **unlawful combination of workmen**. Pitt brought in the first Combination Act (June 1799). It forbade combinations of workmen if these were to try to improve wages or conditions.

In **1800** a second Combination Act forbade strikes, union meetings or the collection of union subscriptions.

Many older societies continued to exist as friendly societies; many of the old and many of the new continued, illegally, to work as unions, trying to get better conditions and pay.

RECOGNIZING UNIONS, 1824

Francis Place, a former breeches-maker and strike-leader and, by 1820, a master tailor, had a shop at Charing Cross. He led the campaign to legalize trade unions.

Joseph Hume was a radical MP and friend of Place. He tried to bring in a Private Member's Bill to legalize unions.

Huskisson would not allow this. But he did put Hume on the Committee concerned with the emigration of workmen (1824).

Place organized workmen to present evidence to this Committee, to show that unions were necessary and not revolutionary.

In **1824** Parliament repealed the Combination Acts. It was now legal to form unions. In 1825, however, a rush of strikes led Parliament to amend the 1824 Act so that strikes were made illegal.

25.3 National Unions

A number of attempts were made to form one huge union for all working men. In particular there were:
▶ **1818** The Manchester Philanthropic Society, set up by Lancashire spinners to include men of all trades.
▶ **1819** A similar society, organized in London.
▶ **1829** The Operative Spinners of Lancashire, set up by John Doherty who went on to form:
● the **Grand General Union of Operative Spinners in the United Kingdom**, and
● the **National Association for the Protection of Labour** (1830).

He then helped Robert Owen to form the **Grand National Consolidated Trades Union** (the GNCTU) to bring together members of all trades.

ROBERT OWEN AND THE GNCTU

Robert Owen had been a workman. He married the daughter of a mill owner and ran the New Lanark Mills where he:
▶ did not employ young children;
▶ set up schools for children of his workpeople;
▶ provided decent housing for their families.

In **1834** Owen took over the leadership of the GNCTU. He:
▶ appointed four officials to run it from a London headquarters;
▶ claimed 500 000 members;
▶ boasted that this 'army' would force government to pass laws on housing, child labour and wages;
▶ argued for the handing over of industry to the workers, which frightened employers into taking strong action against the unions.

EMPLOYERS AND THE GNCTU

Employers fought Owen by:
▶ the **Document** which men were forced to sign in which they promised not to join or in any way support 'the Union';
▶ **the lock out**; employers shut their factories if men formed a branch of the Union;
▶ **blacklegs**, or non-Union men brought in to do the work of the Union members locked out.

THE LAW, EMPLOYERS AND THE GNCTU

Many magistrates were owners or related to owners; most shared the fear of a workers' rising. This was made clear in the case of the **Tolpuddle Martyrs**.

TOLPUDDLE, OWEN AND THE GOVERNMENT

A Tolpuddle labourer, George Loveless, sent for officials of the GNCTU to help form a branch of the Union when, in 1833, farm workers' wages were lowered from 40p a week to 35p, with the news that in 1834 they would be lowered to 30p a week.

In **February 1834** the magistrates posted a notice warning against the forming of a Union branch, and six days later arrested Loveless and the five other leaders.

The trial at Dorchester showed that they had done nothing illegal in forming a Union branch; they had, however, made members take an oath on joining. This, it was said, was illegal under the Mutiny Act of 1797.

The sentence imposed was seven years' imprisonment in Tasmania; **Owen** protested and organized meetings.

Melbourne as Home Secretary congratulated the magistrates. Lawyers and MPs showed Melbourne that the decision was wrong, and in 1836 the men were pardoned.

THE WEAKNESS OF THE GNCTU

▶ **Most craftsmen** refused to join a General Union.
▶ **Too many officials** were dishonest.
▶ **Too little money** was available to pay men on strike or locked out, so that they were forced back to work.
▶ **Communications** between different parts of the country were very poor and made organization almost impossible.

BACK TO POLITICS

With the collapse of the GNCTU after Tolpuddle, men turned to Chartism (pp. 41–2), to the Cooperative Movement (p. 44) or to other self-help systems such as the Mechanics' Institutes.

25.4 Model Unions

CRAFTSMEN IN THE 1850s

As Britain became the workshop of the world (unit 28), some working people began to earn good wages. Carpenters, plumbers, bricklayers and engineers earned £2 a week in the 1850s.

From these wages they could afford to join a friendly society – such as the Rechabites, Hearts of Oak and Foresters – which collected subscriptions and provided social security benefits.

They helped to form **building societies** and saved through Penny Banks or, after 1861, through the Post Office Savings Bank. Mechanics' Libraries with reading rooms and games rooms were set up.

There was an **aristocracy of labour** consisting of craftsmen, of whom there were **very few** – 60 000 bricklayers for example, with similar numbers for the other crafts.

Craftsmen formed their own unions which were:
▶ **Craft unions**, with a separate organization for each craft and with no room for unskilled workers.
▶ **National organizations**, formed from the amalgamation (or joining together) of older local unions. The development of the railway network (unit 26) made this easier.

▶ **Friendly societies** which provided, from their union subscriptions, social security benefits.

WILLIAM ALLEN

William Allen was General Secretary of the Amalgamated Society of Engineers (ASE), from its formation in 1851 until he died in 1874. His new union presented a **model** for other craft unions to follow as regards rules, organization, funds and benefits.

The ASE accepted the economic system and, unlike Owen, did not seek to change it by revolution.

Other unions imitated the ASE. In particular there were:
▶ the **Carpenters and Joiners**, whose national secretary was **Robert Applegarth**;
▶ the **Boilermakers**;
▶ the **Bricklayers**.

25.5 The Formation of the TUC

TRADES COUNCILS

Local officials of craft unions met together from time to time to discuss common problems. This led to the formation of **trades councils** of union officials, designed to deal with these common problems.

THE JUNTA

The national secretaries of the model unions had their headquarters in London and helped to set up the London Trades Council where they met from time to time.

They tried to persuade politicians, journalists and employers that trade unions were to be welcomed since they:
▶ provided working men with a chance to practise self-help;
▶ could negotiate deals with employers which would be kept;
▶ could stop men from striking because of the fear of their being thrown out of the union – with the loss of benefits.

Not all working-class leaders welcomed this development. The remnants of the Chartists and some of Owen's supporters thought that this was too peaceful an approach. They tried to condemn the leaders of the model unions by giving them the nickname of **Junta** – a Spanish word for a controlling group.

TRADE UNION PROBLEMS, 1860–67

▶ **Dishonest officials** sometimes made off with union funds. When unions tried to prosecute such runaway officials, judges decided that unions were not covered by the law on friendly societies, since they were 'in restraint of trade'. Cases brought by the Boilermakers and by the Carpenters were thrown out of Court.
▶ **Employers** remained suspicious of unions. Many tried to prevent their men joining. Lock-outs were common and so was the bringing in of blackleg labour.
▶ **Violence** developed when men tried to stop blacklegs getting to factories. This came to a head at **Sheffield** in 1866 with the bombing of employers' homes and the homes of non-union workers.
▶ **Public opinion** still saw unions as dangerous organizations.

A ROYAL COMMISSION, 1866–69

The government set up a Commission after the Sheffield outrages.

The Junta persuaded the government to extend the terms of the Commission to allow it to examine trade unionism as a whole. The unions wanted legal recognition so that they could prosecute dishonest officials.

The Commission heard from Allen, Applegarth and other leaders about the benefits provided to union members out of their subscriptions. They also heard of the ways in which strong unions controlled their members, so that

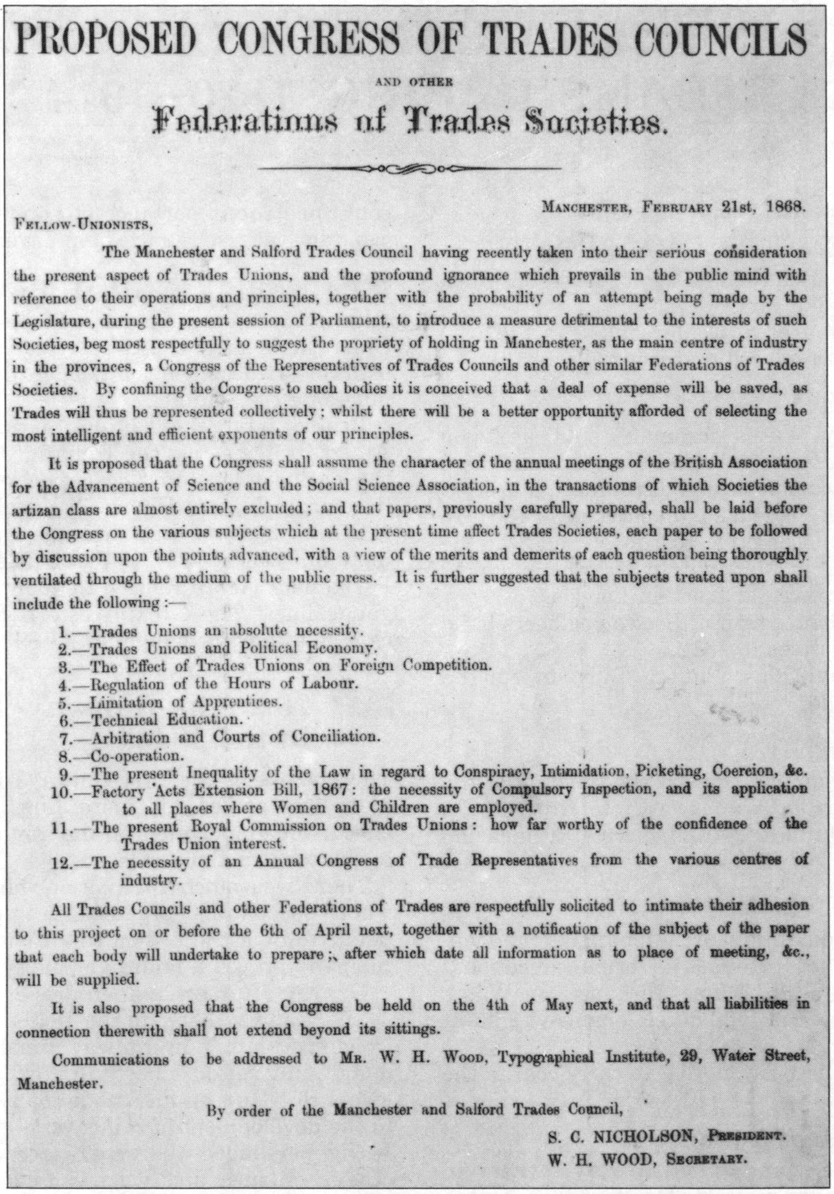

PROPOSED CONGRESS OF TRADES COUNCILS

AND OTHER

Federations of Trades Societies.

MANCHESTER, FEBRUARY 21st, 1868.

FELLOW-UNIONISTS,

The Manchester and Salford Trades Council having recently taken into their serious consideration the present aspect of Trades Unions, and the profound ignorance which prevails in the public mind with reference to their operations and principles, together with the probability of an attempt being made by the Legislature, during the present session of Parliament, to introduce a measure detrimental to the interests of such Societies, beg most respectfully to suggest the propriety of holding in Manchester, as the main centre of industry in the provinces, a Congress of the Representatives of Trades Councils and other similar Federations of Trades Societies. By confining the Congress to such bodies it is conceived that a deal of expense will be saved, as Trades will thus be represented collectively; whilst there will be a better opportunity afforded of selecting the most intelligent and efficient exponents of our principles.

It is proposed that the Congress shall assume the character of the annual meetings of the British Association for the Advancement of Science and the Social Science Association, in the transactions of which Societies the artizan class are almost entirely excluded; and that papers, previously carefully prepared, shall be laid before the Congress on the various subjects which at the present time affect Trades Societies, each paper to be followed by discussion upon the points advanced, with a view of the merits and demerits of each question being thoroughly ventilated through the medium of the public press. It is further suggested that the subjects treated upon shall include the following :—

  1.—Trades Unions an absolute necessity.
  2.—Trades Unions and Political Economy.
  3.—The Effect of Trades Unions on Foreign Competition.
  4.—Regulation of the Hours of Labour.
  5.—Limitation of Apprentices.
  6.—Technical Education.
  7.—Arbitration and Courts of Conciliation.
  8.—Co-operation.
  9.—The present Inequality of the Law in regard to Conspiracy, Intimidation, Picketing, Coercion, &c.
  10.—Factory Acts Extension Bill, 1867: the necessity of Compulsory Inspection, and its application to all places where Women and Children are employed.
  11.—The present Royal Commission on Trades Unions: how far worthy of the confidence of the Trades Union interest.
  12.—The necessity of an Annual Congress of Trade Representatives from the various centres of industry.

All Trades Councils and other Federations of Trades are respectfully solicited to intimate their adhesion to this project on or before the 6th of April next, together with a notification of the subject of the paper that each body will undertake to prepare; after which date all information as to place of meeting, &c., will be supplied.

It is also proposed that the Congress be held on the 4th of May next, and that all liabilities in connection therewith shall not extend beyond its sittings.

Communications to be addressed to MR. W. H. WOOD, Typographical Institute, 29, Water Street, Manchester.

By order of the Manchester and Salford Trades Council,

S. C. NICHOLSON, PRESIDENT.
W. H. WOOD, SECRETARY.

Fig. 25.5 The invitation which was sent out to bring together the first Trades Union Congress.

where they existed and where employers allowed them to negotiate there were fewer strikes, less violence and better industrial relations.

THE TUC, 1868

Trades Councils outside London did not trust the Junta's ability to influence the Commission's opinion.

The **Salford Trades Council** called a meeting of delegates from other trades councils and unions.

The London-based Junta (from the London Trades Council) did not attend, but the first **Trade Union Congress** was held to try to influence the Government and the Commission.

THE COMMISSION'S REPORT, 1869

In view of the outcry at the time of the Sheffield outrages, and of the employers' opposition to trade unions, it was a surprise when the Commission reported favourably on unions. Allen and Applegarth had won the day. The Report:

▶ welcomed the development of trade unions;
▶ argued that where they existed there was less violence;
▶ asked that the legal position of unions be safeguarded in a new Act of Parliament. This, as we shall see, happened under Gladstone's government (unit 29).

Unit 25 Summary

▶ The early development of unions and friendly societies.
▶ The Combination Acts (1799–1800) and their repeal (1824–25).
▶ Robert Owen and the Grand National Consolidated Trades Union.
▶ The Tolpuddle Martyrs.
▶ The growth of 'model' unions under Allen and Applegarth.
▶ The uncertain legal position of trade unions in the 1860s.
▶ The first Congress of trade unions, 1868.

26 RAILWAYS AND STEAMSHIPPING, 1820-1914

26.1 Early Railways

EIGHTEENTH-CENTURY 'TRAM ROADS'
▶ **Wooden rails** were used to make 'tram roads' on which horse-drawn wagons took coal from pits.
▶ **Iron rails** were first used at Coalbrookdale in 1767.
▶ **Wrought iron rails** replaced cast iron rails (1810).

EARLY LOCOMOTIVES
▶ **William Murdock**, Watt's foreman, built a steam engine and ran it along Cornish roads. Watt thought there was no future in such locomotives and discouraged Murdock.
▶ **Richard Trevithick** made a steam carriage in 1801. In 1804 he built the first locomotive to run on rails – at the Pennydarren Ironworks in Merthyr. In 1808 he exhibited an engine running on a circular track in London.
▶ **John Blenkinsop** had a firm of Leed's engineers build him a number of locomotives in 1812.
▶ **William Hedley** built his 'Puffing Billy' to run on colliery lines on Tyneside.

RAILWAY COMPANIES
In **1801** an act of Parliament allowed the building of the Surrey Iron Railway from Wandsworth to Croydon. In South Wales about 150 miles (240 kilometres) of lines had been built by 1811.

GEORGE STEPHENSON, 1781-1848
The son of a colliery fireman in Northumberland, Stephenson began life as a cowherd. He had no formal education.

Working in a colliery, he became an expert on Watt's engine and in **1812** he was appointed engine-wright at Killingworth.

In **1814** he built his first locomotive to carry coal to the Tyne, six miles away.

The Stockton-Darlington Line
By **1821** Edward Pease and other colliery owners in Darlington wanted a cheap method of getting their coal to the coast. They got a Private Act of Parliament to allow them to build a railway and appointed Stephenson as engineer.

The railway was mainly for horse-drawn traffic, although stationary engines were used for gradients. Steam-engines were only used for coal traffic.

Pease asked Stephenson to make the gauge of the track equal in width to that of country carts. These were, on average, 4 feet 8½ inches wide (about 1.42 metres), which became the standard gauge on all British lines.

The Liverpool-Manchester Line
In 1826 Stephenson was appointed engineer of the Liverpool-Manchester line. This was the real start of railway building.

In 1829 the Rainhill Trial was held to choose the locomotive to be used. The competition was won by Stephenson's *Rocket*, which reached a speed of 30 m.p.h.

The line opened in 1830. Its success encouraged others.

ROBERT STEPHENSON, 1801-59
He was the son of George Stephenson, helped his father design the *Rocket* and to lay many of the first railway lines. In 1837 he became chief engineer of the London–Birmingham railway and went on to become a great railway engineer.

LONDON AND RAILWAYS, 1843
By 1843 London was linked to Dover, Brighton, Southampton, Bristol, Birmingham, Lancaster and York. This confirmed the importance of London over other provincial 'capitals' such as Manchester, Liverpool and Birmingham.

ISAMBARD KINGDOM BRUNEL, 1806-59
Brunel was equal in genius to Stephenson. He was appointed Chief Engineer to the Great Western Railway in 1833 and in **1835–41** designed the London-Bristol line, including the mile-long Box Tunnel.

Brunel built the Clifton Suspension Bridge and the Albert Bridge across the Tamar at Devonport. He also built the early steamship *The Great Western* (p. 65) and the harbour at Milford Haven – both failures.

Brunel insisted on a wide gauge of 7 feet (about 2.10 metres), which led to 'the battle of the gauges' until Parliament (1846) refused to allow any more of these wide gauge lines. The Great Western Railway (GWR) did not change to narrow gauge until 1892.

26.2 The Railway 'Mania' in the 1840s

The success of the first railways led to the formation of many companies for more lines. This had some good effects – on employment in the iron and coal industries, and in the construction trades.

There was much speculation, however, and some fraud when speculators organized companies, persuaded the public to invest and then sold their own shares before the company proved a failure, as many did.

George Hudson, a linen draper from York, was known as the 'Railway King' in the 1840s, making a great fortune from speculation in railway companies' shares. He was found guilty of dishonesty in 1849 and his fortune shrank away. But Hudson had made many valuable contributions to the development of railways:
▶ He persuaded the separate companies to allow each other's engines and wagons to go along all lines. This overcame the problem of creating a system of 'through traffic' which had weakened the canal system.
▶ He organized a Clearing House where companies could work out their debts to each other arising from this traffic.
▶ He had shown the value of the railway system to the economy.

26.3 The Railways and the Economy

By 1843 there were 1952 miles (3523 kilometres) of line open; by 1848 about 5000 miles and by 1855 nearly 8000 miles (12 800 kilometres). Nearly all main developments had been completed. This network provided many benefits:
▶ The **iron and coal industries** were greatly expanded to provide the materials to build the lines.
▶ The **coal industry** continued to expand to provide the fuel for the increasing number of engines in use.
▶ **Other industries** had their goods carried quickly and cheaply so that their 'natural' market expanded. Large-scale production became possible; goods became cheaper.
▶ **Employment** expanded in coal, iron, construction industries and in the railway companies.
▶ **Overseas countries** wanted a similar system and employed British contractors such as Thomas Brassey (1805–70) which provided even more employment in British industry.
▶ **Agriculture** benefited as farmers enjoyed wider markets for their perishable goods in distant towns and cities.
Fishing ports such as Grimsby flourished.

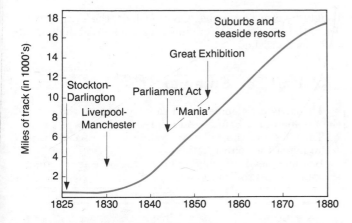

Fig. 26.3 A diagram illustrating the development of railways in the nineteenth century.

▶ **Ports** expanded to deal with increased export trade resulting from the expansion of industry.
▶ **Nation-wide developments** were now possible – and the British soon had national newspapers, unions and political parties.
▶ **Branded goods** on sale in stores throughout the country became commonplace.

26.4 Opposition to the Railways

This came from:
▶ Certain **landowners**, who feared 'the monster'. Some refused to sell land to the railway companies, forcing engineers to make costly detours; the Duke of Devonshire insisted that the line near Chatsworth had to be under cover. Other **landowners** made high profits from the sale of land and saw incomes rise as local agriculture prospered.
▶ **Canal companies**, which feared competition. Many railways were built to compete with existing canals. Some canal companies were bought out by railway companies which allowed the canals to fall into disuse.
▶ **Coaching firms**, which depended on the road system. As railways developed so turnpike trusts were ruined, coaching inns and firms went out of business.
▶ **Certain towns**, which kept the lines away from their 'neighbourhood'. Oxford and Cambridge kept the lines well away from the colleges; Eton College stopped the building of a station at Slough, a mile away.
▶ **Certain writers**, who 'proved' that travellers on railway lines would be suffocated in tunnels, blinded by smoke, have their nerves wrecked by the noise and speed or be injured by flying stones thrown up from the track, and that cornfields and woodlands would be destroyed by fires caused by sparks from the engines and animals would die of fright as trains passed by.

DIFFICULTIES OF RAILWAY BUILDING

Even with this opposition, the development of a railway network went ahead. And this in spite of the difficulties of:
▶ **construction** of tunnels, easily negotiated gradients, cuttings and viaducts without much equipment;
▶ **operation** of primitive signalling equipment by untrained workmen;
▶ **lack of comfort** on second- and third-class carriages, which were open boxes with no seats until the 1844 Act (p. 48) insisted on better conditions.

26.5 The Development of Steamshipping

BRITISH SHIPPING DOMINATED THE WORLD

The history of shipping may be divided into six periods:

Wooden ships, 1800–33

In 1800 all ships were wooden and driven by sails. There were **small ships** of about 100 tons which sailed around the coasts and **larger ships** which were used, for example, to carry timber from the Baltic and to bring goods from India. These varied in size from 600 to 700 ton weight.

American ships were then the largest and best because Americans had plenty of timber and its merchants had to build ships for the long runs along the Atlantic coast. Since they could cut down on (or 'clip') the time taken by British boats, they were known as 'clippers'.

After 1833 the East India Company lost its monopoly of trade with the Far East. British merchants built 'clippers' for this trade. They could go three times as fast as previous East India merchant ships. But wooden ships, if longer than 300 feet, buckled under the strain imposed by the sea, and could not stand the vibrations of the steam-engines used after 1830.

Iron sailing ships

In **1787** Wilkinson built the first iron ship. Iron was stronger and lighter than wood; iron ships could be much larger and carry more cargo. The hulls of iron ships quickly became fouled by the growth of barnacles and other animal life, however, so 'composite' ships were built which had a frame of iron and a skin of planking.

The steam-engine and shipping

▶ **William Symington** built the *Charlotte Dundas* (1802) for use on the Forth-Clyde Canal. Its engine drove it at 6 m.p.h. **The steamship** could sail in a straight line and did not have to 'tack'. This made it suitable for use on a canal.
▶ **Robert Fulton** built the *Clermont* (1806) for use on the River Hudson in the USA.
▶ **Henry Bell** built the *Comet* (1812) to work on the River Clyde. It became the first sea-going steamship when it went out into the Clyde estuary.
Wooden steamships were used for coastal work.

Crossing the Atlantic by steam

Those early steamships had inefficient engines which drove paddles on either side of the ship. The engines used a great deal of coal, which took most of the room below deck. The first steamships concentrated on carrying mail and passengers.

Because of their unreliable engines the first steamships carried sail. In 1819 the American ship, the *Savannah*, crossed the Atlantic in 25 days, using its engines for only 85 hours.

In **1833** a Canadian ship, the **Royal William**, crossed the Atlantic using only steam. It had to stop several times, however, to clear the boilers of the salt drawn in from the sea.

Brunel's *Great Western* (1838) crossed the Atlantic in 15 days, but it carried only 94 passengers. To have been a commercial success it needed the government's mail contract. This went to the American, Samuel Cunard (1838).

Improving the steamship

▶ The **screw** (propeller) **engine** replaced the paddles (1840s).
▶ **John Elder** invented the compound engine (1854) – so called because it had more than one piston and cylinder. The fuel which had driven only one piston now drove a number of pistons, and steamships went much faster. Less **coal** was required. This left more room for cargo.
▶ **Steel** became cheaper with the development of the Bessemer and Siemens processes. In 1859 it had cost £40 a ton; by 1880 it was only £5 a ton. Steel was lighter than iron and the engines used less power to drive the steel ship than similar sized iron ones, allowing them to carry more cargo.
▶ Sir Charles Parson's **steam turbine engine** (1897) made further economies on fuel; ships carried still more cargo.

The Suez Canal, 1869

The opening of the Canal shortened the journey to India, China and Australia. But sailing ships could not use it because it did not provide room for tacking. This gave a boost to the steamship and spelt the end for clippers such as the *Cutty Sark*.

THE BENEFITS OF STEAMSHIPPING

▶ **Freight charges** fell and **imports** were cheaper.
▶ **British industry** benefited because British companies owned about 60 per cent of the world's shipping, since Britain was the world's largest trading country. Ships were bought by other countries. On the Clyde, the Tyne and the Tees the coal, steel, engineering and shipbuilding industries flourished.

Unit 26 Summary

▶ The early development of a railway system; the work of the Stephensons, Brunel and George Hudson.
▶ The effects of the railways system on the economic and social life of the country.
▶ Britain's lead in shipbuilding; the effects of steamshipping on Britain's economy.

---

27 AGRICULTURE, 1846–1914

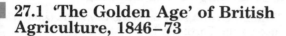

27.1 'The Golden Age' of British Agriculture, 1846–73

In 1846 Disraeli and his supporters had prophesied that the repeal of the Corn Laws (p. 49) would ruin British farming. They were proved wrong and during the next 30 years or so British agriculture enjoyed a 'Golden Age'. The reasons for this were:
▶ **Demand** for food increased with the growth of towns.
▶ The **prosperity** of many industrial workers in the 1850s and 1860s allowed them to afford more and more varied food.
▶ **Foreign competition** could not yet supply the food because of the absence of any efficient method of travel by sea.

British farmers were helped to produce more food by:
▶ **fertilizers**, such as Peruvian guano which was first imported in 1839;
▶ **scientific work** at such centres as the Rothamsted Experimental Station (1842), which led to the development of better strains of seeds, more fertilizers, such as super-phosphate, and better methods of farming;
▶ **drainage,** which was improved by the work of such engineers as the Scotsman, James Smith, who devised a system using broken stones and who invented a special plough for deep ploughing after drainage. In the 1840s the use of hollow-tile drains became commonplace;
▶ **knowledge** of the new methods and systems became more widespread with the promotion of agricultural shows and by the work of the Royal Agricultural Society (founded in 1838);
▶ **changed conditions of leasing**; landowners allowed long leases to their tenants and encouraged them to improve their farms;
▶ **machinery** for threshing and combine-harvesting came into use – although only slowly;
▶ **the railway network** (unit 26).

27.2 Why Did it All End?

Disraeli's gloomy prophesies were realized after 1873 when many sectors of British agriculture were ruined. The reasons for this sudden change in fortunes were:
▶ **bad harvests** because of bad weather in Britain, which ought to have led to high prices to ensure a good income for farmers;
▶ **falling prices**, owing to the high volume of cheap grain from the USA;
▶ **railways** built by British contractors had opened up the prairies of America and brought the grain to the eastern seaboard. British steamships carried this corn to Britain;
▶ imports of **dairy produce** in **refrigerated shipping** coming from Australia, New Zealand and Argentina;
▶ **diseases** which affected British herds and flocks.

NOT ALL SUFFERED

Wheat farmers were ruined, as were the owners of land in wheat-growing areas. **Dairy farmers** were more fortunate, however, since there was still a high demand for fresh milk, cheese and meat.

Vegetable farmers profited from the fall in price of other foods. There was now money to spare for vegetables which could be carried to market on the railway network.

Working-class families gained from the fall in food prices (above). Many men were able to allow their wives not to go to work (unit 41). Many families enjoyed rising living standards (unit 41).

Unit 27 Summary

▶ The golden age of British agriculture – reasons for.
▶ Why agriculture went into a partial recession after 1870.
▶ The benefits of falling prices – for some.

28 INDUSTRIAL PROGRESS AND TARIFF REFORM

28.1 British Supremacy

THE GREAT EXHIBITION, 1851

In 1851 the Great Exhibition took place in Hyde Park where a 'Crystal Palace' was built to house the exhibits. **The reasons for holding the Exhibition were:**
▶ **economic**; British industry welcomed a chance to show its products and to compare them with foreign goods;
▶ **political**; politicians wanted to show that Britain, unlike Europe, was peaceful.

Two men played a major part in the Exhibition: **Prince Albert**, the Prince Consort, who opened it, was the inspirer, and **Joseph Paxton**, once gardener to the Duke of Devonshire, who designed the great building of glass. The idea of having an Exhibition had been **opposed by anti-foreigners**, who feared an inrush of foreign revolutionaries, and by **cranks**, such as Colonel Sibthorpe, MP, who forced Paxton to design the building to include trees growing in Hyde Park.

The success of the Exhibition was seen in:
▶ **the exhibits** from all over the world;
▶ **the visitors** who flocked to see it, aided by the railway network and the cheap day tickets produced for them;
▶ **the profits**, which went to the building of the complex which included the Victoria and Albert Museum.

THE WORKSHOP OF THE WORLD, 1850–70

Britain enjoyed an industrial supremacy based on:
▶ **the railways**, which speeded up industry and trade;
▶ **employment** of millions of people. The 1851 census showed that over half the population lived in towns with populations over 50 000. Britain was the world's first **urban society**;
▶ **the Empire**, which provided the **markets** for goods and the **raw materials** needed to make them;
▶ **internal peace**, which encouraged investment and meant that little production had to be diverted to war goods. In other countries revolutions or, in America, a Civil War, either hindered industrial development or diverted industrial production into the making of munitions and other goods needed to fight a war.

THE EVIDENCE OF BRITISH SUPREMACY

▶ **Coal**; its output increased from 45 million tons in 1846 to 65 million (1856) and 100 million (1863).
▶ **Iron**; the basis for machine making; its output increased from one million tons in 1833 to six million in 1875.
▶ **Steel**; its output increased from 40 000 tons in 1851 to ¼ million (1851) and 1¼ million tons (1880).
▶ **Railways**; there were 2044 miles open in 1843 and 14 000 in 1873.
▶ **Exports**, which continued to expand and to change in character. **Cotton and woollen** textiles made up 60 per cent of British exports in 1850; **coal** went to foreign countries for use by steamshipping; **machinery**, the export of which was forbidden until 1843, became a major export – Britain helped other countries to industrialize.
▶ **Imports** increased as foreigners tried to earn the money to pay for British exports. In particular there was:
● **food**; after 1873 Britain imported over half the cereals she needed and vast quantities of meat, sugar and tea;
● **raw materials**, particularly cotton;
▶ **wool**, from Australia, the main supplier;
● **timber, tobacco** and **metals**;
▶ **The steamship** – see unit 26.

28.2 Britain, The World's Banker

During the period **1830–50** Britain exported more than she imported and so earned a balance of payment surplus – in gold.

Overseas investments were made by British firms using this surplus. They opened mines, developed plantations for rubber and timber, and built foreign railways. **'Invisible' exports** came from the income on those investments and **British shipping**.

During the period **1850–75** imports exceeded exports, but income from 'invisibles' gave Britain a surplus to invest overseas.

By 1914 Britain had invested over £5000 million overseas, helping foreign firms and governments to industrialize.

GAINER OR LOSER FROM OVERSEAS DEVELOPMENT?

▶ **Invisible exports** (interest on loans) enabled Britain to import more, and this allowed a high standard of living.
▶ **British shipping** profited from the carrying of the increased exports and imports.
▶ **British industry** gained. Over 67 per cent of loans were spent on British machinery and products.

However, foreign countries industrialized. So:
▶ **India** developed its textile industry and produced goods more cheaply than Britain.
▶ **America** opened its prairies and British agriculture suffered.
▶ **America and Germany** bought the latest machines and became major industrial challengers after 1870 (see below).

BRITISH INDUSTRIAL PROGRESS

Students spend a good deal of time learning the details about the first stage of the industrial revolution (units 3 and 5). They sometimes overlook the fact that even greater changes took place **after 1830**. In particular there were changes in:

The iron and steel industry

▶ **John Neilson** invented a **hot blast** (1828), which allowed the use of raw coal in furnaces, halved the amount of coal used and led to the growth of the Lanarkshire iron industry.
▶ **James Nasmyth** invented the **steam hammer** (1840), which made possible the manufacture of great iron bars needed for the railways and steamships.
▶ **Henry Bessemer** invented the **converter** (1856), in which the hot blast burned the impurities out of molten pig-iron. By adding carbon to the product Bessemer produced mild steel, bought in great quantities by railway companies. Unfortunately the Bessemer process could not be used with British phosphorus-bearing ores. This lead to the importing of non-phosphorus ores and to the shift of the industry from the iron fields to areas around ports.
▶ **William Siemens** invented the **Open Hearth Process** (1866), which cheapened the cost of producing steel; it too, required non-phosphorus ores.
▶ **Sidney Gilchrist-Thomas** discovered a means of using British ores in the new process (1878). He lined the converter with dolomite limestone, which extracted the phosphorus from the ore and deposited it as a slag. Unfortunately, British firms had invested heavily in the Bessemer or Siemens methods. They were unwilling to invest in the new process. It was used by German and American firms, which overtook Britain in steel production.

Machine tools

The first industrial machines were hand-made, and spare parts also had to be made by hand. The mass production of great numbers of identical articles and parts depends on machine tools, such as the drill, cutting machines and lathes. Their development was due to:

▶ **Joseph Bramah**, who made machine tools to manufacture his invention – a patent lock;

▶ **Henry Maudslay**, who was trained by Bramah. Around 1800 he invented a screw-cutting lathe and a slide-rest to hold the metal-cutting tool;

▶ **Joseph Whitworth**, (one of Maudslay's pupils), who, in the 1830s, built standardized gauges, measuring machines and a machine for making exact screws and screw-threads.

▶ **James Nasmyth**, another of Maudslay's pupils, who invented the steam hammer and built machine tools with Whitworth.

28.3 British Decline

FOREIGN COMPETITION

British agriculture suffered from foreign competition after 1873 (p. 66). By 1881 British industry as a whole faced foreign competition. Britain lost her lead in some industries (coal and steel) and barely entered the race in more modern industries (chemicals, electrical engineering), which were dominated by firms in the USA and Germany. The reasons for this loss of leadership were:

▶ **Failure to innovate**, as in the case of steel. In the expanding **coal industry** there were fewer mechanical aids than in German and American mines, so that British coal became relatively dearer.

▶ **Refusal to change** from the older industries – cotton and coal – to the more modern science-based industries because:

● **management** by the families of men who had 'made' the first industrial revolution did not do as their predecessors had done in their time – change;

● **education** of the managerial classes concentrated on classical studies and ignored science;

● the education of the **working classes** also was deficient; few stayed on at school after the age of 11, even in 1880. In the USA and Germany better systems of education provided industry with workpeople qualified to work in more modern industry.

▶ **Home markets** for American firms and nearby markets for German firms were much larger than the domestic market for British firms. Foreign firms could plan a larger output, with bigger plant and more efficient machinery. This enabled them to produce goods of better quality and at a lower price.

▶ **Tariffs** kept British goods out of many markets.

▶ **Free Trade** meant that Britain allowed the free entry to foreign goods, which flowed into Britain after 1880.

▶ **Peace and political stability** came to the USA with the end of the Civil War (unit 21) and to Germany with the completion of unification (1871). This allowed people in those countries to concentrate on industrial development.

THE EVIDENCE OF BRITAIN'S DECLINE

▶ **Industry expanded** – but at a slower rate.

▶ **Imports increased** – and, significantly, of manufactured goods.

▶ **Unemployment rose** – after 1880 it was 'normal' for about 12 per cent of workers to be unemployed.

28.4 Chamberlain and Tariff Reform, 1900–06

In unit 34 we will see that Joseph Chamberlain was one of the most important politicians in the late nineteenth century. We will see that he was, in turn,

▶ a social reformer;

▶ an ambitious politician;

▶ an active imperialist.

He saw his campaign for Tariff Reform as an aid to his policies and ambitions.

Unemployment

As an industrialist and as President of the Board of Trade, Chamberlain had become aware of the effect of foreign

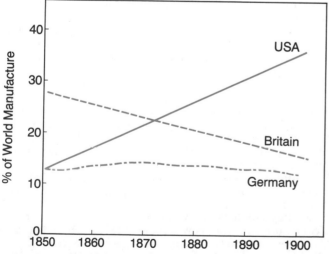

Fig. 28.3 A graph showing the total world manufacture of all types of goods in the period 1850–1900. Notice how Britain's share fell. Examiners expect explanations of the reasons for (i) the growth of and success of foreign competition, and (ii) Britain's decline.

PUNCH, OR THE LONDON CHARIVARI.—December 16, 1903.

PAPA COBDEN TAKING MASTER ROBERT A FREE TRADE WALK.

HISTORY REVERSES ITSELF;

OR, PAPA JOSEPH TAKING MASTER ARTHUR A PROTECTION WALK.

PAPA JOSEPH. "COME ALONG, MASTER ARTHUR. *DO* STEP OUT!"
MASTER ARTHUR. "THAT'S ALL VERY WELL, BUT YOU KNOW I CANNOT GO AS FAST AS YOU DO."

Fig. 28.4 A cartoon showing Chamberlain taking Balfour down the road to Protection, the opposite of the journey which Cobden made Peel take in 1845–46 (inset).

competition. He had seen the slow-down in the growth of British industry and trade, the rise of foreign imports and the resulting unemployment.

Tariffs

He and others knew that foreign countries kept British goods out of their home markets by imposing high import duties (or tariffs) on imports. Britain, as a Free Trade country, allowed the free import of foreign goods.

'Fair trade' was the slogan of a number of societies formed in the 1880s which asked that Britain form its own system of tariffs. This would allow her to exclude other countries' goods and would give her a bargaining weapon in negotiations for lower tariffs.

Imperial Tariffs

Australia, Canada and New Zealand had imposed their own tariffs on foreign imports, largely to provide their governments with the revenue needed to run their countries. These tariffs applied equally to goods from Britain and Germany or any other foreign country.

Imperial Preference

At the 1897 Imperial Conference, Chamberlain asked Empire countries to impose a lower tariff on British goods than on, say, German goods. In this way they would show their preference for British goods. The Conference leaders argued that while this would give Britain a larger share in their markets, it would give them nothing in return. Britain would continue to allow the import of agricultural produce from the USA, Denmark, Russia and other European countries as well as from Canada, Australia and New Zealand. Why wouldn't Britain put tariffs on foreign imports and so show a preference for agricultural goods from the Empire?

Once the Boer War was over, Chamberlain returned to this problem. He saw his Tariff Reform campaign as a means of:

- ▶ **uniting the Empire** in a Common Market;
- ▶ **helping industry** by providing larger markets;
- ▶ **providing funds** (from the British tariff) to finance

pensions, health insurance and housing schemes;
- ▶ **giving the Conservatives** a winning idea for the next Election.

The Cabinet under Balfour after 1902 was badly split over the proposals for a British tariff and Imperial Preference. The **Duke of Devonshire** resigned early in 1903, protesting that a British tariff would increase the price of food and be unpopular with the voters. When the Cabinet rejected Chamberlain's ideas, he, too, resigned in the autumn of 1903 so that he could be free to tour the country and campaign for support for his policy.

The Liberals has been badly split by the Second Boer War with the majority supporting the government once the war had started, while a Radical minority, led by Lloyd George, had opposed the war. But the Conservatives helped to unite the Liberals with the **1902 Education Act** (p. 106) with its proposals for more state aid for Church schools and with the **Tariff Reform campaign**. Asquith, a leading Liberal, followed Chamberlain around the country, addressing audiences who had, the day before, heard Chamberlain explain Tariff Reform.

Big Loaf, Little Loaf

Chamberlain's arguments were well developed, but complicated. Asquith's argument was much simpler; if there were tariffs on food imports, then prices would go up **or** people would get a smaller loaf for the price now paid for a bigger loaf. People understood this more easily than Chamberlain's economic and Imperial unity argument.

Although Chamberlain's campaign failed (either to win Cabinet support or to win national support), it played a major part in the 1906 Election. On this, see unit 35.

Unit 28 Summary

- ▶ Britain's early industrial lead.
- ▶ The volume and nature of British overseas investments.
- ▶ Britain's industrial progress after 1850; the growth of foreign competition.
- ▶ Evidence of and causes of Britain's relative decline.
- ▶ Chamberlain's Tariff Reform programme.

---

29 GLADSTONE: PART I, TO 1874

29.1 Gladstone's Early Career

AN ANGLICAN TORY MP

- ▶ Gladstone was the son of a rich Liverpool merchant.
- ▶ After schooling at Eton he went to Oxford, where he was influenced by the leaders of the Oxford Movement, many of whom became Catholics. Gladstone remained an Anglican.
- ▶ In **1832** he became MP for the 'rotten' borough of Newark.
- ▶ He was author of several books on Greece, Biblical Studies and *The Church and its Relations with the State* (1838).
- ▶ In **1839** Macaulay, a Whig MP, described him as 'the rising hope of the stern and unbending Tories'.

A PEELITE, 1841–46

As **President of the Board of Trade**, 1843–45, he helped

promote Peel's free trade policy (pp. 48 and 49), which pleased the Cobdenites.

In **1845** he resigned over the Maynooth Grant (pp. 48 and 56). In **1846** he supported the repeal of the Corn Laws.

A PEELITE, 1846–65

He was **Chancellor of the Exchequer** in Aberdeen's Whig-Peelite coalition (1852–55), in Palmerston's Whig government (1859–65), and in Russell's government (1865–66).

He completed Britain's move to free trade (p. 50), lowered the duty on newspapers, set up the Post Office Savings Bank (1861) to encourage working-class thrift, and arranged the Cobden Treaty with France (1860).

OPPOSED PALMERSTON

- ▶ He supported Palmerston over Italy (p. 52).

▶ He oppposed him over the Don Pacifico affair (p. 51).
▶ He resigned from office when Britain entered the Crimean War, believing that peace ought to be maintained.
▶ He served under Palmerston after the Crimean War, but differed from him over attitudes towards the American Civil War.

29.2 Gladstone Becomes Party Leader

In 1865 Palmerston died; Russell became Prime Minister. Gladstone, as Leader of the House of Commons, proved an able organizer of Commons' affairs.

Russell became too sick to continue in 1867 and Gladstone became Party Leader because:
▶ **old Whigs** (aristocratic landowners) approved of his education and Anglicanism. They would not have served under Bright or Cobden;
▶ **young Whigs** (merchants and industrialists) approved of his policies on trade and taxation and his opposition to Palmerston. They might not have served under a Whig aristocrat;
▶ **MPs and peers** of all descriptions admired the ability of a man who had held office for many years;
▶ **most people** approved of his idealism which had caused him to resign over Maynooth and the Crimean War.

THE FIRST CLASH WITH DISRAELI, 1866–67

This took place over the question of Parliamentary Reform and we will study this in detail in unit 38. But here you should notice that:
▶ there was a growing demand for further Reform;
▶ Gladstone introduced a Reform Bill in 1866 (p. 93) which Robert Lowe (a Whig) helped to defeat;
▶ Derby formed a government and Disraeli introduced a Reform Bill (p. 93) which got through Parliament;
▶ In the 1868 Election the Whigs won a majority.

29.3 Gladstonian Liberalism

Until 1868 there had been only the Tory and Whig parties. After 1868 people talked about a Liberal Party – the successor to the Whigs. By Liberalism they meant:
▶ **Peace**, which would enable industry and trade to develop and mean less need for increased taxation;
▶ **Retrenchment**, or a cutting back in government spending. Gladstone wanted to 'live to see the day when income tax would be abolished'. Liberals thought that taxation deprived people of the liberty to spend their money as they wished, believing that economic and social development would be best guaranteed by allowing people freedom to spend their money as they wished. Such a policy required the minimum of legislation on such things as Public Health, which would require money;
▶ **Reform** of institutions and laws which prevented people from acting freely. This explains Liberal support for Free Trade which allowed the free working of economic forces.

These three Liberal beliefs were in accord with **laisscz-faire** and **self-help**, a doctrine popularized by Samuel Smiles in *Self Help* (1859). Smiles showed how the great inventors and engineers had succeeded by their own efforts and argued that anyone could succeed if they tried. This belief was supported by:
▶ **the middle class**, whose thrift and hard work led to their enjoying 'the good life';
▶ **the skilled workers** who, by 1860, had good wages (p. 62) and strong unions (p. 62) with social security provided by their own efforts;
▶ **the majority of people** who gained from the rise in living standards in the 1850s and 1860s and from falls in living costs because of cheap food after 1873 (p. 50).

29.4 Gladstone's Ministry, 1868–74

Forster's Education Act, 1870

This is examined in detail on p. 106.

University Entrance, 1871

Until the passing of this Act, every student going to Oxford or Cambridge had to be a member of the Anglican Church. Nonconformists were not allowed to attend. Gladstone knew that the Liberals had the support of the majority of Nonconformists. By abolishing the religious qualification for University Entrance, Gladstone pleased the **Nonconformists** and lived up to the demand for **reform** of institutions when these prevented complete freedom.

Civil Service Reform, 1871

Until the 1850s anyone wanting a job in the Civil Service got it through knowing someone of influence. Government ministers and MPs got jobs for their friends. In the 1850s the British had taken over the government in India (p. 59). Sir Charles Trevelyan had examined the Indian Civil Service and proposed that no one should enter that Service without passing an entrance examination, and that promotion should depend on success in other examinations. The Crimean War had shown the inefficiency of the British Civil Service (p. 54). In 1871 Gladstone's reform said that:
▶ only people who passed an entrance examination should be allowed into the Service;
▶ there would be different standards of examination for different grades, with University standards being set for people entering the Administrative Grade.

THE COLOSSUS OF WORDS.

Fig. 29.1 A cartoon drawn in 1879 showing Gladstone as the equivalent of one of the seven wonders of the world – the Colossus of Rhodes. Notice the way in which Gladstone appears to dominate his surroundings and the cartoonist's use of the main features of Gladstone's policies – Peace, Retrenchment and Reform.

This reform was popular with Liberals because:
- it gave the sons of **the middle class** (without much political influence) an opportunity to get into the Service;
- it would lead to **increased efficiency**;
- it **cost** the government nothing.

The Ballot Act, 1872 (p. 94)

This step on the road of Parliamentary Reform ensured that workers who had gained the vote in 1867 (p. 93) could vote without fearing an employer's anger if they voted against his wishes.

The Licensing Act, 1872

Until 1872 there was no limit to the number of ale houses or beer shops in any town, nor were there any limitations on the hours during which these could open. This Act:
- set up a **licensing authority** in every town; anyone wishing to open a place for the sale of beer or spirits had to apply for a licence to do so;
- put a **limit** on the number of such shops; many previous owners were refused licences;
- limited the opening hours (6.00 am to 11 pm). This:
- annoyed the **brewers**, who wanted as many outlets as possible for their produce;
- annoyed the **licencees**, who feared a drop in income;
- made every beer house a **recruiting ground** for Tories during the 1874 election.

The Judicature Act, 1873

The government reformed the High Court system to make the legal system more efficient.

Army Reform – by Cardwell

The Crimean War had shown the inefficiency of the Army. Cardwell, the Secretary of State for War, brought in reforms:
- The **Commander-in-Chief** of the Army would, in future, be under the control of the Secretary of State for War.
- **Commissions** would no longer be for sale to the highest bidder. In future, officers would be promoted on merit.
- **Recruitment** would be encouraged by the abolition of life service; men could now join for six years on active service, plus six years in the reserves.
- **County regiments** would replace the regiments previously known only by a number (the 58th) or by their founder's name. Each county would provide a regiment with a base which might attract local recruits.
- **Flogging** was abolished.

These reforms were not popular, and Gladstone had to compensate those who had bought their commissions and were no longer going to be able to sell them, and had to ask Queen Victoria to use her Royal Warrant to overcome the delaying tactics of the House of Lords.

Trade union reform

This is examined in detail on p. 95. But here you ought to note that, following the Report of the Royal Commission (p. 63) the government brought in two reforms:
- the **Trade Union Act**, 1871 which allowed unions to register with the Registrar of Friendly Societies and to bring cases to court if they wished;
- the **Criminal Law Amendment Act**, 1871, which forbade picketing.

These reforms succeeded in angering both **the middle classes**, who opposed trade unions and **the working classes**, who opposed the ban on picketing.

Ireland

As we shall see on p. 78 Gladstone came to power in 1868 saying, 'My mission is to pacify Ireland'. He tried to do so by:
- **Disestablishing the Irish Church**, 1869, which pleased the Catholics but angered the Anglicans;
- the **Land Act**, 1870 (p. 78), which angered landowners while it also failed to satisfy the Irish.

The Torrens Act, 1868 (p. 46)

This was the government's attempt to deal with the growing problems of industrial towns. It said that:
- local councils could declare a house as 'unfit for human habitation' because of its lack of services or poor construction;
- councils could ask the owner to repair such housing;
- if owners refused, councils might then condemn the property and order it to be pulled down.

This Act angered property owners, without providing any more housing for the poor. If housing was pulled down the poor had to crowd together in other, often equally inadequate, housing.

Local government

The Local Government Board was set up in 1871 (p. 46).

GLADSTONE'S FOREIGN POLICY, 1868–74

In **1870** Bismarck of Prussia organized a war against Napoleon III of France as part of his plan for uniting Germany. Gladstone remained neutral in this Franco-Prussian War.

Bismarck won Russia's friendship by inviting her to tear up the Black Sea clauses of the Treaty of Paris, 1865 (p. 55). Again, Gladstone took no action.

The **Alabama** had been a cause of dispute in Palmerston's time (p. 52). Gladstone agreed to submit the United States' claim to an international court of arbitration, which decided that Britain should pay £3¼ million to the USA.

He refused help to Sher-Ali, the ruler of Afghanistan.

WHY WAS THE GOVERNMENT UNPOPULAR IN 1874?

As early as 1872 the government seemed to have run out of steam. Disraeli then described the Front Bench as 'exhausted volcanoes'. In the 1874 election the Tories won a majority of seats for the first time since 1867. The government was unpopular because:
- Some of the **rich middle class** switched their allegiance to the Tories.
- **The brewers** were annoyed by the Licensing Act.
- **Many workers**, already angered by the trade union legislation, welcomed Disraeli's promise on sanitary reform (p. 73).
- **Whig landowners** opposed the Irish Land Act and the interference with property by the Torrens Act.
- **Popular opinion**, as seen in popular songs and jingles, was against the 'pacific' policy, which seemed to mean a free hand for the hated Russians and giving-in to the Americans over the Alabama case.

Unit 29 Summary

- Gladstone's early career; a free-trading Peelite.
- Why Gladstone became Party leader.
- Gladstone's liberalism – theory and practice (1868–74).
- Why did Gladstone lose power in 1874?

30 DISRAELI

30.1 His Early Career

Disraeli was born in 1804, the son of a Jewish immigrant who had made a small fortune in business, changed the family name from D'Israeli and had his son baptised an Anglican.

He went only to a local private school – unlike Gladstone, who mixed with the sons of aristocrats at school and at University.

In 1826 he published his first novel, *Vivian Grey*, but his best-known novels, *Coningsby* (1845) and *Sybil* (1846) were published after he became an MP. In these novels he attacked the industrialists for the way in which, under **laissez-faire**, they treated their workpeople, and he suggested that the aristocratic upper class should act as the protectors of the workers.

Disraeli stood in several elections in the 1830s – as a Whig, a Radical and as an Independent. Few people took him seriously, because he was 'a mere novelist', unlike the serious Gladstone.

In 1837 he made friends with Mrs Wyndham Lewis, whose Tory husband controlled the 'rotten' borough of Maidstone. He gave Disraeli the seat when it became vacant in 1837.

In 1839 he married the widowed Mrs Lewis. Her money allowed him to give his time to politics.

DISRAELI AND PEEL

▶ In 1841 Peel did not give Disraeli a government post.
▶ Peel moved towards Free Trade. Disraeli accused him of giving in to middle-class industrialists.
▶ Over Repeal, he accused Peel of:
● betraying the gentlemen of England, whose interests he was supposed to defend as leader of their party;
● destroying the Tory Party again, as he had in 1829 (p. 33);
● handing the future of the country to industrialists who would have no thought but to make profit.

AFTER REPEAL

Peel resigned (p. 49) in 1846. The Peelites tended to support the Whigs and, after Peel's death in 1850, they drifted into Coalition with Whig colleagues. By 1868 as we have seen, Gladstone, the Peelite, was leader of the Whig-Liberal Party.

Disraeli was the leader of a small group of anti-Repeal Tories, who feared that they would never get power again.

30.2 Forming a New Party

If the Tories were to get back into power they had to:
▶ devise **new policies** to win electors' support;
▶ produce the **candidates** to speak on those policies;
▶ have **an organization** to help gain electoral support.

It was Disraeli who was responsible for these changes. He:
▶ taught the small Party that it would be pointless to try to win support for a reversal of a Free Trade policy, which was responsible for a rise in living standards;
▶ converted the Party to acceptance of Reform, so that the electors would not think of the Tories as 'the die-hards';
▶ promoted Reform when in office in minority governments, including an extension of the franchise in 1867 (below);
▶ developed ideas on the need for social reform, about which he spoke at great length without working out what he really intended to do;

▶ appointed his friend, J. A Gorst, to the job of reorganizing the Party machinery. From his headquarters at the Carlton Club in London, instructions went to agents in every constituency on how to register voters, to canvass, to enrol people in the Party and to collect the money needed to run election campaigns;
▶ appealed to the electorate as the spokesman for a Party which would have a strong foreign and imperial policy – unlike that of the Liberals under Gladstone.

HOW SUCCESSFUL WAS HE?

▶ **Between 1846 and 1874** the Tories were in office for only three short periods, and only because of Whig quarrels.
▶ **Between 1874 and 1906** the Tories appeared to be the 'natural government'. The Liberals had an unhappy Ministry between 1880 and 1885, split over the Home Rule for Ireland question in 1886 and resigned after a short period in office between 1892 and 1895.

DERBY-DISRAELI GOVERNMENTS

Although Disraeli developed the ideas and Party policy, Lord Derby was the nominal leader of the Party.

Derby was Prime Minister between February and December 1852 and between February 1858 and June 1859. Disraeli was Chancellor of the Exchequer in both these governments and in Derby's third Ministry, which was formed after the defeat of Gladstone's Reform Bill (p. 93).

Derby became Prime Minister in 1866 but resigned from ill-health in February 1868, and Disraeli became Prime Minister.

30.3 The 1867 Reform Act

There was little importance about the Derby Ministries of 1852 and 1858. But the third Ministry came to office because of Gladstone's defeat over a Parliamentary Reform Bill. We will examine this in detail on p. 93, but here you should notice that:
▶ Gladstone's Bill would have given the borough franchise to the occupier (whether owner or tenant) of a house valued (for rating purposes) at £7 a year, while in the counties the franchise would have been extended to the occupiers of houses valued at £14 a year.
▶ Robert Lowe led a group of Whigs against the Bill.
▶ Disraeli brought in a Reform Bill so that Tories could claim to be the Party of Reform.
▶ His Bill originally contained proposals for 'fancy franchises' to give extra votes to people with certain educational and property qualifications. Cabinet discussions led to radical changes until the Bill proposed the vote for all the ratepayers in boroughs. Almost one million people got the vote, most of them working men.
▶ Gladstone's supporters voted for this solution to the Reform question. Lowe and some Whigs, and Lord Cranborne (later Lord Salisbury) and some Tories voted against it. But the Bill was passed (p. 93).

30.4 The 1868 Election

Disraeli dissolved Parliament in the autumn of 1868, hoping that the new voters would vote Tory. This was not to be so, however.
▶ The **working class** realized that the Act had been passed because of Gladstone's proposals and support.
▶ The **middle class** was basically Nonconformist and would hardly vote for an Anglican Party. They approved of

Gladstone's Free Trade policies and feared that the Tories might go in for some form of Protection.
► **Gladstone and Bright** toured the country and won support. Disraeli only wrote a letter to the electors, as Ministers had always done.
► **The Liberals** had a majority of 112 seats.

IN OPPOSITION, 1868–74

Disraeli did not always oppose Gladstone's proposals. However, he attacked the government on:
► its foreign policy (p. 71);
► its Licensing Act (p. 71);
► the absence of any adequate social reform.

Having appointed Gorst in 1870 (p. 72), Disraeli copied Gladstone and in 1872 went on a countrywide tour addressing large audiences. It was in these speeches that he developed the ideas of a future Tory policy on:
► sanitary reform;
► the need to uphold the Monarchy against the threats of Republicanism by such people as Joe Chamberlain (p. 83);
► the need for a vigorous foreign policy.

He argued that the Liberals represented sectional interests (of industrialists and merchants), while the Tories were 'a National Party' supporting the Church, the Monarchy and the greatness of the country.

30.5 Disraeli's Ministry
SANITARY REFORM

Disraeli appointed **Richard Cross** Home Secretary to bring in the promised reforms. Cross found that 'his chief', having spoken at great length about sanitary reform, had no ideas of his own on the subject. Cross was responsible for:
► **The Artisans' Dwellings Act, 1875** (p. 46) This amended the Torrens Act (p. 71) and allowed councils to condemn whole areas as unfit for human habitation;
► **The Public Health Act, 1875** (p. 46) which brought into one major Act all the provisions of the many small Acts passed since 1848 – on Nuisance Removal, Burial, Refuse Disposal and Water Supply. It also compelled councils to appoint Medical Officers of Health with power to make towns healthier.

Most of the provisions of these Acts were **adoptive**. Councils could use the powers given but were not compelled to. Many did not, being frightened by the cost, **Chamberlain** (p. 83) changed the face of Birmingham by using the powers given.

OTHER DOMESTIC REFORMS

► **The Factory Act, 1878** which was a consolidating Act (p. 44).
► **The Pure Food and Drugs Act, 1875**, which attacked the adulteration of food and increased the powers of Food Inspectors.

► **The Merchant Shipping Act, 1876** was largely the work of Samuel Plimsoll, a backbench MP who attacked dishonest shipowners who made a profit from the insurance paid when their unseaworthy and overloaded ships sank. He demanded that each ship should have a load-line (the Plimsoll line) to show how much cargo a ship could carry safely.
► **The Climbing Boys Act, 1875** (p. 44).
► **Epping Forest** was saved from enclosure and put under the protection of the City of London;
► **The Education Act, 1876**, which slightly amended the 1870 Act (p. 106).
► **Trade Union Law** was improved by:
● **The Conspiracy and Protection of Property Act 1875**, which allowed peaceful picketing;
● **The Employers' and Workmens' Act, 1875**, which said that if an employer or a workman broke his contract, he could be sued in the civil courts. Previously only workmen could be sued – and in the Criminal Courts, where judges could impose prison sentences.

30.6 Disraeli the Imperialist

He showed he was an imperialist in:

Afghanistan

The Russians extended their Empire to the borders of Afghanistan (1875) and seemed to threaten India. Disraeli sent an agent to Kabul (capital of Afghanistan) to look after British interests. On his murder, Disraeli sent an army to take revenge. The Afghans were better-armed and better-led. The British lost thousands of men at Maiwand (1879). In 1880, with Gladstone back in power, Roberts won a victory at Khandahar, but Britain could not control Afghanistan.

India

He persuaded the Queen to accept the title of Empress of India (1876). This impressed the Princes of India, whose support Britain needed against Russia.

The Transvaal

When the Boers were fighting the Zulus, in 1877, Disraeli sent an army to defend them and announced that Britain had annexed the Republic. The British were defeated by the Zulus at **Isandhlwana** but got their revenge at **Ulundi** (1879). This saved the Boers from the Zulus but led to their demand for British withdrawal – and to the First Boer War (p. 86).

The Suez Canal shares

The Khedive of Egypt wanted to sell his shares to get money to pay his debts (1875). The British had played no

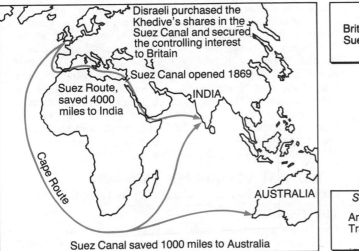

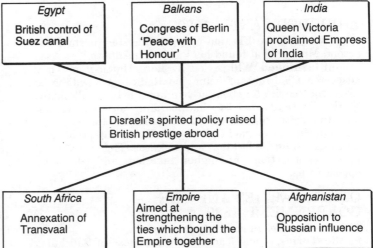

Fig. 30.6 A sketch map and diagram to illustrate Disraeli's foreign and imperial policies.

part in building the Canal. After its opening (1869) it proved to be 'the lifeline of the Empire' cutting the journey to Australia by 1000 miles and that to India by 4000 miles. When Disraeli heard of the proposed sale of shares, he made a secret deal, got £4 million on loan from Rothschilds without Parliamentary approval and bought the shares, which gave Britain a half share in the control of the Canal.

DISRAELI'S FOREIGN POLICY

'Forward' was one description of his imperial policy. He had a similar policy in **the Balkans**, as we shall see in detail in unit 32. Here you should notice that:
▶ **'Jingoism'** was a popular policy, the expression coming from a Music Hall song which went:
'We don't want to fight but by jingo if we do,
We've got the ships, we've got the men,
We've got the money too.'
▶ Palmerston had won popular support with his vigorous foreign policy, and Disraeli wished to do the same.
▶ **The Treaty of San Stefano** (p. 76) gave Russia too much influence in the Balkans;
▶ **The Congress of Berlin** (p. 77) was called to allow the Powers to re-draw the map of the Balkans and to limit Russian power. Disraeli's success at this Congress won him great acclaim.

30.7 The Election, 1880

▶ **His foreign policy** was attacked by Gladstone claiming that a 'forward' policy was bullying and wrong.
▶ **His imperial policy** led to wars in Afghanistan and the Transvaal – and Gladstone appealed to the morality of the electors when condemning both the policies and the wars.
▶ **The economy** had suffered from the effects of the agricultural depression (p. 66) and the onset of foreign competition. Disraeli's government did nothing to alleviate the effects of the depression.
▶ **Ireland** remained a major problem about which the government had done nothing. Irish voters in Britain voted for the Liberal promise to solve the Irish problem.

THE CONSEQUENCES OF HIS POLICIES
Gladstone formed his second Ministry in 1880 and had to cope with the problems left by Disraeli in Afghanistan, the Transvaal and Egypt.

Unit 30 Summary

▶ Disraeli's early career; his opposition to Peel, 1845–46.
▶ The formation of a new Conservative Party.
▶ The importance of the 1867 Parliamentary Reform Act.
▶ Disraeli's ministry, 1874–80; his foreign and imperial policies.

---

31 GLADSTONE: PART 2, 1880–94

31.1 The 1880 Election

THE MIDLOTHIAN CAMPAIGN, 1879
In 1875 Gladstone resigned the leadership of the Party. But anger at Disraeli's policies – in Afghanistan, the Transvaal and at the Congress of Berlin – drew him back. In 1876 he wrote a pamphlet attacking Disraeli's support for 'the unspeakable Turk'. But much more important was his long tour of Midlothian during the winter of 1879–80. In the course of this campaign he delivered a number of long speeches which roused the Liberal conscience against the warlike policies of the Tory government.

A DIVIDED PARTY, 1880
After winning the Election of 1880 Gladstone formed his second Ministry but found his Party divided into:
▶ **old-fashioned Whigs**, led by Lord Hartington. They suspected Gladstone of being too Radical, too willing to 'trust the people', to whom he had appealed in Midlothian;
▶ **the Radicals**, led by Chamberlain, once 'Republican Joe' the reforming Mayor of Birmingham (p. 83), who wanted the government to deal with social problems – housing, old age, education and sickness. This would need government action and higher taxation, and Gladstone opposed this.

OTHER PARTIES AND THE GOVERNMENT, 1880
The other parties in the Commons were:
▶ **the Tories**. Their leader, the Marquess of Salisbury, was in the Lords. In the commons they were led by Sir

Stafford Northcote, who seemed almost afraid of Gladstone;
▶ **the Irish Nationalists**, led by Parnell;
▶ **'the Fourth Party'** which was the nickname given to a group led by the young Lord Randolph Churchill. He, Gorst (p. 72) and A. J. Balfour, Salisbury's nephew, were annoyed at Northcote's leadership. They attacked Gladstone's policies whenever they could.

31.2 Gladstone's Problems

EARLY PROBLEMS
Gladstone's temper and autocratic manner annoyed many people and made it easier for the Fourth Party.
The Bradlaugh case gave them a great opportunity. Charles Bradlaugh, an atheist, was elected MP for Northampton. He refused to swear the oath of allegiance to the Queen on the Bible. The Commons therefore excluded him. Churchill then attacked Gladstone for being illiberal. The electors of Northampton re-elected Bradlaugh. After much argument the government decided to allow him to take his seat provided he **affirmed** his loyalty and allegiance without using the Bible. Churchill and his friends then attacked Gladstone for being in league with atheists – a damaging attack in the God-fearing 1880s.

COLONIAL PROBLEMS, 1880–85
Gladstone inherited the problems left by Disraeli.

The Transvaal
The Boers demanded their independence. Gladstone hesitated about giving way to the Boers. They raised a small army and attacked the British, whom they defeated at

Majuba Hill (1881). Gladstone withdrew the army and invited the Boers to a conference which led to the signing of the **Convention of London** (1884), which gave the Boers their independence. Many people resented this withdrawal.

Egypt

The British and French governments had officials in Egypt to ensure that shareholders in the Canal Company got their dividends each year. In **1881** an Egyptian nationalist, **Arabi Pasha** led a rising against these foreigners. The French withdrew their officials. Gladstone sent an army under **Sir Garnet Wolseley** to restore order. In 1882 he defeated Arabi's army at Tel-el-Kebir and ensured British control of Egypt. Many people condemned this 'forward' policy on behalf of shareholders, and complained of a 'most wanton invasion' words used by Gladstone to condemn Disraeli in 1879.

The Sudan

The Sudan was under the control of the ruler of Egypt. In 1882 Gladstone sent British officials to Egypt, but refused to send any to the Sudan. In 1883 a religious fanatic, **the Mahdi** led the Sudanese in a rising against Egypt. At first Gladstone ignored this rising, which was an Egyptian affair. However, in **1884** he was forced to agree to send in a British army to bring out the Egyptian officials and their families. **General Gordon** was in charge of the expedition. When he got to Khartoum, the capital of the Sudan, he ignored his orders and decided to stay on to defeat the Mahdi and restore order. Gordon was then beseiged in Khartoum. At first Gladstone refused to send in a relief force. But in 1885 he gave in to popular demand to save Gordon. The force arrived too late – Gordon was killed two days before its arrival. The majority of people blamed Gladstone for his death. His nickname of the G(rand) O(ld) M(an) was changed to G(ordon's) O(wn) M(urderer).

IRELAND

Ireland caused Gladstone many problems, as we shall see in unit 33.

He was forced to use **Coercion Acts** to try to stamp out the murderous attacks on landlords and their property. This angered the Irish and did not solve the problem, but roused the anger of many Liberals in England.

He introduced his **Second Land Act**, 1881, which might have solved the land problem if it had been introduced many years before. But by 1880 Parnell and the Irish had come to demand Home Rule and independence.

Parnell led a united group of Nationalist MPs in the Commons. They made life difficult for the government by speaking for hours at a time to stop government business going ahead. This forced the government to bring in **the closure**, often called **the guillotine**, by which the government announces the time when the debate will end and a vote be taken. Many MPs thought this was an interference with the liberty of speech.

31.3 Some Reforms, 1880–85

Because of these many problems the government is sometimes described as 'The Ministry of all the Troubles'. But Gladstone managed to get through some reforms.

The Married Women's Property Act, 1882

Before this, a married woman's property became her husband's even if it was a gift from a rich father. This Act allowed women to keep their own property – a sign that some women, at least, were demanding equality with men.

The Corrupt Practices Act, 1883 (p. 94)

This limited the amount of money that candidates could spend during elections. It also made it illegal for them to buy food or drink for voters. Rich people would thus have less influence at election times.

Parliamentary Reform, 1884

This is explained in detail on p. 94. It gave the vote to millions of men living in county constituencies, who now had the same rights as men living in borough constituencies.

The Redistribution of Seats Act, 1885 (p. 94)

A result of the 1884 Reform Act. It ordered the redrawing of constituency boundaries and a redistribution of seats, so that roughly the same number of voters lived in each constituency.

31.4 The 1885 Election

THE DEFEAT OF THE GOVERNMENT, JUNE 1885

In June 1885 the government was defeated in the Commons by the combined votes of the Tories, the Irish, who were angry at the Coercion Acts, and 70 Whigs led by Hartington, who suspected Gladstone of being too radical.

A MINORITY GOVERNMENT

There could not be an immediate election, because the changes needed by the Redistribution Act had not yet been made.

Salisbury formed a minority government in which Lord Randolph Churchill was a leading member. He persuaded Parnell that the Tories would end coercion in Ireland and provide a solution to the Irish question.

THE ELECTION, NOVEMBER 1885

By November 1885 the new electoral registers were ready and the constituency boundaries had been redrawn. In the election campaign there were four major groups led by:
► **Gladstone**, who promised lower income tax, more education and a chance for people to help themselves to a better life;
► **Chamberlain**, who put forward what became known as **'the Unofficial Programme'** in which he promised that a Liberal government would deal with the problems of unemployment, poverty, old age and housing;
► **Salisbury**, who promised to restore British influence abroad;
► **Parnell**, who demanded Home Rule for Ireland. His followers won 86 seats in Ireland. More importantly, Parnell persuaded the Irish living in Britain to vote for Tory candidates. This gave the Tories about 40 seats.

THE RESULT

The **Liberals** won 335 seats; the **Tories** won 249 seats, and **the Irish** won 86 seats – the difference in number between the two major parties. What would Parnell do when Parliament met in January 1886?

GLADSTONE AND HOME RULE

On the 17th December 1885 Gladstone announced that he intended to bring in a Home Rule for Ireland Bill.

Chamberlain was angered by this announcement. He argued:
► that he had won the votes of many working men with his 'Unofficial Programme', which would be ignored if the government spent its time on Home Rule;
► that the Party Leader ought not to decide party policy without discussing things with the other leading men;
► that Gladstone was out of touch with the needs of the time. The country needed what some called a 'socialist policy' – of help for the old, unemployed and badly housed. Chamberlain called Gladstone a 'Rip Van Winkle' who did

not understand the problems facing the country in the mid-1880s.

BACK IN POWER – THE THIRD MINISTRY

▶ Parliament met in January 1886, and a combination of Irish and Liberal votes defeated Salisbury's minority government.
▶ **Hartington** and the Whigs feared that Chamberlain would have too great an influence over Gladstone. They voted with Salisbury and in time were swallowed up in the Tory Party.
▶ In February 1886 Gladstone became Prime Minister.
▶ The Home Rule Bill was introduced in April 1886. Its terms are given on p. 79.
▶ **Chamberlain** attacked the proposal. He and his followers called themselves Liberal Unionists (because they wanted to maintain the Union with Ireland);
▶ In June 1886 the Bill was defeated in the Commons and Gladstone resigned.

HOME RULE AGAIN

In 1892 the Liberals won the Election. Gladstone, now 83 years old, formed his fourth Ministry, and brought in a second Home Rule Bill. This got through the Commons, but was defeated in the Lords. Gladstone wanted to hold another Election with Ireland as the main issue. The rest of the Cabinet refused to agree so Gladstone resigned (1894), to be succeeded as Prime Minister and Party Leader by Lord Rosebery. Gladstone died in 1898.

Unit 31 Summary

▶ The Midlothian campaign versus Disraeli.
▶ Party divisions in the House of Commons, 1880.
▶ The Ministry of All the Troubles, 1880–85; Bradlaugh; colonies; Ireland and foreign affairs.
▶ Party politics and Irish Home Rule, 1885–86.
▶ Gladstone and Irish Home Rule, 1886 and 1892.

32 THE EASTERN QUESTION, 1870–1914

32.1 Remembering the Question

On p. 53 we saw that the Question had three parts:
▶ the weakness of Turkey;
▶ the ambitions of the major Powers;
▶ the nationalism of the subject races in the Balkans. The Question led to the Crimean War and the subsequent Treaty of Paris (1856) did not solve the problem (p. 55).

A HARDER QUESTION

After 1870 two things made the Question more difficult:
▶ **Austria**, driven from Italy and Germany as they became unified, looked at the Balkans for compensation.
▶ **Russia**, having failed to get her way by helping Turkey in 1833 (p. 53) and by war in 1853 (p. 54) adopted the policy of **Pan Slavism**. (**Pan** means **all**; the **Slavs** are one of the races living in Eastern Europe.) The Russians were the largest Slav group, and after their defeat in 1856 they hoped to get more advantage by helping their fellow Slavs win their independence from Turkey.

32.2 The Bosnian Rebellion, 1875

▶ In 1856 the Slav people had seen how weak Turkey was.
▶ They had seen Rumania gain its independence (1861).
▶ **Turkey** remained cruel, greedy and inefficient.
▶ In 1875 **Bosnia** and **Herzegovina** rose against Turkey.

THE POWERS AND THE RISING, 1875–76

Russia, Germany and Austria wanted the Turks to give Home Rule to the rebels. **Disraeli** would not agree; he feared that a weak Turkey would not halt the Russian advance towards the Mediterranean and the Suez Canal.

Other Slav peoples rose – Serbs, Montenegrins and Bulgarians. It seemed that Turkey might lose its European Empire.

WAR, 1876–78

In **1876** the Turks took revenge on the Bulgarians; the world was horrified by the **Bulgarian Massacres**; Gladstone wrote a pamphlet about it and attacked Disraeli for not taking action on behalf of the Christian Slavs.

Russia sent an army to help the Bulgarians. In **May 1877** Russian troops crossed the Danube; in July they reached **Plevna** where the Turks held out until December 1877. The fall of Plevna allowed the Russians and Bulgarians to sweep on towards Constantinople. Britain threatened to interfere if Russia continued her advance. To give backing to this threat, a British fleet was sent to the Black Sea. In **January 1878** the Turks signed an armistice.

32.3 The Treaty of San Stefano, 1878

The Russians and the Turks negotiated a treaty:
▶ **Turkey** lost most of her European territory.
▶ **Bulgaria** became independent and was given territory which stretched from the Danube to the Aegean Sea. This gave her a long coastline on which to build ports. Russia might use these as outlets into the Mediterranean.
▶ **Rumania, Serbia** and **Montenegro** were all made larger and given their independence from Turkey. This pleased the Slav peoples; the Serbs thought about gaining control of other parts of the Turkish Empire, Bosnia and Herzegovina.
▶ **Russia** gained Kars and Batum in the Caucasus, and recovered part of Bessarabia (lost to Rumania in 1856).
▶ **Rumania** had part of the Dobruja in compensation.

THE POWERS AND THE TREATY

▶ **Disraeli** was frightened by the size of Bulgaria and feared that it would be a Russian puppet.
▶ **Austria** had many Slavs in its Austro-Hungarian Empire and feared that the success of the Southern Slavs might encourage the Northern Slavs (in modern Czechoslovakia) to rise.

▶ **Austria** had many Serbs living in the southern part of its Empire. She feared that Serbia might try to bring these people into a larger Slavonic kingdom based on Serbia.

▶ **Austria**, far from wanting a larger Serb/Slav kingdom, wanted to march south to gain control of parts of the decaying Turkish Empire.

▶ **Germany**, under Bismarck, had no interest in the region, but did not want her Allies (Russia and Austria) to come to war. So Bismarck and Disraeli forced the Russians and the Turks to come to Berlin to make a new Treaty.

32.4 The Treaty of Berlin, 1878

At the Congress of Berlin the Powers redrew the map of the Balkans. The main terms of the Treaty were:

▶ **Bulgaria** was split in three. One part, called **Bulgaria**, was granted self-government but remained part of the Turkish Empire; another part, **Eastern Rumelia**, was to be governed by a Christian governor appointed by Turkey; the third part, **Macedonia**, was restored to Turkish rule.

▶ **Bosnia and Herzegovina** were handed to Austria – not as part of her Empire but for her to **administer**. In 1908 she announced that she had annexed these Slav regions.

▶ **Serbia** and **Montenegro** remained independent but had to hand back some of the territories given them at San Stefano.

▶ Britain gained **Cyprus**.

THE IMMEDIATE SIGNIFICANCE OF THE TREATY OF BERLIN

▶ **Turkey** was larger than after San Stefano.

▶ **Austria** was now involved in the Balkans, and opposed to Russia's claim to be the major Power in the region.

▶ **Britain** had got barriers against Russia, in the shape of a compact Turkey, and Austria. She also took **Cyprus** as a base from which to keep an eye on Russia to the north and the Suez Canal to the south.

▶ **Disraeli**, now Lord Beaconsfield, and his Foreign Minister, **Lord Salisbury** returned to a great welcome from the British people who applauded the 'Peace with honour'.

THE FAILURE OF THE CONGRESS OF BERLIN

In 1885, **Salisbury** admitted that 'We had backed the wrong horse' in Turkey, whose rulers failed to govern well.

▶ **Bulgaria** united with **Rumelia** to form a larger kingdom (1885).

▶ The **Armenian Massacres**, 1894–96, showed again how cruel the Turks were.

▶ In 1897 Austria and Russia, alarmed at the unrest in the Balkans, agreed that they would maintain the **status quo** in the Balkans and maintain the peace there. They renewed this agreement after an uprising in Macedonia (1903) had threatened to lead to an anti-Turkish rising.

▶ Radical Serbs murdered their King and Queen (1903). The new monarch, anxious to win popularity, claimed sovereignty over the five million Serbs and Croats living under Austrian rule.

In 1908 the unrest in the Balkans and the failure of the Berlin settlement were illustrated by:

▶ the rising by radical **'Young' Turks** against the corrupt, cruel and incompetent government of Sultan Abdul Hamid (Abdul the damned);

▶ **Bulgaria's** rejection of the overlordship of Turkey, now torn by revolution;

▶ **Austria's** decision, with Russian agreement, to annex Bosnia and Herzegovina, which she had administered since 1878;

▶ **Russia's** anger when Austria, after her successful annexation, did not honour the agreement by which she was supposed to have supported Russia's claim to have the Straits open to Russian warships.

32.5 The First Balkan War, 1912–13

▶ **The Balkan League** (1912) was formed by Serbia, Greece, Bulgaria and Montenegro for their own self-defence and the protection of their fellow Christians in Turkey.

▶ In **1912** Turkey was attacked and defeated by the League.

▶ In **1913** Grey, British Foreign Minister, called the warring powers to a Conference in London, where Turkey ceded all her territory north and west of the line from Enos to Midia, which left her with a mere strip of European territory.

THE LEAGUE BREAKS UP

The members of the League had united to defeat Turkey, which now had only a strip of European land around Constantinople. But they were unable to agree about the division of Macedonia, the territory running from Greece to Constantinople. The peoples of the region were a mixture of Bulgars, Serbs and Greeks.

▶ **Serbia** wanted either a part of Macedonia, or a part of Albania, to provide her with a port.

▶ **Montenegro** also wanted Albania.

▶ **Italy** wanted Albania to satisfy the desire for an Empire.

▶ **Austria** supported Italy's claims, in an effort to limit Serbia's growth.

The outcome was the creation of a new kingdom of Albania – and Serbian determination to get control of Macedonia.

▶ **Bulgaria** had been given Macedonia at the Treaty of San Stefano, but had lost it at Berlin. If Macedonia was to be divided up in 1913, she wanted the largest part of it.

▶ **Greece** claimed Salonika, part of Macedonia.

32.6 The Second Balkan War, 1913

Bulgaria had made the major contribution to Turkey's defeat in 1912–13 and claimed the largest share of Macedonia; **Serbia, Greece, Montenegro** and **Rumania** (a newcomer to the fray) would not agree.

▶ **Bulgaria** attacked the other states.

▶ **Turkey** joined in hoping to regain some land.

▶ **Bulgaria** was defeated.

THE TREATY OF BUCHAREST, 1913

This Treaty ended the Second Balkan War:

▶ **Bulgaria** had to lose Thrace to Turkey, and part of the Dobruja to Rumania;

▶ **Serbia** was given northern Macedonia, but no coastal strip, so that she remained landlocked;

▶ **Greece** was given southern Macedonia, including Salonika;

▶ **Montenegro** was enlarged.

THE EFFECTS OF THIS TREATY

Serbia saw herself as the champion of the Slav peoples. Having defeated Turkey she thought of defeating Austria and freeing Slav peoples in her Empire.

Austria became more resentful of Serb ambition and growth.

But the crisis had shown that problems could be solved by international conferences. The Big Powers, it seemed, were governed by people who would not willingly go to war but would settle their differences around the Conference table.

32.7 The Eastern Question and War, June–July 1914

In unit 36 we will examine the steps by which Europe divided itself into Armed Camps between 1890 and 1914. Here you should notice that Germany, Austria and Italy were allies on one side, Russia and France allies on the other, with Britain having **Ententes**, but not alliances with Russia and France. Here, too, you ought to see how the Powers were drawn into war by events in the Balkans.

▶ **28th June 1914** Franz Ferdinand, heir to the Austrian throne, was murdered while on a visit to **Sarajevo**, the capital of Bosnia which Austria had annexed in 1908 and which Serbia wanted.

▶ **Austria** claimed that the murder had been planned by secret societies in Serbia. She decided to punish the Serbs.

▶ **Germany** promised to support Austria. Her generals thought that they could defeat France and Russia in 1914, but feared that as time went on these Powers would get stronger.

▶ **23rd July 1914** Austria sent a series of demands to Serbia. Their acceptance would have made Serbia little more than an Austrian protectorate. Serbia was given two days to answer.

▶ **24th July 1914** Serbia accepted most of the demands but asked for time to consider others. Austria refused.

▶ **25th July 1914 Russia** said she would have to mobilize her forces in case she had to go to Serbia's help.

▶ **28th July 1914 Austria** declared war on Serbia.

▶ **30th July 1914** Russia ordered partial mobilization.

▶ **Germany** demanded that Russia cancel her mobilization.

▶ **Russia** refused.

▶ **1st August 1914** Germany declared war on Russia and her ally, France.

Britain was not involved in these negotiations and did not enter the War until Germany invaded Belgium on 4th August. This was a breach of the agreement made in 1839 (p. 50). We will examine Britain's entry into the War on p. 89.

Unit 32 Summary
▶ European Powers and the Eastern Question.
▶ The crisis 1875–8.
▶ The Treaty of San Stefano and the Congress of Berlin.
▶ The Balkan Wars, 1912–13.
▶ The immediate cause of the outbreak of war, July 1914; Sarajevo.

---

33 IRELAND, 1860–1986

33.1 The Irish Problem in 1860

Three of the old problems (p. 55) still remained:

▶ **The land** was owned by English landowners, whose agents charged as big a rent as possible. Failure to pay the rent led to **evictions**, which were often the cause of **violence**.

▶ **Religion:** the majority of the people were Catholics, but the Protestant Church of Ireland was the Established Church.

▶ **Politics:** O'Connell had campaigned for Home Rule for Ireland (p. 56). Although the British gave this to Canada, Australia and New Zealand, they refused it to Ireland. Instead they appointed:

● a **Viceroy** and a **Lord Lieutenant**, who from Viceregal Lodge in Dublin's Phoenix Park, supervised the administration of British law throughout Ireland;

● a **Chief Secretary**, to help the Lord Lieutenant and to control **the Royal Irish Constabulary**, modelled on the Metropolitan Police Force.

After the Famine (p. 56) the old problems were made worse by:

▶ **Irish bitterness** towards the British, who had done too little in the period 1845–50;

▶ **Irish emigrants** in Canada, Britain and above all the USA who carried the bitterness with them and who provided money to support anti-British movements.

THE FENIANS

In **1858** a group of Irish emigrants in the USA founded the Irish Republican Brotherhood (the IRB), to fight for Irish Independence. The Irish for 'alone' is **fein**; the group became known as the Fenians.

They had their own newspapers, societies and organizations throughout the USA to keep alive memories of Ireland.

Some served in the US army in the Civil War (1861–65) and used their experience to train young Fenians. Fenian activity took various forms:

▶ **1866** In May a group raided across the Canadian border.

▶ **1867** 1200 Fenians assembled in Chester and a battalion of guards was sent to guard the castle and its arms dump.

▶ **1867** Attacks were made on army barracks in Ireland.

▶ **September 1867** Two Fenians were rescued from a prison van in Manchester; a policeman was killed.

▶ **December 1867** Twelve people were killed during the attempt to free Fenians imprisoned in Clerkenwell gaol.

▶ **Fenian bombing** of buildings in Britain led to the formation of the Special (Irish) Branch.

33.2 Gladstone's First Ministry, 1868–74

'**My mission is to pacify Ireland**', said Gladstone after winning the 1868 Election.

The Religious Problem

In 1869 Parliament passed the **Irish Church Act**, which said that:

▶ the Protestant Church was no longer the official State Church;

▶ farmers no longer had to pay tithes to Protestant clergy;

▶ the Church had to give up land and other wealth valued at £25 million. Some of this was used to help found schools in Ireland. This Act, and the 'godless Gladstone', angered the **Protestants**.

The Land Problem

The **First Irish Land Act**, 1870, said that:

▶ **evictions** were forbidden if tenants paid rents;

▶ **compensation** had to be made at the end of a lease for any improvements which a tenant might have made.

This act failed to solve the land problem because:

▶ **rents** could be increased at the end of a lease, and people evicted if they refused to pay it;

► **compensation** was often refused, and few tenants could afford the costs of a court case needed to force payment;
► **the depression** which affected farming after 1873 (p. 66) forced down prices and made it impossible for some tenants to pay even a low rent. Evictions were common.

33.3 Further Problems, 1874-9

CHARLES STUART PARNELL

Parnell was a Protestant landowner from County Wicklow. He became convinced that Ireland needed Home Rule. In 1875 he was elected MP for County Meath. When he went to the House of Commons he found an Irish party led by **Isaac Butt**, an Irish lawyer. Butt's policy was to ask Parliament for Home Rule, and when this was rejected, to do nothing until, in another year, he repeated the request. Parnell adopted a different policy:
► by intervening in every debate he held up government business and forced attention on the Irish problem;
► in so doing he became popular with other Irish MPs;
► in 1877 he replaced Butt as leader of the Party and used it to carry out the policy of **obstructionism**, which is also known as **filibustering**.

THE LAND LEAGUE AND MICHAEL DAVITT

Davitt, a Fenian, had spent many years in British prisons. In **1879** he formed the **Land League** to unite tenants who, because of the depression, were threatened with eviction.

The League got money from the USA, formed branches throughout Ireland and seemed to be a threat to government.

Parnell realized the value of the League in uniting the people and organizing them, but he feared that if the land problem was solved, the people might not support the movement for Home Rule.

In 1879, Parnell, already the 'uncrowned King of Ireland', was elected President of the Land League.

CAPTAIN BOYCOTT

In 1879 Parnell toured Ireland telling tenants not to pay until landlords agreed to lower rents. He told them that they should have nothing to do with anyone who took over a farm after an eviction.

Captain Boycott was the first to suffer. His servants and workmen left; people would not serve him in shops. His name added a new word to the English language.

33.4 Gladstone's Second Ministry, 1880–85

Violence was common. Ricks were burned, animals maimed, farmhouses and owners' houses bombed and burned.

W. E. Forster was Chief Secretary for Ireland. To help him, Gladstone pushed through the **Coercion Act (1881)**, allowing arrests without trial. He also passed **the Second Land Act, 1881**. It was an improvement on the First Land Act because:
► **fair rents** would be fixed by judges;
► **free sale** of leases would be allowed to tenants wishing to give up farming during the period of their tenancy;
► **fixed tenancies** had to be arranged between landlords and tenants. This would put an end to evictions. This gave the Irish the '3 Fs' for which the Land League had campaigned. But Parnell wanted Home Rule, and he advised the Irish to continue to refuse to pay their rents; violence continued.

Forster imprisoned Parnell in Kilmainham Gaol and **violence** increased. In May 1882 Gladstone sent **Chamberlain** to make an agreement with Parnell. The so-called **Kilmainham Treaty** said that:
► The government would provide money to pay off the arrears of rents owed by tenants;
► **Parnell** would call for an end to violence and be released – as he was in May 1882.

Forster resigned at this submission to Parnell and was

THE RIVALS.

Fig. 33.4 Gladstone offered Ireland a peaceful solution.

succeeded by **Lord Frederick Cavendish**.

On 6th May, the day after his arrival in Dublin, Cavendish and his Under-Secretary, **T. H. Burke** were murdered as they walked in **Phoenix Park** by a gang called the **Invincibles**, whose actions were condemned by Parnell and other Irish leaders.

Gladstone was uncle to Lady Frederick Cavendish. Angry at the murder of his niece's husband, he:
► brought back the Coercion Act;
► amended the agreement on rent arrears to bring less relief to tenants. So violence continued.

IRELAND AND BRITISH POLITICS, 1885

Parnell used his influence during the 1885 election to help the Tories; after that election he held the balance of power in the Commons and Gladstone supported Home Rule (December 1885) (p. 75).

GLADSTONE'S HOME RULE BILL, 1886

In April 1886 Gladstone's Bill proposed;
► a Parliament in Dublin to deal with Irish affairs;
► to end the representation of Ireland at Westminster;
► to leave control of foreign affairs, defence and external trade in the hands of the British government.

The Bill was rejected by the Commons, however (p. 76).

33.5 Salisbury and Ireland

Salisbury had three policies towards Ireland:
► **Firmness** was shown by the Coercion Acts used by the new Chief Secretary, Balfour, to evict non-payers of rent and to arrest resisters.
► **Parnell's** reputation was attacked:
● by *The Times*, which in 1887 published a series of letters allegedly written by Parnell ordering the Phoenix Park murders;

● in **1889** when Parnell brought a libel case against *The Times*. A Government Minister, the Attorney-General, appeared for *The Times*. In **1890** the case ended in Parnell's favour, when **Richard Piggott** admitted forging the letters;

● by **Captain O'Shea**, one of Parnell's followers whose wife, Katherine, ('Kitty') was Parnell's mistress. In 1890 Chamberlain persuaded O'Shea to bring a divorce action against his wife, citing Parnell as the co-respondent (or 'other man'). Parnell offered no evidence, and his character was torn to shreds in court.

▶ **'Kindness'** was the Tory solution to the land problem. In a number of Land Purchase Acts between 1886 and 1905 the Conservative governments proposed to make £200 million available for loans to tenants who wanted to buy their land from the landowners.

By this policy the government hoped:

▶ to create a body of satisfied Irish proprietors; by 1920 the greater part of the land was owned by the Irish, whereas before 1903 most of the land was owned by the English and the Irish were only tenant farmers;

▶ to weaken the support for Land League and Home Rule.

PARNELL AND THE VOTERS, 1890–91

British voters were shocked by the divorce case. **Gladstone**, who had known about Parnell and Mrs O'Shea since 1880, had to pay attention to the attacks on Parnell in Nonconformist Chapels, newspapers and speeches.

The Irish Nationalists were told that there would be no Home Rule Bill while Parnell remained leader. The Party split. Twenty-six Irish MPs remained loyal to Parnell, while 44 followed a new leader, Justin McCarthy.

The Catholic Church came out against Parnell because of Gladstone's promise to bring in Home Rule if Parnell were rejected. Parnell died, a broken man, in October 1891. His death allowed the two Irish groups to come together again.

33.6 The Development of Home Rule

HOME RULE, 1893

In 1892 Gladstone came back to power. His Second Home Rule Bill differed from the First. It proposed:

▶ to set up an Irish parliament (as in 1886).

▶ to have 80 Irish MPs at Westminster.

This Bill was rejected by the Lords (p. 76).

THE PROBLEMS OF ULSTER

While Catholics formed the majority throughout Ireland, there was a Protestant majority in four counties in the north-east. These feared that under Home Rule, Protestants would suffer as the Catholics had under Protestant rule. The Ulster Protestants, had:

▶ helped defeat Wolfe Tone's rising in **1798** (p. 56);

▶ been used as a threat against Gladstone in 1886. Lord Randolph Churchill had invited them to make civil war if Home Rule came. He coined the slogan 'Ulster will fight and Ulster will be right'.

IRELAND AND BRITISH POLITICS, 1910–12

In 1910 **John Redmond** led the Irish Nationalists. The Liberals needed their votes in the Commons. As the price for the support of the Irish Nationalists, Redmond got:

▶ **the Parliament Act, 1911**; the House of Lords would not be able to prevent the passing of a Home Rule Bill;

▶ **a Home Rule Bill, 1912**, which was passed by the House of Commons but rejected by the Lords. Because of the Parliament Act, it was expected that this Home Rule Bill would become law in 1914.

ULSTER, 1912–14

The Tories led by Bonar Law, son of an Ulsterman, resented the 1911 Act and the power of Irish MPs. **Sir Edward Carson**, an MP, a Protestant lawyer from Dublin, 'played the Orange card'. He:

▶ recruited an 'army' of Ulster Volunteers;

▶ bought guns from Germany;

▶ organized the signing of the **Ulster Convenant**, which 500 000 Protestants signed to pledge to defend their right to remain part of the Union.

▶ **Bonar Law** promised Tory aid to the 'rebels'.

THE BRITISH ARMY AND ULSTER

In 1913, Asquith inserted a clause in the Bill to allow the people of any county to vote it out of a United Ireland, but only for six years. Carson dismissed this as a 'temporary reprieve' and the danger of a Civil War became even greater.

The British Army had many bases in Ireland, the largest being on the Curragh, south of Dublin. In March 1914 Carson, Bonar Law and other leaders met the officers at the Curragh. These agreed that they would 'prefer to accept dismissal' rather than fight against fellow-Protestants.

The War Minister saw Gough, Chief Officer at the Curragh. Gough persuaded him to accept the officers' demand, which was not to use the Army in Ulster.

This 'Curragh Mutiny' led to the resignation of the War Minister, the Chief of the Imperial General Staff and other leading officers. But the doubt remained as to what the Army would do in the event of a Civil War.

THE DIVIDED SOUTH

▶ **Redmond** led the Nationalists and hoped to get Home Rule.

▶ The IRB, now led by Tom Clarke and the poet Padraic Pearse, feared that the British would deny Ireland its freedom.

▶ **The Irish Volunteers**, formed as a response to the Ulster Volunteers, were nominally under Redmond's control. In fact they came under the control of the IRB.

▶ **James Connolly**, leader of the Irish working-class movement, campaigned for a socialist society, which brought him into opposition with the IRB, Redmond and the government which supported the employers during a great strike in Dublin in 1913.

HOME RULE AND THE WAR

In **July 1914** George V held a conference with party leaders to try to get a peaceful settlement. He failed.

In **September 1914** the Home Rule Bill had been passed twice by the Commons and twice by the Lords when the War started in August 1914. In September it was passed for the third time by the Commons and, when signed by the king, became law. It was agreed to suspend its operation until the end of the war.

Redmond persuaded his followers to serve in the forces, but leaders of the **IRB** and **Connolly** took firmer control of the remaining **Irish Volunteers**, and planned an armed rising. Once again, 'England's difficulties would be Ireland's opportunities'.

Sir Roger Casement, a British civil servant, went to Germany to try to get help and to recruit Irish prisoners-of-war into an Irish rebel army. Few joined him; the Germans offered no help, and Casement was captured by the British on his return to Ireland (April 1916).

Most leaders in Ireland decided to call off the proposed rising, but the IRB called for the Easter Rising of 1916 in which they:

▶ proclaimed an independent Republic;

▶ were defeated after a week's bitter fighting;

▶ were jeered at by the Dublin people as they marched to prison.

The British then executed many of the captured leaders. The Irish, having failed to support the rising, now made them into 'martyrs'.

SINN FEIN

Arthur Griffiths was the principal founder of a new political movement, which won support away from Redmond's party. **Irish-Americans** supported this radical movement.

De Valera, a leader of the Easter Rising who had not been executed, was released from prison in June 1917. He won a by-election in Clare and was elected President of Sinn Fein.

THE ELECTION, DECEMBER 1918

- ▶ **Redmond's party** was almost eliminated.
- ▶ **Sinn Fein** won 73 of 105 Irish seats.
- ▶ Sinn Fein refused to go to Westminster. They met in Dublin and formed **Dail Eireann** in January, 1919. **The Dail** demanded:
- ● British withdrawal from the whole of Ireland;
- ● the establishment of an Irish Republic.

33.7 The Emergence of the Irish Free State

THE GUERRILLA WAR, 1919–21

The British would not go beyond what had been agreed in 1914 – with Ireland remaining a part of the Empire. **Ulster** – or at least six counties of the Province – was to be excluded from the new Ireland.

The government had to defeat the Sinn Fein rebels. They tried to do so by using:
- ▶ **the army**, under General Macready;
- ▶ **the Royal Irish Constabulary**, which was an armed force;
- ▶ **the auxiliaries**, a force of ex-officers;
- ▶ **the 'Black and Tans'**, a specially recruited force which wore half-military and half-police uniform.

The guerrillas of the IRB enjoyed:
- ▶ **the sympathy** of the majority of the Irish;
- ▶ **local knowledge**, which allowed them to escape arrest;
- ▶ **the help** of many Irish working for the British;
- ▶ **the sympathy** of many countries;
- ▶ **the support** of many British horrified at the cruelty of the 'auxies' and 'the Tans' in their campaign;
- ▶ **the leadership** of **Michael Collins** and **de Valera**, whose tours of the USA brought in money.

THE GOVERNMENT OF IRELAND ACT, 1920

This set up separate Parliaments in Dublin **and** in Belfast. The Dublin Parliament had power over the 26 counties of **Southern Ireland**. The Belfast Parliament controlled the affairs of the six counties of the North.

In Ulster the Protestants had a solid majority. The omission of the Catholic counties of Donegal and Monaghan (parts of the Province) ensured this.

Sinn Fein rejected the division of Ireland, the need for southern Irish MPs to take an oath of loyalty to the Crown, and Ireland's membership of the Empire.

In the south the guerrilla war went on, so when, in June 1921, George V opened the Belfast Parliament, he appealed for peace throughout the island.

THE TREATY

De Valera agreed on an end to the fighting (July 1921) and took an Irish delegation to meet Lloyd George.

The British offered Dominion status, demanding:
- ▶ Irish allegiance to the Crown;
- ▶ safeguards for British defence in Ireland;
- ▶ Northern Ireland's right to decide on its own future.

De Valera would only accept:
- ▶ 'external association with the Commonwealth', without Irish MPs having to swear allegiance to the Crown;
- ▶ the complete independence for a united Ireland.

In October negotiations were resumed. De Valera stayed in Dublin. Collins and Griffiths agreed (5th December 1921):
- ▶ the formation of an Irish Free State of 26 counties;
- ▶ the setting up of a Boundary Commission to supervise alterations in the boundary between Northern Ireland and the Free State. It was thought that Catholic Tyrone and Catholic Fermanagh would vote to join the Irish Free State.
- ▶ Britain could use five Irish ports as naval bases in wartime.

The **Dail** voted to accept this Treaty (by 64 votes to 57). De Valera rejected acceptance and conducted a civil war against the 'Staters', which dragged on until 1923.

THE IRISH FREE STATE AND BRITAIN SINCE 1922

In **1932** de Valera decided to abandon the war against the independent government of the Free State. His **Fianna Fail** party won a majority in the 1932 election in the Free State.

Having refused to acknowledge the position accorded the British and the Crown in the Treaty, de Valera undertook a tariff war against the British. This lasted until 1936 and, while it harmed British exports to the Free State, it was much more damaging to the Irish farming community which found itself barred from the British market.

In **1937**, having won a majority in a further election, de Valera's government issued a revised constitution which:
- ▶ gave the Catholic Church a special and powerful position in the country;
- ▶ abolished the name of 'Irish Free State' and used the name **Eire** instead.

Eire remained neutral during the Second World War and, while many Irishmen fought in the British forces and many more worked in British factories, the relationship between the governments of the two countries became less friendly.

In **April 1949**, after Britain had acknowledged that the Republic of India could remain part of the Commonwealth, the de Valera government claimed the right to proclaim the Republic of Ireland.

In May 1949 the British government formally accepted that Southern Ireland was independent and no longer a member of the British Commonwealth.

33.8 The Ulster Problem

The Protestant majority in Northern Ireland created a 'Protestant State for a Protestant people', while **the Catholics** supported the idea of a united Ireland.

To safeguard the State, the Ulster government created a para-military force of B-Specials with power to interrogate Catholics and search their homes.

Discrimination against Catholics was practised by:
- ▶ **the government**, which drew constituency boundaries to ensure that few Catholics were elected to Parliament;
- ▶ **local governments**, elected by gerrymandered arrangements, which gave Protestants the priority in housing, education, jobs and contracts;
- ▶ **employers**, including central and local government, who refused to employ Catholics;
- ▶ **the trade unions** in industrial Belfast, where the Protestants formed a majority.

CIVIL RIGHTS, 1968

For over 40 years the Catholics appeared unable or unwilling to do anything. There was little support for the IRA – the revolutionary successor to the IRB – and its campaign of violence against the British and the Protestants. Then in the 1960s there came:
- ▶ **the Race Relations Act, 1965**, by which the British government tried to protect the rights of coloured people in Britain;
- ▶ the formation of the **Civil Rights Movement** in Ulster;
- ▶ marches and demonstrations, in which the Civil Rights

Movement rallied Catholic support;
▶ clashes with the B-Specials.

33.9 Britain and Ulster, 1969–86

Until 1968 Britain paid little attention to Ulster, but the clashes between the Civil Rights Movement and the B-Specials attracted worldwide attention. The invasion of Catholic housing estates by Protestant gangs supported by B-Specials forced the government to send in British forces to defend the Catholics.

Terence O'Neil, the Ulster Prime Minister, tried to bring in reform in answer to the Civil Rights Movement, but a rebellion in his Unionist Party forced him to resign. His successor failed to find a peaceful solution to the problem.

In 1972 William Whitelaw, the then Home Secretary, abolished Stormont, the provincial parliament. Ulster would be governed by British Prime Ministers and officials. Whitelaw tried to get Protestants and Catholics to agree on some form of government-by-committee, on which both would be represented. The Protestants rejected this.

The IRA took advantage of the unrest to come forward as protectors of the Catholics but divided into the **IRA**, the name kept by the traditional members of the long-established movement which wanted unity, and **the Provisional IRA**, which wanted a socialist republic.

The guerrilla warfare threatened to wreck Ulster. Town centres were destroyed, industrialists kidnapped and killed, army barracks attacked. The army set up search blocks, attacked Catholic bases where the IRA had its strength, and arrested many leaders.

At first the IRA leaders were given **political status** in Ulster prisons. The government then took away that status which gave the prisoners the right to wear their own clothing, decide on what work they would do and conduct ceremonies and processions in the prisons. In retaliation prisoners went on hunger strike; a number died. The British government refused to give way to this form of pressure and, in October 1981, the hunger strike was called off.

While the Catholic population tended to support the IRA and the 'Provos', the Protestant majority had its own paramilitary organizations, including the Ulster Volunteer Force (UVF).

The local elections in Ulster in May 1981 showed that the divisions in the community had hardened. **Ian Paisley**, a leading anti-Catholic, won votes from the traditional Unionist supporters. **Sinn Fein** and its allies on the Catholic side, won power from more moderate leaders such as Gerry Fitt. The Ulster problem was as far from a solution in 1981 as in 1914.

There were efforts, on both sides of the religious divide, to try to find unifying and moderate policies. But the failure of the **Alliance Party**, the success of Paisley, and, on the Catholic side, the election of Republican prisoners in parliamentary elections, indicates that there is little support for moderation.

There have also been a variety of 'peace movements', in which people from both sides of the religious divide – and usually women – have tried to organize people into groups pledged to bring an end to the sectarian fighting. Unhappily these have had little long-term success, as is indicated by the present state of tension in the Province.

33.10 The Anglo-Irish Accord, 1986

Politicians and voters in the Irish Republic were divided in their attitudes towards Ulster's problems. Of the political parties in the Republic, Fianna Fail tended to demand the unification of Ireland, as de Valera had done. Some extremists provided aid for the IRA and Provisionals, who found refuge in the South when facing arrest in the North. Fine Gael, however, tended to support a more moderate policy, fearing an upsurge of left-wing movements if the Marxists, in the Provos and other radical groups, succeeded in their struggle in the North.

Under Garrett Fitzgerald, the government pushed through a series of Acts which allowed closer cooperation between the police forces in the North and the South, and the extradition to Britain or the North of people suspected of crimes in those parts of the United Kingdom.

British politicians became increasingly aware of the need to find some solution to the problem of Ulster. Public opinion showed a desire to 'bring the troops home' from Ulster; the financial cost of trying to maintain order was very high and the Thatcher government hoped to cut that cost.

Prime Ministers Thatcher and Fitzgerald signed an Accord, which aimed to please both the Catholics and Protestants.

▶ There was to be no attempt to bring Ulster into union with the Republic until and unless the majority of people in Ulster voted for such unification. This was intended to appease the Protestants.

▶ The government of the Republic was to play a major role in Ulster's affairs; its Ministers would sit on a joint Ministerial Council along with UK Ministers; its civil servants would sit with UK civil servants on joint committees examining and implementing legislation applicable to Ulster. This was aimed at ensuring a Catholic voice in the future government of Ulster.

The Ulster Protestants refused to accept British claims that the Accord would not harm their position. Old militant organizations recruited new members, while new and more extremist organizations sprang up to express Protestant hostility to the Accord. Initially this violent Protestant reaction seemed to be supported by leading Protestant politicians, who encouraged a one-day strike and called for such actions as a 'rates strike'. However, as the violence increased, some of these, notably Ian Paisley and James Molyneux, called for a lessening of the violence, which had led to Protestant attacks on the predominantly Protestant police force.

The Province, which had always been divided on sectarian grounds, now had a major division in the Protestant ranks and its future seems even bleaker than it had been in 1980.

Unit 33 Summary

▶ Irish problems, 1860.
▶ Gladstone and Ireland, 1868–74: Church and Land solutions.
▶ The career and importance of Parnell.
▶ Michael Davitt and the Land League.
▶ Gladstone and Ireland, 1880–85: Land Acts, Coercion and Home Rule.
▶ The fall of Parnell.
▶ The Ulster problem, 1912–14 and 1968–86.
▶ Home Rule Bills, 1912–14.
▶ Sinn Fein and the 1918 Election.
▶ Guerrilla war, 1919–21.
▶ The Government of Ireland Act, 1920 and the Treaty, 1921.
▶ Ulster 1921–86.

34 JOSEPH CHAMBERLAIN

34.1 Chamberlain's Early Career

After leaving University College School, London, Chamberlain (born 1836) worked for a while in his father's office. He went to work with his cousin, Joseph Nettlefold, in Birmingham where he built the family firm into the country's major manufacturer of nuts, bolts and screws. He was able to retire from business while still in his 30s.

34.2 Chamberlain's Political Career

THE RADICAL

Chamberlain was a Nonconformist in religion, and proved to be equally nonconforming in politics.

Education

In 1869 he helped form the Birmingham Education League, through which the Nonconformists campaigned for educational reform. In time this League became the **National Education League**, which campaigned for free, compulsory and religious-free education in state-provided schools. The League put pressure on Forster, whose 1870 Act (p. 106) saw the start of state education.

Political organization

Forster's Act said that school boards had to be elected in each school district. Chamberlain and his ally, Schnardhost, founded the **Birmingham Liberal Association** to make sure that members of the League were elected to the Birmingham School Board. This was the first real political organization.

Local Politics

Having won control of the School Board, Chamberlain used the Association to get himself and friends elected on to the Birmingham Council. In 1873 he was elected Mayor of Birmingham and held that office until 1876. During these three years he used all the powers of Disraeli's adoptive Acts (p. 73) to make Birmingham a cleaner and healthier place.

National Politics

Having succeeded in local politics, he became MP for Birmingham (1876) along with John Bright, the leader of the Anti-Corn Law League and promoter of the 1866 Reform Bill. As an MP during a Conservative Government, Chamberlain won public attention with his attacks on the aristocracy and the monarchy. Having seen how France had become a Republic after the overthrow of Napoleon III in 1870–71, Chamberlain campaigned for a British Republic and earned the nickname of 'Republican Joe'.

THE LIBERAL MINISTER, 1880–85

Gladstone did not like Chamberlain, but he had to recognize the importance of the politician who had now set up the National Liberal Federation based on the Birmingham model. He had several MP colleagues who supported his Radical views, notably Sir Charles Dilke.

In 1880 Gladstone appointed Chamberlain to the post of President of the Board of Trade, where he was in control of the Poor Law system. Chamberlain made several attempts to improve the system, encouraging Guardians to provide work for the unemployed and allowing slight improvements in conditions inside workhouses.

In 1885 he published his *Unauthorized Programme* as his election manifesto (p. 75). He claimed that this helped win a good deal of working-class support during the 1885 election.

Gladstone's rejection of the *Programme* – as 'socialism' – led Chamberlain to call Gladstone 'a Rip Van Winkle' who was out of touch with the real needs of the times.

Gladstone's announcement about Home Rule angered Chamberlain (p. 75). When Gladstone introduced a Home Rule Bill, Chamberlain resigned from the Cabinet, led 40 MPs into the lobby against Gladstone and helped defeat the Bill (p. 76).

THE LIBERAL UNIONIST, 1886–95

For some years Chamberlain refused to join the Conservatives when they were in power. He hoped that Gladstone might retire, so that he might come back into the Liberal ranks as the new leader.

However, he remained opposed to Gladstone, who did not retire until 1894, by which time the division between Chamberlain and the Liberals had widened.

He had become friendly with Salisbury, the Conservative leader, whom he had helped in his campaign against Parnell (p. 80).

When Salisbury came back to power in 1895 he offered Chamberlain any job he wanted in the government. He chose to become the Colonial Secretary – an unimportant position and a surprising choice for the man who had once opposed Disraeli's 'forward' policy (p. 74).

34.3 Chamberlain and Africa, 1895–1903

The scramble for Africa

While Europeans had fought for Empires in Asia in the seventeenth and eighteenth centuries, Africa had remained the 'Dark Continent' until explorers such as Livingstone and Stanley had shown the economic possibilities of its interior.

In the 1880s and 1890s Africa was divided, peacefully, among the European powers, anxious to extend their Empires to obtain:
- ▶ **markets** for the products of their factories;
- ▶ **materials** such as timber, copper and various vegetable oils which could be used in their factories;
- ▶ **men** who would work in their plantations and mines and who might also form part of an Imperial Army;
- ▶ **money** from the high return on the investments in mines and plantations.
- ▶ **political popularity at home** and **greater influence abroad**, which would follow from control of larger Empires.

Chartered Companies, modelled on the now defunct East India Company (p. 57) were given Charters which provided each with the monopoly of trade in a certain region. Thus there were the Royal Niger, British South African and other Companies in which British people invested their money, which was used to develop trade and industry in Nigeria, Bechuanaland, Rhodesia, Nyasaland, Uganda and Kenya.

The government helped these Companies by giving them their Charters, by founding the new Schools of Tropical Science and Tropical Medicine where home-based scientists tried to find ways of making life healthier in Africa, and by providing the armies needed to fight wars when the needs arose. There were two Boer Wars (p. 86), for instance, and there were other wars against the Ashanti and the Zulus.

Government take-over of the Companies' territory came about when the various Companies found it impossible to maintain law and order and to administer the vast regions given to them. Kenya, Uganda and Nigeria were taken over in this way, proving that 'the flag follows trade' and not, as many think, 'trade follows the flag'.

34.4 Chamberlain and the Older, White, Colonies, 1895–1903

Canada, Australia, New Zealand and South Africa were different from British possessions in Asia and most of Africa, in that many emigrants settled in these places, and the British government allowed them an increasing degree of self-government (unit 24).

In 1887 the Prime Ministers of the Australian states, of Canada and New Zealand came to Britain to celebrate the Queen's Jubilee. This allowed the holding of the first Prime Ministers' Conference, during which there was talk about finding some way of uniting the Empire.

The 1897 Jubilee allowed a repeat of such a Conference, with Chamberlain as the Chairman. He was anxious to unite the Empire so that:
▶ British industry would have guaranteed markets, which were badly needed because of the growth of foreign competition (unit 28.3);
▶ the government could speak on behalf of the Empire countries when negotiating with foreign powers. This would give Britain more influence in the world.

There were no firm conclusions to these talks, because the newly independent countries of the 'white' Empire were not anxious to allow the Mother Country too much power.

34.5 Chamberlain and Foreign Policy, 1895–1903

The ambitious Chamberlain not only ran the Colonial Office, he also tried to play a major role in foreign affairs. He tried to organize understanding, if not alliances, with:
▶ Germany and the USA, claiming that the three Anglo-Saxon countries could control the world between them;
▶ France and Russia, once it became clear that Germany was intent on following an anti-British policy (p. 88).

OTHER ISSUES

▶ Tariff Reform; see unit 28.4;
▶ The Election, 1906; see unit 35.

Unit 34 Summary

▶ Chamberlain as (a) Radical and (b) Liberal Unionist.
▶ Chamberlain in government, 1895–1903: African affairs; imperial unity and Tariff Reform; foreign affairs.

---

35 CONSERVATIVE GOVERNMENTS, 1886–1905

35.1 Salisbury

Disraeli resigned the leadership of the Tory Party after the 1880 Election. His place was taken by the Marquess of Salisbury. Salisbury was Prime Minister in a minority government in 1885, took power after the defeat of the Home Rule Bill in 1886 and, after a short period of Liberal government (1892–95) became Prime Minister for a third time. When he resigned in 1902 his place was taken by his nephew, A. J. Balfour.

SALISBURY AND DISRAELI, 1867

Salisbury (then Viscount Cranborne) had been in the Tory government in 1867. He resigned because he was opposed to the Reform Bill (p. 72). In 1868 he succeeded to the title of Marquess of Salisbury on his father's death.

SALISBURY AND DISRAELI, 1874–80

Salisbury was Foreign Secretary in Disraeli's Ministry of 1874. He played a major role in the Congress of Berlin, 1878 (p. 77), but he had little sympathy with the social reforms of this government.

SALISBURY, GLADSTONE AND IRELAND, 1885

In June 1885 Salisbury became Prime Minister of a minority government. An election could not be held until the terms of the 1885 Redistribution Act had been carried out. Parnell and Gladstone hoped that this minority government would, with the support of Gladstone's followers, solve the Irish problem (p. 75). Salisbury refused to do anything, although Lord Randolph Churchill (father of Sir Winston) persuaded Parnell that if the Tories had a

majority government they would solve the Irish problem. This helps to explain the result of the 1885 Election (p. 75).

SALISBURY AND CHURCHILL, 1886

Churchill had played a major role in:
▶ leading the opposition to Gladstone in the Commons, 1880–85 (p. 74);
▶ persuading Parnell to support Tory candidates in the 1885 election (p. 75);
▶ whipping up Ulster opposition to the Home Rule Bill of 1886 (p. 80).

Although Churchill was only 37 years old in 1886, Salisbury made him Chancellor of the Exchequer. In this post he:
▶ argued that the Party ought to follow Disraeli's policies on social reform, although Salisbury was opposed to this;
▶ won the support of the Party workers in the constituencies and tried to get Salisbury to accept that they ought to have a voice in deciding government policy, although Salisbury was opposed to this;
▶ planned a Budget in the winter of 1886 to cut income tax and to give local authorities an extra £5 million to spend on social reform. To make his Budget balance, he wanted cuts in other government spending, including a cut in the spending by the War Office, then under the Minister, W. H. Smith.

Smith refused to make the cuts and Salisbury supported him. Churchill wrote a letter of resignation, hoping to force Salisbury to back him against Smith. Salisbury published the letter, accepted the resignation and appointed a Liberal Unionist, Goschen, as Chancellor. This was, virtually, the end of Churchill's career. He never held office again and died in 1895.

Salisbury's failure to follow Disraeli's policies in social reform was one reason for the rise of the Labour Party (p. 99).

35.2 Salisbury's Domestic Policies, 1886–92

THE LOCAL GOVERNMENT ACT, 1888

This dealt with the government of the country outside the boroughs. It created 62 county councils and made separate county borough councils for towns with populations over 50 000. It also set up the London County Council, the forerunner of the modern Greater London Council.

Education

In 1891 the government abolished school fees for children going to Board Schools (p. 106).

Factory Act, 1891

This said that no child below the age of 11 could go to work, and women workers were not to work more than 12 hours a day.

The Smallholdings Act, 1892

This was an attempt to deal with unemployment in the agricultural sector, following the depression of the 1870s and 1880s (p. 66). Little improvement took place, although it shows that Salisbury was aware of the problems of poverty and unemployment.

The Royal Commission on Labour, 1892–95

The Report of this Commission showed that about half the country's workers earned about 75p a week, but that they needed 125p if they were to have enough to live on. Salisbury ignored this Report and the growth of the new, large and militant trade unions (unit 39). This was another reason for the growth of the Labour Party.

35.3 Salisbury's Domestic Policies, 1895–1902

The Workmen's Compensation Act, 1897

This stated that workers in certain trades and industries who were injured at work, or who caught a disease as a result of their work, could claim compensation from their employers. This was a first step along a long road of workers' compensation.

The Education Act, 1902

This was largely the work of a civil servant, Robert Morant, and of A. J. Balfour in whose ministry (1902–05) it finally became law. For its terms and effects see p. 106.

35.4 Salisbury's Foreign Policy, 1886–1902

Salisbury was his own Foreign Minister.

In **1887** Salisbury saw France as the main threat to Britain. This made him friendly towards the Triple Alliance (p. 88). In 1887 he signed a naval agreement ('the Mediterranean Treaty') with Italy in which both countries agreed that:

▶ no country be allowed to take over any of the islands in the Mediterranean or any of the countries bordering on that sea;

▶ Britain would help Italy if she were involved in a war with France;

▶ Britain would help Italy and Austria if they were involved in a war with Russia in the Balkans.

China

In the 1890s the European Powers began to take an increasing interest in China. There was a danger that they might get involved in a war as each tried to extend its influence in that country. In **1897** Germany occupied the district around the port of Kiao-chow; in **1898** the Russians occupied **Port Arthur**, which led the British to acquire **Wei-Hai-Wei**, midway between the two. Salisbury forced the Chinese government to give Britain an almost complete monopoly of trade in the commercially important **Yangtze** river valley.

The Balkans

Salisbury arranged a series of meetings in which Germany, Russia, France and Britain agreed on the areas in which each should have the major influence. This lessened the danger of war. But Salisbury was aware that Britain could no longer dominate the world. This explains his policy in **the Balkans**. Although he had played a major role at the Congress of Berlin, he later realized that Turkey was incapable of reform and would not provide the necessary bulwark to Russian expansion. 'We backed the wrong horse', he said.

So:

▶ in **1885** he agreed to the reunion of Rumelia with Bulgaria – which he had helped to split in 1878 (p. 77);

▶ in **1895** he tried to get the European powers to act together against Turkey after the Armenian massacres. None of the powers was willing to act, and the Turkish problems remained to trouble Europe (pp. 77 and 89).

The USA

In **1892** Salisbury agreed to submit to arbitration the dispute which existed between Britain and the USA over fishing rights in the **Baring Straits**. The tribunal rejected the Americans' claims and agreed that British seal fishers could fish in the Straits.

In **1895–96** there was a dispute with **Venezuela** over her boundary with British Guiana. The USA threatened to act as a 'big brother' on the side of 'little' Venezuela. Salisbury submitted the case to international arbitration. The case was settled in Britain's favour in 1899.

In **1898** the USA was at war with Spain over **Cuba** and **Puerto Rico**. Salisbury acted as a 'benevolent' neutral, to prevent France and Germany from helping Spain.

In **1901** he agreed to surrender British rights under an 1880 agreement with the USA, in which the Americans had agreed that they would not build a canal across Panama except as a joint venture with Britain. In 1903 this allowed the USA to begin the construction of the **Panama Canal**.

SALISBURY AND BURMA, 1886–92

Britain had first gone to war in Burma in the 1820s and had further extended its conquests in 1852. Salisbury continued this expansion. In 1886, Britain conquered the remainder of Burma and, in 1896, forced the ruler of Siam to grant Britain exclusive rights in north and south Siam. The French were also busily engaged in acquiring an Empire in this area – taking Saigon in 1859, Cambodia in 1863, Annam in 1884, Tonkin in 1889 and Laos in 1893. Anglo-French rivalry in south-east Asia increased the hostility between the two countries.

SALISBURY AND AFRICA

▶ The Chartered Companies (p. 83) were only set up after 1887, when Salisbury had become a committed imperialist.

▶ **Zanzibar** was acquired as part of an agreement with Germany (**1890**) in exchange for Britain handing over the Baltic island of Heligoland to Germany.

▶ **The Zambesi** was accepted as the boundary between British and Portuguese interests in East Africa, by an agreement signed in **1891**.

▶ **Uganda and Kenya** were acquired in 1892 when the East Africa Company faced bankruptcy and it seemed as if France might move in to take these regions over. **Nigeria** was similarly acquired in 1900.

▶ **The Sudan**: Salisbury realized that Britain's control of

Egypt depended, in part, on her control of the Nile Valley. This explains his actions in Uganda and Kenya. It also explains his policy in the Sudan where the **Mahdi** had defeated Gordon in 1884 (p. 75). **Kitchener** defeated the Mahdi's successor at the Battle of Omdurman (1898) and brough the Sudan under Anglo-Egyptian rule.

After Omdurman, Kitchener moved on, and at Fashoda met a French army led by Captain Marchand. The French intended to create an Empire stretching across North Africa, including the Sudan. For a time it appeared that there might be war between the two countries; the Royal Navy was put on a war footing; politicians in both countries made warlike speeches. But in November 1898 the French withdrew and the Sudan was in British hands.

35.5 The Boer War, 1899–1902

Relationships between the British and the Boers had been uneasy for many years. There had been crises because of:

▶ **The Great Trek** (p. 59) when the Boers left the Cape which they had occupied long before it was acquired by Britain in 1814.

▶ **Natal**, the home of the Zulus, which Britain had annexed in 1843 to ensure the safety of the Cape from Zulu attacks.

▶ **Basutoland**, over which Britain had established a protectorate to guard the Basuto people against encroachment by the Boers in the independent Orange River State.

▶ **Griqualand West**, which had been annexed by Britain in 1871 after the Griqua chief had asked for help against Boer expansion westward from the Orange River State. This expansion had been prompted by the discovery of diamonds at Kimberley.

▶ **The annexation of the Transvaal, 1877** (p. 73) The Boer state was badly governed; its attacks on the Zulus provoked an uprising led by warlike Zulu King, Cetawayo. To protect the Transvaal – and to safeguard the Cape and Natal – Disraeli's government annexed the colony, promising the Boers self-government.

▶ **The Zulu Wars, 1879** Cetawayo attacked the Transvaal (p. 73) and was ultimately defeated at Ulundi.

▶ **The First Boer War, 1881**, prompted by:
● a desire for independence and;
● Britain's initial defeat at Isandhlwana by the Zulus. When Gladstone hesitated about giving the Boers their independence they started a war, defeated the British at Majuba Hill (1881), and forced Gladstone to give them the independence they wanted.

But relationships between the British and the Boers then became even worse:

▶ **Cecil Rhodes** was the chairman of the Kimberley diamond mines and Prime Minister of the Cape Colony (1890–96). He wanted Britain to occupy as much of Africa as possible. He dreamed of a united Africa under British rule, extending northwards from the Cape. He planned the construction of a Cape-to-Cairo railway through British Territory.

▶ **Bechuanaland** was acquired when Rhodes persuaded the government to secure it as a Protectorate (1884) to ensure it against German expansion from south-west Africa.

▶ **The British South Africa Company** was set up by Rhodes in 1889 to develop the resources of the country which was later named after him – Rhodesia.

Paul Kruger, Boer leader in the Transvaal, resented British expansion and encirclement of Boer territory. This would have led to a war sooner or later, but the events leading to the war were:

▶ **The discovery of gold in the Witwatersrand, 1886**: the Boers were farmers and the gold-mines were largely run by British immigrants, called 'Uitlanders' (outsiders) by the Boers.

▶ **Kruger's** hostile policy towards the Uitlanders, who soon outnumbered the Boers. They were denied all political rights and were heavily taxed.

▶ **The Jameson Raid, 1895:** Dr Jameson, administrator of Rhodesia and supported by Rhodes, engineered a plot by which the Uitlanders would rise against the Boers, call for British help and so ensure a British Transvaal. The plan was a failure; the Uitlanders did not rise and Kruger was made to appear a saviour to his people. Rhodes was forced to resign office in the Cape; Jameson was brought to trial in London.

▶ **The Uitlanders' Petition** to the British government, that asked for action against a Boer government which refused to grant them any political concessions. Negotiations between the British and Boers broke down owing to the obstinacy of Kruger and the ambitious imperialism of Chamberlain.

▶ **Chamberlain** sent an army to the Cape, which Kruger regarded as a threat; he asked that it be withdrawn. Chamberlain refused and in October the Boers declared war on Britain.

The **Second Boer War** fell almost naturally into three periods:

▶ **October 1899–January 1900:** the Boers had larger forces and took the offensive. They beseiged British forces in Ladysmith (in Natal), Kimberley (in the Cape) and Mafeking (in Bechuanaland). In December 1899 there was a 'Black Week', when British attempts to relieve these towns failed.

▶ **February 1900–August 1900** Lord Roberts and Lord Kitchener led large armies which relieved the besieged towns and captured Johannesburg and Pretoria, the capital of the Transvaal.

▶ **The guerrilla war** Many people thought that the Boers would now give in, but they continued to fight a guerrilla war. Kitchener enclosed large areas inside lines of barbed wire guarded by blockhouses. Behind the wire he destroyed farm houses where friendly families might have helped the Boers. Women and children were interned in concentration camps, where bad hygiene and poor administration caused thousands of deaths among civilians. This period came to an end when the Boers agreed to the Treaty of Vereeniging.

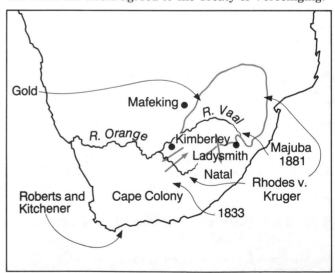

Fig. 35.5 A map of Southern Africa which examiners have used as a basis for questions. You should be able to write a few sentences about each of the names and dates shown in the illustration.

THE TREATY OF VEREENIGING, 1902

In this it was agreed that:
▶ the Transvaal and the Orange Free State were annexed by Britain;
▶ the Boers were promised self-rule;
▶ £3 million was to be paid as compensation for damage to Boer farms.

It was left to a later Liberal government to negotiate with the Boers and to arrive at the settlement which led to the formation of the **Union of South Africa** (1909) in which:

▶ The two British colonies, Cape of Good Hope (with responsible government since 1872) and Natal (which had been self-governing since 1893) were linked with the former Boer Republics of Transvaal and the Orange Free State, which gained self-government in 1907.
▶ All four states adopted common policies on customs, railways and attitudes towards the black population.

SALISBURY'S RESIGNATION

In **1900** Salisbury gave up the post of Foreign Secretary. His successor, Lord Lansdowne, worked to find allies for Britain (unit 36), and Salisbury called an election.

The people voted for the government in this 'khaki', or wartime, election. The Tories won 402 seats and had an overall majority of 134 seats. In 1902 Salisbury made way for Balfour.

35.6 Balfour

BALFOUR'S DOMESTIC POLICIES, 1902–05

▶ **The Education Act, 1902** (discussed on p. 106). Here you should note that it angered Nonconformists and helped reunite the Liberals, who had been divided over the Boer War.
▶ **The Taff Vale Judgment** attacked union power. Balfour rejected union appeals for amending legislation, thus ensuring the growth of the still struggling Labour Party (unit 40).
▶ **Tariff Reform** (p. 68) divided the party, but Balfour refused to come down on one side or the other.

BALFOUR'S FOREIGN POLICY, 1902–05

Lansdowne was Foreign Secretary and he negotiated:
▶ the Anglo-Japanese Alliance, 1902 (p. 88);
▶ the Anglo-French Entente, 1904 (p. 88).
In so doing, he paved the way for the Anglo-Russian Entente negotiated by Grey in the Liberal government (p. 88).

35.7 The 1906 Election

The Balfour government, divided over Tariff Reform, staggered along until the end of 1905, when it resigned to make way for a Liberal government led by Sir Henry Campbell-Bannerman, who called for an election in January 1906.

The Liberals won 377 seats, the Conservatives 157, the Irish 83, Labour 29 and trade unionist Lib-Labs 24. The reasons for this major swing to the Liberals were:
▶ **Tory disunity**, with some candidates supporting Chamberlain and others opposing him;
▶ **Tory unpopularity** because of:
● memories of the inefficiency during the Boer War (p. 86);
● publication of the news that Chinese coolies were being brought to work in South African mines in slave-like conditions, with government approval;
● the Education Act, 1902 (p. 106);
● the Taff Vale case (p. 96).
▶ **Liberal promises** to bring in some social reforms and a Trade Union Bill to undo the harm of Taff Vale.
▶ **A pact** between the Liberals and Labour leaders.

THE SIGNIFICANCE OF THAT ELECTION

▶ The Liberals had a sufficient majority to push through their reforms (unit 37).
▶ Labour had become a major party for the first time.
▶ The Irish did not get their Home Rule Bill until the Liberals were much weaker (p. 92).
▶ Chamberlain had a stroke and retired from politics. Tariff Reform did not go away and it was his son, Neville, who, in 1932 was the Minister in charge of bringing in the British tariffs which ended Britain's traditional Free Trade policy (p. 123).

> ### Unit 35 Summary
> ▶ Salisbury and the fall of Randolph Churchill, 1886.
> ▶ Salisbury's domestic and foreign policies, 1886–92.
> ▶ Africa: the Boer War, 1899–1902.
> ▶ Balfour as Prime Minister, 1902–05.

36 FOREIGN AFFAIRS, 1890–1914

36.1 Bismarck's Alliances

After defeating France in 1871, Bismarck needed a long period of peace so that the newly united Germany might develop her industrial power. He knew that France might wish to take revenge, so he organized a system of alliances.

The Dreikaiser Bund or Three Emperors' League, 1872

In 1872 Bismarck persuaded the rulers of Austria and Russia to join with the German Emperor in a League in which they agreed:
▶ to be friendly towards each other;
▶ to guard against the spread of republicanism from France. This isolated France. Bismarck persuaded her to look for compensation in the form of colonies in Asia and Africa. This brought her into conflict with Britain in southeast Asia (p. 85) and the Sudan (p. 86).

The Dual Alliance 1879

Russia and Austria were rivals in the Balkans. In 1878 at the Congress of Berlin, Bismarck supported Austria's claims and so angered Russia. In 1879 he went further and signed an alliance with Austria, in which it was agreed that:
▶ if Germany were attacked by only one Power (e.g. France), Austria would remain neutral, but would come to Germany's aid if she were attacked by two Powers;
▶ Germany would side with Austria if Austria went to war with Russia.
This secret Treaty was of more use to Austria than to Germany. It was not known to Russia, which therefore agreed to sign, in **1881** and **1884**, the Renewal of the Dreikaiser Bund. Continuing unrest in the Balkans between 1885 and 1887 led to Russian hostility to Austria. However, Bismarck, anxious to maintain peace, persuaded Russia to sign the **Reinsurance Treaty, 1887**, with Germany.

The Triple Alliance, 1882

This brought Italy into alliance with Germany and Austria, because Italy wanted support in her conflict with France, which had seized Tunisia in 1881.

36.2 The Franco-Russian Alliance, 1894

Bismarck was dismissed by the young Kaiser, William II, in 1890 and the Reinsurance Treaty was not renewed. This left Russia isolated – as was France. An alliance between these two was unlikely because France was a democratic Republic, while Russia was ruled by the autocratic Tsar and because France and Russia had clashed over religion and power in 1853–56 (p. 54). But the French realized their need for an ally. The French provided loans to help Russian industrialization and this helped improve relations between the two countries, who went on to sign an Alliance in 1894. Europe was now divided into two Armed Camps.

36.3 Britain and the Armed Camps

In 1895 Britain was more friendly to the Triple Alliance than to the new Dual Alliance because:
▶ the royal families of Britain and Germany were related;
▶ they shared a common form of anti-Catholic religion;
▶ Bismarck had carefully avoided taking any action, in colonies or trade, which might have angered the British.
  Britain's relations with the Dual Alliance showed that:
▶ she feared Russian influence in the Balkans and China;
▶ she feared French influence in south-east Asia and Africa, and almost came to war with France in 1898 (p. 86);
▶ she had signed the 'Mediterranean Agreement' with Italy in 1887 as an anti-French and pro-Triple Alliance move.
  It is perhaps not surprising that in 1898 Chamberlain should have tried to arrange a treaty of friendship involving Germany, the USA and Britain. Germany wanted Britain formally to join the Triple Alliance, but Britain refused to do so.

36.4 Foreign Policy, 1902–07

The British needed the help of colonial troops from Australia, Canada and New Zealand to defeat a small nation like the Boers. The immediate effect of this was to force Britain to look for friends in Europe and Asia.

THE ANGLO-JAPANESE ALLIANCE, 1902

This was Britain's first formal Alliance for many years and came as a surprise to many who did not realize that **Russia** was threatening British influence in China, and that **Japan** had emerged as a major power with her defeat of China, and her powerful industrial system.
  Both countries needed a friend in the Far East, both countries shared a naval interest, and both were opposed to Russia. In the Alliance it was agreed that:
▶ if either country was involved in a war with only one other country, then the other Allied power would remain neutral.
▶ only if one Ally was attacked by two or more Powers would the other Ally come to the aid of her partner.
  Japan could now consider a war with Russia, knowing that she would have the support of Britain if France joined Russia.

ANGLO-GERMAN HOSTILITY, 1895–1904

The traditional friendship between these two countries changed into increasing hostility owing to:
▶ **The Kaiser's attitude**, due in part to his envy of Britain's greater power and to his wish to outshine his mother's native country. This was reflected in:
● **the Naval Bills**, the first of which was signed in 1898 and by which the Kaiser set out to build a powerful fleet. The British needed a large fleet to guard the Empire and trade routes. The growing German fleet could only be intended for use in a war against Britain;
● **the Kruger telegram**, which the Kaiser sent to congratulate the Boers on their success against the Jameson Raid (p. 86);
● **the Damascus speech** in which the Kaiser, on a visit to the Middle East, promised to act as the supporter of Muslims. Britain with its interests in India, Egypt and Persia felt that this was an attack on her;
● **the Berlin-Baghdad railway**, built through the Balkans and Constantinople, was seen by Britain as a German attempt to gain influence in this region. With the defeat of Russia by Japan in 1904, fear of Russia was replaced by fear of Germany in the decaying Turkish Empire.
▶ **Commercial rivalry** due to Germany's increasing industrial power.
▶ **Colonial rivalry** in south-west Africa and the Pacific.

THE ANGLO-FRENCH ENTENTE, 1904

This agreement of friendship (not an alliance) was the result of:
▶ both countries' fear of Germany;
▶ King Edward VII's suspicions of his nephew, the Kaiser. He lent his support to Lord Lansdowne, the Foreign Secretary who tried to improve relations between Britain and France;
▶ Delcassé, the French Foreign Minister, who was anxious to gain friends against Germany;
▶ the ending of French hostility to Britain (over Fashoda and during the Boer War) by a state visit by Edward VII to France, when he praised France as the home of European culture and pretty women. President Loubet came on a return visit to Britain and the Entente was signed in which:
● France recognized British domination of Egypt;
● Britain recognized French domination of Morocco;
▶ long-standing disagreement over Newfoundland fishing rights were settled and would no longer be a potential cause of war.

THE ANGLO-RUSSIAN ENTENTE, 1907

This came about because:
▶ both countries were hostile to Germany;
▶ both had a common friend in France;
▶ the defeat of Russia by Japan (1904–5) showed that Britain had less to fear from Russia than from Germany.
  In this agreement the two countries settled their differences over:
▶ **Persia**, with each agreeing to have a 'sphere of influence' in different parts of the country;
▶ **Afghanistan** and **Tibet**, with Russia agreeing to keep out of these countries, which bordered on British India.

36.5 The Three Crises, 1906–11

1906 Algeciras

The Anglo-French Entente had been signed by the Conservative government. It annoyed the Kaiser because it gave France a friend who might become an ally, and it divided North Africa up without his being involved. He though that the Liberals might not support the Entente.
  In 1906 he tried to break the Entente.
▶ The French had forced the Sultan of Morocco to accept their proposals for a reform of the Moroccan government.
▶ The Kaiser claimed that he would not allow this, and appeared to be a champion of Moroccan rights.
▶ He demanded an international conference to discuss the affair, and made warlike preparations which frightened the French government, who dismissed Delcassé for arranging the Entente.

▶ The conference took place at Algeciras and was a disaster for Germany because:
● Britain and the USA supported France;
● France was given control of the Moroccan bank and police;
● the British and French army staffs started a series of talks in which their generals agreed as to how each would use its forces in the event of a war with Germany. This had not been part of the original Entente but had come about because of German action.

1908 Bosnia and Herzegovina

As if in answer to the signing of the Anglo-Russian Entente, Austria took advantage of the 'Young Turk' revolution and announced the annexation of Bosnia and Herzegovina, which she had administered since the Congress of Berlin (p. 77). This angered Serbia, who appealed to Russia. But Russia, still recovering from the disaster of the war with Japan, was too weak to help. Her ally, France, and her friend, Britain, were unwilling to support her, so that Austria got away with her 'grab', which made her even more ambitious, while it made Serbia even more angry.

1911 Agadir

In 1911 there were a number of risings against the inefficient Sultan of Morocco. France sent an army to Fez to restore order. The Kaiser feared that France might be about to annex Morocco, so he sent a German warship, the *Panther*, to the Moroccan Port of Agadir, claiming that he was protecting German businessmen in the country. This move succeeded in:
▶ alarming the Foreign Secretary, Grey, who feared that Germany might be going to build a port on the Moroccan coast;
▶ angering the pacifist Lloyd George, Chancellor of the Exchequer, who told the Lord Mayor's Mansion House guests that Britain might well have to go to war if her interests were threatened. A conference was called to try to resolve the matter.

In Paris it was agreed that:
▶ Germany should have two slices of the Congo as compensation for not having got anything in the division of North Africa;

Fig. 36.5 A map of North West Africa and South West Europe in the 20th century. You should be able to name the territory marked A, and the towns marked 1, 2 and 3. Examiners will expect explanations of the importance of these places.

▶ the *Panther* was withdrawn and France given a free hand.

More significantly, the British and French started on a series of Naval talks, which led to an agreement which said that:
▶ in the event of a war involving either country, the French fleet would be concentrated in the Mediterranean to guard the south coast of France and British interests in the Mediterranean;
▶ the British fleet would guard France's north coast.

36.6 Britain Prepares for War

Haldane was War Minister in charge of the Army. He had agreed to the talks with the French in 1906. He also set about reforming the British Army by:
▶ creating a **General Staff** to take command of the Army;
▶ setting up an **Expeditionary Force** of six infantry divisions and one cavalry division to be kept prepared to be sent to the Continent once war was declared;
▶ forming the **Territorial Army** of volunteers who met regularly to get some military training. They would defend the country when the regular army was sent overseas;
▶ encouraging the public schools to set up **Officers Training Corps** in which older pupils would get military training while at school. They would be better prepared to become officers in the event of war.

Sir John Fisher was the First Sea Lord. He had seen how the German Navy had grown and had ships which were more modern and better armed than ships in the Royal Navy. He campaigned for a new type of ship, the **Dreadnought**. In 1909 the Navy asked for six such ships; Lloyd George, the Chancellor said the country could afford none; the Cabinet agreed to find the money for four – and then decided to build eight.

36.7 Britain Enters the First World War, August 1914

In unit 32 we examined the Eastern Question. We saw that:
▶ in 1912–13 the countries of the Balkans League fought to defeat Turkey, then fought over the spoils;
▶ the Serbs became more ambitious and aggressive;
▶ Austria decided to teach Serbia a lesson;
▶ Germany, fearing the growing power of Russia and France, decided to back Austria and risk a war with France and Russia, believing that she could win such a war;
▶ the Archduke Franz Ferdinand was murdered at Sarajevo;
▶ Austrian demands to Serbia led to 'war by timetable', in which the main dates were:
● **24th July** Serb acceptance of most of Austria's demands with a request for time to consider the others.
● **25th July** Austria's refusal to grant this time and Russian announcement that she would have to mobilize her forces.
● **28th July** Austria's declaration of war against Serbia.
● **30th July** Russia ordered partial mobilization. Germany demanded that Russia call off her mobilization.
● **1st August** When Russia refused to do so Germany declared war on Russia and on France.

Britain was hardly involved in these negotiations. In spite of the naval agreements with France, Britain did not enter the war until after Germany invaded Belgium. The reasons for the invasion were:
▶ the **Schlieffen Plan** for the speedy defeat of France – which would allow German forces to then turn on Russia;
▶ this Plan, drawn up in 1905, demanded a massive drive across Belgium and Northern France, around Paris and back towards Germany;
▶ on 2nd August Germany asked Belgium for permission to send troops through that country. When this was refused, Germany invaded Belgium on 4th August. Since 1839 Britain had insisted on the neutrality of Belgium (p. 50);

On 3rd August the King of the Belgians asked for British help in the event of a German invasion, and following the German refusal to withdraw on 4th August, Britain declared war on Germany. It is worth noting that Grey, the Foreign Minister, and Asquith, the Prime Minister, had, by their policies and promises, virtually pledged British support to France. It is likely that they would have tried to persuade Parliament to aid France even if Germany had not invaded Belgium.

Unit 36 Summary

▶ Bismarck and European alliances, 1870–1890.
▶ Europe in two armed camps, 1894.
▶ Britain and the armed camps, 1870–1900.
▶ The Anglo-Japanese Alliance, 1902.
▶ The growth of Anglo-German hostility, 1895–1904.
▶ The Ententes with France and Russia.
▶ Three crises, 1906–11: Algeciras, Bosnia, Agadir.
▶ Britain, Belgium and the entry into war, August 1914.

---

37 THE LIBERALS, 1906–14

37.1 'Old' and 'New' Liberalism

▶ **Gladstonian Liberalism** had three main features; Peace, Retrenchment and Reform (pp. 70–1). It was in step with the principles of **laissez-faire** and of the **self-help** preached by Samuel Smiles.
▶ **Chamberlain** had tried, in 1885, to get the Liberal Party to take a more 'socialist' turn by providing state aid for the old, poor, unemployed and badly housed. Gladstone rejected this.
▶ **The Boer War** had divided the Liberals even further, with the leaders supporting the government once war had been declared, while a minority led by Lloyd George were pro-Boer and anti-government.

37.2 Social Problems

In spite of Liberal rejections of 'socialism', and Salisbury's refusal to follow Disraeli's path despite Churchill's insistence, the demand for government involvement in social affairs grew because of:
▶ **The Report of the Royal Commission on Labour, 1895** proved that working people could not earn enough to provide basic necessities (p. 85).
▶ **Charles Booth's** massive survey, *Life and Labour of the People in London* (1891), which proved that about one-third of the people lived in grinding poverty. Booth, a Liverpool shipowner, wanted to disprove the arguments of the 'socialists'. His survey proved how right these left-wingers were.
▶ **Seebohm Rowntree's** *Poverty; a study in town life* (1902). Rowntree, the York chocolate-maker, had read Booth's work and wanted to prove that its findings did not apply to York, where he was the largest employer. His survey showed that, as in London, about one-third of the people lived in grinding poverty, owing to one or more of the following:
● old age;
● unemployment;
● underemployment, so that men only worked for part of a week;
● low wages;
● large families;
● sickness;
● the death of the wage-earner.
▶ **The Boer War**, during which it was found that over half of those who volunteered for the forces failed the simple medical test.

▶ **Surveys, reports and novels** by a variety of authors, including Henry George (*Progress and Poverty*), Robert Blatchford (*Merrie England*), Jack London (*People of the Abyss*), William Booth of the Salvation Army (*In Darkest England* and *The Way Out*), all of which proved the existence of great poverty.

Because of poverty there were accompanying social problems such as:
▶ **ill-health:** many working people were too frequently away from work, thus adding to their poverty.
▶ **inadequate housing:** many people could not afford the rent for decent housing, and consequently became more prone to illness because of the conditions in which they lived;
▶ **the cycle of poverty** first noted by Rowntree, who showed how a child born into a poor family lived in poverty until he was old enough to get a job and leave home. For a few years he might then live above the poverty line, but when he married and had children his family slipped into poverty. This happened because children from poor families had insufficient education, little work-skill and small chance of getting full-time employment at a decent wage.

THE GROWTH OF SOCIALISM

Socialism, for the late Victorians and the Edwardians, meant that the state (or government) ought to compel the people (or society) to cooperate to overcome social problems.

'Gas and Water' Socialism was the term applied to the results of the work of Chadwick (p. 45) and Chamberlain (p. 83) with their environmental reforms.

Many people, including those in societies formed at the end of the nineteenth century, demanded that government ought to develop **personal services** for those whose poverty prevented them from helping themselves. There was a demand for such things as state pensions, subsidized housing, and a state health service.

37.3 New Liberalism, 1906–14

We have seen why the Liberals won the 1906 Election and by how great a majority. Campbell-Bannerman, as Prime Minister, had Asquith as his Chancellor, Lloyd George at the Board of Trade and Winston Churchill as an active Radical Liberal supporting Lloyd George. When Campbell-Bannerman retired because of ill-health in 1908, Asquith became Prime Minister, Lloyd George, Chancellor and Churchill went to the Board of Trade. It was these three who were the main creators of the Liberal reforms of this period.

LIBERAL REFORMS, 1906–08
Workmen's Compensation, 1906

This extended the terms of the 1897 Act (p. 85). Employers were forced to pay compensation to any workman earning less than £200 a year, who might have been injured at work.

Reforms affecting children

▶ **The School Meals Act,** 1906 allowed local authorities to provide a school meals service for the very poor. 'Old' Liberals attacked this as an interference with parental responsibility.

▶ **The Schools Medical Inspection Service,** 1907 was set up to allow doctors and nurses to visit schools regularly to inspect all the children at least once a year. It was hoped that this might allow a better attack on preventible diseases.

▶ **Juvenile Courts** were set up in which magistrates could deal separately with young offenders, for whom Borstals were built.

▶ **Shop Acts** made it illegal to sell alcohol, tobacco and fireworks to children.

▶ **Working hours** for children in spare-time jobs at weekends or after school were limited.

▶ **The Education Act,** 1907 provided opportunities for working-class children to go, free, to secondary (Grammar) schools.

Old age pensions, 1908–09

In 1908 Parliament passed the Old Age Pensions Act by which, from 6th January 1909, people aged 70 or over were to get 5s (25p) a week, payable at the Post Office, provided that they had less than £21 a year from any other source. You should note that:

▶ although it seems a small amount, the first pension was equal to about one-quarter of the unskilled worker's wages;

PUNCH, OR THE LONDON CHARIVARI—January 6, 1909.

THE NEW YEAR'S GIFT.

Fig. 37.3 A welcome for the Old Age Pension.

▶ many books still repeat the error that married pensioners received a total of 7/6d (37½p). This was, in fact, a provision of the original Bill but it was dropped during the debate. Married pensioners received, each, their own 5s (25p).

The Trades Disputes Act, 1906

This undid the damage done by the Taff Vale Judgment (p. 96).

REFORMS MADE BY THE ASQUITH GOVERNMENT, 1909–14

The Trade Boards Act, 1909

This Act set up Boards of Government officials to supervise the conditions of work and pay of people employed in occupations (often called 'sweated industries') not covered by Factory Acts.

The Labour Exchanges Act, 1909

This Act set up a chain of Labour Exchanges throughout the country where, it was hoped:

▶ employers would send information of labour required;

▶ the unemployed would go to get information of work available. With the passing of the National Insurance Act (see below) these exchanges were also used as the offices where the unemployed drew their benefit.

National Insurance, 1911: Part 1, National Health Insurance

You should make sure that you understand the difference between the two parts of this Act, the second of which dealt with unemployment (see below). You should also ensure that you understand how limited the proposals were, so that you do not confuse them with the modern National Health Service, which had its beginnings in 1948. The 1911 Act set up a National Health Insurance scheme, but only for manual workers earning less than £160 a year.

In this scheme:

▶ the insured workman paid 4 pence each week into an Insurance Fund; his employer paid 3 pence and the state added 2 pence; ('9 pence for 4 pence' was a slogan used by Lloyd George; the total of 9 pence was roughly equal to 3½p in present-day money);

▶ the workman was entitled to receive free medical attention from a doctor paid out of the fund;

▶ if absent from work owing to illness, he would receive 10s (50p) a week for a maximum of 26 weeks, after which he could claim a disability pension of 5s (25p);

▶ workmen who became ill owing to tuberculosis (a 'killer' disease at that time) were entitled to special hospital treatment;

▶ wives of insured workers were entitled to a maternity benefit of 30s (£1.50) after the birth of a baby.

You ought now to make a list of the treatments available under the modern NHS which were not covered by the 1911 scheme, and notice also that the scheme did not apply to families, but only to the insured workmen.

National Insurance, 1911: Part 2, Unemployment Insurance

Here again you need to ensure that you understand the scheme and its limitations.

▶ It only applied to men in certain construction industries.

▶ An Unemployment Fund was built up out of contributions by the insured workmen (2½ pence a week) and their employers (2½ pence).

▶ When unemployed, an insured workman was entitled to 7s (35p) a week for a maximum of 15 weeks, payable at one of the Labour Exchanges.

Notice:

▶ how few men were covered by the scheme;

▶ that it was a flat rate scheme which did not take account of workers' families;

▶ that the benefit was paid for only 15 weeks.

The Trade Union Act, 1913

This Act undid the damage done by the Osborne Judgment (p. 96).

37.4 The Budget, 1909

(This was later called **'the People's Budget'**.) In planning for these reforms, the Chancellor, Lloyd George, had to plan for the collection of extra revenue to pay for them. He had also to find the money for the military and naval reforms (p. 89). In his 1909 Budget he proposed:

▶ an increase in income tax from 5p in the £ to just under 7p for those with incomes above £3000 a year;

▶ a super-tax of an extra 6 pence (2½p) for those whose incomes were above £5000 a year;

▶ an increase in the rate of death duties;

▶ a new land tax – which had to be dropped because it was found too difficult to enforce.

THE LORDS AND THE BUDGET

This Budget and its proposals for tax increases, coupled with the social reforms which had already been outlined or passed, aroused the anger of the richer classes and in particular of the House of Lords. The Budget had a rough ride:

▶ **The Commons** debated it from April to November 1909 – an unusually long time for a Budget debate. The Conservatives were determined to try to prevent its passage, but failed.

▶ **The Lords** rejected the Budget on 30th November 1909, the first time that the Lords had ever rejected a Budget.

37.5 Reforming The Lords

THE LORDS AND THE LIBERALS

▶ **Balfour** claimed that, in spite of the Liberals' majority in the Commons, the Conservatives, through their power in the Lords, would continue to run the country.

▶ **The Lords** had either rejected or severely changed Liberal proposals for Education, Licensing and the Welsh Church. It seemed as if Balfour was right.

▶ **The electorate**, which had given the Liberals such a massive majority in 1906 had, by 1909, already begun to turn against them. By-election results showed a swing to the Conservatives.

▶ **The Liberals**, angered by the powers of the Lords and worried at the state of public opinion, decided to take the Lords on in a constitutional struggle.

THE ELECTION, JANUARY 1910

The rejection of the Budget forced the government to call an Election, which resulted in a stalemate, although the Conservatives regarded it as a victory. The Liberals won 275 seats, the Tories 273, with the Irish once again, as in 1885–86, holding the balance, along with the small number of Labour MPs. To ensure the passage of the Budget through the Commons, the Liberals had to win the support of the Irish who demanded:

▶ the promise of a Home Rule Bill;

▶ an Act to ensure that such a Bill could not be rejected in the Lords, as in 1893 (p. 80).

REFORMING THE LORDS BY AGREEMENT

In May 1910 a new King, George V, came to the throne. He called leaders of all parties to a Conference at Buckingham Palace, in the hope that they might agree on solutions to the problem of the Lords and Ireland.

These negotiations broke down and the Liberals then introduced a Parliament Bill which, after passing through the Commons, was rejected in the Lords.

THE SECOND ELECTION, 1910

In December 1910 Asquith was forced to call another Election over the Lords' problem. Again, the result was a stalemate; the Liberals and the Conservatives each won 272 seats.

THE PARLIAMENT ACT, 1911

The Parliament Bill was again passed through the Commons, but again, the Lords seemed likely to reject it. Consequently, Asquith got the King to agree to the creation, if necessary, of enough Liberal Peers to ensure its passage.

Lansdowne, leader of the Lords, persuaded many Tories ('the Hedgers') to abstain, to allow the Bill through rather than have their Peerages devalued by a mass creation; Lord Halsbury, led a small group who wanted to fight to the last ditch ('the Ditchers').

On 4th August 1911 the Lords passed the Bill, which then became law with its main clauses saying:

▶ **Money Bills** passed by the Commons had to be passed by the Lords.

▶ **Other Bills** might be rejected in the Lords. But if a Bill was passed by the Commons in three successive sessions (and note it is not **years** but **sessions**), then, although the Lords might have rejected it twice, it had to be passed on the third occasion. This gave the Lords a **suspensive veto**.

▶ MPs were to have a salary for the first time, £400 p.a.

▶ **Elections** had to be held at least every five years and not, as prior to 1911, every seven years.

This Act was a culmination of a process which had started with the Reform Act of 1832 (p. 38) and which led to the growth of democracy and the power of the Commons over the Lords.

37.6 Other Features of the Liberal Governments

Other units examine in detail the Liberal policies on:

▶ Ireland (unit 33)

▶ Trade Unions (unit 39)

▶ Education (unit 42)

▶ Foreign Affairs (unit 36)

▶ Women (unit 41)

Unit 37 Summary

▶ Meaning of 'New' Liberalism.

▶ The growth of social problems and of 'socialism'.

▶ Liberal reforms, 1906–11, for working people, children, the unemployed, sick and aged.

▶ The 1909 Budget and the Parliament Act, 1911.

38 PARLIAMENTARY REFORM, 1860–1928

38.1 1832, The Final Solution

▶ **Lord John Russell** spoke of the 1832 Act as the final solution to the reform problem. He earned the nickname of 'Finality Jack'.

▶ **Sir Robert Peel** spoke of the 1832 Act as 'a final and irrevocable settlement' in his Tamworth Manifesto (unit 19).

▶ **The Chartists** failed to obtain further reforms.

▶ **Palmerston**, easily the most influential politician in the 1850s and the early 1860s, was opposed to further reform.

38.2 The Pressures for Reform

A new working class had emerged by 1860, largely owing to the continuing industrial revolution. This new class had proved itself to be responsible and deserving of consideration by:

▶ **education**; from their own money, workers provided a network of Mechanics' Institutes with reading rooms, games rooms and lecture halls, where they went to listen to University lecturers;

▶ **savings**; the working class had learned to save part of their money in:

● the newly formed Building Societies;

● savings banks such as the Yorkshire Penny Bank;

● the Post Office Savings Bank set up by Gladstone in 1861. By 1866 over 650 000 of them had Post Office Savings Books;

▶ **political activity**; they had formed responsible trade unions such as the ASE (unit 25), through which they provided their own form of self-help and social security. They had also shown during the American Civil War that they were prepared to support the 'right' cause even if this meant hardship because of the drop in the import of raw cotton from the USA.

Convinced **politicians** such as Bright began to appreciate the changed nature of the working class. In the 1860s Bright used the arguments which had been used by the middle class in 1830–32 when they were asking for the vote, but he used these arguments in favour of giving the vote to the working class. It was Bright who converted Gladstone to the idea of further reform.

In the USA and in many colonies such as Australia, New Zealand and Canada, there was a wider democracy than there was in Britain. The visit of the Italian hero, Garibaldi, was used by the Radicals such as Bright to whip up support for attacks on the existing Parliamentary system.

Palmerston's death in 1865 released a flood of reform — as can be seen from the list of reforms passed during Gladstone's First Ministry (unit 29).

38.3 Gladstone's Bill, 1866

Gladstone proposed that the franchise should be given to all adult males who were inhabitants or owners of houses rated at £5 a year, instead of the £10 a year as agreed in 1832 (p. 38). This proposal would have given the vote to a small number of better-off workers, but was bitterly opposed by **Robert Lowe** and other Whigs. Lowe was afraid that such a reform would lead to mob rule. Bright nicknamed Lowe's followers **'the Adullamites'**, after a Biblical tribe which hid away in the darkness of a cave because it was afraid to face the world as it really was.

The proposal was defeated by a combination of Tory and Whig votes, which led to Gladstone's resignation and to the Derby Ministry in which Disraeli was Chancellor.

38.4 Disraeli's Reform Act, 1867

It may seem surprising that a Conservative government should have brought in a Reform Bill because:

▶ the Party had opposed the 1832 proposals;

▶ Peel had accepted 1832 as a final settlement;

▶ the Party traditionally had been against change.

But Disraeli was an opportunist. He realized that:

▶ Gladstone would come back again with reform proposals;

▶ the Conservatives needed to win a wider support if they were ever to form a majority government;

▶ it was essential to get rid of the idea that the Party was opposed to reform.

In fact, Disraeli had proposed Parliamentary reform when the Derby–Disraeli government held office in 1859. Now in 1867 he brought forward new proposals.

At first Disraeli's proposals were much like Gladstone's, but in Cabinet some people argued that there was no logic in a £5 franchise. Why not £4 or £3? Gradually they came to the point where the Bill contained no mention of money at all.

Lord Cranborne, later Lord Salisbury, who would lead the country and the Party (unit 35), resigned in protest against this wide extension of democracy. In the Commons, Disraeli's proposals were supported by Gladstone's supporters, opposed by Lowe and Cranborne, but accepted by the majority.

In 1867, the Reform Act gave **the vote** to:

▶ every male adult householder living in a borough constituency;

▶ male lodgers paying £10 a year for unfurnished rooms.

This gave the franchise to about 1½ million voters. The Act also dealt with **constituencies**:

▶ boroughs with less than 10 000 inhabitants lost one of their MPs.

PUNCH, OR THE LONDON CHARIVARI.—August 3, 1867.

A LEAP IN THE DARK.

Fig. 38.4 A contemporary cartoon on Disraeli's Reform Bill, 1867. The British people (represented by Britannia) are being carried by the horse (representing Disraeli) towards the hedge of reform. Onlookers appear to be as frightened as the rider.

▶ the 45 seats left available were redistributed by:
● giving 15 to towns which had never had an MP;
● giving one extra seat each to some larger towns – Liverpool, Manchester, Birmingham and Leeds;
● creating a seat for the University of London, which thus came on a par with Oxford and Cambridge;
● giving 25 seats to counties whose population had increased since 1832.

38.5 Other Reforms

THE BALLOT ACT, 1872

The extension of the borough franchise meant that:
▶ It would be very expensive to bribe one's way to victory.
▶ Parties had to set up local organizations to ensure the registration of their potential supporters and the adequate covering of the constituency during election times. Chamberlain (p. 83) and Disraeli (p. 72) were the first to realize this.
▶ Candidates and parties had to offer policies which would win working-class support, since the working class now formed the majority in most borough constituencies.

Employers were still able to use their influence in some constituencies, however, because of the open system of voting. To bring this to an end, the Gladstone government brought in the **Ballot Act**, which set up the secret system of voting which we still use. No employer could now punish workmen for not voting as they had been told.

THE CORRUPT PRACTICES ACT, 1883

This Act specified how much money candidates could spend during election time, and banned such practices as the buying of food or drink for voters. Politicians had now to win support by promoting better policies.

THE THIRD REFORM ACT, 1884

The 1867 Act had dealt with the borough franchise and had said little about the franchise for **county constituencies**. In the 'Ministry of All The Troubles' (unit 31) Chamberlain and Bright campaigned for equal treatment for these constituencies. Salisbury, now leader of the Conservative Party, opposed this campaign because he feared that a wider democracy in the counties might bring to an end the Conservatives' hold on these constituencies.

Gladstone brought in a Bill which:
▶ having passed through the Commons was rejected by the Lords – a sign of the tension between the two Houses;
▶ passed through the Commons again and this time was allowed through the Lords after Gladstone had promised to bring in a further Bill on redistribution of seats;
▶ gave the counties the same franchise as the boroughs – adult male householders and £10 lodgers;
▶ added about 6 million new voters to the voting lists.

THE REDISTRIBUTION ACT, 1885

Seventy-nine towns with populations smaller than 15 000 lost their right to elect an MP, and 36 towns with populations between 15 000 and 50 000 lost one of their MPs and became single-member constituencies.

Towns with populations between 50 000 and 165 000 were given two seats, and larger towns and the county constituencies were divided into single member constituencies.

You should notice that Gladstone's government was defeated shortly after this Act was passed, but that no election could be held until the boundaries had been redrawn. This will help to explain the need for a minority government, under Salisbury in the summer and autumn of 1885 (p. 75).

VOTES FOR WOMEN

After the 1885 Act, about half the **adult males** in the country had the right to vote. Those who did not have the franchise included:
▶ those who shared their overcrowded houses with other families – which meant that they were not householders;
▶ those who lived with their parents – the father alone having the vote.

But all men could hope that one day they would acquire the household right to vote.

In 1867 John Stuart Mill failed to get Parliament to give women the franchise on the same terms as men. Women played little part in the country's **economic** life – they either did not work (if they were middle class or above) or they did menial and lowly paid work. They also played little part in the country's **social** life, as can be seen from:
▶ the small number who went on to higher education (unit 41);
▶ their loss of control of their own property once they were married. Only in 1882 did the Married Women's Property Act allow some of them to keep such property.

Their low economic and social status was reflected in their failure to gain the right to vote. We will examine their changing roles in unit 41.

THE POSITION OF THE LORDS

We still call the Lords the 'Upper House', a reflection of its once great powers in the nineteenth century:
▶ to block the 1832 Reform Bill until threatened with an influx of new Peers;
▶ to prevent the passage of part of Cardwell's reforms, until overruled by a Royal Warrant (p. 71);
▶ to reject the original 1884 Reform Bill;
▶ to reject the Home Rule Bill in 1893.

The growth of democracy in the constituencies and the changing nature of the kind of men who became MPs led to the demand for an examination of the power of the Lords. Gladstone said, in 1893, 'The Lords must amend or be amended'. Unit 37 examined how the amendment took place in 1911.

38.6 Democracy

In later units we will see how, when and why the franchise was extended to:
▶ all adult males by the 1918 Act (unit 45);
▶ women over the age of 30, by the 1918 Act (unit 45);
▶ all adult women, by the Act of 1928 (unit 47);
▶ over eighteens by an Act of 1969 (unit 55).

Unit 38 Summary

▶ The increasing demand for Parliamentary Reform after 1832.
▶ The 1867 Reform Act: 'surprising in its origins, decisive in its effects'.
▶ Minor reforms: Ballot Act, 1872; Corrupt Practices Act, 1883.
▶ Third Reform Act, 1885.
▶ Votes for women.
▶ The House of Lords, 1832–1911: the Parliament Act, 1911.

39.1 The Position in 1867–8

In unit 25 we saw:
▶ The development of the **Model Unions**.
▶ The **benefits** which these paid their members.
▶ The **control** which they had over their members.
▶ The uncertain **legal position** of unions as regards their right to prosecute dishonest officials.
▶ The **middle-class** hostility to trade unions.
▶ The calling of the first **TUC** even though this was not supported by the leaders of 'the Junta'.

GLADSTONE AND THE UNIONS, 1868–74

Some workers gained **the vote** in 1867 (unit 38). This gave them some political influence.
▶ **The Royal Commission on Unions** (p. 62) reported favourably on trade unionism in its Report of 1869.
▶ Gladstone then passed two Acts affecting trade unions:
● **The Trade Union Act, 1871** which permitted the formation of unions, set up a system by which they could register with the Registrar of Friendly Societies and bring cases before the courts when their 'property, right or claims to property' were involved.
● **The Criminal Law Amendment Act, 1871**, which was passed on the same day and which made picketing illegal. This limited the unions' powers to maintain a strike, while some lawyers thought that the Act meant that even to prepare an organization for a strike was forbidden.

UNIONS AND POLITICS, 1871–5

The unions were angered by Gladstone's legislation. The 'Junta' called a TUC to meet in London in March 1871, which set up a **Parliamentary Committee** to watch over legislation concerning trade unions.

Between 1871 and 1874 it campaigned for the repeal of the Criminal Law Amendment Act. In the **1874 Election**, candidates were asked for their views on this Act, and workers were advised to support candidates willing to promote its repeal.

Thirteen candidates were put forward by the Committee and two of them, **Macdonald** and **Burt** were elected, the first working-class MPs.

DISRAELI AND TRADE UNIONS, 1874–80

Following the 1874 Election, and on the advice of his Civil Servants, Disraeli allowed the introduction of two Acts concerning unions.
▶ **The Conspiracy and Protection of Property Act, 1875** made peaceful picketing lawful. It also said that anything which could legally be done by an individual could legally be done by a union.
▶ **The Employers and Workmen Act 1875** said that if an employer or workman broke his contract, he could be sued in the civil courts, where the guilty party could be made to pay damages. Before 1875 only workmen could be so sued, and only in the Criminal courts, where judges could impose prison sentences.

39.2 The Deprived Working Class

▶ **The Model Unions** only catered for a small minority of the working class. In 1888 there were only 200 000 members in 23 craft unions.
▶ **The 1867 Reform Act** had given the vote to only 1½ million working-class men.

▶ **The Post Office Savings Bank** had only 650 000 savers.
▶ The majority of workers in the 1860s and 1870s were:
● unskilled – which meant they earned low wages;
● often unemployed, particularly after the onset of the depression of the 1870s; even when they had work, they were often underemployed since they only worked part of the week or part of the day.

As a result of their poor economic conditions they also suffered from social deprivation as could be seen from:
● **their housing**, as described in Mearns' *The Bitter Cry of Outcast London* (1883) and in the surveys made by Booth and Rowntree (unit 37);
● **their clothing**, which was picked from dustbins and which can be seen in photographs of school children of the time;
● **their high rates of sickness and death**, both of which drove them and their families even further into poverty.

UNIONS FOR THE UNSKILLED – JOSEPH ARCH

In the 1850s and 1860s the skilled workers gave no thought to the unskilled workers. They accepted the principles of self-help, which taught that it was possible for men to get on by their own efforts.

Most of the skilled workers had in fact got on by their own efforts, being the children of less privileged workers, so Model Unions created by the skilled workers did not recruit members from the unskilled – who, in any case, could not have afforded the relatively high fees charged by those unions.

In the 1870s **Joseph Arch** organized a union for agricultural workers, among the least well paid and most deprived, particularly after the onset of the agricultural depression after 1873 (unit 27). Arch, a hedge-cutter and a Nonconformist preacher:
▶ set up the **National Agricultural Labourers' Union, 1872**;
● organized branches of the Union all over the country in 1872–73;
▶ met resistance from employers who refused to recognize the Union and, when the men went on strike in 1874, locked them out from work;
▶ had to admit defeat in 1874–75 when the men, facing starvation because the Union had little money to give them, accepted the employers' terms and returned to work.

Arch's Union collapsed and this seemed a proof that it was not possible to organize unions among unskilled workers, particularly if, like agricultural workers, they were poorly paid and worked in widely separated regions.

SOCIALIST SOCIETIES, 1880–1900

▶ **Self-help** had brought prosperity for the middle class and for a minority of the working class.
▶ **The majority** of the working class, however, received little benefit from the free working of the market, as can be seen from their wages, housing and clothing.
▶ A number of **influential books** showed that it was possible to organize society so that the wealth of the country might be used to provide a decent life for everyone (unit 37).
▶ A number of **societies** were formed to promote some of the ideas developed in these books. There were:
● **The Social Democratic Federation** (SDF) founded by an Old-Etonian Marxist, Henry Hyndman, who hoped to unite all radicals and all workers who wanted a change.
● **The Socialist League** formed by the poet William Morris when he broke away from the SDF in 1884.

● **The Fabian Society**, also formed in 1884, and whose intellectual members hoped that their pamphlets would compel politicians to produce policies aimed at improving social conditions.

UNSKILLED UNIONS, 1888–9

The SDF and other socialist societies were small bodies, but behaved like fervent apostles, preaching at factory gates. Some working-class men joined these societies and learned that life might be better.

Annie Besant, a left-wing journalist and a friend of Bradlaugh, (p. 74) organized the match-girls at **Bryant and Mays**, called a strike and forced the employers to increase the girls' wages to about 1½p an hour.

Will Thorne, a working-class member of the SDF, organized a Gas Workers' Union among the unskilled men at the gasworks of the London Gas Light and Coke Company. When the men threatened to strike, the company reduced their working day from 12 hours to 8 – without a reduction in pay.

39.3 The London Dockers' Strike, 1889

Many thousands of men were employed in London Docks. Some skilled workers had their own unions, but the mass of the workers were unskilled and had no union. Their conditions were deplorable:

▶ they stood at the dock gates waiting for foremen to call a few to come to load or unload a ship;

▶ when called, they received only 4d (less than 2p) an hour – and may have worked for only a couple of hours;

▶ if not called, they received nothing – as was the case for the majority and particularly the older men;

▶ they fought wildly with one another for a chance of a job – low paid though it was.

Ben Tillet, a member of the SDF organized a Tea Workers' and General Labourer's Union at Whitechapel. Tillet demanded that no one be taken on for less than four hours at a time and that labourers' wages be increased to 6d an hour (2½p) (the 'Dockers' Tanner'), with more for overtime.

The employers refused; the men came out on strike and most people expected the union's collapse.

▶ **The craft unions** at the Docks came out in sympathy with the unskilled men.

▶ **John Burns**, also a member of the SDF, organized the 100 000 men and their families on a series of marches through London, which drew attention to their working and living conditions.

▶ **Money** came from public collections, from other unions and from the Australian Dockers, who sent £30 000.

The strike lasted for five weeks. It was ended when the employers agreed to meet a **Mediation Committee**, set up at the Lord Mayor's Mansion House.

Cardinal Manning, as chairman of the Committee, brought the two sides to an agreement by which the men got their 6d (2½p), and **Tillett** became full-time secretary of the Dock, Riverside and General Labourers' Union.

OTHER UNSKILLED MEN

The success of the Dockers led to the formation of other unskilled unions – in the textile trade and in the building industry. There was even a General Labourers' Union for workmen in any or every trade and industry.

But these unions, like the Dockers, had no funds because their members earned very low wages and could not afford 1d a month in fees.

Neither did they have much organization since their officials could not afford to travel around the country.

They were, however, much larger than the craft unions and they were more militant and willing to call strikes to get their way. Between 1890 and 1900 the number of trade unionists doubled reaching two million by 1900.

39.4 The Older Unions Change Policies

The leaders of the craft unions were frightened by the growth of the large, militant, unskilled unions. They feared that at future meetings of the TUC these unions would gain control, because they would have more votes than the smaller, craft unions.

To try to prevent this, the craft unions changed their rules. They recruited unskilled members at lower fees – and smaller benefits. With the continuing depression in the 1890s, however, some craft workers demanded that their unions become as militant as the unskilled workers.

THE NEW UNIONS AND POLITICS

The New Unions (the terms given to the unskilled unions) could only win small wage increases for their members. Unskilled workers could still not afford adequate housing; they were still unable to afford to save for their old age or to take out insurance policies, as could the better-paid workers.

They would need Parliamentary legislation if they were to get state pensions, subsidized housing, unemployment benefit and other social security provisions.

Neither Gladstone's Liberals nor Salisbury's Conservatives were willing to provide such legislation. This drove the leaders of the unskilled workers to help form a new political party, as we shall see in unit 40.

39.5 The Unions and The Law

TAFF VALE, 1900–02

In 1900, members of the Amalgamated Society of Railway Servants (ASRS) – now the NUR – came out on strike against the Taff Railway Company in South Wales. The union later made the strike an official one.

When the strike was over, the Company sued the union, claiming compensation for the damage done to company property and for the losses suffered by the company because of the strike.

The case was finally settled by the Law Lords in the House of Lords who decided that:

▶ the union had to pay £23 000 damages to the company;

▶ it had also to pay £19 000 in legal costs.

This decision meant that unions would be less likely to go on strike. This, in turn, meant that they had little chance of winning an argument with employers.

In unit 37 we saw that it was this decision and the government's refusal to bring in amending legislation which:

▶ made the unions even more anti-Conservative and helped to explain the result of the 1906 Election (p. 87);

▶ drove the skilled workers into the Labour organization, set up largely by unskilled unions (p. 100);

▶ forced the Liberals to promise to bring in a new Act if they won the 1906 Election.

The Trade Disputes Act, 1906 promoted by the newly elected Liberal government said that no cases could be brought against unions for damages done by a strike. This restored the **industrial power** of the unions.

THE OSBORNE DECISION OR JUDGMENT, 1908–9

The 1906 Act had restored the unions' industrial power. By this time, however, they also had **political power** through the Labour Representation Committee, later named the Labour Party.

This party was funded by the unions, which provided the money to pay for:

▶ election campaigns;

▶ propaganda, pamphlets, posters and the like;

▶ candidates' expenses for travelling and hotels;

▶ MPs pay, until the 1911 Act gave MPs a salary (p. 92).

W. V. Osborne was a branch secretary of the ASRS and a Liberal. He objected to his union's use of money to fund the Labour Party, and he prosecuted the union for illegal use of money.

This case was finally settled in the House of Lords which decided that:
► unions could not use their general funds for political purposes;
► unions could set up a political fund into which members might, if they 'contracted in', pay a contribution.

Since few members would voluntarily ask for the forms to contract in, union funding of the Labour Party dropped drastically, so that the **political power** of the unions was threatened.

As part of its price for supporting the Liberals during the controversy with the Lords in 1909–11 (p. 92) the Labour Party got the government to promise to change the law.

The Trade Union Act, 1913 said that:
► the general funds of the unions could not be used for political purposes;
► if members agreed, a separate political fund could be set up by a union;
► every member would have part of his contribution put into that fund, unless he 'contracted out' from making such a payment;
► if anyone contracted out, he was not to lose any other of his union privileges.

Since few men bothered to contract out, union contributions to the Labour Party now grew again.

39.6 Syndicalism

From 1910 the **cost of living** started to rise, after almost half a century during which it had continually fallen. At the same time there was a rise in **unemployment**, largely owing to foreign competition (unit 28).

Unrest in industry was revealed by the number of strikes, the clashes with the police as they tried to allow blackleg workers to get to factories, and by the lock-outs by employers.

Socialist leaders such as Tillett and Mann and a miners' leader, A. J. Cook, talked and wrote about syndicalism. **Syndicalism** was a philosophy which said that:
► **the workers** in an industry ought to control it. Miners should control the coal industry, railway workers the railways and so on;
► **the old owners** ought to be deposed, although they had put up the money to start and develop the industries. Syndicalists claimed that the workers had 'earned' the right to control the industries, which would not have developed without their work.

This doctrine frightened not only employers and Conservatives; it also frightened many Radicals, so that Lloyd George and Churchill, two great reformers (unit 37), became hostile to trade unionism.

THE TRIPLE ALLIANCE

1910–12 saw a series of nationwide strikes by the larger and more militant unions. Dockers, miners, railway workers and others came out on strike. The dockers' hourly pay went up to 8 pence as employers gave way to the strikers. **1912** saw a nationwide transport strike, which collapsed and led many to think that syndicalism would not gain support.

In **1913** the leaders of the three big unions, the Transport Workers' Federation, the National Union of Railwaymen and the Miners' Federation, formed the **Triple Alliance** agreeing that:
● none of them would call a strike without consulting the others, whose members would be affected by such a strike;
● they would act jointly, so that if one was involved in a dispute, the others would come out on sympathetic strike.

39.7 The War and the Unions

In unit 43 we shall see that during the First World War:
► **unions grew** larger as they recruited members;
► **union leaders** were involved at national and local level in committees and organizations formed to help the war effort;
► some leaders (Clynes, Hodges, Barnes) were made members of **government**, while Henderson, the Party leader after MacDonald's resignation, became a member of the **War Cabinet** when Lloyd George became Prime Minister in 1916;
► union members earned **high wages** and learned to enjoy a better standard of living than they had had in peacetime.

This meant that unions became 'respectable', as accepted parts of organized society, while their leaders and members learned to expect that life would be better than it had been in 1913.

But the War led also to the loss of markets for British goods, including coal, and to inflation.

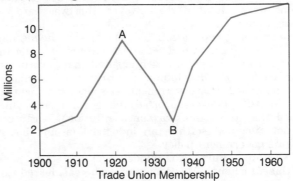

Fig. 39.7 A graph showing changes in trade union membership since 1900. Examiners will expect explanations for the growth (at point A), the fall (at point B) and the great rise in membership since 1940.

39.8 Unions in the Post-War World, 1918–21

1918–20 was a period of 'boom', as the world made up for the development which had not taken place during the War. During this period unions:
► won higher wages for dockers (led by Bevin), railwaymen (led by Thomas) and miners (led by Cook and Smith);
► organized many strikes, including one by policemen in London and Liverpool.

1921–2 saw the end of the 'boom' and the onset of the trade recession which was to last until 1939 and which was to deepen in the 1930s into the 'Great Depression'. In this period, there was:
► the **Geddes Axe**, with its cuts in government spending;
► the return to private ownership of the mines, which had been taken over by the government during the war and whose nationalization had been recommended by a Royal Commission (the Sankey Commission) in 1919;
► mine-owners' announcement of a cut in wages (31st March 1921).

Black Friday (15th April 1921) saw the refusal by the other members of the Triple Alliance to support the miners in their dispute with their employers. The miners lost their strike, went back to work on reduced wages (July 1921) and then saw wages cut in other industries by other employers.

THE COAL INDUSTRY, 1921–6
During **1921–4** European coal output fell because of the French occupation of the Ruhr. In Britain, the industry did well, but the mines were old, unmechanized and badly run.

By **1924–5** the European industry was back to normal and the demand for British coal fell. Owners announced proposals for further cuts in pay after the return to the Gold Standard (unit 47).

In 1925 the miners received the support of the General Council of the TUC (set up in 1920), which threatened to bring out millions of workers if these cuts were made.

Baldwin intervened. He offered the owners a subsidy, so that wages need not be cut while discussions were held about the industry's future by the **Samuel Commission**. **Red Friday** is the name given to the day on which this announcement – seen as a victory for the unions – was made.

In **March 1926**, however, the Samuel Commission reported in favour of a cut in wages and an extra hour's work each day. The subsidy was to end on 1st May 1926. Owners and miners failed to reach agreement on wages and hours, and the government and the General Council of the TUC held discussions on the industry's future.

On **1st May 1926** the mine owners announced the closure of the pits and the 'locking-out' of the men. On **2nd May 1926** talks between the TUC and the government broke down when printers refused to produce the *Daily Mail*.

39.9 The General Strike

On **3rd May 1926** the TUC called the General Strike, and on **4th May 1926** many workers were called out. Because millions were left at work, however, this was hardly a General Strike.

Government preparation had gone on since Red Friday, 1925. The government had set up the Organization for the Maintenance of Supplies, which ensured that government continued, food was distributed, electricity and gas supplies were maintained and a government newspaper was produced.

The **middle class** supported the government, which claimed that the strike was unconstitutional because it was not aimed at settling an industrial dispute but at changing government policy.

The **Labour Party** was divided over the strike. Most politicians, including MacDonald and Thomas, feared that the strike might lead to anarchy, and preferred a political, rather than an industrial, settlement to the problems of coal.

The BBC under Sir John Reith allowed broadcasts by government spokesmen, but refused MacDonald or any Labour leader to speak, and the **Churches** condemned the strike; Cardinal Bourne denounced it as a serious sin, which alarmed many Catholic workers.

Liberal leaders, such as the lawyer Sir John Simon, declared it was illegal and that men faced harsh punishments.

THE END OF THE STRIKE

The moderate leaders of the TUC had no contact with the miners' leaders who had gone back to the coalfields. They feared the possibility of anarchy, the attacks by the Churches and the effects on the Labour Party.

After only nine days they approached the government and called off the General Strike. The miners, left in the lurch, continued with their own strike, but months later were forced to go back to work at lower wages.

THE TRADES DISPUTES ACT, 1927

Baldwin had promised the TUC that he would not take revenge on the strikers. But in this Act:
▶ a General (or sympathetic) Strike was made illegal;
▶ policemen, civil servants and other essential workers were forbidden to go on strike;
▶ civil servants' unions were forbidden to affiliate to the TUC;
▶ union members wishing to pay into the unions' political funds had to 'contract in' – which saw a drop in union financing of the Labour Party (p. 97).

This was the signal for many employers to punish ex-strikers by refusing to take them back.

39.10 Unions, 1927–45

Industrial action had proved disastrous in 1926. The **unions** then turned to:
▶ **Negotiations** with employers, as instanced by the

discussions in which industrialists were led by Sir Alfred Mond and trade union representatives by Ben Turner.
▶ **Political action** through the Labour Party – although this proved to be a disappointment, as we shall see in unit 48.

Membership fell sharply for a while, because of the massive unemployment in the 1930s, but at the same time **new unions** were formed for workers in new and growing industries in a more modern Britain (unit 49).

UNIONS AND THE WAR, 1939–45

As in 1914–18, union leaders were involved in the conduct of the War with **Ernest Bevin**, of the Transport and General Workers Union, who was the second most important member of Churchill's Cabinet.

Union **membership** climbed again, and, for reasons which we shall examine in unit 51, working-class people expected that post-war life would be an improvement on the past.

39.11 Unions in the Post-War World

With the Labour victory in 1945, unions cooperated to ensure that the **Welfare State** should be developed. They also had the satisfaction of seeing their government repeal the 1927 Act. They also demanded **higher wages** for their members.

In the 1950s, unions learned to work with Conservative governments which, under Churchill and Eden, tended to favour negotiations rather than confrontation (unit 53).

In 1961 unions cooperated with the Macmillan government when it formed the National Economic Development Council ('Neddy'), but opposed its proposals for a National Incomes Commission ('Nicky') to regulate wages.

Confrontation between unions and government became a feature of the 1960s and 1970s. In particular there was:
▶ the **Wilson (Labour) government's** withdrawal of its proposals for trade union reform in Barbara Castle's **'In Place of Strife'**;
▶ the **Heath (Conservative) government's** Industrial Relations Act, which led to confrontation with the miners in 1972 and 1973 and to the 'three-day week'. The government climbed down in the face of widespread support for the miners, and lost the 1974 Election;
▶ the **Callaghan (Labour) government's** changing relationship with the unions which:
● supported the government's attack on inflation, even though this meant restrictions on wage increases in 1976, 1977 and 1978;
● rejected a call for a 5 per cent limit on wage increases in 1979, which led to a series of strikes and the 'winter of discontent', which alienated voters and helped ensure the return of the Thatcher (Conservative) government in 1979.

For the relationship between the unions and the Thatcher governments, see unit 55.

Unit 39 Summary

▶ Gladstone, Disraeli and trade union reform, 1868–75.
▶ The unions and politics, 1871–5: the Lib-labs.
▶ Unions for the unskilled; the work of Joseph Arch, Annie Besant, Will Thorne, Tom Mann, Ben Tillett and John Burns.
▶ The London Dockers' Strike, 1889.
▶ 'New' unionism and political development, 1889–1900.
▶ Taff Vale, 1902 and the Trade Disputes Act, 1906.
▶ The Osborne Case and the Trade Union Act, 1913.
▶ Syndicalism and the Triple Alliance.
▶ Unions and the war, 1914–18.
▶ Unions prosper and suffer, 1918–26; the General Strike, 1926, the Trade Disputes Act, 1927.
▶ Unions since 1926.

40 THE RISE OF THE LABOUR PARTY, 1893–1924

40.1 The Failure of the Older Parties

▶ **Chamberlain** wanted the Liberal Party to deal with the social problems in the 1880s, but Gladstone refused to do so (unit 31).
▶ **Churchill** wanted Conservatives to follow Disraeli's policies on social reform, but Salisbury had refused to do so (unit 35).
▶ **Social problems** which needed attention included:
● **poverty** which was well documented by the surveys of Booth and Rowntree (unit 37);
● **unemployment** because of the growth of foreign competition;
● **ill-health** because of the conditions in which so many lived and the lack of medical attention for the poor;
● **housing** – the poor were only able to afford inadequate housing.

THE VOTE, CLASS AND POLITICAL PARTIES

The **Tory** (later called the **Conservative**) party was, traditionally linked with the **land-owning aristocracy**, although it won elections only with the support of people from other classes.

The **Whig** and later the **Liberal** parties were linked with the **merchant and industrial classes**, although often led by members of the aristocracy. It was this party which, in 1832, gave the vote to the **middle clases** (unit 14).

The **1867 Reform Act** gave some working men the vote. Lowe and Cranborne realized that, one day, these working-class people would imitate the aristocrats (and Conservatives) and the middle classes (and Liberals) by forming their own party.

40.2 Early Steps towards a Working-Class Party

In **1868** the TUC formed the **Parliamentary Committee** (unit 39) and in **1869** a group of workers formed the **Labour Representation League**, aiming to get working men elected as MPs.

1874 saw the election of Burt and MacDonald. They won their seats because:
▶ of their own history as union leaders;
▶ they stood for seats where the mass of voters were working men;
▶ the local Liberal Associations encouraged their members to vote for these working men, who were opponents of the Conservatives. **Lib-Labs** was the term used to describe such working-class MPs, whose number increased until, by 1906, there were 24 such members, most of them representing mining constituencies.

THE WEAKNESS OF THE LIB-LAB POSITION

The working men who became Lib-Lab MPs came from craft unions and they accepted the philosophies of **laisser-faire** and self-help.

They supported Gladstone's policies on trade, taxation and opposition to social reform, and had little contact with, or sympathy for, the majority of the working class, who lived in poverty (unit 37).

40.3 Keir Hardie, 1856–1915

Hardie was a self-educated miners' leader who had left school at the age of eight, worked in pits from the age of 10 and who became a miners' leader while still under 20.

In 1888 he asked the Liberal Association in mid-Lanark to nominate him as a Lib-Lab candidate. They refused, and he stood as the Scottish Labour candidate – and came bottom of the poll.

He then formed the **Scottish Labour Party**. Following his example, men in other parts of Great Britain formed local Labour Parties.

In **1892** Hardie won the West Ham seat as an Independent Labour candidate; John Burns won Battersea. Hardie's arrival at the Commons – with brass band, red flag and wearing a cloth cap – caused a commotion.

In **1893** Hardie called a meeting of delegates from various local Labour parties, the SDF and other social societies, and at **Bradford** these delegates formed the **Independent Labour Party** (the ILP).

In the **1895** election, Hardie and Burns lost their seats, but the new party continued to recruit members.

PHILIP SNOWDEN

Having gone to a Board School, Snowden, crippled by a spinal injury, used his illness to educate himself by reading widely.

He got a clerical job in local government and was an early recruit to the ILP (1898).

Politically, he admired Gladstone and his fiscal policies. In the small ILP Snowden became recognized as 'the financial wizard', one of the few who understood economics and finance.

From 1903 to 1906 and from 1917 to 1920 he was Chairman of the Party. He was elected MP for Blackburn in 1906 and although he lost his seat in the 1918 Election he came back to Parliament in 1922 as MP for Colne Valley.

In the Labour governments of 1924 and 1929 he was Chancellor of the Exchequer, a post which he also held in the National Government formed in 1931. He resigned from that government when it abandoned Free Trade (unit 49), and he died in 1937.

HARDIE, THE TUC AND THE ILP, 1895–9

The ILP, like the other socialist societies, was **small**, recruiting members into local branches much as, say, CND or the Friends of the Earth have done in the 1970s and 1980s. It was also **poor**, because its few members had little money to spend on maintaining a political party. Hardie kept himself by writing for newspapers.

The TUC on the other hand represented the unions which were:
▶ **much larger**, particularly after the growth of the New Unions for unskilled workers;
▶ **better organized**, with a network of branches in factories and workplaces all over the country;
▶ **richer** – the older craft unions had relatively large funds, while even the new unions could raise a great deal of money by asking their members for only 1d each.

Bernard Shaw of the Fabian Society, having seen that Gladstone would not begin to tackle the social problems, wrote an open letter (1893) in which he asked the unions to back Hardie's new ILP.

Hardie, as a union delegate, asked Annual Conferences of the TUC to support his new party. But from 1895 to 1898 the Congress voted against this because:
▶ the majority of people at the Conference were from the

craft unions, with their belief in self-help and their opposition to socialism;
► the leaders of the TUC were almost all from these unions, and advised the Conferences to reject Hardie's appeal.

By 1899 the picture had changed because an increasing number of delegates came from the growing number of large new unions, and they supported socialist ideas. Some delegates from the craft unions had become converted to socialism and were, in some cases, members of the SDF; and the continuation of the depression had shown even the self-helpers that there was something wrong with the existing system so that they, too, accepted the socialist argument.

HARDIE, THE ILP AND THE TUC, 1899–1900

In **1899** the Conference of the TUC voted by 546 000 to 434 000 to accept Hardie's motion that a conference be held with interested parties and societies, to see how they could get more working men elected to Parliament. That vote showed the size of the opposition to the idea of the formation of a separate working-class party.

In February 1900 a Conference was held in London with delegates from:
► the various socialist societies – SDF, Socialist League, Fabians (unit 39);
► the Cooperative Society;
► local Labour parties;
► Hardie's ILP;
► representatives from a small number of unions.

This Conference decided to form the **Labour Representation Committee**, which changed its name to the Labour Party in 1906.

40.4 The Craft Unions and the LRC

At first the craft unions refused to support the LRC. However, the **Taff Vale decision** (unit 39) and the government's refusal to bring in amending legislation showed them that they needed a voice in Parliament.

Between 1903 and 1906 many craft unions joined the LRC, bringing with them:
► money;
► organization;
► leaders of a higher quality.

THE ELECTORAL PACT, 1903

The **Liberals** had just begun to recover from the disasters of the Boer War which had split the Party. Their recovery was helped by the 1902 Education Act (unit 42) and by Chamberlain's Tariff Reform campaign (unit 34).

They feared that they might fail again at a General Election, however, particularly if the working-class vote was split between Liberal and Labour candidates.

Herbert Gladstone, Chief Whip of the Liberal Party, wanted an electoral agreement with Labour. **Ramsay MacDonald**, secretary of the LRC was willing to discuss this. **The Pact**, 1903, was an agreement whereby:
► the leaders of the Parties advised local Associations to cooperate during an election;
► they suggested that only one candidate should stand against the Conservative. In some places this would mean that a Liberal withdrew, in others that a Labour candidate withdrew. The Alliance between the present-day Liberals and the Social Democrats, which was signed in 1981, was another such electoral arrangements.

40.5 The 1906 Election

We have seen the reasons for the Conservative defeat at this Election (unit 35). For **Labour** the Election was a triumph:
► 50 candidates were put up by the richer party, now financed by the unions;

► 29 Labour MPs were elected, as well as 24 Miners' candidates – the remnant of the old Lib-Lab group. These joined the Labour Party during the next couple of years so that there were, in effect, 53 Labour MPs in Parliament.

Balfour, the Conservative leader, appreciated the importance of this development, which would force the Liberal Party either to become more left-wing and lose the support of its right-wing Gladstonians **or** to stick with its Gladstonian beliefs and so lose the support of its working-class voters.

THE LABOUR PARTY IN PARLIAMENT 1906–11

The Trades Disputes Act, 1906 (unit 37) was one result of the new power of Labour and the unions. **The social reforms** of the Liberal Government (unit 37) were generally supported by the Party, although it was opposed to the self-financing element in the National Insurance Act. Labour wanted the funds for unemployment and health funds to be provided out of general taxation.

Some **Radicals** outside Parliament agreed with the criticisms made by the Webbs of the Fabian Society that the Labour MPs had failed to dominate Parliament or to carry their socialism into practice. In particular the Webbs argued that:
► the Labour members seemed to be merely a wing of the Liberal party;
► they were fighting among themselves, with Snowden (the sick man with a vile temper and vicious tongue) becoming even more critical of his less able colleagues;
► Hardie was a sick man who no longer had the strength to lead as he had once done;
► MacDonald was a lukewarm socialist and seemed ready to leave the ILP.

THE LABOUR PARTY IN PARLIAMENT, 1911–14

The Parliament Act, 1911, gave MPs a salary of £400 and was a great benefit to Labour MPs, few of whom had the chance to keep a job while being MPs, unlike the journalists, lawyers and bankers in the other parties.

The Trade Union Act, 1913 (unit 39) ensured the union funding for the Labour Party.

40.6 The War, 1914–18 and the Labour Party

We will discuss the political and other effects of the First World War in unit 45.

THE 1918 ELECTION

We will examine this in detail in unit 45, but here you should notice:
► **Lloyd George** led his Coalition government into the election and won 484 seats – 338 Conservatives, 136 Lloyd George Liberals, and 10 other supporters;
► **Labour** won 59 seats, although MacDonald failed to be re-elected because of hostility towards his pacifism in 1914–18;
► **the Asquithian Liberals** won only 26 seats;
► Labour therefore became the second largest grouping in the Commons.

40.7 Labour in Power, 1924

In unit 45 we will examine the political development of the period 1918–24 and the reasons for Labour's successes in the elections of that period. We will also see why and how in January 1924 MacDonald became Labour's first Prime Minister, why his government was unable to achieve very much and why it did badly in the 1924 election.

RAMSAY MACDONALD

Examiners often ask a question on the career and importance of MacDonald.

MacDonald was the illegitimate son of a Scottish fisherwoman and was born at Lossiemouth in 1866. He went to a Board School where he became a pupil teacher (unit 42), and then went to work in London as a clerk and attended evening classes.

In 1888 he became private secretary to a Liberal MP and, after giving up that job, earned his living as a journalist. He joined the ILP soon after it was formed and stood as a candidate in the 1895 election. In 1900 he became secretary of the LRC (some voted for him because they thought that they were voting for 'another MacDonald', that is, a trade union leader).

In 1900 he was a candidate at Leicester, a seat he won in 1906 when he also became chairman of the ILP. He attacked Britain's entry into the First World War, which helped towards his defeat in Leicester in the 1918 election.

In 1922 he was elected MP for Aberavon and was elected Leader of the Party, so that he became the first Labour Prime Minister in 1924. During this government (unit 45) he was both Prime Minister and Foreign Secretary.

In 1929 he became Prime Minister for the second time (unit 48), but his government failed to cope with the problems of the depression (unit 46) and resigned in 1931.

At the invitation of King George V he formed a National Government in 1931 (unit 48) which led to his break with the Labour Party. He resigned in 1935, taking the post of Lord President of the Council.

He lost his seat at Seaham Harbour in the 1935 election, being defeated by Emmanual Shinwell, but he came back as MP for the Scottish Universities.

He died at sea in 1937 when on his way to South America.

Unit 40 Summary

▶ Votes, class and political parties.
▶ The working class 'Lib-Lab' MPs.
▶ Keir Hardie and the ILP: the formation of the LRC.
▶ Craft Unions and the LRC: importance of Taff Vale.
▶ The electoral pact, 1903, and the growth of the Labour Party.
▶ MacDonald: the effects of the war, 1914–18; in power, 1924, 1929–31.

---

41 THE CHANGING ROLE OF WOMEN

41.1 Victorian Middle-Class Women

Most Victorian mothers had large families. In the early nineteenth century most children died before reaching the age of five. Things improved, and it was quite common for the later Victorian families to have seven or more living children.

All middle-class families employed a number of servants, and by 1900 there were over one million of them. Many Victorian homes had a copy of Mrs Isabella Beeton's *Book of Household Management*, with its instructions on running a home, supervising servants and cooking.

Until about 1850 **middle-class girls** were brought up entirely at home and were educated by mothers or governesses. They were taught that their main role was to 'catch' a middle-class husband so that they, in turn, would bring up more middle-class children.

Until late in the century these girls and their mothers had few rights:
▶ If they were householders (e.g. rich widows) **they could vote** in local elections and in elections for the Boards of Guardians and for the School Boards but not in Parliamentary elections.
▶ **They could be candidates** for election to the Board of Guardians and School Boards, but not to the local council or to Parliament.

Until late in the century few middle-class girls, and no middle-class mother, considered going to work (unless poverty drove some to become governesses). Work belonged to the working class.

41.2 Victorian Working-Class Women

Most working-class girls who were born into poor families had to go to work at an early age, earned little money and tended to marry men from their own deprived class. This helped perpetuate the cycle of poverty revealed by Rowntree (p. 90).

Some working-class girls were daughters of skilled workers whose wages were high enough to allow them to stay at school for some time, but even these girls had to go to work at a fairly early age.

The wives of skilled workers were **emancipated** (or freed from going to work) because their husbands earned enough money to keep them in decent conditions.

The differences between the sub-groups in the working class were seen in:
▶ housing; ▶ clothing; ▶ health;
▶ leisure, for it was the prosperous working class who could afford the money for railway excursions, music-hall tickets and lending libraries.

41.3 Emancipation

Those women who fought for emancipation wanted:
▶ to get the same **education** and **jobs** as their brothers;
▶ the right to own their own **property**;
▶ **the vote**, as a sign of equality with men.

REBELS AGAINST SOCIETY

By 1850 it had become clear that about 25 per cent of middle-class girls were not going to be able to marry, because some men:
▶ emigrated to the colonies;
▶ died in the many small wars fought by Victorians;
▶ remained bachelors.

What was their role, since they could not fill the expected role of wives and mothers? It was from the ranks of these single women that the Victorian rebels emerged.

41.4 The Emancipators, the Professionals, and Legislation

The emancipators

If middle-class girls were to get the same sort of job as their brothers, they had to get the same sort of education.

In 1850 **Frances Mary Buss** founded the North London Collegiate School and in 1858 **Dorothea Beale** founded the Cheltenham Ladies College. In these and similar schools the girls were taught by women who prepared them for Civil Service Examinations (p. 70), entry into business and commerce, the Universities or one of the learned professions.

Only progressive fathers spent money on so educating their daughters. Most continued to think of women as 'beautiful pictures in a beautiful golden frame'.

Emily Davies led the fight for Higher Education. In particular she was reponsible for:
▶ persuading the Universities to allow girls to take the same **Certificate examinations** as their brothers – the forerunner to the School Certificate (1917) and Matriculation examinations which, in turn, were the forerunners to O and A Levels (1951) and eventually the GCSE;
▶ opening her own Hitchin College, with six students who were taught by lecturers from nearby **Cambridge University**. This college was soon moved to Girton at Cambridge, the first of the women's colleges. **London University** refused to allow women into the University until the 1870s, in spite of Emily Davies' arguments and influence.

The professionals

Florence Nightingale had organized hospitals in the Crimea (unit 22). On her triumphant return after the War, the 'Lady with the Lamp' used her influence to set up the **Nightingale School for Nurses** (1860). This established nursing as a respectable profession for well-educated ladies.

Elizabeth Garrett (who became Garrett-Anderson after her marriage) had heard a lecture by **Elizabeth Blackwell**, an Englishwoman who had gone to the USA where she had qualified as a doctor. Elizabeth Garrett wanted to become a doctor. She was allowed to enter the Middlesex Hospital as a student, but the male students protested and she finally qualified in Paris. She helped found the Elizabeth Garrett-Anderson Hospital, where all the staff were women and where women could train to become doctors.

Legislation

▶ In **1876** Parliament passed a law allowing medical schools to admit women as students.
▶ By the 1890s a number of women had qualified, but were regarded with suspicion by most men and by many women.

THE CHANGING NATURE OF WORK

Until the middle of the century most jobs required a good deal of **physical strength**, and were deemed unsuitable for women, who were all considered to be too delicate. Even **office jobs** – with heavy ledgers on high shelves – were done by men, as you can see from Dickens' *David Copperfield* and *A Christmas Carol*.

In the second half of the century there was a change in the nature of some jobs because of:
▶ **the telephone** with its switchboard, where many girls got jobs as operators and supervisors;
▶ **the typewriter**, which altered the nature of office work and provided job opportunities for thousands of women;
▶ **legislation** on factories, education, health and housing which led to the expansion of the **Civil Service**, where many women found work. In particular the expansion of **state education** after 1870 provided work for thousands of women in schools and in Education offices;
▶ **chain stores and department stores**, which became a feature of towns in late Victorian Britain. These provided job opportunities for thousands of women – as assistants, buyers and supervisors and in some cases as senior managers, as in Selfridge's, the store opened by an enterprising American.

THE CHANGING ROLE OF THE MIDDLE-CLASS WIFE (See fig 2.6)

In **1870** and **1882** Parliament passed **Married Women's Property Acts**. These allowed a married woman to retain ownership of property which she might have received as a gift from a parent, but which until 1882 had automatically become the property of her husband.

Smaller families became the norm for late Victorian middle-class women because of:
▶ **rising costs of education of sons** at public, boarding schools;
▶ **rising costs of running homes**, largely because of rising standards of expectation as regards the size of the home, number of servants, type of furniture, entertainment and holidays;
▶ **falling incomes** because of the depressed state of industry, which led to the fall in profits and dividends on which many middle-class families lived;
▶ wider knowledge of methods of **contraception** among middle-class families – only in the 1920s did the working classes get this knowledge;
▶ a decline in **religion**, which might otherwise have led women to refuse to agree to contraception.

With smaller families there were:
▶ **a higher living standard** since the family income had to be shared among fewer people;
▶ even **higher expectations** of future standards;
▶ **better health** and a longer **expectation of life** for women – which made it even more desirable to provide them with education and job opportunities. But few married women of the middle classes continued to work after marriage. Indeed women working in the Civil Service, teaching or local government **had** to leave work when they got married.

41.5 Votes for Women

In the 1860s a number of local committees had been formed to organize demands for 'Votes for Women'. In 1897 **Millicent Fawcett** linked these together to form the National Union of Women's Suffrage Societies. She hoped to persuade male politicians to give women the same rights as men had at that time (unit 38).

THE SUFFRAGETTES

In 1903 **Emmeline Pankhurst** formed the Women's Social and Political Union, to take more **violent** action in pursuit of their demands for 'Votes for Women'.

They drew attention to their demands by:
▶ **heckling** at political meetings;
▶ **chaining themselves** to railings at Buckingham Palace and Downing Street;
▶ organizing a **window-smashing** demonstration in Oxford Street;
▶ **Emily Davison's** death at Epsom, when this leading suffragette threw herself under the hooves of King Edward VII's horse during the running of the Derby in 1913 to draw wide attention to the 'cause'.

They were badly treated by males. **Hecklers** were whipped, roughly handled and thrown out of meetings, and **demonstrators** such as the window smashers, were arrested and sent to prison.

THE 'CAT AND MOUSE' ACT, 1913

Women prisoners often went on **hunger strike**, as a protest against their sentences. At first the authorities **forcibly fed** such prisoners, but there was a public outcry against this barbarity.

Parliament then passed an Act which allowed the **release** of a hunger striker, only for her to be **re-arrested** when she had recovered her health.

WOMEN AND THE WAR

We will examine this in some detail in unit 43. Here you should notice that:
▶ Emmeline Pankhurst changed her slogan to 'The right to serve'.
▶ Women did a **wide variety of jobs** and served in the **armed forces** as part of their contributions to the war effort.
▶ In 1918, when giving all adult males the vote, Parliament also gave the vote to **women over the age of 30**. Only in **1928** did women get the vote on the same terms as men.

41.6 Women in Inter-War Britain

In unit 46 we will see that in the middle of the Great Depression of the 1930s Britain underwent a major industrial and social revolution. Women were those who gained most from this.
▶ **Smaller families** became the norm for all classes, so that women were healthier because they had fewer children to bear and rear. (see fig. 2.6.)
▶ **Living standards** rose for most people owing to:
● smaller families;
● falling prices (p. 116);
● government welfare provision;
● technology, which provided new and improved goods such as prepared foods, household goods such as the vacuum cleaner and cheaper clothing and furniture.
▶ **Housing standards** improved, with millions buying their own homes and millions more moving into new council housing.
▶ **Job opportunities** for women multiplied with the technological revolution. There were jobs in:
● **industry** – as skilled, semi-skilled and unskilled machine operators;
● **commerce** – in the increasing number of **tertiary** industries such as insurance, banking, building societies and the like, all of which expanded in this period;
● **government and local government**, with the expansion of the welfare state.

But it still remained true that most married women did not go to work if they could avoid it.

41.7 Women in Post-War Britain, 1945–80

During the Second World War women again made a major contribution to the war effort. Millions of married women went back to work or, in some cases, went to work for the first time.

After the war they continued to work because:
▶ **government policy** of full employment meant that there were never enough workers to fill all the jobs created – hence also the need to bring in immigrant workers, as well as providing jobs for some eight million married women;
▶ **living standards** had risen during the 1930s, and people expected that they ought to continue to rise. To get the income needed to enjoy this rising standard, married women had to go to work to add to the family income;

▶ **job opportunities** increased owing to the continued technological revolution – in industry and in commerce as well as in government service.

It is easier for married women to have two roles (at home and at work) in the modern world because:
▶ **smaller families** mean that women have less work to do than their mothers and grandmothers had;
▶ **healthier women**, having borne and reared only one or two children, are better able to combine these roles;
▶ **homes** are easier to run, since they are smaller than the Victorian home and with the aid of modern gadgets, prepared foods and easier-to-clean clothing, furniture and carpeting, it is relatively easy to run a home.

THE LAW AND WOMEN SINCE 1945

It is untrue that, even today, women have the same rights or opportunities as men. This may be seen in:
▶ the entry into Universities, medical schools and apprenticeship schemes, where there is always a **higher proportion of boys than girls**;
▶ the control of institutions such as Universities, Schools, Colleges and political parties at local and national level – where men predominate;
▶ the small number of women who become councillors or MPs.

Part of the problem lies in:
▶ **parental expectation** – many families still put a higher value on educating boys than girls;
▶ **female expectation** – even women councillors and politicians tend to appoint men rather than women to positions of authority;
▶ **biology** – since women have to give up their careers when they have babies, so that they tend to be further behind their male counterparts when they return to work;
▶ **employers** – who tend to prefer men to women since they are less likely to be away from work because of sick children or are not going to be away from work because of pregnancy.

Parliament passed **the Equal Pay Act, 1969**, which made it illegal for employers not to pay women the same wage as men for doing the same job. But in industry and commerce the average women's wage is still only 75 per cent of men's average wage (1986). **The Equal Opportunities Commission** has been set up, which has the right to investigate allegations of discrimination against women. However, women continue to find it more difficult to get a mortgage, and their income tax forms still have to be filled in and signed by their husbands.

Women have won a number of battles since 1881 but in 1987 there are still more to be fought.

Unit 41 Summary

▶ What emancipation meant to (a) middle-class women; (b) working-class women.
▶ The evolution of women's freedom.
▶ The size of middle-class families; effect on women's struggle.
▶ Votes for women.
▶ Women and the war, 1914–18.
▶ Women in (a) inter-war Britain, 1919–39; (b) post-war Britain, 1945–86; the quest for equality.

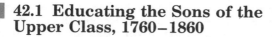
42.1 Educating the Sons of the Upper Class, 1760–1860

Many sons of the nobility and gentry were educated at **home** in the eighteenth century. Others went to **boarding schools**, including the 'Public Schools', of which the most famous were Eton, Winchester, Charterhouse, Shrewsbury, Westminster and Rugby.

Most of their **teachers** were Anglican clergymen and the **syllabus** was almost entirely Classical – Latin, Greek and Ancient History. **Bullying** was common, as we know from the biographies of Gladstone and others, and as shown in *Tom Brown's Schooldays*.

In 1808 the boys at Harrow rebelled against the cruelty of the headmaster and in 1818 the Army had to be brought in to put down a riot at Winchester. There was a drop in the number of boys attending these schools which were, however, saved from extinction by:

▶ the **Industrial Revolution**, which created a rich industrial class, anxious to give its sons the sort of education once only available to the sons of the landed nobility and gentry;

▶ the **railway system**, which made it possible to send boys to far away schools;

▶ the **reforming headmasters**, for example:

● **Samuel Butler** of Shrewsbury who, between 1798 and 1836, taught his pupils to respect learning, to use their leisure time intelligently and to practise **self-discipline**, rather than have it imposed on them by teachers;

● **Thomas Arnold**, headmaster of Rugby from 1828 to 1842, who adopted Butler's idea of a **prefectorial system** of control, made **the chapel** a major feature of school life and enlarged the **syllabus** by introducing modern subjects such as mathematics and languages;

● **Edward Thring**, headmaster of Uppingham between 1853 and 1887, who built a **gymnasium** and **swimming pool**, organized **games** for his pupils, built **workshops** and **music rooms** and created an **old boys' organization**.

So successful were these men and their imitators (many of them men who had taught under one of the reformers) that the schools expanded and many new boarding schools were founded during the nineteenth century. Some of these were:

▶ **former grammar schools**, such as Uppingham, which became well known and found the money to build boarding houses;

▶ **new foundations**, built with money provided by banks, merchant companies, church societies or individuals.

Poorly run boarding schools, which charged lower fees and whose teachers were often ill-educated, also grew to satisfy the demand for boarding school education among the less well-off members of the middle class. Charles Dickens wrote about a real school (in Yorkshire) in his novel *Nicholas Nickelby*.

Other sons of well-off parents went to **local private schools**, as did Disraeli (unit 30).

42.2 The Grammar Schools, 1760–1871

The **grammar schools** were so called because of the **syllabus** which, like that of the public schools, concentrated on the ancient languages, whose grammar had to be learned by the pupils.

They had been **founded** at different times in the past – by monasteries or cathedrals (as in Canterbury and Exeter), by rich individuals anxious to have their memory

perpetuated (as with John Lyon at Harrow and Archbishop Whitgift at Croydon), and by Tudor monarchs who used some of the money stolen from the Church to provide such schools – still named after Edward VI or Queen Elizabeth. Some of them were corporation grammar schools, controlled by the local corporation of a chartered borough (unit 15).

Almost all the grammar schools were small, reflecting the size of the population and the number of people who could afford the fees charged by such schools. Manchester Grammar School, for example, consisted of one large room in 1819.

By 1760 most of these grammar schools had decayed because:

▶ the **corporations** which controlled some of them were corrupt;

▶ the **charters** written at the time of their foundations were often badly written, so that:

● **schoolmasters** had to be paid according to the charter, which often failed to mention the need to teach children. Some masters, therefore, drew their salaries but refused to take pupils;

● **other schoolmasters** were appointed, not because they were capable but because they were related to some trustee – and they failed to maintain standards;

● **classical languages** were mentioned in the ancient charters – whereas the parents of industrial towns such as Leeds wanted to have their sons taught mathematics, modern languages, accounting and other subjects which would be useful in business and trade. But a decision by Lord Eldon, the Lord Chancellor, in 1809, made it illegal for schools to ignore their charters and to provide such modern subjects.

Dissenting Academies were founded by **Nonconformist ministers** (forbidden to teach in the grammar schools or Universities) to provide these modern subjects. Some of these taught to University level; others taught boys until they were 18 years old, and attracted the support of the new industrial middle class.

The grammar schools were saved from extinction by:

▶ the **Municipal Reform Act** (unit 15) which in 1835 reformed local government and provided better trustees for some schools;

▶ the **Industrial Revolution**, which created a large number of families willing and able to pay for their sons to have a grammar school education;

▶ changes in the **law** which allowed the teaching of new subjects;

▶ a system of **examinations**, which began with the Cambridge Local Examinations in 1871 and led on to the School Certificate and modern GCSE examinations.

But even at the end of the nineteenth century there were few such schools, and these catered for the prosperous middle class. There was little, if any, chance for children from the working class to go to such schools.

42.3 Schools for the Working-Class Children, 1760–1830

'Dame' schools were provided by 'genteel' women who charged a penny or so a week and who taught small groups of children to read and write. In *Great Expectations* Dickens shows how the blacksmith's son went to such a school.

Sunday Schools had been set up by Methodist chapels because this was the only day on which working-class children were free. **Robert Raikes**, a Gloucester newspaper owner and industrialist, founded such a school and

Fig. 42.3 Inside a typical monitorial school in 1839. Examiners will expect candidates to be able to write about the pupils who are standing up, the way in which the monitorial system worked and the two men who developed this system.

helped spread the idea, so that by 1800 there were thousands of such schools, with about a quarter of a million pupils. These schools were funded by voluntary collections and the children taught to read the Bible, to learn their religion so that they would be better workpeople, more obedient to their masters and mistresses, and less likely to become criminals when they grew up.

Charity Schools were founded by local Churches and funded by local collections. Many of these came under the supervision of the Society for the Promotion of Christian Knowledge (founded 1699). In these schools children were taught to read, to do simple arithmetic, and (in some) to write. Humanitarians, for example Hannah More (unit 10), founded such schools in various parts of the country. But after 1800 these schools fell into decay because:

▶ **fear of the French Revolution** led to an attack on schools which taught children to read such things as radical pamphlets;

▶ **the children** tended to go to work in the expanding industries.

Monitorial Schools, in which a teacher taught older pupils ('monitors') who then taught younger children, were **founded** at roughly the same time (1811) by two different men:

▶ Andrew Bell, an Anglican vicar, whose supporters founded the **National Society** to supervise the many National schools in which, in addition to reading, writing and arithmetic, children were also taught the Anglican catechism;

▶ Joseph Lancaster, a one-time Quaker, whose supporters founded the **British and Foreign Society** to supervise the B & F Schools in which, in addition to the 'three Rs', children were taught religion, without any bias towards Anglicanism. This pleased Nonconformist parents but angered the Anglicans.

Monitorial Schools were **funded** by voluntary subscriptions made by individuals and by collections at churches, and by fees charged for school attendance.

42.4 The Government and the Education of the Poor, 1830–70

The growth of towns made it impossible for the two Voluntary Societies to provide enough schools for all children.

The Industrial Revolution created a demand for workpeople with at least a little education, and in **1833** the government made a grant of £20 000 a year, to be divided between the two Societies to help them build more schools.

By **1860** this grant had increased to over £500 000 as other Societies were founded by Wesleyans, Jews, Catholics and other religious groups which built schools for children from their churches.

In **1839** the government set up a Cabinet Committee to supervise the spending of this grant (then raised to £30 000). **Kay-Shuttleworth** was the first secretary of this Committee which:

▶ appointed inspectors to supervise the schools;

▶ set up teacher-training colleges in the 1840s;

▶ encouraged the Societies and Churches to set up their own teacher-training colleges.

The Newcastle Commission, 1858, examined the education of working-class children and reported that:

▶ **many children** did not attend school at all; indeed there were not sufficient school places for all the children in the country;

▶ **school children** entered school at different ages, depending on their families' financial position and interests; they also left at different ages as the need arose for some to go to work. This meant that children might have one, two, four or six years at school;

▶ **attendance** fluctuated with the weather, the state of trade, the demand for labour by local farmers and with the state of health of children and their families;

▶ there was a need for **local boards of education**, with power to collect a school rate to build more schools. This was turned down by Parliament.

Robert Lowe was appointed to take charge of the Education grant. He devised a new system, or **Revised Code**, (1862), of financing and supervising the schools, which has become known as **Payment by Results**. Any school which wished to receive a government grant had to:

▶ undergo a **yearly examination** by a visiting Inspector;

▶ accept a **common syllabus** in the 'three Rs' which the Inspectors could easily examine in all the schools;

▶ agree to have their grant varied according to:

● the number of children registered as present on the day of the inspection;

● the success of the children in the examination.

This system, said Lowe, would ensure that the government got value for money spent on education which, after the Crimean War, it wanted to cut if possible. In fact this system led to:

▶ **rote learning** of tables, pages of reading and other matter, with little if any understanding;

▶ the removal from the syllabus of non-examinable subjects such as science or history, until the Revised Code gave grants for such subjects (after 1867);

▶ condemnation of working-class children to **an inferior form** of education which, said Lowe, would fit them for 'their station and business in life' but would not 'raise them above their station', nor allow them a share in that **superior form** of education available to the middle class.

THE FORSTER ACT, 1870

In **1867** some town workers received the franchise. Lowe then declared, 'We will have to educate our masters', meaning the new voters.

In **1869** The Birmingham Education League, led by Chamberlain (unit 34) and other similar Leagues or Societies were demanding an extension and improvement in state education for the poor because:

▶ Germany, the USA and France had better-developed systems of state education and were proving to be industrial rivals (unit 28);

▶ industry needed even better-educated workpeople as it became more technologically and scientifically based;

▶ the government needed more and better-educated workpeople to work in the enlarged Civil Service and in the Post Office.

In **1870** Parliament passed the Education Act which said that the country was to be divided into about 2500 **school districts**, in each of which **Schools Boards** were to be elected by the ratepayers of the district.

The Boards were to examine the provision of elementary education in their district, provided then by the Voluntary Societies.

If, as was likely, they found that there were not enough school places for the number of children in their district, the Boards would then levy a school rate and build and maintain **Board Schools** out of the rates.

Boards would be empowered to make their own by-laws which would allow them to charge **fees**, of, if they felt it necessary, to allow children in without payment, and to insist on **attendance** if they wished. London made attendance compulsory for children between the ages of 5 and 13. Only in 1880 did the Mundella Act make attendance compulsory, and only for children between 5 and 11.

In Board schools the **religious lesson** would be either the first of the day or the last, and attendance at such lessons was not to be compulsory. This was a compromise aimed at satisfying the competing demands of the Nonconformists and Anglicans. It is often referred to as the Cowper-Temple clause, after the men responsible for it.

42.5 The Development of Elementary Education, 1870–1902

The 1870 Act is an important landmark in the history of English education. The setting up of schools which were independent of religious bodies and which were maintained with public money, local and national, spurred the voluntary bodies, particularly the Anglicans and the Catholics, to make greater efforts so that their children might be taught in schools providing for the teaching of their particular Catechism (or body of religious belief).

The 1870 Act was followed by a series of Acts which helped create a national system of education:

▶ **Sandon's Act, 1876** said that in areas where there was no School Board, the ratepayers were to elect School Attendance Committees.

▶ **Mundella's Act, 1880** made schooling compulsory, by forcing School Boards and Attendance Committees to make by-laws to compel attendance.

▶ An Act of **1891** gave parents the right to demand free schooling for their children.

▶ An Act of **1893** fixed the school-leaving age at 11. In **1899** this was raised to 12. Although the dates lie outside the scope of this unit, it is worthwhile noting that the school-leaving age was raised in 1918 (to 14), in 1947 (to 15) and in 1966 (to 16).

42.6 Problems of State Education, 1870–1900

The voluntary schools had more children than did the country's Board Schools, even in 1900, but these schools had to rely on church collections, fees and a small government grant, whereas the Board Schools had the local rates for their support. By 1900 it was evident that the standards of equipment and furniture (in laboratories, domestic science and woodwork rooms) were much lower in voluntary schools. There would have to be a change in their financing.

Higher classes were being run by some Board Schools to cater for more able children, whose parents were willing to let them stay on after the school leaving age (raised to 12 in 1899). This was an illegal use of the school rate, as was proved by the **Cockerton Judgment** of 1901. Something would have to be done about these illegal classes.

County Councils, set up in 1888 (unit 35), provided technical education out of funds obtained from the Science and Art Department attached to the Kensington Museums, and from the Board of Agriculture. But there was no link between Board Schools and County Technical Schools. There would have to be a reform to provide this link.

The Civil Service, now more efficient after the Gladstonian reform (unit 29) was led, in 1900, by highly educated and able men. Some of these helped Lloyd George to organize the Insurance Scheme (unit 37). One of them, **Robert Morant**, was responsible for the **1902 Education Act** which **Balfour** guided through parliament. This Act abolished the School Boards and created **140 Local Education Authorities** (LEAs) run by county and borough councils which were to be responsible for:

▶ elementary education (the former Board Schools became County Schools);

▶ technical schools and colleges (formerly run by the counties);

▶ secondary (grammar) schools which they were empowered to build, while they could also take-over existing grammar schools whose governors asked to be taken over;

▶ teacher-training colleges.

The Act provided some of the money needed by the **voluntary schools**, which previously got money directly from the government grant. This angered the Nonconformists, who complained of 'Rome on the Rates' in their attack on the rate funding of Church Schools. This attack helped unite the Liberals (unit 28).

42.7 Education Acts since 1902

THE 1907 ACT

In 1907 Parliament passed an Act which said that one-quarter of all the places at **rate-aided grammar schools** had to be kept as **free places** for children who had gone to elementary schools. This decision created the **eleven-plus system**, whereby elementary schoolchildren competed for the small number of places open to them.

A ladder of opportunity was provided for clever working-class children, particularly in counties which went beyond the 'one-quarter' and offered a larger number of free places. This led many **middle-class parents** to take their children from private schools in the hope that, from the elementary school, they might get a free place at the grammar school.

THE FISHER ACT, 1918

This Act said that:

▶ **nursery schools** should be founded for three-year-old children;

▶ **county colleges** should be founded to which young work-people could go for a day or so every week to continue their education;

▶ **the school leaving age** was to be raised to 14. The last point was put into law, but employers, local education authorities and the government combined to stop the other reforms being put into practice on the grounds that in the depressed state of industry and trade, the country could not afford the cost.

EDUCATION IN THE INTER-WAR YEARS

In 1926 a government Committee (the **Haddow Committee**) reported on the system of state education. It suggested an examination at the age of 11 for all children, and the setting up of a new kind of secondary school for the children who did not then pass on to grammar school. In these secondary 'modern' schools, teachers were to be encouraged to start new subjects in the classroom.

By 1939 over two-thirds of the nation's children were in such 'Modern' Schools.

THE 1944 ACT

As in 1918, wartime led to an interest in education. **R. A. Butler** was responsible for the 1944 Act which raised the **school leaving age** to 15 (achieved in 1947) and said that it was to be raised to 16 as soon as possible, and abolished fee-paying for secondary (grammar) schools, so that all the places would now be open to competition. It went on to create the three part **(or tripartite)** system of secondary education by dividing 11-year-olds into:
▶ the academic, who passed the eleven-plus and went on to the **grammar school**;
▶ the practical, who, although failing the eleven-plus, did well enough to go to a **technical school**;
▶ the majority, who went on to **secondary modern** schools.

42.8 The Debate over the Comprehensive School

Many parents were disappointed by the way in which the 1944 Act worked, with children from the same families and streets going to different kinds of schools at the age of 11.

Many reports showed that the eleven-plus examination did not really work because:
▶ many 'successes' at 11 left school at 15 without taking any of the Certificate examinations for which they were supposed to be fitted;
▶ many 'failures' at 11 got a number of subjects in the Certificate examinations for which, at 11, they were said to be 'unfit'.

Some LEAs could not afford to create three kinds of schools – notably rural areas such as Devon and Anglesey. These created the one large secondary school where all the children from the area went. London County Council also created such 'comprehensive schools', although allowing a number of children to go to local existing grammar schools on passing the eleven-plus.

In the 1950s and 1960s there was an expansion of the comprehensive system, although different LEAs introduced variations on the system with, for example:
▶ **middle schools**, so that children went to a primary school until they were 9 or 10, then to a middle school until they were 13 or 14, then to a high school for the last years of schooling;
▶ **Sixth Form Colleges**, which recruited the senior pupils from all the local secondary, comprehensive or high schools.

But the **grammar school** remained a major feature of secondary schooling.

In 1965 the Minister of Education in the Wilson government, **Anthony Crosland**, issued a document compelling LEAs to submit their plans for the abolition of the eleven-plus and for the introduction of a system of comprehensive

schooling. Many did so, and went ahead with reorganization. Others dragged their feet, but were forced to take action when in 1974 Labour came back to power and the Minister, **Shirley Williams**, insisted on reorganization. A small number of LEAs continued to resist the Minister's demands, but in 1980 most of these had climbed down and the country now has a network of comprehensive schools.

42.9 Technology and Education, 1950–86

Modern industry continues to be more complex and more science-based. This creates a demand for a better-educated workforce.
▶ **The Colleges of Advanced Technology** were opened in the late 1950s to provide highly educated **technologists**. They developed into the modern Polytechnics.
▶ **Colleges of Further Education**, often based on older **Technical Colleges**, have developed to provide the **craftsmen and craftswomen** needed in industry and commerce.
▶ **Colleges of Higher Education**, based on the former teacher-training colleges, have expanded and changed so that they now provide a wide education for teachers, social workers and others involved in the **humanities**, as well as providing so-called **vocational courses** for those who want qualifications in business studies, science, catering, tourism and other such occupations.
▶ **The Universities**, many of which were founded in the 1950s and 1960s, have expanded to take in and educate a larger proportion of people to help provide more of the educated workforce needed by an industrialized nation.

SIR KEITH JOSEPH, 1979–86

The Conservative Prime Minister, Mrs Thatcher, had formerly been Minister of Education. Some people hoped she would support an expansion of spending on education. Sir Keith Joseph, her Minister of Education, showed in his early speeches and writings that he understood the importance of education to Britain's industrial future.

Financial cuts, however, affected educational development. Schools received less money (in real terms) for books and materials and teachers' salaries fell relative to wages in the private sector. A long and damaging strike (1985–86) led to some improvement in their position, but left behind a legacy of bitterness between employers and teachers and between teachers and some parents.

Another aspect of the cuts was that universities received grants which failed to take full account of inflation. Keith Joseph imposed additional cuts on some universities, so that there was a fall in the number of undergraduates. These cuts were particularly harmful when applied to universties, such as Salford, which specialized in technological education.

The introduction of the GCSE may be seen as Joseph's major contribution to educational reform, although he also tried to improve teacher-training.

Unit 42 Summary

▶ Upper-class education, 1760–1860; the work of Butler, Thring and Arnold.
▶ Grammar Schools and Dissenting Academies, 1760–1871.
▶ Working-class education, 1760–1830; the work of Raikes, More, Bell and Lancaster.
▶ Monitorial schools.
▶ Elementary education, 1830–70; the work of Lowe and Forster.
▶ The beginnings of state-provided education, 1870–1902: Education Acts, 1902, 1907 and 1918.
▶ The 1944 Act; the demand for comprehensive schools.
▶ Technology and education, 1950–1986.
▶ The 'reign' of Keith Joseph, 1981–86.

43.1 The German Plan

In 1905 a German commander, **Schlieffen**, drew up a plan to be used in the event of Germany's being involved in a war against both France and Russia. Under this plan seven armies were to drive through Belgium and Northern France. According to a strict timetable, they were to link up with German armies at Strasbourg within 48 days, having surrounded and occupied Paris on the way.

Within days of the declaration of war, the **British Expeditionary Force**, commanded by **Sir John French**, was in Belgium. Their task, agreed with the French, was the defence of Mons.

Mons was directly in the path of the German advance, and in late August the British Army had its first taste of the war. British **rifle fire** was so rapid that the Germans believed they were armed with machine guns, but **British losses** (1600 dead in nine hours) were high, with some regiments (e.g. the Cheshire) losing almost all their men.

The German plan was delayed by the battle, and by the planned retreat from Mons which gave the French armies time to prepare. At **Ypres** the Army, commanded by **Sir Douglas Haig,** made another stand in another bloodbath. **The Russians** mobilized more quickly than Germany expected, and **Moltke**, the German commander, took men from France to reinforce the troops on his Eastern front.

The delay at Mons which had put the timetable out of gear, and the withdrawal of troops by Moltke, meant that **Von Kluck**, the German commander in France was forced to abandon the Schlieffen Plan.

The German Armies turned south, but instead of going to the west of Paris, tried to link up with their Strasbourg-based armies by marching to the east of the capital. Von Kluck's failure to seize the Channel ports on the French coast allowed British reinforcements to be sent to fight in France.

At the **River Marne**, a few miles from Paris, French armies, reinforced by civilians and troops brought to the front in Parisian taxis, were commanded by **Joffre**. The British were commanded by **French** and the Allied armies drove the Germans back over the **Aisne** and saved Paris.

43.2 Trench Warfare

By December 1914 the opposing armies were dug in, and trenches ran from Switzerland to the Channel coast. On both sides the generals wanted to break through enemy trenches, but failed because of:
▶ the **defensive barricades** of barbed wire;
▶ the **machine guns**, which gave defenders an advantage over attackers;
▶ the **failure of artillery** bombardments to break either the wire or the morale of the enemy – who were, however, warned by such heavy bombardments, so that they were better prepared for the forthcoming attack.

During the winter months of each year of the war men lived a miserable life in muddy, waterlogged trenches, struggled through the mud of no man's land (between the opposing trenches) to attack the enemy, and drowned in the mud if they slipped off the duckboards laid for the advance.

In spite of continued failures, opposing generals continued to order major battles. There were:
▶ **the Somme 1916**, on the first day of which (in July 1916) 60 000 British soldiers died, out of a force of 100 000; by the time this battle ended in November 1916, Britain had suffered 400 000 casualties in 'the Graveyard of Kitchener's Army;

▶ **Ypres**, 1915 and 1917, the latter battle being better known as **Passchendaele**, and September 1918;
▶ **Loos**, 1915;
▶ **Verdun**, 1916;
▶ **Messines, Vimy, Cambrai** – all in 1917;
▶ **St Quentin**, 1918.

NEW WEAPONS

To try to break the deadlock both sides introduced new weapons.
▶ **Gas** was first used by the Germans at the **Second Battle of Ypres** (1915).
▶ **The tank**, travelling at 3 m.p.h., was first used by the British at **the Somme**, where the heavy vehicles got bogged down in the mud or were destroyed by enemy artillery.
▶ **The aeroplane** was, at first, a slow moving, inefficient and unarmed machine used mainly for observation of enemy movements. During the war both sides increased their production of planes and improved the machines by:
● developing **more powerful engines**; some machines had four engines. After the war, an aeroplane made the first transatlantic crossing;
● developed **interrupter gear**, which allowed machine guns to be fired through the revolving propeller.

By the end of the war, planes were playing a role in land battles, attacking enemy troops in their trenches.

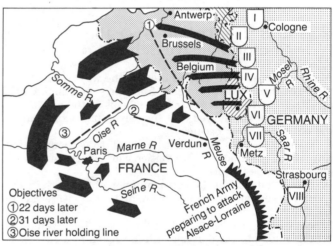

Fig. 43.1 The German attack on France as (i) planned by Schlieffen and (ii) as it actually developed in August 1914. Notice the differences. You should be able to explain why the plan was changed.

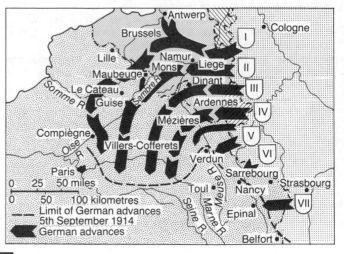

43.3 War on Other Fronts

The Western Front in France was the main theatre of war, but the **Turkish Front** became important when Turkey entered the war on Germany's side (October 1914). This:
▶ closed the route through which Allied aid could get to Russia;
▶ led to the unsuccessful attack on the Dardanelles (March 1915) by a fleet of old battleships;
▶ led to the **Gallipoli** campaign, designed to take Constantinople from the rear. This failed because:
● **the army** was too small;
● **the commander**, Ian Hamilton, delayed the attack;
● **the Turks** were well prepared and well led by Mustapha Kemal (later Kemal Ataturk).

The Gallipoli campaign led to the deaths of thousands of **colonial troops** from Australia, Canada and New Zealand (the ANZAC forces) and resulted in the resignation of **Churchill**, who had argued for the attack on the Dardanelles and Gallipoli.

In November 1916 **Bulgaria** joined the war on Germany's side, and this led to the defeat of **Serbia**. At **Salonika**, in northern Greece, the Allies kept a force of 600 000 as a sign that they had not abandoned the Eastern Front.

The **Palestine campaign** was aimed at preventing Turkey from invading Egypt, while the British advance from the Persian Gulf into **Mesopotamia** was meant to protect Britain's oil supplies. In this campaign:
▶ the Turks defeated the British at **Kut-el-Amara** (1916);
▶ the British captured **Baghdad** and **Jerusalem** (1917) and in September 1918 General **Allenby** made a triumphal entry into **Damascus**;
▶ **T. E. Lawrence** ('of Arabia') played a role in bringing the Arab tribes on to Britain's side against their Turkish overlords.

43.4 The War at Sea

During this war, as during any major war, **the role of the Navy** was to:
▶ protect British trade routes and ensure imports of essential food and goods;
▶ blockade enemy ports to try to prevent such imports getting there;
▶ convey troops to the Continent and other theatres of war;
▶ protect imperial possessions against enemy attack.

The development of a large and powerful **German Navy** (unit 36) made it likely that there would be major battles. In fact there were few naval battles of any size. The only major one was at **Jutland** (May 1916) where, after a day of fighting, the Germans withdrew and their fleet never came out to action again. This battle was claimed as a British victory because of the German withdrawal, but is now seen as at least a partial defeat, because of the heavier losses suffered by the British. The Germans had:
▶ better armour to protect their ships;
▶ better armaments which inflicted damage on British ships;
▶ better technical and naval awareness.

Modern writers suggest that this reflected the state of industry and of education in the two countries.

SUBMARINE WARFARE

The Germans developed the **submarine** (or U-Boat) to attack British shipping. Losses were very heavy:
▶ February 1917–266 ships sunk;
▶ March   1917–338;
▶ April   1917–430.

Supplies of food ran low (in April 1917 there was only six weeks supply of corn in the country).

The **convoy system** was then forced on an unwilling Navy by a dominant Prime Minister, Lloyd George. Naval ships protected merchant vessels sailing in groups. This led

to fewer losses of British ships, and by March 1918 the German U-boats were suffering heavy losses as they were attacked by armed naval vessels.

43.5 The End of the War

In April 1917 the **Americans** entered the war in response to the attacks on American ships by submarines, and to the 'Zimmermann telegram', promising German aid to Mexico if she attacked the USA.

The British naval blockade had led to food shortages in Germany (1917), and **Ludendorff**, the German army commander, realized that if Germany did not win the war in the winter of 1917–18 the home front would collapse and lead to demands for a peace.

In March 1918 the Germans made a series of attacks on the Western Front:
▶ the British were attacked at **Arras** and **Amiens**– March, 1918;
▶ the German attack then switched to the north (April) and once again the Flanders' fields around **Ypres** were the scenes of great slaughter. By the end of April this attack had been halted.

The Germans then attacked and defeated the French at the **Aisne**, made their way to the **Marne** and the roads to **Paris**. **American troops** were thrown into the battle to defend Paris, and the Allied counter-attack was led by a supreme commander, **Foch**, who had been imposed against the wishes of the British generals, Haig and Robertson, to take control of the entire front. This attack was led by tanks and aircraft and broke the German lines, for the first time since 1914.

At **Amiens** the British defeated the Germans on 'the blackest day in the history of the German army', and by the end of September the whole Allied line was advancing.

On 4th October Ludendorff asked for a truce. The Allied reply was **Wilson's Fourteen Points**, which was rejected by the Germans.

After a further Allied advance the **Kaiser** abdicated on 9th November and German politicians proclaimed a Republic, willing to accept the Fourteen Points as terms for an Armistice which ended the fighting at 11.00 am on 11th November 1918.

43.6 The Effect of the War at Home

WORKERS AT HOME

Trade union leaders were involved in national and local committees set up to help increase industrial production. The **unions** gave up their right to strike, and also agreed to 'dilution', whereby unskilled workers did work previously only done by skilled workers. The numbers of workers in unions grew. Hodges, Barnes, Clynes and Henderson were invited to join the **government**, which gave Labour both 'respectability' and experience of government.

STANDARDS OF LIVING

Many wartime homes had a higher income than they had had in 1913:
▶ there was more regular employment at higher wages;
▶ many married women went to work and added to family income;
▶ soldiers had to send regular 'allotments' of money to their families.

As a result of this, more people enjoyed a better diet of meat, fruit and vegetables than they had been able to afford in 1913, and they enjoyed improved health, as reflected in the reports from school medical inspections.

THE GOVERNMENT AND INDUSTRY

The **coal** and **railway** industries were taken over by the government to ensure an adequate supply of coal and the organized transport of men, goods and materials.

The government controlled many British factories by:

▶ controlling the **supply of materials** – released only to factories which produced goods needed by the government;

▶ insisting on **better book-keeping systems**, so that government would know what prices to pay for factory output;

▶ persuading industry to accept **new machinery** brought from the USA, and **improved methods** of production to ensure an adequate supply of munitions and other essential goods.

The Corn Production Act (1917) guaranteed farmers a price for their crop, and many farmers ploughed up land which had been left untouched since the onset of the depression in the 1870s (unit 27).

THE WAR AND THE LABOUR PARTY

Hardie and MacDonald became unpopular for opposing British entry into the war, and **Henderson** replaced MacDonald as party leader (1914) and became a member of the Cabinet in 1915. In 1918 Henderson and Webb produced a new constitution.

The party grew **richer** because of the increased union membership, and **the Representation of the People Act, 1918**, gave the vote to all adult males and to women over the age of 30, increasing the possibilities of Labour winning more seats.

After the war, when people became disillusioned with the War Premier (Lloyd George) and with the war itself, many turned to the Labour Party because of MacDonald's original opposition to the war.

THE WAR AND THE LIBERAL PARTY

Morley resigned from the government as soon as war was declared. Others were to do so within a short time. Some Liberals opposed the government take-over of industry, the extension of its control over other parts of industry and with its fixing of prices paid to farmers. All this was an interference with the philosophy of **laisser-faire** (p. 38).

Conscription

Conscription proved a major breaking point for many Liberals. Originally, Kitchener had relied on volunteers (1914–15), but the slaughter of 1914–16 proved too much for this system, and the Generals wanted even more men.

Between June 1915 and May 1916 Parliament debated this issue, before deciding that every man between the ages of 18 and 40 had to register for service. Millions were conscripted into the forces; 27 Liberal MPs voted against this drastic interference with personal liberty.

Munitions

War Munitions provided another major strain. The generals called for even more shells, but in 1914 and 1915 private industry failed to produce enough. In May 1915 Lloyd George became Minister for Munitions. He was responsible for the **Munitions of War Act**, 1915 which gave the government powers to limit the profits made by munitions firms, and to take over some firms and open new government-run munitions factories.

The results were good and the supplies of shells increased, but many Liberals disagreed with this 'socialist' industrial policy.

Rationing

Food rationing provided yet another strain on Liberal loyalties. By 1918 the government had taken control of the country's scarce food supply, establishing a rationing system to ensure a fair distribution of food (rather than allow it to be shared out by higher prices, which would have benefited only the better-off).

The weekly rations were eight ounces of sugar; five ounces of butter and margarine; four ounces of jam; two ounces of tea; eight ounces of bacon.

Many Liberals believed that the government ought to have allowed market forces to work freely – even if this led to higher prices and an unfair distribution of the scarce food.

THE FALL OF ASQUITH, DECEMBER 1916

In May 1915 Asquith asked the Conservatives to join the Liberals **in a Coalition government**. By December 1916 many Conservatives were dissatisfied with Asquith's running of the war as he lacked energy, control over the generals and new ideas on how to improve things.

Lloyd George asked Asquith to set up a **War Cabinet** of four men to run the war, of whom Asquith would not have been one. The Prime Minister refused and Lloyd George resigned.

On 5th December 1916 Asquith also resigned, hoping to prove that only he could command Liberal loyalty and support. He suggested that the King ask the Conservative leader, Bonar Law, to form a government, hoping that he would fail. Law refused, but suggested that the King send for Lloyd George, the Minister for Munitions. Lloyd George became Prime Minister in December 1916 and proved to be a dynamic leader.

THE MAURICE DEBATE, APRIL 1918

In April 1918 there was a debate on whether the Lloyd George government was doing enough to help the Western Front.

Some generals wanted more men and attacked Lloyd George through their friends in the Commons. One, **Sir Frederick Maurice**, wrote a letter to the papers accusing the Prime Minister of 'starving the Front of the men and materials needed'.

In the ensuing debate, Lloyd George defended himself by quoting figures supplied to the government by Maurice's own Military Department. But in this debate many Liberals voted against Lloyd George to get their own back on him for Asquith's overthrow. This split marked a division in the Party which never really healed.

Lloyd George won through with Conservative support.

THE COUPON ELECTION, 1918

As soon as the war ended in November, Lloyd George called an election. He sent out a letter to every candidate he supported, which Asquith nicknamed **'the coupon'**. Few of those who had voted against him in the Maurice Debate received this support.

In the feverish mood of the time most candidates and voters supported Lloyd George – Asquith was heavily defeated.

The election result was:

▶ Coalition MPs 484 (Lloyd George Liberals 136; Conservatives 338); Labour and other supporters of the Coalition 10;

▶ Labour, 59 seats;

▶ Asquithian Liberals, 26 seats.

It was the Lloyd George Coalition government which had to make the Peace Treaties with the various enemy countries, and which had to cope with the domestic effects of the 'Great War'.

◼ Unit 43 Summary ◼

▶ The abandonment of the Schlieffen Plan.
▶ Life in the trenches.
▶ War in the Middle East.
▶ War at sea; the submarine campaigns.
▶ Reasons for Germany's defeat.
▶ Social, political, economic and industrial effects of war.
▶ The rise of Lloyd George; the Coupon Election, 1918.

44 PEACEMAKING: THE EFFECTS OF THE WAR ON BRITAIN

44.1 Wilson's Fourteen Points

In January 1918 President Wilson issued his Fourteen Points on which a peace settlement should be based. The Germans finally accepted this in November 1918 and signed the Armistice.

In December 1918 Wilson went to Paris to meet **Orlando** of Italy, **Clemenceau** of France, and **Lloyd George** of Britain.

The 'Big Four' dominated the Conference at Versailles and the three European leaders forced Wilson to modify:
▶ **Point 1:** by meeting in secret, contrary to the open diplomacy Wilson had promised;
▶ **Point 2:** by refusing to give up the right to search shipping trading with enemy countries during wartime;
▶ **Point 3:** by maintaining tariff barriers;
▶ **Point 4:** by not guaranteeing disarmament;
▶ **Point 5:** by ignoring the rights of colonial peoples;
▶ **Point 6:** by sending armies to attack the Bolshevik government of Russia;
▶ **Point 9:** by not settling the boundary of Italy;
▶ **Point 13:** by creating a Poland which contained over two million Germans;
▶ **Point 14:** by creating a League of Nations which they refused to allow to work as Wilson intended.

44.2 The Conference at Versailles, 1918–19

This was only one, although the most important, of the peace-making Conferences. It led to a Peace Treaty with Germany. Other Treaties arranged a settlement with Austria (**St Germain**); Bulgaria (**Neuilly**); Hungary (**Trianon**) and Turkey (**Lausanne**).

At Versailles there were 1037 delegates from 32 victorious powers, who had 60 committees of experts to help investigation of special problems.

The Conference and its decisions were really determined by the 'Big Four' who reached their decisions in secret. They had to take into account the violent nationalism of many European peoples and the angry public opinion in their own countries which called for 'revenge' against Germany and which made finding solutions even more difficult.

Germany was not represented at the Conference, nor were any other of the defeated powers (Austria–Hungary, Bulgaria and Turkey).

Russia, although an Ally in 1914, was not represented, because the Allies refused to recognize the Bolshevik government of Lenin.

THE TREATY OF VERSAILLES, 28TH JUNE 1919

Germany had to accept, or reject, the terms without discussion.
▶ **German losses in Europe**
● **Alsace-Lorraine**, seized in 1870, was restored to France with its valuable industrial and mineral wealth.
● The **Saar**, an important coalfield, was to be administered by the League for 15 years, when its future would be decided by a plebiscite among its inhabitants.
● The new countries of **Poland** and **Czechoslovakia** were given portions of German territory.
● **Danzig**, an important German port, was declared a 'free city' to be administered by the League of Nations, while **Memel**, another important port, was given to Lithuania.
● **Belgium** and **Denmark** were also given small portions of German territory.

Fig. 44.2 The makers of the Versailles Treaty.

● **The Rhineland**, although not lost permanently, was to be occupied by Allied troops for 15 years. In all, Germany lost over six million inhabitants (about 10 per cent of its population) and large areas of valuable and strategically important territory.
▶ **German colonies** were ceded to the Allies, who agreed to run them as Mandates of the League of Nations, with Germany losing all her trading rights with these territories:
● **Britain** controlled Tanganyika (German East Africa).
● **France** controlled the Cameroons.
● **New Zealand** controlled Western Samoa.
● **South Africa** controlled German South-West Africa, which it now treats as part of its own territory, having failed to carry out the terms of the Mandate (to help the native populations to attain independence).
▶ **German military strength** was weakened by the Treaty, which said:
● the German **air force** had to be disbanded;
● the German **navy** and **army** were to be reduced in size and strength, tanks and submarines being banned;
● Germany was never to build **fortifications** on the banks of the Rhine and the Rhineland was to be occupied by the Allies for 15 years.
▶ **Reparations** were imposed to provide for the damages caused by the war. At first the Allies talked of getting:
● £6600 million in cash;
● the surrender of the merchant navy (to Britain);
● large quantities of coal (to France) and cattle to Belgium.

Keynes, a leading economist and one of the British 'experts' at the Conference, pointed out that:
▶ to get that amount of money, Germany would have to export masses of goods and so ensure unemployment in most other industrialized countries;
▶ she would, in fact, never be able to manage to provide the goods or the cash.

The French were more insistent on reparations than were the British (who had suffered less). When Germany fell behind with her payments, the French occupied the **Ruhr** industrial region in 1923 – so ensuring that Germany would fall even further behind, while also helping the British coal industry to enjoy a false boom (unit 46).

MacDonald, as Labour Prime Minister and Foreign Secretary helped to organize a plan named after the USA Minister, **Dawes**. The **Dawes Plan** (1924) modified the reparations payments, as did the **Young Plan** (1929).

Reparations were finally abandoned in 1932, by which

time Germany had repaid only the money borrowed from the Allies after 1919. But by this time the reparation question had created economic problems for the world, and had helped Hitler to rise to power as the spokesman for the German antagonism towards reparations.

▶ **War guilt:** in Clause 231 of the Treaty the Germans were forced to accept total responsibility for the outbreak of the war.

▶ **The League of Nations** was established.

GERMAN REACTION TO THE TREATY

There was widespread criticism, led by Keynes, of the harsh Treaty in Britain. In Germany the reaction was much stronger, and the **politicians** who signed the Treaty were denounced as traitors, while the **German Army** leaders argued that they had been 'stabbed in the back', ignoring the fact of their defeats and retreats.

Germans claimed, rightly, that the Treaty ignored the **Fourteen Points** on which they had assumed it would be based, and the **loss** of German people and territory to Czechoslovakia, Poland, Denmark and Lithuania, was a future cause of war.

Germany was excluded from the **League of Nations**, which Germans then saw as an Allied 'club' for the maintenance of the Treaty.

44.3 Other Territorial Arrangements

Austria–Hungary was divided into two small, landlocked countries, and both countries suffered major territorial losses:

▶ **Yugoslavia** was formed from the old Serbia and from the Southern Slavs who had lived in Hungary.

▶ **Rumania** was enlarged by Bessarabia (from Russia) and Transylvania (from Austria–Hungary).

▶ **Czechoslovakia** was formed from the old German kingdom of Bohemia and from the Northern Slavs of the old Austria–Hungary.

New countries were created. In addition to **Yugoslavia** and **Czechoslovakia**, they were:

▶ **Poland,** formed with the additions of Posen and Silesia from Germany and of Galicia from Austria and of West (or 'White') Russia from Russia.

▶ **Finland, Estonia, Latvia** and **Lithuania,** formed from former Russian territory.

Turkey lost her former Empire with:

▶ **Britain** gaining control of Palestine as a Mandate;

▶ **France** gaining control of Syria as a Mandate;

▶ **Arab** countries gaining their political independence, although they became economically and diplomatically dependent on the Allies.

44.4 The League of Nations

This had been proposed in Wilson's Fourteenth Point. **The Covenant** (or solemn agreement) of this League was included in all the treaties signed by the Allies and the defeated nations.

The League consisted of:

▶ **The Assembly**, which met annually. Each member nation had one vote (a recognition of the principle of democracy) and could air its grievances. Decisions had to be unanimous, which meant that the Assembly rarely reached a decision.

▶ **The Council**, which met three times a year. There were, originally, eight members:

● the four Great Powers – Britain, France, Italy and Japan, each had a permanent seat;

● four (later increased to 11) seats were held by smaller nations in rotation.

▶ **The Secretariat**, or international Civil Service, of permanent officials who administered the business of the League.

▶ **The International Labour Organization**, developed in conjunction with the League, which also had its headquarters in Geneva. Representatives of government, employers and workers worked to improve conditions of life and work for the world's population.

▶ **The International Court**, which grew stronger as a result of the founding of the League. Founded in 1900, the Court had originally been ignored by the Powers. In 1922 the first Permanent Court of Justice was founded at the Hague and (although it had limited powers) by 1939 its 15 judges had considered almost 70 cases, while over 400 treaties had been made containing agreements to refer disputes to the Court.

▶ **Commissions**, set up by the League, achieved a good deal of success. These included Commissions on Mandated Territories, health, drug traffic, equal rights for women and social and economic problems with international repercussions.

ATTITUDES TOWARDS THE LEAGUE

France wanted the League to be a strong body with power to act to safeguard French security against Germany.

Britain supported the idea of a League where disputes could be settled. However, unlike France, Britain's main interests lay outside Europe, and she did not support the idea of armies being sent into Europe in the event of negotiations breaking down.

The USA refused to join the League, although it had been created as a result of Wilson's insistence. In 1918 the Republicans had won control of the Senate, which rejected the Democratic President's proposals for joining the League.

Germany saw the League as an Allied 'club' from which she was originally excluded, and **Russia** was originally excluded from the League by the anti-Bolshevik powers. Although she later joined, she always regarded it with suspicion as a 'Capitalists' Club'. She was expelled in 1939 for her invasion of Finland.

44.5 The Results of the War for Britain

Britain made certain **territorial gains** (Tanganyika and Palestine).

In unit 43 we saw that the war had affected:

▶ trade unions;

▶ living standards and people's expectations;

▶ government control of industry;

▶ the Liberal and Labour Parties;

▶ the role of women in society and politics.

The increased **government power** – over industry, farming, taxation, manpower and national supplies of such things as food and raw materials – might have been used after the war to alter radically the nation's economic and social life. This was what some people hoped that Lloyd George intended to do, after his use of slogans such as 'homes fit for heroes to live in'. Some new Ministries were set up (Health and Transport), which some saw as a sign that 'the Welsh wizard' meant to carry out his proposed radical programme. We will see in unit 45 that he did not do so.

Economically Britain suffered a great deal because of the war. Millions of tons of **shipping** were lost and although these had been more than replaced by 1920, it was at great cost.

Many **men** were killed or seriously injured so that they never contributed to the nation's wealth, as otherwise they might have done, and many overseas **markets** were lost to British exporters unable to supply goods during wartime. Other countries learned to manufacture goods themselves, or had to import from other countries, so that the USA and Japan became industrially very powerful and proved successful rivals to Britain in the post-war world.

45 DOMESTIC AFFAIRS, 1918–24

45.1 Four Prime Ministers

During this period there were four Prime Ministers:
▶ **David Lloyd George**, the leader of the wartime Coalition government, was Prime Minister until the rebellion by some Conservatives in 1922.
▶ **Bonar Law**, leader of the Conservatives in 1910 (unit 37), had helped form the wartime Coalition, had remained in the government after the 1918 election but had retired from ill-health in 1921. He came back into politics in October 1922 to lead the Conservative rebellion against Lloyd George and became Prime Minister for a short time, but ill-health forced him to retire in 1923.
▶ **Stanley Baldwin**, a Minister in the Coalition government, helped organize the Conservative rebellion in 1922, succeeded Bonar Law as Prime Minister, but resigned after the 1923 election. However, he was Prime Minister again from 1925 until 1929 and from 1935 until 1937. Examiners often ask questions on the importance of his career, and you will find part of the answer to that question in this unit.
▶ **Ramsay MacDonald** became Labour's first Prime Minister in 1924, was Prime Minister in a second Labour Government in 1929 and led the National Government from 1931 until 1935. In unit 40 you will find a summary of his career, a favourite subject with examiners. In this unit you will find some development of the answer to the question on MacDonald's career, importance and achievements.

45.2 Lloyd George

LLOYD GEORGE'S EARLIER CAREER

Lloyd George was born in Manchester in 1863 and brought up by an uncle in Caernarvonshire; after schooling at the village school he became a solicitor (1884), spoke for the Liberals and became a Liberal County Alderman (1889).

He was elected an MP in 1890, and became nationally famous for his opposition to the Boer War (unit 35).

Minister

▶ 1905 President of the Board of Trade;
▶ 1908 Chancellor of the Exchequer, responsible for the 1909 Budget (unit 37) and the 1911 Insurance Act (unit 37);
▶ 1915 Minister of Munitions;
▶ 1916 (June) succeeded Kitchener as War Minister;
▶ 1916 (December) formed Coalition government.

Wartime Prime Minister

▶ **Generals** disliked him because he stood up to them (Haig and Robertson) and insisted on a unified command led by Foch (unit 43);
▶ **Admirals** disliked him because he insisted on the convoy system, which ensured Britain's overseas supplies (unit 43);

▶ **Unions** cooperated with him on dilution of labour, women workers and abandonment of right to strike (unit 43);
▶ **Old-fashioned Liberals** disliked his ruthless prosecution of the war with what they criticized as illiberal policies on industry, agriculture, rationing and conscription (unit 43).
▶ **The electorate** saw him as the 'war winner' and voted for the Coalition government in the 1918 election (unit 43).

An 'uneasy' Liberal

During **the Boer War** he quarrelled with the Party's leaders who supported the government's war effort, and between **1905 and 1911** he upset old-fashioned Liberals with his Budget, Insurance Act and attacks on the Lords (unit 37).

In **1912** he proposed a Coalition government to help overcome the problems of Ireland and the Lords and in **1915** he supported the formation of Asquith's Coalition government, even if this meant the dismissal of his friend, Churchill. In **December 1916** he formed the Coalition government following the resignation of Asquith. This split the Liberals.

In the **1918 Election** he had refused to send the 'coupon' to Asquithian Liberals, most of whom lost their seats (unit 43). From **1918** to **1922** he led a government which was dependent on Conservative votes (see below).

He had his own **Lloyd George Fighting Fund** (see below) which he used to maintain his own wing of what he still called the Liberal Party, which made an uneasy alliance with Asquith in 1924 but which won fewer and fewer seats at elections (unit 48).

In 1931 he officially left the Liberal Party to form an Independent Liberal Party, but rejoined the Liberals for the 1935 election.

Before and during the Second World War he favoured a settlement with Hitler (unit 50).

He died in 1945 just after becoming an Earl.

LLOYD GEORGE'S GOVERNMENT, 1918–22
Versailles

Lloyd George was Britain's main representative at the peace-making Conference (unit 44).

Russia

In February 1917 the Tsarist government had been overthrown by a Russian revolution, and in October 1917 the resulting democratic government was overthrown by the Bolshevik revolution.

Lloyd George and many others feared that this might be the start of a world-wide revolution. Britain, France and the USA sent troops to Russia to help the anti-Bolsheviks during the Civil War (1918–22).

Lloyd George remained an anti-Communist and helped persuade many people that Labour was a Bolshevik Party.

Homes fit for heroes

This was one of the slogans used by Lloyd George as part of his promise to make post-war Britain a better place in which to live.

Addison, Minster of Health, 1919, piloted a Housing Act through Parliament. This Act gave local authorities power to build houses and promised a government subsidy of £260 for each council house built. Councils could charge less for the rent of the houses and so help the poor to become better-housed.

Failure

In the post-war boom of 1919–20, prices of timber, glass, bricks, copper and rubber rose sharply. This pushed up the price of housing. Councils had to charge high rents even for the subsidized houses, so that only the better-off workers could afford to live in council houses.

Trade unions

The trade unions welcomed Lloyd George's Unemployment Insurance Act (unit 46) and enjoyed the industrial boom of 1919–20, during which most of their members had jobs and many unions won wage increases. The **railway workers**, in a government-controlled industry, resisted an attempt to cut wages (September 1919) when J. H. Thomas, their leader, threatened a strike. The government climbed down and postposed the cuts.

The **miners**, led by Robert Smillie, won a wage increase from the government (March 1920), and the **transport workers**, led by Ernest Bevin, had a favourable report from a Commission of Inquiry set up by the government and won a wage increase.

The end of the boom

The post-war boom came to a sudden end in the autumn 1920. By early 1921 there were two million unemployed– over 20 per cent of the people insured under the Insurance scheme.

The coal industry, which had made a profit for the government in 1919 and 1920, was handed back to private owners as prices fell from £6 a ton to £1 a ton.

The Triple Alliance

In unit 39 we saw that the miners, railwaymen and transport workers reached agreement as to joint action by the three unions.

Coal owners, facing a sharp fall in price, announced wage cuts to start 31st March 1921. The **miners** refused to accept the proposed cuts, went on strike (1st April 1921) and called on their fellow unionists in the Triple Alliance to support them.

Thomas and **Bevin** promised to bring their men out on 15th April 1921, but **Lloyd George** met the leaders of the three unions and trapped **Hodges**, the miners' leader, into agreeing that he would accept a government promise to maintain miners' wages while discussions went on with government, owners and miners. The miners were angry and refused to accept this, but Thomas and Bevin claimed that their threat of a strike had forced the government to offer this concession and that the miners were unreasonable not to accept it. Thomas and Bevin called off their threatened strike on what became known as **Black Friday** (15th April 1921). The miners remained on strike until 1st July 1921, when they were forced back to work on the owners' terms.

The Geddes Axe, 1922

Sir Eric Geddes was appointed to make cuts in government spending, to make up for the extra spending being made on the Unemployment Insurance Fund (unit 46).

Geddes made cuts in spending on:
▶ the **Army** and **Navy**;
▶ **Education**, closing the few County Continuation Schools opened under the Fisher Act (unit 42);

▶ **Health** and **Welfare Services**;
▶ **Council housing**.

Geddes was successful; the government spent less, but this led to a rise in unemployment (fewer people employed on house building and in education).

Ireland, 1918–22

The Home Rule Act had been suspended in 1914. Some Republicans had organized the Easter Rising, 1916 (unit 33).

In the 1918 election 73 Sinn Feiners were elected as MPs for Irish constituencies. They set up the Dublin Parliament and declared Ireland a Republic. There followed the anti-British war, with the British employing the 'auxies' and 'the Black and Tans' (unit 33).

Lloyd George pushed through the **Government of Ireland Act** 1920, which set up separate Parliaments in Dublin and Belfast.

The Civil War went on until June 1921 when Lloyd George invited leaders from Dublin and Belfast to come to London.

Collins led the Sinn Fein delegation and reluctantly agreed to accept a peace Treaty giving Ulster its independence. This set up the Irish Free State for the 26 counties of the South of Ireland (unit 33) and, as far as Britain was concerned, ended the Irish problem – until 1968 (unit 33).

Many people in Britain opposed this solution, claiming that Lloyd George had given in to the rebels in the South.

Chanak, 1922

By 1922 Lloyd George's power was weakened because of:
▶ **Irish policies** (of **terrorism**, which angered the Liberals, and of **peace-making**, which angered the hardliners);
▶ **unemployment**, which was rising;
▶ the **Geddes Axe**, which betrayed wartime promises;
▶ the **'honours scandal'** arising from the sale of titles and other honours, bringing money to Lloyd George;
▶ German failure to pay **reparations**.

In **Asia Minor** armies of Greeks and Turks faced each other as their governments fought to gain control of Constantinople and Anatolia. Lloyd George spoke of favouring a Greek victory but Kemal Ataturk (unit 43) led Turkish troops which swept the Greeks out of Asia Minor and advanced on the Dardanelles, where Allied troops were stationed at Chanak.

France and Italy withdrew their troops; Britain had only six battalions at Chanak and when Lloyd George asked for reinforcements from the Dominions these were refused. Conservatives in the Cabinet were alarmed that Britain might find herself engaged in another war with no ally.

The Turks withdrew and the feared war did not break out, but many people condemned the brinkmanship of Lloyd George.

▉ 45.3 The Carlton Club Meeting, October 1922

Bonar Law had led the Conservatives into the wartime Coalition with Lloyd George and into the 1918 election. In 1921 he retired because of ill-health. **Austen Chamberlain**, eldest son of Joseph (unit 34) then led the Conservatives in the Coalition government.

Conservative MPs began to demand an end to the Coalition when Lloyd George became less popular in 1922. **Chamberlain** summoned all Conservative MPs to a meeting at the Party headquarters, the Carlton Club (unit 30) for 19th October 1922.

At that **Carlton** meeting **Chamberlain** demanded the loyal support of all Conservatives for the Coalition, fearing that Lloyd George would be able to win an election and sweep them from the Commons.

Baldwin argued that the Party had a majority in the Coalition (and could do without Lloyd George) and would be blamed by the electorate for the failure of the government. He wanted them to break with the Coalition and fight an election as an independent Party. **Bonar Law** came from a sick bed to back Baldwin, and by 187 votes to 87 the MPs voted for an end to the Coalition.

Lloyd George resigned that afternoon and a few days later Bonar Law became Prime Minister.

THE 1922 ELECTION

Bonar Law called an election in which:
► **Conservatives** won 347 seats;
► **Labour** won 142 seats;
► **Liberals** won 117–divided into 65 Asquithian Liberals, 52 Lloyd George Liberals.

MacDonald, who had lost his seat in 1918, came back as MP for Aberavon and was chosen as Leader of the Labour Party. Bonar Law retired again in May 1923 and Baldwin became Prime Minister, knowing that:
► **the Coalition Conservative Ministers**, led by Chamberlain, refused to serve under him;
► **Lloyd George** was angling to make a new Coalition, based on Tariff Reform and anti-Bolshevism;
► **unemployment** was a major problem.

In October 1923 Baldwin spoke of the need for a Tariff which would, at one and the same time help British industry, bring Chamberlain back into the Party, and defeat Lloyd George's attempts.

Baldwin argued that Bonar Law had promised in 1922 that there would be no tariff reforms without another election, so an election was called in December 1923.

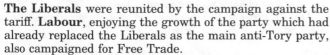

45.4 The 1923 Election

The Liberals were reunited by the campaign against the tariff. **Labour**, enjoying the growth of the party which had already replaced the Liberals as the main anti-Tory party, also campaigned for Free Trade.

The result of the election was that:
► Conservatives won 258 seats;
► Labour won 191 seats;
► the united Liberals won 158 seats.

Some **Conservatives** wanted Baldwin to make a Coalition with Asquith, in order to keep Labour out. **Baldwin** argued that if he could not form a government, then the King ought to send for the leader of the second largest Party and ask him to form a government. **Labour** would then, perhaps, form a government. Baldwin argued that since this would be a minority government it would be:
► **dependent** on support from at least the Liberals, but perhaps also from the Conservatives, if it was to get its work done in Parliament;
► **too weak** to do anything 'Bolshevik';
► **overthrown** whenever the Liberals and Conservatives united;
► **an experience** for Labour ministers who would, one day, form a majority government. Baldwin argued that it would be good for them to learn how to govern, run the Civil Service, prepare a Budget and get Bills through Parliament, while still being controlled by the Conservatives and Liberals.

Asquith agreed with this and promised to support Labour provided that it did nothing rash.

THE FIRST LABOUR GOVERNMENT, 1924

Ramsay MacDonald was both Prime Minister and Foreign Secretary. He was successful in:
► persuading France to evacuate **the Ruhr** (unit 50);
► helping to organize the **Dawes Plan** (unit 50);

► persuading nine countries to sign the **Geneva Protocol**, in which they agreed to use their forces to back League decisions. It was not his fault that, in the 1930s, they did not do so.

Philip Snowden (unit 40) was Chancellor of the Exchequer. He dominated the Cabinet in discussions on economics and:
► supported **Free Trade**;
► followed another Gladstonian policy on **taxation**, believing that lower taxes would enable people to spend their own money in a way which would stimulate employment;
► did nothing to help lower the level of **unemployment**;
► raised **Unemployment Benefit** slightly.

John Wheatley, a Scottish MP, was Minister of Health and responsible for the **Housing Act** (1924) which increased the subsidy to councils which built houses for letting and which was responsible for the building of about half-a-million new homes.

THE FALL OF THE GOVERNMENT

Anti-Bolsheviks in the Liberal and Conservative parties were alarmed by MacDonald's Russian policy in which he **recognized** the Russian government and made a **trade treaty** with Russia. 'Russian lover' was one attack on the moderate MacDonald.

J. R. Campbell, editor of a communist paper, *The Daily Worker*, wrote articles appealing to British soldiers not to fight against the working class, should the British revolution start. **Patrick Hastings**, Attorney General, first decided to bring a case against Campbell ('incitement to mutiny'), then decided that the government could not prove its case and announced that there would be no prosecution.

The Liberals supported Baldwin in a vote of censure on the government (October), which was defeated. MacDonald resigned and called for a fresh election.

45.5 The 1924 Election

This was the first election in which politicians used 'the wireless'.

The Daily Mail, strongly anti-Labour and fearful of Bolshevism, produced a **Zinoviev letter**, now known to be a forgery, but which the Foreign Office accepted as a letter from a Russian leader to the British Communist Party, showing it how to gain control of the Trade Union movement and bring about a workers' revolution. This was used to show the danger of having a Russian-loving Labour government.

The Labour Party suffered little harm–it gained half-a-million more votes than it had had in 1923, but it had lost support among those who had hoped for a solution to unemployment.

The result of the election was:
► Conservatives 419 seats;
► Labour 151 seats;
► Liberals 40 seats–a sign of continued decline and a poor reward for having helped bring down Labour.

Unit 45 Summary

► Lloyd George in power, 1918–22; boom and slump.
► The 1922 Election; Bonar Law, 'the unknown Prime Minister'.
► Baldwin and the 1923 Election.
► MacDonald and the first Labour government; its failure.

46 INDUSTRY AND TRADE, 1919-39

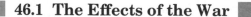

46.1 The Effects of the War

Markets were lost because of the wartime drop in exports (unit 43). Former customers learned to import goods from elsewhere, or to manufacture goods for themselves; many countries became industrialized for the first time or expanded their existing industries.

New industrial giants emerged (Japan and USA) relatively unaffected by the war and which had time, industry and energy to devote to their own industrial expansion and to export goods into former British markets.

Tariffs were imposed by countries which wanted to protect their own growing industries and wanted to gain a better balance of payments situation.

As many countries had to pay interest on wartime loans ('invisible imports') they cut down on their visible imports, which included British goods.

Primary prices – of food and raw materials – had risen during the war because of wartime demand by the warring nations for raw materials such as minerals and wool, and because of a fall in the supply as countries were overrun by enemy troops.

But with the end of the war there was a sharp drop in prices because demand fell as governments cancelled contracts, and supply was enlarged by the return of the once war-torn countries to the market, and by the materials and food provided by the enlarged output of the war-free countries which had expanded production during the war.

This fall in prices and incomes led to a drop in the demand for British goods.

British prices were increased by the return to the Gold Standard at a pre-war parity (1925) (unit 47).

COAL, A SPECIAL CASE

In 1913 British miners had produced almost 300 million tons of coal, almost 100 million being exported. After the war, **demand declined** because of:
▶ the increasing use of **oil**, particularly in shipping;
▶ the increasing use of **electricity** in homes and industries;
▶ greater **efficiency** in industry, where boilers consumed less to produce the same total units of efficiency of heat;
▶ greater **economy** in homes because these were smaller than the Victorian homes and because builders installed smaller, more efficient grates.
▶ British **prices** were too high, especially after 1925.
Supply increased, as mining increased in:
▶ the USA;
▶ Germany (once she had started to recover);
▶ Poland (one of the new industrial nations), where pits were more mechanized than British ones, so that men produced more per shift (and so more cheaply) than British miners.

SHIPBUILDING, ANOTHER SPECIAL CASE

In 1913 British shipyards built about two-thirds of the world's ships. These yards, on the Tyne, Wear and Clyde, provided demand for the iron and steel industries of these areas.

During the war they had been busy turning out new ships to replace those sunk by submarines (unit 43), but after 1918 there was a fall in demand for such replacements.

The supply had increased as Japan, the USA, Greece and Poland (new industrial nations) all turned out large numbers of ships.

British yards found it impossible to sell, so that yards were closed and unemployment rose in the neighbouring industries – coal, iron and steel.

Jarrow, a town totally dependent on one yard (Palmer's) became the 'town that was murdered', when that yard was closed in 1934.

46.2 The Depression

STRUCTURAL UNEMPLOYMENT

In the nineteenth century, industry had developed around the **coal fields**.

Certain areas became heavily dependent on one or a number of interrelated industries. Coal, iron and steel industries in the North-East grew with the growth of the shipbuilding industry.

The decline in the demand for coal, ships, textiles and other **staple industrial products** led to large scale unemployment in those industries.

DEPRESSED AREAS

▶ **Lancashire**, dependent on coal and textiles, suffered mass unemployment.
▶ **South Wales**, dependent on coal, iron and steel also suffered.
▶ **Central Scotland**, dependent on coal and shipbuilding, was another area of mass unemployment.
▶ **The North-East**, dependent on shipbuilding, coal and iron and steel, included Jarrow.

THE DEEPENING OF THE DEPRESSION

The depression started in 1920 with the end of the post-war boom, and by 1922 over two million were out of work (unit 45).

The return to the Gold Standard in 1925 made exporting difficult, and the Wall Street Crash, 1929 (unit 48), led to a disruption of world trade and made exporting even more difficult. Note, however, that this did not cause the British depression; it only deepened it, as can be seen from the unemployment figures of the 1920s and 1930s.

Government policies made matters worse:
▶ **The Geddes Axe**, with its emphasis on cuts in government spending, led to less employment in building and other industries.
▶ **Churchill's** cuts in spending on the armed forces (unit 47) led to lower demand for munitions, and less employment in the coal, iron and steel and munitions industries.
▶ **Snowden's demands** for balanced budgets in 1924 and 1929–31 (units 45 and 48) led to lower government spending.
▶ **Neville Chamberlain**, Chancellor from 1932 to 1937, was responsible for further cuts in government spending on roads, bridges, housing and education, which led to less employment in the construction and other industries (unit 49).

46.3 New Industries amidst the Encircling Gloom

Older history books tend to concentrate on the **depressed areas** and on the large-scale unemployment in those areas. But more modern research draws attention to the growth of new industries and to the rise in living standards during the 1930s.
▶ **Electricity** was linked with the growth of a number of new industries, producing electrical goods (Hoover for example) and the equipment needed to produce the electricity.

► **Motor vehicles**, mass produced, by Morris and Austin in particular, and sold in their millions in Britain and overseas, provided employment for skilled and semi-skilled workers in a variety of factories. This employment included assembling cars and producing the plugs and other components needed to assemble cars. Jobs were also created in related industries – selling and maintaining cars, producing petrol and oil.

► **Food producing** had developed in wartime, with the mass production of corned beef and tinned jams. After the war this industry expanded with the production of such items as cornflakes and custard powder, leading to an increased demand for **tins** and an expansion of such firms as Metal Box, which produced the tins.

► **The petro-chemical industries** expanded to produce not only the oil and petrol needed for the motor vehicles, but also the paints, drugs and other chemicals which have become part of our lives.

► **Tertiary industries** expanded. These industries are so called because they are not **primary** (producing food, minerals and raw materials) nor **secondary** (which use the raw materials to manufacture goods). They include:
● insurance, banking, hire purchase;
● repairs and installation of radio, TV and other household equipment;
● personal services – such as hairdressing;
● entertainment – an industry which vastly expanded in the depressed years with the growth of the film-making industry and the opening of a number of cinemas;
● hotels and restaurants;
● holiday camps, such as that opened by Butlin (1937) and Pontin (1938).

WHAT WAS 'NEW' ABOUT THESE NEW INDUSTRIES?

The new industries were **powered** by electricity or oil, and not by coal. This made them cleaner to work in and freer to chose a location. The nineteenth-century industries had been forced to develop near coal fields. Modern industry (making food, motor-cars or aeroplanes) can develop wherever it likes, because of the development of the nation-wide electricity grid (unit 47).

The new industries sold most of their products in **Britain**, and were not export-orientated, as were the textile and other older industries. This meant that when choosing their location, industrialists considered their market, one-sixth of which would be in or near London, and accordingly chose to build most of their factories in or near London.

Since most industries grew up in the south and south-east there was:
► a shift of population into these areas and away from the traditional industrial areas (which then became even more depressed, since younger people tended to move out);
► the growth of towns and suburbs in the south and south-east, providing employment for housebuilders and for suppliers of household equipment and furnishings;
► the creation of 'three nations' living in:
● the **depressed areas** of large-scale and long-term unemployment;
● the '**boom**' **areas** of the growing towns around the new industries;
● the '**twilight**' **areas** where people feared that unemployment might spread to them.

46.4 The Government and the Unemployed

In unit 49 we shall see how the government tried to cope with unemployment by:
► abandoning Free Trade in 1932;
► appointing Commissioners to try to bring industry into the depressed areas;
► helping the older industries to reorganize, so that in each industry there would be fewer, but larger and more

powerful firms, better able to compete with German, Japanese and US firms;
► its rearmament policy, which led to employment rising in the coal, iron and steel and shipbuilding industries late in the 1930s.

THE GOVERNMENT AND UNEMPLOYMENT BENEFIT, 1919–39

The **1911** Insurance Act provided unemployment insurance for a small number of workpeople (unit 37). During the First World War the government widened the existing scheme to bring in munition workers. Since these were rarely out of work, the Fund had a large surplus each year.

In **1919–20** the scheme was further extended to take in:
► former soldiers. These were allowed to claim benefit even if they had not belonged to the scheme before (this was the first use of the **uncovenanted benefit** or **dole**);
► non-insured industrial workers who lost their jobs as industry turned from making war goods to peace-time production.

In **1920** there was a high level of employment in 'booming' Britain. Lloyd George brought in a new Unemployment Insurance Act. It said that all workers, except domestic servants, farm workers and Civil Servants, earning less than £250 a year, had to be insured.

Workers, employers and government each paid into an Insurance Fund. After having paid for 12 weeks, a worker was entitled to unemployment benefit of 15 shillings (75p) a week for a maximum of 15 weeks in a year while out of work.

In 1920 there were fewer than a million out of work, and Lloyd George hoped that his new Act would not only be self-financing but would leave a surplus in the Fund each year. The end of the boom in 1921 meant that:
► over two million were unemployed by December 1921;
► they could only draw benefit for 15 weeks;
► the government had to bring in a new scheme to provide for them once they had run out of 'covenanted benefit'. This new scheme provided that after receiving insurance benefit for 15 weeks, the unemployed would continue to receive the same total sum, but not from the Insurance Fund. They would be paid from government taxation, which then had to be increased.

In **1927** Neville Chamberlain was the Minister of Health in Baldwin's government (unit 47). He pushed through a new Unemployment Insurance Act, because the payments out of the Fund were much greater than payments into it. This Act:
► reduced the benefits paid to the unemployed and the payments made into the Fund by workers and employers;
► extended the time during which benefit would be claimed – in place of the 15 weeks, Chamberlain's scheme provided for an indefinite period during which the unemployed could claim benefit. This ended the 'dole' but meant that the claims on the Insurance Fund rose very sharply. The government had to pay increasing amounts to the Fund, and by 1930 it was paying £50 million a year.

In his **1929** reform of Local Government (unit 47) Chamberlain abolished the Boards of Guardians who had run the Poor Law system since 1834 (unit 15) and appointed Public Assistance Committees (PACs) from the county boroughs and county councils to run the system.

In **1930** the government passed a new Unemployment Insurance Act, which made it easier for workers to claim benefit. Workers no longer had to prove that they were 'genuinely seeking work'. This Act also dealt with the problem of men who had never worked and had never paid into the Insurance Fund. They had been allowed to claim 'transitional' benefits until they found a job. In future they would claim alongside men who had paid into the Fund.

The Fund in crisis, 1930–31

The terms of the 1930 Act led to increased claims on the Fund and to an increase in government contributions to that Fund as the level of unemployment rose;

▶ October 1929 – 1 200 000;
▶ March 1930 – 1 600 000;
▶ July 1930 – 2 100 000;
▶ August 1931 – 3 100 000
          (23 per cent of the working population).

Government finance in crisis, 1930–31

While paying more into the Fund, government was getting less revenue from taxation, since fewer people were at work and paying income tax. This led to a **deficit**, an unfavourable balance in government finance.

Snowden wanted to wipe out that deficit by cutting employment benefit and so reducing the government contribution to the Insurance Fund, by cutting the wages and salaries of public service workers (so that teachers would lose 15 per cent of their salary), and by tax increases.

The Labour Cabinet split over this and MacDonald resigned (unit 48).

The National Government and unemployment benefit

Benefit was cut so that a married man with two children received £1.36 a week instead of £1.50. But as prices had fallen by about 30 per cent, it was argued that the unemployed did not really suffer. Few of them agreed.

A means test was introduced. Claimants for benefits had to declare all a family's sources of income – wife's earnings, children's wages, parents' pensions and interest on any savings. If this income was sufficiently high, an unemployed man might get no benefit, while he would get lower benefit if his family had a certain amount of income. There were fights at Labour Exchanges when men were refused the benefit to which they felt they were entitled.

LIFE FOR THE UNEMPLOYED

In families not affected by the Means Test (because there was no other family income), life was hard, as could be seen from:
▶ diet, clothing, housing, furniture;
▶ lack of money for such things as school outings, entertainment and insurance contributions;
▶ declining standards of health.

For families affected by the Means Test, life was equally hard but additionally there was often:
▶ tension between unemployed husbands and employed wives, who saw their wages being the cause of lower benefit for which, unfairly, they blamed their husbands;
▶ tension between parents and employed children, who resented having to make up for the cuts in benefit;
▶ many examples of broken marriages and broken homes.

You may read about life for the unemployed in such works as George Orwell's *The Road to Wigan Pier* or Walter Greenwood's *Love on the Dole*.

Unit 46 Summary

▶ The effect of war on British industry and trade.
▶ The decline of the coal and shipbuilding industries.
▶ The depression of the 1920s.
▶ The growth of new industries.
▶ Unemployment benefit and the 'dole'.
▶ Life on the dole.

---

47 BALDWIN AND THE GENERAL STRIKE

47.1 Stanley Baldwin's Earlier Career

▶ The son of a leading steel-maker in the Midlands, he was educated at Harrow and Cambridge.
▶ On his father's death he inherited the Bewdley seat in the Commons.
▶ In 1917 he became Financial Secretary to the Treasurer (with Bonar Law as Chancellor of the Exchequer).
▶ In April 1921 he became President of the Board of Trade.
▶ In October 1922 his speech to the Carlton Club meeting of Conservative MPs led to overthrow of Lloyd George's government (unit 45).

47.2 Prime Minister, 1923

In unit 45 we saw how:
▶ Bonar Law became Prime Minister in 1922;
▶ Baldwin succeeded him in 1923;
▶ he decided to appeal to the country on the issue of Protection in order to:
● have a weapon against unemployment;
● win back the Conservatives led by Chamberlain;
● trump Lloyd George's attempt to re-form a Coalition.
▶ he helped bring Labour to power.

47.3 Prime Minister, 1924–29

In this government the leading Ministers were:
▶ **Austen Chamberlain**, Foreign Secretary, eldest son of Joseph Chamberlain and leading Tariff Reformer;
▶ **Neville Chamberlain**, half-brother to Austen, an energetic Minister of Health;
▶ **Winston Churchill**, Chancellor of the Exchequer, given this surprising post to ensure that he did not team up with his friend, Lloyd George, to form a Centre Party.

Neville Chamberlain

He pushed through 25 major Acts during this period.
▶ **The Local Government Act, 1929** was a major Act which:
● abolished the Poor Law Guardians (unit 15);
● compelled county and borough councils (unit 35) to elect Public Assistance Committees (unit 46);
● gave the councils increased powers to deal with public health, hospitals, child welfare, roads and town and country planning;
● entitles Chamberlain to be remembered as one of the founders of the modern Welfare State.
▶ **National Insurance** was affected by his Unemployment Insurance Act, 1927 (unit 46);
▶ **The Widow's, Orphans' and Old Age Pensioners' Act (1925)** provided pensions for:
● over 65s, who received 10 shillings a week (50p);
● widows, who also received 10 shillings a week as well as an allowance for dependent children.

Austen Chamberlain

▶ signed the Locarno Treaties, 1925 (unit 50);
▶ signed the Kellogg Pact, 1928 (unit 50);
▶ was an advocate of the League of Nations (unit 44);
▶ was hampered by Churchill's insistence on the Ten Year Rule (p. 125) that governments should assume that there would be no war for the next 10 years, rolling the 10 years on year by year. This led to:
● cuts in spending on the services;
● the threat of the abolition of the RAF;
● a weakening of the power of the Foreign Secretary to deal with foreign powers.

Winston Churchill

As Chancellor of the Exchequer, Churchill was:
▶ a supporter of Neville Chamberlain's work, some of which (on Pension and Welfare) cost a lot of money;
▶ an opponent to Labour and the trade unions, whom he suspected of being tools of the Bolsheviks against whom he had helped to send British troops in 1918–19;
▶ responsible for the revaluation of the pound, 1925 (see below);
▶ violently opposed to the General Strike (see below).

A Reforming Government, 1924–29

In addition to the work of Chamberlain, the government was also responsible for:
▶ the **Electricity Act**, 1926, which set up the Central Electricity Board to distribute power on a National Grid. This Act of nationalization showed that, in some ways, the government was aware of the right answers to some problems;
▶ granting a charter to the reformed **BBC**–another example of the setting up of a public corporation (see unit 56);
▶ the **Equal Franchise Act, 1928**, which gave women the vote on the same terms as men.

But the government is best remembered for:
▶ the General Strike (see below);
▶ its failure to deal with rising unemployment;
▶ its loss of the 1929 election, which allowed Labour to form a second government.

▇ 47.4 The Return to the Gold Standard, 1925

Before 1914 Britain had lent a good deal of money to foreign firms and governments (unit 28). Much of this money had been spent in Britain, and so provided employment for millions of people in the country.

The interest paid on the loans and the repayment of the loans by annual instalments were 'invisible exports' for Britain, helping provide a surplus on the Balance of Payments, allowing Britain to lend even more money overseas (unit 28).

After 1920 British firms exported less (unit 44) and earned less foreign money, but Britain continued to import vast quantities of food and raw materials. Even with the 'invisible exports', Britain did not always earn a surplus to lend abroad.

Foreigners continued to come to London, asking for loans–out of tradition and because British financiers had created the system to provide such loans. British bankers borrowed money from overseas banks (in the USA and France) at low rates of interest and loaned this to other overseas countries at higher rates of interest.

Montagu Norman, the Governor of the privately owned Bank of England, supervised the working of this financial system. Norman seemed unaware that the war had changed things; he still thought of Britain as the world's leading banker. No did he appreciate the changed value of the pound because of:
▶ the abandonment of the gold standard 1914 (and of the promise of the bank note to exchange the note for gold);

▶ the subsequent over-issue of bank notes and Treasury Notes which led to:
● inflation, or higher prices;
● foreigners offering less of their money for the more plentiful pound notes. In 1913 the £1 was worth 4.86 American dollars; in 1918 it was worth only 4.20 dollars.

This fall in the value of the pound led to a fall in export prices; a shipment of £1000 of coal would have cost 4860 dollars in 1913 and only 4200 dollars in 1918. This was good for British exporters. It also led to a rise in import prices; 4860 dollars worth of tobacco would have cost £1000 in 1913, but would have cost almost £1400 in 1918. This was good for the British car and other industries.

Norman seemed not to appreciate these benefits. He wanted the pound to be as strong as it had been in 1913. He persuaded Churchill to revalue the pound so that it was restored to its pre-war value (or **parity**). This increased export prices and lowered import prices, which was bad for British exporters and for industries producing for the home market against foreign competition.

THE COAL INDUSTRY AND THE REVALUED POUND

John Maynard Keynes, a leading economist, (unit 44) was one of the few critics of the decision on revaluation. He pointed out that it would lead to lower exports, more unemployment, and a decision by employers to try to force men to accept lower wages, which would be resisted.

The coal industry was already unable to export as much as it would have wished, for reasons explained in unit 46. **Owners** then announced (1925) that wages would have to be cut and hours of work extended.

Cook, secretary of the Miners' Union, coined the slogan 'Not a penny off the pay, not a minute on the day'. **The Triple Alliance**, which had betrayed the miners on Black Friday 1921 (unit 45), now agreed to support the miners with a sympathetic strike.

Baldwin did not want a strike yet. He agreed on 31st July 1925 ('Red Friday') to pay a subsidy to the owners so that wages could be maintained at their existing levels, and **Sir Herbert Samuel** was appointed to head a Commission to examine the coal industry. **Churchill**, who had to find the money for the subsidy, was anxious that it should be ended as soon as possible.

The Samuel Commission, the sixth to examine the coal industry since 1918, reported in March 1926 that:
▶ the industry ought to be reorganized, as had been proposed by the Sankey Commission in 1919;
▶ the subsidy ought to be ended, because it was unfair to other industries which had to meet part of the cost via taxation;
▶ wages ought to be cut and the working day extended from seven to eight hours.

Baldwin announced that the subsidy would end on 30th April 1926, and the **owners** announced new wage rates, lower than those proposed by Samuel.

The **miners** refused to accept these proposals and asked for the support of the other unions. **The TUC** agreed to support the miners and gave its General Council powers to negotiate with the government and, if needs be, to call out other unions on strike.

The subsequent history of the General Strike has been examined in unit 39.

▇ 47.5 The 1929 Election ▇

The election was held in May 1929. Baldwin hoped that the bitterness of the Strike would have died out and that the new women voters ('the flapper vote') would support the Conservatives, who had given them the vote.

Baldwin campaigned on the slogan **'Safety First'** showing:
▶ the government's record on welfare and housing;
▶ the dangers of 'socialism' under a Labour government;

Fig. 47.5 A Conservative election poster, 1929. MacDonald, the Labour leader, is shown as climbing to power (and a policy of nationalization) on the back of the Liberal leader, Lloyd George.

▶ the threat of inflation from Lloyd's George's programme (see below).

Lloyd George, using some of his Fund (unit 45) made a final attempt to win back power by:

▶ employing experts, such as Keynes, to produce pamphlets and other propaganda;

▶ having a programme which called for large government expenditure on roads, bridges, houses and other 'public works' to create employment in the construction and other industries;

▶ promising to abolish unemployment within 12 months.

Labour, again supported by the unionists who had tried the industrial weapon (of the General Strike) produced its own programme, **'Labour and the Nation'**, promising that it would solve the country's economic problems.

The result of the election was:

▶ Labour won 287 seats;

▶ the Conservatives won 261 seats;

▶ the Liberals won only 59 seats.

Labour was now the largest Party in the Commons for the first time. But, as in 1924, it could only form a government with the support of the Liberals.

In May 1929 MacDonald became Prime Minister for the second time, in the government which had to deal with the effects of the Wall Street Crash (unit 48).

Unit 47 Summary

▶ The career of Baldwin.
▶ Conservative government, 1924–28.
▶ The return to the Gold Standard, 1925; why; its effects.
▶ Keynes on the inevitable depression.
▶ The General Strike, 1926.
▶ Why Baldwin lost the 1929 Election.

---

48 THE SECOND LABOUR GOVERNMENT, 1929–31

48.1 The Important Ministers

▶ **Ramsay MacDonald** was, again, Prime Minister. For his career see unit 40. You will find further development of part of that career in this unit.

▶ **Arthur Henderson**, a former trade union official, member of Lloyd George's Coalition government in 1916–18 and part-author of the Party's constitution of 1918 (all in unit 43). He was Foreign Secretary.

▶ **Philip Snowden** (unit 43) was Chancellor of the Exchequer. His attitudes remained what they had been in 1924 (unit 45) when he had shown himself to be:

● Gladstonian as regards **Free Trade**;

● orthodox as regards **balanced budgets**;

● lacking in ideas on how to deal with **unemployment**.

▶ **J. H. ('Jimmy') Thomas**, another trade union leader (see unit 45) was made Lord Privy Seal, with special responsibility for developing plans for dealing with unemployment.

▶ **Margaret Bondfield** was appointed Minister of Labour, the first woman to hold a Cabinet post.

48.2 The Government's Achievements, 1929–31

▶ **Unemployment** remained the most important problem (see below).

▶ **The Coal Mines Act**, 1930, which:

● reduced the working day to seven and a half hours;

● set up a commission to plan the reorganization of the industry.

▶ **The House Act**, 1930, which was the government's attempt to revive the subsidies given under the Wheatley Act, 1924 (unit 45).

▶ **Unemployment Insurance Act**, 1930 (see unit 46).

▶ **Foreign Affairs** are examined in unit 50.

48.3 Plans for Unemployment

J. H. Thomas, Lord Privy Seal, had no Ministry to look after. His job was to provide plans to bring down the level of unemployment.

Oswald Mosley, was junior Minister attached to Thomas's office. Mosley had been:

▶ a successful officer during the War;

▶ a Conservative MP in 1918;

▶ a Labour MP after breaking with Baldwin because of his government's unwillingness to tackle unemployment;
▶ a popular speaker, a successful Olympic fencer and a very rich man.

Public works

▶ is the term used to describe work done (out of government expenditure) on building roads, houses, schools, hospitals and amenities such as welfare clinics, libraries, museums and parks;
▶ provide employment, directly, for the people engaged on their construction and, later, for the people employed in the amenities and on the maintenance of roads and parks;
▶ provide employment, indirectly, for those who supply the machines and materials used in their construction;
▶ provide further employment, indirectly, as the newly employed spend money on consumer goods.

Snowden allowed Thomas to spend £42 million on such works, only to find that delays, planning problems and lack of energy by local authorities meant that the money was not always spent as quickly as government wished.

Snowden would not allow further expenditure, because he realized that this spending had to be matched by taxation. He agreed with most economists at the time who thought that tax increases would lead to lower consumption since people would have less to spend – and so unemployment would increase; and that taxation ought to be decreased during a depression as an encouragement to people to 'spend their way out of the depression'.

THE MOSLEY MEMORANDUM

Mosley agreed with the ideas put forward by Lloyd George during the 1929 election (unit 47). Both of them had got some of their ideas from Keynes, who was on his way to proving that:
▶ depressions were caused by a fall in demand;
▶ demand could be most easily increased by **increasing government expenditure** on public works, on increased pensions and other allowances; by **increasing bank credit** (or loans) to promote expansion and by public (or government) direction (or control) of industry.

Such increased expenditure would be best met by having a budget deficit, so that the government would not match its expenditure by equal increases in taxation. He ignored the danger that this might lead to inflation, arguing that the real enemy was unemployment and the misery it caused.

You should notice that, in different ways and without having read Keynes's work, both Hitler in Germany and Roosevelt in the USA arrived at the same conclusion, and used government money on public works to help reduce unemployment.

Mosley wanted a vast expenditure on public works, and on:
▶ good pensions for older workers, so that they might retire to make way for younger unemployed workers;
▶ a system of tariffs to protect British industry from unfair foreign competition.

He put these ideas to the government which, under Snowden's influence, rejected them.

He took them to the Party Conference in 1930, where, although he received a standing ovation, his plans were rejected on the advice of the Party's leaders.

He then resigned to form the New Party which in time became the British Fascist Party. He saw himself as the Hitler-like leader who would save Britain from depression.

48.4 The Wall Street Crash, October 1929

The British government's problems were made worse by this Crash.

During the 1920s the US economy had grown rapidly and many companies had vast profits. Shareholders in such companies received high annual dividends. This encouraged others to try to buy them; share prices shot up – seemingly continuously.

Banks lent money to clients anxious to buy shares and the New York Stock Exchange (Wall Street) allowed 'buying on the margin', so that people had only to put down 10 per cent of the price when buying shares, the rest not being required for another month. This gave people the chance to buy shares ('on the margin'), sell them at a higher price, and make a profit.

People ignored the fact that in 1928 and 1929 companies made lower profits than they had done earlier in the 1920s, largely due to **overproduction** which led to firms failing to sell their goods.

In 1929 unemployment in the USA rose and **farm prices** fell owing to overproduction, with wheat being cheaper than it had been for over 400 years. This brought down the cost of living but it meant that farmers:
▶ had lower incomes;
▶ bought fewer goods;
▶ could not support their local shops, many of which closed down, leading to a fall in demand for industrial products which led to increased unemployment.

The bankers were the first to realize the serious situation. They:
▶ asked their clients to repay their loans;
▶ forced them to sell their shares to get that money;
▶ drove down the prices of shares, as there were millions of people trying to sell and few anxious to buy.

The Crash took place in the last week of October 1929, when millions of shares were sold at fractions of their previous value.

This fall in prices led to:
▶ ruination for many individual shareholders;
▶ thousands of bank failures, when they failed to get back the money they had loaned to clients to buy shares;
▶ closure of shops and factories whose owners were bankrupted by the fall in prices of shares they had owned;
▶ ruin of many people who had left their money in banks, only to find now that they could not get it back;
▶ the recall of overseas loans made to German and Austrian banks and firms, which led to the spread of the depression to those countries;
▶ a drop in the US demand for overseas goods, which helped to spread the depression world-wide;
▶ a further drop in the demand for British goods throughout the world;
▶ a sharp rise in the level of unemployment in Britain.

48.5 Unemployment in Britain, 1929–31

Primary prices fell because of the world-wide depression. This brought down the cost of living for those at work and helps to explain the rise in living standards in the 1930s. But it also led to:
▶ **lower incomes** for primary producers – for Australian wool farmers, New Zealand dairy farmers and Rhodesian copper miners;
▶ a lower demand by them for British goods;
▶ rising unemployment in export-based industries.

The Insurance Fund (unit 46) required ever greater subsidies from the Government:
▶ if there were 940 000 unemployed, the money coming into the Fund (from the workers) equalled its outgoings;
▶ in 1929, 1930 and 1931 unemployment continued to rise, reaching 3 100 000 in 1931 (unit 46);
▶ the government had to put more money into the Fund.

In 1929 the Conservative government had put in £12 million. In 1930 the Labour government had put in £37 million and in 1931 another £55 million – nearly five times as much as was put in by the government in 1928.

THE BUDGET, 1930–31

The subsidy to the Insurance Fund had to come out of taxation. In February 1931 Snowden warned the country about the danger of this, explaining that there could either be a deficit (and inflation as the government printed more money), increases in taxation, or cuts in expenditure.

A committee, under Sir George May, was appointed to examine this problem and to report by August 1931.

THE BANKING PROBLEM, 1930–31

In 1931 European bankers feared that the Labour government ('Russian-lovers') (unit 45) might not be willing to tackle the problem of the budget deficit.

They feared that the government might devalue the pound (the opposite of Churchill's action of 1925) (unit 47). This would have given them fewer pounds in return for the loans they had made in response to Norman's policy (unit 47).

The collapse of many European banks in July 1931 led to increased fears for the British banking system. On 16th July European bankers began to take their money (gold) out of London. By 31st July the Bank of England had to ask the leading banks of France and the USA for special loans to have gold to repay earlier loans.

48.6 The May Committee Reports 1st August 1931

On 31st July Parliament went on holiday until October. On 1st August the Report of the May Committee was issued showing:

▶ government spending exceeded tax revenue by £120 million a year;

▶ the need for a slight increase in taxation **and** large cuts in government spending;

▶ that spending on unemployment ought to be cut severely.

European bankers read the Report, feared that the government would not do as it suggested and took their money from the Bank of England at an increasing rate. The loan of £50 million ran out by the middle of August and the Bank had to apply for further loans. These requests were refused until the government made up its mind about the May Report.

Montagu Norman broke down, under the strain of a crisis which was largely of his making, that is, his policy of trying to ensure that London would be the world's financial centre (unit 47). His deputy had to ask MacDonald for his decision on the May Report (11th August 1931).

THE GOVERNMENT AND THE MAY REPORT

MacDonald called his Ministers back from holiday. He and Snowden argued for acceptance of the Report's suggestions. Henderson, who was not only a Cabinet Minister but was also speaking for the TUC, argued for devaluation as an alternative policy.

On the **22nd August** the government voted to accept a watered down version of the Report. Leaders of the Conservative and Liberal Parties promised MacDonald that they would (but only grudgingly) support this if it were brought to the Commons.

The King consulted all Party leaders, knowing that Henderson and others might refuse to accept the Report in its entirety.

On the **23rd August** news came that the foreign bankers would not give the extra credits unless the May Report was completely accepted. **The Cabinet** split over this demand for the acceptance of the Report and its demand for a cut in unemployment benefit.

On the **24th August** MacDonald went to the King, resigned and accepted his invitation to form a National (or Coalition) government with the promised support of Baldwin (Conservative) and Samuel (Liberal). His critics accused him of merely wanting to stay in power. He argued that the forming of a Coalition was the only way to win public confidence, which would lead to a rapid solution to the economic and financial problem.

THE MASTER CHEMIST.

Professor MacDonald. "Now if only these rather antagonistic elements will blend as I hope, we'll have a real national elixir."

Fig. 48.7 MacDonald shown as 'the chemist', trying to form his National Government.

48.7 The National Government

▶ **Labour** ministers in the National Government included MacDonald, Snowden and Thomas – the majority of Labour ministers and MPs refused to support it.

▶ **Conservative** ministers included Baldwin and Chamberlain, while all Conservative MPs supported the government.

▶ **Liberal** ministers included Samuel, although Lloyd George (who was absent through ill-health at this time) refused to support the government.

The following cuts asked for by the May Report were made:

▶ **salaries** of teachers, policemen, Civil Servants and members of the Armed Forces were reduced by, on average, 10 per cent.

▶ **unemployment benefit** was cut by 10 per cent.

The budget was then balanced; the bankers gave the loan of £80 million, but the crisis did not end. A mutiny at the naval base at Invergordon against the pay cuts led foreigners to fear this government's climb down, and more bankers took their money from Britain.

On 21st September the government cut the value of the pound from 4.86 American dollars to 3.40 dollars, which bankers had claimed would lead to ruin when suggested by Henderson and others earlier in the year.

THE 1931 ELECTION

The National government had been formed to save the pound, which it had failed to do. MacDonald had promised that once the crisis was over, normal party politics would be resumed and that there would be no election until then.

In October 1931 MacDonald called an election asking for a 'Doctor's Mandate' to cure the nation's problems.

The result of the election was:

▶ National government 554 seats being:
- Conservatives – 473   ▶ Labour 52
- National Liberal – 68   ▶ Lloyd George Liberal 4.
- National Labour – 13

It was this government and the Conservative-dominated Commons which set about dealing with the domestic and foreign problems facing the country.

Unit 48 Summary

▶ The Labour government and unemployment; Mosley versus Thomas.

▶ The Wall Street Crash, 1929; its effects on industry and trade.

▶ The financial crisis, 1930–31.

▶ The fall of the Labour government, 1931.

49 DOMESTIC AFFAIRS, 1931–39

49.1 The Abolition of Free Trade

Devaluation (a fall in the value of the pound) was the result of the abandonment of the Gold Standard, before the 1931 election. This helped to lower export prices and to put up import prices of manufactured goods, which helped British domestic industry.

Neville Chamberlain, younger son of Joseph Chamberlain (unit 34), became Chancellor of the Exchequer after the election; **Snowden** became a Viscount and went to the House of Lords.

The Import Duties Bill (February 1932) was introduced by Chamberlain. This:
► imposed no tariff on most food and raw material imports;
► put a tariff of between 10 and 20 per cent on about a quarter of the goods imported;
► put a higher tariff on other goods (making up about half of Britain's imports).

The effect of this abolition of Free Trade was:
► to put up import prices of foreign goods. This helped British industries, e.g. motor-vehicles and electrical goods, to sell their goods in Britain;
► to put up import prices and so increase the cost of living. But because world prices were falling (unit 48), prices were lower than they had been in the 1920s.

EMPIRE FREE TRADE – A FAILURE

Chamberlain had carried out one part of his father's proposed programme (unit 28). **Imperial Preference** had also been part of that programme.

An Imperial Conference was held at Ottawa, Canada, in the summer of 1932. **Chamberlain** hoped the Empire countries would put lower tariffs on goods bought and sold within the Empire. But:
► Canada and other countries wanted to protect their own developing industries against British imports;
► Canada wanted to develop trade with the USA and refused to hamper that trade by putting tariffs on US goods.

Trade treaties between Britain and several countries in the Empire were a poor substitute for Imperial Preference which meant:
► Britain agreed to buy a stated amount of their goods;
► in return, the other country agreed to buy a stated amount of British exports (often coal) or to impose a lower tariff on British exports in general.

Similar treaties were signed with other countries in the Baltic, South America and with Russia. These agreements helped some industries (notably coal) to maintain exports, but they were an interference with the free flow of world trade, which had unfortunate results for Britain:
► Other countries followed Britain's example, which meant that they and their treaty partners imported less from Britain.
► When the bilateral (or two-sided) agreement between, say, Britain and Argentina, excluded Polish coal from Argentina, Poland had less money to spend on imports, including those she might have bought from Britain.

49.2 Changes in the Government, 1932

Snowden, whose bitter attack on the Labour Party helped to win the 1931 election, resigned over the abandonment of Free Trade.

The Liberals were divided over this issue:
► the Samuelites, led by Sir Herbert Samuel, resigned;
► others, led by Sir John Simon, opposed the abandonment of Free Trade, but stayed in the government. These Simonite National Liberals became Conservative in all but name.

THE GOVERNMENT'S MONETARY POLICY

Chamberlain, as Chancellor, followed Snowden's policy of balancing the budget – government spending was equalled by tax revenue.

In 1934 he had a higher revenue than expenditure, which allowed him to increase the level of **Unemployment Benefit** and to raise the **salaries** which had been cut in 1931 (unit 48).

Expenditure was cut in order to get that balance right. This meant:
► less money for building of bridges, roads and houses;
► a lower demand by contractors for machinery and other materials they would have needed;
► less employment in a number of industries.

Germany and the **USA** followed a different policy and had budget deficits (unit 48), because expenditure was higher than tax revenue. This meant that:
► those countries developed their motorways in the 1930s when labour and materials were cheap. Britain began to do this in the 1950s when costs were much higher;
► they also provided employment for more people.

The interest on the National Debt (money borrowed by past governments, see unit 7) took a large part of tax revenue. If this could be cut, Chamberlain could lower taxes. In February 1932 he announced that instead of paying 5 per cent interest on its past borrowing, it would only pay 3½ per cent. The lenders (or stock-holders) accepted this because:
► the Bank of England had brought down its interest rate from 6 to only 2 per cent;
► other borrowers (Building Societies and industry) offered lower rates – 2½ to 3 per cent;
► if they had taken their money out of government stock (as Chamberlain offered to let them do) they could not have reinvested it at a higher rate of interest.

Lower interest rates saved the government about £3 million a year and ought to have tempted industrialists and local authorities to borrow money for development – which would have lowered the level of unemployment. Following the example of the central government, however:
► **local authorities** spent less on roads and houses;
► **industry** spent less on new factories and machinery;
► **British industry**, lacking modernization and mechanization ever since 1870 (unit 28), missed a chance to re-equip and catch up with the foreigners.

THE GOVERNMENT AND INDUSTRY

Protection of some industries by a tariff wall was a major part of government policy towards industry.

Failure to develop new industries or to modernize the old ones was the result of the belief that the depression would last a long time and could not be solved by government.

Reorganization of some industries followed from the belief that there ought to be fewer, but larger firms, better able to compete with foreign firms. So the government helped to set up:
► the **British Iron and Steel Federation** run by the owners of iron and steel companies. This Federation:
● closed down certain works as uneconomic;
● planned the building of new, larger works;

Fig. 49.2 Only the start of a rearmament campaign in 1936 provided a hope of work for the millions in the depressed areas.

● benefited from the tariff against imports;
● expanded output from five million tons of steel in 1931 to 13 million tons in 1937;
● refused to allow the construction of a new works planned for Jarrow – the area of highest unemployment.
▶ **National Shipbuilders Security**, formed in February 1930 and which got its money from the **Bankers Industrial Development Corporation**. This:
● bought up shipyards and closed them down until the number of yards equalled the volume of work available;
● was responsible for the closing of Palmer's at Jarrow in 1934.

Aid to industry, apart from the **tariff** and (indirectly) the **lower interest rates** was provided by loans such as the £9½ million provided to help in the building of ships for the North Atlantic service. This money helped to pay for the building of the *Queen Mary*, which provided work on Clydeside until its launch in 1936.

GOVERNMENT AND THE LOCATION OF INDUSTRY

The old industries were depressed and the areas dependent on them became **Depressed Areas**.

The new industries – motor-vehicles, electrical goods, petro-chemical and food processing – grew in the 1930s and provided many jobs. The owners of the new industries did not build their factories in the old industrial areas because:
▶ **Power**, provided by the electricity from the National Grid (unti 47), was available everywhere and, unlike the old industries, the new ones did not need coal.
▶ **Labour** for the new industries had to be skilled or semi-skilled and did not need to have the physical strength of the workers in the old industries. This labour was easily available anywhere.
▶ **Markets** for the goods from the new factories were mainly in the populated south-east and Midlands. It would have been foolish to have built a Mars-producing factory in Scotland and to have had to carry most of the output to the south.
▶ **'Green and pleasant land'** was a better description of, say, Weybridge (where an aircraft industry grew up) or Oxford (where the Oxford-born William Morris built his cars) than it was of the old industrial areas.
▶ **Industrial relations** in the older areas were scarred by bitter memories. Owners of new industries hoped for better industrial relations in new areas.

The Special Areas Act, 1934 was an Act which:
▶ appointed two Commissioners for the whole country;
▶ provided £2 million to spend on trying to attract new industry into the old areas;

▶ failed to persuade industry to move from the pleasant south to the grimmer industrial areas;
▶ led to the building of some industrial estates in some old areas – but where factories often required the work only of women or unskilled machine-minders.

▪ 49.3 The Better-off Areas and People

Falling prices were the result of the world depression. Between 1929 and 1933 the cost of living fell by 15 per cent. During the same period, **wage rates** remained fairly static – on average they fell between 1929 and 1933 by only 5 per cent, so **rising living standards** were the result of the combination of falling prices and steady wages.

Cheap money, the result of the fall in the Bank Rate and of government interest rates (above) led to:
▶ lower interest rates from finance houses and hire purchase firms;
▶ easier terms from such houses and firms;
▶ more people buying goods on hire purchase (HP);
▶ increased employment in firms producing these goods.

Tertiary industries, providing a 'service', grew to cater for the demand created by the rising living standards.

Signs of prosperity

▶ **Cinemas** were built in every town (unit 56).
▶ **Newspapers sales**; only in the 1930s did the mass of the people first begin to take a daily paper.
▶ **Shops** were opened by Woolworth, Marks and Spencer, and others to provide goods for the millions who had money to spend.
▶ The new **'wireless'** was bought by better-off people and by 1939 there were 11 million in British homes.
▶ **New housing**, see below.

THE HOUSING BOOM, 1931–39

Evidence of the housing boom

▶ **1920–29** Councils built one million houses for letting, while **private industry** built half a million for sale;
▶ **1930–39** Councils built only 700 000 houses for letting (because of cuts in government and local authority spending); **private industry** built two million for sale.

Who bought the houses?

Most of them were built in the new, prosperous areas surrounding the new industrial developments. Workers in the new industries had money to spare for house buying.

Why could they afford to buy?

▶ **Falling costs** – of food and clothing, meant that families had money to spare for other things, including housing.
▶ **Steady wages** and the assurance of future employment in growing industries encouraged spending on housing.
▶ **House prices** fell as the prices of materials fell. Houses costing £1200 in 1920 cost only £320 in 1933.
▶ **Building societies** offered lower interest rates after 1932 and extended the term of repayment from 10 years to 20 years. This led to low weekly or monthly repayments and made it easier for people to buy.
▶ **Hire purchase firms**, charging lower interest rates, made it easier to buy goods to furnish and equip houses;
▶ Woolworth and other chain stores provided **cheap goods**.

▪ 49.4 People and Politics, 1932–39

▶ **The Communist Party**, founded in 1920, remained a small party, with its main strength in the old, **depressed** industrial areas.

► **The Fascist Party** led by Mosley (unit 48) from the amalgamation of a number of right-wing groups was more important. It had:
● regiments of blackshirted men, attracted by the pay, food, uniform and prospect of gaining power;
● Mosley's ability as a mass orator, which attracted many followers and was best seen at mass demonstrations, the most notorious of which was the 1934 Olympic Rally at which there was fighting between Fascists, Communists and police;
● street marches to attract support. In 1936 Mosley organized a mass march through London's East End with its large Jewish community. The police cleared the streets and the Communists tried to prevent it from taking place so that there were many fights, including the 'Battle of Cable Street' in which the police fought against Mosley's followers on one side and the anti-Fascists on the other.
► **The law** was changed to ban such demonstrations and the wearing of para-military uniforms.
► **The unemployed** demonstrated in local rallies and marches, and in nationwide marches demanding 'the right to work'–but to little avail.
► **The Peace Pledge Union** founded by Canon Dick Shephard in 1934:
● had its members sign a pledge renouncing war as a means of settling international disputes;
● recruited 130 000 followers by 1937;
● frightened the government into a more pacifist policy (unit 50).

The 1935 election

► **MacDonald** resigned as Prime Minister and became Lord President of the Council in May 1935, just after George V's Silver Jubilee;
► **Baldwin** became Prime Minister in his place;
► **Lansbury**, the pacifist leader of the Labour Party, was forced to resign when the Party Conference voted for re-armament (1935);
► **Attlee** took his place;
► **October 1935** Baldwin called an election which took place in November and in which:
● Conservatives won 387 (compared with 454 in 1931);
● National Liberals won 33;
● National Labour (the remains of MacDonald's followers) won only eight;

● Labour won 154 (compared with only 52 in 1931);
● **MacDonald** was defeated at Seaham by Emmanual Shinwell; another seat was found for him and he remained a member of the government until May 1937, when Chamberlain succeeded Baldwin.

49.5 The Year of the Three Kings, 1936

George V died in January 1936 and **Edward VIII** came to the throne to popular acclaim because of:
► his work as Prince of Wales when he had won worldwide renown on his tours of the Empire and the USA;
► his modern approach to life, reflected in his dress, tastes in music, attitudes towards such such things as aeroplanes and industrial development;
► his youthful appearance compared to his father, although Edward was over 40 in 1936.
The Abdication in December 1936 was the result of:
► Edward's wish to marry a twice-divorced Mrs Wallis Simpson;
► Baldwin's insistence that the people would not accept her as their Queen;
► the opposition of Labour and Liberal leaders and parties to the proposed marriage;
► the opposition of the governments of the Dominions.
Churchill, Rothmere and Beaverbrook tried to form a **King's Party** aiming to win popular support for the King, on the grounds that he had the right to marry 'the woman I love', and to overthrow Baldwin, whom they disliked.
George VI, the former Duke of York, came to the throne in December 1936 when Edward finally abdicated, which he had planned to do at the beginning of November if he were not allowed to marry Mrs Simpson and have her as Queen.

Unit 49 Summary

► The National Government and the end of Free Trade.
► Cheap money–why, and its effects.
► Industrial reorganization and more unemployment.
► Depressed areas and the location of new industries.
► Rising living standards, 1931–39; the housing boom.
► The Abdication, 1936.

50 FOREIGN AFFAIRS, 1919–39

50.1 Optimism, 1919

The League had been set up (unit 44) and people hoped international disputes would be settled peacefully.
Memories of the First World War led many to believe that politicians would never again expose their peoples to war.
The **costs** of war were rising with the introduction of the aeroplane and larger warships. People hoped that politicians would settle things peacefully rather than face the high expenditure needed for modern war.

BRITAIN, VERSAILLES AND PACIFISM

Keynes, the first critic of the Treaty (unit 44) argued that:
► **reparations** would not be paid;
► **Germany** would seek revenge;

► the **Treaty** needed to be re-written.
In the 1920s many people came to demand a softening of the harsh treatment which Germany had been dealt. This angered the French.
Churchill, Chancellor from 1925–29 (unit 47), wanted lower taxation. He persuaded the Cabinet that:
► wars were too costly to contemplate;
► no country would make war in the future;
► every year the government should have a 'Ten Year Rule' that for the next 10 years there would be no war;
► military spending would be cut. He starved the RAF of money for new aircraft.
Chamberlain, Chancellor from 1932, continued this policy, insisting that depressed Britain could not afford to re-arm. Only after 1935 did this policy slowly begin to change.

Pacifism was widespread and was shown by:
▶ the **Oxford Union** debate, February 1933, when students voted by 257 to 153 not to fight for 'King and Country';
▶ the **Peace Ballot**, 1934 organized by the League of Nations' Union, showed a vast majority in favour of:
● the League of Nations; ● disarmament;
● peaceful settlements of disputes.

50.2 Foreign Policy, 1924–31

MACDONALD'S FOREIGN POLICY, 1924

MacDonald was Prime Minister and Foreign Secretary in 1924. **Russia** had been excluded from Versailles and later attacked by some western powers, including Britain. In her isolation she had signed the **Treaty of Rapallo**, 1922, with her former enemy, Germany, who was also isolated from the rest of Europe. In this the two countries reached agreement about:
▶ the renunciation of reparations;
▶ the resumption of diplomatic relations;
▶ the resumption of economic relations – Germany helped to rebuild Russian industry;
▶ the illegal training of German troops and airmen on Russian soil.

MacDonald wanted to end Russia's isolation and:
▶ recognized the Bolshevik government;
▶ provided loans for Russian economic developments;
▶ signed a trade treaty between Russia and Britain.

Germany was helped by MacDonald's work for the acceptance of the **Dawes Plan**; the figure for reparations was lowered and the French left the Ruhr.

The Geneva Protocol was signed by Britain and eight other leading European countries. These agreed to use their armies and navies to enforce League decisions if necessary.

BALDWIN'S FOREIGN POLICY, 1924–29

Austen Chamberlain was Foreign Minister in this period.

The Locarno Treaties 1925, attempted to satisfy the demands of the German Chancellor (Stresemann) and the French Foreign Secretary (Briand). In these treaties, Britain, France, Germany, Belgium and Italy:
▶ guaranteed to maintain the existing frontiers between Germany and her western partners (France, Belgium and Italy);
▶ accepted treaties arranged between Germany and Poland and Germany and Czechoslovakia, without offering the guarantee offered to the western frontiers of Germany;
▶ suggested that Germany's eastern frontiers were not the concern of the western Powers, so that Germany might seem to have a free hand to alter hers by treaty or by war;
▶ Germany agreed that she would not use force against her neighbours;
▶ the Powers agreed to set up a Conference on Disarmament under the supervision of the League of Nations.

In **the Rhineland**, a start was made in 1925 to end the occupation of the region by Allied forces, and **Germany** became a member of the League of Nations in 1926.

The Kellogg Pact, 1927, put forward by the US Secretary of State with the support of Briand of France, was signed by Britain and 64 other nations who agreed never to use war as an instrument of foreign policy.

LABOUR'S FOREIGN POLICY, 1929–31

Henderson was Foreign Minister in this government. **MacDonald** played a large part in foreign affairs.

▶ The Conservatives had broken off relations with the USSR in 1927;
▶ Labour restored diplomatic relations, October 1929.

At the **London Naval Conference, 1930**, Britain, America and Japan agreed to limit their navies, and the '5:5:3' rule was accepted, with Britain and the USA being allowed five ships for every three Japanese vessels.

In **1930** Allied troops were finally removed from the Rhineland (unit 44), a sign that the Allies believed Germany would be a peaceful neighbour. **Disarmament** as a means of reducing tension and government spending was a major policy:
▶ in **1930 and 1931**; preparations were made for a major Conference to try to agree the reduction in the size of armies, navies and air forces;
▶ in **Geneva**, 1932, at the Disarmament Conference where:
● **Germany** (which had joined the League in 1926) wanted forces equal in size to those of France;
● **France**, opposing this, asked for firm guarantees against German aggression;
● it was clear that nations did not really believe in the documents they had signed renouncing war.

Hitler became Chancellor of Germany in 1933 and took Germany out of the Conference and the League, October 1933.

50.3 The Failure of the League, 1919–30

France did not believe the League would work. She took unilateral action when she occupied the Ruhr (1923) to try to force Germany to pay her reparations.

Italy, a permanent member of the Council (unit 44), defied the League in 1923 when she seized the island of **Corfu**, which belonged to Greece; refused to accept a League demand that she should hand it back, and held on to Corfu.

The Locarno Treaties were signs that the major Powers did not really believe in the League. Why were such non-League agreements needed if the League was really expected to work? **The Kellogg-Briand Pact** was another extra-League agreement which would not have been needed if people really accepted the powers and decisions of the League.

Germany, even under Stresemann but more so under Hitler, did not accept the terms of Versailles as regards her eastern frontier. Her withdrawal from the League (1933), followed by that of Japan (1933) and by the USA's refusal to become a member, made the League that much weaker.

The breakdown and failure of the Disarmament Conference (1934) marked a further failure of the League, even though Russia became a member (1934).

THE MANCHURIAN AFFAIR, 1931

China had been torn by civil war since 1911 when Sun Yat Sen had set up a Republic. **The Chinese Republic** (1912) had to fight:
▶ warlords who wanted local power for themselves;
▶ after 1927, the Communists.

Japan had long had aims in China. In 1894, having defeated China, she had taken Formosa, and in 1902, after the defeat of Russia, she had taken the southern half of Sakhalin and Port Arthur as well as Korea. She saw China as a major market for her goods.

Manchuria was claimed by the Japanese, who invaded it. **China** appealed to the League in January 1932 and **the Lytton Commission** sent by the League examined the dispute. It condemned Japan, who left the League. **Japan** then invaded China itself, having set up 'independent' Manchukuo (a re-named Manchuria).

The League took no action, because neither Britain nor France was willing to go to war in the middle of the post-Wall Street depression (unit 48).

50.4 The National Government's Foreign Policy, 1931–35

▶ **Disarmament**, which would allow lower taxation, was a major policy; the government played a part in the Conference until it collapsed in 1934.
▶ **Hitler**, having withdrawn from the League, set about rearming, in defiance of the Versailles Treaty (unit 44).

▶ **The Stresa Front**, 1935 was formed by Britain, France and Italy who agreed to resist attempts to revise the Treaty of Versailles.

▶ **The Anglo-German naval agreement**, 1935, said that Hitler's Germany would have a navy which would be 35 per cent as big as Britain's.

This agreement:

● was contrary to the Versailles Treaty;
● went against the terms of the Stresa agreement;
● angered France and Italy;
● led France to make a defensive alliance with Russia.

The Abyssinian crisis, 1934–36

Mussolini had come to power in 1922, and in 1925 his government sponsored Abyssinia as a member of the League, In 1935, Mussolini signed the Stresa Agreement, out of fear of German ambitions in Austria.

Abyssinia was invaded by Italian troops in October 1935, and the **League** condemned Italy (7th October 1935).

League members agreed to stop trading with Italy. These **economic sanctions** were meant to make it impossible for her to get the materials to wage a war. **Oil**, however, was specifically excluded from this agreement, the most important material needed in a modern war.

Mussolini appealed, in 1935, to his Stresa allies, to allow him a free hand in Abyssinia. **Sir Samuel Hoare**, Foreign Secretary, went to meet Laval, Foreign Minister of France, December 1935; they drew up the 'Hoare-Laval Pact' which would have allowed Italy to take two-thirds of Abyssinia.

Public outcry led to Hoare's resignation. Eden became Foreign Secretary.

By May 1936 Italy had conquered Abyssinia, and had become less friendly with Britain and France.

The League had failed, and **Hitler** renounced the Locarno Treaties.

50.5 British Foreign Policy, 1936–39

The Rhineland crisis, March 1936

The Versailles Treaty created a military-free zone between Germany and France. On the 7th March 1936, German troops invaded the Rhineland, breaking the Treaty and the Locarno Treaties.

Eden and the French Foreign Minister were equally unwilling to take action against Hitler; both pointed to the domestic problems which might follow from a declaration of war, while also arguing that it was Russia and not Germany which was Europe's main problem.

Chamberlain opposed military action, and Hitler held on to the Rhineland.

The Spanish Civil War, 1936–39

In July 1936, Franco led a Spanish army from North Africa to an attack on the Republican government of Spain. Germany and Italy sent supplies to Franco; German and Italian airmen had a chance to try out their 'planes and ideas during the fighting they did for Franco.

Britain and France called for 'non-intervention' by other nations, which served only to help Franco, who gained control of Spain in 1939.

While, officially, Britain was neutral, there were many collections to provide money and other aid for the Republicans.

Eden's resignation, 1938

Chamberlain became Prime Minister in 1937. He was anxious to maintain peace. He feared Russia and Communism and he hoped to be able to negotiate with Hitler and Mussolini. In 1938 he reopened negotiations with Mussolini, but Eden was opposed to this, and resigned when the Prime Minister insisted on going ahead with the talks with Mussolini.

Austria, 1938

In January 1938 Hitler tried to overthrow the Austrian socialist government under Schuschnigg, but failed.

Schuschnigg was then called to a meeting with Hitler, who forced him to appoint an Austrian Nazi, Seyss-Inquart as Chief of Austrian Police.

Schuschnigg proposed an Austrian referendum to ask the people whether they wanted a union with Germany. Hitler was afraid that this might show an anti-German result and he rushed troops to the border, called Schuschnigg to another meeting and made him resign to make way for Seyss-Inquart, who invited Germany to occupy Austria.

On 12th March German troops invaded. Chamberlain sent a note of protest but took no further action against this breach of the Versailles Treaty (unit 44).

Hitler announced **the Anschluss**, or union of Germany and Austria, which had the effect of hemming in Czechoslovakia.

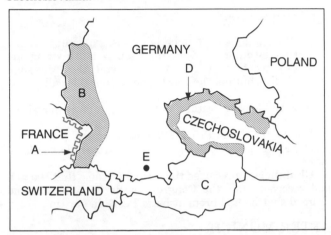

Fig. 50.5 A sketch map of Central Europe before the Second World War. Examiners expect candidates to be able to name the fortifications marked A, the area marked B, the country marked C, the area marked D and the city marked E. They will also expect explanations about the importance of each of these places marked on the map.

CZECHOSLOVAKIA, 1938

This was a new state created at Versailles, a portion of which had once been part of Germany (unit 44). The Czech Germans (known as the Sudeten Germans) were led by a Nazi, Henlein, who asked the Czech government for a separate Sudeten-German state. This was refused.

In September 1938 Hitler threatened to take it by force. Chamberlain sent Lord Runciman to examine the problem.

Many in Britain thought that Germany had some claims to this land and its people, torn away at Versailles (unit 44).

On **15th September 1938** Chamberlain flew to meet Hitler at **Berchtesgaden** where:

▶ Hitler, Daladier (French Prime Minister) and Chamberlain met Czech representatives;

▶ the Czechs were told they would have to make 'sacrifices'.

On **22nd September 1938** Chamberlain flew to meet Hitler at **Godesberg** where he persuaded Hitler not to act until Britain had imposed certain terms on the unwilling Czechs. Hitler threatened to invade Czechoslovakia on 1st October 1938.

THE AIR RAID PRECAUTIONS ACT, 1937

▶ These compelled local authorities to draw up plans for the safety of civilians against the expected air attacks.

▶ **Rearmament** had started during 1936–37 with £185 million being made available for such machines as the **Hurricane** which first flew in 1935 and the **Spitfire**, which first flew in 1936.

▶ **Radar**, the name given to the method of detecting approaching enemy aircraft, had been first designed by a team headed by Robert Watson-Watt in 1935. A chain of radar stations was built around the coast.

▶ **The Army** was given some new weapons, including an improved **Cruiser** tank, but its officers gave it a poor welcome, preferring to plan for cavalry attacks.

▶ **The Navy** got a number of new ships, including the *Hood*, the fastest and most powerful battle-cruiser afloat, new battleships, such as *Rodney* and *Nelson*, new submarines, aircraft carriers and escort vehicles.

September 1938

Air-raid precautions were put into effect;
▶ sandbags were issued for protection of newly dug slit trenches in public parks;
▶ radar stations were put on 24-hour duty;
▶ barrage balloons appeared above town and cities;
▶ advice was given to protect against bomb-blast, and many houses had their windows protected with strips of sticky paper;
▶ gas masks were issued to the civilian population.

MUNICH, 1938

On 28th September Chamberlain was explaining to the Commons the danger of war. Hitler sent a note inviting him to a third meeting. At **Munich** he met Hitler, Mussolini and Daladier, but not the Czech leaders, nor their allies, the Russians.

On 29th October Britain and France gave Hitler all he wanted.
▶ **Benes**, the Czech Prime Minister, resigned.
▶ **Hitler** declared that he had no further demands to make.
▶ **Chamberlain** received the sort of welcome that Disraeli had received after the Congress of Berlin (unit 32) and claimed that he had brought back 'Peace in our time'.

AFTER MUNICH

▶ **13th March 1939** Hitler forced the Czechs to accept a German takeover of the rest of the country.
▶ **15th March 1939** Chamberlain complained.
▶ **April 1939** the **Conscription Act** forced everyone between the ages of 18 and 42 to register for service in the forces.
▶ French and British military staffs held conversations.
▶ **April 1939** Britain gave a guarantee to Poland, promising to come to her help if she were attacked by Germany.
▶ **The Oxford Union** voted by 423 to 326 in favour of conscription.

50.6 The Polish Crisis

East Prussia had been separated from the rest of Germany by the creation of 'the Polish Corridor', to give Poland access to the sea. **Hitler**, having torn up other clauses of the Treaty (the Rhineland, rearmament, Austria and Czechoslovakia) was determined to get back this part of former Germany – as part of his 'March to the East', in search of space, grain, oil and empire. **Russia**, under Stalin, feared German expansion and an attack. She had made an alliance with France (above).

Chamberlain, the anti-Communist, refused to make such a Russian alliance until August 1939, when he sent a low-level delegation to discuss a possible alliance.

Stalin was convinced after Munich that the western powers would not fight. **Hitler**, fearing a war on two fronts, and conscious that France and Britain might honour their agreement with Poland, sent his Foreign Minister, Ribbentrop, to make an agreement with Stalin (August 1939), in which they agreed to remain neutral if either was involved in a war.

THE OUTBREAK OF WAR

▶ On 1st September 1939 German troops invaded Poland.
▶ Britain and France waited until 3rd September before declaring war. The policy of appeasement had failed.
▶ Russian troops invaded Poland from the east (17th September).

50.7 The Creation of the Commonwealth

In 1914 all the countries of the Empire entered the war along with the Mother Country.

In 1917 the leaders of the Dominions, Australia, New Zealand, Canada and South Africa met in London and formed the **Imperial War Cabinet**. They demanded that after the war they be given a voice in formulation of foreign policy.

At Versailles they had their own representatives, signed the Treaty and were given some of the Mandated Territories (unit 44).

In 1926 Balfour, as Chairman of the Imperial Constitution Conference, re-defined the Dominions as 'autonomous communities ... equal in status ... united by a common allegiance to the Crown, freely associated as members of the British Commonwealth of Nations'.

In 1931 the Statute of Westminster recognized the new equality of status for the Dominions, which could now pass their own laws and choose their own foreign policies.

OTHER EMPIRE COUNTRIES
Egypt

▶ 1922 saw the end of the British protectorate, with Egypt becoming an independent kingdom in alliance with Britain.
▶ 1936 saw a special treaty involving arrangements for British control of the Suez Canal. It was this treaty which was broken by Nasser in 1956 (unit 54).

India

▶ **The Government of India Act**, 1919, gave the Indians less independence than they had hoped for after the part played in the war.
▶ **Rioting** led to disastrous reaction, especially at **Amritsar** where Gurkhas commanded by General Dyer shot 1500 civilians (1919).
▶ **Gandhi** persuaded the Indians not to rise in armed rebellion, but to practise 'civil disobedience' as a way of undermining British power. Gandhi:
● was jailed as an agitator;
● on release continued with his policy;
● broke the salt-tax laws with his march to the sea at Dandi where he broke the laws by gathering salt on the seashore.
▶ **The Government of India Act, 1935:**
● was the result of a series of London Conferences ('the Round Table Conferences') between British and Indian leaders;
● gave the Indians an increased share in Provincial governments and some share in national government;
● failed to present a solution to the religious division between Muslims and Hindus.

In September 1939 the Viceroy announced that the government of India, in which Indians had little share, had declared war on Germany. Many Indians protested and were imprisoned.

Unit 50 Summary

▶ The growth of anti-war feeling; optimism about the League.
▶ The Treaties of Rapallo and Locarno.
▶ German reparations.
▶ The failure of the League of Nations – and of its members.
▶ The Manchurian crisis, 1931.
▶ The Stresa Front and the Abyssinian war.
▶ The German occupation of the Rhineland and Austria.
▶ The Czech crisis, 1938–9.
▶ Munich.
▶ War over Poland, 1939.

51 THE SECOND WORLD WAR, 1939–45

51.1 The 'Phoney War'

Britain declared war on 3rd September, prepared for the bombing which had been forecast. **The BEF** sailed to France. The French, in their **Maginot Line** and the Germans behind their **Siegfried Line**, seemed prepared to sit it out. The first British soldier was killed in December.

Poland was quickly conquered by the 'blitzkrieg' in which:
- dive-bombers terrified the population;
- paratroopers landed behind Polish lines to occupy strategic positions;
- tanks, invented by the British but ignored by most military staffs except the Germans, rolled through enemy lines.

51.2 The Naval War, 1939

U-boats (or submarines) were used to attack:
- **merchant and passenger shipping** such as the *Athenia* sunk on the day of British entry into the war;
- the naval base at Scapa Flow (October 1939) sinking the *Royal Oak*.

German surface raiders, notably the *Graf Spee*, attacked shipping in the Indian and Atlantic Oceans.

The *Graf Spee* was scuttled in Montevideo on 20th December 1939 after a running fight with three cruisers, *Ajax*, *Achilles* and *Exeter*, in what became known as the Battle of the River Plate.

51.3 Defeat in the West, April 1940

Denmark and Norway were invaded on 9th May; the Danes put up no resistance; the Norwegians, in spite of betrayal by a politician, **Quisling**, fought with the help of British troops who landed in the north around **Narvik**. **Holland and Belgium** were conquered by a 'blitzkrieg', and **the Maginot Line** did not prevent a German advance through the Ardennes and on towards the Channel.

Dunkirk was the escape route for British troops cut off by the advance. From 24th May to 3rd June 1940 the 'little ships' evacuated 337 000 troops, in spite of German air attacks.

France capitulated, and **Britain**, alone against Germany, waited for an invasion.

CHURCHILL, THE WAR LEADER

On **10th May 1940**, after the disasters in Norway, Belgium and Holland, Chamberlain resigned in the face of criticism in the Commons.

Churchill and not Halifax (Chamberlain's nominee) became Prime Minister, leader of the Conservative Party and head of a Coalition government (see below).

His speeches raised the morale of the people, while expressing their determination. On 10th May he made one such speech in which he promised that Britain would fight 'on the beaches . . . in the fields . . . in the streets . . . . We will never give in. . . .'

51.4 The War in the Air

THE BATTLE OF BRITAIN, JULY–SEPTEMBER 1940

The RAF had 45 squadrons of **Hurricanes** and **Spitfires** in July 1940; factories were turning out about 500 a month.

'Sealion' was the code name for Hitler's planned invasion, for which:
- **the German army** had assembled 13 divisions in northern France;
- **the British** had a poorly armed army back from France and a Local Defence Volunteer force (later called the Home Guard);
- **Germany** had to gain control of the Channel and of the landing places in Britain.

Goering launched the Battle of Britain which fell into four stages:
- **10th July–7th August**; coastal convoys, vital inland targets and some cities were attacked and river estuaries mined; the Germans lost many planes;
- **8th–23rd August:** large scale attacks on RAF airfields;
- **24th August–6th September:** the bombing of military targets defended by RAF fighters, which lost more men and planes than did the Germans; airfields and factories were destroyed or damaged;
- **7th–30th September:** all RAF fighters were placed in the south to protect the country against the feared invasion. Huge raids by day ended after the 'Battle of Britain' when Germany lost 60 planes. These raids were called off and the Germans went back to bombing airfields and, at night, London.

The RAF lost over a thousand planes, while over 700 pilots were killed or wounded.

Night bombing replaced day-time raids (in which the RAF had proved to be invincible), and the British had to endure the 'blitz' of 1940–41.

THE 'BLITZ'

Night-time bombing attacks saw the dropping of:
- high-explosive bombs;
- incendiaries which caused widespread fires;
- parachute mines which could demolish a street of houses.

The civilian population was partially protected by:
- **Anderson shelters**, set in the earth and covered with soil;
- **Morrison shelters**, which were indoor steel boxes;
- **Communal shelters** and, in London, the underground stations.

Heavy damage and many casualties nevertheless led to:
- an increased communal spirit;
- an increase in volunteers to the various voluntary services.

Coventry was raided three times, started on 14th November; ports were attacked constantly. The attacks on Merseyside lasted for eight nights in May 1941, during which 2000 people died.

Churchill discovered that 'the blitz' damaged morale – but only for a time. He insisted that the RAF should prepare a huge bomber force, under 'Bomber' Harris, to attack German towns.

THE RAF ATTACKS AFTER MAY 1942

Cologne was attacked by 1000 planes; 39 were lost. The **Halifax** and the **Lancaster** became important weapons, although they did not achieve the object of destroying German industry or German morale.

After the entry of the USA into the war (see below) their Army Air Force had **Fortresses** and **Liberators** as bombing aircraft and **Thunderbolts** and **Mustangs** as escort-fighters.

The combined forces of the RAF and the USAAF continued to bomb German cities and towns until May 1945.

51.5 The Battle of the Atlantic – and another Role for the Navy

Hitler called off his planned invasion ('Sealion'). Like Napoleon and the Kaiser, he decided to attack Britain's overseas trade on which Britain depended for food and raw materials and for foreign war materials.

Convoys had been organized from the start of the war. Crossing the Atlantic took about 15 days. **U-boats** in **wolfpacks** waited until the convoys had little cover from air or from surface vessels then sank a number of ships.

Condors, German heavy bombers, attacked convoys in British waters, and **mines** in estuaries and harbour entrances were a final obstacle.

The battleship *Bismarck* and the cruiser *Prinz Eugen* were another menace. They:
▶ came into the Atlantic from the Baltic in May 1941;
▶ were attacked by *Hood* ('the pride of the Navy'), *Prince of Wales* and aircraft carrier *Ark Royal*;
▶ sank the *Hood* (only three survived of its crew of 1429);
▶ drove off the *Prince of Wales*;
▶ were attacked by **Swordfish** planes from *Ark Royal* which crippled *Bismarck* and left her an easy target for *Rodney* and the *Duke of York*, battleships which had joined the battle.

Bismarck was sunk by torpedoes from *Dorsetshire* (27th May 1941); *Prinz Eugen* escaped.

WINNING THE BATTLE OF THE ATLANTIC

Many ships were lost: in 1941 and 1942 800 000 tons of shipping was lost each month.

Escort vessels became better equipped with:
▶ Asdic and radar, which located the U-boats;
▶ bomb-throwers armed with explosive charges.

Better quality escort vessels appeared in the shape of:
▶ faster frigates;
▶ corvettes, which could ram or otherwise destroy submarines when they came to the surface.

Bomber planes played their part in 1942 and 1943.

In 1943 the number of U-boats being sunk rose sharply from an average of 10 a month (1942) to over 50 a month (1943). At the same time the losses of shipping went down sharply, with an average monthly loss of less than 100 000 tons.

OTHER ROLES FOR THE NAVY

▶ To protect convoys to Russia after December 1941 along the dangerous route around northern Norway.
▶ To protect troop convoys to Africa and, when invasions started, to Italy and France.
▶ To protect troops and materials coming from India, Australia and New Zealand (around the Cape), from North America and from Latin America.

51.6 The Extension of the War, 1941–42

Russia was invaded on 22nd June 1941 in Operation **Barbarossa**. **The Germans:**
▶ **delayed** their attack to help the Italians in their invasion of Greece and Yugoslavia;
▶ enjoyed their **early success** because of their 'blitzkrieg';
▶ reached the outskirts of **Moscow** by September 1941;
▶ were halted by 'General Winter' and fanatical defence;
▶ reached **Stalingrad** on 15th September 1942 where winter came to the aid of the Russians.

Italy entered the war on the German side on 11th June 1940:
▶ from Abyssinia, Italian troops occuped British Somaliland;
▶ from Libya, Italian troops attacked Egypt;
▶ from Albania they attacked Greece.

North Africa June 1940–September 1942
▶ **Wavell** with a small force drove the Italians to Benghazi;
▶ **British Somaliland** was liberated (early 1941);
▶ **Haile Selassie** was restored to the throne of **Abyssinia**;
▶ British forces were withdrawn to **Greece**;
▶ **Rommel** ('the Desert Fox') was sent to help the Italians;
▶ **Greece** was conquered by Germany (April 1941) and used as a base for an attack on Crete, captured May 1941;
▶ Rommel drove the British from Libya, except Tobruk;
▶ **Auchinleck** replaced Wavell, conquered Cyreneica and relieved Tobruk. German forces were starved of supplies because of the Russian campaign;
▶ the German airforce, using Italian bases, attacked **Malta** and **convoys** carrying supplies to North Africa.

In **May 1942** Rommel received supplies; he succeeded in attack by tanks against the weakened British force, drove them from Libya and deep into Egypt. This was a threat to the Suez Canal ('lifeline of the Empire') and to British oil supplies from the Middle East.

In July 1942, Rommel was held at El Alamein. Alexander replaced Auchinleck and Montgomery was appointed to command troops at El Alamein – the Eighth Army of 'Desert Rats'.

By October 1942, Montgomery was better supplied and equipped than Rommel (with American Sherman tanks and self-propelled guns). Battle commenced on the 23rd October; by the middle of November superior air power and tanks forced a German retreat.

In **Operation Torch**, November 1942, Americans invaded Morocco and Rommel was caught in a pincer movement of US forces plus 8th Army. Rommel flew home and in May 1943 250 000 Germans surrendered; North Africa was cleared of enemy troops.

Japan

Japan had an alliance with Germany and Italy – the Rome-Berlin-Tokyo Axis, and had been at war with China since 1937 (unit 44). In 1940, after the fall of France, the French were forced to allow the Japanese occupation of Indo-China.

Japan planned an invasion of Indonesia and Malaya to get rubber and oil supplies; control of the sea was essential for this to succeed and on 7th December 1941, Japanese planes sank most of the American Fleet in **Pearl Harbor**.

Japanese seaborne troops then conquered naval bases at Guam and Wake Island, naval forces sank the *Prince of Wales* and *Repulse* sent to defend Malaya and Singapore, and captured Hong Kong (Christmas 1941).

Japanese forces then took Manila (January 1942); Singapore (February 1942), captured the Dutch East Indies (March 1942), and defeated the Americans in the Philippines and the British in Burma (May 1942).

The USA

America had been determined to keep out of the war, 1939, and had sold supplies to whoever had gold to buy them.

By December 1940, Britain had no more gold, but Roosevelt persuaded Congress to pass the Lease-Lend Act (March 1941) which:
▶ permitted lease or lend of supplies to any government whose defence was thought to be vital to the USA;
▶ was applied to supplies for Britain alone, until Russia entered the war, when it was extended to Russia.

Roosevelt had earlier (January 1941) spoken of 'four freedoms':
▶ of speech;   ▶ from want;
▶ of worship;   ▶ from fear.

The Atlantic Charter was drawn up at a meeting between Roosevelt and Churchill off the coast of Newfoundland, in which they expressed their reasons for opposing tyranny and their hopes for peace, freedom and liberty everywhere.

After a US trade ban on Japan in July 1941 and Pearl Harbor, Americans did badly at first, because they had not prepared for war, unlike the Japanese, and it took time to mobilize forces and resources.

The USA became the 'arsenal of the free world' because it:
▶ built new factories and adapted existing ones for producing war materials;

▶ developed new, better-built and better-armed ships, planes and tanks in large numbers;
▶ sent men to fight in North Africa (above), Europe (below) as well as against Japan.

51.7 Turning Points, May 1942–February 1943

▶ At **El Alamein** Rommel's forces were halted (July 1942) and defeated (November 1942), before the British attack which led to the surrender of German forces, May 1943.
▶ At **Stalingrad** German forces had been halted (September 1942) then destroyed by a combination of:
● weather and the wrong equipment;
● Russian stubborness and bravery;
● Hitler's refusal to allow a withdrawal, which led to the surrender of German forces in February 1943.
▶ **The Coral Sea and Midway Islands** were the scenes of the first US naval victories over Japan. From June 1942, US troops 'island-hopped' towards Japan; in August 1942 began a six months' battle for Guadalcanal whose capture (early 1943) gave the US forces a springboard for further attacks.
▶ The Battle of the Atlantic was won by May 1943.

51.8 The Allies on the Attack

Russia began to retake captured cities in May 1943 as the Germans were driven into retreat by forces which were:
▶ supplied by US material carried on British convoys;
▶ better led than the German armies;
▶ inspired partly by patriotism (reborn under Stalin in 1941) and partly by fear of:
● Germany's aim of enslaving the Slavs;
● Stalin's use of the prison camps for failures.

Sicily was invaded on 10th July 1943 by US and British troops. On 25th July the Fascist Grand Council advised the king to dismiss Mussolini.

Italy was invaded on 3rd September from Sicily and Mussolini's successor, Badoglio, surrendered. The Germans seized power and continued the fight against the Allied advance.

France was invaded on D-Day, 6th June 1944, in **Operation Overlord**. This operation was helped by:
▶ **the Pipe Line Under The Ocean** (PLUTO), which carried oil supplies across the Channel;
▶ **the Mulberry Harbours**, designed by British and US scientists, built in Britain and towed, complete, across the Channel to replace harbours destroyed either by bombing or by enemy action;
▶ the superiority of **Allied forces** at sea and in the air;
▶ help provided by **French Resistance** workers.

THE END

Russian troops drove the Germans from Russia and then from the countries of Eastern Europe, all of which, except Yugoslavia, owed their liberation to the Red Army, which meant that Russia was able to impose Russian-dominated governments on those countries.

Allied troops drove the Germans from Italy and France, Belgium and Holland and on into Germany itself. Unlike 1918 there were no Fourteen Points; the Allies insisted on 'unconditional surrender'.

On 30th April Hitler committed suicide. His successor, Admiral Doenitz ordered an end to German resistance (7th May 1945). The eighth of May was celebrated as V-E Day.

The Americans in the Pacific and the British in Burma and Malaya continued their wars against the Japanese.

On 6th August the first atomic bomb was exploded at **Hiroshima** and this was followed by the second atomic attack, on **Nagasaki** (9th August 1945). The Japanese government ordered an end to Japanese resistance (14th August) and McArthur took the Japanese surrender in Tokyo Bay, while Mountbatten took their surrender in Singapore.

51.9 The Effect of the War on Britain

Government and manpower

Conscription had started in the summer of 1939, before the outbreak of war. **Essential workers** were not taken into the Forces, but were subject to 'direction of labour', forced to leave non-essential work to go to factories producing war materials.

Ernest Bevin, once the leader of the Dockers in 1919 (unit 45) and the Transport Workers at the time of the General Strike (unit 47), was brought into Churchill's government as Minister of Labour. It was he who imposed the 'direction of labour' and brought in the second Conscription Act, 1941, which forced unmarried women to join one of the forces or go to work in one of the essential industries.

The government and industry

Industry was quickly brought under government control, and officials were appointed to run the railways, road transport system and docks. The Ministry of Fuel and Power was set up in 1942 to direct the coal industry, which remained in private ownership.

The government took steps to produce war material by control of power supplies and raw materials, which were not given to firms which refused to comply with government regulation, and by direction of labour away from such firms.

Workers were not only subject to 'direction'. They were also:
▶ persuaded by Bevin to allow 'dilution', so that unskilled people did work previously done by skilled workers;
▶ persuaded by Bevin to give up their 'normal' working day and to work longer hours, so that more munitions might be produced.

The expansion of the aircraft industry

Beaverbrook, owner of the *Daily Express* and a friend of Churchill, was made Minister of Aircraft Production in 1940 to help ensure a plentiful supply of aircraft. He:
▶ cut through inessential regulations to allow supplies to reach firms building 'planes';
▶ persuaded motor car firms to turn to producing aircraft;
▶ cooperated with Bevin to get unions on his side.

Government and the nation's supplies

There was a shortage of many goods because of government direction of industry and the U-boat attacks. Food, petrol and raw materials were in short supply which led to:
▶ rationing of petrol (September 1939) – only those who could prove a need received a ration book;
▶ rationing of food (January 1940) so that everyone was entitled to a small amount of meat, sugar, butter, fats and other basic foods, as well as sweets;
▶ rationing of less basic foods by a system of 'points';
▶ rationing of clothing by a system of 'coupons'.

Lord Woolton was appointed Minister of Food, to control the rationing system and, with the Ministry of Agriculture, persuaded people to 'grow more food'. New kinds of food were introduced, such as dried egg.

Government powers

In 1929 Snowden attacked Keynes' ideas of 'spending our way out of the depression', and in the 1930s the government refused to find the £100 million demanded by Mosley's Memorandum (unit 48). But during the war:
▶ £105 million was spent each week;
▶ income tax was raised from its peacetime level of 22½p in the pound to 37½p (1939) and to 50p (1942);
▶ purchase tax was imposed on luxury goods, so that richer people paid even more tax if they bought those goods.

Emergency Powers Acts were introduced in 1939 and 1940 to allow:
▶ arrest and imprisonment without trial of German nationals and some British Fascists, such as Mosley;
▶ control of newspapers; for a time the Communist *Daily*

Worker was closed down, while the *Daily Mirror* was threatened with a similar fate when it became critical of the government.

A destructive war

▶ Three million homes were destroyed or damaged; ports, railways and factories were also destroyed and damaged.

Few, if any, repairs could be made to any but the essential things, and there was little modernization or replacement of ageing equipment during the war, which is described as a 'notional' cost – because we can only have a notion of how much might have been done if there had been peace between 1939 and 1945.

▶ **Overseas investments** were sold to buy goods in America – North and South.

▶ **Overseas debts** built up as government borrowed abroad to help to pay for the war.

▶ **Prices** of imports would be higher after the war because of the destruction of:

● supply sources in Asia, Europe and Russia;

● so much housing and industrial building throughout the world, which would lead to a high demand after 1945, and so higher prices, of building materials.

Social change

Evacuation of children and families from cities threatened by bombing into safer rural areas revealed the social divisions between better-off and poor, and led to demand for social reform by many of those comfortably off. Labour won many 'middle-class' seats in the 1945 election.

Government committees reported on the need for change in the post-war world. There were Reports on:

▶ **Full Employment** – to be achieved by government adoption of the ideas once put forward by Keynes, Lloyd George and Mosley.

▶ **Redistribution of Industry and Population** – to ensure the end of the Depressed Areas and of the urban sprawl in the south-east. This, too, would require government action and legislation.

▶ **National Health**, proving that the country needed a government-controlled system to run hospitals and other services.

▶ **Coal** and other industries, pointing to the need for some essential industries to be brought under government control by nationalization.

Government Acts increased the claims to social change and raised expectations of further changes:

▶ **Education Act**, 1944 (unit 42);

▶ **Family Allowance** Act 1945 helped increase family income – a most important reform for the less well-off families.

▶ **The Beveridge Report**, 1942, explained how the five 'giant evils' of Want, Ignorance, Squalor, Idleness and Disease could be overcome by a state-provided system of social insurance, allied with government determination to maintain full employment.

The Army Bureau of Current Affairs ran classes for troops during their off-duty hours. Lecturers and teachers showed how the Government Commissions' recommendations and Beveridge's suggestions could be put into practice, and how this would help improve life for the majority of the people.

Full employment was achieved during the war, as everyone had a job or was in the Forces. People expected that after the 'Victory over the Germans' there might be a 'Victory over unemployment'.

THE END OF THE WAR AND THE COALITION GOVERNMENT

Churchill had invited Labour's leaders into his government. **Attlee** was the efficient chairman of most Cabinet meetings as Churchill's Deputy; Bevin was the important Minister of Labour; Morrison, Home Secretary, was in charge of home affairs; Dalton was at the Board of Trade.

When the Germans surrendered (May 1945) Churchill asked Labour's leaders to agree to fight the next election as a Coalition. The Labour Party's Annual Conference rejected this (June 1945).

Parliament was dissolved on 15th June; polling day was 5th July but, to allow for the return of the votes of men serving overseas, the counting day was 25th July.

51.10 The Election

Churchill was popular, and most poeple thought that he would win the election, but he made several mistakes:

▶ he refused to adopt the Beveridge Report;

▶ he suggested that the mild-mannered Attlee would bring in some sort of secret police and concentration camps if Labour won;

▶ he insisted on wearing a uniform, which upset many men who had had their fill of officers and uniforms.

He was also unfairly blamed, as a Conservative, for having been responsible for:

▶ the effects of the General Strike;

▶ the depression of the 1930s, when the Conservatives had controlled Parliament and done little.

Labour also had the support of people anxious for social reform, and many 'first time' voters, of whom there were many millions, since there had not been an election since 1935.

THE RESULT OF THE 1945 ELECTION

▶ Labour won 393 seats.

▶ The Conservatives won 213 seats.

▶ The Liberals won 11 seats.

▶ There were 22 other MPs including two Communist MPs.

Labour had a majority over all other parties combined of 147, and Clement Attlee formed Labour's first majority government which had to tackle the many problems facing post-war Britain.

Unit 51 Summary

▶ The reasons for Germany's early successes, 1939–40.

▶ The Battles of Britain (and the bombing blitz) and of the Atlantic (including submarine warfare).

▶ The German attack on Russia.

▶ The Japanese attack on Pearl Harbor and early successes, 1941–2.

▶ Turning points: El Alamein, Stalingrad and Coral Sea.

▶ Reasons for Allied victories.

▶ Effects of the war on life in Britain.

▶ The Labour victory in the 1945 Election.

52.1 The 1945 Government

LABOUR'S MINISTERS, 1945

▶ **Clement Attlee**, Prime Minister, had been Party leader since 1935 (unit 49). For a summary of his career see below.
▶ **Ernest Bevin**, Foreign Secretary, had been a major Trade Union leader (unit 47) and Minister of Labour during the war.
▶ **Hugh Dalton**, Chancellor of the Exchequer, had been in the 1929 government (unit 48). He resigned in 1947 because of a budget leak.
▶ **Herbert Morrison**, Lord Privy Seal, had been in the 1929 government, but had lost his seat in the 1931 election (unit 48). He came back as an MP in the 1935 election, but found Attlee in the chair as the accepted party leader. When ill-health forced Bevin's resignation in 1950, he became Foreign Secretary.
▶ **Stafford Cripps**, a famous barrister and an extreme left-winger, was President of the Board of Trade until 1947, when he became Chancellor in place of Dalton. Ill-health forced his resignation in 1950 and he was succeeded by Hugh Gaitskell.
▶ **Harold Wilson** entered the Cabinet as President of the Board of Trade in 1947.
▶ **Aneurin Bevan**, an extreme left-winger and war-time critic of the Coalition government, was Minister of Health and Housing.

THE AIMS OF THE ATTLEE GOVERNMENT, 1945

▶ **The rebuilding** of war-damaged Britain.
▶ The return to normal of British **overseas trade**.
▶ The implementation of the **Beveridge Report**.
▶ The implementation of **other promises of the wartime government**, as promised in Labour's Manifesto 1945, on full employment, location of industry and housing.
▶ **To raise living standards.**

THE DIFFICULTIES FACING THE GOVERNMENT, 1945–50

▶ The effect of the war (already examined in unit 51). Here you should recall:
● **the lost markets;**
● **the destruction** and the need for rebuilding;
● **the overseas investments** sold;
● **the overseas debts** incurred;
● the loss of 25 per cent of **British shipping**;
● the **'notional loss'**, or 'what might have been done'.
▶ **Post-war demand** for food, raw materials and machinery;
● in **Britain**, to achieve Labour's aims (above);
● in **Europe**, where destruction was worse;
● in **Asia**, after the Japanese had been defeated.
▶ **Post-war supply** of food, raw materials and machinery was scarce, because of the devastation of war, and made scarcer by:
● **Argentina's** drought, 1946, which meant less wheat and beef at higher prices;
● **Antartica's** poor whaling season, 1946, which led to a shortage of cooking oils;
● **India's** refusal to export ground nuts to Britain, which increased the shortage of vegetable oil;
● **Germany's** food shortage, 1945–46. Attlee sent wheat and potatoes from Britain, which had to bring in rationing of these items, which had been ration-free during the war.
At first imports were mainly **only available from the**

USA, which had not suffered wartime destruction. But how was Britain to pay for these imports after 1945?
Higher prices for most imports were the result of high world demand and scarce supply. Britain had to pay these high prices which led to:
▶ **balance of payments** problem (below);
▶ **inflation**, as manufacturers and shopkeepers were forced to put up their prices;
▶ **higher wages**, as workers demanded more to enable their families to buy the more highly priced goods.
In unit 28 we saw that in the nineteenth century Britain earned enough to pay for her imports **and** to lend money to overseas borrowers. In unit 47 we saw that after 1918 Britain continued to be a lender overseas. We also saw that the payment of interest and capital by overseas borrowers helped to pay for much of British imports. After 1945:
▶ **exports** were down in volume and value until 1948, when they began to recover;
▶ **imports** were up in price and, if everyone had been allowed to do all they wanted (building, furnishing, clothing and eating), they would also have been up in volume;
▶ the **balance of visible trade** was bound to be unfavourable. In the past this had been made up by a favourable balance on 'invisibles';
▶ **'invisible imports'** were up because of Britain's debts;
▶ **'invisible exports'** were down because of loss of shipping and the sale of overseas investments;
The balance of payments on current accounts was therefore in deficit. Britain was trying to spend more than she earned. This could be overcome by:
▶ **increasing exports**, which took time but which was achieved, so that in the 1950s exports exceeded imports;
▶ **cutting imports**, which led to severe rationing, imposition of restrictions on building so that only the essential was done, and which also led to the term 'The Age of Austerity' to describe Britain in 1945–50;
▶ **borrowing from abroad** – see below.

THE USA AND THE LABOUR GOVERNMENT, 1945–50

The Americans had thought that Churchill would win the election. They feared that Labour would be 'soft on Communism', and they stopped Lease-Lend aid, refusing to 'finance socialism'.
Keynes was sent (1945) to negotiate loans from the US and Canada – totalling about £1000 million to pay for the food, raw materials and equipment to rebuild Britain.
Higher prices meant that the money was spent by 1947–48 and not, as Keynes had planned, by 1950. **Marshall Aid**, introduced as a form of US help to Europe, provided Britain with £2400 million by 1951, and saved Britain from collapse.

INCREASING EXPORTS, 1945–50

By **1947**, exports had begun to rise as factories (rebuilt and modernized) began to turn out goods (rationed to home buyers).
Devaluation of the pound in September 1949 was one of Cripps' solutions to the export problem. He cut the value of the pound from 4.03 US dollars to 2.80 dollars. This lowered export prices, and so helped to make it easier to sell British goods and to earn dollars. Cripps also:
▶ cut **rations** in 1948 and 1949 (becoming known as 'Mr Austerity');
▶ persuaded **unions** to hold back their wage demands so that:
● export prices could be held down;

● home demand could be held down to allow goods to be exported.

By **1950** exports were twice their 1938 level, while imports had hardly gone up (because of rationing). This allowed the government to begin to improve life at home by abolishing the rationing system of bread, petrol, clothes and potatoes.

THE GOVERNMENT AND THE UNIONS, 1945–50

The unions felt that this was 'their' government. **The Trade Union Act**, 1946, undid the damage done to them by the 1927 Act (unit 39), and the unions cooperated with Cripps by holding back **wage demands** in 1948 and 1949. They refused to do so in 1950 because:

▶ **devaluation** put up **import** prices; there was a rise in the cost of living; unions wanted wage increases to take account of this;

▶ **profits and prices** were not being held back or controlled.

The unions welcomed the government's policies on:

▶ nationalization – see below;

▶ social reform – see below.

NATIONALIZATION – OR STATE OWNERSHIP OF INDUSTRIES

This was already a feature of British life.

▶ The **Post Office** had been state-controlled since it started.

▶ Baldwin had nationalized the **BBC** and the generating of **electricity** (unit 47).

▶ **British Overseas Airways Corporation** (BOAC) had been a publicly owned company since 1940.

During the war there were Reports which called for the state ownership of:

▶ **coal**; the **Reid Committee** showed (1945) that if the industry was to survive, it would need large-scale investment, which existing owners could not provide;

▶ **transport** by rail and road, so that it could be integrated and, run by a National Corporation, would be used efficiently. The railway system had been run down by its private owners and would need massive investment to help it to recover;

▶ **gas supply**, which would allow for the best economic uses of raw materials (coal) and methods of output.

Economists such as Keynes had taught that increased government spending (on investment in railways and mines) was the best cure for depression. The government intended to use the nationalized industries to ensure investment and to avoid a depression.

"ALL I ASK IS THAT YOU GET IT PROPERLY BALANCED"

Fig. 52.1 The Labour Government overloaded the British economy after 1945 because of their ambition to build up the Welfare State and, at the same time, to maintain British military power.

Socialists hoped that nationalization would lead to a 'happier' people – the workers would feel a 'new' pride in 'their' industry and consumers would feel an equal pride in the industries which they 'owned'. Few people share those beliefs today.

Profits made from state-controlled industries would be used either to reduce taxation or to increase spending on welfare provision. In fact, most nationalized industries have had to be subsidized by the taxpayer.

Between 1945 and 1951 the government nationalized:

▶ the Bank of England, 1946;

▶ coal, electricity supply and civil aviation, 1947;

▶ gas supply, 1948;

▶ railways and road transport, 1948;

▶ the iron and steel industry, 1949.

By 1950 the government controlled about 20 per cent of British industry.

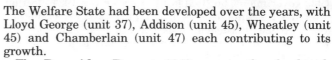 52.2 The Welfare State

The Welfare State had been developed over the years, with Lloyd George (unit 37), Addison (unit 45), Wheatley (unit 45) and Chamberlain (unit 47) each contributing to its growth.

The **Beveridge Report**, 1942 was another landmark (unit 51). Labour implemented Beveridge by:

▶ **The National Insurance Act, 1946**, by which all adults, except married women, had to pay weekly contributions to cover themselves against sickness, unemployment and retirement.

▶ **The Industrial Injuries Act, 1946**, which replaced the older Workmen's Compensation Acts and provided state pensions for men injured or disabled at work.

▶ **The National Health Service Act, 1946**, which ensured free medical attention for everyone, no matter what their income. This came into operation in April, 1948.

The state could now claim that it looked after people 'from the cradle to the grave', with maternity grants, family allowances, sickness and unemployment benefits, retirement pensions and death grants.

The National Assistance Board was set up in 1949 to replace the old Public Assistance Committees (unit 46), to provide help for those who 'slipped through the welfare net' – the handicapped, deserted or unmarried mothers and the wives of criminals. The Board also paid grants to those whose weekly incomes were too low to give them a 'minimum standard of living'.

HOUSING

Bevan was the Minister of Health and Housing. The high demand for housing came from:

▶ the **need to rebuild** damaged towns and cities;

▶ **rising expectations**; people living in older housing wanted houses with proper water supplies and sanitation;

▶ **rising incomes**; people could afford decent housing.

That demand could not be met, because of the imports/balance of payments problems. There was a strict licensing system, which limited the amount of private housing.

Housing for letting, mainly built by councils, increased after 1945, and in 1950 200 000 houses were being built – a sign of the improvement in the imports situation (see above).

By 1950 Britain had built one million post-war homes – a much higher figure than had been achieved after 1918, but much lower than people had come to expect after the boom of the 1930s (unit 49).

NEW TOWNS

In 1946 Parliament passed the **New Towns Act**. This allowed the creation of **Development Corporations**, which used government money to build new towns with offices, shops, factories, schools and other amenities, as well as housing. This was an improvement on pre-war council estates built on the fringes of existing towns.

Sixteen new towns were planned – eight to take people from overcrowded London, the rest to take people from other cities such as Cardiff, Glasgow, Liverpool and Birmingham.

EDUCATION

The government implemented the 1944 Act (see unit 42).

52.3 The 1950 Election

Between 1945 and 1950 Labour had not lost a single by-election, a record not equalled by any other post-war government. It had achieved what R. A. Butler described as 'the greatest social revolution in our history' (1948).

In February 1950 Attlee called an election:
► the Labour vote went up – to 13¼ million;
► many middle-class seats, won in 1945, reverted to the Conservatives because of hostility towards:
● continued rationing and restrictions;
● high taxation;
● the feeling that middle-class living standards had fallen relative to those of working people – there were fewer servants and people had fewer and cheaper holidays.

The result was:
► Labour 315 seats;   ► Liberals 9;
► Conservatives 298;   ► Irish Nationalists (from Ulster) 2.

THE SECOND ATTLEE GOVERNMENT, 1950–51

Many of its Ministers were tired or ill: Cripps retired in October 1950, and Bevin was replaced by Morrison, because of ill-health, and died within a month of giving up the Foreign Office (1951).

The Korean War will be examined in unit 54 but here you should note:
► many feared that it was the start of a Third World War;
► this fear led to a high demand for raw materials, the price of which rose sharply, so increasing Britain's imports bill and leading to a balance of payments problem;
► the government decided to re-arm; £1 500 000 000 would be spent each year. This would impose strains on:
● **exports**, because materials and labour would be diverted into munitions;
● **imports**, which would have to provide the raw materials and machinery;
● **inflation**, because there would be more money (through wages to munition makers), but no increase in goods in the shops.

Gaitskell, the new Chancellor, had to find money to pay for the ever-rising costs of the National Health Service and for the re-armament programme. He decided to impose small charges for some welfare services – dental treatment and prescription charges.

Bevan, angered at the appointment of 'young Gaitskell', called this a betrayal of the 'free' service, created in 1946.

He resigned, along with Wilson, and three other leading left-wingers. Attlee was in hospital at this time and unable to play his normal 'soothing' role.

Morrison, Foreign Secretary, had to deal with the crisis caused by Mossadeq's nationalization of the Anglo-Iranian Oil Company (which will be examined in unit 54). You should note that Britain failed to prevent the nationalization and Morrison refused to use force.

52.4 The Election, October 1951

The divided government had an overall majority of only six. Attlee feared that it might be overthrown at any time.

The King, George VI, was due to go on a world tour in the autumn of 1951 and Attlee feared that the government might be defeated while he was away – and therefore unable to dissolve Parliament, so he called the election before the King's expected departure.

This was a bad time for the government because of:
► **rising prices** – the result of the Korean War;
► **rising taxes** – because of re-armament;
► **the divisions** caused by the 'Bevanites';
► its weak **foreign policy** (unit 54).

Churchill and the Tories were much stronger than they had been in 1945 because:
► **R. A. Butler** had created a 'Think Tank' at the Conservative Head Office, which produced pamphlets outlining radical policies;
► **Lord Woolton** (unit 51) had helped to rebuild the Party machinery in the country – with election agents in most constituencies and with active workers in the growing Young Conservative organization;
► the electors saw that the Conservatives would not 'undo' the welfare provisions of the Labour government, but expected that it would have a firmer foreign policy.

THE RESULT, 1951

► Conservatives 321 seats;
► Labour 295;   ► Liberals 6;

It was a Conservative government which came to power in October 1951, promising to 'set the people free' – of rationing, controls and socialism.

Unit 52 Summary

► Labour's aims and the country's problems.
► The export drive and the government's relationships with trade unions.
► Nationalization – which industries and why.
► The development of the Welfare State.
► The effects of the Korean War on Labour plans and policies.
► The Elections of 1950 and 1951.

53 CONSERVATIVE GOVERNMENTS, 1951–64

53.1 The Four Prime Ministers

Winston Churchill

Winston Churchill's career is a favourable subject with examiners. You should note:
► **pre-1906** – a soldier, journalist, author;

► **1906–12** – Radical Liberal at Board of Trade (unit 37);
► **1914–15** – First Lord of Admiralty, blamed for Dardanelles (unit 43);
► **1922–24** – he slowly drew back to being a Conservative;
► **1925–29** – Chancellor of the Exchequer (unit 47);
► **1929–39** – when he was wrong about India (opposing the

trend to self-government) and the Abdication (unit 49), but right about Hitler and the need to re-arm;

▶ **1939–45**–when he became the great war leader, remembered for:

● great speeches;

● his friendship with Roosevelt, which helped ensure US aid even before American entry into the war;

● the formation of a Coalition government in which Labour leaders were given major roles (unit 51);

● his fear of Stalin's future policies, but his inability to convince Roosevelt of the Russian danger.

▶ **1945–55**–when as Party Leader and, after 1951, as Prime Minister he was responsible for:

● the work of Woolton and Butler (unit 52);

● convincing the people that 'Tory Freedom' was worth supporting;

● not undoing the welfare work of Labour;

● promising a more vigorous foreign policy in the aftermath of the withdrawal from Iran (unit 54).

Anthony Eden

Later Viscount Avon, Eden's career covered:

▶ **1935–38**, Foreign Secretary, supported the League and non-intervention in Spain, resigned in 1938 (unit 50);

▶ **1940–45**, wartime Foreign Secretary subject to Churchill's power, influence and energy; attended wartime Conferences;

▶ **1951–55**, Foreign Secretary and 'heir' to Churchill;

▶ **1955–57**, Prime Minister, resigned after illness following Suez disaster (unit 54).

Harold Macmillan

▶ A Radical Tory MP, opposed to Baldwin and Chamberlain and a supporter of Keynes' ideas on unemployment (unit 48);

▶ wartime Minister responsible for North Africa and for Greece; became friendly with Eisenhower in North Africa;

▶ **1951–54**, Minister of Housing, who called for 300 000 houses a year;

▶ **1955–57**, Chancellor in succession to Butler; he first supported the invasion of Suez, then saw the economic dangers following US condemnation, and advised withdrawal;

▶ **1957–63**, Prime Minister.

Sir Alec Douglas Home

Home had been Foreign Secretary in Macmillan's government (as Lord Home) and was replaced by Edward Heath.

▬ 53.2 Economic Recovery and Slow Progress

By 1953 **Tory freedom worked** in that:

▶ **exports** had recovered (unit 52);

▶ **new works** were producing the steel, petro-chemicals and aeroplanes;

▶ **the Korean War** ended and the prices of imports fell as sharply as they had risen when it started (unit 52);

▶ Britain's **import bill** fell, allowing the government to permit the import of more goods;

▶ **rationing** and **licensing** ended.

Full employment was a feature of life and was the result of:

▶ **government policies**;

▶ **investment** in nationalized industries and in buildings for welfare services;

▶ **housing**, with a 50 per cent increase in building under Macmillan's urging, 1952–55;

▶ the **welfare services**, which needed more workers of all sorts;

▶ **exports**, which had doubled by 1951 and continued to expand and so create employment;

▶ **welfare spending** by people who received pensions and other allowances and which created a demand for goods and labour;

▶ **industrial demand** for labour, which was high because;

● many **new factories** were being built;

● **housing** development expanded;

▶ **consumer demand** was high because most families could afford more goods.

NEW KINDS OF WORKERS

Women found it easy to get work and many **married women** combined two roles–of workers and housewife (unit 41). This gave many families at least two incomes.

Immigrants

It became increasingly difficult to find people to do the lowest-paid jobs, because of the attraction to other work by higher wages in the 'full employment' society, so employers brought workers from Malta and Cyprus; in the early 1950s workers began to arrive from the West Indies and Pakistan.

Macmillan's boom (see below) attracted 56 000 immigrant workers (1960) and 136 000 more in 1961. By 1964 there were over one million coloured immigrants in Britain. There were also the first of the 'second generation'–the British-born children of immigrant parents.

Limiting this immigration became government policy in response to fears that parts of the country might be 'swamped' and that there might be racial violence. This limitation was achieved by:

▶ The Commonwealth Immigration Act, 1962;

▶ Labour's stricter Act, 1968.

Race Relations sometimes exploded into violence. The government tried to improve matters with:

▶ **The Race Relations Act**, 1965, which forbade discrimination against people on account of colour;

▶ Conservative **rejection** of Enoch Powell's demands for stricter controls and for repatriation

▶ **acceptance** of reports such as that issued by Lord Scarman after the Brixton riots of 1981.

THE LOCATION OF INDUSTRY SINCE 1945

The **depressed areas** continued to have higher than average levels of unemployment. In response to a wartime Report successive governments have tried to bring industry to those areas by:

▶ insisting on **licensing** for new factory buildings and by trying to persuade industrialists to build in depressed areas;

▶ offering a number of **'carrots'** to attract firms into these areas–low interest loans, tax concessions and help with housing for key workers;

▶ setting up Development Agencies. The **depressed areas** became **development areas**, with officials set to work to attract new industry. These areas were South Wales, West Scotland, the North-East and North-West of England.

While these policies have had some success, the development areas still have high unemployment and critics argue that:

▶ the policy is **very costly**;

▶ **firms close down** works in the development areas as soon as recession starts.

▬ 53.3 The 1955 Election ▬

Butler, as Chancellor since 1951, had been able to:

▶ **lower taxation**–because:

● there was less spent on re-armament than had been originally planned by the Labour government (unit 52);

● there were more tax payers (owing to full employment) so that each had to pay slightly less;

▶ end the **rationing** and **licensing**;

▶ allow Macmillan to build **300 000 houses a year**.

The government was very popular. Eden, who took over from Churchill, wanted his own mandate and called an election in which the result was:

▶ Conservatives 344 seats;

▶ Labour 277 seats; ▶ Liberals 6 seats.

ATTLEE RETIRED AS LABOUR'S LEADER, DECEMBER 1955

Examiners sometimes ask for an account of his career, in which you should note:
▶ an Oxford graduate and son of middle-class parents, he became a member of the Labour Party before 1914.
▶ Elected MP for Stepney, London, 1922. He was a junior minister in MacDonald's two governments (units 45 and 48).
▶ He retained his seat in 1931 (unit 48) while most leaders lost theirs, so that he was the most experienced MP after Lansbury's resignation before the 1935 election (unit 49).
▶ During **May 1940–July 1945** he was a member of the Coalition government and Deputy Prime Minister from 1943.
▶ He led Labour to victory in 1945 and by 1951 had shown his ability to:
● hold together a strong team of Ministers;
● lead the 'greatest social revolution' (unit 52);
● sack inefficient Ministers in a ruthless way.
▶ His illness (1951) was a cause of the Labour split (unit 52). After 1951 he and his colleagues seemed to have run out of ideas – what was Labour to do next? This helped the Conservatives to win the 1955 election.
▶ He held on to power to help Gaitskell (and not the experienced but older Morrison) to become his successor.

INFLATION AFTER 1955

Cost-push inflation is the term used to describe the rise in prices caused by:
▶ higher import prices, 1945–53 (unit 52);
▶ higher wage demands to meet rising costs;
▶ higher taxes, such as Purchase Tax.
Demand-pull inflation is the term used to describe the rise in prices caused by too high a demand for the goods available because of:
▶ home demand; ▶ export demand.
Rising wages were a result of cost-push and a cause of demand-pull inflation. They continued to rise in the 1950s because:
▶ employers, including government, tried to attract the workers they needed away from other employers;
▶ unions used the opportunity to get higher wages;
▶ employers, including government, paid up.
Rising imports was one result of higher family incomes. There was a rise in the volume of **raw materials** to make the goods, and of **manufactured goods** brought in to meet home demand. **Balance of Payments'** deficits then became a permanent problem as the nation bought more from abroad than it earned by exports.
These twin problems, inflation and payments' deficits, were attacked in the 1950s by:
▶ **credit squeezes**, with higher interest rates, which made it more expensive to borrow money – and so cut down on the demand for goods at home;
▶ **HP regulations** which were changed to force people to repay their debt in a shorter time;
▶ **higher purchase taxes**, which increased prices;
▶ **government exhortation** to workers.

53.4 The Macmillan Boom – or 'Never had it so good' Period

Macmillan replaced Eden after the Suez disaster. He had to:
▶ **re-unite the Conservative Party**, which was divided into pro-Suez 'hardliners' and anti-Suez 'softies';
▶ win **electoral popularity** after Suez;
▶ defeat the new Labour leader **Gaitskell**, who was popular with the middle classes.
He allowed his Chancellor, Thorneycroft, to resign when he wanted a balanced budget in 1957, asking for further cuts or tax increases. Heathcott Amory became Chancellor and went on to: ▶ lower the rates of interest;

▶ ease the HP regulations;
▶ have a budget deficit, so that government spending could go up without a tax increase to pay for it.
This created the economic boom of the years 1958–60 and pulled more women into work, thus increasing the 'affluence' of many families. It also pulled in more immigrants (above).

THE 1959 ELECTION

For the first time in this century a Party won a third consecutive election. The result was:
▶ Conservatives 365 seats;
▶ Labour 258 seats; ▶ Liberal 6 seats.

THE PROBLEMS OF TORY FREEDOM, 1960–63

Balance of Payment crises continued, and **inflation** made British goods more expensive, so that:
▶ Britain imported more foreign manufactured goods;
▶ British exporters found it increasingly difficult.
Trade Unions claimed that 'Freedom' gave them the right to demand ever higher wages, and there was **slow growth** of the nation's annual output. Foreign competitors produced at a higher rate, so that their people grew more wealthy more quickly. This was because:
▶ **investment** in European industry had been better-planned and was larger than British investment. Workers produced goods more cheaply and for higher wages;
▶ European governments had not developed the same welfare system as Britain. Their equivalent system was paid for by payments made by employees and employers who:
● were forced to think up labour-saving methods so that they paid less into the welfare fund;
● kept more of their money at the end of the week because income tax was much lower.

53.5 The End of 'Freedom' and the Start of 'Planning', 1961

Macmillan feared national bankruptcy and less valuable money. In 1961 he made three major changes in policy:
▶ he decided to apply for membership of the EEC (unit 54);
▶ he set up the **National Economic Development Council** (NEDC or 'Neddy') where government Ministers, representatives of employers and of unions met to work out plans for the future of the economy;
▶ he set up the **National Incomes Commission** (NIC or 'Nicky') to regulate the pattern of wage increases.
These steps had mixed fortunes:
▶ Britain was not allowed into the EEC (unit 54);
▶ 'Neddy' produced valuable discussion papers, but little real change took place before the 1964 election;

Fig. 53.5 Tory Freedom had collapsed by 1961 and Selwyn Lloyd, the Chancellor of the Exchequer (begging a lift) and Prime Minister Macmillan had started to create a planned economy. The Labour leader Harold Wilson (on the motor cycle) claimed that this was Labour's policy and that it ought to be operated by a Labour Government.

▶ 'Nicky' was ignored by the new Chancellor Selwyn Lloyd who, in July 1961, imposed a credit squeeze, and a wages pause in which:

● no wage increases were allowed to government employees;

● private industry was advised to follow this example.

But the government failed to make this wages freeze stick – it had to give in to the electricians in the government-controlled Central Electricity Board, who threatened to strike if they did not get their pay increase.

THE END OF THE MACMILLAN ERA, 1962–63

▶ Unemployment rose after cuts in spending by government and consumers (after the wage freeze and credit squeeze).

▶ **By-elections** were lost in 1962–63 as people turned to the Liberals or to Labour.

▶ **Scandals** involving spies, such as Vassal, and ministerial involvement in the Profumo case led to criticism.

▶ Macmillan retired in the summer of 1963.

THE MAUDLING 'BOOM', 1963–64

Maudling, Chancellor in the government led by Sir Alex Douglas Home, tried to restore popularity by 'buying our way to prosperity'. His policy was to:

▶ lower the interest rates;

▶ cut taxes;

▶ hope that this would encourage industrialists to invest in new machinery.

He was **successful** in making the government more popular, as the 1964 election showed, but he **failed** to get industry moving. Most of the increased income (from lower taxes) went on foreign goods. This led to a Balance of Payments' problems in 1964.

THE 1964 ELECTION

Labour was led by Harold Wilson after Gaitskell's death in 1963. Wilson, an economist, promised that Labour could get the country back on its feet. People believed him.

The result was:

▶ Labour won 317 seats;

▶ the Conservatives won 304 seats;

▶ the Liberals won 9 seats.

Unit 53 Summary

▶ Reasons for, and effects of, economic recovery.
▶ More women at work and increased immigration.
▶ The location of industry debate.
▶ Inflation and deficits on the balance of payments.
▶ 'Never had it so good'.
▶ Economic decline and the need for economic planning.

---

54 FOREIGN AND IMPERIAL AFFAIRS, 1945–88

54.1 The Cold War

Europe was divided by agreements at wartime Conferences, and **Eastern Europe** was ruled by Russian-controlled governments. **Russia** remained suspicious of the West because of:

▶ **intervention** by Western Powers in 1918–19 (unit 45);

▶ **appeasement** of Hitler;

▶ **atomic power** developed by Britain and the USA, but not shared with their wartime ally.

The Western Powers feared Russia because of:

▶ the repeated hopes for **'world revolution'**;

▶ Russia's control of **Eastern Europe**;

▶ the size of Russia's **armed forces**;

▶ Stalin's brutal treatment of **dissidents**;

▶ **Russian opposition** to attempts to retore Europe.

'The iron curtain' was Churchill's description (March 1946) of:

▶ **Russia's advance** into previously independent States;

▶ **her unwillingness** to allow access to or from the West;

▶ **Europe's** need for US help for defence.

THE COLD WAR IN ACTION – GREECE

Greece was part of Britain's 'sphere of influence'. **Since 1944**, when Greece had been liberated, **Greek communist forces**, anxious to set up a Russian-controlled government, had clashed with other **Greek forces** anxious to maintain Greek independence. These were helped by British troops.

Bevin feared that if Greece fell to the Communists, **Turkey** would go next and Russia would threaten **British interests** in the Mediterranean.

Britain's **economic difficulties** (unit 52) made it difficult

Fig. 54.1 *The Daily Mail's* cartoonist's view of Churchill's *Iron Curtain* speech. You should know (i) when and where it was made, (ii) who was the *Joe* referred to; (iii) why the *curtain* was brought into place.

to hold on to Greece, and in **March 1947** Britain announced her decision to evacuate. **Truman**, President of the USA, then issued what became known as the **Truman Doctrine**, by which the USA was committed to:

▶ helping the **Greeks and Turks** by giving military aid;

▶ **containing Russia** to its present areas of influence;
▶ aiding any **'free peoples'** threatened by the Russians.
This speech and US intervention in Greece heightened the tension between East and West.

BERLIN

Germany was divided into four Allied zones. As an indication that Germany was still regarded as a potential enemy, there was the **Treaty of Dunkirk** in March 1947, in which Britain and France agreed that they would help each other in the event of either of them being attacked by Germany.

Berlin, the capital of pre-war Germany, but in 1945 deep in the Russian zone, was also divided into four zones. The **Western Allies** were allowed to use roads, canals, railways and air space through the eastern (Russian) zone of Germany.

The **Western Allies** decided to help the Germans to rebuild their country by:
▶ allowing them free elections;
▶ creating a new currency;
▶ undertaking other economic reforms.
Stalin saw this as a threat to Russia and the eastern zone.

Czechoslovakia was brought firmly under Russian control in 1948; Prime Minister, Benes, 'committed suicide'.

The Berlin Blockade began when the Russians closed the road, rail and canal links from the west to Berlin. **The Berlin Airlift** was organized to maintain supplies to the people in the three western-controlled zones in Berlin. In this:
▶ British and US 'planes carried supplies to the airfields in the western-controlled zones;
▶ Berlin was more than amply supplied;
▶ Russia's attempt to drive the Allies from Berlin failed.
Stalin called off the Blockade in May 1949.

THE NORTH ATLANTIC TREATY ORGANIZATION (NATO), APRIL 1949

Stalin had rejected a US offer of Marshall Aid. The 'rape' of **Czechoslovakia** showed Russian determination to expand if she could, and **the Berlin Blockade** showed how she might achieve this. **European countries** were too weak to stand up to Russia, so **Bevin** helped to create NATO in which:
▶ Britain, the USA and (initially) 10 other countries pooled their military forces in Europe;
▶ the USA became committed to the defence of Western Europe.

THE COLD WAR HOTS UP – KOREA, 1950–53

China had come under Communist rule in October 1949. **Russia**, having failed to expand further in western Europe, turned her attention to the East, where she helped to organize:
▶ anti-British rebellions in Malaya and Singapore;
▶ anti-Dutch risings in Indonesia;
▶ the first anti-French risings in Indo-China.
Korea, once part of the Japanese Empire (unit 50), had been divided between Russia and the USA in 1945, the border between their zones being the 38th parallel of latitude.

Russia rejected proposals for elections in a unified Korea, and **the North Koreans** invaded the south in June 1950.

The Security Council of the United Nations condemned the invasion; Russia was boycotting the Council because of its refusal to admit Communist China as a member. This gave the USA the chance to push through a resolution calling on the UNO to fight against the invasion.

The UN forces in Korea were largely from the USA, although the British and Commonwealth troops made a large contribution to the war in which:
▶ **North Korean** troops had occupied most of the south by September 1950;

▶ **MacArthur**, the US commander of the UN forces, organized a seaborne landing at Inchon, drove the North Koreans back over the border and invaded the North. China then came into the war;
▶ **Chinese armies** drove the UN forces back to the south and led MacArthur to suggest the dropping of an atomic bomb on China: **Attlee** flew to persuade Truman not to follow this advice and MacArthur was sacked in April 1951.
▶ **Peace negotiations** had started early in 1951 but did not really get under way until July 1953 when both sides signed an armistice at Panmunjon, although they have not (yet) signed a peace treaty.

▓ 54.2 British Foreign Policy 1945–59

BRITAIN AND THE EMPIRE, 1945–50

▶ **India** gained its long-promised independence in August 1947 after negotiations between:
● Mountbatten, the last Viceroy;
● Nehru, the leader of the Hindus, who wanted a united India;
● Jinnah, the Muslim leader, who insisted on a separate Muslim state–Pakistan.
▶ **Burma** became independent and left the Commonwealth (January 1948).
▶ **Ceylon** became independent (February 1948) inside the Commonwealth.
▶ **Eire** left the Commonwealth (1949).
▶ **Palestine**, a British Mandate since 1918 (unit 44) was a country in which British forces fought against:
● **Jewish forces**, anxious to get that homeland promised by the Balfour Declaration, 1917;
● **Arab forces** opposed to a Jewish state.
There was an influx of Jewish settlers escaping from the ruins of Europe after 1945; the British tried to halt this immigration and eventually **Bevin** handed the problem to the UNO.
This withdrawal was to lead to a series of Jewish–Arab wars, and was another sign of Britain's economic weakness.

IRAN, 1951

The Anglo-Iranian Oil Company controlled Iran's oil.
Saudi Arabia received 50 per cent of the profits of its American-controlled oil industry, and **Iran** asked for similar treatment, but was refused.
Mossadeq, Prime Minister, nationalized the Company in April 1951. **Morrison**, Labour's Foreign Secretary, sent warships to the Gulf, but **the government** decided that the Company had acted foolishly and that there was no case against nationalization.
In **October 1951**: all British workers were evacuated from Iran. **Public opinion** condemned Labour's weakness.

EGYPT AND THE SUEZ PROBLEM, 1951–56

A treaty (1936) allowed British troops to be stationed in bases along the Suez Canal. In **1951** Egypt cancelled that treaty; British civilians withdrew but the forces remained, attacked by Egyptian terrorists.
In **1952** King Farouk was overthrown by an army revolt led by General Neguib, but controlled by Colonel Nasser.
Nasser negotiated with **Eden**, and in 1954 British troops left the Canal bases.
The Aswan High Dam was Nasser's scheme for the control of the water of the Nile, to produce electricity and irrigation. The USA and Britain promised aid.
Nasser wanted to be the leader of a 'greater Arab' nation. He supported the anti-French movement in Algeria and, being an anti-Israeli, bought arms from Russian-dominated Czechoslovakia.
Dulles, US Secretary of State, withdrew the US offer of help for the Dam, and forced Britain to withdraw also. Nasser nationalized the Canal Company, claiming that income from the Canal would finance the Dam.

Eden, accused of being a weak Prime Minister, wanted to teach Nasser a lesson. He and Foreign Minister Lloyd:
▶ negotiated with the French and the Israelis and planned a tri-partite attack on Egypt;
▶ ignored anti-war opinion in the Commonwealth;
▶ did not consult Eisenhower, who was standing for re-election in the autumn of 1956.

After Israel had attacked Egypt, Eden:
▶ sent British forces from Cyprus and Malta to land along the Canal and at Suez and Port Said (31st October 1956);
▶ claimed that he merely wanted to separate the warring forces;
▶ was condemned by the USA and Russia;
▶ was forced to halt the fighting (7th November) and to withdraw to make way for a UN peacekeeping force.

The Canal was blocked – which led to increased prices of British imports coming the long way around the Cape.

After a period of illness Eden resigned (January 1957).

CYPRUS

Cyprus became important as a base after the Suez disaster. Britain said Cyprus would 'never' gain independence, but Greek rebels, influenced by Archbishop Makarios, fought a guerrilla and terrorist war against the British.

Makarios was sent into exile, condemned by British opinion as 'a murdering priest'. The fighting continued; Britain had to negotiate with Makarios and with the Turkish minority in Cyprus, which gained its independence (1959) inside the Commonwealth.

Fighting between Turks and Greeks led to the intervention of the UN and to the division of the island (1964).

The mainland Greek government smuggled troops into Cyprus. The mainland Turkish government threatened to invade the island to defend the Turkish Cypriots. This, and the demands of the USA, forced a Greek withdrawal.

In 1971 Greek extremists declared war on Makarios; Greek forces invaded the island and Turkish troops were sent to defend their portion of the island.

In 1983 the Turkish Cypriots made a UDI, announcing that their northern portion of the island was an Independent Republic. In 1985, with the aid of the UNO, talks were held to try to find a solution to Cyprus's problems. It is too soon to say whether these will succeed.

54.3 Britain, a Nuclear Power

Economic weakness had led to British withdrawal from the Empire and Greece and the failure of the Suez venture.

Successive governments seemed determined that Britain should keep its own nuclear power:
▶ Churchill's government planned to use **Blue Streak** bombers, then decided to develop the Blue Streak **rocket missiles**;
▶ Macmillan's government scrapped this and decided to buy the US **Skybolt** missiles (1960);
▶ The US government scrapped **Skybolt** (1962);
▶ Kennedy and Macmillan negotiated the Nassau Agreement (1962), the US agreeing to supply **Polaris** missiles for use in British-built nuclear submarines;
▶ Wilson's government maintained **Polaris**;
▶ the Thatcher government is planning to develop **Trident** as a more modern form of nuclear deterrent.

Being a nuclear power gives Britain 'a place at the top table', able to help to negotiate a Test-Ban Treaty with the USA and Russia (1963).

Russia and the USA ignored Britain in:
▶ the **Cuba crisis**, when Russian determination to build rocket-launching sites in Cuba almost led to a nuclear war;
▶ the Strategic Arms Limitation Talks, usually called the **SALT talks**, which continued through the 1970s as the two Powers try to reach agreement on arms limitation.

People question whether Britain should spend such a high proportion of her output in this way, and the morality of nuclear weapons is challenged by campaigners in anti-nuclear movements such as the Campaign for Nuclear Disarmament (CND).

Britain, and other NATO countries, have agreed to allow the USA to site Cruise and Pershing missiles in Europe. CND has supported the anti-Cruise campaigns, organized mainly by women, such as the 'Greenham women', so-called after the camp which some of them have built and lived in outside the US Air Force base at Greenham Common, Berkshire.

54.4 The Continued Withdrawal from Empire, 1951–84

Churchill declared that he 'had not become the King-Emperor's Prime Minister to preside over the liquidation of the Empire'. Nevertheless, **independence** was granted to:
▶ **Ghana**, formerly the Gold Coast (1957);
▶ **Malaya** (1957);
▶ the **Sudan** (1956);
▶ **Cyprus** (1958);
▶ **Nigeria** (1960);
▶ **Tanganyika and Zanzibar** (1960);
▶ **Sierra Leone** (1961);
▶ **Kenya** (1963), after the Mau Mau rising.

The Central African Federation of South Rhodesia, Zambia and Nyasaland had been united to form a new country in which white settlers might continue to dominate. It broke up in 1963 and:
▶ Zambia and Nyasaland (later Malawi) became independent.
▶ Southern Rhodesia remained a colony (see below).

Negotiations were held to try to solve the problems of:
▶ Hong Kong: Britain and China reached agreement (1984) on the future of the island. It will return to Chinese control, but will be allowed to retain some of the freedoms which its people have enjoyed as a British colony.
▶ Gibraltar: Britain and Spain are in dispute as to the future of the 'Rock'. To try to force Britain's hand, Spain closed the frontier between Spain and Gibraltar. This only increased the friction between the two countries and harmed the economies of Spain and the colony. Nevertheless, there are signs that the two countries may be willing to start negotiations to try to find a solution to the problem of Gibraltar.
▶ The Falkland Islands: Argentina has long claimed these islands, although the British settlers on the islands are unwilling to accept rule by Argentina. In April 1982 Argentinian forces invaded the islands. Britain sent forces to drive them out. The Falklands War ended with British forces in control of the islands, but with Argentina still claiming them. Britain has to keep forces on the islands, at great cost, as a deterrent to Argentina. It may be that negotiations will resume about the future of these islands and their inhabitants.

'THE WIND OF CHANGE'

Macmillan, visiting Africa in 1960, told the South African parliament of 'the wind of change' which had swept through the continent, and warned the whites that they might not be able to maintain their power under the system of **apartheid**, or separate development, which allowed whites to rule South Africa.

Black movements grew up and were crushed by police action. Individuals were arrested without trial, severe sentences were passed on those brought to trial and found guilty, and leaders, such as Mandella, were banished.

Unrest continued and led to the **Sharpeville** affair (1960), where 69 black demonstrators were shot by police. The Prime Ministers' Conference condemned South Africa (1961), which left the Commonwealth.

Campaigns against South African policies have continued – some nations banning trade with South Africa, others accepting a UN motion not to supply her with arms, while individuals (such as Peter Hain) and groups (such as the Anti-Apartheid Movement in Britain and elsewhere) have led demonstrations against South African sportsmen visiting overseas.

RHODESIA – FROM COLONY TO ILLEGAL INDEPENDENCE

Rhodesia was dominated by white power – political and economic. The whites feared the growth of black political movements, their fears being confirmed by the savagery which followed Congolese independence and by the corruption and economic breakdown which took place in Ghana and Uganda.

Ian Smith, leader of the Rhodesia Front, declared Unilateral Independence in 1964 when Labour came to power in Britain. Talks to resolve the affair failed; sanctions only worked slowly, and by 1977 Rhodesia was still a powerful country.

Portuguese colonies in Angola and Mozambique became independent, exposing Rhodesia to more attacks, and in 1979 Smith held talks with black leaders and announced free elections, which led to a Parliament dominated by blacks, who chose Bishop Muzorewa as their first black Prime Minister.

Nationalist rebels refused to accept this Smith-imposed settlement. The Civil War continued. Lord Carrington, Foreign Minister in the Thatcher government, called a conference of all Rhodesia's leaders. This led to another election and to Robert Mugabe (a former guerrilla leader) becoming Prime Minister in 1980.

54.5 Britain and the European Economic Community

The European Coal and Steel Community was set up in 1950. The governments of Germany, Italy, France, Belgium, Holland and Luxembourg agreed that the coal, iron and steel industries of their six countries should, in future, be controlled by an authority which was outside the direct control of governments. Britain refused to join a Community in which a supranational body controlled major industries of member countries.

In 1956 **the Six** held talks which, in 1957, led to the formation of the European Economic Community (EEC) in which the member countries:

▶ **abolished tariff barriers** inside the Community;
▶ shared a **common external tariff** against imports;
▶ devised an **Agricultural Policy** to safeguard the incomes of farmers;
▶ aimed at **political unity**.

Britain refused to continue as a member of the team discussing such a Community because:

▶ she enjoyed free trade with the **Commonwealth**. This would have to be given up on entry into the Community;
▶ she had her own **agricultural policy** – an improvement on the one devised for the Community;
▶ she feared the loss of **political sovereignty** as the institutions of the Community grew powerful;
▶ she thought that her **special relationship** with the USA would be weakened if she entered the EEC.

Britain proposed a **Free Trade Area**, in which the Six would be one member, with no tariff barriers inside the Area, each country being free to maintain its own external tariffs and trade relations.

The Community rejected this, and Britain formed a smaller **European Free Trade Area** of six other countries, whose populations and industries were too small for it to rival the Six. The continued growth of the economies of the Six and the continued decline of Britain forced her to reconsider the question of entering the Community.

Macmillan (1961) started negotiations with the EEC, Heath being Britain's chief negotiator. At the same time, Macmillan held talks with the Americans about Britain's purchase of nuclear weapons from the USA. Kennedy and Macmillan reached agreement during talks which took place in 1962 in the Bahamas. They signed the **Nassau Agreement**, by which the USA agreed to supply **Polaris** nuclear missiles for use in a fleet of nuclear submarines which Britain would build.

The Nassau Agreement convinced President de Gaulle of France that Britain was not yet sufficiently 'European-minded' and he vetoed the British application in 1963. Wilson repeated the application, only for de Gaulle to repeat his refusal (1966).

De Gaulle resigned in 1969 and Heath began fresh negotiations. Britain finally joined the Community in 1971.

Opposition to British membership continued, even after Wilson held a referendum which showed popular support for membership.

The benefits of membership have been less apparent than the rise in prices, increase in imports from Europe and increase in the payments of large sums into the Community's budget – mainly to maintain an inefficient system of farming. It is, however, foolish to blame Britain's present economic difficulties on British membership of the EEC. These are rather the result of long-standing failure to improve British industry and, more recently, of the deep world recession.

European elections were held in 1979 and it is likely that the Euro-MPs will demand more power over the ministers and institutions of the EEC, which may well lead to a further decline in the power of the British Parliament, which already is obliged to accept, without debate, whole batches of European regulations.

The Thatcher governments succeeded in negotiating a lowering of the British contribution to the Community Budget and in forcing the Community to reconsider the Common Agricultural Policy. In 1984–5, farmers were forced to accept lower quotas in the hope that this would, in time, lead to a fall in the size of, and cost of, the surpluses of milk, meat, wine and fruit.

Unit 54 Summary

▶ The Cold War: the Berlin crisis, 1948; formation of NATO.
▶ The Korean War, 1950–53.
▶ The problems of Iran and Palestine.
▶ The Suez war, 1956.
▶ The problem of Cyprus.
▶ Britain's armaments' policies.
▶ 'The wind of change' and continued withdrawal from Empire.
▶ The Falklands War, 1982.
▶ The problem of Rhodesia–Zimbabwe.
▶ Britain and the EEC.

55 DOMESTIC AFFAIRS, 1964–79

 55.1 The Wilson Government, 1964–66

THE ECONOMY

The government had to deal with the problems of inflation and a Balance of Payments' deficit, made worse by:
▶ the £800 million deficit left by 'Maudling's boom';
▶ foreign fear that Labour would devalue the pound – as in 1931 and 1949 (unit 52);
▶ foreign withdrawal of money out of London, and the driving down of the value of the pound.

The International Monetary Fund (IMF) agreed to lend £1000 million while the government put things right.

The aims of the government were:
▶ to bring down the rate of **inflation**;
▶ to increase **exports**;
▶ to pay off Britain's **overseas debts**;
▶ to build up **the economy**, so that Britain could compete with foreign countries and become wealthier.

Planning – a path to the cures

The Department of Economic Affairs was created as a new Ministry to deal with the economy. **George Brown**, Labour Deputy Leader, in charge of this powerful Ministry, persuaded employers and trade unions to sign:
▶ acceptance of the **National Plan** for industrial modernization and expansion;
▶ the **Declaration of Intent**, by which they agreed to hold down wages and prices.

Regulation – another path to the cures

▶ A **Prices and Incomes Board** was set up; wage and price increases would have to be approved;
▶ the **Industrial Reorganization Commission** was set up to help firms to merge to form large bodies. It helped Leyland to merge with the British Motor Corporation to form a larger organization, better able to compete with foreign firms – it was hoped.

Minor reforms, 1964–66

▶ **prescription charges** were abolished;
▶ **rate rebates** were introduced for the less well-off;
▶ Crosland, the Minister of Education, sent out a Circular asking LEAs to submit plans for the reorganization of secondary schools on comprehensive lines (unit 42).
▶ **The Open University**, originally known as 'The University of the Air' was first described in a White Paper of February 1966. This University, now centred on Milton Keynes, provides degree courses for adults who wish to study in their free time. In addition to course notes and study aids, the University uses radio and television to teach its courses. Many hundreds of thousands of students have enrolled on its courses and the concept of 'The University of the Air' has been copied by other countries. This may be seen as the most long-lasting of the reforms of this government.

THE 1966 ELECTION

The government gave the impression of tackling the nation's economic problems – and gained in popularity.
The Conservatives:
▶ got the blame for the £800 million deficit;
▶ found it hard to argue against Labour's policies;
▶ had a new leader, Edward Heath, still relatively unknown to the public.

Living standards rose as workers gained higher wage increases, before the Incomes Board got to work. **Inflation** and the falling value of the pound abroad were, generally, ignored by most people.

Wilson called an election early in 1966. The result was:
▶ Labour 363 seats;
▶ Conservatives 253 seats;
▶ Liberals 12 seats.

55.2 The Wilson Government, 1966–70

The economic situation became worse because many workers:
▶ forced employers to give them wage increases – in spite of the decisions of the Incomes Board;
▶ went on strike, particularly in the car industry, in spite of their leaders' signatures on the **Declaration of Intent**;
▶ kept ahead of inflation – but ensured that it became even worse.

James Callaghan, Chancellor of the Exchequer, introduced:
▶ **a prices and incomes freeze**, allowing no increases at all;
▶ a Budget, 1966, which included:
● **Selective Employment Tax**, which forced employers to pay a tax for each worker employed. It was hoped to force employers to modernize, so as to reduce their SET payments;
● **a credit squeeze**, including cuts in government spending, higher interest rates and tougher HP regulations. This made it harder to sell goods in Britain and forced firms to export.

Strikes – and particularly a long strike by seamen – made things worse:
▶ **exports** fell because of the seamen's strike;
▶ **imports** arrived in foreign ships;
▶ the **balance of payments** position worsened.

1967, a year of disaster

▶ the **National Plan** was abandoned;
▶ the **IMF** was asked for an even bigger loan;
▶ cuts in **government spending** included cuts in spending on housing, schools and other public works;
▶ the **credit squeeze** was made tougher;
▶ **De Gaulle** pointed out that Britain was too weak a country to be allowed into the EEC (unit 54).

Getting it right, 1967–69

Devaluation (1967) brought the pound down to 2.40 US dollars, which helped exporters but increased prices of imports. **Roy Jenkins**, the new Chancellor, announced in the autumn (1968) an even more severe credit squeeze, and sharp increases in taxation.

On course again, 1970

Exports rose 1968–70, while imports were held steady. In 1970 Britain earned £800 million more than she spent on imports.

1970s problems

▶ **inflation**; prices were 18 per cent above 1964 level;
▶ **Jenkins** abandoned the wages freeze;
▶ **unions** won massive wage increases;
▶ this would push up the future rate of inflation.

Government unpopularity, 1970

Labour voters were angry at the 'Tory policies' used to fight inflation. **Many people** resented the wages freeze imposed by the government which allowed gas, electricity and other prices to rise, so reducing their living standards.

Barbara Castle, Minister of Employment, had brought in a White Paper, **In Place of Strife** (1969). This Paper:
▶ angered union leaders with its proposals to limit union power;
▶ was withdrawn in the face of union threats not to support Labour in the next election;
▶ lost Labour the support of many moderate voters who wanted action taken against militant unions.

PEOPLE AND PROBLEMS, 1968–70

Immigration became a major problem when Asians, holding British passports, were expelled from Kenya by a government in which Africans held a majority and which wanted to bring to an end Indian domination of Kenya's economic life. Labour had opposed the Immigration Act, 1962 (unit 53), but brought in a new Immigration Act, 1968, which was meant to forbid immigrants to settle unless they already had family connections in the country. It was amended to allow the free entry of Kenyan Asians. This angered Enoch Powell, who began to make even more controversial speeches about coloured immigration.

Ulster became a problem in 1968 when the **Civil Rights Movement** was founded. The **Protestant majority** refused its demands. For the outcome of this problem see unit 33.

Regional nationalism grew, because unemployment remained higher in Wales and Scotland than in England.
▶ **Plaid Cymru** saw its leader, Gwynfor Evans win a seat at a by-election in Carmarthen.
▶ The **Scottish National Party** (SNP) saw Winnie Ewing win a seat at Hamilton (1967).

Heath promised that the next Conservative government would give Scotland its own Assembly or Parliament.

THE 1970 ELECTION

Labour was unpopular with many of its own supporters (credit squeeze; wages freeze; cuts in spending; falling living standards 1967–69; Castle's White Paper). **Labour** was also unpopular with many moderates (the economic problems were worse than in 1964; the withdrawal of Castle's White Paper; devaluation).

Young voters had opposed Labour's 'Tory policies' and had turned to **direct action**, such as the Anti-Apartheid Movement and the Stop-the-Tour campaign against South African cricketers (1970).

Heath promised that he would bring down the rate of price increases, which many thought meant a reduction in prices. **Conservative policies** (credit squeezes, high interest rates and cuts in spending) would be best applied by a Conservative government and not by Labour.

The result of the Election:
▶ the Conservatives won 330 seats;
▶ Labour won 287 seats;
▶ the Liberals won 6 seats.

 ## 55.3 The Policies of the Heath Government, 1970–72

Government spending was cut by:
▶ ending the provision of free milk for children over seven years old;
▶ increased charges for medical and dental treatment;
▶ the abolition of aid to the Development Areas.

Tax cuts could be made because of this reduced spending. **Government hoped** that these cuts would lead to **increased consumer spending, more employment**, and more **investment** by industrialists and by companies, whose profit taxes had been reduced.

Government disappointment followed, because industrialists did not invest and consumers bought more foreign goods.

Fig. 55.3 A cartoon of 31st March 1972, showing (from left to right) Sir Alec Douglas Home, Lord Carrington, John Davies, Robert Carr and William Whitelaw trying to plug holes in the dyke marked *Tory Policies*. After only two years the policies of the Heath Government had been shown to be either unworkable or unacceptable to the majority of British voters.

THE GOVERNMENT OF THE U-TURNS, 1972–73

Upper Clyde Shipbuilders had been getting government aid since 1950. In 1970 this aid was cut. This led to:
▶ the firm's decision to close four yards;
▶ fears of rising unemployment on the Clyde;
▶ workers' occupations of the yards;
▶ delegations of workers meeting the Prime Minister and other Ministers (June 1971);
▶ a government decision to increase the aid from £6 million paid by Labour in 1970, to £40 million.

Prices continued to rise because:
▶ The Brazilian **coffee crop** was ruined by frost (1971);
▶ **the world's sugar crop** was damaged at the same time, so that there was both a rise in price and a shortage of sugar, which had to be 'rationed' by shopkeepers;
▶ **wheat prices** rose after the US decision to sell a large part of its crop to Russia.

Unemployment rose because of cuts in government spending started by Labour and continued by the Heath government. **Rolls-Royce** faced bankruptcy and closure because of its failure to meet a contract with Lockheed. Thousands of workers faced unemployment. The government stepped in and nationalized the firm, paids its debts to supplier firms and provided the money needed to produce the engine promised to Lockheed.

Development Areas were provided with more money than in 1970, and **government spending** was increased without increases in taxation. Barber 'printed' £4000 million to pay for new roads, houses and schools—and ensured that inflation roared away at even higher levels.

HEATH AND THE UNIONS

The Industrial Relations Act, 1972

Unions had to register with the Registrar of Friendly Societies, who had power to examine their rules and the ways they spent their income.

Many Unions refused to register, and lost certain tax concessions.

The Industrial Relations Court had power to forbid a union to call a strike without a 'cooling off' period to allow further discussions, and could insist on secret ballots of members before a strike was called.

Union leaders refused to appear before the court; six striking London dockers were sent to prison for refusing to obey the Court—but were released on government instruction.

Wages policies

Heath had promised the abolition of wage freezes and of government control of wage increases, and Labour's Prices and Incomes Board was abolished.

Unions took advantage of this freedom, 1970–71, to win large increases and to fuel inflation. A new Prices and Incomes Board was set up in 1972.

HEATH AND THE MINERS, 1972–74

The economy was in poor shape in 1972 owing to
► rising rates of **inflation** as a result of:
● Barber's budgets and £4000 million spending;
● unions' winning of **wages increases:**
► balance of payments problems, because of:
● rising world prices – coffee, sugar and oil (below);
● British **failure to export**;
● consumer **spending on imports**.

Heath's solution to this was a wages policy operated by his Prices and Incomes Board.

In January 1972 the government told the National Coal Board to refuse the miners' demand for a wage increase. The miners' strike led to a fuel shortage at generating stations. The government climbed down and the miners got their increase.

Oil prices rose sharply in 1973 which led to:
► increased petrol prices – up from 35p to 70p a gallon;
► increased industrial costs – and prices;
► increased imports' bill and a worsening of the Balance of Payments position.

In January 1974 the miners demanded another wage increase. Again the government told the NCB to refuse it, and the Prices and Incomes Board was asked to examine the claim.

The miners went on strike which led to:
► a cut in the output of electricity;
► closure of shops, offices and industry to save fuel, which led to the 'three-day week'.

55.4 The Election, February 1974

Heath had a large majority in the Commons, but he declared:
► the country ungovernable owing to the strike;
► the problem of inflation 'insoluble'.

He called for an election. During the campaign his Incomes Board declared in favour of the miners' pay award.

Wilson promised to get the country back to work.

The result was:
► Labour 301 seats;
► Conservatives 297 seats;
► Liberals 14 seats.

Heath tried to negotiate a coalition-type arrangement with the Liberals, but finally resigned and Wilson became Prime Minister. Since he did not have a majority in the Commons, he knew that he would have to call another election within a short time.

THE ELECTION, OCTOBER 1974

Wilson allowed a wages free-for-all and **unions** won wage awards of up to 30 per cent increases in pay. **Living standards** rose while people ignored the fact that prices would, at this rate, double every three years or so.

The miners went back to work and the three-day week ended.

The election result was:
► Labour 319 seats;
► Conservatives 277;
► Liberals 13;
► SNP and Plaid Cymru won some seats in Scotland and Wales.

GOVERNMENT AND INDUSTRY

The National Enterprise Board (NEB) was set up with money to spend on helping British industry. It saved:

► British Leyland, with £2800 million;
► Chrysler, with about £200 million;
► Ferranti, the electronics firm;
► the micro-processor industry.

Workers' cooperatives, set up by former employees in bankrupt firms, received help but failed to make good, and **inflation** grew at an alarming rate owing to:
► the Barber-led inflationary push;
► rising wages costs;
► rising world prices, above all of oil;
► the falling value of the pound.

The Balance of Payments' position worsened so that the government had to ask the IMF for a loan of £3000 million. **Cuts in government spending** were demanded by the IMF; **Denis Healey**, the Chancellor under Callaghan, cut:
► £1000 million off the plans for building houses and schools (1976);
► another £2500 million (1977).

Unemployment grew to 1 500 000 in 1978 and went on rising. **Wages policies** were tried, again, to help halt inflation:
► **1976** Wage increases were limited to £6 a week – which particularly helped the lower paid;
► **1977** Government and unions agreed to limit increases to four per cent;
► **1978** Unions refused the government request for a 10 per cent limit on increases. The government imposed this on their employees, but private industry paid higher wages so that, on average, wages increased by about 14 per cent.
► **Inflation** came down from 15 per cent (January 1978) to 8 per cent (January 1979) – a vast improvement on 1973 and 1976.
► **1979** Unions refused the government request for a 5 per cent limit in wage increases, which would have kept the rate of inflation below 8 per cent and so helped exporters to sell their goods.

THE WINTER OF 1979

The government tried to impose a 5 per cent limit on pay increases for its employees. **Private industry** paid more; Fords paid 15 per cent, lorry drivers got 20 per cent and drivers of petrol tankers got even more. **Public servants**, e.g. firemen, ambulance drivers and teachers, saw living standards fall, while those of other workers rose.

Strikes between January and March 1979 forced the government to pay higher wage awards (about 9 per cent) and to set up a Comparability Board, which had power to compare wages in government and private industry. The government promised to honour the decisions of the Board.

Inflation crept up again because of the higher wages, reaching 10 per cent in May 1979.

THE ELECTION, MARCH 1979

Referendums in Wales and Scotland showed that the majority of their people did not want separate Parliaments, and **the government** refused to bring in the promised Scottish Parliament Bill.

MPs in the **Scottish Nationalist Party** voted to bring the government down.

The **campaign** showed:
► **the Conservatives**, now led by Margaret Thatcher, promising a repeat of Heath's programme of 1970–72 with tax cuts, cuts in spending, no interference with wage bargaining, and less aid to industry and to the Development Areas;
► **Labour** suffering because its traditional supporters felt, as they had in 1970, that the government had failed to behave as they expected a Labour government to behave – with cuts in spending, wages freezes, falling living standards as wages failed to keep up with inflation and a rise in unemployment.

The result:
► the Conservatives won 339 seats;
► Labour won 268 seats; ► The Liberals won 11.

Unit 55 Summary

▶ Labour governments, 1964–6 and 1966–70.
▶ The problems of inflation and immigration.
▶ Conservative government, 1970–73 and changes in policies.

▶ The three-day week, 1973 and the miners' strike.
▶ Labour governments, 1973–9, under Wilson and Callaghan.
▶ Callaghan versus the unions; the winter of discontent, 1978–9.

56 THE THATCHER DECADE

56.1 Aims of the Three Governments

Margaret Thatcher led three governments after winning elections in 1979, 1983 and 1987. They all hoped:
▶ to bring down the rate of inflation;
▶ to reduce the role of government in the nation's economic life. This led to privatization (Unit 56.8): it also led to the end of government subsidies to loss-making industries (e.g. steel, coal and railways);
▶ to cut the level of income and company taxation: it was hoped that this would create the 'climate' for industrial expansion, a growth in exports and the creation of new jobs in expanding industries;
▶ to attack what the governments saw as 'the too great power of local councils': limits were fixed on councils' spending, on rate increases and on councils' activities (Unit 56.9);
▶ to weaken the power of the trade unions (Unit 56.5);
▶ to develop a renewed belief in the 'market forces' which, it was argued, had made Britain 'great' in the nineteenth century.

56.2 Economic Policies, 1979–83

Geoffrey Howe was Chancellor of the Exchequer in this first Thatcher government. He:
▶ cut income taxes in the 1979 budget;
▶ increased the level of VAT, to make up for the revenue lost by cuts in direct taxation;
▶ had to borrow more heavily from the money market: this led to higher interest rates and increased the value of the pound (Unit 56.3);
▶ cut planned government spending on roads, housing and welfare services, which led to further rises in unemployment;
▶ had to further increase government spending and borrowing because of the inflation caused by VAT increases and to pay the higher volume of unemployment benefit;
▶ allowed, and sometimes forced, nationalized industries to raise their prices so that some (e.g. British Gas) became even more profitable and gave the government the huge sums collected from customers; while others (e.g. the Electricity Boards and British Rail) became more self-financing, requiring less of a subsidy from the government.

56.3 The Effects of Policies, 1979–83

The government's aim to 'roll back socialism' and to undo what it saw as the 'mistakes of the past' was at the root of many of its policies during this period. It is not surprising that this often had painful effects.

The unduly high value of sterling led to unduly high prices for British exports. Firms were unable to sell their goods abroad and many were forced to shut down. Regions which had once been prosperous (e.g. the Midlands) suffered high unemployment (15-20 per cent); regions which had always had high rates of unemployment became even more depressed (the North-East, Merseyside and Scotland).

The total of unemployment rose to nearly 4 million. The government adopted a number of schemes (e.g. YTS) to take young people off the unemployment register and to provide some form of industrial training. Unemployed people obviously had less income than they had when they worked. This meant they bought less, which led to further rises in unemployment in some domestic industries.

56.4 The Balance of Payments 1979–84

In this period Britain was an oil-exporting country. The growth of the North Sea oil industry meant that Britain did not have to spend money on oil imports (which lowered our imports' bill by £10 billion a year), and earned money (about £7 billion) from oil exports.

With the rise in the value of the pound sterling, British export prices rose relative to those of other countries. So, while Germany increased her exports to the USA by 55 per cent and Japan increased hers by 45 per cent, Britain saw her exports to the USA fall by 7 per cent.

The rise in the value of the pound also led to lower prices for foreign imports into Britain. This led to a continual rise in imports of manufactured goods (e.g. cars) and so to more unemployment in British industry.

56.5 Governments and the Unions

The government believed that trade unions had gained too much power in post-war Britain. Heath, Wilson and Callaghan had each tried, but failed, to limit this power. After 1979 the government pushed through a number of Acts to curb union power, and the power of their leaders:
▶ Picketing by strikers was to be allowed, but workers were not allowed secondary picketing. This meant that striking miners could picket coal mines, but not, for example, coal-using power stations. Unions which allowed secondary picketing were liable to prosecution and, if guilty, to fines.
▶ Strikes were allowed, but only after unions had held

ballots of members. Unions which called strikes without ballots could be prosecuted and fined.

▶ Industrialists were allowed to prosecute unions to recoup losses suffered as a result of illegal strikes.

▶ Unions had to ballot their members to get their agreement on the levying of, and use of, the political levy.

The government was directly involved in conflict with some unions with workers in the nationalized industries. As these industries suffered the effects of cuts in government spending and attempts to limit wage increases, union leaders organized massive strikes. Some leaders, notably Scargill of the National Union of Mineworkers (NUM), claimed that they were as much interested in bringing down the government as in maintaining their members' living standards and jobs. The government defeated, in turn, unions in the steel, rail and coal industries. This provided the example for private employers to resist demands for wage increases, and for industrialists to push through plans for modernization, which led to falls in the numbers of workers employed. Subsequent Thatcher governments passed more anti-union legislation and, in January 1989, planned to abolish the closed shop. It was the policies of this first government which had ensured that, by 1989, union power had become a mere shadow of what it had been in the years before Thatcher came to power.

56.6 The Election, 1983

Opinion polls carried out in the winter of 1981–82 showed that the government was very unpopular because of:
▶ rising unemployment;
▶ high interest rates;
▶ the effects of attempts to cut government spending.

However, the Labour Opposition failed to take advantage of this unpopularity. It's most important mistakes were:
▶ the continuing internal 'war' with the left-wing calling for extremist policies which were unpopular with the majority of voters;
▶ its support for hard-line union leaders, such as Scargill, who were unpopular with the voters;
▶ its support for the costly and inefficient local councils.

In April 1982 the Falklands War began (Unit 54.4). This provoked an upsurge of 'patriotism', much to the surprise of liberal and left-wing commentators. This 'Falklands factor' helped to explain the Thatcher victory in the 1983 election. The election saw the emergence of a new political force, the Alliance between the Liberals (led by David Steel) and the Social Democratic Party (SDP). The SDP had been formed in 1981 by a 'gang of four' former Labour Ministers: David Owen (who came to lead the new party in 1984), Shirley Williams, William Rodgers and Roy Jenkins. The SDP recruited some 40–50 000 members: some from the right-wing of the Labour Party, who were discontented with the extremism of their former Party; some from voters who had never belonged to any party in the past. It gained about 25 per cent of the total votes cast in the election: its candidates gained second place in over 100 seats, but failed to gain many seats outright.

56.7 Lawson's Economic Policies, 1983–87

Nigel Lawson succeeded Howe as Chancellor in 1983, and pursued many of Howe's policies (Unit 56.2). He was more fortunate than Howe in some ways (below) and, with the assistance of other countries' Finance Ministers, he was able to bring about a lowering of interest rates.

North Sea oil was now a major factor in the economic structure of Britain. As well as the savings on imports and the addition to exports (Unit 56.4), taxes on the oil industry produced about £10 billion a year in government revenue. This enabled the Chancellor to lower other forms of taxation or to use the oil taxes to pay for unemployment benefit which, otherwise, would have demanded higher income tax (see Unit 56.10).

Lawson was also helped by the privatization programme (Unit 56.8). The proceeds from the sales of 'the family silver' also allowed either tax reductions or spending which, without privatization, would have led to higher taxes.

Lawson hoped to cut government spending; however, partly because of inflation, and partly because of on-going plans in welfare policies (and a growth in the number of pensioned people), spending increased. There were increases in the amount of spending on unemployment benefit, and increases in spending by the Defence Ministry and by government departments which employed workers who asked for, and got, wage increases to match the rate of inflation.

The value of the pound sterling on foreign exchanges was linked with the value of North Sea oil. As the price of oil fell (Unit 56.10), so did foreigners' notions of the value of the pound. A falling pound helped British exporters, but increased the prices of imports and so increased the rate of inflation. To try to bolster the value of the pound, the government was forced to have high interest rates which attracted foreign money to Britain. These rates had to be higher than those offered by other countries. Thus, while Britain had a rate of 14 per cent, the USA had a rate of 12 per cent and Germany of 6 per cent. Lawson persuaded the Finance Ministers of the world's leading countries to implement lower interest rates to a commonly agreed level. This allowed him to lower British interest rates which led to:
▶ lower mortgage rates, so that housebuyers had more money to spend on other things (which helped to create jobs in some industries);
▶ more industrial investment, which was more attractive with lower interest charges;
▶ lower rates for bank loans and hire purchase agreements, which led to a massive increase in borrowing and spending (and so to more jobs), and increases in house prices.

56.8 Privatization

Thatcher and her supporters in government thought that public services tended to be inefficient, expensive, and run more in the interests of the workers than of customers whose needs were ignored. Even many of those who didn't support the Conservatives had to agree on this. Private businesses (or enterprises) led to more competition, lower prices, more efficient use of resources, better quality of product or service, more customer satisfaction and greater independence for owners, workers and customers. In Unit 56.9 you will see how these views affected the government's attitude towards Local Government. Note that the government sold to private shareholders some of the industries which were nationalized by post-war Labour governments (Unit 52.1), and others which had been nationalized before and after that time.
▶ British Telecom took over the telecommunications system once run by the Post Office;
▶ Britoil took over the government interest in North Sea oil;
▶ Gas was de-nationalized, so too were British Leyland, British Airways, The British Airports Authority, British Steel, and the once-nationalized transport industry became the privately owned National Freight Corporation. The government's plans for 1989 included the sell-off of the water supply industry, plans to sell off British Coal and the electricity supply and generating industry, and tentative plans to sell off British Rail.
▶ Local authorities (Unit 56.9) were forced to allow private firms to tender for street cleansing, refuse collection, hospital food supplies and services, and local transport services, while they were also forced to sell-off council housing.
▶ Many people feared that Kenneth Baker's educational

reforms were intended to lead to a greater degree of privately-funded education while others thought that Kenneth Clarke's reforms of the NHS would lead to the growth of private health provision and a general decrease in government spending on health services.

Much of the above suggests that the government's privatization policy had philosophical roots and economic and social effects. It should be noted that, when a government sells an industry to private shareholders, it collects many billions of pounds: the idea behind plans for the sale of the water industry, for example, was to raise an expected £9 billion. Such additions to government revenue allow Chancellors to lower taxes in general and direct (income) tax in particular.

This policy had many critics, notably from the left-wing of the Labour Party. However, it should be noted that this Thatcherite policy has also been followed by socialist governments in France and Spain, and may have been seen at work even in Communist Russia and China. The more moderate 'new' Labour Party, led by Neil Kinnock, made it clear that, when elected to power, it would try to re-nationalize the now privately-owned industries. It seemed that Thatcherite privatization would be a future norm, just as increased government control was taken as the norm in the not too distant past.

56.9 Local Government and Finance

In 1985, local council spending was responsible for 27 per cent of all public spending by central and local governments. This made councils important factors in the economy. 77 per cent of councils' spending went on staff and materials (current expenditure); 15 per cent was spent on buildings and equipment (capital expenditure); 8 per cent of council spending went to pay off old debts. When Thatcher came to power in 1979, inflation had fallen from a high of 25 per cent to about 8 per cent. Industry, as well as central and local government, was forced to pay higher wages, and so, even, were the loss-making industries (e.g. coal, steel and shipbuilding) subsidized by the government. This tended to increase the rate of inflation, as can be seen in the 'model' below, in which 1980 is taken as a base year and a 10 per cent rate of pay increase is assumed.

	Money supply	Goods in shops	Price level
Assume that in 1980	100	100	100
Now increase public spending in 1981 e.g nurses pay	110 (say)	100 (nurses do not increase no. of goods in shops)	110
If we repeat the exercise for 1982	120	100	120

The 'model' shows that because of inflation, there are increased wages for government employees, and so higher taxation is necessary to pay for those wages. Because of increased taxes, higher prices are charged by business and industry, resulting in the loss of export markets, and unemployment in export-based industries.

Thatcher wanted to cut public spending so that taxes could be reduced, so that people had more freedom to spend their money as they wished, so that employers (with lower taxes) would give lower wage increases and charge lower prices, which would increase the chances of exporting and of employing more people.

As part of that policy she cut the subsidies to loss-making industries. One result of this was the closing of loss-making mines and shipyards – and a further rise in unemployment. She also tried to limit wage increases to public servants – nurses, teachers, etc – and demanded cuts in local government spending, or, at least, limits to the increases they may

have planned to make. This brought her into conflict with left-wing local councils who claimed that they were fulfilling their promises to their voters by providing improved services and more jobs. When the government passed laws to allow it to control levels of rate increases, some councils ignored the law (some councillors were brought to court, fined and banned from standing for future election). Others diverted money which was supposed to go on capital spending and used it for staff pay increases: this led to further deterioration in the conditions of roads, housing, schools, etc.

Acts were passed to compel local councils to allow council tenants to buy their homes on favourable terms. The government planned to eventually sell off almost all council housing, if not to unwilling individual tenants, then to Housing Action Companies which would become the new landlords instead of councils. The government claimed that the 'rolling back' of the role of councils led to increased efficiency (even in areas which were merely under threat of privatization), a lowering of costs in real terms, and greater public satisfaction. However, not everyone agreed with this verdict.

The government made its most serious attack on local authorities by replacing the rating system with the Poll Tax. The rating system had been long criticized because:

▶ it took no account of a householder's ability to pay; retired widows paid the same rates as did the neighbour who might have had three or more wage earners in the house;

▶ business people had no vote (except as householders) in local elections and felt that they had no control over the taxing authority.

The Poll Tax was meant to provide the local authorities with about 18 per cent of their income. Another 25 per cent would come from a Business Rate fixed by central government (thought to be friendly to business) and the rest would come from direct grants made by the central government. In theory everyone over the age of 18 would pay a Poll (or head) Tax.

▶ This increased the number of local taxpayers well above the numbers who paid rates. In theory everyone should have paid less.

▶ But local authorities used this new tax as an excuse to overspend in 1990 (when the tax came in).

▶ Some occupiers of small (and lowly-rated houses) had to pay more than they had paid in rates;

▶ owners of highly-rated homes paid much less;

▶ the Business Rate turned out to be very high.

This tax raised widespread criticism of the government; many Tory MPs protested; popular demonstrations led to clashes with the police; thousands of people refused to pay; some were fined, others sent to prison but most escaped arrest. This, it seemed, was 'a change too far'.

56.10 Cheap Oil?

The Organization of Petroleum Exporting Countries (OPEC) had pushed up oil prices in:

▶ 1973 during the Yom Kippur War (the fourth Arab–Israeli war). By 1974 oil prices were four times what they had been in 1972;

▶ 1979, after small increases between 1973 and 1978.

In 1979 oil (which had cost 2 dollars a barrel in 1972) sold at 35 dollars a barrel. The industrialized nations of the world found that:

▶ their imports bills rose: this led to cuts in other imports as they tried to solve their balance of payments problems. But one country's import is another's export. Cuts in exports led to rising unemployment, particularly in Britain because of its dependence on trade.

▶ their costs rose as industry, transport, commerce and private individuals had to pay more for fuel. For some people and firms this led to bankruptcy, since they could not sell their more expensive goods; for others it led to hardship, as they tried to cope with increased costs. The outcome, again, was increased unemployment throughout the industrialized world. Since the unemployed buy fewer goods than the employed, this led to even lower demand – and more unemployment.

However, the power of OPEC was shaken by:
▶ the discovery of non-OPEC oil: the North Sea provided Britain with her own source – and a valuable export. Other, non-Middle Eastern countries, e.g. Mexico, also began to develop their own oil industry;
▶ the expansion of production in some OPEC countries, anxious to take advantage of the increased prices;
▶ cuts in demand from the West, partly because of the depression, and partly because of successful fuel-saving campaigns and the increased use of substitute fuels. By 1983 oil prices had fallen to 27 dollars a barrel. Saudi Arabia, the leading producer, attempted to bring some order into the market as she tried to persuade other OPEC countries to cut their output to match the decreased demand. When some, such as Nigeria, refused, Saudi Arabia volunteered to cut her output from 8 million barrels a day to only 2 million, if others would agree to smaller cuts. This faced her with a major economic problem: she had started on an economic expansion policy based on oil prices of 35 dollars and with oil at only 27 dollars and with output severely cut, Saudi Arabia suffered a balance of payments problem. To try to compel other OPEC countries to fall into line, Saudi Arabia increased her output again, so that in 1985–86 oil prices slumped to 15 dollars (December 1985) and then to 10 dollars (March 1986). This affected Britain because of the importance of oil to her Balance of Payments situation (Unit 56.4). However, cheaper oil prices allowed reduced industrial costs, less consumer spending on fuel and increased spending on non-oil goods. This aided the economic recovery which was a feature of Lawson's Chancellorship. (Unit 56.12)

56.11 The Election, 1987

In 1987 Mrs Thatcher led her Party to an historic election victory. She was the first Prime Minister to win three successive elections, and her Party was the first to win such successive victories since 1919. Her success was due to:
▶ the economic recovery (Unit 56.12). People felt confident about the future and credited the government accordingly;
▶ approval of her success against the militant unions and hard-left local councils. Even the defeated Labour Party blamed 'loony-left London councils' for the defeat;
▶ the division of the anti-Thatcher vote between Labour and a vigorous Alliance (Unit 56.6); many people preferred Owen and/or Steel to Kinnock;
▶ the failure of Kinnock's 'soft-sell' and media-inspired election campaign to overcome people's doubts about important features of the Labour campaign. Would left-wing union leaders force a Labour government to backtrack on Thatcher policies and so allow a resurgence of union militancy and selfishness? Would Kinnock be able to push through a sensible defence policy in the light of left-wing demands for unilateral nuclear disarmament, e.g. as demanded by Ron Todd of the Transport Union? Would a future Labour government try to 'roll back Thatcherism' as regards local councils and allow increased, wasteful spending?

56.12 Lawson's Economic Successes, 1985–88

Lawson was fortunate in that the Reagan government in the USA adopted an expansionist policy, spending much more than it collected in taxes, so encouraging a boom which led to increased imports and a growth in world trade in general. The demand for British goods increased.

He was also fortunate in the drop in oil prices (Unit 56.10) and in having persuaded other governments to adopt lower interest rates' policies (Unit 56.7) which further stimulated world-wide economic activity as was shown by:
▶ annual increases in British export levels (4 per cent);
▶ falling unemployment (down from 4 million to 2 million);
▶ higher wage rates (up annually 9 per cent) which allowed more spending, increased demand for goods (and the creation of jobs) and electoral satisfaction;
▶ increased productivity by industry (up about 8 per cent annually) which allowed the payment of higher wages without equally high increases in the rate of inflation. Productivity also made British industry more competitive, and able to regain a greater share of world trade;
▶ the restoring of confidence in the Midlands and other regions which had suffered during the 1981–83 recession;
▶ continued increases in the volume of industrial and commercial development.

However, his policies also contained the seeds of future problems. In particular:
▶ there was an unhealthy growth in the volume of borrowing by private consumers. In 1988 they borrowed £40 billion from banks and other institutions as they went on a spending spree;
▶ there was an equally unhealthy fall in the rate of private saving as people preferred to spend;
▶ there was a greater growth in imports than in exports so that, in 1988, there was a balance of payments deficit of £14 billion. In proportion to national output, this was much greater than the USA's deficit which had already alarmed the world;
▶ economic expansion showed that there were shortages of skilled people in many fields: the failure to invest in industrial training became increasingly evident.

56.13 Economic Difficulties, 1988–92

In October 1987 the world's stock markets crashed, much as they had done in 1929 (Unit 48.4). Many people feared that the 1987 Crash would be followed by depression, as the 1929 Crash had been (Unit 48.4–5). To help avoid such consequences Lawson persuaded the Finance Ministers of the world's leading industrialized countries to:
▶ lower their interest rates, and so promote borrowing by industry and by private consumers;
▶ lower their tax rates, so allowing consumers and industrialists to have more money to spend;
▶ avoid import-cutting legislation which might have led to a trade war.

Lawson also adopted his own policies, which included the lowering of British interest rates. This reduced rates for, in particular, borrowers and housebuyers. One outcome was the rise of the already sharp rate of house price increases. Many people found that they were 'sitting on a fortune', and were encouraged to borrow against their houses and to spend the loans on various consumer goods. The boom was good for industry and employment. Another of Lawson's policies was to cut £4 billion off direct taxes in his 1988 Budget. This encouraged the increased spending already under way.

By the summer of 1988 it was clear that the economy was running ahead of itself: there was an alarming trade deficit, wage rates were rising too rapidly and inflation had begun to rise again from 4 to 5 per cent. In response, Lawson proposed to allow the exchange rate to control his policy. He wanted to link the value of the pound to the value of the German mark, a very strong currency. If the latter rose, so too, would the pound; if the mark fell, so would the pound. Mrs Thatcher, on the other hand, disliked this step which she saw as Lawson's method of pushing her into linking sterling with the European Monetary System which she refused to join. She demanded that interest rates should be used to control the economy. There took place the 'battle of

Downing Street' which Thatcher won: Lawson was forced against his better judgement, to increase interest rates which reached 13 per cent late in 1989. This led to some effects welcomed by government:

▶ there were cuts in house prices, or at least in the rates at which prices increased. People felt less confident about borrowing against their property;

▶ mortgage rates rose, so that housebuyers had less money to spend on other goods;

▶ there was a slight easing of the trade deficit, which still remained a major problem.

However, there were less beneficial effects:

▶ the pound rose in value so that, as in 1981–83, export prices became less competitive, while import prices fell, so encouraging that very rise in imports which Lawson wished to avoid;

▶ the government came under political pressure for having promoted spending in the Budget only to have to apply economic brakes later in the year.

The fall in consumer spending and in exports led to more unemployment and greater government unpopularity. This was reflected in Conservative losses in the EEC elections (June 1989). Thatcher's unpopularity increased following the EEC summit at Madrid (December 1989) where Lawson and Foreign Secretary Howe failed to persuade her to accept greater Community integration and British entry into the EMS.

There was great criticism of the privatisation of both electricity and, later, water; both were seen as more beneficial to shareholders than customers. Tory education policy was also criticized. Under successive ministers:

▶ City Technology Colleges were set up. Meant to be supported by industry and urban-based, the few that started were heavily funded by government and suburban-based;

▶ the Local Management of Schools forced Local Education Authorities to hand control of schools' budgets to heads and governors. This was meant to limit the power of local authorities and increase that of parents. Critics noted the low level of school funding, the increased class sizes, the deterioration of school buildings and the lack of money for spending on books and equipment;

▶ schools were encouraged to opt out of all control by local authorities and become grant maintained, getting their budgets directly from central government. Ministers hoped that this would further weaken the power of left-wing councils. In fact the few opted-out schools were in Tory-controlled areas;

▶ a National Curriculum in all subjects had to be followed by all state schools, a reform generally welcomed.

▶ a system of nation-wide school tests were announced. The tests for 7-year-olds were held in 1991; similar tests for all 9, 11, 14 and 16-year-olds will be held in future years. The results of these tests have to be published so that schools can be compared and, it is argued, parents will be led to demand improved performance in 'bad' schools.

There was more criticism of Health Service reforms:

▶ some doctors were given control of their budgets, free from Health Authority control. Many welcomed this freedom to buy hospital care for their patients. Others noted that such preferential treatment created a two-tier system;

▶ hospitals were encouraged to become Trusts, funded by government. Some welcomed this freedom: critics noted that the level of funding was too low and feared that this Trust system might be a step towards Health Service privatisation.

Too few people noted the problems for a Service which, because of the development of medicine and skills, could perform once unheard of operations (at great cost) and which had to cope with an ageing population.

56.14 Government Changes

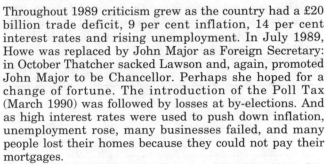

Throughout 1989 criticism grew as the country had a £20 billion trade deficit, 9 per cent inflation, 14 per cent interest rates and rising unemployment. In July 1989, Howe was replaced by John Major as Foreign Secretary: in October Thatcher sacked Lawson and, again, promoted John Major to be Chancellor. Perhaps she hoped for a change of fortune. The introduction of the Poll Tax (March 1990) was followed by losses at by-elections. And as high interest rates were used to push down inflation, unemployment rose, many businesses failed, and many people lost their homes because they could not pay their mortgages.

At the same time, Labour became more popular because:

▶ its policies were more generally acceptable: no re-nationalization; no promises of high public spending; no repeal of Tory anti-union laws;

▶ Kinnock won general support for his continued attack on MPs and members who belonged to Militant;

▶ a series of reforms of the Party's organization and structure weakened the power of trade unions and of left-wing constituency elements;

▶ a young, able and moderate group of front-bench MPs produced moderate policies and suggested that they would be well able to form a government if elected to power.

56.15 Thatcher Out

In August 1990 Iraq invaded Kuwait and Thatcher backed US President Bush's moves to get the UNO to condemn Iraq and to support the preparation of military forces to drive Iraq out. Maybe she hoped for a re-run of the Falklands factor which had helped her in 1983 (56.6). But many Tory MPs decided that they would not win a future election with her as Party leader. In November 1990 she lost the leadership contest and was replaced by John Major.

56.16 Major's Government, 1990–92

▶ He followed many of Thatcher's policies – on inflation, education and health;

▶ he had a gentler style than Thatcher and allowed some moderation of social policy;

▶ he abolished the Poll Tax – but not until 1993;

▶ as inflation fell he allowed a fall in interest rates, but unemployment, business failure and house repossessions still continued to rise;

▶ he took a pro-European line at the EEC summit at Maastricht in 1991 but strongly opposed plans for a federal Europe and a common currency;

▶ he developed Thatcher's policy on Northern Ireland (Unit 33) which led to the signing of the Anglo-Irish Agreement. Under this Agreement, British and Irish ministers and officials meet to discuss common problems, notably Northern Ireland.

56.17 The Election, 1992

Major might have called an election:

▶ in November 1990 when he became Prime Minister and might have won 'a sympathy vote';

▶ in February 1991 once the Gulf War had been won. He waited and suffered from the continuing recession which showed little sign of ending. Meanwhile the Labour Party continued to show its moderate (and vote-catching) face, although even in March 1992, it had not managed to gain a definite lead in opinion polls, in spite of the government's poor economic record.

In Scotland voters showed that they looked for some form of Scottish Home Rule: some wanted complete independence and a break up of the Union; others wanted the sort of regional government which Ulster had once enjoyed. Tories opposed to any such moves lost popularity.

Unit 56 Summary

▶Thatcher governments, inflation, unemployment, privatization, trade unions, poll tax.
▶The Liberal – SDP Alliance.
▶The effects of cheap oil, 1986.
▶Major's government.

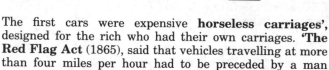

57 MODERN COMMUNICATIONS, 1900–88

57.1 Travel and Communications, 1900

▶ The development of the railways (unit 26) and the **steamship** had, in their time, revolutionized travel.
▶ **The postal system,** devised by Rowland Hill (unit 15) had benefited from the speed of rail and steamship travel.
▶ But most present methods of communication have developed only in this century.

HORSE-DRAWN TRAFFIC

Horse-drawn carriages carried people from place to place in the towns; the rich had their own, the middle class hired theirs from livery stables, the lower middle class caught hansom cabs, while the working class took horse-drawn omnibuses.

Horse-drawn wagons and carts delivered goods in towns, though errand boys were beginning to use bicycles.

THE BICYCLE

Until the 1880s this was a heavy, clumsy machine. The 'penny-farthing' (1879) was lighter than the older 'bone shaker', but still weighed about 50 lbs.
The 'safety' bicycle was produced in the 1880s with the diamond-shaped frame, lower saddle, wheels of equal size and pneumatic tyres developed by the Belfast chemist, J.B. Dunlop.
Mass production brought down the price, which meant the bicycle became a popular means of transport for **men** going to work, **women** going shopping and for **people** to get out into the country.

THE ELECTRIC TRAM

The first electrically drawn tram appeared in 1885. By 1901 many towns had abolished the horse-drawn tram in favour of the electric tram which:
▶ was cheaper – with fares of one penny and two pennies instead of the one shilling (12 pennies) charged by horse-drawn trams and buses;
▶ was cleaner, larger and carried more people;
▶ allowed people to live further away from their places of work, and led to the building of suburbs.

THE PETROL ENGINE

A German, **Otto,** perfected a four-stroke engine in 1878.
   A German, **Daimler,** used petrol in an engine, 1885.
   A German, **Benz,** used a petrol-engine to drive a tricycle, 1885
   Daimler drove the first motor-car, 1887.
   Lanchester built the first British car 1896, and by 1903 there were about 20 000 motor cars licensed to travel on Britain's roads.

57.2 The People's Car

The first cars were expensive **horseless carriages',** designed for the rich who had their own carriages. **'The Red Flag Act** (1865), said that vehicles travelling at more than four miles per hour had to be preceded by a man waving a red flag to warn people of the approaching danger. Its abolition (1896) is commemorated in the London–Brighton run, the first of which was made in 1896.
   William Morris, later Lord Nuffield, made cars available to less well-off people by:
▶ the **mass production** methods of the **assembly line,** already used in the bicycle industry and by Ford in the US. Morris introduced this method into the British car industry;
▶ buying most of his components from **specialist firms,** which also used mass production methods to produce cheaper plugs, tyres, brake systems and other parts of the car, which Morris **assembled** rather than made;
▶ **lowering the price,** so that by 1930, Morris, Herbert Austin and Ford were selling cars for only £100. This was possible because:
▶ **mass production** led to lower unit costs;
▶ **prices** of materials fell in the 1930s (unit 46);
▶ **wages** were held down in the depressed 30s.
▶ aiming to create a **motor-buying public** by ensuring that:
● they knew about the car through advertisements;
● could be ensured of servicing and repairs at easily available service stations.
   The number of cars licensed for use on British roads increased to two million in 1939 and, after 1950, went on increasing, so that today there are some 13 million licensed cars.
   The economic effects of this development are:
▶ **employment** in the car and component industries;
▶ **employment** in the steel-making and other related industries;
▶ **employment** in tertiary industries – servicing, selling, advertising and insuring cars;
▶ **employment** in road-building firms and in local and central government to supervise the development of the road systems.
   The social effects of the spread of car ownership include the following:
▶ **travel** has become commonplace. Unlike people in 1900, almost everyone today has been on journeys to the countryside, seaside and, in many cases, abroad;
▶ **holidays** have become different from what they were in 1900 where there was, for those who enjoyed holidays, only the seaside or the country house;
▶ **equality** has become more of a reality since the working man in his second-hand Ford can get to the same places as the wealthy man in his Rolls Royce;

The reasons for the spread of ownership are:
► the work of **Morris** and other manufacturers, who brought down prices;
► the rise in **living standards** (unit 49), because of lower prices in the 1930s and ever-increasing real wages since 1945;
► the development of **HP firms** which make it easier for people to afford to buy cars by monthly instalments.

57.3 Communications

RADIO

Marconi, an Italian living in Britain, first sent a message across the Channel to France in 1899. In **1901** he sent a message from Cornwall to the USA, and by 1912 many shipping lines had radios on their ships, which was a help at the time of:
► the sinking of the *Titanic*, whose appeals for help were picked up by other ships which raced to the rescue;
► the arrest of Dr Crippen (1910), a wanted murderer, who was recognized by the captain of the liner *Montrose*. A radio message to Scotland Yard led to Crippen's arrest when the liner docked in Newfoundland.

Wireless sets were mass produced by many firms in the 1920s. **The British Broadcasting Company** (1922) was formed by these firms, and got permission from the Post Office to send out programmes. The number of licensed sets increased from about 80 000 in 1923 to about 9 million in 1939, largely owing to:
► falling prices, a result of mass production;
► HP firms – as with the motor cars (above);
► rising real wages during the depressed 1930s (unit 49).

The British Broadcasting Corporation was formed in 1926 when Baldwin's government (unit 47) took the control of this new method of communication out of the hands of private firms.

The **transistor,** a product of the development of the computer industry, has replaced the bulkier valve, brought down the price of radios, and allowed a much wider ownership.

The effects of the radio have included:
► in the 1920s and 1930s particularly, an educating of public taste by a variety of programmes, music, documentary, drama and discursive, which brought music and ideas to people who would never otherwise have heard or thought about them;
► the spread of employment in a number of industries and occupations; producing, advertising and servicing radios;
► the development in the 1960s of the 'pop' record industry which, in turn, led to:
● pirate commercial stations in the 1960s;
● the development of local BBC radio;
● the emergence of legal commercial radio.

NEWSPAPERS

Until the 1880s, most papers were locally produced and sold. By this time many nationally owned firms were mass-producing and selling their goods – Cadbury's, Fry's, Lipton's and Beecham's were household names.

William Harmsworth, later Lord Northcliffe, revolutionized the newspaper industry by:
► persuading these and other firms to advertise in his newspaper, the *Daily Mail* (first produced in 1896);
► using the income from advertisments to:
● keep down the price of the paper (to one old halfpenny) so that almost everyone could afford to buy it;
● employ reporters and staff to produce a lively paper which would attract a wide readership;
► realizing that the newspaper was merely a portable advertising board and not, as the older papers had been, a serious presentation of news only.

Newspaper production had been revolutionized in the late nineteenth century by machines which allowed the production of thousands of copies per hour; printing, typesetting and folding machines enabled men to do much more than workers previously.

Newspaper buying became more common after 1900 because more people had money to spare for such 'luxuries' and, after the 1870 Education Act (unit 42), were able to read.

The 'Battle of the Press' was a feature of the 1920s and 1930s when, for the first time, most people bought a daily paper. This 'battle' was:
► dominated by 'Press Lords' such as Northcliffe, Beaverbrook (of the *Daily Express*) and Rothermere;
► the cause of the continued low price of the papers;
► the cause of much advertising and 'reader-catching' schemes.

Since the emergence of commercial television, newspapers have tended to lose some advertising revenue and many have closed down.

THE CINEMA

Silent films were shown before 1914, and **stars** such as Charlie Chaplin, Mary Pickford and Rudolph Valentino were world famous by 1928. **'Talking pictures'** first appeared in 1928, making films even more attractive.

Cinemas were built throughout the country during the 1930s – a reminder that many people had money to spare for entertainment during the depression. **Glamorous names** for cinemas (e.g. Plaza, Majestic, Granada and Alhambra) helped increase the sense of escapism provided by the films and by their stars, and by the decor inside the cinemas.

Cinema-going was commonplace. By 1939 over half the population went once a week, and one quarter went twice a week. This declined after the war. In 1946 there were 4650 cinemas in Britain, by 1967 only 1900 and today there are almost daily announcements of further closures as a result of:

► **alternative forms of leisure** for the motor-owning and more affluent people;
► **fall in quality of films,** with an emphasis on 'horror';
► **television,** which allows 'talkies' in the home.

57.4 Air Travel

AIR TRAVEL BEFORE 1939

There had been many worldwide experiments aimed at finding a way of enabling people to fly, and the development of the petrol engine allowed more successful experiments.

The Wright brothers made the first flight in a heavier-than-air machine at Kitty Hawk in 1903. In 1909, **Louis Blériot,** a Frenchman, won the *Daily Mail* prize of £1000 for the first person to fly across the English Channel.

During the war, 1914–18, aeroplanes were improved as regards:
► engine capacity;
► strength of frame;
► size of aircraft.

Alcock and Brown, two former RAF pilots, flew in a converted bomber from **Newfoundland** to Ireland, and became the first men to fly non-stop across the Atlantic, after the war.

The world's first **passenger service** was opened in 1919 between London and Paris, for a fare of £25.

In the 1920s aviators such as Alan Cobham proved that it was possible to fly from Britain to such parts of the world as South Africa, India and Australia. **Imperial Airways** was formed in 1924 to provide services to most parts of the Empire.

By 1939 aircraft were more powerful, luxurious and safer than they had been in 1919 but there was still no regular Transatlantic service.

AIRCRAFT AND THE SECOND WORLD WAR, 1939–45 (unit 51)

Wartime development led to **aircraft** in which:
► **frames** were made of metal, which is rigid and strong and has lower production and maintenance costs than the older wooden frames;
► **engines** were more powerful, able to drive the larger planes and carry heavier loads:
● In **1939** the Wellington bomber had a range of about 750 miles and carried about 1814 kilos (4000 lbs);
► By **1945,** Lancaster bombers carried 6800 kilos (15 000 lbs) and had a range of 1400 miles;
► only **one pair of wings** was needed, because of the stronger metals used in the fuselage. This cut down air resistance and made planes more efficient and comfortable;
► **streamlining** was used to lessen wind resistance; cockpits were covered, as were gun turrets;
► **undercarriages** were made retractable, with wheels tucked into the wings when the plane was in flight.
   Flying aids were developed which included ground-to-air control by the radio telephone, and air-to-air contact between aircraft in flight.

Radar

Radar (unit 51) was developed by Robert Watson-Watt working at Farnborough. He showed that aeroplanes gave out an echo as they flew through a radio beam, and this echo enabled observers to estimate the plane's distance, speed and direction.
   By 1936 he had picked up echoes from planes over 75 miles away, and by 1939 he had supervised the construction of a chain of radar stations around the coast. Post-war development of radar had been of major importance, allowing controllers to tell pilots:
► what to do in any circumstances, as they plot the progress of planes on a radar map;
► the position, speed and direction of other planes—essential when planes fly at supersonic speeds;
► how to land their planes even when visibility is very low.

THE JET ENGINE

Frank Whittle a cadet at the RAF College at Cranwell, 1927, wrote an essay describing flights of 500 mph—when few planes could reach 200 mph.
   In 1930 he developed the **gas turbine jet engine** but it was 1936 before he found financiers to back his idea, the RAF having rejected it.
   The Gloster E28/39, the first British jet plane, first flew in 1941, although a German jet plane, the Heinkel 178, had flown in 1939. In 1947 a US plane broke the sound barrier in a level flight.
   The Comet, the first commercial jet plane, first flew in 1950, marking Britain's world lead in aviation. It went into service in May 1953. A series of crashes as a result of metal fatigue led to its withdrawal, however. By 1958 a larger, safer **Comet** was available from De Haviland, but by then US firms had produced cheaper aircraft of similar design and greater capability. Britain never recovered its lead.
   Concorde, the joint Anglo-French supersonic plane, was the result of an Anglo-French agreement signed in November 1962. It went into service in 1973 and was hailed as a great triumph and emphasized the ability of British technologists.

■ 57.5 Other Developments ■

Christopher Cockerell, had been an electronics engineer before becoming a boat builder.
   In 1955 his idea for a new vessel had been accepted by the Admiralty, which classified it as 'secret' and stopped any commercial development. In 1957 a Swiss engineer produced plans for a similar machine.

Cockerell got Admiralty permission to ask the National Development Corporation for finance to help Saunders Roe (a plane building firm) to produce the Hovercraft for commercial, rather than military purposes.
   In July 1959 the first trans-Channel trip was made—50 years after Blériot's crossing by plane.

RAIL TRAVEL

Little improvement was made to stock or lines during the period 1880–1939, and times taken by trains hardly changed.
   The nationalization of the railways (unit 52) led to the development of:
► new steam locomotives, which first appeared in 1951;
► diesel and electric locomotives which were cleaner, more efficient and required less servicing than steam engines which they replaced;
► the electrification of parts of the railway network and the announcement, in 1981, that more of the system will be electrified.
   The drop in the amount of freight and of passengers carried by post-war trains has been the result of the development of road transport, aided by:
► the new motorway system;
► the development of larger lorries (the 'juggernauts').
   This drop in income for the railways has led to the closure of many lines, particularly when Dr Beeching was appointed by the Macmillan government. His report (1962) on railway profitability led to the closing of 5000 miles of lines.
   Many unprofitable lines are maintained today by subsidies from local and central government, which realize that closure would lead to even more congestion on roads and to further isolation for certain communities in the country.

TELEVISION

John Logie Baird and **Isaac Schoenberg** were the pioneers of the development of television. In 1936 the world's first television service was opened at Alexandra Palace although:
► it only served an audience in the neighbourhood of London;
► the nine-inch wide screen gave a poor picture;
► sets cost about £350 in the depressed 1930s.
   In 1950 there were still only 3000 licensed sets in the country. In the 1950s and early 1960s:
► manufacturers, aided by technological development, produced cheaper and larger sets;
► the BBC increased its output both in quality and quantity;
► more people could afford the lower prices charged for TV sets.
   By 1965 there were over 13 million licensed sets.
   In 1954 the government had ended the BBC's monopoly by creating the Independent Television Authority to supervise the new television companies (Granada, Westward, etc). The BBC gets its income from the licence fees; commercial companies get theirs from advertising which:
► is a sign of British affluence;
► led to a drop in income for newspapers (above).
   Television, like the earlier cinema, produces its 'stars' although, unlike the cinema, these tend to have a much shorter 'public' life.

■ Unit 57 Summary ■

► Urban transport—the bicycle and the tram.
► Wider travel—the motor car and railway system.
► Radio and the transistor revolution.
► Newspapers.
► The rise and fall of the cinema industry.
► Air travel.
► TV.

58 EXAMINATION QUESTIONS

58.1 Structured questions based on one or more pieces of evidence

Candidates are not asked to make any evaluation of this evidence: source-evaluation questions can be found in **58.2** and **58.3**.

Questions may require, as answers:
(a) one word (e.g. question **9(a)** and **(b)**);
(b) a sentence (e.g. question **1(a)(i)** and **(ii)**);
(c) more extended writing (e.g. question **10**).

Candidates for the **London East Anglian Group** and for the **Midland Examining Group** should note that they have to do a longer essay as part of their answer. See questions **1(b)** and **2(c)**.

1 Population Changes 1860-1986

(a) Study the tables below and then answer questions **(i)** to **(v)** which follow:

UNITED KINGDOM BIRTH RATE
(approximate figures)

1920	25.4
1930	16.3
1950	16.2
1960	17.5
1970	16.3
1980	13.1

UNITED KINGDOM INFANT MORTALITY RATE
(approximate figures)

1920	100
1930	67
1950	31
1970	18
1980	13

(i) Write a sentence to explain what is meant by the term 'birth rate'. (2)
(ii) Write a sentence to explain what is meant by 'infant mortality rate'. (2)
(iii) Write one or two sentences to suggest possible reasons for the sharp drop in the birth rate between 1920 and 1930. (3)
(iv) Write one or two sentences to suggest possible reasons for the sharp drop in infant mortality between 1930 and 1950 (3)
(v) Using the information given in the tables and your own knowledge, describe and explain the main trends in British population growth in the period from 1950 to the present day. (5)

ESSAY QUESTIONS

(b) EITHER
(i) Describe and account for the main changes in the size, distribution and occupations of the population of Britain between 1870 and 1914. (15)
OR
(ii) In the period 1870-1914 various attempts were made to improve conditions in British cities. How important in this process were the work and ideas of Joseph Chamberlain? (15)

LEAG, 1990

2 The Agricultural Revolution, 1760-1820

Read the extract and then answer the questions which follow.

> 'Enclosure of the open fields was no new thing in the eighteenth century. Where there was just a single landowner he could enforce enclosure. More often there were also some smaller freeholders or leaseholders. Sometimes it was possible to secure voluntary agreement between all the landowners concerned. However, in most cases it was necessary to force enclosure on some landowners who expected to lose form such a change.'

(a) What do you understand by the following terms:
   (i) open fields; (2)
   (ii) 'freeholders; (1)
   (iii) leaseholders? (1)

(b) How and why was it possible to force some landowners to accept enclosure against their will? (6)

(c) 'Only a small minority of people lost from enclosures.' Do you agree? Explain your answer fully. (15)

MEG, 1990

3 The Industrial Revolution, 1760-1860

Read the extract and then answer the questions which follow.

> 'As the eighteenth century progressed the demand for iron increased and more ironmasters began to use coke. The greatest expansion in the eighteenth-century iron industry took place in South Staffordshire and Shropshire. Among the ironmasters who set up works there was John Wilkinson. 'Iron-mad' Wilkinson was of great importance in the development of the industry. In 1774 he invented a new method of boring cannon. He followed this by supplying James Watt with the accurate parts he needed for his steam engine. His interest in iron was almost fanatical. He built the first iron boat in 1787, erected an iron chapel for his workmen, and insisted that he should be buried in an iron coffin.'

(a) **(i)** As the eighteenth century progressed, why was coke increasingly used as a fuel by the ironmasters? (2)
   (ii) Name one other ironmaster, apart from Wilkinson, and give one reason why this ironmaster was famous. (2)

(b) Why was the greatest growth in the eighteenth-century iron industry in South Staffordshire and Shropshire? (6)

(c) 'The Industrial Revolution was founded on iron.' Do you agree? Explain your answer fully. (15)

MEG, 1990

4 The Industrial Revolution, 1760-1860

Look carefully at the illustration below showing machinery in a cotton spinning mill, and answer the questions which follow.

(a) Explain why many accidents happened in cotton mills. (4)

(b) Did the appointment of inspectors make the 1833 Factory Act a success? Explain your answer. (6)

(c) 'The increased demand for cloth from the rapidly growing population was the main reason for the decline of the domestic system of textile manufacture.' Do you agree with this statement? Explain your answer fully. (15)

MEG, 1990

5 Transport, c1760-c1870

(a) Study this extract from an account of the history of the Liverpool and Manchester Railway and then answer questions **(i)** to **(v)** which follow:

'At the time of the Rainhill Trials the *Rocket* went up the Whitson gradient, with a carriage holding twenty to thirty passengers, at a speed of 15 to 18 miles per hour, and the ease and regularity with which this was done produced confidence that even up the gradients the locomotives would provide the necessary power.'

(i) Write a sentence to explain the term 'locomotive' (2)

(ii) Write a sentence to explain the meaning of 'Rainhill Trials' (2)

(iii) Write one or two sentences to explain why the Liverpool and Manchester Railway was important in the history of railways. (3)

(iv) Write one or two sentences to describe the conditions of rail travel for the various social classes in early Victorian England. (3)

(v) Write a paragraph to explain the importance of the work of Isambard Kingdom Brunel to the development of railways in England. (5)

ESSAY QUESTIONS

(b) EITHER

(i) Transport by road was slow and dangerous in the middle years of the eighteenth century. To what extent were **(a)** turnpike trusts and **(b)** road engineers responsible for improving this situation during the years 1760-1830? (15)

OR

(ii) Give reasons to explain the rapid development of canals in the late eighteenth and early nineteenth centuries. Why had the use of canals begun to decline by the 1840s? (15)

LEAG, 1991

6 The American War of Independence

(a) Study the passage below and then answer questions **(i)** to **(v)** which follow:

'Many colonists were coming to regard themselves as free Americans and not as subjects of a far away king. It was at this stage that the British government chose to tighten the reins. In 1763 George III forbade further emigration to the West; in 1765 came the Stamp Tax. From the English point of view, there were good reasons for these moves, but the colonists did not see things in this light. "No taxation without representation" became the cry.'

(i) Write a sentence to explain what the Stamp Tax taxed. (2)

(ii) Write a sentence giving one reason why emigration to the West was forbidden in 1763. (2)

(iii) Write one or two sentences to explain why British governments decided to tax the American colonies in the 1760s. (3)

(iv) Write one or two sentences to explain what the colonists meant by 'No taxation without representation'. (3)

(v) Write a paragraph to explain why British governments were unwilling to allow as much freedom as many colonists wanted in the years after 1763. (5)

ESSAY QUESTIONS

(b) EITHER

(i) Between 1763 and 1775 many people in British and the American colonies wanted peace. Why then did armed rebellion break out in 1775? (15)

OR

(ii) In the early part of the war the American forces seemed to have little chance of defeating the British, yet in 1781 the British army surrendered to the Americans. Why did the course of the war change so completely? (15)

LEAG, 1990

7 The Poor Law, 1790-1850

Study the extract below and then attempt all parts of the question.

'Poverty was a serious problem in the late eighteenth and early nineteenth centuries. In rural areas, mainly in the South, farm labourers were very poor. In urban areas, mainly in the North, there were periods of great poverty for labourers.

The Old Poor Law System was unable to cope with this situation. Various schemes were tried to deal with the problem. One was the "Speenhamland System". This and, indeed, other attempts to help the poor were much criticised.'

(a) Why was there so much poverty in 1790? (10)

(b) 'The adoption of the "Speenhamland System" shows that the landowners had much sympathy for the poor.' Do you agree or disagree with this opinion? Explain your answer. (10)

(c) Do you think that the disadvantages of the 'Speenhamland System' were greater than its advantages? Explain your answer. (10)

SEG, 1991

8 William Pitt the Younger

Look at this cartoon of 1794 which contrasts the prosperity of the middle class with the poverty of the working class as a result of the wars with France. Then answer the questions which follow.

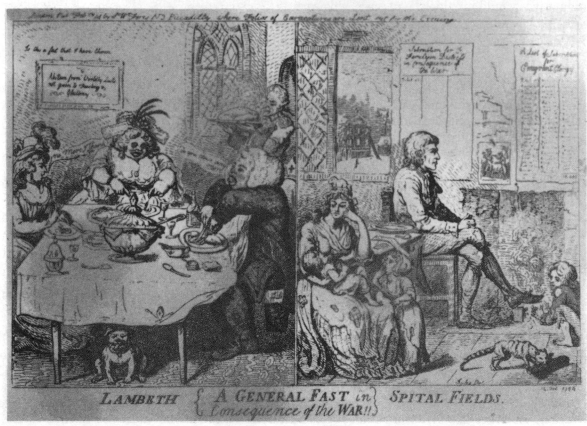

(a) (i) Name two taxes which had been introduced or increased in the ten years before 1800. (2)
   (ii) Give two reasons why new taxes had been introduced. (2)
(b) Why did the British government pass laws to restrict the rights of individuals from 1793 to 1801? (6)
(c) 'The wars with France created great poverty and distress in Britain between 1793 and 1815.' Do you agree? Explain your answer fully. (15)

MEG, 1991

9 The Defeat of Napoleon

Read the passage below which is a description of Nelson written by Wellington after the one occasion they met in September 1805. Then answer the questions which follow.

> 'He did not know who I was, but at once began to talk about himself, in a vain and silly way. I was surprised and almost disgusted. He went out of the room for a moment. When he came back he was completely different. He talked sensibly about the state of the country and the Continent. In fact he talked more like an officer and a statesman. I don't know that I ever had a conversation that interested me more.'

(a) (i) Name the sea battle which prevented Nelson and Wellington meeting again after the occasion described in the passage. (1)
   (ii) Name one of Wellington's victories in the Peninsular War. (1)
   (iii)Give two reasons why Corunna was important in the Peninsular War. (2)
(b) How did Napoleon hope the Continental System would help to defeat Britain? (6)
(c) 'Britain's contribution to the defeat of Napoleon owed more to Wellington than to Nelson.' Do you agree? Explain your answer fully. (15)

MEG, 1991

10 Religion and society, 1750-1820

Study the extract below and then attempt all parts of the question.

> 'John Wesley spent much of his life preaching the Christian message. He expected his followers to be members of the Church of England, but a complete break with that Church occurred, and a separate Methodist Church was formed soon after his death. By 1815 there were nearly a quarter of a million Methodists in Britain.

The growth of Methodism had important social and economic results. Methodist virtues became widely accepted and played an important part in Britain's growing prosperity. Wesley's work and the growth of Methodism also had important effects for other churches including the Church of England.'

(a) Why did Methodism develop in the second half of the eighteenth century? (12)

(b) What effects did the growth of Methodism have on people's lives? (8)

(c) Did the Church of England change as a result of the growth of Methodism? Explain your answer (10)

SEG, 1991

11 Domestic policies, 1815-70

(a) Study this extract from Cobbett's *Weekly Political Register* of March 1817 and then answer questions **(i)** to **(v)** which follow:

'Countrymen and Friends
Before this letter will reach your hands, Acts of Parliament of the most tremendous importance to us all will probably be passed which will most deeply affect our liberties and lives. One of these is the suspension of the Habeas Corpus Act.'

(i) Write a sentence to explain what is meant by 'habeas corpus' (2)

(ii) Write a sentence giving one reason why the Government passed laws which Cobbett thought 'will most deeply affect our liberties and lives' in the years after 1815. (2)

(iii) Write one or two sentences to explain why the Government disliked such newspapers as the *Weekly Political Register*. (3)

(iv) Write one or two sentences to describe the March of the Blanketeers in 1817 and its outcome. (3)

(v) Write a paragraph to describe how the local magistrate dealt with the meeting at St Peter's Fields, Manchester, in 1819 and how the Government reacted to these events. (5)

ESSAY QUESTIONS

EITHER

(i) The Chartist movement caused concern to governments in the late 1830s and the 1840s. What factors explain the growth of Chartism and why did its methods alarm governments at this time? (15)

OR

(ii) Describe the creation and growth of the Co-operative Movement during the years to 1870. How important was the Co-operative Movement in the history of working-class movements during these years? (15)

LEAG, 1990

12 Parliamentary Reform

Study the newspaper extract below and then attempt all parts of the question.

'We have often told the poor that the Reform Act would do them no good. That is not to say it is of no use. What we want to point out is that, unless the new, "liberal", parliament gives all householders the vote, the Reform Act will be worse than useless.'

from *The Poor Man's Guardian*, (December 1832)

(a) The 1832 Reform Act did not give the vote to the poor. Why, therefore, did many of them support the Act? (9)

(b) A further Reform Act was passed in 1867. Did this Act help the poor? Explain your answer. (7)

(c) The 1884 Reform Act gave all male householders the right to vote in parliamentary elections. Why did it take so long to achieve this right? (9)

SEG, 1991

13 The Whig Reforms in the 1830s

(a) Study the passage below, which is about the 1832 Parliamentary Reform Act, and then answer questions **(i)** to **(v)** which follow:

'...each of the boroughs marked [A]...shall from the end of this Parliament cease to return any members to serve in Parliament...
Each of the places marked [C]...shall from the end of this Parliament return two members to serve in Parliament.
[A] Amersham, St Mawes, Corfe Castle, Minehead, Dunwich, Gatton, Bramber, Borough-bridge, Old Sarum.
[C] Stockport, Devonport, Sunderland, Greenwich, Bolton, Blackburn, Manchester, Finsbury, Tower Hamlets, Stoke-upon-Trent, Brighton, Birmingham, Leeds.'

(i) Write a sentence explaining the meaning of the term 'parliamentary borough'. (2)

(ii) Write a sentence to explain the meaning of the term 'freeholder'. (2)

(iii) Write one or two sentences giving one reason why the places listed after [A] were losing their members of parliament. (3)

(iv) Write one or two sentences explaining why the places listed after [C] were gaining members of parliament. (3)

(v) Write a paragraph to explain how voting and the election of MPs was changed by the 1832 Reform Act. (5)

ESSAY QUESTIONS

(b) EITHER

(i) In 1833 slavery was abolished in the British Empire. In what ways did abolition affect Britain and the Empire? (15)

OR

(ii) In 1834 the Poor Law Amendment Act was passed. In what ways did this Act change poor relief in Britain? (15)

LEAG, 1991

14 Education

(a) Study the passage below and then answer questions **(i)** to **(v)** which follow:

'During the early 1800s, two church societies were founded. Their aim was to provide an elementary education for children ... Joseph Lancaster set up the British and Foreign Schools Society. The Church of England founded the National Society. Its leader was Andrew Bell ... Both of these used a new method of teaching. It was known as the Monitorial System. In 1833 the first parliamentary grant was given to education. The sum was ú20,000. The money was divided equally between the two church societies...'

(i) Write a sentence to explain the meaning of the term 'elementary education'. (2)

(ii) Write a sentence to explain the meaning of the term 'Monitorial System'. (2)

(iii) Write one or two sentences to explain why the 'Monitorial System' was sometimes criticised at the time. (3)

(iv) Write one or two sentences to explain why the church societies took so much interest in the education of the poor at this time. (3)

(v) Write a paragraph to explain why parliament gave a grant of £20,000 to education in 1833. (5)

ESSAY QUESTIONS

(b) EITHER

(i) In what ways did public schools change in the years from 1815 to 1867? (15)

OR

(ii) James Kay-Shuttleworth and Robert Lowe were important figures in education. Show in what ways the work of both of these men affected education in this period. (15)

LEAG, 1991

15 The Poor Law Amendment Act, 1834

Study the picture below and then attempt all parts of the question.

A new ward at Marylebone Workhouse, 1867 (an illustration produced at the time).

(a) This picture shows a workhouse in 1867. Why did some poor people live in workhouses? (7)

(b) How successful was the Poor Law Amendment Act of 1834 in dealing with the problem of poverty? (8)

(c) 'The way the poor were treated altered greatly between 1834 and 1880.' Do you agree or disagree with this statement? Explain your answer. (10)

SEG, 1991

16 Chartism, 1832-69, and its results

Study the extract below and then attempt all parts of the question.

> 'Working class people were bitterly disappointed by the Reform Act of 1832. In the 1830s the London Working Men's Association drew up the six points of the Charter. People flocked to support Chartism. Three petitions, the last in 1848, were presented to Parliament. All were rejected.
>
> Chartism virtually ended in 1848. None of the points of the Charter had at that time been achieved. However, Chartism was certainly not a complete failure.'

(a) Explain why working class people were so disappointed by the Reform Act of 1832. (10)

(b) 'Chartism collapsed in 1848 because of an improvement in economic conditions.'
Do you agree or disagree with this opinion? Explain your answer. (10)

(c) Was Chartism a complete failure? Explain your answer. (10)

SEG, 1991

17 Conditions in Mines and Factories

(a) Study the pictures below and then answer questions **(i)** to **(v)** which follow:

PICTURE A: (a trapper and a putter working in a coalmine)

PICTURE B: (children working in a textile mill)

(i) Write a sentence to explain the work done by a 'trapper'. (2)

(ii) Write a sentence to explain the work done by a 'putter'. (2)

(iii) Write one or two sentences to explain two reasons why young children were employed in textile mills. (3)

(iv) Write one or two sentences to explain two of the dangers always present in coalmines. (3)

(v) Write a paragraph to explain the ways workers gained and lost by the introduction of the factory system. (5)

ESSAY QUESTIONS

(b) EITHER

(i) The Earl of Shaftesbury devoted his life to improving working conditions for children and women in factories and mines. How important was the part he played in this movement? (15)

OR

(ii) Why were reforms in working conditions in mines and factories so slow in coming about and what progress had been made by the 1860s? (15)

LEAG, 1990

18 Public Health and Population, 1760–1870

(a) Study the plan below showing court dwellings in the early nineteenth century and then answer questions **(i)** to **(v)** which follow:

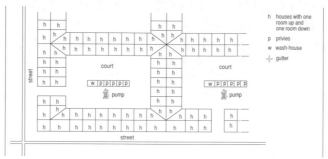

(i) Write a sentence to explain what is meant by the term 'court dwellings'. (2)

(ii) Write a sentence to explain why houses for workers were often built in this way. (2)

(iii) Write one or two sentences to explain why sanitation and hygiene would present difficulties to the occupiers of such dwellings. (3)

(iv) Write one or two sentences to explain the possible link between the planning of houses of this type and the spread of cholera. (3)

(v) Write a paragraph describing other ways in which the planning of this area might have created social and health problems. (5)

ESSAY QUESTIONS

(b) EITHER

(i) Describe the efforts which were made by individuals and by public bodies to improve public health during the period 1840-70. Show how far Edwin Chadwick was responsible for the success of these efforts. (15)

OR

(ii) 'The period 1760-1830 saw revolutionary changes in the size, composition and distribution of the population of Britain.' What were the changes and what reasons help to explain why they occurred? (15)

LEAG, 1991

19 Medical Science, Public Health and Leisure, 1760–1870

(a) Study the print below which shows a doctor engaged in vaccination against smallpox and then answer questions **(i)** to **(v)** which follow:

(i) Write a sentence explaining the meaning of 'smallpox'. (2)

(ii) Write a sentence to explain the meaning of 'vaccination'. (2)

(iii) Write one or two sentences to explain why some doctors in the late eighteenth and early nineteenth centuries thought vaccination was dangerous. (3)

(iv) Write one or two sentences to explain why surgery in the early nineteenth century had to be carried out rapidly. (3)

(v) Write a paragraph to show how far the work of James Simpson made surgery safer. (5)

ESSAY QUESTIONS

(b) EITHER

(i) The period 1760-1870 saw a number of far-reaching improvements in the treatment and care of the sick. How important were each of the following in bringing about these improvements:

    (a) Florence Nightingale;

    (b) Louis Pasteur;

    (c) Joseph Lister. (15)

OR

(ii) Describe the leisure activities of the various social classes during the period 1760–1870. To what extent did the nature of these activities change during this period? (15)

LEAG, 1991

20 Sir Robert Peel

Study the extract below and then attempt all parts of the question.

> 'When the Tories returned to power under Peel in 1841, a new type of party appeared. This party was much more prepared to carry out reforms and was aware that the electorate was much larger than before 1832. In 1846, however, this party split into two groups. Disraeli gathered the party together and built a new Conservative Party from it.'

> an historian's view, (1989)

(i) Why did a new type of Tory Party emerge in 1841? (7)

(ii) Why did the Tory Party split into two groups in 1846? (6)

(iii) 'Peel, not Disraeli, was the man who built the new Conservative Party.' Do you agree or disagree with this opinion? Explain your answer. (12)

SEG, 1991

21 Agriculture, 1760-1870

(a) Study the extract below, taken from a speech made in the 1830s by Richard Oastler about the Corn Laws, and then answer questions **(i)** to **(v)** which follow:

> 'Whenever I hear a British workman shout "cheap foreign corn", I always fancy that I see his wife pulling his coat and hear her crying, "low wages, long labour and bad profits". Is not that the case? And when I hear a large millowner coaxing his workpeople with a promise of "cheap foreign corn", I fancy I see him shrugging his shoulders and saying "More work for less money, that's all!"'

(i) Write a sentence to explain what is meant by the term 'Corn Laws'. (2)

(ii) Write a sentence to explain why both the workmen and the millowner were calling for 'cheap foreign corn' in the 1830s. (2)

(iii) Write one or two sentences to explain in your own words why people like Richard Oastler viewed the demand for 'cheap foreign corn' with suspicion. (3)

(iv) Write one or two sentences to explain he effectiveness of the methods used by the Anti-Corn Law League during the early 1840s. (3)

(v) Write a paragraph describing the events of 1845-46 which led to the repeal of the Corn Laws. (5)

ESSAY QUESTIONS

(b) EITHER

    (i) Describe the procedure for bringing about an enclosure of agricultural land and explain how the enclosure movement encouraged the use of new farming methods, selective breeding and new technology. (15)

OR

    (ii) What impact did the Revolutionary and Napoleonic Wars (1793-1815) have on:

        (a) landowners and farmers, and

        (b) farm labourers? (15)

LEAG, 1990

22 Ireland, 1760-1860

(a) Study the passage below and then answer questions **(i)** to **(v)** which follow:

'Attempts to achieve free trade for Ireland met with difficulties. That unhappy country continued to be affected by poverty, absentee landlords, a parliament which represented only the Protestants, and insufficient religious liberty for Roman Catholics. Grattan had tried during the American War to gain some concessions from the British Government...Wolfe Tone seized the opportunity offered by the French War to rise in revolt, but his forces were brutally crushed. The government sought the solution already tried with Scotland - an Act of Union.'

(i) Write a sentence to explain the meaning of the term 'absentee landlords'. (2)

(ii) Write a sentence to explain the meaning of the term 'free trade' for Ireland in the 1770s. (2)

(iii) Write one or two sentences to explain the concessions which Grattan had gained from the British Government during the American War. (3)

(iv) Write one or two sentences to explain why 'Attempts to achieve free trade for Ireland met with difficulties'. (3)

(v) Write a paragraph to explain the aims of Wolfe Tone's revolt of 1798 and why it failed. (5)

ESSAY QUESTIONS

(b) EITHER

(i) The Act of Union between Britain and Ireland was passed in 1800. Why did the government consider that this Act would improve Anglo-Irish relations? (15)

OR

(ii) What grievances did the Irish have against the English between 1780 and 1800? In what ways did these grievances change after 1800? In what ways did they remain the same? (15)

LEAG, 1991

23 Trade Unions 1760-1867

(a) Study the passage below and then answer questions **(i)** to **(v)** which follow:

'The Repeal of the Combination Acts in 1824 and the Amending Act which followed in 1825 left the trade unions with very limited powers. The failure of the GNCTU in 1834 another blow to the movement and little real progress was made until the formation of the national craft unions or New Model Unions in the 1850s such as the ASE.'

(i) Write a sentence to explain the meaning of the term 'combination'. (2)

(ii) Write a sentence to explain the meaning of the term 'craft union'. (2)

(iii) Write one or two sentences to explain why the repeal of the Combination Acts was an important event for trade unions. (3)

(iv) Write one or two sentences to explain why trade unions often found it difficult to take effective action after the Acts of 1824 and 1825. (3)

(v) Write a paragraph to explain how trade unions developed between 1825 and 1834. (5)

ESSAY QUESTIONS

(b) EITHER

(i) What were the aims of Robert Owen's Grand National Consolidated Trade Union (1834) and why did it fail? (15)

OR

(ii) The New Model Unions of the 1850s were a great improvement on the earlier unions. Explain why this was so and give details of the changes in the law these unions campaigned for. (15)

LEAG, 1990

24 Railways, 1820-1914

Read carefully the passage below which relates to the development of railways, and answer the questions which follow.

'The glories of 'The Bear', where a good twenty minutes were allowed to the traveller to eat three or four shillings worth of boiled fowls and ham to make sure he was not hungry during the night, are fast fading away forever. This well-known hostelry is about to be permanently closed as a public inn because of the development of railways.'

From a newspaper in 1842

(a) **(i)** On which method of road transport did innkeepers depend? (1)

(ii) According to the extract, which group of people other than innkeepers would suffer from the coming of the railways? (1)

(iii) Name two industries where employment increased as a result of railway development. (2)

(b) How did working-class people benefit from the passing of the 1844 Railway Act? Explain your answer. (6)

(c) 'The growth and development of railways up to 1850 was mainly due to the work of George Stephenson.' Do you agree with this statement? Explain your answer fully. (15)

25 Gladstone's First Ministry 1868-74

(a) Study the passage below and then answer questions **(i)** to **(v)** which follow:

'Gladstone's First Ministry was one of the great reforming ministries of the nineteenth century with major reforms in education, the army and the trade unions. In Forster's Education Act, Board schools were set up, but the Cowper-Temple clause caused argument. Nevertheless, his party, the Liberals, were to lose the next general election in 1874.'

(i) Write a sentence to explain what 'Board schools' were. (2)
(ii) Write a sentence to explain why the 'Cowper-Temple clause caused argument'. (2)
(iii) Write one or two sentences to explain how entry to the Civil Service was changed by Gladstone. (3)
(iv) Write one or two sentences to explain why the trade unions were pleased with parts of the Trade Union Act of 1871. (3)
(v) Write a paragraph to explain how the British army was improved by Cardwell's army reforms. (5)

ESSAY QUESTIONS

(b) EITHER
(i) Gladstone's record in foreign affairs during his first ministry was by no means bad, but it was still attacked by many. Do you consider these attacks were justified? Explain your answer by careful consideration of his foreign policy. (15)
OR
(ii) Gladstone suggested that the Licensing Act was the main cause of the Liberal defeat in the 1874 election. Do you agree? Explain your answer by reference to his policies in the period 1868–74. (15)

26 Disraeli

(a) Study the cartoon below, which is about the purchase of shares in the Suez Canal, and then answer questions **(i)** to **(v)** which follow:

(i) Write a sentence to explain the meaning of the term 'empire'. (2)
(ii) Write a sentence explaining how Disraeli got the chance to buy shares in the Suez Canal. (2)
(iii) Write one or two sentences explaining why Disraeli was so keen to buy the shares. (3)
(iv) Write one or two sentences explaining why this purchase led to criticism of Disraeli in the House of Commons. (3)
(v) The lion in the cartoon represents Britain. Write a paragraph explaining why the lion is shown holding a key. (5)

ESSAY QUESTIONS

(b) EITHER

(i) In the years after 1876 Britain became heavily involved in Egypt and the Sudan. What were the results for Britain of this involvement? (15)

OR **(ii)** Gladstone and Disraeli often differed over their policies towards the British Empire. Explain in what ways their policies differed. (15)

LEAG, 1991

27 Relations between Britain and the Boers in South Africa

(a) Study the map which shows South Africa in 1890 and then answer questions **(i)** to **(v)** which follow:

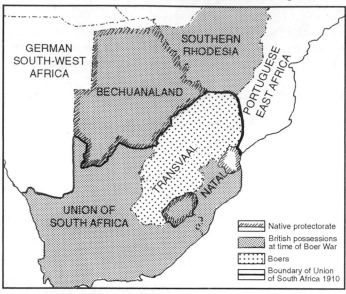

(i) Write a sentence to explain who the Boers were. (2)

(ii) Write a sentence to explain who the Uitlanders were. (2)

(iii) Write one or two sentences to explain the circumstances in which the Boers in the Transvaal regained their independence in 1881. (3)

(iv) Write one or two sentences to explain how the discovery of gold in the Transvaal in 1886 caused problems for the Boers. (3)

(v) Write a paragraph to explain the ambitions of Cecil Rhodes in South Africa in the late nineteenth century. (5)

ESSAY QUESTIONS

(b) EITHER

(i) Why did war break out between the British and the Boers in 1899? (15)

OR

(ii) The British eventually won the Boer War which lasted from 1899 to 1902. Why did the British find the task of defeating the Boers so difficult? (15)

LEAG, 1991

28 The Liberals, 1906-14

The following extract concerns the laws passed by the Liberal governments of 1906-1914.

'In these years a number of laws extended the welfare service. They only slightly reduced the misery existing among the poor, and the problems that needed to be dealt with but they do mark an important stage in the growth of the Welfare State.'

(a) (i) Who was Prime Minister in the years **(a)** 1906–1908 and **(b)** 1908–1914? (2)

(ii) Explain briefly the term 'Welfare State'. (2)

(b) Why did the Liberals pass laws to help children and old people? (6)

(c) 'The Liberal reforms only slightly reduced the misery existing among the poor. Therefore, they were not important.' Do you agree? Explain your answer fully. (15)

MEG, 1990

29 Parliamentary Reform, 1860-1928

(a) Study the passage below and the cartoon and then answer questions **(i)** to **(v)** which follow:

'Not until 1867 was the franchise extended, but the hustings still remained. One view of the 1867 Reform Act is shown in the cartoon from that year.'

A Leap in the Dark

(i) Write a sentence to explain the meaning of the term 'franchise'. (2)

(ii) Write a sentence to explain the meaning of the word 'hustings'. (2)

(iii) Write one or two sentences to explain which classes still dominated the House of Commons after the 1832 Reform Act (3)

(iv) Write one or two sentences to explain how demands for further parliamentary reform were kept alive between 1832 and 1867. (3)

(v) Write a paragraph to explain why the 1867 Reform Act was described as 'Shooting Niagara' and as 'A Leap in the Dark'. (5)

ESSAY QUESTIONS

(b) EITHER

(i) It was thirty-five years after the Great Reform Act of 1832 before the next reform of parliament. Give reasons for this long delay. (15)

OR

(ii) How did Disraeli's successful Reform Act in 1867 differ from the proposals put forward by the Liberals and why had Disraeli and the Conservatives taken up the cause of reform? (15)

LEAG, 1990

30 Parliamentary Reform, 1860–1928

The cartoon and the extract are concerned with the House of Lords.

THE NEW GUY FAWKES PLOT:

OR, THE BEST ADVERTISED CONSPIRACY IN THE WORLD.

[The First Autumn Meeting of the Cabinet has been summoned for the Fifth of November, Guy Fawkes Day]

'The action of the House of Lords in refusing to pass into law the Budget is a breach of the Constitution and a seizure of the rights of the House of Commons.'

H H Asquith, the Liberal Prime Minister, speaking in the House of Commons on 2 December 1909, two days after the Lords had rejected the Budget.

(a) **(i)** Name the man who is shown pushing the wheelbarrow in the cartoon.   (1)

(ii) In the cartoon, the man walking in front of the wheelbarrow is Campbell-Bannerman. What position did he hold in the government at that time?   (1)

(iii) Name two Bills that were defeated by the House of Lords between 1906 and 1909, other than the Budget of 1909.   (2)

(b) Why did the House of Lords refuse to pass the Budget in 1909?   (6)

(c) 'The reason why the House of Lords' powers were limited in 1911 was that the Lords had used them in an irresponsible way.' Do you agree? Explain your answer fully.   (15)

MEG, 1990

31 Trade Unions, 1867-1980

'The social conditions of the 1880's produced the 'new unionism'. Union membership was no longer restricted to skilled craftsmen but began to spread among ordinary workers. There was an outbreak of strikes - over 500 in 1888. In 1889 the dockers struck for a minimum wage. The strike lasted for six weeks. Their victory in winning the "Dockers Tanner" was an outstanding success for unskilled workers and showed the value of organisation and industrial action.'

(a) **(i)** Name one other major strike of unskilled workers which occurred in 1888–9.   (1)

(ii) What were the differences between the 'new unionism' and older unions such as the New Model Unions?   (3)

(b) Why was there an outbreak of strikes in the late 1880s?   (6)

(c) How effective were trade unions in helping to improve the conditions of poor people between 1851 and 1914?   (15)

MEG, 1990

32 The Rise of the Labour Party

Study the cartoon below and then attempt all parts of the question.

FORCED FELLOWSHIP

WORKING MAN: "ANY OBJECTION TO MY COMPANY, GUV'NOR?
I'M AGOIN' YOUR WAY"—*(aside)* "AND FURTHER."

A cartoon, (1909) by Bernard Partridge.

(a) By 1914 the Liberal Party was in decline. Why was this? (8)

(b) This cartoon is from 1909. It shows the growing strength of the socialist movement. Why, then, did it take until 1924 for the socialists to form the first Labour Government? (7)

(c) 'The Labour Party did not achieve very much in the 1920s and 1930s.' Do you agree or disagree with this opinion? Explain your answer. (10)

SEG, 1991

33 Votes for Women

(a) Study the passage below, which describes a suffragette being force-fed, and then answer questions **(i)** to **(v)** which follow:

> 'On Saturday afternoon the wardresses forced me onto the bed and two doctors came in with them. While I was held down a nasal (nose) tube was inserted. It is two yards long, with a funnel at the end. There is a glass junction in the middle to see if the liquid is passing. The end is up the right and left nostrils on alternate days. Great pain is experienced during the process, both mental and physical.'

Mary Leigh, a suffragette

(i) Write a sentence explaining the word 'suffragette'. (2)

(ii) Write a sentence explaining why some suffragettes were force-fed. (2)

(iii) In 1913 Parliament passed the 'Cat and Mouse Act'. Write one or two sentences explaining how this Act changed the ways in which suffragettes could be treated. (3)

(iv) Write one or two sentences describing the actions of suffragettes in the years from 1903 to 1914. (3)

(v) Write a paragraph explaining what methods other than suffragette activity were used to try to get women the vote in the years before 1914. (5)

ESSAY QUESTIONS

(b) EITHER

(i) Why did many people oppose giving the vote to women in the years before 1914? (15)

OR

(ii) In what ways did the First World War affect the position of women in British society? (15)

LEAG, 1991

34 The Role and Status of Women, 1880-1930

Study the extract below and then attempt all parts of the question.

> 'Women's status in political life was very different in 1930 from what it had been at the beginning of 1918. Perhaps more significantly, there was an improvement in the status of women in the family and in society. There were many reasons for this. One reason was the First World War itself. Women's freedom extended to sport, but perhaps the most obvious change in the life of women between 1919 and 1930 was in women's fashion. As women's freedom grew, so divorce became easier.
>
> These freedoms did not, of course, reach all women. Working-class women were still bound by poverty.'

(a) 'The First World War was an important cause of change in the lives of women.' Do you agree or disagree with this opinion? Explain your answer. (10)

(b) In what ways did the part played by women in politics change between 1918 and 1930? (8)

(c) Was there a general improvement in the position of women in the family and in society between 1919 and 1930? Explain your answer. (12)

SEG, 1991

35 Education since c1870

(a) Study the extract below, which is taken from an account of his schooldays in the 1920s, written by an old age pensioner in the 1970s, and then answer questions **(i)** to **(v)** which follow:

> 'I passed the free place scholarship exam when I was in the elementary school. But my mother warned me that it was no good me hoping to go to a grammar school because she and my father would not be able to afford the money for me to go there. They would not be able to afford the uniform and, on top of that, they could not pay to keep me there until I was 16.'

(i) Write a sentence to explain the meaning of 'free place scholarship exam.' (2)

(ii) Write a sentence explaining the meaning of 'elementary school' (2)

(iii) Write one or two sentences to explain how this man's education was different since he was unable to go to 'a grammar school'. (3)

(iv) Write one or two sentences to explain how the situation described by the author in this extract had changed by the 1950s. (3)

(v) Write a paragraph describing the main changes brought about by governments in secondary education between 1965 and the present day. (5)

ESSAY QUESTIONS

(b) EITHER

(i) The period between 1870 and 1902 saw important changes in education. In what ways did government policy towards Board Schools and Voluntary Schools change during these years? (15)

OR

(ii) What is meant by the term "public school"? Describe the ways in which public schools have changed since 1870 and the ways in which they have remained the same. (15)

LEAG, 1991

36 First World War

(a) Study the photograph below which shows crowds in London welcoming the declaration of war in August 1914, and then answer questions **(i)** to **(v)** which follow:

(i) Write a sentence to explain the meaning of the word 'patriotism'. (2)

(ii) Write a sentence explaining why many British people were excited and enthusiastic about the First World War in its early stages. (2)

(iii) Write one or two sentences explaining why British civilians were generally much less enthusiastic about the war from 1916 onwards. (3)

(iv) Write one or two sentences showing why British troops became less enthusiastic about the First World War. (3)

(v) Write a paragraph to explain why so much warfare on the Western Front was 'trench warfare'. (5)

ESSAY QUESTIONS

(b) EITHER

(i) During the First World War the British government spent a great deal of effort on propaganda directed at the home front. What forms did this propaganda take and why was it so important to he government? (15)

OR

(ii) What was 'conscientious objection' and why did it become a controversial issue? (15)

LEAG, 1991

37 The First World War

Study the extract below and then attempt all parts of the question.

> 'The Schlieffen Plan depended on a knock-out blow against France. The Germany army began by attacking Belgium. At first the Plan seemed to be working and the German army rolled on into France. By the end of August the Germans were only fifty miles from Paris, but there the plan went wrong.
>
> The following three years on the Western Front saw massive offensives against enemy trenches by artillery and infantry. At most, a few miles of land were gained.'
>
> from *World Conflict in the Twentieth Century*, (1987), by S Harrison

(a) Why did the German army fail in its attempt to achieve a 'knock-out blow against France' in 1914? (10)

(b) During the years 1915-17 'the Western Front saw massive offensives against enemy trenches by artillery and infantry'. Why did these offensives fail to break through the enemy lines? (10)

(c) The breakthrough eventually came in 1918. In that year the deadlock on the Western Front was broken. What had changed by 1918 to make this possible? (10)

SEG, 1991

38 The Problems of the Peace Settlement and Post-war Britain

(a) Study the photograph below and then answer questions (i) to (v) which follow:

(i) Write a sentence to explain the meaning of the term 'mandate' as used in the Treaty of Versailles. (2)

(ii) Write a sentence to explain the meaning of the term 'reparations' as used in the Treaty of Versailles. (2)

(iii) Write one or two sentences to explain why the attitude of many people in Britain was hostile to Germany in 1918. (3)

(iv) Write one or two sentences to explain what happened to the Germany navy at the end of the war. (3)

(v) Write a paragraph to explain the gains made by Britain in the Treaty of Versailles. (5)

ESSAY QUESTIONS

(b) EITHER

(i) What part was played by Lloyd George at the Versailles peace conference? (15)

OR

(ii) What were the main problems at home and overseas which faced Lloyd George as Prime Minister in 1918 and how did he set about solving them? (15)

LEAG, 1990

39 Industry and trade, 1919-1939

Study the extracts below and then attempt all parts of the question.

Extract A

'Jarrow is dead. It is a derelict town. One out of every two shops appeared to be permanently closed. Wherever we went there were men hanging about, not scores of them but hundreds and thousands of them.'

from *English Journey*, (1933) by J B Priestley

Extract B

'Years of living in Yorkshire have fixed forever my idea of what a factory should be. It should be a grim, blackened rectangle with a tall chimney at one corner. Yet these decorative buildings I see here in the South, all glass and concrete and chromium plate, seem to my mind to be playing at being factories. Actually they are evidence to prove that the new industries have moved south.'

from *English Journey*, (1933) by J B Priestley

(a) Why was there such high unemployment in the 1930s? (7)
(b) How successful were government attempts to deal with unemployment in the 1930s? (8)
(c) 'It is wrong to call the 1930s the time of the Great Depression for all in Britain.' Do you agree or disagree with this opinion? Explain your answer. (10)

SEG, 1991

40 The General Strike, 1926

Extract A

'The workers' response has exceeded all expectations. The first day of the General Strike is over. They have shown their determination and unity to the whole world. They have resolved that the attempt of the mineowners to starve three million men, women and children into submission shall not succeed.'

The British Worker, 5 May 1926

Photograph B

Office girls travelling to work by lorry during the General Strike.

(a) (i) What was meant by the term 'General Strike'? (2)
(ii) What was 'The British Worker'? (2)
(b) Why did some office girls travel to work by lorry? (6)
(c) 'The only reason for the collapse of the General Strike was the firm stand taken by the government.' Do you agree? Explain your answer fully. (15)

MEG, 1990

41 The Labour Government, 1929-31

'On August 23rd 1931 MacDonald decided he must resign and went to inform the King. He later returned to the Labour Cabinet to announce that he had agreed to remain as Prime Minister with a National government of "personalities". The Labour Party regarded this as treachery.'

(a) (i) Name the King referred to in the source. (1)
(ii) Why did MacDonald have to inform the King of his resignation? (1)
(iii) Give two reasons why MacDonald had decided to resign. (2)
(b) Why did the Labour Party view MacDonald's acceptance of the post of Prime Minister of a National Government as 'treachery'? (6)
(c) How did the formation of the National Government affect the Conservative, Labour and Liberal parties in 1931? Explain your answer fully. (15)

MEG, 1990

42 Britain during the Second World War

(a) Study the poster on the next page and then answer questions **(i)** to **(v)** which follow:

(i) Write a sentence explaining the meaning of the term 'Home Front'. (2)
(ii) Write a sentence explaining why this poster was aimed at women. (2)
(iii) Write one or two sentences describing one other method used to try to make sure that food supplies were used as effectively as possible. (3)
(iv) Write one or two sentences explaining the ways in which women helped the war effort. (3)
(v) This is a government poster. Write a paragraph explaining the other methods used by the government to persuade people to play a more responsible part in the war effort. (5)

ESSAY QUESTIONS

(b) EITHER
(i) From August 1940 to the end of the war, Britain was frequently attacked by Germany from the air. What forms did these attacks take? How successful were the British government and people in defending themselves against air attacks? (15)

OR

(ii) In what ways did Germany try to attack Britain by sea from 1939 to 1945? How effectively did Britain defend itself against these attacks? (15)

LEAG, 1991

43 The Labour Government 1945-1951

(a) Study the passage below and then answer questions **(i)** to **(v)** which follow:

'In the 1945 election, Labour won 393 seats out of 640 and so gained an overall majority for the first time. Attlee's government faced a mammoth task. Britain was deeply in debt, many towns had suffered appalling damage. Food and clothing and fuel were in short supply. Yet people demanded "social security from the cradle to the grave".'

(i) Write a sentence explaining the meaning of the phrase 'overall majority'. (2)
(ii) Write a sentence to explain the phrase 'from he cradle to the grave' as used in the passage. (2)
(iii) Write one or two sentences explaining why the Labour Party won the 1945 election. (3)
(iv) Write one or two sentences explaining why 'Britain was deeply in debt' in 1945. (3)
(v) Write a paragraph explaining the ways by which the Labour Government of 1945 to 1951 tried to tackle the problem of bomb damage. (5)

ESSAY QUESTIONS

(b) EITHER
(i) In 1948 the National Health Service came into being. Some people were very much in favour of this change; others were very much against. Why did people disagree so much over this policy? (15)

OR

(ii) In what ways did the Labour Governments of 1945 to 1951 try to rebuild Britain's industry and trade? How successful were they? (15)

LEAG, 1991

44 Politics in Britain 1951 to 1979

(a) Study the figure below and then answer questions **(i)** to **(v)** which follow:

Conservative and Labour parties in the House of Commons. The shaded areas show the winning parties.

(i) In the late 1950s the Prime Minister Harold Macmillan said that many British people 'have never had it so good'. Write a sentence explaining what he meant. (2)

(ii) The Labour government elected in 1964 had frequent difficulties in the House of Commons. Write a sentence giving one reason why this was so. (2)

(iii) Write one or two sentences explaining why there were two General Elections in 1974. (3)

(iv) The Labour government from October 1974 to 1979 could not be sure of an overall majority in the House of Commons. Write one or two sentences explaining how it tried to strengthen its position. (3)

(v) The General Election of 1979 was held after the so-called 'Winter of Discontent'. Write a paragraph explaining the meaning of this term. How did the 'Winter of Discontent' affect the result of the General Election? (5)

ESSAY QUESTIONS

(b) EITHER

(i) During the years 1964-1979, Trade Unions often had great political influence. In what ways did they try to influence the government? How successful were they? (15)

OR

(ii) Choose either the Labour government of 1966 to 1970 or the Conservative government of 1970 to 1974. How successful was the government you have chosen in trying to solve the problems that it faced? (15)

LEAG, 1991

45 Britain's World Role

(a) Study the cartoon below, which is about the Suez Crisis of 1956, and then answer questions **(i)** to **(v)** which follow:

(i) In 1956 Colonel Nasser, the Egyptian leader, announced the nationalisation of the Suez Canal Company. Write a sentence to explain what this 'nationalisation' meant. (2)

(ii) Write a sentence giving one reason why Britain was concerned about Colonel Nasser's actions. (2)

(iii) Write one or two sentences describing the ways in which Britain intervened in Suez in October 1956. (3)

(iv) Write one or two sentences describing the ways in which the USA reacted to Britain's actions in Suez. (3)

(v) Write a paragraph explaining the ways in which Sir Anthony Eden was criticised in Britain for his actions. (5)

ESSAY QUESTIONS

(b) EITHER

(i) Between 1945 and 1980 the part played by Britain in world affairs changed. Choose two events (excluding Suez) and use them to explain why this change has taken place. (15)

OR

(ii) In the 1960s and 1970s Britain's relations with many members of the Commonwealth changed. Explain how Britain's relations with any two Commonwealth countries changed during this period. (15)

LEAG, 1991

46 Race Relations in Britain

The following extract concerns the development of racial equality in Britain.

'Wilson's Government introduced the first of Britain's Race Relations Acts in 1965. The ministers were aware that the law can do little to remove prejudices, but they hoped that the law would encourage equality. The Labour Government extended this law with a second Race Relations Act in 1968, which made it illegal to treat a person less favourably on the grounds of colour, race or national origins.'

(a) (i) Name the two areas of the Commonwealth from which most immigrants came to Britain in the 1950s and 1960s. (2)

(ii) Why did the British government welcome many immigrants in the 1950s? (2)

(b) Why did the Labour Government feel it was necessary to pass a second Race Relations Act in 1968? (6)

(c) 'Government legislation has helped a great deal in the creation of a society in Britain, in which people are treated equally regardless of colour, race or national origins.' Do you agree? Explain your answer fully. (15)

MEG, 1991

47 Developments in Transport between the Wars

(a) Study the statistical tables below and then answer questions **(i)** to **(v)** which follow:

TABLE A

Private cars in use in Britain

1914	132,000
1924	474,000
1934	1,308,000
1938	1,944,000

TABLE B

British steamships in use

	number	tonnage
1912	12,382	10,992,000
1922	12,787	11,223,000
1932	9,248	9,774,000
1938	7,491	7,819,000

(i) Write a sentence to explain the meaning of the term 'mass production' in the car industry. (2)

(ii) Refer to Table A. Write one or two sentences explaining why the number of cars on British roads rose so sharply at this time. (3)

(iii) Write a sentence to explain what sort of craft airships were. (2)

(iv) Write one or two sentences to explain the advances made in passengers flights. (3)

(v) Write a paragraph to explain the main developments in rail travel. (5)

ESSAY QUESTIONS

(b) EITHER

(i) The motor car began a revolution in everyday life, but its coming had pleasant as well as unpleasant effects. Write an essay to explain the good and bad effects between the wars of the increased use of motor cars. (15)

OR

(ii) Refer to Table B. Why did the shipping industry go through very great difficulties between 1918 and 1939? Were there any important advances in the shipping industry at the same time? (15)

LEAG, 1990

58.2 Questions based on one or two pieces of evidence which require some evaluation of sources

Up to and including 1991 such questions were set only by the **Southern Examining Group** and all the examples which follow come from that Group's papers. However, other Boards may well decide to adopt this method of questioning.

1 The Eastern Question, 1821-56

Study the source below and then attempt all parts of the question.

'The Cabinet agreed yesterday that it would not do to let Mehemet Ali declare himself independent and separate Egypt and Syria from the Turkish Empire. If it is necessary and if the Sultan demands it, we are prepared to give him naval aid against Mehemet. We intend to order our fleet immediately to go to Alexandria in order to prove to Mehemet Ali that we are determined to stop his actions.'

from a letter, (1838) from Palmerston to Lord Granville

(a) Why was Palmerston so concerned about Mehemet Ali's action? (10)

(b) Does this source prove that Palmerston opposed Mehemet Ali's action? (5)

(c) How useful is this source as historical evidence about the Eastern Question in the period 1821-56? (5)

(d) 'The Straits Convention of 1841 solved the Eastern Question in the period to 1856.'

Do you agree or disagree with this opinion? Explain your answer. (1)

SEG, 1991

2 The Indian Mutiny

Study the source below and then attempt all parts of the question.

THE HOUSE WHERE OUR WOMEN WERE SLAUGHTERED BY ORDER OF NANA SAHIB, 16 JULY 1857

The massacre at Cawnpore, 1857 - from a drawing made 'on the spot' in 1857

(a) Why were many British women killed in India in 1857? (10)

(b) 'As this source was drawn on the spot, it is of great value as historical evidence about the Indian Mutiny.' Do you agree or disagree with this opinion? Explain your answer. (6)

(c) What other types of evidence could be used to find out about the massacre at Cawnpore in 1857? (4)

(d) 'The Indian Mutiny had little long-term effect upon British rule in India.' Do you agree or disagree with this opinion? Explain your answer. (10)

SEG, 1991

3 Forster's Education Act of 1870

Study the sources below and then attempt all parts of the question.

Source A

'The Act of 1870 aimed to provide school places where none already existed. It was for that reason alone that School Boards were created. The Act of 1870 successfully carried out this great, if limited, aim.'

from a speech made by Balfour in the House of Commons in 1902

Source B:
Numbers of pupils attending Board and Voluntary schools in 1902

Board Schools	5,700 schools	2,500,000 pupils
Voluntary Schools	14,500 schools	3,000,000 pupils

from official figures

(a) Source A says that the 1870 Act provided more school places. Do the figures in source B prove this? Explain your answer.   (4)

(b) Source A was part of a speech made by Balfour just as his government were introducing a new Education Act. Does this mean that source A is unreliable as evidence about the 1870 Act? Explain your answer.   (6)

(c) 'In 1870 the Government did not want to change education a great deal.' Do you agree or disagree with this opinion? Explain your answer.   (10)

(d) How successful was the 1870 Education Act?   (10)

SEG, 1991

4   Changes in Education, 1918-1944
Study the sources below and then attempt all parts of the question.

Source A

'Most elementary schoolchildren will not benefit from secondary education because of the weakness of their mental powers. The benefit of such an education for the masses has been exaggerated. The vast majority will be manual workers who have no need for such an education'.

from *Mass Education in England*, (1928) by J H Garrett

Source B

'Public education shall be organised into three stages called primary education, secondary education and further education. Local authorities are required to provide secondary education. The school leaving age shall be raised to 15.'

from the 1944 Education Act

(a) The Education Act of 1944 (the Butler Act) was passed only 16 years after source A was written.
Does this mean that source A is unreliable as evidence about public opinion towards education in Britain? Explain your answer.   (5)

(b) How useful is source B to an historian studying the history of education in Britain in the twentieth century?   (5)

(c) Why did many people not want any further changes to education after 1918?   (10)

(d) 'The Education Act of 1944 provided free, compulsory education to age 15. It therefore ended a series of changes which had begun in 1870.' Do you agree or disagree with this opinion? Explain your answer. (10)

SEG, 1991

5   The First World War
Study the sources below and then attempt all parts of the question.

Source A

'It is no use being miserable for I tell you we are bound to win with the men we have got. I have just seen a battalion of them, going into the trenches. I tell you the boys of Britain cannot be beaten.'

from a letter sent from the Front Line in 1917

Source B

'That night passed quietly but it was cold and damp in our trench. We were hungry and bad-tempered. Why was something not being done on our side? What were the Staff Officers doing? Probably they were still in bed filled with pride. We hoped that, whatever did happen, we would miss the next attack.'

from *Ypres 1917*, (1967) by N Gladden

(a) Sources A and B were both written about 1917, by men who were at the Front. Explain why they differ. (10)

(b) By 1917 there had been stalemate on the Western Front for three years. Why was this?   (10)

(c) 'The main reason for the defeat of Germany on the Western Front was the courage of the British soldier.' Do you agree or disagree with this opinion? Explain your answer.   (10)

SEG, 1991

58.3 Questions based on a number of sources of various kinds requiring candidates to evaluate and interpret the material.

1 Population Changes

Study sources A, B and C and then answer the questions (a) to (d) which follow.

Source A

Population Figures of Britain 1700–1851
(in millions)

1700	5.5
1750	6.5
1780	8.0
1801	10.5
1811	12.0
1831	16.0
1851	21.0

Source B

'In the second half of the eighteenth century there was more fresh meat and vegetables, and the supply of food improved so that fewer people died of starvation or diseases caused by malnutrition. Transport improved, so that food shortages in a particular area could be avoided. New houses, though poor by our standards, were built of bricks and mortar, instead of timber and mud; they had slate roofs instead of thatch, and the effect of these changes was to reduce pests which carried disease. Personal cleanliness was improved by an increase in the production of soap and of cotton clothing.'

From A J Holland *The Age of Industrial Expansion*, 1977

Source C

Population Figures of Britain 1931–1991
(in millions)

1931	45.0
1951	49.0
1961	51.0
1971	54.0
1981	54.0
1991	56.0 (estimated)

(a) Study source A. How reliable are these population figures? Give reasons for your answer. (5)

(b) Does source B fully describe all the reasons for the changes in population shown in source A? (10)

(c) Using source C, what has happened to the population of Britain since 1931? Explain why this has taken place. (7)

(d) Describe and explain the nature of, and the reasons for, immigration into Britain in the twentieth century.

NEA, 1991

2 The Domestic Policy of the Younger Pitt

The following sources give evidence of some Scottish reactions to the news of the French Revolution. Source A is part of a report which appeared in the *Caledonian Mercury* on September 2, 1790, dealing with an address to the National Assembly in Paris from the Whig Club of Dundee. The Whig Club's interest lay in reforming Britain's political system.

Source A

'The triumph of liberty and reason over despotism is an interesting event to the most distant spectators...That some disturbances and even acts of violence should have attended this great Revolution is in no way surprising; that these have not been more numerous is the wonder of every politician. Our hopes are that your example will be universally followed, and that the flame you have kindled will consume the remains of despotism and bigotry in Europe. We congratulate you on having an army of citizens and a wise monarch.'

Source B is part of a letter written by Henry Dundas, to the Home Office in London, describing the reactions of some people in Scotland to events in France.

Source B

'The success of the French Democrats has had a most mischievous effect here. If it went no further than to give occasion for triumph to those who entertain the same sentiments here there would be little harm, for they are few in number, and only two or three of them possess any considerable influence or respectability. But it has led them to think of forming societies for reformation in which the lower classes of people are invited to enter...'

(a) What were the reactions in Scotland to the events of the Revolution in France?

Source C is from a report on the death of Louis XVI in *The Morning Chronicle*, on 24th January, 1793.

Source C

'The murder of the late French King, an act of such complicated injustice, cowardice, cruelty and impolicy, as is scarcely to be paralleled, will serve to make a war with France popular...'

Source D is from Lord Cockburn, in *Memorial of his Times (1779–1850)*, and is about changing attitudes towards events in France.

Source D

'Somewhat less was said about Jacobinism and sedition, though still too much. Napoleon's obvious progress towards military despotism opened the eyes of those who used to see nothing but liberty in the French Revolution; and the threat of invasion, while it combined all parties in the defence of the country, raised the confidence of the people in those who trusted them with arms, and gave them the pleasure of playing at soldiers. Instead of Jacobinism, Invasion became the word.'

(b) Do you agree that the execution of the French King was the most important factor in causing the growth of anti-French feeling in Britain in the 1790s?

SCE, Credit Level, Unit 2 A, 1990

3   Conditions in the textile industry, 1830s

Study carefully the sources below and then answer the questions that follow.

Source A

Hand-loom weavers

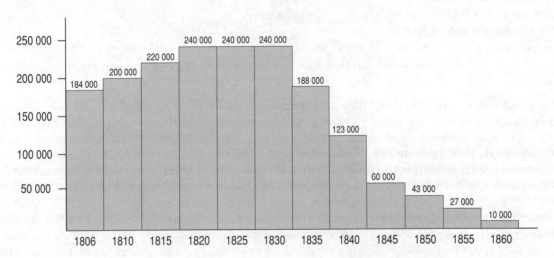

From a graph published in Cook and Stevenson,
Longman Atlas of Modern British History, 1978

Source B

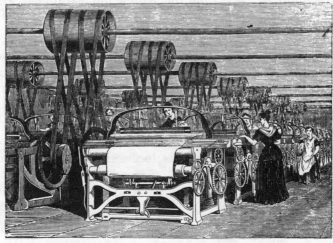

A mill scene about 1840

Source C

'On Monday, I spent the whole morning in my examination of the works: I find them in the highest order, and every arrangement that could be desired for the comfort and welfare of the people. A great many of the workers have houses belonging to themselves, which they have purchased out of their savings: I visited several of them, and was struck by their extraordinary neatness, cleanliness and handsome furniture. One of the mechanics (those who make and mend the machinery) a man of forty years of age who earns twenty-five shillings (£1.25) a week, lives in a house which cost him £200 and which he paid for out of his savings. It is of two stories, with a nice garden, full of fruit trees and vegetables, and the rooms are most handsomely furnished. I do not think there can be a happier population, and it is quite delightful to see Mr. Buchanan (the owner of the factory) among his people, who seem to look up to him as a father.'

Memoir of Leonard Horner (a factory inspector) written in 1832

Source D

'You are a weaver?   Yes.
What are your wages?   Seven shillings and sixpence (37½p) a week.
How long have you been a weaver?   Twenty-three years.
What did you earn when you began work?   I was only a boy then, but I could earn 12/– (60p) a week.
How does the fall in wages affect you?   It robs me of all the comforts of life. I can get nothing but the worst of food and less of it than I used to.
What do you do for clothing?   As well as I can. Sometimes I have some and sometimes very little... When I was a young man I did get more wages. I had three suits of clothes, and a good watch in my pocket, and two or three pairs of shoes, and one or two good hats...
What do you do for furniture?   I have never bought any in my life.
How does your wife do for clothes?   Just as I do – quite as bad.
Have your children any stock of clothes?   No, they have just enough to put on clean on Sunday, they have one dress on and off.
What does your wife earn?   About 5/– (25p) per week.
Does she go to a cotton factory?   Yes.
Is it not painful to you to have to send your wife to a factory?   Yes, it causes great grief to me.'

Evidence of John Brennan before the Select Committee on Hand-loom Weavers, 1834

Source E

'The conditions under which men and women worked in these mills have horrified later generations. However, we must be careful when comparing conditions today with those of 1800. Actions and conditions that seem brutal and callous (heartless) to us now would not have seemed harsh at that time. The employers and workers of that age did not know any better. Factory owners made their own rules. They built factories to their own standards. The employed women and children because everyone else did. Some owners were brutal but others were kindly. What they all did have in common was the wish to make profits.

The factories brought great changes in their wake. In the new mills the owners insisted on strict discipline. Absenteeism and irregular attendance at work were punished, often by dismissal. Hours of labour often exceeded twelve a day, and apart from the odd day at Christmas and Easter there were no holidays. Lateness, talking, drunkenness and sleeping at work were punished by fines or dismissal...

Factory owners deliberately employed large numbers of women and children. Women were valuable. They did not strike or riot for more money; they did not agitate for trade unions; and they could be paid low wages. Similarly, the low wages and nimble fingers of children made them valuable too ...

Not every employer was cruel or vindictive...In some mills efficient work was rewarded with higher pay, a bonus, long-term contracts or promotion. Some employers built schools, chapels and shops for their work-people. Others refused to allow corporal punishment and even organised trips to the sea or countryside.'

Alan Jamieson, *The Industrial Revolution*, 1971

(a) In what ways does source A show that the textile industry was changing during the period concerned?   (3)
(b) How does source B provide an explanation for the change shown in source A?   (3)
(c) Why do sources C and D, both written in 1834, present contrasting views of the changes that were taking place in the textile industry at the time?   (5)
(d) How does the author of source E agree and disagree with the views expressed in sources C and D?   (5)
(e) Consider the strengths and weaknesses of each of the sources as evidence for an understanding of the changes that were taking place in the textile industry. What other evidence would you need to consult in order to provide a more complete explanation?   (9)

WJEC, Syllabus C, 1991

4 The Working Classes, c1760 – c1870

Study carefully the sources below, and then answer the questions which follow.

Source A

'Any workman who shall at any time enter into any combination to obtain an advance of wages, or to lessen the hours of working, or who shall persuade, intimidate, influence or force any workman to leave his work; or who shall hinder any manufacturer from employing such workmen as he shall think proper; or who shall refuse to work with any other workmen...shall be committed to and confined in the common Gaol or House of Correction.'

From the *Combination Act*, 1799

Source B

THE PIONEER;

OR, GRAND NATIONAL CONSOLIDATED

TRADES' UNION MAGAZINE.

"THE DAY OF OUR REDEMPTION DRAWETH NIGH."

No. 34.　　　　SATURDAY, APRIL 26, 1834.　　　　[Price 2d.

Printed by B. D. Cousins, 18, Duke Street, Lincoln's Inn Fields, London.

GREAT PUBLIC MEETING OF THE LONDON MEMBERS OF THE GRAND NATIONAL
TRADES' UNION, ON MONDAY, APRIL 21, 1834.

*The above view was taken by a member of the Miscellaneous Lodge, from the upper part of Copenhagen-fields.
The procession consisted of from forty to fifty thousand unionists, was between six and seven miles in length; and it is estimated
that no less than four hundred thousand persons were assembled on the occasion.*

The Pioneer, 26 April 1834

Source C

'Article 6: That the main aim of the Masters' Union shall be by all legitimate means to separate their workmen from the Unions to which they belong, and give encouragement and protection to those who have persisted in refusing to enter into such combinations.

Article 7: That a register shall be kept of all the names and addresses of all workmen, distinguishing the members of the Unions from others, recording the character of each for industry, honesty and skill.'

From *The Poor Man's Guardian*, 1834

Source D

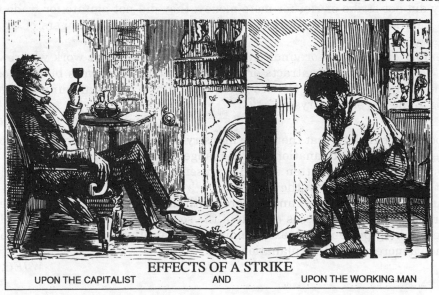

EFFECTS OF A STRIKE

UPON THE CAPITALIST　　　AND　　　UPON THE WORKING MAN

From *Punch*, 1852

Source E

A Royal Commission was set up to 'enquire into the organisation and rules of Trades Unions' in general...since the legal position of the trade unions was far from clear.

The trade unions urged that the law be changed and took the opportunity to present a well-founded case for trade union reform...

The outcome of the Royal Commission was the new Trade Union Act of 1871 giving the unions the legal recognition they wanted...but the Criminal Law Amendment Act (1871) made picketing illegal – to be modified four years later when the Conspiracy and Protection of Property Act of 1875 restored the right to peaceful picketing.

P.Sauvain, *British Economic and Social History, 1700–1870* , 1987

(a) Explain the meaning of the words underlined in source A and source E   (2)

(b) Why was the Combination Act (source A) passed in 1799? Explain your answer by reference to the source and your own recalled knowledge.   (4)

(c) In your opinion, do sources B and C explain the importance of the events of 1834 in the history of the trade union movement? Explain your answer.   (5)

(d) In what ways do sources D and E present contrasting views of the trade union movement? Explain your answer.   (5)

(e) Consider the usefulness of each of the sources as evidence for the study of the trade union movement in England and Wales. State briefly one important development which is not mentioned in the sources. Give reasons for your answer.   (9)

WJEC, Syllabus C, 1991

5   The Reform Bill of 1832

The following sources give evidence about the parliamentary system in Scotland and England before and after the 1832 Reform Act.

In source A, the historian T.C. Smout writes about the Scottish electoral system before 1832.

Source A

'In 1820 the voters' roll for the county constituencies of Scotland held only 2,889 names, or one voter to every 625 members of the population. In Cromarty the member was returned by 9 voters. Ayrshire had the biggest electorate in the country with 240 voters. In the burghs the situation was worse: the member for Edinburgh, for instance, was returned by 33 voters who were all town councillors with the right of choosing their own successors: the population of the capital of Scotland in 1821 was 138,000.'

T.C. Smout, *A History of the Scottish People 1560–1830*, published 1986

Source B: A map of the British Isles showing parliamentary representation

KEY

All English and Irish counties: 2 members each

All Welsh and most Scottish counties: 1 member each

Scotland 4 000 electors

England 150 000 electors

45 members

100 members

Sunderland

YORKSHIRE

Bradford • • Leeds

Bolton •

Manchester • • Sheffield

• Stoke

RUTLAND

More than half of the 203 boroughs were in the southern counties, which elected 50% of the House of Commons

These six counties elected one quarter of the members - more than Scotland and Ireland combined

(a) How useful are sources A and B in understanding the demand for reform of the franchise before 1832? Give reasons for your answer.

(b) In what ways were Scotland and Ireland treated differently from England over representation in parliament before 1832?

In source C, a modern author describes the Reform Act, 1832.

Source C

'The Reform Act redistributed the constituencies, abolishing 56 rotten boroughs and giving their seats instead to the industrial cities. It also gave more seats to the counties with the largest populations.

In addition the rules specifying who was eligible to vote were changed. For the first time the law laid down that all voters had to be male, over 21, and (in the towns) be the owners of property, or tenants of a house with a rent of at least £10 per year. This was a substantial sum of money for those days – equivalent to a year's pay for a cook or maid. As a result only the educated middle classes gained the vote.

The Reform Act had little effect on the voting ambitions of the working class – something that angered them when they realised the Act was not going to alter Parliament overnight. Altogether about another 300,000 people got the vote, making the proportion of voters in England and Wales about one person in very 30.

The Members of Parliament elected to the new industrial constituencies were manufacturers and industrialists not workers. The working classes were little better off after the passing of the Act than before. But there was one big difference. Parliament had at last overcome its resistance to changing the system which elected members of the House of Commons. Change would be much easier from that point on.'

P. Sauvain, British Economic and Social History, published 1987

Following the 1832 Reform Act, what problems remained unsolved in Britain's progress towards democracy?

SCE, Credit Level, Unit 1A, 1990

6 Agriculture, c1760-c1870

Study sources A, B, C and D, which are concerned with the enclosure movement of the late eighteenth and early nineteenth centuries, and then answer questions **(a)** to **(d)** which follow:

Source A An aerial photograph of a village taken in the 1960s

Source B

'I am well informed about the progress and present state of agriculture in all parts of the kingdom, and can say that we owe the spread of every great and beneficial practice such as marling, turnips, hoed, clover drilling and horsehoeing beans, all to great farmers; and what further improvement we may look for must be gained by the same means.'

From a letter written by Arthur Young in the late eighteenth century

Source C

'The results became more and more oppressive to the poorer people, and above all to those who could advance no clear title to their land. These poorer people were driven from their tiny holdings, deprived of their rights of common, driven to become hired labourers or to seek work in the towns or in the coal mines.'

A view about enclosures expressed by two historians writing in the 1930s

Source D

'It was once thought that enclosure meant the end of the small farmer. But detailed study has shown that although their number went down in the early eighteenth century it actually went up during the main period of enclosure. Enclosure did not create a massive army of rural poor forced to flock to towns in search of work, although many writers have condemned enclosures on these grounds. There may have been cases where workers were harshly treated or thrown out of their homes. Only where beef was profitable did the acreage shrink and the number of jobs decline. Otherwise enclosure increased the jobs.'

A view of enclosures held by the historian R B Jones writing in 1977

(a) Study source A.
   (i) What evidence is there in source A to show that the system of farming in this area has changed at some time in the past?　(2)
   (ii) How useful are sources such as this to someone studying this period and topic? Explain your answer.　(3)
(b) Study source B.
   (i) Using source B and your own knowledge, show how far you think Arthur Young was justified in claiming that he was 'well informed'.　(2)
   (ii) To what extent could the improvements mentioned by Young only have taken place on enclosed land?　(4)
(c) Study sources C and D.
   What reasons could explain the different views of the effects of enclosure shown in these two sources?(4)
(d) Source B is a contemporary source and source D a modern source. Compare the strengths and weaknesses of these two sources as historical evidence.　(5)

LEAG, 1991

7   Transport 1750-1830

Study the material below and then attempt all parts of the question and answer questions **(a)** to **(d)** that follow.

'Roads were much improved in the late eighteenth and early nineteenth century and a canal network had been built by 1830. However, probably the greatest advance in the period 1750 to 1875 was the development of the railway. The period after 1830 is often called the Railway Age.'

Source A

A drawing of Stephenson's 'Rocket', (1829)

Source B One reaction to travelling on the Liverpool-Manchester Railway

'I had the satisfaction, for I can't call it pleasure, of taking a trip of five miles, which we did in just under a quarter of an hour. It is impossible to get rid of the idea of instant death to all upon the least accident happening. It gave me a headache which has not left me yet.'

From comments made in 1830 by Thomas Creevey

(a) Do you think that the skill of the road engineers was
  (i) the main reason,
or **(ii)** one of many reasons,
or **(iii)**not a reason,
  for the improvement of the road system between 1760 and 1830? Explain your choice. (8)
(b) In what ways did the growth of canals change British industry? (6)
(c) 'The development of railways had a disastrous effect on other forms of transport.' Do you agree or disagree with this opinion? Explain your answer. (6)
(d) Source A is a picture of the 'Rocket'. source B is the opinion of one person. Is one more useful than the other as historical evidence? Explain your answer. (5)

SEG, 1991

8 The Textile Industries 1750–1850

Study the Introduction and sources A to E below and then answer all the questions. To answer the questions, use only the information given. In your answers, you should refer to the sources by letter.

Introduction

'The textile industries, especially cotton, grew in size in the period 1750-1850. It was a period which saw the introduction of machinery and the growth of the factory system. The industries were increasingly located in the north of England. Lancashire became the centre of the cotton industry.'

Source A The condition of handloom weavers before 1803

'The period 1788-1803 was the golden age of this great trade. Crompton's Mule, the Water Frame and the Spinning Jenny created a great demand for cloth, which meant that weavers were much needed, along with space for their looms.

Their houses and small gardens were clean and neat. All the family were well clad - each man with a watch in his pocket, and the women well dressed too. Every house was well furnished with a clock, tea services and ornaments. Many families had their cow.'

from The Origin of the New System of Manufacture, by W Radcliffe

Source B A threat from the Luddites

'Sir,

Information has just been given in that you are an owner of those hated machines. I have been asked by many men to give you a warning to pull them down. If they are not taken down by the end of next week, I shall send at least two hundred men to destroy them and burn down your buildings. If you fire at my men, they have orders to murder you.

Go to your neighbours to inform them that the same Fate awaits them if their machines are not taken down. We will never lay down our arms until the House of Commons passes an Act to destroy all the machinery hurtful to the people.

Signed by NED LUDD,
from a letter sent to a Huddersfield mill-owner in 1812

Source C The condition of apprentices in a Lancashire mill

'Evidence of John Moss, master of the apprentices at a Lancashire mill in 1816.
Q What were the hours of work?
A From 5 o'clock in the morning until 8 at night all the year through.
Q What time was allowed for meals?
A Half an hour for breakfast and half an hour for dinner.
Q Would the child sit or stand at work?
A Stand.
Q The whole of the time?
A Yes.
Q Were they usually very tired at night?
A Yes.
Q Did you inspect their beds?
A Yes. There are always some of them missing, some might be run away, others I have found asleep in the mill, on the mill-floor.
Q Were any children injured by machinery?

A Very frequently. Very often fingers were crushed and one had his arm broken.

Q Were any children deformed?

A Yes, several. There were two or three that were very crooked.'

From evidence to the Factories Inquiry Commission, (1816)

Source D Raw cotton used in Britain, 1800–49 in millions of pounds weight (lbs)

1800–09	594
1810–19	934
1820–29	1,664
1830–39	3,208
1840–49	5,263

From *Factory Reform*, (1968) by K Dawson and P Wall

Source E Population growth in three towns, 1750–1801

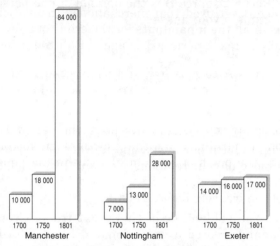

From *A Social and Economic History of Industrial Britain*, (1987) by J Robottom

(a) What can you learn about the textile industries from source A? (5)

(b) Of what use is source B as historical evidence about the textile industries? (5)

(c) Sources A and C give different accounts of the effects of changes in the textile industries. Why do you think these sources differ? (6)

(d) 'The introduction of machinery brought benefits to working people in the period 1750–1850.' Do sources A to E provide evidence to support this opinion, or not? Explain your answer. (7)

(e) How useful are sources A to E in accounting for the growth of the factory system? Explain your answer. (7)

9   American Independence, 1760–1784

Look carefully at sources A to F. Then answer all the questions that follow.

Source A

'There is not the smallest thought for the health, the comfort, the happiness, the wealth, the growth, the population, the agriculture, the manufacture, the commerce, or the fisheries of the American people. All these are sacrificed to British wealth, British commerce, British domination, and the British navy.'

John Adams, a colonist, describes the Acts of 1763–64

Source B

An American Loyalist cartoon of Rebels 'tarring and feathering' a tax-collector

Source C

'After meeting together, they passed the time in speech-making, hissing and clapping, cursing and swearing until it grew near to darkness, then the signal was given, to act their deeds of darkness. They crowded down to the wharves where the tea ships lay, and began to unload. They then burst the chests of tea, when many persons filled their bags and their pockets with it; and made a tea pot of the harbour of Boston with the remainder; and it required a large tea pot for several hundred chests of tea to be poured into at one time. It is said that some of the inhabitants of Boston would not eat fish caught in their harbour, because they had drunk the East India tea. After the affair was over, the town of Boston, finding that it was generally condemned, said it was done by a group of Mohawk Indians.'

> Peter Oliver, the nephew of the Chief Justice of the colony of Massachusetts, December 1773

Source D

'By blocking up the harbour of Boston, you have involved the innocent trader in the same punishment as the guilty who destroyed your merchandise. Instead of making an effort to find the real offenders, you punish all the inhabitants for the crime of a few lawless people.

This country had no right to tax America. It is against all the principles of justice and could never be justified.'

> From a speech by the Earl of Chatham to the House of Lords in May 1774

Source E

Mr Strahan   Philadelphia, 5 July 1775

You are a Member of Parliament and one of that majority which has doomed my country to destruction. You have begun to burn our towns and murder our people. Look upon your hands! They are stained with the blood of your relations! You and I were long friends. You are now my enemy.

And

I am

Yours,

B Franklin

> A letter from Benjamin Franklin to his old friend William Strahan

Source F

'Even if the colonies do have large number of men, what does that matter? They are raw, indisciplined, cowardly men. Believe me, my Lords, the very sound of cannon would carry them off as fast as they could run.'

> From a speech made by the Earl of Sandwich to the House of Lords in 1775

(a) (i) Read source C. What name is normally given to the event described in this source? (1)

    (ii) By what name was the Earl of Chatham (Source D) previously known? (1)

(b) Look at source B. Why are the Rebels treating the tax-collector in this way? (2)

(c) Read source C. How can we tell from this source whether Peter Oliver supported or opposed the actions of these people of Boston? (6)

(d) Read sources D and F. Both these sources are from speeches by British politicians. Explain and account for the differences between them. (8)

(e) Look at all the sources. How far do these sources show why American grievances eventually led to war? Explain your answer fully. (12)

> *MEG, 1990*

10 The Wesleys and Religious Change

Look carefully at sources A–E. Then answer all the questions.

Source A

'Several disorderly persons, calling themselves Methodist preachers, go about causing riots, and are to be brought for questioning before the Magistrates.'

> A Staffordshire warrant of 1743

Source B

'The magistrates were known to be unfriendly towards the Methodists, so disorderly mobs were violent towards them. Why was this? Many people no doubt disliked the strictness and discipline for which Wesley stood. He was against the use of alcohol at a time when London and the big towns were drinking themselves into disease and death with cheap gin. He condemned smuggling, or even dealing in smuggled goods, when a large proportion of the tea drunk in the country had never paid duty. Keepers of ale-houses, smugglers, and all those who could persuade poor folk to waste their money on unnecessary goods had no love for Wesley and his preachers. It was easy for these men to start rumours when they came to preach.'

> A modern historian comments on hostility to the Methodists

Source C

The Holy Club

Source D

'Jan 31 1870

In the evening Sam spoke in favour of the Methodists, rather too much I think. We did not play cards this evening as we usually do.

Jan 28 1787

I read Prayers and preached this morning at Weston…not above 20 people in all at Church…the weather being extremely cold and severe with much snow on the ground.

Oct 12 1792

John Buck, the Blacksmith, who was lately informed against for having a smuggled tub of gin in his house, was pretty lightly fined. Dinner today boiled tongue and turnips and a fine couple of ducks roasted.

Oct 23 1792

Had a tub of brandy and a tub of rum brought this evening.

Feb 22 1795

I fully intended to go to church and do my duty this afternoon but the weather was still severe, and much snow on the ground. I thought it too dangerous for me to go into a damp church after walking through snow. I therefore sent word to my parishioners, that there would be no service.'

Some extracts from the diary of a Church of England parson

Source E

'23 February 1745 (on his way to Newcastle)

We found the roads much worse than they had been the day before. Not only were the snows deeper, which made the pathways in many places impassable, but the hard frost, following the thaw, had made all the ground like glass. We often had to walk, it being impossible to ride. It was past eight in the evening when we got to Gateshead Fell, which appeared a great pathless waste of white. The snow filling up and covering all the roads, we were at a loss how to go on when an honest man of Newcastle overtook us and guided us safe into the town.

'5 April 1771

In the morning I preached at eight, to as many as the house would contain. At noon, because of the numbers, I was forced to preach in the street. I preached at Manchester in the evening, but the house was far too small; crowds had to be turned away.'

Entries from John Wesley's Journals

1   What was 'The Holy Club' (source C)?   (2)
2   Read source A. What does this source tell us about the Staffordshire authorities' attitude towards the Methodists?   (2)

3 Read source B. How far does this source give us an account of Methodists beliefs and practices? (6)

4 Read sources D and E. Explain and account for the differences in attitudes between the Church of England parson and John Wesley. (8)

5 Look at all the sources. 'By 1771 John Wesley had become a respected figure, and the Methodists were no longer seen as a threat.' To what extent do these sources support this statement? Explain your answer fully. (12)

MEG, 1990

11 Britain 1815-1830

Study sources A, B and C and then answer questions **(a)** to **(d)** which follow:

'In 1815 Lord Liverpool's government, which largely represented the landowning interests, passed the Corn Law. This banned the import of foreign corn until British corn had reached 80 shillings (£4) a quarter.'

Source A From a petition by the occupiers of farms in Cleveland, February 1815

'That the great and sudden drop in the value of the produce of their farms has reduced many of the petitioners to a situation of great difficulty and distress: unless some effective remedy is applied, many of the petitioners will no longer be able to pay their rents and taxes...a great proportion of their labourers and servants will be thrown out of employment...they believe the import of foreign corn has caused their distress...the petitioners humbly believe it is unfair...to allow these foreigners to have command of the British market...corn should be properly classified in the same way as other British goods and deserves to be protected on the home market at the same rate.'

Source B Annual average price of British wheat per quarter, 1801-30

1801	119 shillings	1811	95 shillings	1821	56 shillings
1802	70 shillings	1812	126 shillings	1822	45 shillings
1803	59 shillings	1813	110 shillings	1823	53 shillings
180	62 shillings	1814	74 shillings	1824	64 shillings
1805	90 shillings	1815	66 shillings	1825	68 shillings
1806	79 shillings	1816	78 shillings	1826	59 shillings
1807	75 shillings	1817	97 shillings	1827	58 shillings
1808	81 shillings	1818	86 shillings	1828	60 shillings
1809	97 shillings	1819	74 shillings	1829	66 shillings
1810	106 shillings	1820	68 shillings	1830	64 shillings

Source C A cartoon by Cruikshank about the Corn Law of 1815. The men in the boat are French traders.

(a) Study source A: In your own words, explain the argument put forward by the petitioners to improve their present situation. (4)

(b) Study sources A and B:

(i) Do the figures in source B support the opinion in lines 1 – 2 of source A? Explain your answer. (2)

(ii) Do the prices of British wheat for the years 1815–30 suggest that the Corn Law was a success? Explain your answer using source B and your own knowledge. (4)

(c) Study source C: Explain what message the cartoonist is trying to put across about the Corn law of 1815. (4)

(d) Study sources A, B and C: What are the advantages and disadvantages of the types of evidence represented by sources A, B and C to someone studying the Corn Law of 1815 and its effects? (6)

LEAG, 1991

12　The Poor Law, 1815–50

Study sources A, B, C and D and then answer the questions which follow.

Source A

'There is only one farmer in the north of Hampshire who owns nearly 8,000 acres. He grows 1,400 acres of wheat and 2,000 acres of barley. Is it any wonder that the number of poor people increase? What little land they had, they have lost!'

From W Cobbett, *Rural Rides*, 1821

Source B

'An important change has taken place in industrial areas because of the change from hand-loom to power-loom weaving. For some time the changes in the cotton trade meant that many workers who had lost their jobs as hand-loom weavers were found jobs in the new factories. But soon there was a fall in demand for woven cloth and even cheaper ways of weaving were brought in. These two factors led to high unemployment and terrible poverty.'

From a Parliamentary Committee Report, 1827

Source C

'That the present state of the poor does require further assistance than has been generally given them.

Resolved,

　　that the magistrates will make the following calculations and allowances for the relief of all poor and industrious men and their families.

　　That is to say,

　　When the Gallon loaf weighing 8lb 11oz (4kg) shall cost 1s (5p),

　　Then every poor and industrious man shall have for his own support 3s (15p) weekly, either produced by his own or his family's labour, or an allowance from the poor rates, and for the support of his wife and every other member of his family, 1s 6d (7½p).'

　　　　　　A resolution made by the magistrates responsible for the Poor in Reading, 11th May 1795

Source D

A Women's ward in a workhouse in the 1840s.

(a) Do the reasons described in sources A and B fully explain why poverty was increasing at the beginning of the nineteenth century? Explain your answer. (8)

(b) Source C describes the Speenhamland System. How successful was this system in providing poor relief in the early nineteenth century? Give reasons for your answer. (7)

(c) How useful is source D as a piece of historical evidence about conditions in the workhouse? Explain your answer. (7)

(d) 'Much was achieved in the first ten years after the Poor Law Amendment Act of 1834.' Give reasons why you might agree or disagree with this statement. (8)

NEA, 1991

13 The Poor Law 1834-1890

Look carefully at sources A to F. Then answer all the questions.

Source A

Extracts from Baxter's *Book of the Bastilles*, which was a collection of pieces of information, all of which were chosen to show the new Poor Law in a bad light.

(i) A little boy having been separated from his mother in the Nottingham Union raged in despair and tore off his hair by the handful.

(ii) At Bourne, a poor man applied to the Guardians for relief. They offered him a place in the workhouse, but he refused. A week later he was found dead in a field, having chosen death by starvation rather than enter a workhouse under the present system.

Source B

The Chairman of the Sheffield Board of Guardians in 1855 commenting on the benefits of the workhouse for its inmates.

> 'They rise to the minute, they work to the minute. They must be clean, respectful, hard-working and obedient. In short, the habits impressed upon them in the workhouse are precisely those which would have prevented them becoming inmates in the first place.'

Source C

Dr Edward Smith in the Report to the Poor Law Board on the Diet of Inmates of Workhouses, 1866

> 'There can be no doubt that the object for which workhouses have been established is more fully achieved now than it has been at any former period. Able-bodied people are now scarcely at all found in them during the greater part of the year. At present those who enjoy the advantages of these institutions are almost solely those who deserve them, namely the aged and inform, the destitute sick, and children.'

Source D

From a history of Preston written in 1883

> 'This workhouse has an imposing external appearance. The interior is very spacious, substantial and conveniently arranged: and a striking air of order and cleanliness fills the establishment. There are workrooms and a school, a dining hall capable of accommodating, at one sitting, 670 persons, and chapel facilities for Protestants and Roman Catholics.'

Source E

The Rev J L Davies, a Guardian of Marylebone workhouse (in London) in 1888

> 'I know, and I am glad, that they dislike extremely to go to the workhouse as a rule.'

Source F

Photograph of a dinner in a late nineteenth-century workhouse

1   Read source C.
(a) What was meant by 'able-bodied'?   (1)
(b) What was the main 'object for which workhouses were established'?   (1)
2   Read sources A(i) and A(ii). Give two aspects of the new Poor Law which these two sources illustrate.(2)
3   Read source D and look at source F. To what extent do these sources give similar impressions about workhouses? Explain your answer.   (6)
4   Read sources B, C and E. Do these sources give a reliable view of the attitudes which existed towards the very poor from 1834 to the end of the nineteenth century? Give reasons for your answer.   (8)
5   Use all the sources. How far would these sources enable an historian to write a balanced account of how well the workhouse system worked after 1834? Explain your answer fully.   (12)

MEG, 1991

14   The Chartist Movement

Study the Introduction and sources A to D and then attempt all parts of the question.

Introduction

'The Chartist movement began after the 1832 Reform Act failed to give the vote to the working man. The Charter itself demanded six political points, but the Chartists were also interested in improving conditions for the working classes. The Chartist leaders had different ideas of how to achieve their aims. The two main leaders were William Lovett and Feargus O'Connor. O'Connor edited the Chartist newspaper called *The Northern Star*.'

Source A

'Physical force is harmful to the movement. Guns are not what are wanted, but education for the working people.

Violent words do not kill the enemies but the friends of the movement. All this violent opposition can only lead to the destruction of Chartism.'

from *The Life and Struggle of William Lovett*, (1876) by William Lovett

Source B

'Fellow citizens, shall we allow it to be said that four million of us men, who are capable of bearing arms and defending our country against foreign invasion, allowed a few tyrants from inside our own country to defeat us?

We have decided to obtain our rights peaceably if we can, but forcibly if we must. Those who begin to fight against us or who forcibly attempt to stop our peaceful requests for change should look out.'

from *The Northern Star*, (1847)

Source C

'Moral force and physical force are labels that have been given to the Chartists since 1838. Lovett was always one of the moral force and O'Connor one of the physical force. More recently this simple difference has been questioned. A close investigation of their public speeches shows some provocative talk by Lovett and some peaceful talk by O'Connor. This does not mean that the labels are useless. There was undoubtedly a split between the Chartists about the use of violence.'

from *Politics and the People*, (1972) by K Randell

Source D

'A physical force chartist arming for the fight that never was'

A cartoon from *Punch*, (1848)

(a) Do sources A and B show that the Chartists held different views? Explain your answer. (5)

(b) How far are the views expressed in source C supported by the evidence in sources A and B? Explain your answer. (6)

(c) 'Source C is secondary and is therefore not reliable as historical evidence about the Chartist movement.' Do you agree or disagree with this opinion? Explain your answer. (5)

(d) 'Source D is a cartoon and is therefore of little use as historical evidence about the Chartist movement.' Do you agree or disagree with this opinion? Explain your answer. (6)

(e) 'Because the Chartists were so divided, their attempts at reform were not taken seriously.' Does the evidence in the Introduction and in sources A to D support this view? Explain your answer. (8)

SEG, 1991

15 Chartism

The following sources give evidence about parliamentary reform in Britain between the 1830s and the 1860s.

Source A A Chartist meeting in the 1840s

Source B is a description of this meeting, published in the Illustrated London News at the time.

Source B

'The wagon waiting for the delegates was inscribed on the right side with the motto, "The Charter. No surrender. Liberty is worth dying for", on the left, "The voice of the People is the voice of God", while on the back was inscribed, "Who would be a slave that could be free? Onward we conquer, backward we fall". Banners were inscribed "The Charter", "No vote: no muskets", "Vote by ballot", "Annual Parliaments", "Universal suffrage", "No property qualifications".'

(a) Describe the aims of the Chartists and the methods they used to try to achieve these aims.

In 1867 the Second Reform Act extended voting rights and altered the right of some boroughs to be represented in parliament.

Source C is a description of some of the terms of the 1867 Act.

Source C

'The Second Reform Act granted the franchise in the boroughs to all householders and £10 lodgers, and in the counties to £12 leaseholders. Boroughs of less than 10,000 population lost at least one of their MPs, the resulting forty-five parliamentary seats going to the counties and the big new towns.

The Act practically doubled the existing electorate. The household franchise in the towns meant that many of the working class now enjoyed the vote for the first time. The possible consequences of this caused some alarm – Carlyle, for instance wrote of "Shooting Niagara", and Derby spoke of "a leap in the dark".'

D. Richards and J.W. Hunt, *An Illustrated History of Modern Britain*

In the first General Election following the 1867 Act, a majority of Liberal MPs were returned. In source D, Friedrich Engels, friend and supporter of the Communist leader Karl Marx, gives his view of the election.

Source D

'What do you say to the elections in the factory districts? Once again the proletariat (working class) has discredited itself terribly.

　　Everywhere the workers are the rag, tag and bobtail of the official parties. If any Party has gained from the new votes it is the Tories.

　　The parson has shown unexpected power.

　　Not a single working-class candidate had a ghost of a chance, but Lord Tumnoddy could have the workers' votes with pleasure!'

(b)　In what ways was democracy extended by the Second Reform Act?

(c)　Does Source D give a fair assessment of the effects of the Act? Explain your answer.

SCE, Credit Level, Unit 1B, 1990

16　Public Health, 1815-75

Study sources A, B and C and then answer the questions which follow.

Source A

Growth of population in British towns 1801-1851. (The figures are given in thousands.)

Towns	1801	1821	1831	1851
Birmingham	71	102	144	233
Bradford	13	26	44	104
Chester	15	20	21	28
Exeter	17	23	28	33
Glasgow	77	147	202	345
Leeds	53	84	123	172
Liverpool	82	138	202	376
Manchester	75	126	182	303
Swansea	10	15	20	31

Source B

A nineteenth century Glasgow 'court'.

Source C

'Most of the districts occupied by workers do not even have common sewers. The houses are badly drained, often poorly ventilated and do not even have privies. The streets which are narrow, unpaved, and worn in deep ruts become full of mud, refuse, and disgusting filth. The district is surrounded on every side by some of the largest factories of the town, whose chimneys vomit forth dense clouds of smoke which hang heavily over this unhealthy region.'

From J P Kay, *The Moral and Physical Condition of the Working Classes in Manchester*, 1832

(a) According to source A, which was the largest British town in 1851? (1)

(b) What does source A tell us about the growth in population of British towns in the first half of the nineteenth century? Give reasons for your answer. (6)

(c) Do sources B and C describe all the conditions which resulted from the growth of Victorian towns? Explain your answer. (8)

(d) How successful was the Public Health Act of 1875 in improving conditions such as those shown in source B and C? Explain your answer. (7)

(e) The death rate in Birmingham fell from 25.2 per thousand between 1871 and 1875 to 20.7 per thousand between 1880 and 1885. How important was the work of Joseph Chamberlain and the Cadbury family in achieving this success? Give reasons for your answer. (6)

NEA, 1990

17 Medicine and Health, c1760–c1870

Study sources A, B and C, which are concerned with the care of the sick in the nineteenth century, and then answer questions **(a)** to **(d)** which follow:

Source A

A drawing by the artist Rowlandson of a ward in the Middlesex Hospital, 1808

Source B

'The sick lay on wretched beds, fit only for tramps, and were nursed mainly by old pauper women of the lowest possible class. I visited an enormous workhouse...where there were nearly 500 sick and infirm patients. The matron told me..."I never nursed anybody, I can assure you, except my 'usband before I came here. It was misfortune brought me to this."'

Francis Cobbe writing about a visit to a workhouse infirmary in 1859

Source C

'I entered as a first year student at the newly erected St Thomas's Hospital. The building cost £600,000, a large sum of money for those days. But what was the result of all this expense? As afar as surgery was concerned, practically nothing, for the old enemy, blood poisoning, was as common as ever. We students were allowed to go from the post-mortem room to attend midwifery cases. The ways of the operating surgeon seem almost incredible. An old sister, who had spent her life in the service of the Hospital, once sadly said to me, "I really think the surgeons do as much harm as they do good."'

Memories of St Thomas's Hospital, recalled by J Leeson in 1865

(a) Study source A.
   (i) What evidence is there in source A to suggest that condition in the Middlesex Hospital were not typical of hospital conditions in the early nineteenth century?   (4)
   (ii) Name two types of evidence (other than those represented by sources A, B and C) which might be used to check the accuracy of source A.   (2)
(b) Study sources A and B.
   (i) In what ways does the situation described in source B differ from that shown in source A?   (2)
   (ii) Using both sources and your own knowledge, give reasons which could explain these differences in hospital conditions.   (4)
(c) Study source C. What evidence is there in source C to explain why, despite improvements, hospitals were still unhealthy places for patients?   (3)
(d) Sources B and C are both descriptions written many years after the situations they describe. In the light of this, how much can they be relied on by someone studying hospital conditions in this period? Give reasons to support your answer.   (5)

LEAG, 1990

18   Free Trade, 1760-1850

Study sources A, B, C and D and then answer the questions which follow.

Source A

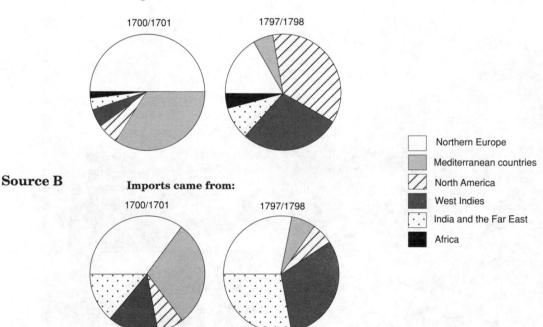

Trading customers 1700–1800

Exports went to:

1700/1701   1797/1798

Source B   **Imports came from:**

1700/1701   1797/1798

Northern Europe
Mediterranean countries
North America
West Indies
India and the Far East
Africa

Source C

'In the first place we want Free Trade in corn because we think it is fair. We require it at the natural price of the world's market, even if it becomes dearer with Free Trade. We do not believe that Free Trade in corn will harm the farmer. Neither do we believe it will harm the farm labourer since it will enlarge the market for his labour and give him an opportunity of finding employment. We believe that Free Trade will increase the demand for labour of every kind.'

From a speech by Richard Cobden in 1844

Source D

'The evil of the potato blight may be much greater than present reports show. We must be prepared for a great disaster.'

Sir Robert Peel writing in 1845

(a) Using sources A and B, and your knowledge of the period, explain how the pattern of Britain's overseas trade changed during the eighteenth century.   (8)
(b) Does source C describe all the arguments in favour of Free Trade? Give reasons for your answer.   (6)
(c) How important was the event outlined in source D in contributing to the repeal of the Corn Laws in 1846? Give reasons for your answer.   (8)
(d) 'Membership of the European Community has had very little impact on British trade since 1973.' Explain whether you agree or disagree with this statement.   (8)

19 The Crimean War, 1854-56

Study the sources below and then attempt all parts of the question.

Source A Lord Cardigan leading the Charge of the Light Brigade

A *Punch* cartoon, (1854)

Source B

> 'Cardigan played the part of a hero but not a general. He led like a general but, having led his men up to the guns, he felt he had done all that was required of him. He retreated gradually and slowly back up the valley. On meeting another officer he said, "I have lost my brigade." He pointed to a tear in his own uniform and complained that it would not now keep out the cold.'

from *Battles of the Crimean War*, (1962) by W B Pemberton

(a) Source A suggests that Cardigan was the hero of the Light Brigade. source B gives a different impression. How do you explain the difference? (10)

(b) The Charge of the Light Brigade showed that some British officers during the Crimean War were not very able. What effect did this have on Britain's war effort? (10)

(c) 'The Crimean War was a disaster for Britain.' Do you agree or disagree with this opinion? Explain your answer. (10)

SEG, 1991

20 Ireland, 1815-1870

Look carefully at sources A to E. Then answer all the questions.

Source A

> 'Her overcrowded population totally depends on agriculture. Ireland lacks those sources of wealth which develop with civilisation. The people live on the most basic diet and would starve if the potato crop fails. This dense population lives in extreme distress. The Established Church is not their Church. The richest members of the aristocracy live in England. In Ireland you have a starving population, an absentee aristocracy and a foreign church. In addition you have the weakest government in the world. That is the Irish Question.'

Disraeli explaining in a speech to Parliament
what he understood by the 'Irish Question', 1844.

Source B

This picture, 'Breeding poultry to pay the rent', was drawn for an English newspaper in about 1845.

Source C

Two different views of the Irish problem were given in 1846.

'The problem of Ireland is totally beyond the powers of men. The cure has been directly provided by an all wise Providence. Though unexpected it is likely to be effective.'

A letter written by Trevelyan, the English Secretary of the Famine Relief Committee

'In spite of her wealth England cannot keep her children from perishing by hunger. How can the Government allow patient subjects to starve to death while there is a penny in the Treasury?'

An editorial from an Irish newspaper

Source D

This passage was written by an Irishman, after he had visited England in 1850.

'They were almost totally ignorant of the real situation in Ireland. This was partly because they lacked accurate historical information and partly because they had never lived in Ireland. No English gentleman can begin to understand what makes Ireland poor and discontented.'

Source E

In 1870 Queen Victoria wrote a letter to the Prime minister Gladstone about his Irish Land Bill.

'The Queen's only comment is about the lack of sympathy it shows for the landlords. She does not think it fair to blame them entirely for the present state of things. The grievances of the tenants may be very real, but this should not encourage them to think that they are justified in using violent means to seek relief.'

1   Read source E. Give two examples of the 'grievances of the tenants' in the period from 1815 to 1870.   (2)
2   Read source A. What did Disraeli mean when he said that 'Ireland lacks those sources of wealth which develop with civilisation'?   (2)
3   Read source D. How useful is this source as an explanation of British attitudes to Ireland?   (6)

4 Read source C. Explain the similarities and differences between these two views of how the Irish famine should be dealt with. (8)

5 Look at all the sources. 'Solve the Land Question and you will solve the problem of Ireland.' Do these sources provide enough evidence to show this is true? Explain your answer fully. (12)

MEG, 1991

21 Trade Unions, 1760-1867

Study sources A, B, C and D, which are concerned with the organisation of trade unions in the 1820s and 1830s, and then answer questions **(a)** to **(d)** which follow:

Source A

'We, the manufacturers, having seen the distress of the workers at Stockport stirred up by trouble-makers to strike, and having seen that this distress is made worse by help being given by our workers to the strikers in that town, do hereby agree to cut by 10% every fortnight the wages of our workers who refuse to sign a declaration that they will not be members of a union or contribute to the support of any strikers.'

> Evidence given to a Parliamentary Committee in 1831 concerning a strike held in Stockport in 1829 over wages. During the strike the manufacturers published this declaration.

Source B

'We the undersigned...do hereby declare that we are not in any way connected with the General Union of the Building Trades and that we do not and will not contribute to the support of such members of the said union as are or may be out of work as a result of belonging to such a union.'

> From a Declaration or, as it was sometimes called,
> *The Document* which was in use in the Building Trade in 1833

Source C

> A modern artist's impression of the admission of a new member to a trade union in the early nineteenth century

Source D

'Good men must combine when the wicked plot against them. Working men who live by their own labour must unite to protect themselves when the capitalists, who live in luxury out of the labour of others, are banded together to starve the honest industrious worker.'

> Adapted from J R Stephen's commentary on the trial
> of Glasgow cotton-spinners for illegal combination, 1838

(a) Study sources A and B.
  (i) What evidence is there in these sources of the tactics used by the employers to break strikes? (2)
  (ii) To what extent do these sources support the view that employers were becoming increasingly concerned about trade union activity in the 1820s and 1830s? (3)

(b) Study sources A, B and C.
  (i) To what extent does the evidence of sources A and B explain the need for secrecy and loyalty such as that shown in source C? (3)

   (ii) Source C is a modern reconstruction of a trade union ceremony. What are its limitations to someone studying trade unions in this period?   (4)

(c) Study sources A, B and D. To what extent are Stephens's comments in source D supported by the evidence of sources A and B?

(d) Using all these sources, as well as information of your own, explain the purposes of trade union activity in the period 1820-1840.   (5)

LEAG, 1991

22 Railways, 1840-1914

Look carefully at sources A to E. Then answer all the questions.

Source A

(i) These figures show the effect of the development of railways on the supply and sale of coal in London between 1845 and 1875. They show an annual average for each five-year period.

five-year period	tons supplied by sea	tons supplied by rail
1845-9	3,279,000	19,000
1850-4	3,379,000	451,000
1855-9	3,167,000	1,195,000
1860-4	3,407,000	1,750,000
1865-9	3,001,000	3,064,000
1870-5	2,940,000	4,609,000

(ii) These figures give the approximate length of railway line open and in use by the public.

Year	miles in use
1843	2,000
1848	5,000
1853	6,800
1858	8,400
1863	10,600
1868	12,700
1873	14,000

Source B

'From the great superiority of the locomotive engine, railway companies may be taken for all practical purposes to possess a complete monopoly as far as regards the carrying of passengers. This is not the case to the same extent for movement of goods because railways experience effective competition from canals. The saving of time does not give such a superiority over the older method of transport.'

Part of the Report to Parliament on the Railways, published in 1844

'In considering the improvement of goods traffic, it is very difficult to make a real comparison with the past. The growth of the railway system has entirely altered all the conditions of that traffic. They have allowed industry and trade to spring up, which without railways could not have existed.'

A comment made by the Royal Commission on Railways which reported in 1867

Source C

'If house rents twenty miles from the city, and travelling by rail, were no more expensive than house rents in crowded streets in town, would the factory worker not be persuaded to exchange the dirty suburbs for the pure atmosphere of the countryside? Who would prefer to live in Paddington, if he could for the same cost live in Stanmore, Epsom or Reigate? These pleasant sites are all accessible by railway and are within half an hour's ride of the capital.'

An article published in *The Railway Times* on 29 June 1850

Source D

'Manchester used to be the centre of the factory system, containing more mills than any other place; but the number of factories has gradually decreased. The opening of fresh railway branches to every little village has put the factories on the same footing as though they were in Manchester itself.'

An extra from *Murray's Handbook for Shropshire*, Cheshire and Lancashire published in 1870

Source E

'For all practical purposes, railways are the only public highways available in the kingdom.

Townspeople are as dependent upon the Railway system for transport over any distance beyond five or six miles, as they would be if all of the Turnpike roads and public highways were closed. Railway Companies have control of all the highways of the country. They also control the entire carrying trade. This practically gives a Railway Company absolute power over the welfare and prosperity of the district it controls.'

Part of the records of Liverpool City Council for the years 1871-72

1 Read source E. Why did 'Railway Companies have control of all the highways of the country'? (2)

2 Read source D. Why did the opening of the railways put factories in the villages on the same footing as those in Manchester? (2)

3 Study source A. Explain and account for the trends shown in these figures. (6)

4 Read source B. These two extracts are taken from Reports of Parliamentary Committees and yet they contradict each other. Does this meant that one or both are unreliable? Explain your answer. (8)

5 Look at all the sources. To what extent do the sources show that the development of the railway network between about 1850 and 1873 transformed the economic, industrial and social life of Britain? Explain your answer fully. (12)

MEG, 1990

23 Agricultural Development Since 1850

Look carefully at sources A to E. Then answer all the questions.

Source A: Farm machinery at the Great Exhibition, 1851

Busby W, UK, 2 or 4 horse plough, horse-hoe on the ridge, ribbing corn drill, and cart.

Crosskill W, UK, Norwegian harrow, meal mill, cart, clod crusher, and gorse bruiser.

Garrett & Sons, UK, horse hoe, general purpose drill, four-row turnip drill on the flat, improved hand barrow drill for grass seeds, steam engine and threshing machine.

Hornsby and Sons, UK, corn and seed drill, two-row turnip drill on the ridge, oil cake bruiser, steam engine.

McCormick C H, United States, reaping machine.

Source B: Output of wheat in bushels per 100 acres

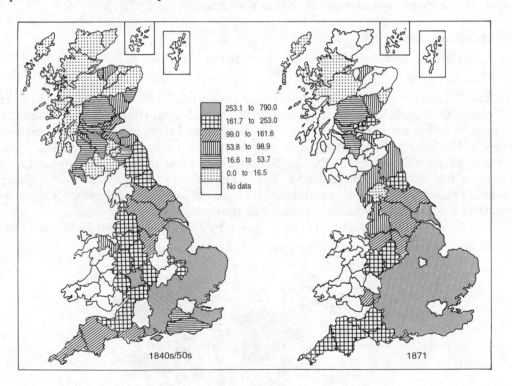

253.1 to 790.0	
161.7 to 253.0	
99.0 to 161.6	
53.8 to 98.9	
16.6 to 53.7	
0.0 to 16.5	
No data	

1840s/50s   1871

Source C

'The most striking feature of agricultural progress within the last 20 years has been the general introduction of reaping machines and the steam plough. But with the exception of these and other implements and machines there is really little that is new in the practice of the last quarter of the century. In my account of English agriculture written in 1850, I find descriptions of good farming in nearly every part of the country, the details of which differ very little from the practice of the present day.'

From a report written by James Laird in 1872.
He had been asked by *The Times* to write a report on English agriculture

Source D

'Mowing by machinery is not so often practised as might be expected. Some farmers keep a machine to safeguard themselves against unreasonable demands as to prices and wages, in time of pressure, rather than from preference for this method of cutting the grass crop. Some will say that they are unwilling to quarrel with their labourers who look with an evil eye on that which they consider (however unjustly) an interference with the rights of labour.'

Taken from an account of farming near London published in 1869

Source E High farming and golden years, 1850-75

'British farming had a "golden age" from about 1850 to about 1875. The land was peaceful. There were rich harvests and a rising demand for agricultural products.

Those who lived at the time called the methods they used "high farming". This meant that they aimed to gain large profits for the land, and were willing to make large investments to do so. New buildings, drainage, machines, fertilisers and good labour all cost money.

Farming, forestry and horticulture employed over two million people; more than ever before. Rents rose by 20%, farmers' incomes by 100% between 1850 and 1870. Prices rose by about 25% over this time, leaving a clear profit. It looked as if high farmer almost guaranteed success.'

Taken from a recent school textbook

1　Read source E.
   (a)　Give one reason or a 'rising demand for agricultural products' during the period 1850-75.　(1)
   (b)　Name one fertiliser brought into general use in farming during this period.　(1)
2　Look at source B. Using these maps, give two statements which can be made about developments in wheat production between 1840 and 1871.　(2)
3　Read sources C and E. What are the similarities and differences between these two sources as evidence about the 'Golden Age' of farming (1850-75)? Explain your answer.　(6)
4　Read sources A and D. Could a historian reach reliable conclusions about the use of machinery in farming between 1850 and 1875 from these sources? Explain your answer.　(8)
5　Look at all the sources. How far do these sources show that the period 1850–75 was one of great agricultural advancement and prosperity? Explain your answer fully.　(12)

MEG, 1990

24　The Irish Question, 1867-1918

Study sources A, B, C and D and then answer questions **(a)** to **(d)** which follow:

Source A

'The national demand in plain and popular language is simply this, that nothing can ever satisfy Ireland until Irish laws are made and administered upon Irish soil by Irishmen.

Our claim to self government rests, not just on right and title, but also, fellow citizens, upon the failure of the British government in Ireland for the last hundred years…Take…population: while in every civilised country in Europe the population has increased, in Ireland, in the last sixty years, it has decreased by one half. Take…civil liberty. There has been a Coercion Act every year…Take…industrial development…a history of industry deliberately suppressed by British acts of Parliament…Now such a record as that cries out for vengeance…'

Adapted from a speech by John Redmond in Dublin on 4 September 1907

Source B A cartoon showing some problems facing Redmond in the 1900s

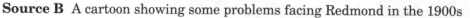

Source C

'Being convinced in our own minds that Home Rule would be disastrous to the wealth of Ulster as well as the whole of Ireland, undermining our civil and religious freedom, destroying our citizenship and dangerous to the unity of the Empire, we show names are written below, men of Ulster, loyal subjects of His Gracious Majesty King George V, humbly relying on the God whom our fathers in days of stress and trial confidently trusted, do pledge ourselves in solemn Covenant...to stand by one another in defending for ourselves and our children our position of equal citizenship in the United Kingdom and in using all means which may be found necessary to defeat the present plot to set up Home Rule Parliament in Ireland...

God Save the King'

Covenant = contract or promise   Adapted from Ulster's Solemn League and Covenant

Source D

An artist's impression showing the Ulster Volunteer Force unloading arms at Larne Harbour, 1914

(a) Study source A:
    (i) In your own words, explain why John Redmond considered that Ireland should be given self-government or Home Rule.   (3)
    (ii) What chance had John Redmond of achieving his aim in 1907 when he made his speech?   (3)

(b) Study source B: What point is the cartoonist trying to make about the problem facing John Redmond in trying to achieve his aim?   (3)

(c) Study source C: What arguments are put forward in this source? Comment on the tone of the language used to express these arguments.   (5)

(d) Study source D: source D is an artist's impression of the scene at Larne. Does this make it more or less reliable as historical evidence than a photograph or a cartoon of the same event would be? Explain your answer.   (6)

LEAG, 1991

25 Foreign Affairs, 1890-1914

Look at sources A to E carefully. Then answer all the questions.

Source A

    (i) 'We belong to the community of Europe and we have no right to avoid those duties to look after the interests of the whole community. There is a big difference between trying to get on well with your neighbours and that mood of superior isolation which we proudly like to call "non-intervention".'

                              from a speech made by Lord Salisbury in 1888

    (ii) A recent book puts forward Lord Salisbury's view about alliances with other countries in Europe.
        'Lord Salisbury, the British Prime Minister, believed that no government based on a parliamentary democracy could enter into a permanent alliance with a foreign power. He said this because a later government under a different political party could ignore the promises made by an earlier government.'

Source B

The following cartoon was printed in a British magazine on Christmas Day 1901. Britannia and Colonia represent Britain and her Empire. The other three figures represent Germany, France and Russia.

Source C

A recent book looks at relations between Britain and Germany at the beginning of this century.

'Germany produced half as much steel as Britain in 1860, was level by 1900, and was to produce twice as much by 1914. So, although Germany was Britain's biggest customer, she was also regarded as Britain's biggest rival in trade. Therefore, Britain was ready to welcome friendly approaches made by France in 1903.'

Source D

A recent historian describes Britain's diplomatic position in 1914.

'There can be no doubt that Britain's diplomatic position in 1914 was dangerously misunderstood. British military and naval officers expected to be drawn into a war between France and Germany; but many politicians and the general public were unaware of the obligations Britain had agreed with France.'

Source E

Part of a note written during a Cabinet meeting on 30th July 1914 by the Prime Minister, Herbert Asquith, to a close personal friend, Venetia Stanley.

'We have no obligation to help France or Russia...We mustn't forget the tie created by our friendship with France...It is against British interests that France should be destroyed as a great power.'

1 Read source C. Give two other ways in which Britain considered Germany a 'rival'. (2)
2 Read source C.
   (a) What is the name of the 'agreement' which was made as a result of 'friendly approaches' made by France to Britain in 1903? (1)
   (b) Which other country joined Britain and France in this 'agreement' in 1907? (1)
3 Read source A(i) and A(ii). What similarities are there in the statements about Salisbury's foreign policy given in these two sources? (6)
4 Read source A(i) and source E. source A(i) and source E are statements made by British prime ministers. Does this mean they are of equal value to the historian? Explain your answer. (8)
5 Look at all the sources. 'Britain's policy of "Splendid Isolation" only existed in population imagination, not in practice.' How far do sources A to E show this to be true? Explain your answer fully. (12)

MEG, 1990

26 Parliamentary Reform, 1867-1928

Study sources A, B, C and D and then answer the questions which follow.

Source A

The Six Points
OF THE
PEOPLE'S
CHARTER.

1. A VOTE for every man twenty-one years of age, of sound mind, and not undergoing punishment for crime.

2. THE BALLOT.—To protect the elector in the exercise of his vote.

3. NO PROPERTY QUALIFICATION for Members of Parliament—thus enabling the constituencies to return the man of their choice, be he rich or poor.

4. PAYMENT OF MEMBERS, thus enabling an honest tradesman, working man, or other person, to serve a constituency, when taken from his business to attend to the interests of the country.

5. EQUAL CONSTITUENCIES, securing the same amount of representation for the same number of electors, instead of allowing small constituencies to swamp the votes of large ones.

6. ANNUAL PARLIAMENTS, thus presenting the most effectual check to bribery and intimidation, since though a constituency might be bought once in seven years (even with the ballot), no purse could buy a constituency (under a system of universal suffrage) in each ensuing twelve-month; and since members, when elected for a year only, would not be able to defy and betray their constituents as now.

The People's Charter, 1837

Source B

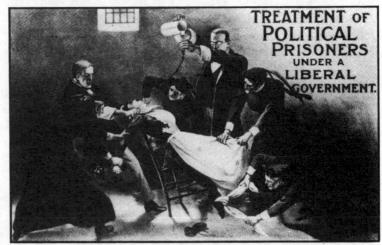

A Suffragette Poster.

Source C

'Frustrated by the Government, suffragette militant action increased. On March 1st 1912 groups of smartly-dressed women began smashing shop windows in the West End. During the next eighteen months, post-boxes were set alight, and empty houses burnt down, and Lloyd George's new house was destroyed.'

From *Britain since 1800*, H Martin, 1988

Source D

Factory workers during the First World War

(a) Source A shows the demands of the Chartists. How far were these demands achieved between 1867 and 1918? Explain your answer. (8)

(b) How reliable is source B as a piece of historical evidence about the way Suffragettes were treated in prison? Explain your answer. (7)

(c) Sources C and D refer to the actions of women in the early years of the twentieth century. Which of these actions was more likely to help women to achieve their aims? Give reasons for your answer. (7)

(d) If the Representation of the People Act of 1918 was successful in giving women the Vote, why then was it necessary to pass another Act in 1928? Give reasons for your answer. (8)

NEA, 1990

27 The London Dock Strike of 1889

Study the Introduction and sources A to F and then attempt all parts of the question.

Introduction

'In 1889 the dockers in London went on strike demanding a wage increase from fivepence to sixpence an hour. They were unskilled workers, who did not belong to a union. The strike was organised by Ben Tillett, the leader of a small union of tea warehousemen. There was a great deal of sympathy for the dockers both in Britain and abroad. Australia sent a huge donation to help the strikers.'

Source A

'To obtain employment men are driven into a shed, iron-barred from end to end. A foreman or contractor walks up and down outside, like a dealer in a cattle-market, picking and choosing from a crowd of men. In their eagerness to obtain employment, they trample each other under foot and they fight like beasts for a day's work.'

from *Memories and Reflections*, (1931) by Ben Tillett

Source B

'Remember the match girls who won their strike and formed a union. Take courage from the gas stokers who only a few weeks ago won an 8-hour day.'

from a speech made to the dockers in 1889 by John Burns, who was a socialist leader

Source C

'When the strike was announced a fortnight ago, the number of strikers was about 10,000. Now it is 100,000 or even more. The dockers themselves had no organisation. If they had been left to fight alone, the strike would soon have collapsed. A strike committee directed the strikers and soon every industry was at a standstill. Tens of thousands of tons of food was rotting in ships lying in the River Thames. All this was the result of labour interests working together.'

from a British newspaper, (1 September 1889)

Source D

'I cannot say what the cost of granting the dockers' demands would be, but it would be at least £100,000. That would mean we would have to raise our charges. We cannot afford this, for it would mean either not paying the shareholders of the dock company any profit, or driving ships away from the port. When the final pinch comes, the hopes of the dockers will receive a severe shock and I should be surprised if there is any fight left in them.'

from an interview given by the Chairman of the Dock Directors in August 1889

Source D

'The casual dock labourer was one of the lowest type of labourer. He had neither skill nor strength and was unable to improve his situation by forming a union, as so many men have done'.

from *The Times*, (August 1889)

Source F

A view of the dockers' plight in 1889

"The Secret of England's Greatness: fivepence an hour."

A cartoon from an
Australian newspaper, (1889)

(a) How useful is source A in explaining the background to the London Dock Strike? (6)

(b) Source E gives one view of the dock labourer. Do sources B and C agree with this view? Explain your answer. (5)

(c) Source D is the view of the Chairman of the Dock Employers. What does this source suggest about his attitude towards the dockers? Explain your answer. (5)

(d) Source F is biased and is therefore unreliable as evidence about the docker's plight. Do you agree or disagree with this opinion? Explain your answer. (6)

(e) Without union support the dock strike could not have succeeded. Do sources A to F support this statement. Explain your answer. (8)

SEG, 1991

28   The Rise of the Labour Party, 1890-1924

Study the sources A to H and answer the questions which follow.

Source A: Keir Hardie as shown in a political cartoon of 1892.

Source B

'The respectable citizens of London were shocked when a carriage, with Hardie on top surrounded by laughing, cheering, singing supporters, draw up at the gates of Westminster. They were horrified to see him enter the House of Commons dressed in a checked, tweed suit and a cap. That was just not done; a black suit and top hat was the proper dress there.'

From H Shapiro, *Keir Hardie and the Labour Party*, 1971

Source C

'The hopeless way in which the Independent Labour Party ran its election campaign contributed to its overwhelming defeat.'

From a speech at the 1895 Trade Union congress

Source D

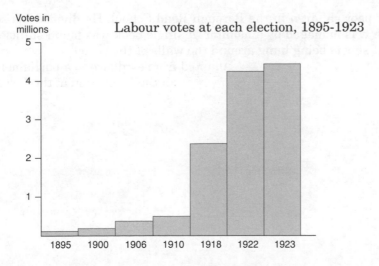

Labour votes at each election, 1895-1923

Source E

'The money difficulty does not exist for unions. A penny a week from every member of a trade union would produce £300,000. The larger unions alone could provide enough to finance 50 Labour candidates.'

From G B Shaw, *Fortnightly Review*, November 1st 1893

Source F

'In the general election of 1895 all the Independent Labour Party candidates, including Keir Hardie, were defeated. Its most serious failure was its inability to convert the Trade Union movement to socialism.'

From C P Hill, *British Economic and Social History 1700–1975*, 1977

Source G

'The Osborne case of 1909 was a shattering blow to the finances of the Labour Party. It cut off the subscriptions of trade unionists and therefore it deprived the Party of much of its income.'

From P Gregg, *A Social and Economic History of Britain 1760–1972*, 1973

Source H

'The Labour Party received many recruits whose heads were as soft as their hearts, whose 'Socialism' amounted to little more than a desire to see the lives of their poorer neighbours improved.

From J A R Marriott, *Modern England 1885-1945*, 1946

(a) Study source A.
  (i) What part did Keir Hardie play in the early history of the Labour Party?   (3)
  (ii) What does source A tell us about Keir Hardie?   (5)
(b) Study sources A and B. Is source B more useful than source A to an historian studying the work of Keir Hardie? Explain your answer.   (10)
(c) Study sources C, D, F and G. Do sources C, F and G provide sufficient information to explain source D? Give reasons for your answer.   (7)
(d) Study sources E, F and G. The progress of the Labour Party was closely related to the Trade Union movement. Do sources E, F and G agree with this view? Explain your answer.   (7)
(e) Study sources A, C and H. Would a modern historian writing about the Labour party consider these three sources to be reliable? Explain your answer.   (8)

NEA, 1991

29 State Education, 1760-1986

Study sources A, B, C, D and E and then answer questions **(a)** to **(e)** which follow:

Source A

Morning	*Class One*
9.15	Religious Instruction
9.30	Read and spell to the master
10.00	Repeat tables - spell from the cards
10.30	Read and Spell to the monitor
11.00	Spell on the cards to the monitor
11.30	Write in copybook, girls sew
12.15	Repeat religious instruction - fill in registers

Adapted from the timetable of a National School in 1818

Source B

'Joseph Lancaster taught poor children in the Borough Road School. He divided his school into eight forms, each of which was managed by a monitor. A single book was found sufficient for the whole school, the different sheets being hung around the walls of the school.'

Adapted from evidence to a parliamentary committee
on the Education of the Lower Classes, 1816

Source C: A print of Borough Road School

Source D

'The poor should be objects of care and attention from the higher classes; if they grow up in ignorance and vice, a fearful responsibility will lie upon those who might have prevented it. The education provided in an elementary school inspires them to virtue and to control. The middle and upper ranks of society now depend upon the labour and skill of the poor.'

Adapted from the *Manual of Teaching* published by
the British and Foreign Schools Society in 1821

Source E

'Giving education to the poor would lead them to be dissatisfied with their lot in life. Instead of making them good servants in agriculture and other employments it would make them insolvent to their superiors.'

Adapted from a speech in Parliament in 1807

(a) Study source A: What can you learn from this source about the education provided in National Schools? (3)

(b) Study sources B and C: These sources both give details of the Borough Road School. Is one likely to be more reliable than the other? Explain your answer. (3)

(c) Study sources A, B and C: How trustworthy and accurate a picture of the Monitorial System at work is provided by these sources? (4)

(d) Study sources D and E: In what ways do these sources differ about the value of educating the poor? (4)

(e) Study all the sources: In the years from 1815 to 1830 the education of the poor became a more and more important issue. How useful are these five sources in helping you to understand why this was so? (6)

LEAG, 1990

30 Industry and Trade, 1910–1939

Look carefully at sources A to F. Then answer all the questions.

Source A

'There is a huge and until now untapped public which will buy, and is beginning already to buy from foreign sources, a really good cheap car. If a valuable market is not to be lost at the outset, the British manufacturer will have to set himself seriously to work to produce small cars as good and as cheap as those now imported from abroad.'

Extract from *The Times* in 1912

Source B

'Herbert Austin walked up the shopfloor and found these two men not working. So he went and found the foreman and Austin said, "Sack these two men, they're doing nothing". The foreman said, "They are waiting for parts to come through". To which Austin replied, "Sack these two men, they're doing nothing".

He was a bit of a bully. Everything had to be done quicker and cheaper all the time.'

A worker at the Austin factory in the 1920s.

Source C

	1932	1937
Building	29.0	13.8
Motor vehicles	20.0	4.8
Electrical engineering	16.3	3.1
Food industries	16.6	12.4
Coal industry	33.9	14.7
Cotton	28.5	11.5
Shipbuilding	62.2	23.8

Official statistics on unemployment in selected industries (figures are percentages)

Source D

'One of the most important of the new industries was electrical engineering, together with the supply of electricity. It was a symbol of the new industrial Britain, freeing other industries from dependence on the coalfields of the North and West and enabling people to move to the Midlands and the South-east. Backward technically until 1918, by the late 1930s the industry was close, if not equal, to its foreign rivals.'

From a recent history of British industry between the wars

Source E

'They are the British disease, the Trade Unions. Their attitudes towards progress are really bad. There is a small portable hand welding machine - in Sweden, Germany and France one man works 4 machines; in Britain one man works one machine.

They build tankers on the continent with 20% less man hours than we can build them, purely because of British trade union practices.'

The manager of a British shipyard speaking in the 1970s

Source F

Unemployed men queuing outside the gramophone Company at Hayes, near London, which was taking on workers in 1932.

1   Read source D.
    (a) Why did people move to the Midlands and the South-east?   (1)
    (b) How was electrical power distributed throughout the country?   (1)
2   Read source A. What was done in Britain to produce 'a really good cheap car'?   (2)
3   Read sources C and D, and look at source F. Does source F support the information given in sources C and D? Explain your answer.   (6)
4   Read sources B and E. What would be the advantages and disadvantages of these sources to a historian trying to work out reasons for success and failure in British industry between 1918 and 1980?   (8)
5   Look at all the sources. 'These sources explain why it is misleading to talk only about the decline of British industry after 1918.' Do you agree? Explain your answer fully.   (12)

MEG, 1990

31 The 1930s

Study sources A, B, C and D, which are concerned with the Depression of the 1930s, and then answer questions **(a)** to **(e)** which follow:

Source A: unemployment figures 1930-1940

1930	1,911,000
1932	2,843,000
1934	2,124,000
1936	1,731,000
1938	1,885,000
1940	709,000

Source B

'We made up our minds to send into the worst-affected areas investigators who would look into the whole situation on the spot. Their reports made a number of extremely valuable suggestions.

We have decided to appoint two Commissioners who will devote their whole time to schemes to help economic development and social improvement in distressed areas. They will have to be given funds – £2 million at first.'

From a speech by Neville Chamberlain, Chancellor of the Exchequer, in 1934.

Source C

A cartoon from the *Daily Express*, 1936

'Work at last'

Source D

'The total population of Wigan is a little under 87,000...more than one person in three...is either drawing or living on the dole...And Wigan is not especially badly off as industrial towns go. Even in Sheffield, which has been doing well for the last year or so because of wars or rumours of war, the proportion of unemployment is about the same...To study unemployment and its effects you have ... to go to the industrial areas. In the South unemployment...is scattered and not obvious. There are plenty of rural districts where a man out of work is almost unheard of...'

(From *The Road to Wigan Pier* by George Orwell, 1937)

(a) Study source A. When, according to this Table, did unemployment reach its highest point in the 1930s? Briefly explain why unemployment was then so high. (3)

(b) Study source B. 'The Government failed to appreciate the extent of the problem of unemployment in the 1930s.' Using source B, and information of your own, comment on the truth of this statement. (3)

(c) Study source C. What message is the cartoonist trying to convey in this source? (3)

(d) Study sources A, B, C and D.

  (i) In what ways to the figures in source A support the evidence of sources C and D? (3)

  (ii) Does the evidence of source D help to explain the Government's actions outlined in source B? Give reasons to support your answer. (3)

(e) What is the value of each of these sources to someone studying unemployment in the 1930s? (5)

LEAG, 1991

32 The National Government, 1931-39

Study the Introduction and sources A to F, and then attempt all parts of the question.

Introduction

'In the summer of 1931 the British Labour Government was faced with a grave financial crisis. The value of the pound could only be kept high by foreign loans. Foreigners, particularly the USA, would not lend the money unless Britain cut her government spending. This appeared to make cuts in unemployment benefit unavoidable. When most members of the government found this solution unacceptable, the Prime Minister, Ramsay MacDonald, went to the King to resign but was persuaded to lead a new National Government drawn from all parties. Only three Labour ministers joined him. His action was widely regarded in the Labour Party as unnecessary and treacherous. A General Election soon followed. It gave the new National Government a huge majority.'

Source A A newspaper comments on the change of government

'Those Labour colleagues who opposed MacDonald's decision come out of it all very badly, in particular Mr Henderson, the Foreign Secretary. He is their ringleader, and yet, as Foreign Secretary, as a member of a previous national government (during the 1914-18 War), and as a party manager, he should have understood the seriousness of the present crisis.

He has chosen to lead the Labour rebels rather than be wise in remaining loyal to his leader. It looked at one time as though he might emerge from this Parliament with more credit than some of his colleagues. Now, however, his time as Foreign Secretary is likely to be remembered for his lack of concern for his country's position in the world.'

From *The Times*, (25 August 1931)

Source B A magazine comments on the change of government

'Mr MacDonald's decision to form a government with the Liberals and Tories seems to us a mistake. He will inevitably find himself at war with the working classes. He will also be opposed by those in all classes who believe that it is silly economics to cut spending power when there is a surplus of goods.

On the personal side we may respect Mr MacDonald's position. He has nothing to gain from his action, and he is drifting away from his party. He will find himself out of sympathy with the views of most members of his new Government.'

From the *New Statesman*, (29 August 1931)

Source C British General Election results: (number of MPs)

1929:   Conservative 260, Labour 288, Liberal 59
1931:   National Government: Conservative 473, Labour 13, Liberal 68.
        Opposition: Labour 51, Liberal 4, others 6.

from official figures

Source D

WE MUST THINK OF OUR SAVINGS AND OUR HOME THAT'S WHY I'M VOTING FOR THE NATIONAL GOVERNMENT

A poster published by the National Government, October 1931

Source E
A view of the fall of the Labour Government, 1931

'When they faced the financial crisis in the summer of 1931, MacDonald and his Labour colleagues were utterly incompetent. In 1931 only boldness could have saved them, but they chose the weak course of giving in when any powerful interest criticised their actions.

They were guilty of the lunacy – or worse – of appointing a committee of their political and financial opponents, the notorious 'May' Committee, to judge their financial policy. The May Committee produced such an alarmist and grossly exaggerated report that foreigners rushed to withdraw their money from London.

The government, instead of standing up to the financiers, argued among themselves. Most of them had little idea of what all the fuss was about. The Labour leaders – MacDonald and Snowden (Chancellor of the Exchequer) – were already determined to betray their followers and go over to the capitalist side.'

From *The Common People*, (1938) by G D H Cole and R Postgate

Source F
A view of MacDonald

'Late in August 1931, a National Government was formed "to save the pound". MacDonald – "in the national interest" – remained Prime Minister and thus earned the lasting contempt of his party. Having risen from the humblest circumstances, he perhaps enjoyed being Prime Minister more than most. Scurrying through St James Park, hopping in and out of comfortable cars, talking with ladies of fashion, he perhaps no longer cared for the party which had brought him to office.'

From *Europe and the Modern World*, (1973) by J and G Stokes

(a) The Introduction explains why the National Government was formed. Is this explanation supported by the evidence in sources B, E and F. Explain your answer. (6)

(b) Study the attack on Henderson in source A and the attack on MacDonald in source F. Do these attacks differ? Explain your answer. (5)

(c) The National Government won a huge majority in the 1931 General Election. Do you think that the National Government's Election poster (source D) would have helped to win that majority? Explain your answer (5)

(d) 'The authors of source E make very clear where their sympathies lie.' Do you agree or disagree with this opinion? Explain your answer, referring to source E. (6)

(e) 'These sources are full of personal opinions, so historians should not use them.' Do you agree or disagree with this opinion? Explain your answer. (8)

SEG, 1991

33 British Foreign Policy 1930-39

Study sources A, B, C and D and then answer questions **(a)** to **(e)** which follow:

Source A

'When the Assembly of the League met in September 1935 the British Foreign Secretary, Sir Samuel Hoare, called attention to Italy's activities. He declared that Britain would support the League of Nations in resisting acts of aggression. Laval, the French Foreign Secretary, agreed. When Mussolini's forces crossed into Abyssinia, the League's Council declared Italy to be an aggressor and imposed economic 'sanctions'. However, as coal, oil, iron and steel were not among the prohibited goods, Italy was not seriously hindered...Thus, in spite of the declarations, Hoare and Laval made a secret proposal to bargain with Italy over land in Abyssinia.'

Adapted from a school textbook

Source B

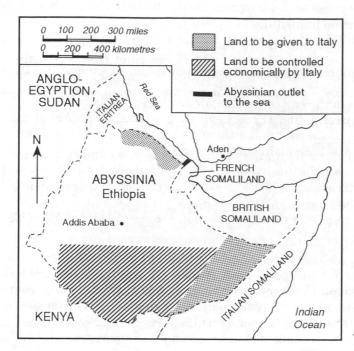

0   100   200   300 miles
0   200   400 kilometres

Land to be given to Italy

Land to be controlled economically by Italy

Abyssinian outlet to the sea

ANGLO-EGYPTION SUDAN

ITALIAN ERITREA

Red Sea

Aden

FRENCH SOMALILAND

ABYSSINIA
Ethiopia

Addis Ababa

BRITISH SOMALILAND

N

KENYA

ITALIAN SOMALILAND

Indian Ocean

A map of the Hoare-Laval proposal

Source C

Winston Churchill's summary of the immense international consequences of the Abyssinian crisis. Churchill was not in office when he wrote this.

'Ever since the Stresa Conference Mussolini's preparations for the conquest of Abyssinia had been apparent. It would be evident that British opinion would be hostile to such an act of Italian aggression. Those of us who saw in Hitler's Germany a danger not only to peace but to survival dreaded the movement of a first class Power, as Italy was then rated, from our side to the other.'

Source D

THE AWFUL WARNING.

FRANCE AND ENGLAND (*together?*).

"WE DON'T WANT YOU TO FIGHT,
BUT, BY JINGO, IF YOU DO,
WE SHALL PROBABLY ISSUE A JOINT MEMORANDUM
SUGGESTING A MILD DISAPPROVAL OF YOU."

A Punch cartoon of 1936, showing Britain and France warning Mussolini about Abyssinia

(a) Study sources A and B; Do you see any differences in the British Foreign Secretary's declaration in September 1935 and the actions he finally took? Explain your answer.   (4)

(b) Study source C: Does Winston Churchill give any reason for this apparent change in policy? Explain your answer.   (3)

(c) Study sources A and B: Use source B, and your own knowledge, to explain the Hoare-Laval proposal mentioned in source A.   (3)

(d) Study source D: Is the sarcasm in the cartoon deserved? Explain your answer.   (4)

(e) Study sources A, C and D: sources C and D represent their authors' opinions and observations on the Abyssinian Crisis at the time. Does this make them more likely to be biased and exaggerated than source A which was written in 1961? Explain your answer.   (6)

LEAG, 1991

34 Britain and World War II

Look at sources A to E carefully. Then answer all the questions.

Source A

A recent book explains why the RAF organised heavy bombing raids over Germany.

> 'The RAF believed Germany could be bombed into surrender, but these night raids cost dearly in terms of men and planes and left them weak elsewhere. The raids seem to have had little effect, because they mostly failed to hit industrial and military targets. They succeeded only in destroying large parts of Berlin and other cities, with much loss of life. On 14the February 1945, 2,000 planes bombed Dresden in a raid known as 'Thunderclap'. Estimates of the number killed vary from 25,000 to 250,000.'

Source B

In June 1941, following Germany's invasion of Russia, the Prime Minister, Winston Churchill, said in a radio speech:

> 'We shall bomb Germany by day as well as by night. We shall make the German people taste each month a sharper dose of the miseries they have showered upon mankind.'

Source C

(i) VICAR WANTS TO SEE BERLIN IN FLAMES

> 'I hope and pray that the Russian advance will not stop until Eastern Germany is laid waste and Berlin is in flames. Once and for all Germany must be taught a lesson and she must realise in her own country the dreadful meaning of war,' declared Rev T Chadwick, Vicar of All Saints Church, Darlaston.

The Midland Advertiser and Wednesbury News in February 1942

(ii) The Bishop of Chichester made a speech in the House of Lords in February 1944 referring to the RAF's policy of bombing civilian targets.

> 'Can't the Cabinet see that this steady devastation of cities is threatening the roots of civilisation?'

Source D

Sir Arthur Harris wrote to the Prime Minister in November 1943

> 'We can wreck Berlin from end to end if the US Air Force will join us. It will cost between 400 to 500 planes. It will cost Germany the war.'

Source E

(i) Churchill sent this note to the Chief of Air Staff on 28 March 1945, after the raid on Dresden.

> 'The time has come to reconsider the question of bombing German cities simply for the sake of increasing terror. Otherwise we shall take over an utterly ruined land. We shall not be able to get building materials or our own needs because we will have to build homes for the Germans themselves. If feel we must concentrate more precisely on military targets, rather than on mere acts of terror and widespread destruction.'

(ii) A photograph of the ruins of Berlin, May 1945.

1 **(a)** Name one make of British plane which was used in the bombing of Germany. (1)
  (b) Read source D. What official position was held by Sir Arthur Harris in 1943? (1)
2 Read source A. Give two reasons why estimates of the numbers killed at Dresden varied so widely. (2)
3 Look at sources B and E(ii). How far does the photograph (E(ii)) show that Churchill's intentions in source B were carried out? (6)
4 Read sources C(i) and C(ii). How useful would these sources be to an historian writing about British attitudes to the bombing of Germany? (8)
5 Look at all the sources. 'The bombing of German cities was carried out just to satisfy the desire of the British for revenge.' Do these sources provide enough evidence to show this to be true? Explain your answer fully. (12)

MEG, 1991

35 The Labour Government, 1945-50

Study the sources A to H and answer the questions which follow.

Source A

'Social insurance may provide income security; it is an attack upon Want. But Want is only one of five giants on the road of reconstruction. The others are Disease, Ignorance, Squalor and Idleness.'

From a government report, Social Insurance and Allied Services, 1942

Source B

'My mother used to sit embarrassed on the edge of a chair in the consulting room on the rare and desperate days when one of us had to be taken to the doctor – opening and shutting her purse, waiting for the right moment to extract the carefully saved coins which could not really be spared. Sometimes the doctor would shout at my mother for not having come before, like the time we had to wait for my sister's throat to turn unmistakenly into something really serious before she was pushed off in a pram to his surgery.'

From a woman's memories of the 1930s, written in 1964

Source C

'On Monday morning you will wake to a new Britain, in a State which "takes over" its citizens six months before they are born, providing care and free services for their early years, their schooling, sickness, workless days, widowhood and retirement. Finally it helps to pay the cost of their burial. All this, with free doctoring, dentistry and medicine, for a weekly deduction from your pay packet.'

From the Daily Mail, July 1948

Source D

'The doctors began by voting not to join the National Health Service. They feared they would be told where to work and would end up with poorer incomes. The government got them to join by agreeing to allow doctors to work only part-time for the National Health Service and to have pay-beds in hospitals for their private patients.'

From J Rowbottom, A Social and Economic History of Industrial Britain, 1986

Source E A cartoon from *Punch* magazine, 1947

"It still tastes awful."

Source F

A complaint made by a doctor when the National Health Service started in July 1948.

'You would think that the people had saved up their illnesses for the first day.'

Source G

The cost of the National Health Service for Britain as a percentage of the nation's wealth.

1949	3.7
1951	3.5
1952	3.6
1953	3.4
1954	3.3
1955	3.3
1956	3.3
1957	3.3
1958	3.4

Source H

'Everyone expected health care standards to go on rising. Each year new hospitals were built and old ones were modernised. But improved health meant increased costs, and this was made worse by the growing proportion of old people.'

From J Rowbottom, A Social and Economic History of Industrial Britain, 1986

(a) Study source A.

    (i) Name the person responsible for the report quoted in source A. (1)

    (ii) What did the report mean when it said that it was intended to 'provide income security'? (3)

(b) Study sources A, B and C. According to these sources, how was the introduction of the National Health Service meant to improve the lives of the poor? Explain your answer. (8)

(c) Study sources D, E and F. Is there sufficient information in the sources to show what the attitudes of the doctors was towards the National Health Service? Explain your answer. (9)

(d) Study source F. How reliable is source F to an historian studying the National Health Service? Explain your answer. (10)

(e) Study sources G and H. source H suggested that health care costs have increased. Does source G support this view? Explain your answer. (9)

NEA, 1991

36 Britain's Changing World Role since 1945

Study sources A, B, C and D which refer to Britain's application to join the EEC in 1963, and then answer questions **(a)** to **(d)** which follow:

Source A

'In 1961 Britain applied to join. Some Europeans were keen to have Britain. Some however still had doubts. They felt that Britain was a half-hearted European and would drag its feet in the move to unity. One of these was De Gaulle. He felt that Britain was too isolated still, too closely linked to the USA and anyway would threaten his leadership of Europe. To De Gaulle Europe was a third force in the world, between America and Russia, with himself as a leading figure. He vetoed the application.'

From a school textbook

Source B

'One might sometimes have believed that our English friends were beginning to transform themselves...Will it be so one day? Obviously only England can answer...after a profound change. Polaris does not serve the principle of having our own deterrent to use as we want. To put our weapons into a multilateral force under foreign command would be against this principle.'

Adapted from a speech made by President De Gaulle in January 1963, soon after Britain had agreed to operate Polaris nuclear missiles in partnership with the USA

Source C

'*Interviewer*: Do you agree with Harold Macmillan's verdict that the veto was used because De Gaulle always looked back to the past, and thought that British membership would destroy the chances France had of leading Europe?]

Heath: I don't think so. De Gaulle must have realised that German strength was greater than French strength. There were many things in which France could give leadership, but he could not possibly have expected to dominate Europe.'

From a conversation with Edward Heath, later Prime Minister of Britain

Source D
From a cartoon published in the *Daily Express* in 1967

Prime Minister Harold Wilson's attempt to gain British entry to the EEC in 1967 is blocked by President De Gaulle of France.

(a) (i) Use source A to explain why Britain's application to join the EEC was vetoed. (3)
    (ii) Study source B. Does this source support the conclusions of the author of source A? (3)
    (iii) Study source C. Does this source support the conclusions of the author of source A? (3)
(b) These sources give the views of the French leader who opposed British entry (source B), a leading British politician who supported it (source C), and an historian (source A). What do these sources show about the difficulties of finding out why Britain's application to join the EEC was vetoed? (4)
(c) Study source D, which refers to the application of 1967. Does this source seem to support the view of any of the other sources? Explain your answer. (2)
(d) Describe and explain Britain's progress towards membership of the EEC after 1963. (5)

LEAG, 1990

INDEX

GCSE REVISE HISTORY (1750–1992)
Review Form

We'd really appreciate your comments, criticisms and suggestions as a user of this study aid - so that we can make the next edition even better and more helpful to you and your fellow students. So please answer the following questions as honestly and specifically as you can.

I **Please rate this book on the following factors:**

(a) on a scale of A (excellent) to E (very bad); and

(b) on a scale of 1 (very important to you) to 5 (of no interest to you).

Add your own comments and suggestions on each point, if you'd like to.

1. Coverage of the topics you need for your assignments/exams

Ⓐ B C D E   ① 2 3 4 5

2. Up-to-dateness of topic coverage and exam questions

A B C D E   1 2 3 4 5

3. Presentation of material in general: attractiveness and distinctiveness of cover, use of space, colour, diagrams, illustration etc.

A B C D E   1 2 3 4 5

4. Presentation of material for ease of reference: locating specific areas/points, headings, index, contents pages etc.

A B C D E   1 2 3 4 5

5. Extent and type of illustrative questions and exam question practice

A B C D E   1 2 3 4 5

6. Provision of advice on studying and revision techniques

A B C D E   1 2 3 4 5

7. 'Tone of voice' of the text - for ease of reading and personal preference

A B C D E   1 2 3 4 5

GCSE REVISE HISTORY (1750–1992)
Review Form

II   **How do you know about Letts Study Aids?**

☐ Teacher   ☐ Letts advertisement in _____   ☑ Bookshop

☐ Friends   ☐ Other _____

III   **What time of year did you buy your Letts Study Aid?**

☐ Start of school year   ☐ Beginning of exam term   ☐ Just before exams

☐ Other _____

IV   **How have you mainly used your Letts Study Aid?**

☐ Backup to school work   ☐ Long term revision   ☐ Last minute revision

☐ Other _____

V   **Do you find the term 'Study Aid' helpful as a description of a book like this one?**

What term do you think would describe it best?

☐ Study Aid   ☐ Study Guide   ☐ Course Companion   ☐ Revise Guide

☐ Revision Aid   ☐ Other _____

Name: _____   Exam being taken: _____

Address: _____   Examining board: _____

_____

_____   Date of exam: _____

Signed: _____

Thank you for your help.